READERS FROM AROUND THE WORLD TALK ABOUT *INSIDE ADOBE PHOTOSHOP*

"Two weeks ago I bought your book Inside Photoshop 4, *and I am amazed.* **It is like a Bible if you don't know how Photoshop works.** *I have the feeling I can actually do something with it even after just two chapters.* **When the new version [of your book] hits the shelves in Holland, I will be the first to buy it."**

—Natan Tazelaar

"I am one of the persons you have helped a lot through your book Inside Adobe Photoshop 4. *I was able to purchase the book off the stands in one of Hong Kong's bookstores, but I live in Manila, Philippines where I have my own desktop publishing business that me and my wife have put up.* **I consider your book my MOST vital reference when the need arises."**

—Paco Arespacochaga

"I am working in IAB, which is 43 years old in photography. I am heading the Digital Imaging outfit here and we are equipped with the latest hardware. **I was looking for a good reference book, and at last I found** Inside Adobe Photoshop 4. *We were doing our job in a crude way. But after reading this book, we were able to work in a professional way."*

—P. Vijay Kumar

"I've been following your tutorials in Photoshop 3 and 4 by way of the Inside *books. They've helped me over several hurdles in my classes.* **The books are always close at hand and are getting a little dog-eared..."**

—Kim O'Connor

*"I scanned about eight different Photoshop books before choosing yours. [**Inside Adobe Photoshop 4] is the one thing in all this confusion which gives me hope.** It seems very sensible and straightforward and appears to have been written by real people (I wonder about some of the others)."*

—Roey Fitzpatrick

*"I am learning, and your book is fantastic. I have used CorelDraw 7, and find through your book, Adobe Photoshop has more to offer me, a novice. **I had purchased another, and returned it to exchange for yours.**"*

—Marilu Bishop

*"Before I purchased your book I used maybe 10% of Photoshop's capability. A month later I feel an incredible sense of power and creative enjoyment when I use the program. I recommend your book to anyone who wants to get past merely "playing" with the program. **I read many computer "how-to" books, but never found any that produced the speed of results as your did.** The style and the use of examples is perfect. More than that, though, is yours and the folks behind the scenes' ability to convey complex ideas in an understandable manner. I consider your book to be **one of the best purchases I've ever made**."*

—Mike Steffanos

*"**The** Inside Photoshop **projects are some of the most exciting I've ever found.** They're clearly written, aesthetically pleasing, and best of all, they make it easy for my students to learn Photoshop. I'm looking forward to using the new projects in the* Inside Photoshop 5 *edition in my classes."*

—Christine C. Frey

"Your publication Inside Adobe Photoshop 4 *is absolutely fantastic. In fact,* **I had already ordered it before its release in South Africa.** *I am looking forward to the possibility of Photoshop 5.0 (Who knows?)."*

—Andrew Kirkland

"I study in Beijing Printing Institute, and my major is Information Engineering. I am a crazy Photoshopper. I bought your book a few weeks ago. I will be honest, it makes me so excited. **I had never read a book about Photoshop as good as yours.** *I almost spend all my time in reading your book these days."*

—Zhang Ning

"Thank you for a very enjoyable and useful book. **[Your book] accompanied me to the Norwegian mountains this Easter** *and was much more pleasant than our dreadful weather."*

—Patrick Gaffney

"I love your books, first Inside Adobe Photoshop 3 *and now* Inside Adobe Photoshop 4. *I want to* **thank you for the special care and loving attention you have given** Inside Adobe Photoshop 4. *Thank you very much for all the thousands of hours you and your wife must have spent on these fine books."*

—Steve & Li Mei Campbell

"The more and more I used Photoshop, the more interested I became in the software and tried as best I could to read the Japanese manuals. However, having no English background in digital art terminology, I was completely lost! **I therefore asked for the most complete instruction book available on Photoshop 4.0 to be sent to me from the States.** *Even though I use the Japanese version of Photoshop, I was able to follow along with no problems. Your book is well organized, easy to understand, and loaded with valuable information."*

—Jim Wiley

"You have heard this before, but I just want to tell you how much I loved Inside Photoshop 4. **I have never found a book that had sooo much information. This book will remain at my side every time I load in Photoshop!"**

—Kurt M. Warnstaff

"Got your book Inside Photoshop 4 Limited Edition. *Just started it and* **am impressed with layout, humor, techniques, and CD goodies.** *When I saw your book was published by New Riders, I grabbed it. New Riders has the best graphic design books and the best tech help. Hey, you guys did reeeal good. Out of all the Photoshop books I have purchased, this is one of the most informative books.* **All the info/lessons on the CDs and step-by-step instructions guided me to a better understanding of how to apply what I have learned to future projects for my clients."**

—Ellen Morrison

"I am enjoying the exercises in your book, and **I have already gotten compliments on my work for restoring/retouching photos** *(from family). Nevertheless, your book has helped greatly."*

—Dennis Rios

"I live in Pakistan and am a proud owner of your Inside Photoshop 4. *You have really written* **a great book and it has helped me tremendously in learning to use Photoshop."**

—Ali Aamir

"I am a photographer specializing in architecture and interiors. **Your book Inside Adobe Photoshop 4 has been very informative and has graced my bedside table for a month or so. (It was, by far, the most highly recommended text.)"**

—Elton Pope-Lance

"I have been using your new Inside Adobe Photoshop 4 *book and love it! I am not a hard-core graphics artist but need to use a quality program for web graphics design. I found that **with your book I was able to get up and running in Photoshop in no time at all!**"*

—Steven Kremesec

*"Thank you for such **a wonderful book and CD-ROM.** It has been such a help in my Adobe Photoshop applications."*

—Garry Bass

*"I just wanted to say a big thank you for putting together a great book, that is not only **easy to use**, but also **a pleasure to read**."*

—Maarten Dijkstra

"I would like to congratulate you on the excellent job you've done putting together Inside Adobe Photoshop 4. *I've found it **an invaluable aid** so far. I particularly like the idea of being able to follow the examples in the book with identical images from the companion CD. **All guides should be as straightforward as this.**"*

—Sandy Tomlinson

INSIDE ADOBE® PHOTOSHOP 5
Limited Edition

GARY DAVID BOUTON

BARBARA MANCUSO BOUTON

GARY KUBICEK

New Riders

201 WEST 103RD STREET, INDIANAPOLIS INDIANA 46290

INSIDE ADOBE PHOTOSHOP 5, LIMITED EDITION

Copyright © 1999 by New Riders Publishing

International Standard Book Number: 1-56205-951-3

Library of Congress Catalog Card Number: 98-86040

Printed in the United States of America

First Printing: November 1998

00   99   98   4   3   2   1

EXECUTIVE EDITOR
Beth Millett

ACQUISITIONS EDITOR
Karen Whitehouse

DEVELOPMENT EDITOR
Jennifer Eberhardt

MANAGING EDITOR
Patrick Kanouse

PROJECT EDITOR
Rebecca Mounts

COPY EDITOR
Gail Burlakoff

INDEXER
Rebecca Salerno

TECHNICAL EDITOR
Gary Kubicek

SOFTWARE DEVELOPMENT SPECIALIST
Adam Swetnam

INTERIOR DESIGN
Louisa Klucznik

COVER DESIGN
Nathan Clement

LAYOUT TECHNICIAN
Mark Walchle

COVER ILLUSTRATOR
Gary David Bouton

TRADEMARKS

All terms mentioned in this book that are known to be trademarks or service marks have been appropriately capitalized. New Riders Publishing cannot attest to the accuracy of this information. Use of a term in this book should not be regarded as affecting the validity of any trademark or service mark. Photoshop and the Photoshop logo are registered trademarks of Adobe Systems Incorporated.

WARNING AND DISCLAIMER

Every effort has been made to make this book as complete and as accurate as possible, but no warranty or fitness is implied. The information provided is on an "as is" basis. The authors and the publisher shall have neither liability or responsibility to any person or entity with respect to any loss or damages arising from the information contained in this book or from the use of the CD or programs accompanying it.

CONTENTS AT A GLANCE

TABLE OF CONTENTS

PART IV: EXTENDED USES FOR PHOTOSHOP

PART V: PUBLISHING AND BEYOND

18 OUTPUTTING YOUR INPUT

ABOUT THE AUTHORS

Gary David Bouton is an author and illustrator who adopted the personal computer after 20 years of creating artwork at a traditional drafting table. *Inside Adobe Photoshop 5, Limited Edition* is Gary's eighth book about Adobe Photoshop. In addition to being a contributing author for three books on CorelDRAW, he has written seven other books about computer graphics for New Riders Publishing. These titles include *Inside Extreme 3D 2*, *Photoshop Filters & Effects*, and *CorelDRAW Experts Edition*. He also wrote the book *The Official Multimedia Publishing for Netscape* for Netscape Press.

Gary has won four international awards in desktop publishing and design and was a finalist in the 1996 Macromedia People's Choice Awards. A contributing writer to *Corel Magazine* and other publications, Gary is also moderator of the CorelXARA discussion list on i/us (`http://www.i-us.com/xara.htm`).

In his spare time, Gary is working on a plug-in filter that will change limericks into square dance calls.

Gary can be reached at: `Gary@TheBoutons.com`.

Barbara Mancuso Bouton has co-authored all editions of *Inside Adobe Photoshop* and was the editor of the *New Rider's Official World Wide Yellow Pages*. She is also the author of Netscape Press' *Official Netscape Power User's Toolkit*. Barbara is a publishing and electronic/Internet document production professional and is a systems consultant for a number of Fortune 500 firms.

"Photoshop 5 is a breath of fresh air for both the professional designer and those who are only beginning to get into computer graphics," said Barbara. "Version 5's emphasis is on design tools, of which there are many new and unique ones, but at the same time, Photoshop's value to prepress and production people remains unparalleled. The true challenge to following up the previous *Inside Photoshop* books with this one was 'where do we begin?' There will surely be a number of our readers who are familiar with Photoshop's traditional features, and there are some who will be coming to Photoshop for the first time. We've tried very hard to integrate new features with the traditional ones, to present Photoshop 5 as a whole to users of all skill levels. We want you to be able to get right down to work—or play—with this new version and this new book."

Barbara can be reached at `Barbara@TheBoutons.com`, or at `bbouton@dreamscape.com`.

Gary and Barbara maintain their own Internet site (`http://www.TheBoutons.com`) as a repository of book listings, corrections and updates to currently available books by the Boutons (`http://www.Boutons.com/updates/updates.html`), and essays on computer graphics, and as an art gallery of current images.

Gary Kubicek has been a contributing author for five Macmillan books on Photoshop; he has also been a technical editor for eight books. A professional photographer for more than 20 years, Gary was an early adopter of Photoshop and the "digital darkroom" as an extension of the self-expression he finds in his traditional photographic work.

"The limitations and confines of conventional photography led me to electronic imaging," says Gary. "If you come from a traditional imaging background, you will have the time of your life in Photoshop 5."

Gary is also a digital imaging consultant, owner of a photo restoration business, and trainer for a variety of clients using Photoshop, PageMaker, and Office97.

Gary Kubicek can be reached at: gary@kubicek.com. His Web site address is http://www.aiusa.com/gary.

DEDICATION

This book is dedicated to those in the world who are wanting, in ways both large and small. If you have a favorite charity, please support it, and if you don't—please find one, or two. If you have a gift, whether it's song, ballet, painting, whatever—please don't hesitate to share your experience with those who are far behind you. The authors don't hide anything or pull any punches when it comes to documenting Photoshop and other programs, because knowledge is something to share, without the fear of creating competition. It truly does our hearts good to see the people who have read our books excel at Photoshop, so much so that we would like to ask questions of them! It means that we've succeeded in doing what we set out to do—to educate.

Simply share your good fortune; we only get one chance to do so in life.

ACKNOWLEDGMENTS

It's not the principal author—or even the "gang of three"—who is solely responsible for the book you hold before you, or for the success of the book. Whenever authors receive applause for their work, some of the clapping *must* be heard by the people "backstage." Editors, production people, and even the folks who drive the distribution trucks to the bookstores, play an integral part in what you will get out of this book. The authors want you to know, in the best way we can provide, the names and contributions of the talented individuals who, together, delivered valuable Photoshop information to you.

We'd like to thank, from the bottom of our pens:

- Macmillan Computer Publishing, who allowed us the time and creative latitude to tell a very complex story in a very informal way.

- Executive Editor Beth Millett, whose support and confidence in this book made it a pleasure to write. Thanks, Beth.

- Development Editor Jennifer Eberhardt, who realized the scope of this book from the beginning, and made every effort to accommodate our professional and occasionally personal needs. We couldn't have asked for a more supportive editor, nor a more enthusiastic reader, of the tome presented to you.

- Copy Editor and sideline cheerleader Gail Burlakoff. Gail has been editing Gary's work since the Photoshop 2.5 book, about a billion years and many upgrade editions ago, and it's gotten to the point where it's hard to tell where Gary's writing ends (usually with, "okay," or "Cool, huh?") and Gail's expert editing begins. Thank you, Gail, for being a friend, and for seeing a book in a larger way than mere sentences and paragraphs.

- The Boutons thank Gary Kubicek, Technical Editor and co-author, for the superb editing work and clear focus on the book, at times when everything seemed like "press Ctrl(⌘)+H to hide from the real world for a while"! Thanks also for posing for many of the example images in the book, such as the "Aliens in Plaid" guy (not the alien), regardless of how ridiculous the instructions must've seemed at the time.

- Special thanks to John Leddy, Christie Evans, and Peter Card at Adobe Systems for providing us with inside information about Photoshop as the development process progressed. Thanks also for Illustrator, PageMaker, and Adobe Dimensions, which were all used for the ads in the back of the book, and for the PDF documents on the Companion CD and the *Limited Edition* CD-ROM.

- MCP Design and Production, for bringing the documentation to physical format, and for allowing the authors to contribute to the book's finished appearance.

- Adam Swetnam, software specialist, for ensuring that the Companion CDs were mastered correctly, and that the contents are easy to access on both the Macintosh and Windows platforms.

- A tip of the hat to Charles Moir and Dave Matthewman at XARA, Ltd., for access to the advance versions of XARA 2, which was used to illustrate and annotate many of this book's figures, as well as to create the advertisements you'll see.

- Ted Alspach at Extensis, for providing full-working demo versions of PageTools, PhotoFrame, Intellihance, Mask Pro, and (Macintosh) VectorTools for our readers on the Companion CD.

- Rose Ann Alspektor at the VALIS Group, for the working copy of Flo' on the Companion CD.

- John Henderson at Three-D Graphics, for allowing us to offer a working version of Texture Creator, for both Mac and Windows, on the Companion CD.

- Thanks to CEO Robert Batty and Eric Lacy at XAOS|tools for allowing us to offer demo versions of their products on the *Limited Edition* CD-ROM.

- Many thanks to Michael, Jeff, and Skip at Alien Skin for the demo version of Eye Candy 3 for the Macintosh and Windows.

- Antoine Clapier at RAYflect for the demo version of Four Seasons shown in Chapter 25.

- Barry Burns and Sumeet Pasricha at Andromeda Software for the 3-D demo filter and the Shadow filter on the *Limited Edition* CD-ROM.

- Thanks to John Niestemski and Susan Bird at Graphic Masters, the folks who bring you the offer in the back of this book for exceptional film recording work (see Chapter 18) from your Photoshop files. For 25 years, Graphic Masters has been the professional choice of designers for getting 35mm and larger format film copies of their work, and for good reason. It's called *quality.*

- Our ISP, Scott Brennan, President of Dreamscape On-Line, PLC., for the type of bandwidth and service we needed to get massive amounts (we **are** talking larger than a floppy here!) of work to Indianapolis faster than overnight. Dreamscape's success here on the East Coast is rooted in personal service, and Scott is yet another business professional we've had the pleasure of calling a friend.

- Mike Plunkett, for playing the lifeguard who rescues "The Gigantic" in Chapter 5. Thanks, Mike...you did it well, and without even a symphony orchestra and choir behind you.

- Gary Kubicek thanks Muriel Buerkley, Tammy Austin, and Daniel Lash for allowing the use of images "Cheers," "Dad-son," and "Family" (respectively). Your photos helped me make Chapter 8 everything I wanted it to be. And special thanks to Jaci Gills for posing as the bench "twin" in Chapter 23. Jaci, as soon as you get an email address, I'll Photoshop it across your shirt. And thanks to Ed Gills and Sue Furletti for assisting in Chapter 23's photographic session.

- Gary Kubicek would also like to give a special thanks to his family (Terri, Rachael, Bethany, "Grandma Mary," and "Uncle Mark"), Jean Weisburg, Taffy McKeon, Mike Tarrenova, Amy Tewksbury, Jerry O'Dell, LaToya Pickett, Tim DeVolve, and Bill Ehrhardt.

- Thanks to David Bouton, closely related to Gary and Barbara, for playing Senator Dave in Chapter 7 and the guy in front of the Tudor home in Chapter 21. Dave, you get your picture in these books more often than *we* do. What's your secret? Thank you, brother!

- Gary and Barbara Bouton want to thank their parents, Jack, Eileen, John, and Wilma, for doing the interior and the landscaping of our new house while we tapped away into the wee hours on "that Photoshop stuff." In fact, you take better care of the house than *we* have! You've consistently told us that what we're doing is important, and it is your faith in our talents that makes you all that much more dear to us. Thanks, Mom. Thanks, Pop.

TELL US WHAT YOU THINK!

As the reader of this book, *you* are our most important critic and commentator. We value your opinion and want to know what we're doing right, what we could do better, what areas you'd like to see us publish in, and any other words of wisdom you're willing to pass our way.

As the Executive Editor for the Graphics and Desktop Publishing team at Macmillan Computer Publishing, I welcome your comments. You can fax, email, or write me directly to let me know what you did or didn't like about this book—as well as what we can do to make our books stronger.

Please note that I cannot help you with technical problems related to the topic of this book, and that due to the high volume of mail I receive, I might not be able to reply to every message.

When you write, please be sure to include this book's title and author as well as your name and phone or fax number. I will carefully review your comments and share them with the author and editors who worked on the book.

Fax: 317-817-7070

Email: desktop_pub@mcp.com

Mail: Executive Editor
            Graphics and Desktop Publishing
            Macmillan Computer Publishing
            201 West 103rd Street
            Indianapolis, IN 46290 USA

ADOBE PHOTOSHOP: THE UNCOMMON HOUSEHOLD WORD

Pepsi, Scotch tape, Kleenex tissues, and Adobe Photoshop. As registered or trademarked brands, all share something in common: they are "name brands" that epitomize a product. Let's choose Adobe Photoshop from the list, because that program is what this book is all about. Two groups of people recognize this brand name: those who use the program, and those who have heard *of the program and its role in complex image editing. Photoshop has almost become a* verb, *as in, "I Photoshopped the piece."*

Ironically, the people who don't use computers but who have heard of Photoshop never truly see the results of the program because the best Photoshop retouching work is completely *invisible*. What someone who doesn't use Photoshop *does* realize on occasion is that even though an image is completely impossible—Adobe has a classic advertisement of a channel swimmer making his way down an interstate highway—the viewer can detect no tampering, no phony aspects within the image. Reality that can't possibly be real is one of the unofficial trademarks of Photoshop, and this is what makes the program a most uncommon household word.

Those of us who use Photoshop tend to take for granted that one cannot get better results—whether retouching a photograph to restore it, or to create a believable fantasy composition—than by using the world's most popular image editing program.

Inside Adobe Photoshop 5, Limited Edition is a fully guided tour of the behind-the-scenes magic this program can produce. The authors take you through comprehensive steps in each chapter to show you how to produce award-winning work, photorealistic or otherwise. Our approach is a straightforward and simple one: it is our belief that every attention-getting image has to begin with a *concept*. The user then chooses the tools to complete the goal, and through a set of procedures, finishes the work. Because we believe there is a definite timeline and series of actions that bring the designer from beginning to end, you'll find that the tutorials in this book were created with the same concept (albeit a little whimsical at times) and actions you'd use for a composition of your own. It is our intention to show you a task, to examine what needs to be done, and then to provide the steps needed to bring the piece to completion. By structuring the book in this way, we make it possible for you to be able to apply the "methodology" shown in this book to a multitude of personal and professional assignments. Oh, yes, and along the way, we'll show you tricks, shortcuts, and advanced techniques that you'll want to use and to store away for future use on a particularly difficult assignment.

AN OMNIBUS APPROACH PROVIDES HELP FOR ALL CLASSES OF DESIGNERS

Photoshop 5 has a streamlined interface, much more logically laid out than previous versions. The program also features commands and palettes you'll also find in other Adobe products, so, for example, a seasoned PageMaker or Illustrator user can get down to work in Photoshop 5 more quickly. At the same time, Photoshop 5 contains many new, sometimes hidden features.

The authors have therefore chosen to presume practically *nothing* in teaching you this new program. Naturally, you need to feel comfortable with your computer's operating system, you need to know how to save, copy, and move a file, and proficiency with a mouse or a digitizing tablet will get you where you're going in Photoshop 5 more quickly than if you unpacked a computer from a box moments ago! The authors have chosen to take a "step back" approach from Photoshop 5, to better include users who might be unfamiliar with such things as anti-aliasing, interpolation, alpha channels, and other computer graphics terms.

As the flow of the book goes, we provide information on computer graphics in general in the first chapters, move on to customizing Photoshop and an explanation of the way selections are defined, and then we integrate what you've learned to move on to more complex image editing by the end of the book. *Everyone* is new to Photoshop 5; it's an adventure for the pro and the beginner alike, and we didn't want to leave out anything in the steps, the notes, the text, or the discovery process. Do not take the attitude of, "Yeah, yeah, I know about the Lasso tool so I'll skip this section." There are new features on the Lasso tool flyout on the toolbox, and you'll be missing out on valuable information if you "gloss" a chapter. The authors didn't presume anything, so as a reader, you shouldn't either!

Let us make learning Photoshop 5 an excursion, an adventure. As most adventures go, you must pack a few things first, such intangible things as a positive attitude, a concept, a proficiency with your computer, and an eagerness to learn. And last but not least, you should have a map, so you don't travel too many side roads, as interesting and valuable as they might be. The authors have provided the map (it's called 'this book'!), and the following sections describe this map, by way of explaining the *structure* of *Inside Adobe Photoshop 5, Limited Edition.*

PUSH DOWN AND TWIST: THE DIRECTIONS FOR ACCESSING THIS BOOK

Most of the examples described in the book are documented in a step-by-step format. If you follow along, your screen should look exactly like this book's figures, except that your screen will be in color. Each chapter leads you through at least two or three sets of numbered steps, with frequent asides explaining why we asked you to do something. The figures show the results of an action, and we explain what the effect should look like.

Most of Photoshop 5's tools have different, enhanced functions when you hold down the Shift, Alt, or Ctrl keys (Shift, Opt, ⌘ Command keys, for Macintosh users) while you click with the mouse or press other keyboard keys. These *modifier keys* are shown in the steps as Ctrl(⌘)+click, Alt(Opt)+click, Ctrl(⌘)+D, and so on. *Inside Adobe Photoshop 5, Limited Edition* is a multiplatform documentation of the application; Windows key commands are shown first in the steps, followed by the Macintosh key equivalent (enclosed in parentheses). UNIX users will also find the steps easy to follow; the primary difference in Photoshop 5 across platforms is the "look" each operating system lends to interface elements.

To show you how easy it is to follow along in this book, here's how we tell you how to access the Feather command:

1. Press Ctrl(⌘)+Alt(Opt)+D (Select, Feather), and then type **5** in the pixels field. Click on OK to apply the feathering.

The translation? You hold down the first key while you press the second and third keys (then release all three keys to produce the intended result), or you can access the command the "hard way" through the menu commands we frequently provide after the key commands in parentheses. The authors are trying to get you comfortable with modifier keys rather than menu commands because this constant reinforcement, highlighted throughout the book, will eventually make you work more efficiently in Photoshop 5. Function keys appear in this book as F1, F2, F3, and so on.

If the steps in an application that's available in both Windows and Macintosh formats are significantly different, we fully explain the steps used in this book.

As mentioned earlier, the Photoshop interface itself is practically identical on all operating platforms. The only real differences lie in the system "padding"—the screen elements that the Macintosh OS and different versions of MS-Windows add to windows, palettes, and menus—and the system font used to display text. In Figure I.1, you can see the Windows NT presentation of Photoshop 5, which is nearly identical to Windows 95 and 98.

FIGURE I.1 *The Windows NT "look" of Photoshop 5.*

Figure I.2 shows the same document you see in Figure I.1, but loaded in the PowerPC version of Photoshop 5, running under System 8.

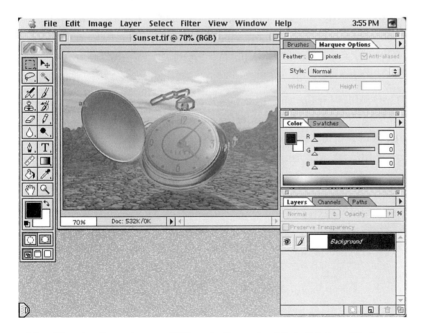

FIGURE I.2 *Photoshop 5 running on a PPC, under System 8, with the "platinum" look.*

If you compare these two figures, you'll note that there is a nominal difference between the two interfaces; there is no difference in the *features* offered in the two versions of Photoshop, however.

Okay, here's a list of the *real* differences in features between the Windows and the Macintosh versions of Photoshop 5:

- When you are in full-screen mode without the menu or title bar on an image, in Windows, you can still access the menu because a flyout button appears at the top of the toolbox.

- On the Macintosh, you can roll up the toolbox at any time by double-clicking on the palette tab at the very top of the toolbox. A second double-click rolls the toolbox down.

- The Document Sizes field and the Zoom Percentage field, on the Macintosh version of Photoshop, are located at the bottom of the current image window. In Windows, the Document Sizes and Zoom Percentage field are on the Status Line at the bottom of the screen, where you can also see options displayed for the currently selected tool.

- Under Windows NT, the Adobe Gamma control panel does *not* automatically load when you install Photoshop 5. You can find and run this utility that globally changes the degree of contrast in the midtones onscreen by double-clicking on the Photoshop 5 folder, Goodies, Calibration, Adobe Gamma.cpl. This utility on the Macintosh auto-installs under the Apple menu, Control Panels. In Windows 95, Adobe Gamma is located under the Start menu, Settings, Control Panel.

- The profiles for opening PhotoCDs and embedding ICC color information are located in Windows under Windows/System/Color. On Windows NT, the files are located in WinNT/System32/Color. On the Macintosh, the same files are in System/Preferences/ColorSync Profiles.

The figures in this book were taken in Windows NT; there simply isn't room in this book to show all the versions of Windows, UNIX, and Macintosh interfaces! Again, where there is a significant difference in the way something is accomplished on a specific platform, this book details specific steps to be used.

A Note to Southpaws

This book was written a little chauvinistically, in that we assume you are right-handed. The Macintosh platform uses a single-button mouse, and which hand you use to click with an onscreen cursor makes no difference. The context menu in Photoshop 5 can be accessed in Windows by clicking on the secondary mouse button, however, and the steps in this book's chapter are written on the assumption that this is the right-mouse button. If you are left-handed and have specified reverse ordering of the primary and secondary mouse buttons, the term *right-click* in the chapter steps means *click on the secondary mouse button*. Support on the Macintosh for this extended feature is performed by holding Ctrl and clicking. Every function in the Windows and Macintosh versions of Photoshop is equal, but certain features are not accessed identically.

Terms Used in this Book

The term *drag* in this book means to hold down the primary mouse button and move the onscreen cursor. This action is used in Photoshop to create a marquee selection, and to access tools on the toolbox flyout. On the Macintosh, dragging is also used to access *pull-down menus* in version 7.x of the OS; Windows users do not need to hold the primary mouse button to access flyout menus and main menu commands.

Hover means to move your cursor onscreen without holding a mouse button. Hovering is most commonly used in Photoshop with the Magnetic Pen and Magnetic Lasso tools, and also with the Eyedropper tool when you're seeking a relative position in an image and the color value beneath the tool (the Info palette, F8, must be displayed to determine the values the Eyedropper reads). Hovering is also a new feature to the Macintosh System 8, where you no longer need to drag on menu items to reveal submenus.

Click means to press and release the primary mouse button once.

Double-click means to press quickly the primary mouse button twice. Usually you double-click to perform a function without the need to click an OK button in a directory window. Additionally, when you double-click on a tool in Photoshop's toolbox, the Options palette appears.

Shift+Click means that you should hold down the Shift key while you click with the primary mouse button.

CONVENTIONS USED IN THIS BOOK

Throughout this book, several conventions are used to clarify certain keyboard techniques and to help you distinguish certain types of text (new terms and text that you type, for example). These conventions are described next.

SPECIAL TEXT

Information you type is in **boldface**. This rule applies to individual letters, numbers, and text strings, but not to special keys, such as Enter (Return), Tab, Esc, or Ctrl(⌘).

New terms appear in *italic*. Italic text is used also for emphasis, as in "*Don't unplug your computer at this point.*"

CASE MAKES NO DIFFERENCE WITH MODIFIER KEY COMMANDS

In this book, you're often asked to use modifier keys instead of digging through the main menu structure of Photoshop 5 to access a command. Although you'll frequently find the shortcut listed with an uppercase letter (for example, "Press D to change the color selection boxes on the toolbox to their default values"), lowercase letters provide the same results. So when you see, "Press Ctrl(⌘)+V to paste the contents of the clipboard to a new layer", you can *indeed* use a lowercase "v"—there's no sense in holding Shift in addition to the *other* keys you'll need to hold with shortcuts!

WE USE NICKNAMES FOR WELL-KNOWN PRODUCTS

Inside Adobe Photoshop 5, Limited Edition would be an even larger book than it already is if every reference to a specific graphics product or manufacturer included the full brand manufacturer, product name, and version number. For this reason, you'll occasionally see Adobe Photoshop 5 referred to as simply "Photoshop" in the text of this book. Similarly, Adobe Illustrator is referred to as "Illustrator," and other products are mentioned by their "street names."

New Riders Publishing and the authors acknowledge that the names mentioned in this book are trademarked or copyrighted by their respective manufacturers; our use of nicknames for various products is in no way meant to infringe on the trademark names for these products. When we refer to an application, it is usually the most current version of the application, unless otherwise noted.

CONTENTS AT A GLANCE

The authors recommend that you use *Inside Adobe Photoshop 5, Limited Edition* as a reference guide, but it was also written as a sequential, linear, hands-on tutorial. And this means that you might benefit most from the information in the book by reading a little at a time, from the first chapter to the last. We are aware, however, that this is not the way everyone finds information—particularly in an integrating graphics environment such as Photoshop's, where one piece of information often leads to a seemingly unconnected slice of wisdom. For this reason, most chapters offer complete, self-contained steps for a specific topic or technique, with frequent cross-references to related material in other chapters. If you begin reading Chapter 6, for example, you will learn a complete area of image editing, but you can build on what you've learned if you thoroughly investigate Chapter 17, as well.

PART I: STROLLING BEFORE RUNNING

In Chapter 1, "Getting Acquainted with Computer Graphics and Terms," you'll become familiar with *why* things work the way they do in Photoshop 5 and other programs. What is a pixel and how do you measure one? What is anti-aliasing and why is it good for your Photoshop work? These and dozens of other questions are answered for both the novice and the experienced user who never had the time to dig deeply into calculus and geometry before getting into Photoshop. Once you understand what's "under the hood," you can make Photoshop do practically anything you want it to do.

Chapter 2, "Getting Stock Images," shows you how to get real-world images into your computer in digital format. It's fun painting in Photoshop, but it's even more fun to retouch a picture of Uncle Fred, or enhance an enchanted sunset scene. This chapter covers the most basic of digital image acquisition methods, from PhotoCD to digital cameras.

Chapter 3, "Customizing Photoshop 5," deals with the reality that Adobe Systems can't predict the working preferences of Susan or Mike. Therefore, you can turn Photoshop 5 into your *personal* Photoshop 5 by investigating the options for cursor display, clipboard output, palette arrangement, unique and personal brush tips, global gamma correction, ICC profiles, and more. Everything you need to know to make Photoshop 5 as comfortable as your favorite sofa can be found in Chapter 3.

In Chapter 4, "The Photoshop Test Drive," the authors invite you to experiment with an image, and in the process, learn about the traditional and new features in Photoshop. As the title suggests, you're driving in this chapter without totally familiarizing yourself with the tools and options. But that's okay; the image you'll use can't be permanently ruined because it's on CD (a read-only medium), and we've prefaced this excursion with the recommendation that there's no right or wrong way to experiment. Discovery is the key concept in this chapter, thinly covering a healthy serving of *fun*!

PART II: BASIC MAGIC USING PHOTOSHOP

Chapter 5, "Working with New Features," is devoted to finding, and then putting to practical use, the features that are new to Photoshop. Learn about the enhanced Type Tool dialog box, the Freeform Pen tool, the History palette, Layer Effects, and more. Also learn what these new features and tool are good *for*, through step-by-step assignments.

Chapter 6, "Selections, Layers, and Paths," is a must-read for users of all skill levels. Selections can be created in at least five different ways in Photoshop 5, and choosing the best method for a specific image can be a design challenge. Work through this chapter, and you'll have a good 50 percent of Photoshop's power tucked under your belt.

Chapter 7, "Retouching a Photograph," highlights the tools and features that can produce a dramatic change in an image. Did you ever think that you could flawlessly remove a finger from the face of someone who is posed awkwardly? This chapter begins the discussions of and techniques used in invisible image retouching. Don't miss it.

PART III: INTERMEDIATE MAGIC AND PHOTOSHOP

You know the basic tools by the time you reach this part of the book, so it's time to move on and experiment with the sort of image manipulation that could earn you a prize.

Chapter 8, "Restoring Heirloom Photographs," takes a look at three photos that were taken years ago. Each image has something wrong with it, from liquid stains to cracks in the photo's emulsion. Learn how to cope with these precious yet flawed images, and bring them back to present-day beauty using the techniques described in Chapter 8.

In Chapter 9, "Creating Surrealistic Images," you step into a different world of imaging, specifically that of photographic, surreal compositions. Learn techniques that make the seemingly impossible an everyday reality. Show your audience that an image sometimes needs to be examined at different levels, all because you know how to twist reality—in a convincing way—using Photoshop's features.

Chapter 10, "Working with Mixed Media," explores the use of physical media as the foundation of a digital creation. We take a humble pen-and-ink drawing in this chapter, pass it through a scanner, clean up the image in Adobe Streamline, and finally embellish the artwork by using paint and sampled textures. This chapter represents the state-of-the-art with respect to traditional cartooning, so don't miss out on the fun!

Chapter 11, "Using Different Color Modes," reaches beyond the typical RGB image to show you different color modes and how to make the best manual conversions between color modes. Need a Duotone for an assignment? Do you need to accurately convert an RGB image to grayscale mode? How about a sepiatone or rotogravure-style image? See how to accomplish different effects through different color modes in this chapter.

Chapter 12, "Creating a Photorealistic Fantasy," shows you how to integrate modeled images with photographic ones to make an out-of-this-world movie poster with laser pistols and ugly aliens…the whole nine yards. Also gain experience with selection tools and Photoshop's Layer Mask feature.

In Chapter 13, "Creating a 'Perfect' Image," you're treated to some techniques for performing something so obvious and yet dramatic, the results can be described as nothing short of flawless. Get into the "invisible mending" train of thought as you replace a boring sky in an otherwise beautiful image, to come up with the *perfect* photo.

PART IV: EXTENDED USES FOR PHOTOSHOP

Chapter 14 is a mind-blowing, fantasy documentation on "Making Things Appear Small." If you've ever wanted to reduce the size of a person (such as your boss) in an image, do *not* miss the steps in this chapter. Advanced selection techniques and color correction are only two of the highlights in this fun, fantasy chapter.

Chapter 15, "Working Between Applications," addresses the reality that professional designers own more than a single application. How do you make Illustrator, for example, work with Photoshop to retouch a "text heavy" composition? The secrets and the steps are shown in this chapter for making applications work together, to arrive at a piece that displays the best features of all the applications used.

Chapter 16, "Creatively Working with Filters," is *not* your typical ride through all of Photoshop's filters (there are 92 of them in version 5, BTW). So what's this chapter all about? You'll learn how to match the best image to the right filter, how to partially apply a filter to an image, and basically put *yourself*, not a filter, in the driver's seat when you're creating something.

In Chapter 17, "Special Effects and Photoshop," you'll learn how to take a person out of his clothes (*in an image*, okay?), to create an "invisible man" effect. Additionally, you'll see how to graft a face—belonging to a man who tendered a model release to the author and you—onto the body of someone we'll pretend did *not* sign a model release. You can do really weird things when you place a face on a different body, and this chapter encourages you to do this!

PART V: PUBLISHING AND BEYOND

Chapter 18, "Outputting your Input," concentrates on the methods and techniques for getting the very best hard copy from an onscreen image. Your work should often lie outside the computer, so you're going to need to know about dot gain, PostScript output, film recorders, color separations, and Photoshop options for outputting your creative input.

Chapter 19, "Creating Graphics for the Web," shows you how Photoshop can be a powerhouse for creating onscreen documents. This chapter takes you through creating seamless tiling textures, making navigation buttons, and the concept process of what makes a Web site an attention-getting one.

Chapter 20, "Building Animations," is for the ambitious designer who wants to tap into Photoshop's Actions capability to edit still frames from an animation. Helper applications—animation *compilers*—are provided on the Companion CD, as are still frames you can work with in Photoshop. Follow the examples, and before you know it, you'll have an AVI or QuickTime movie prepared!

Part VI: Advanced Photoshop Techniques

In Chapter 21, "Simulating the Depth of Field in an Image," you'll learn how to put the finishing touches on a composition consisting of three different images—all of them in perfect focus. Sometimes, getting selections trimmed down to perfection and color balancing are not enough to create a convincing scene. Often, as you'll see in this chapter, selectively throwing the background and foreground of a composition out of focus makes the piece look as though it was photographed using a medium aperture lens setting. Create your own f-stops, using the tricks in this chapter!

Chapter 22, "Creating Reflections and Shadows," concentrates on another important aspect of photorealism and how to achieve it in your work. Shadows and reflections are as important to a photorealistic design as color, perspective, and composition. Learn about exciting new third-party filters for automating shadow creation, and get the scoop on how to make a reflection of an object on a shiny surface.

"Playing with Perspective" is both the title and the theme of Chapter 23. In this chapter, art meets photography, and they both win! See how to create an image in the style of M.C. Escher, where the "correct" perspective is relative to the people in the scene, and not to the viewer of the scene. Learn in this chapter how to create the impossible while retaining absolute photographic realism.

Chapter 24, "Making Your Own Chrome Lettering," is a study in painting in Photoshop. Learn why reflective objects such as chrome lettering appear the way they do, and then get hands-on guidance on how to replicate the "Chrome Look" by using Photoshop's tools. Your work will be an eye-catcher and you'll gain valuable insights into photorealism in this chapter.

In Chapter 25, "The Authors' Favorite Third-Party Plug-Ins," you'll see how some traditional third-party plug-ins for Photoshop can be used to produce outstanding work. You'll also work with advanced technology filters to produce image backgrounds of skies with only a click or two. And you'll learn how to trim around a person's hair accurately and effortlessly, and how to make a photorealistic composition using only one plug-in and Photoshop 5's set of features. Chapter 25 is a comprehensive "book" in and of itself on the hows, whys, and whens of third-party plug-in filters.

PART VII: THE BACK O' THE BOOK

Don't you hate reaching the end of a good book, only to find that the authors skimped on the research they put into it?! Everyone who works with a computer has a natural curiosity about where to learn more, where to find the best sources for more tools, and what stuff means when they read it out of context.

This is precisely what the *Inside Adobe Photoshop 5 Companion CD* and the *Limited Edition CD* are all about. On the CDs, you will find a number of important resources for your continuing adventures in Photoshop, long after you've poured through the pages in this book:

- **Resource files for the chapter examples.** We recommend that you work through the steps shown in this book, using files (carefully prepared by the authors) that demonstrate specific procedures and effects. The files, located in the EXAMPLES folder on the Companion CD, are platform-independent and can be used on any Macintosh or Windows system with Photoshop 5 installed. Sorry, Photoshop 5 itself is *not* included on the Companion CD! You need to bring *some* ingredients in the recipe for imaging fame and fortune to the party yourself!

- **The Inside Adobe Photoshop 5 Online Glossary.** This Acrobat PDF file contains color examples, shortcuts, definitions, and other material pertaining to this book, to Photoshop, and to computer graphics in general. We recommend that you install the OnLine Glossary on your system, and then launch Adobe Acrobat Reader 3 when you need a quick explanation of a technique or interface element in your Photoshop work.

- **Fonts, textures, and scenes in Windows and Macintosh formats, a stupendous collection of resource materials, and more.** The authors have produced a fairly extensive collection (in our opinion) of frequently needed items for Web pages, traditional publication, and other types of media construction. Check out the documentation and the license agreement—FST-7.pdf—in the BOUTONS folder on the Companion CD; these are completely unique, one-of-a-kind, Photoshop-oriented files and programs.

- **The "Fonts, Scenes, Textures, Clip Art, and Close-Ups collection," Volume 8 on the Limited Edition CD.** The Boutons folder on the *Limited Edition CD* contains over 250 MB of ready-to-use 3D clip art, new fonts, new textures—everything to experiment with after you've exhausted the volume *7* files on the *Inside Photoshop 5 Companion CD*! Check out the FST-8.pdf Acrobat document in the BOUTONS folder to see thumbnails of all the goodies in this folder.

- **Shareware, demo versions of working programs, and utilities provided on the Companion CD are hand-picked items the authors have used and that we recommend.** There are certain restrictions on some of the shareware, and please don't confuse "shareware" with "freeware." If you find something on the Companion CD that is useful in your professional work, please read the Read Me file in the folder where you found the utility or file, and register (pay a small fee) to the creator of the program.

- **In the Appendix, instructions for installing Acrobat Reader 3 for the Macintosh and Windows.** You'll be missing out on a lot of fun, useful stuff on the Companion CD if you don't install or already own Acrobat Reader 3. Make sure that this folder is one of the first you visit on the CD.

Last, but certainly not least, don't overlook the special discount offers you'll find at the back of the book. These offers can save you hundreds of dollars!

No One is Perfekt

Forget the disclaimer in this book that says that the information is presented to you "as is." "As is" doesn't do you, the reader, any good if we've made a slip-up in this book, or other books by The Boutons. So what we've done is created a branch of The Boutons' Web site that is exclusively devoted to corrections for *all* our books. The address is http://www.boutons.com, and then click on the Updates button. The corrections are posted as soon as we learn of an error and, as written on our site, the updates include text surrounding the error, so finding the error in the book is very easy. You might want to print the Updates page, fold the pages in half, and tuck them in the book.

All of the above does *not* mean Macmillan and The Boutons are going to leave corrections to their online format. We will get corrections into our books as soon as there is a future printing of a book. We simply want you to have the goods as soon as possible, and the Web makes this effort a reality.

FOLKS JUST LIKE YOU

Chapter 3 is intended to help you prepare Photoshop 5 for your personal use, and we think it's only fair to tell you what *the authors* used to prepare this book and the CDs. Nothing out of the ordinary—we used Photoshop 5, a few outside applications, and systems configured to what we believe go from high-end to modest specifications. For the photographic images, we used available lighting most of the time, a 35mm SLR camera, and family and friends as patient subjects. We believe that business professionals will see where these examples can lead in their own work, and that the novice won't be intimidated by a super-polished compendium of imaging work. The systems include a dual Pentium II 266 mHz with 256 MB of RAM running Windows NT; Pentium 166 mHz machines with 128 MB of RAM, running Windows NT and Windows 95; and a PowerMacintosh 8500 with 96 MB of system RAM, running System 8. All machines have 200–500 MB of empty hard disk space on hard disks of different sizes.

Electronic imaging is such a wonderful, magical thing that it's impossible to keep the child in us quiet. For that reason, many of the examples in this book are a little whimsical—they stretch reality a tad, in the same way you'll learn to stretch a pixel or two, using Photoshop. We want to show you some of the fun we've had with a very serious product, and hope that perhaps we will kindle or fan the flame of the creative spark in you, as well.

Got your Pepsi, your Scotch tape, Kleenex, and Photoshop 5 handy? Let us get started, then…

PART I

STROLLING BEFORE RUNNING

CHAPTER 1

GETTING ACQUAINTED WITH COMPUTER GRAPHICS AND TERMS

This chapter is not a glossary, nor is it intended to insult your intelligence. It is not "the beginner's chapter," nor is it a collection of hands-on tutorials that explain a principle behind Photoshop.

Terrific. So what is this chapter? There are very few professional designers who attended school to master computer graphics. Most of us, like the author, attained a certain level of proficiency with Photoshop, PageMaker, Illustrator and other applications through the process known as bootstrapping. Bootstrapping is where you're in the middle of a process, you don't quite know how to reach the end of the process, the answers aren't in your past experience, but somehow you intuitively figure out an answer. "Trial and error" is the vehicle for bootstrapping.

Let's suppose you don't have the time for bootstrapping yourself into mastering Photoshop or the field of computer graphics in general.

Wouldn't a chapter that explains fundamental concepts be worth your time? That is exactly what this chapter is all about—an attempt at filling in, right from the beginning, the answers to questions that will come your way as you read more of this book!

WHAT TYPES OF COMPUTER GRAPHICS ARE THERE?

Essentially, there are two different types of computer graphics:

- *Vector graphics* are resolution-independent, get their form through parametric equations, consist of an outline and a fill, and must eventually be displayed as a bitmap, whether shown onscreen or printed to a page. The reason they must be displayed is that equations mean nothing unless we can see the product of those equations. You'll find vector graphics in such programs as CorelDRAW and Adobe Illustrator.

- *Bitmap graphics*, also called *raster graphics*, are a "quilt" of pixels that make up a recognizable image. Bitmap graphics are *resolution-dependent*; any given bitmap image contains a finite number of pixels. You'll find bitmap graphics in such programs as Adobe Photoshop and Paint Shop Pro.

In Figure 1.1 you can see an example of a small bitmap graphic and a vector line that was determined by a simple math equation.

Bitmap graphic   **Vector graphic**

FIGURE 1.1   *Bitmap and vector graphics belong to two different types of computer graphics.*

With the exception of paths in Photoshop, which are nonprinting, freeform vector guides, everything you do in Photoshop belongs to the bitmap family of computer graphics. The concentration in this chapter, therefore, is on bitmaps: how they are created, what they are constructed of, what amount of color you can place in them, and so on. Our travels begin with the building block of the bitmap graphic, the pixel.

THE PICTURE ELEMENT PLACEHOLDER

The *pixel*, short for *pic*ture *el*ement, is the smallest whole unit of bitmap graphics you have to work with. A pixel has two distinguishing characteristics:

- It has a position relative to other pixels in a bitmap image.
- It has a color capability that we measure in bits.

With the exception of certain television broadcast standards, pixels are square in shape. The size of a pixel is completely relative. Asking how large a pixel is compares to asking how large a slice of pizza is; it depends on how many slices make up the whole pizza.

IMAGE RESOLUTION

To better quantify a pixel's place in a bitmap image, we often refer to the *resolution* of an image. This fractional amount is usually expressed as *pixels per inch*. The resolution tells us how many pixels are in an inch, and if we know the dimensions of an image, then we can tell precisely how many pixels are in the image. For example, if an image is one square inch, and the resolution of the image is 8 pixels/inch, we can conclude that there are 64 pixels in the entire image. If there are 16 pixels per inch, the same sized image would contain 256 pixels. Neither 8 nor 16 pixels per inch can create meaningful artwork because the resolution is too low for our eyes. In Figure 1.2 you can see an enlargement of a ruler, and how pixels are measured to come up with the resolution of an image. Note that the image at the far right was created at 72 pixels/inch, the resolution of monitor screens—and it looks fine.

In order to tell a co-worker or a pressman how large a bitmap image is, you need to describe both the physical dimensions and the resolution. Which leads us to the three ways to describe the size of a bitmap image.

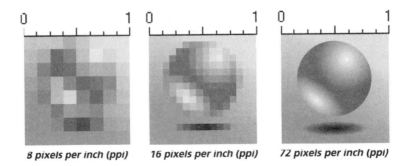

8 pixels per inch (ppi)   16 pixels per inch (ppi)   72 pixels per inch (ppi)

FIGURE 1.2   *The resolution of a bitmap image can be expressed as the number of pixels per inch.*

NOTE

The author somewhat chauvinistically chose the American unit of inches to define resolution, but pixels per centimeter is an equally legitimate means of measuring resolution.

HOW MANY PIXELS ARE IN AN IMAGE?

For high-quality reproduction work, images need to be large. How large? It depends on the line screen of the printing press and also on the physical dimensions of the image. For example, an image that is 2" high and 3" wide, printed at 266 pixels per inch, must be 532 pixels high and 798 pixels wide, for a total of 424,536 pixels in the image. So far, we have two different expressions for the image:

- The resolution and dimensions
- The absolute pixel count for the image

Photoshop will tell you the resolution and number of pixels in an image if you hold Alt(Opt) and click on the Document Sizes field on the status line (Macintosh: on the bottom left of the image window scroll bar).

There is a third method for describing the size of an image, and this is the *saved file size*, as measured in KB or MB. The only catch here is that the file size of an image depends on that image's color capability. A grayscale image, for example, is one third the file size of an equivalent RGB color image, or one quarter the size of a CMYK file. So, in describing the saved file size of an image, we must go back to the second of the pixel's two qualities: the amount of data stored in the pixel.

COLOR DEPTH (COLOR CAPABILITY)

There are several different color depths that we use with images every day. Associated with color depths are the "street names" for the organization of this color data; Photoshop calls different color organizations *color modes*, or *color spaces*. Do not confuse color capability with color mode; a *color depth* is the maximum amount of data a pixel can store, whereas a *color mode* expresses the maximum amount of color data that can be saved to a file format. Think of color mode as a container into which you put color-capable pixels. You can, for example, save a small amount of color data in a large container, but you cannot save a large amount of color data in a small container.

Figure 1.3 is a chart of the color modes you'll find easily accessible in Photoshop; in the right column, you can see the color capability of pixels found in each mode.

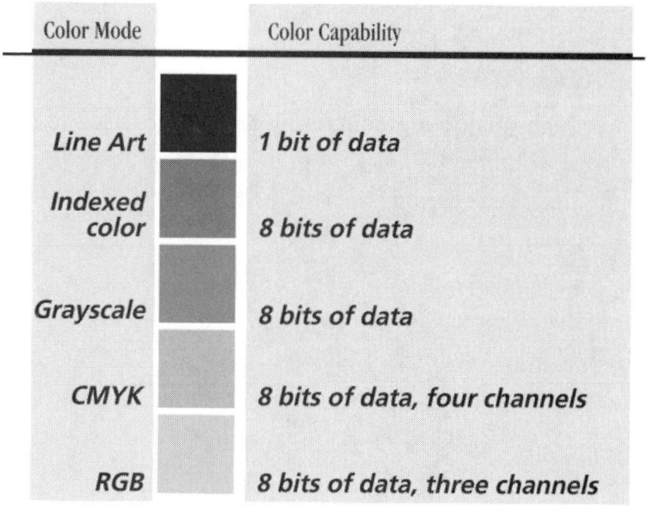

Color Mode	Color Capability
Line Art	1 bit of data
Indexed color	8 bits of data
Grayscale	8 bits of data
CMYK	8 bits of data, four channels
RGB	8 bits of data, three channels

FIGURE 1.3   *Color modes all have a specific color capability.*

Let's examine color capability from the ground up, beginning with the smallest amount of data a pixel can hold.

LINE ART

You might recognize the name *line art* from a scanner setting. This color capability is precisely one bit per pixel. Another name for line art is *bitmap*—literally a map of pixels, each of which contains one bit of color information. If we think about this one, a single bit of information can indicate either an on or an off state; the electrical current is there, or it's not. This means that there are two possible colors for a line art image—white (the current is on) or black (the current is off).

Line art is commonly thought of as consisting of diagrams, pen-and-ink draw-ings, and so on. Photoshop, however, can reduce *any* type of image to line art, with options as to how the conversion is performed. In Figure 1.4 you can see a photographic image of a gumball machine that is now line art; although our eyes tend to visually integrate the data to see some shades of gray, there are either white or black areas in the image. The image was reduced to line art by a process called *error diffusion*, which is something we'll get to later in this chapter.

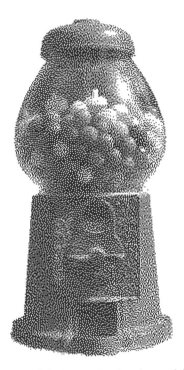

FIGURE 1.4 *Line art, or bitmap mode for images, has the color capability of 1 bit per pixel...on or off.*

Obviously, there is more to computer graphics than line art bitmaps. In the fol-lowing section we'll take a look at the next rung up on pixel color capability, the indexed color image.

INDEXED COLOR

More than a decade ago, a need to be able to send and receive high-quality images through bulletin boards (BBSes) and online services such as CompuServe and

AOL was identified. Indexed color images have a maximum color capability per pixel of 8 bits. If we take the binary "on/off" switch of 2, to the power of 8, we see that the maximum number of colors for an indexed color image is 256.

But indexed color images are not simply another color mode. The structure of an indexed color image is as follows:

- A header in the image file contains a look-up table.

- The pixels in the image are assigned an index number that corresponds to explicit color values in the file's look-up table.

This arrangement makes the file size of an indexed color image quite small, ideal for passing along computer-to-computer communications. A description, in PlainSpeak, of the way an indexed color image works might go something like this:

"Hi, I'm an indexed color image. I'm about to be deciphered by Photoshop. Photoshop looks in the header of my file and sees that, for example, color register #212 for the image is a mixture of Red equal to 63 on a brightness scale of 0 to 255, Green equals 189, and Blue equals 177. Color register #212 is a pale sea green, and everywhere in the image that a pixel is tagged with the number 212, Photoshop will display this color."

In Figure 1.5 you can see an enlarged image that is indexed. The callouts tell us (and the application reading the image) which color values correspond to specific color register numbers.

You can see the economy with which an indexed color image is constructed; there is no need for the host application to look up a complex string of color values. The application takes a look at the index, takes a look at what a specific color is made of, and then displays the color.

The downside of indexed color images is twofold:

- Photoshop's tools are uncooperative when working with a limited palette of 256 colors. Many tools, such as opacity and soft-tipped brushes, will not work at all on an indexed color image. This is because a greater palette of colors than 256 is required for Photoshop to perform sophisticated, complex image editing.

- Most pictures you take in the real world consist of many more colors than 256. An indexed color image is a fair, yet intrinsically inaccurate representation of what you can see in life.

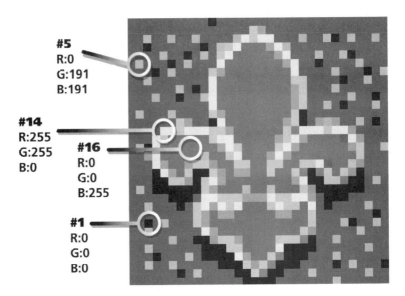

#5
R:0
G:191
B:191

#14
R:255
G:255
B:0

#16
R:0
G:0
B:255

#1
R:0
G:0
B:0

FIGURE 1.5 *An indexed color image is sort of a "paint by the numbers" scheme for arranging and decoding color values.*

Now, a 256-color image header (look-up table) in a file seems to be of a comfortable size for quick display of the indexed color image and for sending it across the Internet. It was decided that a look-up table of more than 256 colors would present some problems, however; the header of the file would become ungainly in size, and any speed issues would be negated. Therefore, a different type of organization for images, called the *color channel image,* was created. Let's begin exploring color channel images with the smallest of them, the grayscale image.

THE GRAYSCALE CHANNEL IMAGE

Grayscale images fit into a category of their own. Although they can contain only 256 different brightness levels, they are not organized as indexed color images are. A grayscale image has a single "color" channel called Black, and all the tones you see in the image are represented by 256 different intensities of black. A grayscale image has a bit depth of 8 bits/pixel.

As a user, you will find that except for color application features, all of Photoshop's tools work the same with grayscale images as they do with other color channel images. Feathering, anti-aliasing, soft-tipped brushes—everything you can do to a color channel image you can do to a grayscale channel image.

THE COLOR CHANNEL IMAGE

Channels are an interesting phenomenon within the structure of high-quality images. Instead of indexing specific color values to be displayed, color channel images are divided into separate "layers" of brightnesses, each corresponding to a primary color. For example, an RGB color image contains three color channels, each of which can contain up to 256 brightness levels. Because color is additive, the composite, the "sandwich" of these color channels, displays the complete color image.

Because each color channel in an RGB color image can contain 2 to the 8th power of different tones, and there are three channels, we often refer to RGB images as 24-bit/pixel images (2 to the 24th power is 16.7 million unique colors).

Two other color modes in Photoshop use color channels in their color organization: LAB color, and CMYK color both use channels of brightnesses to form a composite image. In Figure 1.6, you can see the "sandwich" of color channels that go into the composite of the flower image.

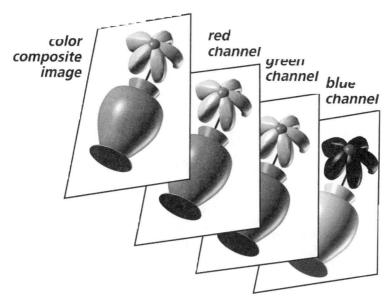

FIGURE 1.6   *Color channel images use the combined brightness of the channels to create the composite image.*

If you'd like to check out the color arrangement in Photoshop, follow these steps:

1. Load the Flower.tif image in Photoshop.

2. Press F7 to display the Layers grouped palette, and then click on the Channels tab.

3. Click on each of the color channel thumbnails to see what contributions each channel makes to the overall image.

Bear in mind that color is additive; this means, for example, that the gold flower in the image is a combination of red and green channel brightnesses. Blue doesn't weigh into the composite color of the flower; therefore, you'll see black in the blue channel over the area of the flower. Conversely, you will see brightness, signifying color contribution, in the same areas in the red and green color channels.

Figure 1.7 is intended to demonstrate how primary, RGB colors blend to make up the composite color. Note that when full intensity of red, green, and blue coincide, white is the resulting color.

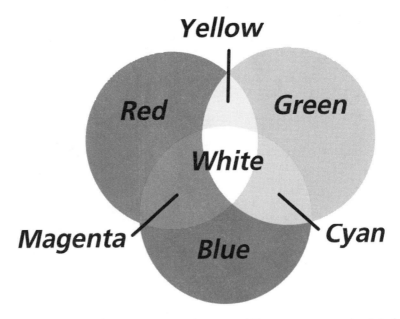

FIGURE 1.7   *Your eyes and your monitor use red, green, and blue components to make all shades of colors. The RGB color mode is closest to the way we see light, and it is an additive color model.*

CMYK COLOR MODE

Cyan, magenta, yellow, and black are the printing inks used to make high-quality color publications. Photoshop enables you to preview and to convert an RGB image to CMYK color mode, but you might notice a reduction in color quality when you do this. The reason? Although CMYK color mode uses four channels, each of which contains 256 brightness levels, the *color space* of CMYK color is not as large as that of RGB color. Printing inks cannot fully capture everything you see in RGB mode. So even though more capability for colors is expressed in CMYK mode, it is not as visually rich as RGB.

CMYK is sort of a funny color mode to display on a monitor. CMYK color mode is based around subtractive pigments; you mix all the colors together and you get black. A monitor's phosphors emit light and are additive in nature, however, so when Photoshop shows you an image in CMYK mode, it's only a simulation of what the image would look like if it were printed to paper, using inks. Black is always a key plate when printing to CMYK; cyan, magenta, and yellow do not truly make black because of intrinsic inconsistency in physical pigment. Therefore, the "colors" we are really talking about in CMYK mode are cyan, magenta, and yellow.

Figure 1.8 shows the CMY color model and the resulting colors when the primary colors overlap.

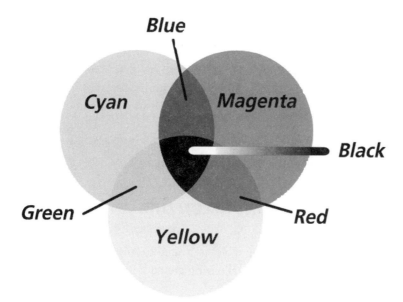

FIGURE 1.8 *CMYK color mode is subtractive. Adding all the primary colors together results in black.*

LAB COLOR

Photoshop offers another color space, LAB color, which is a color channel-type image but is built entirely differently than RGB color. LAB color consists of three channels, each containing yet pixels of 256 different tone capabilities, but the channels are not split into a "user friendly" order. LAB color mode consists of a Lightness channel and two chromacity channels, A and B. You'll see in Chapter 11, "Using Different Color Modes," how the Lightness channel comes in handy for converting color images to grayscale mode.

LAB color is a device-independent color space; theoretically the same colors that you see on your monitor can be expressed in LAB mode on a color print, or even on a silk-screen design. LAB color is slightly larger in its color space than RGB color. When Photoshop performs conversions between RGB, CMYK, and other color modes, it uses LAB color as the intermediate phase because LAB's color space engenders all other color modes; no color is lost when colors are converted through LAB mode.

COLOR REDUCTION METHODS

If you take a close look at a GIF or some other indexed color image, you might notice one of two things:

- The image has a faint pattern running through it.
- The image has pixels scattered through it.

Both of these visual phenomena are caused by a process called dithering. *Dithering* is a method by which colors that cannot be displayed in a limited color palette are "faked"; neighboring pixels tend to blend in the mind's eye and produce a color that isn't actually in the image. If you're considering posting a GIF image on a Web page, please read on, so that you can decide for yourself which method of color reduction is best for your work.

THREE METHODS FOR PALLETIZING AN IMAGE

When an image goes from a high color capability to a low one, colors must be discarded, and a palette (look-up table) is created for the new image. The form of color reduction and the type of palletizing are addressed here as separate issues. First, the color reduction.

Photoshop offers three methods by which you can reduce the number of colors in an image:

- Nearest color (also called *None*, or *no dithering*)

- Pattern dithering

- Diffusion dithering

It would be good if you'd work through the following set of steps because the screen figures in this book cannot show you what happens to color when it is reduced using these methods. Figure 1.9 is an image called Primitiv.tif, a 24-bit image you'll find in the Chap01 folder of the Companion CD; each object in this image has a unique color.

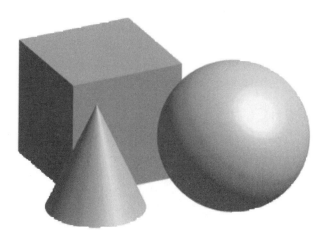

FIGURE 1.9   *The colors in this image need to be reduced to fewer tones. Which method will produce the most eye-pleasing results?*

Follow these steps to see which of the color-reduction methods Photoshop offers will produce the best image:

REDUCING COLOR IN AN IMAGE

1. Open Primitiv.tif from the Chap01 folder of the Companion CD.

2. Choose Image, Mode, and then choose Indexed Color.

3. In the Palette drop-down box, choose Uniform. Adaptive is generally the palletization method of preference, but a Uniform palette will help exaggerate the results you'll see here.

4. Choose None from the Dither Options drop-down list shown in Figure 1.10.

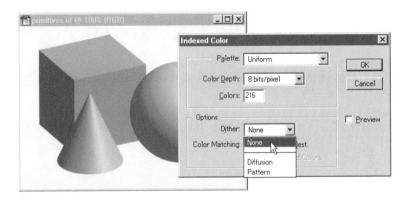

FIGURE 1.10 *No dithering forces the palletization of the image to the nearest neighboring colors—the closest match between the new palette and the original color space of the image.*

5. The colors in the image take on banding and do not represent the original image all that well, as shown in Figure 1.11.

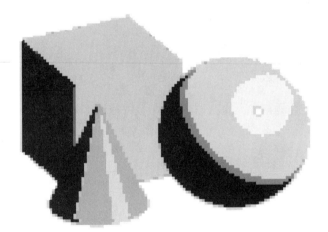

FIGURE 1.11 *Harsh banding is the result of reducing smoothly shaded image areas to the closest matching color in an indexed palette.*

6. Choose Pattern from the drop-down list and look at the image. Although Pattern dithering is a more sophisticated method of color reduction than no dithering at all, the pattern is somewhat of a distraction; the eye concentrates on the pattern more than on the visual content of the image, as you can see in Figure 1.12.

7. Choose Diffusion from the drop-down list. Diffusion dithering, also called *error diffusion*, provides a soft, inaccurate, but eye-pleasing version of the original image. As shown in Figure 1.13, diffusion dithering is clearly the most aesthetic of the color-reduction methods for images of this type.

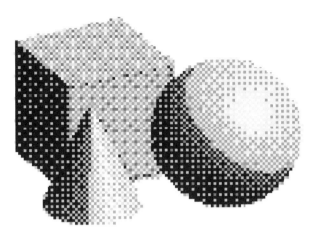

FIGURE 1.12 *Pattern dithering arranges available pixel colors into patterns that simulate the colors that are missing from the original.*

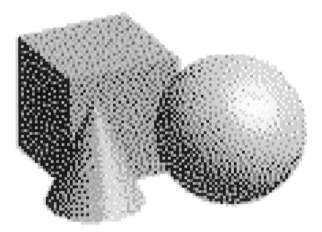

FIGURE 1.13 *Diffusion dithering scatters the "error" in color identity across the image, providing a "ground glass" sort of look for the Indexed color image.*

8. If you'd care to keep the image open, the following is a discussion of the palletizing methods Photoshop offers. You can preview them yourself onscreen.

DIFFERENT PALLETIZING OPTIONS

With the exception of Adaptive palletizing, covered later in this section, every palletizing option you have in Photoshop becomes a "forced fit" for the image you want to color reduce. Why? Because the palette options already have colors predefined for the image, and the color-reduction procedure simply tries to make the best match between the available palette colors and the original image colors.

SYSTEM PALETTE

This palette is different for Windows and the Macintosh. Each system has its own assortment of 256 predefined colors that it uses to display images and interface elements. In general, you should not use your system palette if you know that you're going to be editing or outputting your images on multiple platforms. The Macintosh has a hard time reading the Windows color palette and vice versa.

WEB

If you're designing for the Web, this choice of palletizing will provide the least amount of dithering. Both Netscape Navigator and MS-Internet Explorer have agreed on standard colors for the WWW's palette, and matching your image to this indexed palette of 216 colors ensures that your audience sees your piece the way it was created.

UNIFORM

The Uniform palette gives equal emphasis to every color in the spectrum. This is fine if you have a picture consisting of confetti or dozens of paint cans, but let's suppose that you have a moody sunset picture you want to palletize. The sunset picture will most certainly have heavy golds and oranges. Because the Uniform palette stresses all colors equally, however, there is bound to be more dithering in the image as the color-reduction process attempts to display all the glorious nuances of a sunset with a very limited number of unique golds and oranges.

ADAPTIVE

As the name implies, an adaptive color palette is not a fixed palette. When you use Adaptive palletization, the color palette will emphasize the predominant tones in the original image. In a picture of a sailboat on a lake, for example, there will be a small white sail and many, many different tones of water. The Adaptive palette will write as many different shades for the water as the palette will hold, and will not sacrifice color slots for colors that are not in the image (red or purple, for example).

If you're going to convert an image to indexed color, the best general way to go is to use an Adaptive palette and diffusion dithering. Depending on the image, the audience might not even know that they're looking at 256 unique colors or less!

ANTI-ALIASING AND RESAMPLING ARTWORK

Before you can understand anti-aliasing, you need to know what the term aliasing means in your work. Aliasing is the false presentation of visual data, and is the result of an application rendering an image area without enough visual information. In Figure 1.14, you can see a spaceship (the one at the top) whose outline is aliased—there are supposed to be curved and smooth diagonal lines around its outline, but instead there are stairsteps. *Anti-aliasing*—shown applied to the same spaceship at the bottom of Figure 1.14—is a method for accurately representing image data. This chapter takes you through both a working definition and the methods by which anti-aliasing is added to your work.

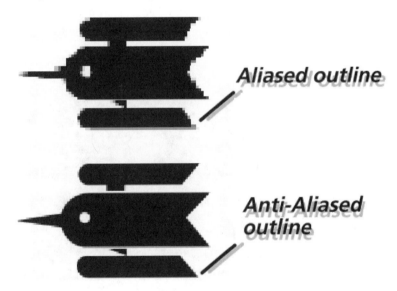

FIGURE 1.14   *Examples of aliased and anti-aliased artwork.*

IMAGE RESOLUTION AND GRANULARITY

The visual example of a checkerboard that extends into the horizon better demonstrates the effects of aliasing and anti-aliasing. To remove user input and simply show how an application handles anti-aliasing, let us say that this checkerboard scene is being rendered in a modeling application—you define the scene, and the application does the rendering work. The squares that are closest to the viewer are white or black; there is no ambiguity about the color of the large squares. As the squares diminish in size toward the horizon, however, each square is perceived using a fewer photoreceptors in the eye, until the horizon appears to be a solid tone instead of alternating colors. Your eye cannot distinguish clearly which squares are white and which are black because the *granularity*—the number of photoreceptors in your eye—is a fixed amount.

When this checkerboard scene is rendered by a computer application to bitmap format, the application performing the rendering has two choices to make: to alias the horizon, choosing either white or black at any given pixel, or to anti-alias, averaging the color for a given pixel to create an image area closer to the way a human eye would see the actual scene.

In Figure 1.15, you can see a checkerboard extending into the horizon. Let's imagine that the square next to the call-out is a single pixel, a pixel whose size cannot change and can contain only one color.

FIGURE 1.15   *How can a single image pixel faithfully represent more than one color?*

The visual content at this point in the picture, however, consists of *more* than one color—there can be a number of white and black squares close to the horizon, with only a single image pixel to represent them. So, what's it going to be: a black or a white pixel? To make such a decision is called *aliasing*; if you fill this pixel with white, you're negating the black squares in this sample area. To reconcile the impossibility of filling a single pixel with more than one color, anti-aliasing of the scene fills the pixel with a shade of black, because in reality the pixel sample area should contain a blend of both black and white sample information.

Anti-aliasing can be added to artwork by most graphics applications on the following three occasions:

- When you make a brush stroke.

- When a brush stroke is made for you, as with a modeling/rendering application.

- When pixels are added to or deleted from an image. This is called *resampling*.

Anti-aliasing does more than simply reconcile pixel colors when the image information is too large to fit in a single pixel. The next section explores the way curves and diagonal lines—geometry that cannot realistically be displayed on a monitor—can be made smooth in appearance by anti-aliasing.

ANTI-ALIASING AND BRUSH STROKES

Curves and diagonal lines are particularly difficult for a monitor to display with image fidelity because a monitor, and the pixel framework of digital images, have no mechanism for displaying anything beyond a rectangular quiltwork of image elements. To keep edges of these geometric shapes smooth in appearance, anti-aliasing is used by applications to place pixels of different opacity along "problem areas" of curves and diagonal lines.

In Figure 1.16 you can see a pair of diagonal lines; the one at left has several pixels of different opacity that "fill in" the abrupt edges where the line is not perfectly parallel to the grid of pixels that make up the image. At right, an aliased version of the diagonal line shows harsh, unappealing "stairsteps."

A fair question at this point would be, "How does the application know where to put the different anti-aliased pixels?" The answer lies in averaging image area tones, and interpolating the correct shade of pixel to lie on the edge of the line or curve. We'll get into the various methods of interpolation shortly. In Figure 1.17, you can see a close up of a rounded shape, with and without anti-aliasing. At a close view, the outline of the anti-aliased shape looks fuzzy, but at 1:1 viewing resolution, the curve is both crisp and soft.

NOTE

Super-sampling is a term used in modeling applications to describe yet another type of anti-aliasing. The mechanism for super-sampling works like this: the user defines a specific size for the scene to be rendered. The application images the scene two times the requested size, holds the image in memory, and then creates the image at the requested size while averaging tones for the image's pixels from the larger image in memory. This super-sampling process can use more than one image in memory; you could request that an 8x image, a 4x image, and a 2x image should be used to average and calculate final pixel colors.

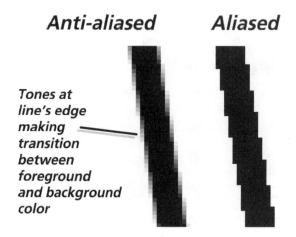

Anti-aliased   **Aliased**

Tones at line's edge making transition between foreground and background color

FIGURE 1.16   *Anti-aliasing makes a transition between foreground and background colors.*

Anti-aliased   **Aliased**

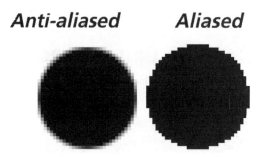

FIGURE 1.17   *Anti-aliasing interpolates—averages—the correct edge color for round shapes.*

If you zoom very closely to a diagonal line whose edges are anti-aliased, you will observe the following phenomenon: pixels at the edge of the line gradually comprise less line color and more image background color, the farther those pixels are from the line. In Figure 1.18, you can see callouts for the percentage mixture of anti-aliased pixels on the edge of a vertical line.

The idea behind anti-aliasing a shape you create is to make a smooth transition between the interior of the shape and its background.

In addition to the anti-aliasing that goes on in modeling and painting programs, a third type of anti-aliasing occurs when you resize a bitmap image. Applications are not quite intelligent enough to "know" what color to make additional pixels in your artwork, nor do they have the artistic intelligence to know how to reassign pixel colors when pixels are deleted from an image. In the following section we'll look at interpolation, and how color averaging can help keep artwork smooth in appearance when it's resized.

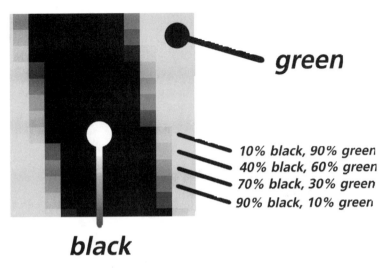

green

10% black, 90% green
40% black, 60% green
70% black, 30% green
90% black, 10% green

black

FIGURE 1.18 *Anti-aliasing is made up of a combination of foreground and background colors.*

INTERPOLATION AND AVERAGING

Suppose that you have a beautiful miniature painting made up of only nine pixels, three pixels on a side. You decide that you want to make the image twice its original size—twice its original height and width—to six pixels on a side, 36 pixels total. There are three methods by which an application can "think up" new pixels to go into the image:

- By creating pixels that are the nearest neighbor in color to the original pixel

- By sampling surrounding pixels in both a horizontal and vertical direction, and then creating a color average of the total sums for new pixels

- By sampling pixels in horizontal, vertical, and diagonal directions, and using a weighted average of the total colors for any given new pixel

Adobe Photoshop calls these three methods of interpolation *nearest neighbor,* *bilinear,* and *bicubic interpolation.* Other applications might have different names for these interpolations, but these are the three names we'll use here.

NEAREST NEIGHBOR

Nearest Neighbor calculation isn't actually a method of interpolation. The program chooses the same color value for neighboring pixels in an enlarged image as the original color found at any given pixel. Therefore, if the center of our hypothetical 3-by-3-pixel painting is 50% black, and we enlarge the painting to 200% size through nearest neighbor calculation, the center of the painting would contain four pixels that are 50% black. No anti-aliasing is produced by using nearest neighbor calculations because no color averaging—no new pixel colors— is added to the new image. You can see how this calculation is performed by a program in Figure 1.19.

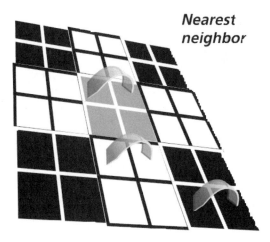

FIGURE 1.19 *Nearest neighbor calculation for new pixels uses the simplest math for reassigning picture elements.*

Nearest neighbor calculation is perfectly fine if your composition is rectangular, and you enlarge the image in multiples of 2 (200%, 400%, and so on). A more sophisticated procedure is required, however, when you're working with large images whose visual content is organic or photographic, and you want to enlarge or reduce the image to, say, 148% of its original size. Most modern image editing applications offer something called *bilinear interpolation*, described in the following section.

BILINEAR INTERPOLATION

A single pixel in a painting that is enlarged using bilinear filtering gets its destination color from the top, left, right, and bottom of its original position. These color readings of neighboring pixels are added together and divided by 4, and then the resulting color is applied to the new pixels in the image. In Figure 1.20 you can see how bilinear interpolation "looks" for new color information in our 3-by-3-pixel painting.

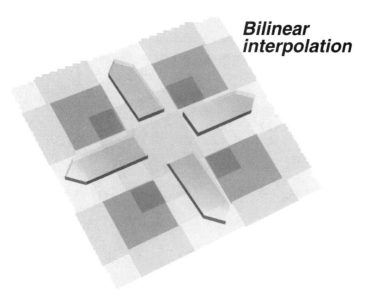

FIGURE 1.20   *Bilinear interpolation creates new pixels based on color averages from both the horizontal and vertical neighbors of the area to be resized.*

Bilinear interpolation produces what we'd call anti-aliased pixels within the new, enlarged image, because whole number values for new pixels are not possible. The resulting new pixels should, from an artistic as well as a mathematical point of view, represent *blends,* percentages, of neighboring pixels.

Although bilinear interpolation produces good anti-aliased pixels, it is not the most sophisticated interpreting method for resizing images. *Bicubic interpolation,* the most advanced method of calculating pixel color, is covered in the following section.

BICUBIC INTERPOLATION

If we think of the nearest neighbor assignment of pixels as being a one-dimensional sampling technique, then bilinear interpolation would be a square function—it looks across two dimensions for pixel data. *Bicubic interpolation* goes one step further in calculating new pixels: a pixel is assigned a new value based on information taken in horizontal, vertical, and diagonal directions, and then the sum is averaged with a preference for the predominating tones in the area—a *weighted* average.

Bicubic interpolation is the most processor-intensive resizing method, because it involves the most calculations, and the aesthetic results are also the most faithful to the original image. Whenever you resample an image, there will be some loss of focus within the image, but bicubic interpolation provides the most faithful of any method for creating new image date, or deleting and reassigning pixel colors. Figure 1.21 shows how bicubic interpolation works.

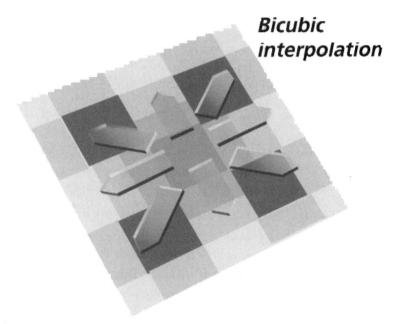

FIGURE 1.21 *Bicubic interpolation is the most artistically pleasing method for resampling an image.*

NOTE

Of the three methods for creating or deleting pixels during resizing, only bilinear and bicubic interpolation produce anti-aliasing. If your computer has the horsepower, and your application offers interpolation choices, choose bicubic for the best results, and then apply minor sharpening filtering if you feel it's necessary.

PROGRESSIVE CHANGES AND ANTI-ALIASING

There is a problem with resampling an image or image area too many times, and this problem is only partially connected to anti-aliasing. Pixel-based images are constructed of a finite number of placeholders, and whenever you change the total number of pixels you also create a change in the artwork. This type of change is progressive—as you resample, you build change upon change and there is no real path back to your original design.

In Figure 1.22, you can see a close-up of a very small sphere design at left. At right, the sphere has been resized (resampled) twice, and it's an out-of-focus blob.

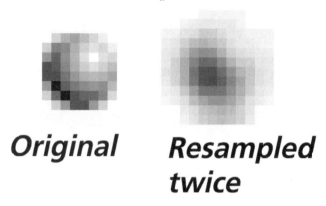

Original   **Resampled twice**

FIGURE 1.22   *Regardless of resampling techniques, multiple resampling progressively deteriorates the sharpness of an image.*

You will not witness such a great amount of deterioration when you resample larger images, but the change in pixel count will still tend to throw the design out of focus due to the averaging the application performs to add or discard pixels. The best strategy for keeping images you resample crisp in appearance is to know in advance what the final size of the image should be, and allow Photoshop to interpolate the selected area only once.

Anti-aliasing is necessary for creating refined artwork, because pixels are rectangular but the content of your artwork most likely is not rectangular. Anti-aliasing also reconciles the impossibility of a single pixel having more than one color value by averaging the colors into a composite tone. Finally, anti-aliasing intelligently reassigns image pixel colors when you enlarge or reduce an image, so that there are no abrupt color transitions, creating *artifacts* (false aliased samples) in your work.

SUMMARY

Color modes, pixels, anti-aliasing, color reduction, resampling images—all are part of your everyday work in Photoshop, although you seldom give it a second thought. But when you hit a creative stumbling block, it's nice to know why things work the way they do (or don't), and hopefully you've found some answers in this chapter to questions you might not even have asked yet.

Photoshop is fun, but it's not nearly as much fun when you don't have some images of your own to work with. Come along to Chapter 2, "Getting Stock Images," to see how you can get images from the outside world into that box in front of you!

Chapter 2

Getting Stock Images

Photoshop is most often used to enhance or combine existing images. The most obvious way to get the images you work with into Photoshop is to open an existing file or to buy some artwork in digital form from a stock agency, another artist, or a photographer. But what if the source materials you want to work with are not already in a digital format? How would you go about "converting" a physical thing, such as a photographic print or a button from a favorite dress, into the collection of pixels that make up a Photoshop document? As you'll learn in this chapter, there are at least five ways to move imagery taken from the real world into Photoshop.

- If you are an accomplished painter, you could use Photoshop's tools to paint a likeness of a physical object. This is perhaps the most basic method of getting an image into Photoshop, but it requires a great deal of time and skill to produce results that are both artistically pleasing and photorealistically accurate.

- You can use a common flatbed scanner to digitize artwork, a photograph, or even small objects. This option is discussed at length in this chapter.

- You can use a digital camera to acquire a digital image. We'll discuss this compara-tively new piece of technology in this chapter.

- You can use a transparency scanner to digitize a slide or a negative of a photograph. This method yields perhaps the best quality image to work with in Photoshop, but you cannot digitize artwork by using a transparency scanner.

- You can have photographs you've taken or commissioned put on a Kodak PhotoCD. This is the most common procedure for getting high-quality color or black-and-white images digitized at a low price, and PhotoCDs deserve attention in this chapter.

Because raw artistic talent is the primary element involved in painting images in Photoshop, this chapter covers only the four mechanical digitizing methods for bringing an image into Photoshop. This levels the playing field, and almost anyone, even with a modest budget, can afford the hardware required to "hook up Photoshop to the real world."

THE "RULES" FOR ACQUIRING AN IMAGE

Whether you use a scanner, a digital camera, or a transparency scanner, there is a common set of guidelines for acquiring an image that you should keep in mind before hitting the Scan button or clicking the shutter:

Your input should approximately equal your output.

What does this mean? It means that there is no point in "overscanning"—sampling more pixels than can possibly be rendered—to your output device. If you're unsure of what the dimensions and resolution of your output will be, it would be a good idea to ask the service that is outputting your file for guidance, or to check the documentation that came with your laser or inkjet printer for recommendations on how large a sample you need to take. You can also consult Chapter 18, "Outputting Your Input," for additional information on the resolution requirements of common output devices.

In the meantime, take a look at the following table to get a general idea of the settings you would use to get good printed results from printers of varying capabilities. Higher dpi values in column one correspond to more refined and better-looking output from common laser printers to expensive printers and printing presses. The table also assumes that you are scanning something that is approximately 4" by 6" in physical dimensions and that you want to output the image at a 1:1 size ratio. A 1:1 ratio means that the dimensions of the printed image are the same as the object you scan.

VARIOUS OUTPUT AND INPUT RESOLUTIONS

RESOLUTION OF PRINTED WORK	LINES PER INCH OUTPUT DEVICE USES	RECOMMENDED SCANNING RESOLUTION	FILE SIZE
300 dpi	45 lpi	90–100 samples/inch	570KB
600 dpi	95 lpi	170 samples/inch	1.99MB
1200 dpi	125 lpi	225 samples/inch	3.48MB
2450 dpi	133 lpi	266 samples/inch	4.86MB

As you can see, the sampling rate for input needs to be far less than the resolution of the output. The most common mistake users make when scanning images is to equate a pixel to a dot of toner or ink. As the chart indicates, the scanning resolution should be more or less two times the frequency of the *line screen* used to create commercial printed work. The only exception to this "times 2" rule is when your output is to a film recorder.

Unlike printers and presses that use line screens to print half-tone images created from dots of ink, film recorders produce continuous tone images by exposing film to light. Consequently, the total amount of information captured by the scanner is measured in saved file size, and saved file size is what determines the quality of film recorder output. The author has found that you can get a very decent 35mm slide from an image file that is at least 4 MB in size; the higher the saved file size, the better the image you receive. With larger-format film recorders that render, for example, a 4"×5" transparency, you should seriously consider scanning an image to yield at least a 14 MB file.

Acquiring images destined for the Web or other onscreen presentations requires far fewer of your computer's resources. This is because the resolution of the image file created only needs to match that of a monitor, which is typically 72 pixels/inch. A full-screen, RGB color mode graphic that measures 640 pixels by 480 pixels and is 72 pixels/inch is only 900 KB when saved to disk. The same image saved as a Grayscale mode image would only be a third that size—300KB.

When scanning, always scan to meet the requirements of your intended output device. For example, if you want to output the image to a printer or a film recorder, and use the image on a Web page, scan the material three times—once for each device. One size *never* fits all! As the saying goes in the imaging trade, "Get it right in the camera," which means "photograph only what you need through the lens." Similarly, you should get it right when you scan. You should not depend on Photoshop to resize images; resized bitmap images always suffer some loss of focus that can never truly be restored, even with Photoshop's magical sharpening filters.

Let's take a look first at the most common piece of hardware used for getting an image photo into Photoshop: the flatbed scanner.

EXAMINING THE FLATBED SCANNER

There was a time, only a few years ago, actually, when flatbed scanners were only for the richest of users, with scanner prices starting at about $1,200. These scanners were slow and noisy because three passes were required to sample an RGB image, one pass for each individual RGB component color—red, green, and blue. They were also extremely delicate. Bump the scanner and the scanning heads could come out of alignment, and your RGB scans would look as sharp as a comic book graphic.

Times have changed; you can now buy a single-element color scanner for around $200 (or less). And the quality of these scanners is terrific because they contain the same electronics as the more expensive scanners of a generation ago. The economics of all computer hardware is that the "early adopters" pay for the research and development of technology, and if you wait, you pay a significantly lower price for identical or even superior technology.

UNDERSTANDING REFLECTIVE SCANNING: SCANNING PHOTOS USING A FLATBED SCANNER

As remarkable as these new scanners are, the advice we are about to give may seem startling. The advice? Don't scan photographic prints. You should only use a flatbed scanner as a last resort, such as when the client does not have the negative of an image.

The problem with flatbed scanners is that they use a *reflective scanning* method to sample images. In short, flatbed scanners use a two-step process to gather samples. First, they direct a light source toward the opaque artwork, and then the scanner's "camera"—its array of photo-sensing sampling elements—records the pattern and characteristics of the light that has bounced (been reflected) back from the artwork. Figure 2.1 illustrates how light travels with reflective, flatbed scanning.

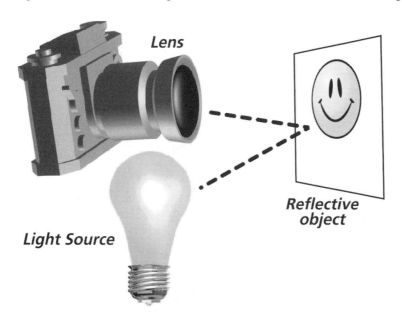

FIGURE 2.1   *Reflective scanning technology bounces light off the target image, and the light is then passed along to the digitizing element in the scanner.*

It's not immediately obvious that reflective, flatbed scanning presents a degraded version of the original image. This is because the print you scan isn't the original source—the *film negative* that was used to create the printed photograph is the true source. If you compare the digital image created by the flatbed scanner to one created by a transparency scanner that scans the actual negative, you'll find that scanning the negative produces superior results.

Brilliance is the name of the game. A scan of a photo of a brilliant flower cannot hope to look as bright onscreen as the same photo looked at as a 35mm slide. Why? Because reflective scanning loses color in the process, as light needs to travel twice as far to the digitizing element in the scanner. Additionally, you're a generation away from the original film when you scan a print. If you allow light to pass *through* the target image, brilliance is retained—you're actually *directing* light, colored light to be precise, at a photosensitive element.

You can see for yourself in Figure 2.2 how the flatbed scan stands up to the image produced by scanning a film negative. The top image was carefully scanned from a good photograph. The bottom image was taken from a PhotoCD. (A PhotoCD is made by scanning film negatives and then storing the image files in a proprietary file format on a CD-ROM disk.) Even though these images are in black and white, you can immediately see the difference. Compared to the PhotoCD image, the reflective flatbed scan suffers from blocked-in darker tones, and the whites are overpowering—delicate areas of near-white have been wiped out. You might say that the scan, and even the print of the negative of this image, has exagger-ated the contrast of the photo. And when contrast is increased, image content and detail are lost.

**Dock1.tif,
from a flatbed
scanner**

**Dock2.tif,
from a PhotoCD**

FIGURE 2.2 *Reflective scanning emphasizes the extremes in tonal distribution within a photograph, whereas transparency scanned PhotoCD images retain clarity in the tonal extremes as well as a good tonal balance in the midtones.*

If you'd like to witness the qualitative difference between a reflective scan and a transparency scan, open (in Photoshop) both the Dock1.tif and Dock2.pcd images from the Chap02 folder on the Companion CD. Dock1 is from a flatbed scanner, and Dock2 is from a PhotoCD.

Now, let's say that your client does not have the negative to Dock1.tif. You are forced to work with this image in Photoshop. Don't despair; with a few cosmetic touch-ups you can bring some life to the image, as you'll learn in the following steps:

ADJUSTING TONE, BALANCE, AND FOCUS FROM A SCANNED IMAGE

1. Open the Dock1.tif image from the Chap02 folder on the Companion CD. You might also want to open Dock2.psd as a reference for your work; open it at 512 by 768 pixel size.

2. With Dock1.tif in the foreground, press Ctrl(⌘)+L to display the Levels command.

3. Drag the midtone slider until the middle Input Levels field reads about 1.19, as shown in Figure 2.3. Doing this "opens up," *expands* the range of the midtones in the image. Most of the image's visual content is located in the midtones. In essence, you're allowing more of the midtone detail to show through in the picture, and also allowing for more color to be added to the overall picture later.

TIP

The first time you open a PhotoCD image in Photoshop, you'll be asked for a Source and a Destination. Click on the Source button, and choose pcd4050e.icm (.pf), click on OK, then click on Destination, and choose Adobe Monitor Settings.icm (Apple Standard), and click on Okay. This is the last time you'll need to specify these settings to open a PhotoCD file.

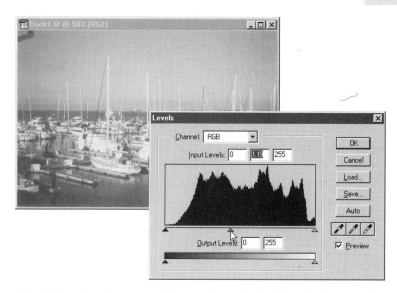

FIGURE 2.3 *The midtones in a scanned photograph are often blocked in, hiding image detail. The Levels command helps redistribute pixels in this zone to allow less contrast and thus greater detail.*

4. Click on OK, and then press Ctrl(⌘)+B to display the Color Balance command. The Dock1 image has an unwanted bluish cast that needs to be eliminated.

5. With the Midtones button clicked, drag the Yellow/Blue slider until the far-right Color levels box reads –33 or so.

6. Cyan is also unwanted in the image. Drag the Cyan/Red slider until the first Color Levels field reads +18, as shown in Figure 2.4. You've created a dramatic change in the overall feeling of the scanned photo; it's much more realistic now. Click on OK to apply the change.

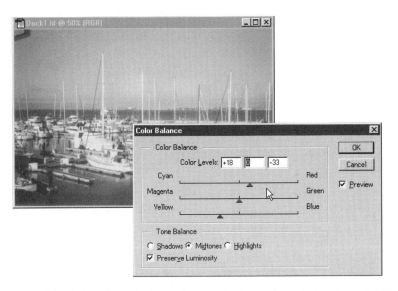

FIGURE 2.4 *Color shifts in the midtones can dramatically change the warmth and overall feeling of a color picture. Use the sliders in the Color Balance command to remove unwanted, predominant color casts.*

7. Press Ctrl(⌘)+U to display the Hue/Saturation command.

8. Drag the Saturation slider to about +23, and then drag the Lightness slider to about +3, as shown in Figure 2.5. There is plenty of denseness in this scanned print, and lightening the image, overall, helps bring out a little additional detail in the shadow areas. Notice that you can now see the reflections of some of the masts. Click on OK to apply the changes.

9. The focus of this image is pretty pathetic because the photo finisher didn't focus the negative properly on the photographic paper, and because the picture wasn't perfectly flat against the scanner's *platen* (glass imaging surface). Choose Filter, Sharpen, and then choose Unsharp Mask.

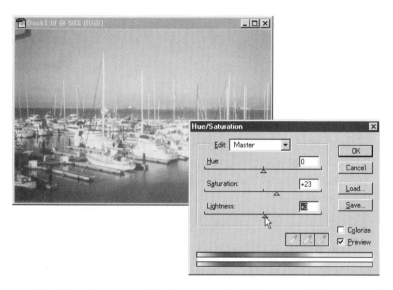

FIGURE 2.5 *Saturation and tonal density are a trade-off. Because you lightened the midtones in the image using the Levels command, there is now more "space" in the midtone pixels to add (to saturate) color.*

10. Drag the Amount slider to 39%, type **0.9** in the pixels field, and then type **1** in the Threshold field. These settings are the author's secret recipe for gently sharpening images that are 1.5 MB and lower in file size. In Figure 2.6, you can see the correct settings. Click on OK to apply the sharpening.

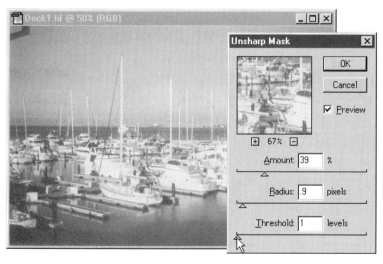

FIGURE 2.6 *The Unsharp Mask filter provides a small but necessary amount of sharpening to the image, with little change in image content.*

11. You're finished! The scan looks much better now, but not as good as the PhotoCD version of the scene. Look at both images onscreen. You've done all that you can to improve the scanned image, short of finding the negative and scanning it. You can save the image, or discard it now by closing it without saving.

WARNING

Naturally, every image is different—every photo has different visual content. Therefore, *do not* for a moment write down the values used in the preceding example as "the way" to fix a bum scan. Instead, use the procedures, the principles behind each command, and the commands, as used, in sequence.

Unfortunately, visual information that is not in a photo will definitely not be acquired through scanning, and if you compare Dock1 to Dock2, you'll see that the whites in Dock1 are so blown-out, there's no visual information beyond a pure white. The names and numbers on the boats can be seen in the PhotoCD version, but not in the scan.

In spite of all the bad things said about reflective scanning up to this point, it is important to keep in mind that there are some things you'll want to do that only a flatbed scanner can do for you. For example, Chapter 10, "Working with Mixed Media," absolutely depends on flatbed scanning of pen-and-ink work that can be embellished by using Photoshop. No one would reasonably photograph a drawing and then scan a photograph of the drawing into Photoshop!

You can also use your flatbed to scan *three*-dimensional objects. Direct scanning of physical objects is fun, innovative, and can provide you with better results than you'd expect. In the next section, you'll see how your flatbed scanner can be used as a digital camera.

DIRECT SCANNING DO'S AND DON'TS

Direct scanning, as the name implies, is the scanning of objects placed on the scanner's imaging surface. You're essentially treating the scanner like an expensive color photocopier machine, except that the results are in far better focus, and the objects scanned can be of different resolutions (different sampling rates).

Naturally, there is a practical limit to the overall size, weight, and depth of the objects you can scan on a flatbed scanner. Generally, the objects you place on the scanner's platen should not be any deeper than 1/2" or so. Here's a brief list of things you can scan; you can decide on the theme of the layout that features the scan:

- Crayons (as long as identifying trademarks on the paper don't show. Better still, remove the paper).

- Flowers, artificial grass, moss.

- Floor tiling made from natural materials such as slate, marble, granite. Don't use synthetic tiles that have a pattern applied to them. That pattern belongs to the company that makes the tile!

- Buttons (which are used in the next example).

- Generic candy. This would include candy corn, but not something like a Tootsie Roll, which has trademarked graphics on the wrapper.

- Generic cereal, such as puffed wheat or rice. You cannot, however, acquire such distinctive, trademarked cereal shapes such as Lucky Charms.

- Sponges. Sponges produce really interesting textures when scanned at high resolutions.

- Feathers. Craft stores carry a wide supply of dyed feathers.

- Clip art from royalty-free clip art books, such as those that Dover produces. In these physical books, which can be picked up at any art supply store, you can find ornamental type initials, borders, and other artwork. The only thing you cannot do with these clip art images is scan them and then sell the electronic versions under your own name. The clip art is okay to use as an element in a page layout, however.

- Pasta. This includes those spiral shapes, shells, spaghetti, elbow noodles, and so on.

WARNING

Do not scan any of the afore-mentioned items without reading this entire chapter first. Some of the objects we've mentioned can leave particles of lint or other debris on your scanner's imaging surface that can ruin your equipment over time.

We'll get to a sure-fire strategy for safely scanning all sorts of things later in this chapter.

Here's a list of objects for which you would need permission from the manufacturer, or that you should not scan at all:

- American currency.

- Trademarked food items and drugs, such as aspirins.

- Textiles, wallpaper, gift wrap that have patterns. You should not, for example, scan a Hawaiian shirt, for the design most certainly is protected by either a trademark or a copyright.

- Trademarked art supplies such as scissors, pencils, rulers, and drafting paraphernalia. You can, however, scan these items and then carefully clone over identifying trademarks, but only if the *shapes* of such objects don't have trademark, patent, or copyright protection. For example, a Bic pen has a trademarked design, and you can't scan and use an image of the pen commercially without the manufacturer's consent, even if the name "Bic" doesn't appear in the scan.

The best guideline for acquiring images directly is to stay away from items that you think have a trademarked shape, or that carry a prominently displayed logo.

LETTING A LAYOUT DICTATE A SCAN

Let's suppose that you're an art director for a publication, and you need to come up with an image to accompany an article on the history of buttons, "All About Buttons." To feature an image of buttons on the page is a natural decision, but before you design the page you must ask yourself:

- What's the best design idea I can come up with?
- How much RAM and scratch disk space do I need, and do I really need to cover an 8 1/2" by 11" page with buttons?

Image size, as measured in megabytes, truly is a consideration when you create a page design. You'll notice very few full-page ads or articles with photos or scans because an 8 1/2" by 11" area, at commercial printing quality, which is 266 pixels per inch, weighs in at 18.9MB! But wait, the news gets worse. Bleed pages— pages with images that run right up to the corner of the printed page—usually need to be trimmed from a larger size paper. This is because bleed pages need space for the printing press gripper to hold onto the page as it passes through the printing plates. This also means that the photo or scan *must* occupy the full size of the printed page before it's trimmed down (to *trim size*, 8 1/2" by 11" in this example). If the pressman tells you, for example, that bleed runs 1/4" outside the trim size, then the image you must scan will be 9" by 11 1/2", or 21MB in file size. And to top it off, these are the RGB sizes; when you finish editing your work and convert the images to CMYK for printing, the files sizes will increase by another 25 percent.

Photoshop needs three to five times the image size in system RAM and hard disk space to run at a comfortable clip and not swap data out to scratch disk. So to create the bleed-size buttons page, your system needs at least 64MB of RAM and an equal if not larger amount of free scratch disk space. (For information about memory settings and specifying scratch disk space, see Chapter 3, "Customizing

Photoshop 5.") If you don't have sufficient RAM for the task, you have three options:

- Buy more RAM. A good suggestion in today's technology market, because RAM can be had for as little as $5 a MB as of this writing. So to add another 32MB to your existing system would cost about $160, less than a cheap meal and two tickets to a Broadway play.

- Define as much uncompressed space on your hard disk(s) as possible for Photoshop to use as scratch disk space. Again, see Chapter 3 for configuring scratch disk and memory allocation. This is not an optimal solution for working with large files; swapping to disk space takes an order of magnitude more time than swapping in and out of RAM.

- Rethink your design. Can you accomplish the same goal—to make a stunning page layout with text and graphics—by using more "white space" on the page, and less image? Can a smaller image be used more effectively than a large one? The answer is yes.

Let's examine the most ambitious layout design first, keeping the scanning requirements within reason so that any user with 24MB of system RAM or more can play along in this layout game. In Figure 2.7, you can see the full-page layout of "wall-to-wall" buttons—the dotted line in the image represents the trim size for the page. This layout is also in the Chap02 folder of the Companion CD, as Buttons1.eps, in case you'd like to view it in Illustrator, CorelXARA, or CorelDRAW as an editable vector design. You'll import the layout to Photoshop shortly, to give you a guide for the finished layout. Don't worry—you'll only be scanning to inkjet output, not to commercial output, so the file you'll be working with will be about 8MB.

You'll notice that the buttons are larger than 1:1 in the design layout. This means that the *physical* area you'll be scanning will be less than 9" by 11 1/2", but the resolution times the physical dimensions will still need to come out to 9" by 11 1/2", which means that we'll need to show you how to set up in your scanner's interface to scan at larger than 1:1 resolution.

FIGURE 2.7   *For this colorful, ambitious page layout, you must scan 9" by 11 1/2" of buttons.*

Here's how to fulfill the layout requirement for a page, bleed size, of buttons:

CREATING A DIRECT SCANNED, AMBITIOUS BUTTON LAYOUT

1. Go to a fabric store and buy a big bag of assorted buttons; we bought two one-quart containers of buttons. Alternatively, you can ask your mother or spouse (if they're into sewing) for a fistful of assorted buttons. If they ask why, tell them, "It's technical."

2. In Photoshop, create a new image that is 9" by 11 1/2" at a resolution of 170 pixels/inch. Click on OK to create the new file.

3. Choose Image, Image Size, and then drop the Width and Height measurement boxes down, and choose pixels.

4. The Width should be 1530, and 1955 should be the Height. Write these numbers down, in case your scanner measures in pixels instead of inches.

5. Cover the scanner's imaging surface with buttons, to within an inch or so of the edges. You will not need to cover the full width and height of the scanner's imaging surface, because you'll be cropping the image at a larger than 1:1 resolution.

6. Choose File, Import from the menu. Choose TWAIN_32 if you are using Windows 95, or Windows NT 4 or later. If you are using a Macintosh, choose File, Import, Twain Acquire. The scanner interface will load on top of Photoshop's workspace.

7. Set the scanner to RGB color, Reflective type scanning, and 170 pixels/inch scanning resolution.

8. Drag a crop box in the image, watching the pixel measurements until the Width reads 1530 and the Height reads 1955. Now, all scanner interfaces are different and they have different features. On the UMAX scanner the author used, the percentage field had to be adjusted until the correct pixel amount for height and width was attained. On some scanners, you can type the width, height, and resolution of the scan directly into fields. Figure 2.8 gives you a view of this particular scanner's interface as well as an idea of the way the buttons were arranged and what the scanner settings look like for this assignment.

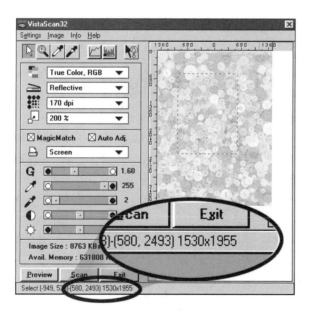

FIGURE 2.8 *Adjust the Width and Height in inches or in pixels, and specify the resolution you want for the scan.*

9. Click on Scan (or OK, or whatever launches the scan on your model of scanner). In a moment, the scanned image will appear in Photoshop. You can close the scanner interface now.

10. Save the file as Buttons1.tif to your hard disk. Keep the file open.

EDITING A SCANNED IMAGE

According to the EPS layout shown in Figure 2.7, a circle needs to be knocked out of the center of the page, to create a space for the headline and body copy. Here's how to overlay the layout on the image and finish the graphics part of the page layout:

NOTE

If you'd like to participate in this direct scanning layout adventure but don't have a scanner, Button1.tif is in the Chap02 folder on the Companion CD and can be used in the following steps.

EDITING THE BUTTON IMAGE

1. Choose File, Open, and then choose the Buttons1.eps file from the Chap02 folder on the Companion CD.

2. In the Rasterize Generic EPS Format dialog box, type **170** in the Resolution field, choose Grayscale (Grayscale takes less time to interpret than RGB color), and then click on OK as shown in Figure 2.9.

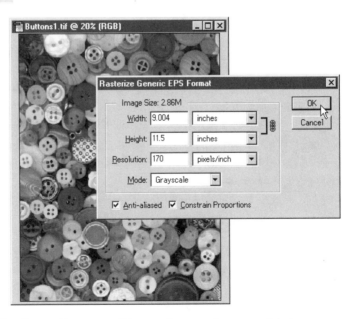

FIGURE 2.9 *Create a bitmap copy of the vector layout to place on top of the image.*

3. Press Ctrl(⌘)+A to Select All, and then press Ctrl(⌘)+C to copy the layout to the Clipboard.

4. Close the Buttons1.eps file without saving it.

5. Press Ctrl(⌘)+V to paste the layout as a new layer into the Buttons1.tif image, as shown in Figure 2.10.

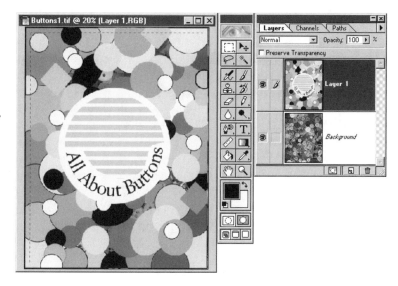

FIGURE 2.10   *Copy the layout to a new layer in the Buttons1 image.*

6. Choose Edit, Purge, and then choose Clipboard. This removes the copy of the layout stored on the Clipboard, and returns much-needed resources to Photoshop and to your computer.

7. With the Rectangular Marquee tool, drag to select the area that is contained within the dotted lines in the layout.

8. Deselect the Eye icon for Layer 1, and click on the Background layer title to make it the current editing layer.

9. Press **D** (default colors) and then press X to make the current foreground color white.

10. Choose Edit, Stroke. In the Stroke dialog box, type **3** in the Pixels field, click on Center in the Location field, and then click on OK. As you can see in Figure 2.11, you've now marked where the trim will be on this page, a convenient reminder for your boss or anyone else who will be looking at this proof copy of the page. Press Ctrl(⌘)+D to deselect the marquee.

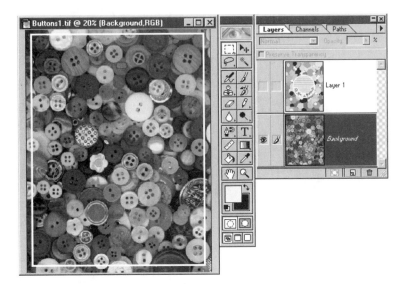

FIGURE 2.11 *Create a guideline in the image indicating where the bleed will be trimmed.*

11. Click on the Eye icon space next to the Layer 1 title, and then click on the title to make the layout layer the current editing layer. Press Ctrl(⌘)+R to display rulers in the image window. You won't be measuring anything, but you need the rulers visible to drag guides out of them.

12. Drag a vertical guide out of the vertical ruler, placing it so that it touches the left of the circle in the image, and then drag a horizontal guide out of the horizontal ruler so that it touches the top side of the circle, as shown in Figure 2.12. If you need to adjust the placement of the guides, press V to switch to the Move tool. The Move tool is the only tool that can adjust guides that have already been placed.

13. With the Elliptical Marquee tool, hold Shift (constrains the tool to producing circles), and then drag, beginning where the two guides intersect, down and to the right, until the marquee touches the bottom and right of the circle on the layout.

14. Drag the Layer 1 title on the Layers palette into the trash icon.

15. Press D (default colors), and then press Delete (Backspace). You've created a clear area in the image that is the same size and in the same location as the circle in the layout, as shown in Figure 2.13.

16. Press Ctrl(⌘)+D, and then press Ctrl(⌘)+S. You can close the image at any time now. The file can be imported to PageMaker or Quark to have the text added, and the layout can be printed to a large format inkjet printer at optimal resolution.

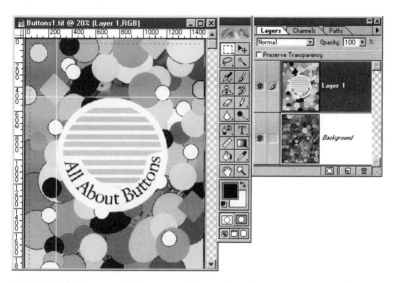

FIGURE 2.12 *Mark the top and left extremes of the circle so that you can create a selection marquee.*

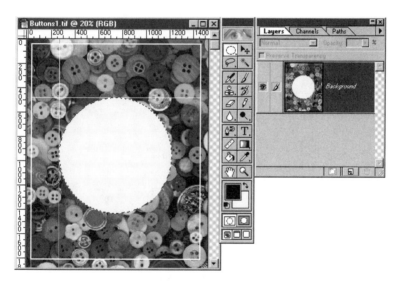

FIGURE 2.13 *Create a hole of 100% white by deleting the contents of the marquee selection.*

Whew! Working with an 8.5MB image in addition to the 2MB layout in Photoshop is quite a strain on systems with a modest amount of RAM and hard disk space. And it's not exactly a picnic for users with plenty of RAM. In the next section, you'll take a look at a layout that conveys the same message as the preceding one but requires less RAM and hard disk space to execute.

THE VERTICAL STRIP LAYOUT

In Figure 2.14, you can see an alternative layout to "All About Buttons."

This layout is different from the first in two significant ways:

- The page is white, and therefore the images of the buttons against white can be floated on the page.

- The page is not a bleed page, so you, the designer, do not have to whip up a huge 9" by 11 1/2" file.

FIGURE 2.14   *This layout demands fewer system resources because it uses a smaller graphic than the first layout.*

NOTE

Again, if you do not own a scanner, Buttons2.tif is in the Chap02 folder of the Companion CD and can be used in the steps that follow.

Because this layout was deliberately designed to require less of your scanning input, let's pretend, in the next set of steps, that this layout is destined for a magazine printed on a commercial press. Magazines are usually printed on presses that have a resolution of 2540 dots per inch and use a line screen of 133 lines/inch, which means that your artwork needs to have a resolution of at least 266 pixels/inch.

Here's how to size up the resolution requirements for the direct scan:

IMPORTING A LAYOUT

1. Choose File, Open, and then choose the Buttons2.eps file from the Chap02 folder on the Companion CD.

2. In the Rasterize Generic EPS Format box, shown in Figure 2.15, set the increments to Inches, choose Grayscale Mode, and type **266** in the Resolution field. Click on OK to render the file to bitmap format.

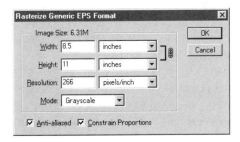

FIGURE 2.15 *Specify 266 as the resolution when importing a file that will be printed on a high-quality commercial press.*

3. On the Layers palette's menu flyout, choose Flatten Image; then, with the Rectangular Marquee tool, drag a rectangular selection around only the buttons in the layout, as shown in Figure 2.16; leave only a little white space outside the buttons.

4. Choose Image, Crop, and then save the file as Buttons2.psd, in Photoshop's native file format.

5. Zoom in to a 100% view of one of the button drawings, and then choose the Measure tool. Press F8 to open the Info Palette, if it is not already open.

6. Hold Shift and drag a line across the widest part of the button, leaving a little white space to the left and right sides, as shown in Figure 2.17. As you can see on the Info palette, the buttons need to be scanned at a width of about 524 pixels at 266 pixels/inch.

7. Line up five buttons on your scanner's imaging surface. It'll help your work here if the buttons are aligned vertically as they are in the layout (a physical ruler can help you do this), but the amount of vertical space between the buttons is not important when you scan because you can tighten or loosen the spacing in Photoshop.

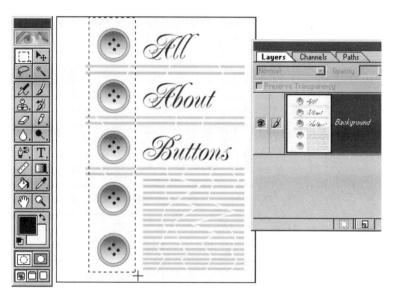

FIGURE 2.16   *Crop around only the area you'll need to measure for your scanning work.*

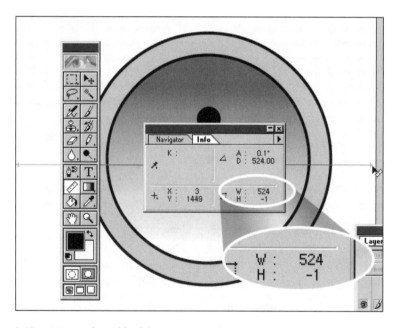

FIGURE 2.17   *Measure the width of the image in pixels.*

8. Choose File, Import, and then choose TWAIN_32 (Mac: Twain Acquire). The scanner's interface opens.

9. Drag the crop box around the buttons and then adjust the scaling and resolution so that the width of the buttons (plus some white space) is approximately 524, as shown in Figure 2.18. Click on Scan (OK, or whatever launches the scanner).

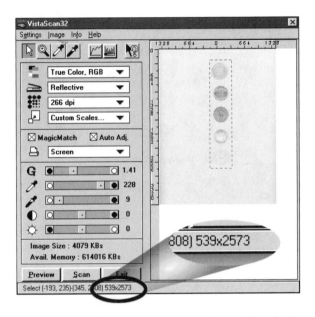

FIGURE 2.18 *Make the marquee selection of the buttons equal in width to the layout you measured.*

Chances are that the background of the buttons is not 100 percent white, because buttons have depth and allow some ambient coloration to seep between the lid of the scanner and the imaging surface. This is easily corrected....

10. Save the file as Buttons2.tif. Press Ctrl(⌘)+L to display the Levels command.

11. Choose the White Point eyedropper and then click in the image, toward the image edge, where the tone should be white. As you can see in Figure 2.19, doing this brings the white point up to paper white and brightens the buttons. Click on OK to apply the change.

12. Click on the title bar of Buttons2.psd, choose Image, Mode, and then choose RGB color.

13. With the Rectangular Marquee tool, drag a selection around the top button in Buttons2.tif, and then while holding Ctrl(⌘), drag inside the selection marquee and toss the selection into the Buttons2.psd window, as shown in Figure 2.20.

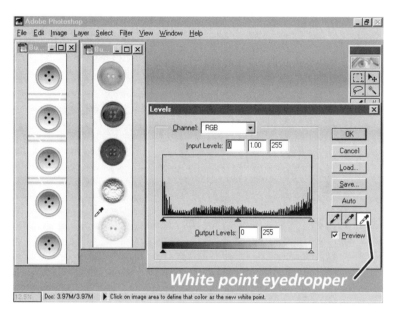

FIGURE 2.19   *Set a new white point in the image by using the White Point Eyedropper tool.*

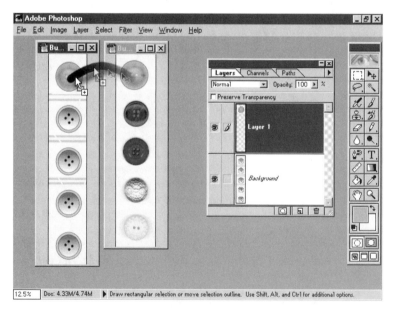

FIGURE 2.20   *Hold Ctrl(⌘) and drag the selection into the Buttons2.psd window to copy the selection.*

14. On the Buttons2.psd Layers palette, drag the Opacity down to about 50% for this new layer; then, with the Move tool drag on the layer to align the button image with its underlying layout counterpart. After the button is aligned, press 0 (zero) on your keyboard to restore the button image to 100% opacity.

15. Choose Flatten Image from the Layers palette's menu flyout to conserve file size.

16. Repeat steps 13–15 with the remaining four button images. Then clear away any of the layout that might remain in the Buttons2.psd image. You can do this by choosing the Lasso tool, encompassing an unwanted area, and then pressing Delete, as shown in Figure 2.21.

17. Choose File, Save As, and save the image as Buttons2 Finished.tif, in the TIFF file format. You can close both images now. You can also turn Buttons2 Finished.tif over to the Production department, along with the layout, so that they can add the text.

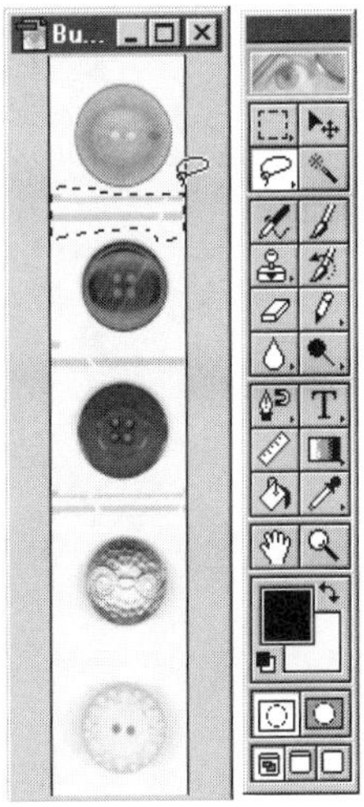

Figure 2.21 *Delete areas of the image that you do not want to appear in the publication.*

SIMPLICITY OF DESIGN AND ECONOMY OF SCANNING

In Figure 2.22, you can see a third layout for the article on buttons. You'll notice that only one huge button is used against white, and that it's a component of an exclamation mark (the headline and text are the stem).

This stark but imaginative design is an eye-catcher. Best of all, you need to scan only one button at larger-than-life size.

If you don't own a scanner, Buttons3.tif is in the Chap02 folder on the Companion CD and can be used with the following steps.

FIGURE 2.22 *Good use of white space and a powerful graphic can sometimes drive the point home better than a wall-to-wall graphic.*

Here's how to measure up and scan the artwork for the third layout:

MEASURING AND SCANNING A SINGLE DESIGN ELEMENT

1. Open the Buttons3.eps file from the Chap02 folder on the Companion CD. In the Rasterize Generic EPS Format dialog box, change the units to inches, type **266** in the Resolution field, specify Grayscale mode from the drop-down list, and then click on OK.

2. When the EPS image appears in Photoshop, use the Rectangular Marquee tool to loosely select the area that encompasses the button in the design, as shown in Figure 2.23, and then choose Image, Crop.

3. With the Measure tool, drag across the widest part of the button, leaving some white space to the left and right. As you can see from Figure 2.24, you need to scan a button (with a border) to produce an image that's about 743 pixels wide.

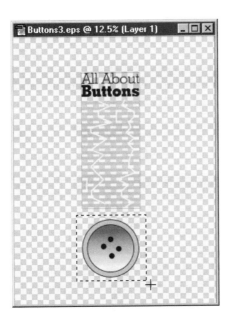

FIGURE 2.23   *Keep only the part of the page layout that requires measuring.*

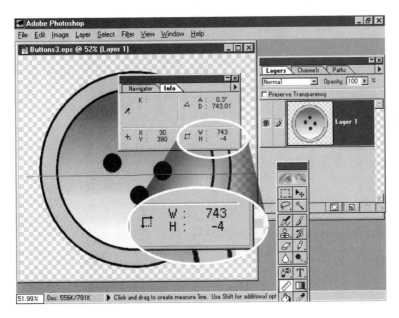

FIGURE 2.24   *Your target image size for the scan of the single button is 743 pixels.*

4. Close the file without saving, and then choose File, Import, TWAIN_32 (Mac: Twain Acquire).

5. Place a button on the scanner's imaging surface, close the lid, and then use the scanner's interface features to create a marquee selection around the button at 266 pixels/inch and about 743 pixels wide, as shown in Figure 2.25. Click on Scan.

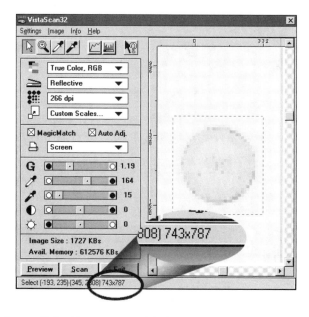

FIGURE 2.25   *Leave a little white space around the button you scan.*

6. After the scan is complete, close the scanning interface and save the image as Buttons3.tif, in the TIFF file format.

7. Use the same technique you used with the Buttons2 image and the Levels command to make the background of the button 100% white.

8. Close the file, and send it off to Production.

So you see, dumping common household objects on a scanner is not a frivolous pastime. A flatbed scanner can be a lifesaver when you don't have the time for conventional photography, and most of the time you'll capture more detail with a scanner than with a camera.

A Warning about Scanning Everything on Earth

If you dislike white spots in photographs (a result of not properly cleaning the negative) you've received from a photo-finisher, then you will *detest* getting scans that contain dust, lint, hair, and other particles that show up in your beautiful image. Guess who would be to blame for these goodies in your work? That's right; it would be you.

Flatbed scanners usually have a plastic gasket that holds the glass imaging plate in place as the scanning head passes across the underside of the glass. This gasket is meant to hold the glass and to buffer the glass against the vibration caused by the machine's components, but the gasket *is not* airtight. Therefore, if you were to scan, say, a bunch of flowers, the pollen and dirt left on the scanning surface might well remain lodged in the edges of the gasket, even though you wiped off the particles after you scanned the flowers. And with time, these particles will eventually get under the gasket, and then you'll have particles *inside* your scanner, placing dots all over your future work. There's really nothing you can do at that point except send the scanner in for repair.

To alleviate this pollution problem and still allow you to scan freely whatever comes to mind, the author recommends taping a sheet of acetate over the entire imaging surface of the scanner, as shown in Figure 2.26. The acetate will also protect the glass from scratches and nicks.

The author has scanned practically everything in the office and the fridge in recent years, even a sloppy tomato slice, by keeping the acetate over the scanner's platen. The scan is good, the acetate is disposable, and the scanner remains in perfect condition optically.

Try to buy the thinnest acetate you can from a commercial art store. We use .003" acetate sheets from a 14" by 17" pad. We recently purchased a 25-sheet pad of acetate for around $12. Be sure to get clear, glossy acetate and not prepared acetate that has been finely sanded to accept paints and oils or, for obvious reasons, tinted acetate.

Take reasonable care of your scanner, and protect the glass and scanner with an acetate sheet when you're scanning sooty, dusty, or pollen-bearing objects, or any object that might scratch the glass. If you always remember to use the acetate, your scanner will thank you and you'll be able to look forward to many years of creating fun and innovative designs, using direct-scanned images.

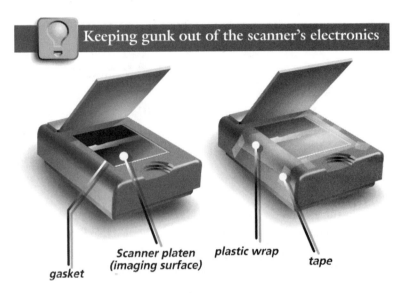

Keeping gunk out of the scanner's electronics

gasket

Scanner platen
(imaging surface)

plastic wrap

tape

FIGURE 2.26 *Tape a large sheet of acetate over the scanning surface to prevent particles from entering the mechanics of the hardware.*

NOTE

PCD writers are a combination of negative scanner and file writer. After each negative is scanned, the PCD writer (a very expensive piece of hardware) writes a single PhotoCD file for that image. The PhotoCD file format is a proprietary compressed format that Photoshop and many other graphic applications can read.

THE KODAK PHOTOCD

If you don't have a negative scanner, or don't want to take the time to scan all your negatives, there is an excellent alternative. You can take your film or negatives to a photo-finisher and ask them to transfer the media to a Kodak PhotoCD. The processing lab will then use Eastman Kodak's proprietary PCD writer to scan your negatives and write the images to a CD-ROM that can be read by your computer's CD-ROM player. So with only a 35mm camera, a CD-ROM drive and a willingness to write a check for PhotoCD processing, you can get good-quality digital image files of your photographs. In 1998, there is hardly a photo-finisher in the world who does not offer PhotoCD writing as a service.

The following section takes a look at how to get a PhotoCD made and how to load a PhotoCD image into Photoshop, and then examines the quality of a PhotoCD image compared to such other input methods as flatbed scanning and negative scanning, using a Nikon CoolScan.

WORKING WITH PHOTOCD IMAGES

A photo-finisher might or might not actually have a PhotoCD (PCD) writer on its pre-mises. As mentioned earlier, the PCD hardware is extremely expensive, so don't expect a "mom and pop" photo-finisher or even a big retailer like Target or Wal-Mart to have this machine at its store. Usually when a local photofinisher offers PhotoCD service, the film you give them is shipped to a large custom pro-cessing plant that does have a PCD writer. Because the processing probably won't be done locally, you might have to wait 10–14 days to get your finished PhotoCD back from your local photo-finisher.

On your end, ordering a PhotoCD is simple. You bring either a roll of undevel-oped film or negatives to the photo-finisher (slides will cost extra because of the extra time required to handle each individual slide), and tell the clerk you want a PhotoCD made of the images. If you send undeveloped film out to be written to a PhotoCD, you will be charged an additional fee for developing. A single PhotoCD can contain about 120 images. It's a good idea to bring several rolls or several strips of negatives to the photo-finisher, because doing this conserves space on the PhotoCD. You can also have images added to a partially filled PhotoCD you already have, but this decreases the overall space on the PhotoCD. You have the option to have your images written to the PhotoCD in a specific sequence, either on a frame-by-frame basis or roll by roll. On average, it costs around 80 cents for every image you have transferred to PhotoCD.

When you bring the PhotoCD back from the photo-finishers, all you need to do is plop the CD into your CD-ROM player and launch Photoshop. There is noth-ing special about a PhotoCD; physically, it is the same as any other CD you might load. What makes a PhotoCD special is the file format the images are stored in, and the compression format, which is part of the file format.

Each image on a Kodak PhotoCD is stored in a single file called an *image pac*. The following five sizes (resolutions) of the image can be opened from a single image pac:

- 72KB (128×192 pixels)
- 288KB (256×384 pixels)
- 1.13MB (512×768 pixels)
- 4.5MB (1024×1536 pixels)
- 18MB (2048×3072 pixels)

The image pac file itself actually only contains the file at 4.5MB. An application's PhotoCD import filter uses a proprietary method of interpolation, along with special hinting information found in the image pac, to produce the other sizes from the 4.5 MB file.

Because the five different sizes of the image are not actually stored in a PCD file, a combination of compression/decompression and interpolation must take place when you choose to open the image in Photoshop at the 72KB, 2.88KB, 1.13MB, or 18MB size. The author recommends that you choose to work with the 4.5MB size image whenever practical. The 4.5 MB image will have the sharpest focus. The reason? Even the best interpolation (resizing) reduces the focus of an image as pixels are added or removed to create a new image size.

NOTE

Keep the contact sheet(s) when sending the CD in for more transfers. The lab doesn't need the sheets and are trashed after the new contact sheet is printed to update the contents of the CD. At least you'll have a backup of the CD contents before the latest transfer when you keep the index print, and pack off the PhotoCD and new images.

The PCD writer prints out an *index print* to go along with every PhotoCD they make. The index print, which is made up of very tiny, numbered thumbnails of all the images stored on the PhotoCD, is not something you'd want to lose because from the outside, every PhotoCD looks identical. The numbers next to the thumbnails on the index print correspond to each image file on the PhotoCD—the first image on a PhotoCD is Img0001.pcd, the second is Img0002.pcd, and so on. Because the thumbnails are so tiny (and as added insurance in case you lose the index print), you might want to take advantage of Photoshop 5's new Contact Sheet feature, described in Chapter 5, "Working with New Features," to create your own, more legible digital contact sheet.

Again, there is nothing special about the physical PhotoCD itself; PhotoCD image files can be copied from the PhotoCD and stored on hard disk, removable media like Zip or Jaz cartridges, or even written to another CD-ROM disk. In fact, the Chap02 folder on the Companion CD contains PCD images that you'll work with in the rest of this section. In the following two sets of steps, you'll load two different-sized images and use the PhotoCD import filter's Destination controls to specify what color space the images will be brought into. The first set of steps shows you how to load and view a PhotoCD image:

LOADING A PHOTOCD IMAGE

1. In Photoshop, choose File, Open, and then choose Img0042.pcd from the Examples\Chap02 folder on the Companion CD.

2. In the Kodak ICC Photo CD dialog box, click on the Image Info button. The Image Info dialog box will tell you that the medium of the original picture is a color negative. This is important news you'll use for defining a source for opening the PhotoCD image. Click on OK to close the dialog box.

3. Click on the Source button, and then, in the Color (Macintosh: the ColorSync Profiles) folder, click on the pcdcnycc.icm (Macintosh: pcdcnycc.pf) file, as shown in Figure 2.27. As you can see in the information window, the DeviceModelDesc(ription) is a color negative, and the color space (not shown in the Macintosh information window) is YCC, which is similar to the breadth and structure of LAB color space. Click on Open to return to the Kodak ICC PhotoCD dialog box.

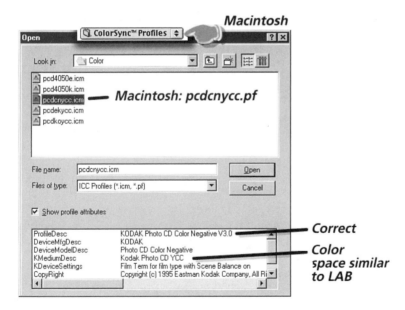

FIGURE 2.27   *Choose a Source profile that matches the medium that was originally used to capture the image.*

4. Click on the Destination button, and then in the Color (ColorSync Profiles) folder, choose pslabpcs.icm (pslabpcs.pf), as shown in Figure 2.28. Again, in the information box you can see that the image will open in LAB mode, which is a wider color space than RGB color, and that the profile is version 2, and not the version 1 file (pslabint). The difference between these two profiles is that the pslabpcs one appears to produce slightly brighter colors with a little more contrast than the version 1 LAB profile. Click on Open.

FIGURE 2.28   *Choose a Destination profile whose color space is compatible with the Source profile.*

5. Choose a file size for the PhotoCD image. As mentioned earlier, the 4.5MB file on PhotoCDs has the best focus because all other sizes are interpolated versions of the 4.5MB file. Choose 1024×1536 from the drop-down list, as shown in Figure 2.29, and then click on OK.

6. That's it! You now have the highest-quality (sharpest focus) image from this file. The file is currently in LAB mode, so keep the image open, and you'll see shortly how to perform minor Gamma corrections while the image is in this mode (color space).

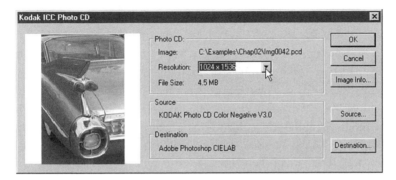

FIGURE 2.29 *Although you can choose from any of the five available sizes for a PhotoCD image, it is recommended that you choose the 4.5MB, 1024×1536 version for the best focus.*

CORRECTING THE GAMMA OF AN IMAGE ACQUIRED FROM A PHOTOCD

Although Kodak has improved in recent years by offering the folks who operate the PCD writer additional color balance data *(profiles)* they can use to tweak the scans they create, a little bit of history can shed some light on why many PhotoCD images are brighter and more washed out than you might expect them to be. Kodak originally developed the PhotoCD as a consumer technology. The idea was that you'd rent or buy a special PhotoCD player that plugged into your TV set, plop the PhotoCD you had made of your vacation into the player, and gather all your friends and family around the TV to watch a high-tech version of the dreaded family slide show.

Unfortunately, the *Gamma* of television sets—the brightness versus voltage output—is not the same as that of computer monitors. Originally, the Gamma of all PhotoCDs was written to 2.2, the Gamma of television tube circuitry, but the Gamma of Macintosh and Windows machines can be anywhere from 2.0 to 1.4. Now, the Gamma of a newly written PhotoCD depends on which settings the operator of the PCD writer chooses. Most still choose a Gamma of 2.2, even if you ask them to use a computer-friendly Gamma profile.

Fortunately, there's a very simple way to Gamma-correct PhotoCD images that you want to save as TIFFs or PSD images. As you saw in the previous section, PhotoCD images are written to a unique color space known as *YCC*; one channel of brilliance and two channels of color make up the YCC gamut of color. Photoshop's CIELAB color space embraces the YCC color space, and the two are quite compatible. To decrease the Gamma (lower the midtones) of a PhotoCD image without disrupting the colors in the image, you now have Img0042.pcd in Photoshop in LAB color mode, and you can use the Lightness channel in the LAB color space to correct the Gamma.

Here's a quick and easy set of steps you can perform to bring a PhotoCD image back into the acceptable range of color expression that computer monitors display:

ADJUSTING GAMMA THROUGH LAB COLOR MODE

1. The picture you've just opened from PhotoCD probably lacks visual snap (contrast), and the midtones seem a little blocked in. On the Layers palette, click on the Channels tab, and then click on the Lightness channel, as shown in Figure 2.30. This is the channel that needs work.

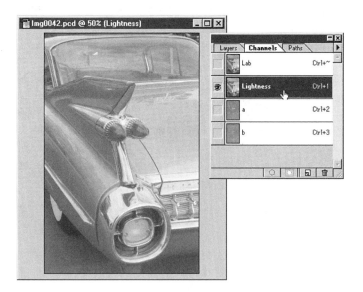

FIGURE 2.30   *Click on the channel that contains only lightness information about the photograph.*

2. Press Ctrl(⌘)+ L to open the Levels command dialog box. Drag the black point slider up to about 35, and drag the midtone slider to the left so that the middle Input Level box reads about 1.15, as shown in Figure 2.31. Doing this makes the shaded areas of the picture a little more dense, and makes the midtones a little lighter, so that you can see more visual detail in the midtones.

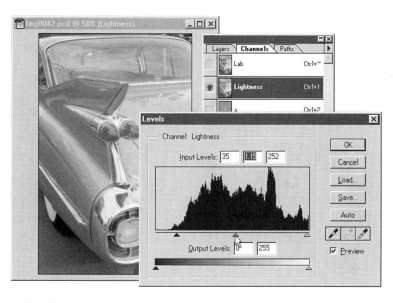

FIGURE 2.31   *Treat the Lightness channel in a LAB mode image as you would treat a grayscale image. If it looks good in black and white, it'll look superb in color.*

3. Click on OK to apply the changes, and then press Ctrl(⌘)+~(tilde) to move your view back to the color composite of this image.

4. Choose Image, Mode, and then choose RGB Color. You will not notice a color change, but many other applications cannot read a file saved in LAB mode.

5. Save the image to your hard disk in the TIFF file format, as Car.tif. You can close the image at any time now.

TRANSPARENCY SCANNING

Unlike the reflective scanning method that flatbed scanners employ, the transparency scanner uses the same first step that goes into making a PhotoCD image: negative scanning. Light is passed through a negative or a slide and captured by photo-sensitive cells that record the color with all the life and brilliance seen by the human eye. Monitors are the counterpart to transparency scanners, in a way, because they emit light. In contrast, when we look at a magazine, our eyes are performing reflective scanning, and the magazine appears duller than if we were looking at a file of the same magazine cover on our monitors.

In Figure 2.32, you can see the basic principle behind transparency scanning. A light behind the source passes the colors of the source, through a lens system, to an array of sensing devices that produces the digital information needed to write a computer file.

Lens **Transparent object** **Light Source**

FIGURE 2.32 *Transparency scanning preserves the luminosity of the original image.*

Because a transparency scanner, such as a Nikon CoolScan, is a pricey item (the street price of the entry-level model we use is about $900), there are no formal tutorials in this section. We will walk through the process by which a negative is scanned, however. The results of the scan made with the Nikon CoolScan are on the Companion CD, which gives you the opportunity to compare, with your own eyes, the results you can expect from using a desktop transparency scanner versus the image produced by CoolScan.

Here's how the Nikon CoolScan works:

TRANSPARENCY SCANNING

1. Power on the transparency scanner and restart your computer. Most computers need to see devices attached to the computer on startup to make use of them. Additionally, scanning can tax your system's resources, and it's a good idea to start with maximum resources available.

2. Start Photoshop.

3. Place the strip of negatives that contains the image you want scanned into the scanner's transparency holder, and close the holder firmly. Insert the transparency holder into the scanner, following the instructions in the scanner's owner's manual. Figure 2.33 illustrates the components of the transparency scanner.

4. From Photoshop's menu, choose File, Import, and then choose Select TWAIN_32 Source (Twain Select). In the Select Source dialog box, choose Nikon CoolScan (32), and then click on Select. The Select Source box closes.

5. Choose File, Import, and then choose TWAIN_32 (Twain Acquire).

6. The TWAIN interface for the Nikon CoolScan appears.

7. To make this a fair contest between PhotoCD technology and scanning negatives yourself, we've chosen 512 by 768 pixels as the size of the scan. This is the exact size of the "base 1" PhotoCD image. Choose Color Neg from the drop-down list, and then click on Preview, as shown in Figure 2.34.

8. Click on Scan, and then close the TWAIN interface. The unnamed image is now in Photoshop's workspace, and it's sideways because the images on a strip of negatives are scanned in portrait mode. (If you scan 35mm slides, you can decide on the orientation.)

9. Choose File, Save As, and then save it to hard disk as Dock3.tif, in the TIFF file format.

WARNING

An *extremely* important part of scanning film is to make sure that your negatives are dust, hair, and fingerprint free! If there is *any* foreign substance on the either side of the negative the scanner will see it and add it to your image. This is definitely not a case where more is better.

It is highly recommended that you invest in a pair of cloth film handling gloves to wear before you even think about taking your negatives out of their sleeves and that you blow the dust off both sides of the film with a compressed-gas duster such as Dust-Off® by Falcon. The gloves and the compressed gas can be found in most photo stores.

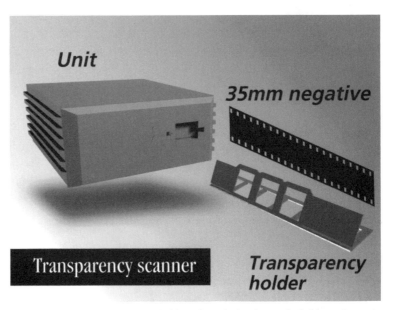

FIGURE 2.33 *Place the film strip in the holder, adjust the bracket on the holder to frame the image you want, and then insert the holder into the unit.*

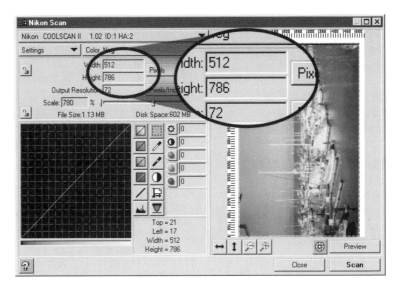

FIGURE 2.34 *Specify the same dimensions for the transparency scan as one of the images in a PhotoCD image pac.*

10. If you don't own a transparency scanner, open image Dock2.psd at 512 by 768 pixel resolution from the Chap02 folder on the Companion CD, and then open Dock3.tif in Photoshop. Compare the quality side by side. Close the images at any time now.

You will notice that the color is far more accurate with the transparency scan, the focus is a teensy bit sharper in the transparency scan, and there appears to be less of an overall "haze" to the transparency scan image. Also, there's no lint on Dock3.tif because the authors took the time to clean the negative before scanning it.

If you're a professional photographer who develops your own film, you might want to search around in that checkbook for the price of a transparency scanner. Demanding photographic work necessitates a hands-on, personal approach.

THE DIGITAL CAMERA

The filmless digital camera is not exactly new, but the number of manufacturers has increased exponentially in the past two years. And along with new manufacturers come different makes and models, each with different features, and each with a different price tag.

There are advantages and drawbacks to be found with all digital cameras. The biggest advantage is that of immediacy; a newspaper photographer, for example, can use a digital camera to capture the moment, upload the images through a cellular modem, and the pictures are ready to be placed and printed before the photographer even gets back to the newsroom. And the photographer doesn't need to wait for developing to see the image; images can be previewed on the LCD screen that most digital camera's sport. And then there's the feature that benefits everyone on earth—because the process is digital, there's zero percent environmental impact from developing chemicals and silver.

The largest drawback to today's digital cameras is the price-versus-features equation. It is difficult to find all the features you want and need in a single digital camera, and those cameras that "have it all" currently cost at least several thousand dollars. In the next section, we briefly explain how a digital camera works, we make recommendations on features you'd want to look for, and we take a look at three models: an inexpensive one, a medium-priced one, and a high-priced model. Keep in mind that because the information on pricing, features, and specific camera models very well may be different when you read this book, it should be read as an overall guide or baseline to what you may actually find in the market. It is impossible to offer timeless recommendations for digital cameras, an area that—like computer technology—seems to changes faster that the click of a shutter.

THE PIPELINE OF DIGITAL PHOTOGRAPHY

In Figure 22.35, you can see an illustration of one of the Olympus cameras on the market in early 1998, which is perhaps most representative of medium-priced digital cameras.

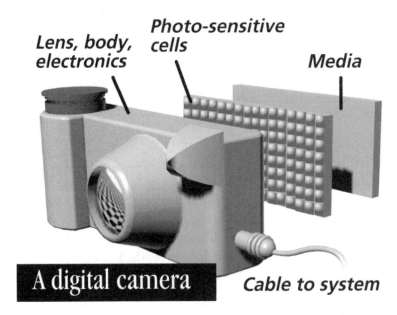

FIGURE 2.35 *From lens to imaging surface to storage, the digital camera takes and saves pictures without using chemicals.*

You will see many odd-shaped digital cameras at stores and in the mail-order catalogs. Some look like the classic "Brownie" camera, others look like a paperback book, and still others look like a science-fiction weapon of sorts. There are a couple of reasons for all the different shapes:

- The manufacturer is trying to come up with the least intrusive viewfinding system. Some digital cameras use the typical rangefinder method, some use a liquid crystal display (LCD) that's actually a tiny monitor, and the most expensive cameras offer single-lens reflex (SLR) viewing through the camera lens *and* LCD display.

- Film doesn't pass through the camera, so the notion of winding and needing spools to wind a physical medium are obsolete. Therefore, engineers can concentrate more on the cosmetic look and the ergonomic feel and balance of the digital camera.

For the most part, all digital cameras operate as the illustration in Figure 2.36 shows. There is a pipeline from images captured by the lens to images you can work with in Photoshop. The process goes like this:

1. The electronic shutter is opened for a brief amount of time, and light is passed through the lens system.

2. The lens focuses and organizes light to be passed onto an imaging surface consisting of hundreds of thousands (and with more expensive cameras, millions) of photo-receptors.

3. The visual information gathered is passed to and stored on some kind of fixed or removable storage media within the camera. Removable media is the most flexible and is often referred to generically as a "flash card." A clear standard for removable storage has not yet been adopted. Today's digital camera is usually designed to use only one of three current "flash card" formats. Flash cards in any of the three formats can usually be found, with capacities ranging from 2MB to 40MB. The type of flash card and capacity that can be used in any particular camera depends on the camera's design.

4. The images stored on the camera's storage media are downloaded in one of two ways to your computer. The quickest way to transfer the files to your computer's hard disk is to attach an internal or external card reader to your computer. The card reader and the flash card itself must of course be compatible with one another, and card readers normally read only one kind of card. The second, more conventional method, is through an "umbilical cord," a cable that connects the camera to a serial or parallel port on the PC,

and through which information is transferred from the flash card to the system's hard drive. This method is slower than a direct "dump" from a flash card. Camera manufacturers are working on a variety of other transfer methods to make the process either faster or easier to use, or both. Some methods being worked on are infrared transfer and transfer via the floppy disk controller.

Several factors will influence your decision to invest in a digital camera, and the following sections take a look at the details.

WHAT ARE YOU GETTING YOURSELF INTO WITH A DIGITAL CAMERA?

Today's digital camera is both like and unlike a traditional film camera. If you're a professional photographer, you should know in advance that you'll be handling a digital camera a little differently, unless you pop for the top-of-the-line models. Here are the features you should consider when you plunk down some serious cash for a digital camera.

FILM SPEED

Traditionally, the speed of film—its ISO number—determines the depth of field (f-stop) you can use, and amount of light necessary to take a picture. Surprise; the digital camera doesn't use film, so ISO *equivalencies* have to be built into the camera itself. In other words, the success with which you take an indoor picture depends a great deal on the camera's ISO capability and whether you need flash photography support to take the image.

On the inexpensive end of digital cameras, the author has seen an ISO as low as 100, equivalent to ISO 100 film in a traditional camera. This 100 ISO means that your best pictures can be taken outdoors on a very sunny day, without the need for a flash. On the high end of the digital camera market, some cameras offer a flexible ISO that can be specified from 200 to 1,600, the upper limit being faster than any film available today.

In general, if you can find a camera whose ISO is at least 400, then you can take pictures indoors without the need for flash photography.

THE LENS SYSTEM

The optics of almost all digital cameras provide good, sharp images, but the real difference in the price you pay among models lies in the flexibility of the lens system.

Most models under $1,000 offer a fixed lens system with automatic exposure control. A fixed lens system means that the camera is essentially "point and shoot"; you cannot zoom in, you cannot change the focus of the lens from foreground to midground, and your creative adventures with the camera are artistically hampered due to the fixed lens. Not all Photoshop users are professional photographers, however, and if you simply want to get a waist-up image of a person, a landscape, or a picture with loose framing of the gang, a fixed lens system is an adequate solution. Fixed lens systems essentially have an f-stop of about 1.5 feet to infinity, and you must be a minimum distance from your subject to get a focused picture.

As you move up in price, you will find auto-focus, auto-exposure cameras that provide more flexibility in your work. These lens systems are more akin to the $300+ 35mm film cameras that are popular with travelers today, and provide good focus and acceptable distances from your subject.

More expensive are the 2x and 3x zoom lenses on digital cameras. These offer greater creative control because you can set the framing (the distance) through the lens. On the high end of digital cameras (you'll read of one later in this chapter), the lens system is identical to that of an SLR film camera. You can focus automatically or manually, you have zoom and macro options, you can exchange lenses, and you can set the f-stop.

TYPES OF COMPRESSION AND THE STORAGE CARD

If you're planning on an all-day outing, it is wise to invest in several cards that fit your model of digital camera. Like film, it's a bummer to run out of memory in your camera just when that once-in-a-lifetime sunset comes by.

Memory capacity has two trade-offs: the size of the picture you're storing, and what sort of compression, if any, the camera system uses. JPEG is a very popular compression format for photographic images, and many digital cameras, both cheap and expensive, sometimes offer on-the-fly JPEG compression of your work to enable you to store either larger images or more images. The author does not recommend JPEG compression, especially not with your one-and-only image, because JPEG is *lossy* compression—some visual information is averaged (discarded) during the compression process.

The author's recommendation is to buy a camera that does not offer a JPEG subsystem (or one whose JPEG capability can be turned off), and to find a model of camera with the features you want plus the capability to take storage cards with large storage capacity.

AMOUNT OF SAMPLES

Because a digital camera operates with memory as storage, there is another trade-off to be made when considering a purchase. Some less expensive cameras take 640 by 480 pixel images. And the card can hold a lot of them. But a 640 by 480 image is only 900KB; you do get a full-screen image on a monitor running 640 by 480, but consider the size when printed. An Epson Stylus Color inkjet printer, for example, can write about 700 dots per inch, and can optimally take an image that is about 150 pixels per inch. The author's done the math for you here: a 640 by 480 pixel image can be optimally printed from an Epson at 4" by 3"—a little small for framing on the wall!

The next step up in expense as well as image quality are cameras that can take 1024 by 768 pixel images, which is equivalent to a 2.2MB file, or approximately a 5" by 7" image when printed to a 700dpi printer. This resolution would be good for a postcard-sized image to mail to friends, but you'd need a camera that can capture at least a 4.5MB file to fill an inkjet printer page with adequate resolution, and that will cost a lot more.

The author's advice is to choose the highest-resolution camera you can afford, and invest in several storage cards to pack along on your trips. Using multiple storage cards is much easier and safer than lugging a laptop around with you on a photographic session.

THREE RANGES OF CAMERAS

As mentioned earlier, books have a longer shelf life than magazines or the latest news release on the World Wide Web. It is inevitable that the following information will be dated, because prices and technology change at a breathtaking pace. It is our intention in the next three sections to describe three digital cameras, in three price ranges, that you can use as a baseline comparison to what is available to you when you go shopping. No doubt you will be able to buy more capable cameras at lower prices than those described here. Please note that we are not specifically endorsing these cameras. We picked them out of a host of cameras made by great companies with a long history of producing either fine traditional cameras or electronics, because these models seem representative of what is available in the market today.

OLYMPUS D-500L (STREET PRICE: $799)

This affordable model can take images up to 1024 by 768, or 850,000 pixels, to yield a 2.2MB file. This is good for 5" by 7" prints from a 600–750 dpi printer. Also, you have the option of taking images at the smaller 640×480 pixel size. The D-500L has a 3x zoom lens (35mm to 150mm equivalent), and a fast ISO 180 equivalent. This is an auto-focus digital camera with manual focus override, center-weighted focus, f 2.8 with a single-lens, reflex-type viewer. The camera has an exposure compensation of plus or minus 3 f-stops. The Olympus also has a focus lock. Close-ups can be taken from 11.8" to 2 feet. Standard focus is 1.97 feet to infinity.

The D-500L comes with a 2MB storage media card that can hold 3 to 25 images. There is a 1.8" back panel LCD for viewing as many as nine of the images stored on the flash card, and the camera has an individual or erase-all feature, plus an erase lock for individual images. The imaging surface is a single-pass CCD (charged-couple device), which eliminates ghosting, and images can be downloaded through either a serial or high-speed parallel port to a Macintosh or Windows computer. The D-500L is TWAIN-compliant, has a Photoshop plug-in for the Macintosh, and has four flash modes for different lighting conditions. Flash distance is up to 15.7 ft.

The D-500L features manual spot metering for backlighting conditions, and a date and time stamp for images.

And if you're reading this book and haven't purchased Photoshop yet, the Olympus D-500L ships with a copy of Adobe PhotoDeluxe, Adobe's entry-level image editing program.

OLYMPUS D-600L (STREET PRICE: $1,300)

This medium-priced camera features a through-the-lens, reflex-type viewfinder, and a 3x zoom lens (36–110mm). Its 7-element glass lens, with an f2.8 design, has macro capability (11.8" to 23.6"). Standard focus range is 23.6" to infinity. The D-600L can take either 1280 × 1024 or 640 × 512 pixel images; this means that you can take 3" by 5" magazine-quality, 266 pixel/inch images. The 4 MB SmartMedia card that comes with it can store between 4 and 50 images, depending on the size of the images you take and the amount of compression you specify. You can also purchase an 8 MB SmartMedia card. You have the option of Standard quality, High quality, and Super high for image size and amount of compression used.

The D-600L features an ISO of 100 and comes with a built-in flash that can operate in four modes, depending on existing lighting conditions. Spot metering is a feature, as well as exposure control and plus and minus 3 f-stop increments are onboard. The camera features a CCD imaging surface of 1.4 MegaPixels gross.

There is a 1.8" back panel LCD for reviewing images, an erase function as well as an image lock function for individually editing images, and a complete erase function for clearing the memory card after you've downloaded your images.

The media cards are easily downloadable via a serial cable, PCMCIA adapter, or through a 3.5" floppy disk adapter for the Macintosh and Windows. The Olympus D-600L weighs 16.5 oz.

THE POLAROID PDC-3000 (STREET PRICE: $2,000–$3,000)

One of the unique advantages of this camera is that it features four compression modes: no compression at all, 2:1 lossless compression, 5:1 lossy, and 10:1 lossy compression. The PDC-3000 comes with an f2.8 lens, equivalent to a 38mm lens, with a focus of 10" to infinity. You can also purchase a 60mm f2.8 lens with focus range of 24" to infinity. The ISO equivalents on this camera are 25, 50, and 100. The scanning aperture shutter is microprocessor controlled and has a speed of 1/25 to 1/500 of a second. The aperture is f2.8 to f.11. The camera has automatic exposure control, electronic auto-focus, and a built-in flash that casts up to 15 feet.

The Polaroid has its own digital file format (software is included for saving and translating file formats) called Polaroid Digital Negative (PDN). You have the option of opening the image on your computer in one of two sizes: the 1600 by 1200 pixel native format, or the smaller 800 by 600 pixel format. The PDN format is proprietary to the camera, and although you are not required to save in this format, Polaroid claims that the PDN format written to your hard disk saves space.

System requirements for the Polaroid for the Macintosh are a PowerPC, System 7 or later, 16MB of RAM recommended, and 20MB of free hard disk space. For Windows, a Pentium or better is required, a SCSI card, Win 95 or later (or Windows NT), 32MB of RAM recommended, and 20MB of free hard disk space.

The Polaroid can produce a 5.6MB file (1600 by 1200 pixels), and at a lower resolution, a 1.4MB file. It comes with a 20MB memory card, a SCSI II interface for the Macintosh or Windows, and a flash card PCMCIA card adapter.

You can take a picture every 4 seconds without flash and every 12 seconds with flash. The PDC-300 weighs 2 lbs. and has a magnesium body.

We must conclude that for the price of a modest digital camera, the resulting images are good for proof prints. And at the size capability for the images, Web design work becomes a snap. If you're looking longingly at a midpriced camera, anywhere from $1,500 and up, you have an alternative. If you find the immediacy of digital photography to be of prime interest, go for the midpriced camera. But if you want sharp, larger digital images, buy a traditional 35mm SLR, get a transparency scanner, and pocket the change. For the most serious of photographers, whose career depends on accuracy and speed, the high-ticket digital camera is the logical selection. The *highest*-priced cameras ($10,000 and substantially higher) are essen-tially a high-end 35mm lens and body with data acquisition and storage hardware wrapped around them. This means that you can swap lenses, adjust the ISO and the f-stop, tweak the focus manually as well as automatically, and the camera will hook up to the lighting equipment you've invested in, so there's a sort of backward compatibility with what you already own.

SUMMARY

What digital acquisition means to the Photoshop user is the capability to bring the real world into the computer for manipulation. As with anything, the trade-off we as designers must all face is quality versus price. If you have no negatives to work with in your profession, a flatbed scanner is a must. You've also seen in this chapter how you can do creative things by direct-scanning with a reflective scanner. If your budget is tight and you have a little wait time, PhotoCD technology offers crisp, small to large images at a pittance of a price per image, and PhotoCDs keep the large number of images you'll take in your career out of precious hard disk space. For the demanding traditional photographer, a transparency scanner fits the bill. You can scan transparencies to any resolution you like, and you get better quality pictures than PhotoCDs, and in less time. If you need real-world photography at a moment's notice for Web work or personal reasons, you can easily afford one of the less expensive models of digital cameras. On the opposite end of the spectrum, the high-end digital cameras provide absolute photographic quality compared to conventional film cameras, and we strongly suspect that if your profession demands a megacamera, you probably work for a large company, and *they* should buy one for you to use!

Chapter 3 takes us back to the menus, palettes, and features of the world's most popular imaging application. If you've been wondering how to work more efficiently in Photoshop, and how to calibrate your monitor, look no farther than the next page. You'll see how to make Photoshop into *your* Photoshop.

CUSTOMIZING PHOTOSHOP 5

One key to creating a successful product is to feature customization. Imagine buying a car without adjustable seats, for example—no one would even take it out for a test drive! Adobe Systems realizes that Photoshop users think and work differently, and wants to allow you, the creative individual, to make Photoshop your personal imaging environment.

Placed throughout the program, you will find numerous options you can set to your liking. Some of these options are on palettes, and others are tucked away in flyout menus, but the majority of optional settings can be found under Preferences. Our first stop in customizing Photoshop 5 is the Preferences dialog box(es).

THE PREFERENCES DIALOG BOX

Press Ctrl(⌘)+K (File, Preferences) to display the Preferences dialog box. This is the place to start when you are prepared to make Photoshop your *own* work environment. From this dialog box, shown in Figure 3.1, you can specify what cursors look like, which colors represent transparent areas, the color and divisions of the gridlines, location of scratch disks, and so on. Each set of preferences can be accessed by pressing Ctrl(⌘)+1, 2, 3, and so on, or you can go sequentially through the list (as you read this chapter) by pressing N. First on the menu is the set of General preferences.

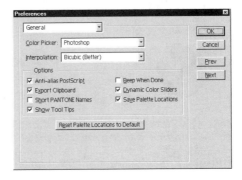

FIGURE 3.1　*The Preferences dialog box is where most of the global settings are located.*

SETTING THE GENERAL PREFERENCES

General preferences is where you specify how the clipboard holds information, how color sliders are displayed, what type of color picker you want to use in Photoshop, and what type of *interpolation*—the reassigning of pixels in an image—you want to use.

COLOR PICKER

If you use Windows, you want Photoshop's Color Picker, plain and simple. With the Photoshop Color Picker, you can select from the entire color spectrum, based on four color models, and choose from several custom color matching systems, such as TRU-MATCH and PANTONE. In contrast, the Windows color picker features only basic colors, allowing 16 custom colors based on two color models.

On the Macintosh, System 8 has six color pickers, including one for the Web. The dialog box and four of the color pickers can be seen in Figure 3.2. Although the Macintosh system color picker offers more selections, the author recommends sticking with Photoshop's Color Picker, for the simple reason that PANTONE and other electronic color-matching specifications exist in Photoshop's Color Picker system, and not in the Macintosh color picker selections.

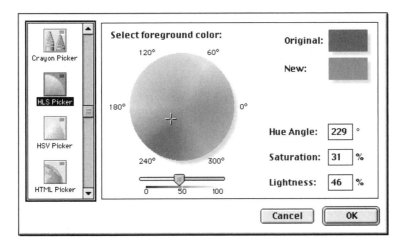

FIGURE 3.2   *The Macintosh user can select from six color pickers, including one for the Web.*

INTERPOLATION

When you change the number of pixels in an image by using the Image Size or Layer Transform command, Photoshop creates or deletes pixels based on the *interpolation* (interpretation) method you have chosen.

Nearest Neighbor, as mentioned in Chapter 1, "Getting Acquainted with Computer Graphics and Terms," is the lowest quality of the three choices. This method gives modified selections a jagged appearance.

Bilinear interpolation is a trade-off between speed and quality. Many applications use bilinear interpolation when they resize images, and although the process is good, it is not the most aesthetically pleasing nor accurate method of reassigning pixels.

Bicubic interpolation is the most precise form of interpolation. Though the slowest of the choices, tonal gradations are the smoothest. Refer to Chapter 1 for a graphical representation of the bicubic interpolation process.

ANTI-ALIAS POSTSCRIPT

To remove the aliased outlines from a pasted or placed selection from EPS files, leave this box checked. If you work with line art, you might want to turn off this feature to maintain the line's hard edges as the line art is rasterized.

NOTE

Any changes you make to the Preferences settings are saved *only* when you exit Photoshop (crashes excluded). These settings are written to the Preferences folder in the System Folder on the Macintosh, and to the PHOTOS40.PSP file in the Prefs subdirectory in the Photoshop directory in Windows. If you want to reset all preferences to their defaults, delete your Preferences file.

Also, if you should run into problems launching Photoshop at any time, those problems probably occur because the Preferences file is corrupted. Trash this file, restart Photoshop (your preferences will be lost), and then rebuild your preferences.

EXPORT CLIPBOARD

With Export Clipboard checked, anything copied to the system clipboard will remain there when you close Photoshop. This feature is a welcome one if your system doesn't have the RAM needed to run both Photoshop and a host application for the contents of the clipboard. You can close Photoshop, freeing up system resources; the image is still on the clipboard, and you can then paste the image into PageMaker or QuarkXPress, for example.

On the other hand, with Export Clipboard *un*checked, the clipboard contents will be purged when Photoshop is closed, thus freeing up system resources.

SHORT PANTONE NAMES

Some applications, such as Adobe PageMaker, cannot read *long* PANTONE names. Checking Short Pantone Names ensures that PANTONE color names will match the naming conventions in other applications, and you can work with the same colors as those specified in Photoshop. This feature is particularly handy if you're exporting Duotones or EPS files that contain a PANTONE spot color.

SHOW TOOL TIPS

When Show Tool Tips is checked, a short description will appear when you hover the cursor over a tool or palette element. For toolbox items, the keyboard shortcut is given after the name. This feature is especially handy for the new Photoshop user.

BEEP WHEN DONE

Photoshop can sound a beep when it finishes performing a task. The beep is useful if you are away from your system during the task. If beeping simply isn't your thing, Photoshop has two visual indicators of task progress: the hourglass (Macintosh: the wristwatch) and the progress bar, located on the status bar in Windows.

DYNAMIC COLOR SLIDERS

When this box is checked, the slider colors on the Color palette change as you drag. The only time you want this feature turned off is when you want to manually enter the color's values and improve Photoshop's performance by an imperceptible amount.

SAVE PALETTE LOCATIONS

With Save Palette Locations unchecked, Photoshop will open with all palettes in default positions. If you break apart a grouped palette, create a new palette group, hide or show only certain palettes, and want Photoshop to open with this view, be sure to check this option.

RESET PALETTE LOCATIONS TO DEFAULT

Clicking this button will do exactly what the title implies—it returns all palettes to their default locations. This is useful if you work on a multiuser machine or have "lost" some palettes. This button affects only palette locations, not settings you've entered in those palettes.

SETTING THE FILE-SAVING PREFERENCES

Figure 3.3 shows the Macintosh Preferences for Saving Files. PC users should note that this dialog is available on the Macintosh only.

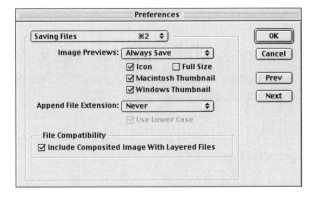

FIGURE 3.3   *The Preferences choices for Saving Files on the Macintosh.*

IMAGE PREVIEWS

Image Previews are the thumbnails in the Open dialog box or icons on the desktop (Macintosh). They are useful for quickly identifying a file by sight. The choices are Never Save, Always Save, and Ask When Saving.

On the Macintosh, you have four kinds of image previews to choose from:

- **Icon.** Saves a preview icon of the image for the desktop or file folder.

- **Macintosh Thumbnail**. Creates a thumbnail for preview in the Open dialog box on the Mac platform.

- **Windows Thumbnail**. Check this box if the image will be used cross-platform and you want a preview in the Windows Open dialog box. Adding a Windows thumbnail will also add about 50 KB to the file size.

- **Full Size**. This preview is for other applications that open Photoshop images for placement at 72 pixels/inch. This is not an option for EPS files.

FILE EXTENSION

On the Mac, this is called Append File Extension. You can choose to add the three-character file extension that denotes the file's format. This is useful if you use the file on a Windows system.

In Windows, you can choose whether the file extension is upper- or lowercase. Lowercase file extensions are usually easier to read than uppercase.

FILE COMPATIBILITY

Checking File Compatibility will allow your image to be opened by applications that support only Photoshop 2.5 files. If you know you will not need this feature, turn it off. Otherwise, you will needlessly add to the saved file size.

SETTING DISPLAY & CURSORS PREFERENCES

The display and cursor preferences for both the Mac and the PC are the same, and we cover these options in the following sections.

DISPLAY

There are four items in the Display field:

- **Color Channels in Color**. Allows you to view the color channel in its respective color rather than in black and white. The color view is more memory intensive, so check this only if you are proofing problem areas (such as saturation and coverage) in CMYK mode images.

- **Use System Palette**. Unless your video card displays a maximum of 256 different colors at one time, leave this option *un*checked. Using the system palette with a video card whose memory is 512 KB RAM or less (which is virtually impossible to find in 1998) causes the displayed image in Photoshop to use only system palette colors, and colors the video system cannot reproduce will be dithered.

- **Use Diffusion Dither**. Diffusion Dither minimizes dither patterns you would see onscreen when working with a 256-color video card. Leave this unchecked if your card supports more than 256 colors.

- **Video LUT Animation**. You want to check Video Lookup Table Animation; the only situation in which you'd want this turned off is with a card (a very old card) that does not support LUT Animation. LUT Animation allows instant viewing of any color or contrast changes you make to an image. Otherwise, you would not see the change you made in the Hue command, for example, until you clicked OK.

CURSORS

If you are new to Photoshop or easily forget which tool you are using, choose Standard as a reminder. Standard displays the symbol for the tool—a paintbrush for the Paintbrush tool, for example. Many Photoshop users find greater accuracy with Precise or Brush Size selected. Precise gives you a cross-hair cursor, and Brush Size shows a circle that indicates the actual size of any painting tool (regardless of zoom factor!). You can see the Display & Cursors dialog box in Figure 3.4.

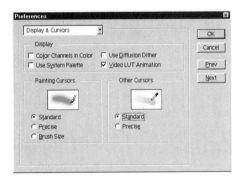

FIGURE 3.4   *From Display & Cursors, you can determine the appearance of your mouse cursor.*

SETTING THE TRANSPARENCY & GAMUT PREFERENCES

Transparency refers to what you see in an image window of a layer image when you've erased part of the background. *Gamut* refers to the color space you're working with. If, for example, your image is in CMYK mode, there can be colors you'll use in the image that will be "out of gamut"; they fall outside the range of colors that can be expressed in the given color space.

TRANSPARENCY SETTINGS

From the Transparency Settings field, shown in Figure 3.5, you can change the color and grid size of the transparent areas in an image that has layers. The default gray-and-white checkerboard is useful in most design situations, unless you are editing an image with lots of small black-and-white areas. If you're editing a gray-and-white checkered tablecloth image, for example, you would want to choose different transparency colors and the Photoshop grid to contrast against the colors in your image.

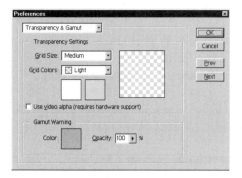

FIGURE 3.5   *The Transparency & Gamut Preferences dialog box.*

GAMUT WARNING

Gamut is the range of colors in a color system that can be displayed or printed. The purpose of a gamut warning is to notify you of a color that is visible onscreen but cannot print in the CMYK model because there is no equivalent color. This warning feature is valuable if you want to replace out-of-gamut color with the color of your choice. Otherwise, when you convert the image to CMYK, Photoshop will bring out-of-gamut colors into gamut, and you might not like Photoshop's choice. To check for any out-of-gamut colors (you might need to change the default gray to a color that contrasts with colors in your image), choose View, Gamut Warning. To bring these areas back into gamut, you might try the Sponge tool in Desaturate mode; go over the highlighted out-of-gamut areas until the out-of-gamut preview color goes away.

SETTING UNITS & RULERS PREFERENCES

The Units & Rulers Preferences enable you to change the ruler's unit of measurement and specify the width of columns and gutters.

RULERS

Six units of measurement are available: pixels, inches, cm, points, picas, and percent. You can make the Rulers display along the edges of an image window by pressing Ctrl(⌘)+R, or choose View, Show Rulers. The rulers appear along the left and top of the image window. To call up the Units & Rulers Preferences box shown in Figure 3.6 directly from the workspace, double-click anywhere on the rulers. If you select Show Rulers in one image, all subsequent images you open will also show rulers until you choose Hide Rulers.

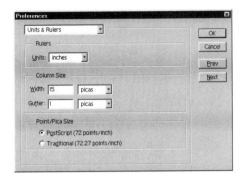

FIGURE 3.6   *Units & Rulers offer six units of measurement for the rulers.*

COLUMN SIZE

A rarely used feature for the average Photoshop practitioner, unless you work for a publisher who requires you to size your images according to columns, is the Column Size feature. As an example of when you would use the Column Size option, say that your publisher wants an image that's two columns wide; each column is 12 picas wide, with a gutter of 3 picas, so you enter those values here. Now, the image you are preparing to send must fit these dimensions. From the Image Size dialog box, choose Columns from the Width drop-down menu and enter **2** for the width. Click OK, and the image is sized to your publisher's specifications.

POINT/PICA SIZE

If you work with points and picas, and output to either a PostScript or traditional device, you need to specify which kind of output you will use. The author recommends that you click the PostScript button, which specifies that there are 72 points to an inch, because fewer and fewer commercial presses use physical layouts and the traditional physical unit specification of 72.27 points to the inch.

SETTING THE GUIDES & GRID PREFERENCES

Guides and a grid can be used to help you position elements in your image. Figure 3.7 shows four guides and a grid placed over an image; Figure 3.8 shows the dialog box.

FIGURE 3.7 *The grid and guides help you to place objects in precise locations.*

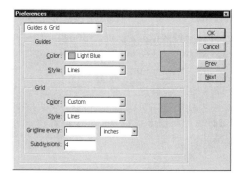

FIGURE 3.8 *The color and style of guides and grid are specified in this Preferences box.*

GUIDES

Guides are lines you drag from the rulers into the document window. Guides do not become part of the image, nor do they print. You can move, remove, and lock guides from the View menu. You can also assign any color to guides and choose between solid or dashed lines.

Guide placement and visibility are specific to each image—if you place a vertical guide at 2", this guide will not appear in the next image you open.

GRID

A grid lies on top of your entire image and is helpful when you need precision while you're working with multiple elements. You can choose any color for the grid and make it appear as Lines, Dashed Lines, or Dots. With the Gridline every and Subdivisions boxes, you determine the frequency of lines in the grid. You can show or hide the grid from the View menu. Similar to Rulers, if you select Show Grid in one image, all subsequent images you open will also show the grid until you choose View Hide Grid, whose keyboard shortcut is Ctrl(⌘)+" (quotation marks). Although this option in not in the dialog box, you can also choose Snap to Grid—a time-saving way of aligning objects across layers—by pressing Shift+Ctrl(⌘)+" (quotation marks) anytime you are working in the Photoshop workspace.

SETTING THE PLUG-INS & SCRATCH DISKS PREFERENCES

The Plug-Ins & Scratch Disks options enable you to specify the location of these items, as shown in Figure 3.9.

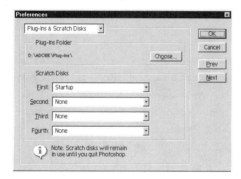

FIGURE 3.9 *Photoshop 5 offers four locations for scratch disks.*

PLUG-INS

Plug-ins are filters, developed by Adobe and third-party vendors, that work within the Photoshop environment. By default, most third-party plug-in filters are installed in Photoshop's Plug-Ins folder (all native filters are located here also). If you prefer to keep a folder containing your plug-ins elsewhere on your hard disk, you can use Choose to tell Photoshop where to look for that folder. The author recommends keeping with the default of the Photoshop Plug-Ins folder. If you move third-party filters, you must also move Photoshop's native plug-ins (which makes no sense unless you're running out of hard disk space); Photoshop cannot load plug-in filters from two different locations in one session.

SCRATCH DISKS

When you exceed the available RAM on your machine, Photoshop will write to the *scratch disk*, which is a temporary space defined on your hard disk(s). This feature enables you to continue working in Photoshop without crashing your machine, although there will be an obvious decrease in performance. RAM speed and hard disk speed are a magnitude of difference in speed—RAM's much faster at reading and writing.

New in Photoshop 5 is the option to assign four locations for scratch disks (one reason Adobe created this option is the memory-intensive History palette). When you exceed the allocated RAM during a Photoshop session, information is written to the first scratch disk. When the first scratch disk is full, Photoshop writes to the second scratch disk, and so on. You want to assign the disk with the most space (uncompressed and defragmented!) to the First field. Work your way down to Fourth, if your system has a third or fourth hard disk location, assigning First to the disk with the most free space, and Fourth (last) to the disk with the least amount of free space. Be sure to have more scratch disk space allocated than RAM, measured in megabytes. Photoshop will use only the amount of RAM equal to the amount that you have in scratch disk space. For example, if you have 128 MB RAM, yet only 30 MB scratch disk space, Photoshop will use only 30 MB of RAM. And in this scenario, you are severely (and needlessly) impinging on Photoshop's performance.

You can monitor whether your scratch disks are being used by clicking on the Document Sizes flyout menu button, located on the status bar, and choosing Efficiency. On the Macintosh, the Document Sizes field is at the bottom of the scroll bar in each image window. To the left of the flyout icon is a percentage of the amount of RAM Photoshop is using. At 100%, Photoshop is using only RAM to perform the operations. A display under 100% indicates that Photoshop is using the scratch disks.

SETTING THE MEMORY & IMAGE CACHE PREFERENCES

Proper settings for memory are imperative for optimum performance in Photoshop. Figure 3.10 shows the Windows version of the Memory & Image Cache preferences.

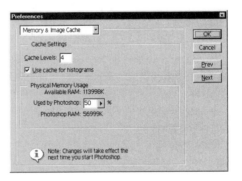

FIGURE 3.10 *The Windows Memory & Image Cache Preferences dialog box.*

CACHE SETTINGS

Photoshop uses image caching to speed the screen redraw during editing. Image caching holds several copies of the document in memory to update the screen quickly when operations such as applying color adjustments and Layer Transform are performed. Cache Settings of 2 or 3 are best for a file under 10 MB, and 4 is good for images of around 10 MB. The maximum setting is 8, and you'll want to experiment with the settings if you work with files larger than 10 MB. Be aware that the higher you set the cache, the more it will drain your system resources.

The Use cache for histograms option is best left unchecked for complete and consistent histogram readings. When checked, the zoom ratio and any previous histograms during that session will influence the histogram.

PHYSICAL MEMORY USAGE

The amount you enter for Physical Memory Usage will affect Photoshop's performance more than the scratch disk and cache settings. Macintosh and Windows each have a different method for specifying memory usage.

On the Macintosh, click on the Photoshop icon and then choose File, Get Info from the Apple menu to view the Info box, shown in Figure 3.11. The Suggested Size is the amount of RAM Photoshop needs. The Preferred Size field is where you can enter a specific amount of RAM to dedicate to Photoshop. How much can you allocate to Photoshop? Follow these steps:

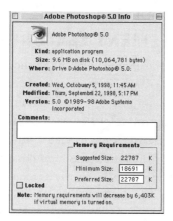

FIGURE 3.11   *To specify the amount of RAM for Photoshop on the Macintosh, use the program's Info palette.*

DEFINING PHOTOSHOP MEMORY ON THE MACINTOSH

1. Open all applications that you must use at the same time as Photoshop. Be aware that the more you open, the less RAM you'll have for Photoshop.

2. Choose About This Computer from the Apple menu.

3. Notice the value in Largest Unused Block. This is the amount of memory currently available and you can allocate no more than 90% of this value to Photoshop. Do the math and proceed to step 4.

4. With Photoshop closed, click once on the Photoshop icon. Press ⌘+I to bring up the Info box and enter the amount from step 4 in the Preferred Size field.

5. Close the Info window.

NOTE

Even if you think you'll never need an application running outside of Photoshop, you cannot allocate 100% of Physical Memory Usage to Windows 98, 95, or NT. The Windows operating system prohibits an application from stealing all system resources. So you can type 100% in this box, but all the memory that will be allocated to Photoshop will actually be about 85%.

On the Windows platform and in the Physical Memory Usage field, you can enter the amount of RAM you want to dedicate to Photoshop. The default setting of 50% is a good trade-off between draining your system by yielding all resources to Photoshop and not yielding enough. During Photoshop sessions, if the Efficiency readout (as described under Cache Settings) rarely or never drops below 100%, you can increase the percentage in the Physical Memory Usage field.

PHOTOSHOP'S NEW COLOR MANAGEMENT FEATURES

In order to accommodate all Photoshop users (who have a broad range of production needs), the simple File/Color Settings/Monitor Setup command is gone. Color management in Photoshop now consists of three related entities: Gamma control, color settings for different types of color spaces, and ICC profiles. This is clearly going to take a little learning if you're new to Photoshop, and it's going to require some rethinking to get the best output if you're a seasoned Photoshop user. We *strongly* recommend that you read the following sections carefully; if you don't, you risk ruining the data in an image file, and you'll be working with an onscreen image that's darker or lighter than you want.

LATE-BREAKING NEWS ON VERSION 5.0.2

As you are reading this, Adobe has already released a patch, version 5.0.2, for version 5. Aside from a number of fixes to the Type tool, layer effects improvements, and support for Illustrator version 8 data, Adobe has made it easier for novices and professionals alike to ensure accurate screen representation of images and faithful output.

The following sections walk you through setting up color management in version 5.0.2. Because the authors are working with an early prototype of version 5.0.2, the information was accurate at the time of this writing, but might not be when you attempt this. Please check out our Web site at http://www.TheBoutons.com/updates/ for the most current information on Photoshop 5.0.2, and if you don't already have the upgrade to 5.0.2, check Adobe's site at http://www.adobe.com to learn how you can get the update.

THE ADOBE GAMMA CONTROL PANEL

When using the Adobe Gamma control panel, you should define a Gamma for your monitor based upon what your eyes tell you, and not the presets the program offers. First of all, "what is Gamma?" might be a good question to ask yourself before engaging in the Gamma utility's wizard (the Assistant on the Macintosh). Gamma is the *non-linearity of signal to brightness*; all monitors have their particular characteristics, but generally, as voltage increases through the video circuitry to the monitor, there will be a falloff in the monitor's brightness, especially noticeable in the midtones of what you're viewing. This voltage versus brightness curve is called the *Gamma curve*, and to compensate for the non-linearity of voltage versus brightness, everyone has a different Gamma displayed on their monitors. Typically, the Macintosh has a Gamma of 1.8, and Windows machines display a Gamma of 2.0. Regardless of what you might read in online Photoshop documentation, these are the values for the respective operating platforms; if you trust the author on this one, you'll have a much easier time calibrating your system to match different outputs. It is the author's advice to avoid using the Gamma control panel unless you feel that all your images in all your applications are displaying too light or too dark. There are things you want to do first to calibrate the tonal scheme of images displayed in Photoshop and other applications:

- Wipe the monitor screen with a damp cloth to remove particles from the air that have been attracted by static electricity.

- Adjust the room lighting. If you're in an office environment, try to explain your need to your boss; if she says "No can do," get on a ladder and unscrew the fluorescent tubes in the ceiling fixture. It's important to have some ambient, indirect lighting where you work, but indirect lighting on your screen. You should not, for example, see the lights in your room reflected in the monitor.

- Adjust the Brightness/Contrast controls on your monitor. Rule number 1 in professional imaging is to avoid changing the image data; change your viewing conditions instead. The reason for this rule is that lighting and monitor contrast can be changed, and then changed back again. But once you change the appearance of, for example, a TIFF file, you can never change its tones or colors to their original state again. Changes made to bitmap images are progressive changes—you can only make changes on top of changes, on top of changes, on...

If none of the recommendations improves the tonal balance of an image, then by all means run Adobe Gamma. If you're unhappy with the results of Adobe Gamma, the saved setting is a file (in Windows with the *.icm extension) in the System Color folder; you can delete the file, and your default monitor settings will be restored. Similarly on the Macintosh, at the end of the Adobe Gamma setup, you're asked to name the saved settings, and the file can be found in the System/Preferences/ColorSync folder.

RUNNING THE ADOBE GAMMA CONTROL PANEL

The Adobe Control Panel can be found under the Start menu, Settings, Control Panel on Windows 95. The Adobe Gamma control panel in Windows NT is located under Photoshop/Goodies/Calibration/Adobe Gamma.cpl. Double-click this file to open the step-by-step Gamma Control dialog boxes. On the Macintosh, you choose the Apple menu, Control Panels, Adobe Gamma.

In Figure 3.12, you can see the opening screen for the Adobe Gamma utility.

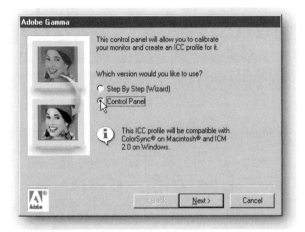

FIGURE 3.12   *Monitor and Gamma settings adjustments are performed in the Adobe Gamma Control Panel.*

On the opening screen, you have your choice of Step By Step mode of calibration or going directly to the Control Panel to perform tonal corrections. Click the Control Panel button and then click Next.

You can see in Figure 3.13 that if there is a specific color profile you want to use, you click Load in the ICC Profile field and locate the profile. Otherwise, use the default Adobe Monitor Settings.icm (default System Profile on the Macintosh). All the settings you enter will write to this profile.

Brightness and Contrast settings are performed by adjusting screen elements in this dialog box via your monitor's dials (or buttons). First you need to adjust the contrast of your monitor to the highest setting, which is the easiest part of performing a Gamma calibration. Next turn the brightness level all the way up, and then turn it down until the gray boxes (located between the black boxes) become as dark as possible, keeping the white area (immediately below the gray and black squares) as white as possible. A word of caution: The longer you look at the white box, the more your eyes will adjust and the harder it will be to notice if the white is still as bright as it should be. Perform this step within a few seconds and don't hesitate to move the brightness back to the highest settings and start again.

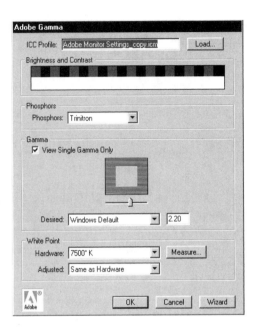

FIGURE 3.13 *Monitor and Gamma settings are entered in the Adobe Gamma dialog box.*

The phosphors that make up the red, green, and blue of your monitor's picture can vary with each manufacturer. Check the documentation that came with your monitor and select the appropriate phosphor from the Phosphors drop-down menu. If you are unsure of the phosphors used on your screen, you might as well choose Trinitron; Trinitron tubes and their equivalents are used in most monitors today.

Adjusting the Gamma slider can be as tricky as working in the Brightness and Contrast field—your eyes can adjust quickly, making the correct setting difficult to notice. Move the slider back and forth until the center box fades into the immediate background. A solid color will obviously not fade into a stripe pattern, but what you are looking for is the point where the box is least noticeable within the background. Squinting at the box helps you evaluate a match. You can uncheck View Single Gamma Only and individually adjust each of the RGB colors. A Gamma of 1.8 is the default on the Macintosh, 2.0 is the Windows 95 default. As mentioned earlier in this chapter, these default settings might look wrong when your monitor is displaying images—if it looks wrong, it is wrong. In this case, skip the default setting and use what your eyes tell you is correct while adjusting the Gamma control(s).

Click Measure if you know the setting for Hardware is incorrect in the White Point field. An alert box with directions appears—be sure to read and understand those directions before clicking OK (Next) to continue. For your next step, the screen will go black, displaying three gray squares. You should be able to click the square that contains the most neutral gray within the first few seconds. Again, the longer you look at the screen, the more your eyes will adjust, thus making an objective choice more difficult. Press Esc when you think you've chosen the most neutral color box.

Finally, you are probably best off leaving the Adjusted options at their default of Same as Hardware. In Windows, click OK to finalize your Gamma corrections and to close the Control Panel; click Save in the attention box that appears after clicking OK; you're finished. On the Macintosh, click the Close box, click the Save button in the attention box, and you're finished.

COLOR SPACE

Adobe has taken the position, and rightly so, that color space as saved within an image file is not the same as the color space your monitor and video card are capable of displaying. In fact, colors saved to an image file can have a greater *gamut*—an expressible number of unique colors—than your monitor can display. For this reason, Adobe has created a number of RGB settings that you can customize to define Photoshop's display of color space, for any particular image, that works best for you.

USING THE COLOR MANAGEMENT WIZARD

When you open an image for the first time in Photoshop 5.0.2, you are presented with a Color Management Wizard—a step-by-step series of dialog boxes that guides you through specifying the color setting that Photoshop uses when displaying an image in the workspace. After experimenting with the same image, using five different machines (and monitors and video cards), the authors believe there are two reasonable options in the Color Management system: Use Default Settings (5.0.2) and Imitate Photoshop 4.0 Color Handling. Figure 3.14 shows the second dialog box you'll reach after pressing Next when the Color Management Wizard starts; this is where you make a choice.

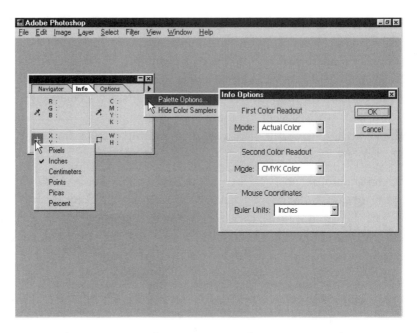

FIGURE 3.14 *These two options result in onscreen images that are consistent with previous versions of Photoshop and the display of the images in other applications.*

If you choose the Photoshop 4.0 settings, images opened in Photoshop display the same color space as when they were created in Photoshop 4.0 (or in other programs). If you choose this option, you are presented with a long string of subsequent dialog boxes that warn you that you are choosing to disable certain color-management features of version 5.0.2, most notably, the ICC Profile feature (which you get to shortly). This option is for users who never deal with CMYK conversions (for pre-press work) and want to work with Photoshop's new features without adjusting the tonal and color controls in Photoshop, and whose work is either for the Web or for film recorders. The monitor color space on the Macintosh varies depending on what type of monitor you use; in Windows, the color space, oddly, is Apple RGB (but this is actually a good option for Windows users).

If you choose Use Default Settings (5.0.2) in the Color Management Wizard, the next dialog box features the Finish button—and images you open in Photoshop 5.0.2 basically appear the same as if you were using the Photoshop 4.0 color settings. The big difference is that by choosing this option, you can now use Photoshop's ICC color profiles in your work.

You can go back to the Color Management Wizard at any time by choosing Color Management from the Help menu and then change your options.

RGB COLOR SETTINGS

If you choose to go with the Photoshop 4.0 Color Settings, Windows users can get right to work in version 5.0.2. In Figure 3.15, you can see the settings that are entered in the File, Color Settings, RGB Setup dialog box, and unless your images look drastically wrong in Photoshop's workspace, you do not need to change the settings in this box.

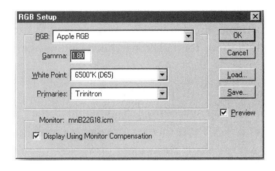

FIGURE 3.15   *These are the RGB color settings if you choose to use Photoshop 4.0's method of color handling.*

However, if you choose Photoshop's 5.0.2 default color settings, there are some tweaks that you will want to perform in the RGB Color Setup box. To better understand what you're getting yourself into, let's briefly describe a couple of the profiles that are used in the RGB Color Setup box.

By default, the workspace color space is sRGB ("*standard*" or "*simplified*" RGB). This breadth of color expression is close to, but a little smaller than, your monitor and video circuitry's capability to display color. Why cheat yourself out of the extra color space that can be shown? Let's straighten out all these options so you have both an accurately calibrated monitor and the opportunity to embed ICC Profiles should you want to in the future.

COLOR SETTINGS FOR WINDOWS

The monitor Gamma you use has already been defined earlier in this section, and it can be any name you choose. We recommend the Adobe RGB (1998) as the

RGB choice in RGB Setup, a Gamma of anywhere from 1.8 to 2.0, a White Point color temperature of between 5500° and 6500° Kelvin, and Adobe RGB (1998) in the Primaries field.

COLOR SETTINGS FOR THE MACINTOSH

When you use the Gamma Control Panel on the Macintosh, the Apple 13" RGB Standard is a very easy choice for the ICC profile—you can choose this by clicking Load, which is to the right of the ICC Profile field. This does not mean that you have to use a 13" monitor—the name of this file comes from the first standard display offered by Apple Computers, so the filename is in fact a misnomer. This profile is compatible with Photoshop's environment and should display accurate consistent color onscreen. Once you're done with the Gamma Control and are back in Photoshop, the following choices should be made in the RGB Setup box:

- RGB—Choose Adobe RGB (1998). This used to be called "SMPTE-240M," and the color space is much more broad than a monitor can display. The reasoning here is that you might be proofing CMYK images or acquiring scans that are in excess of 24 bits/pixel. If you're not doing either one of these things, it still doesn't hurt to have an application color space that's wider than your computer's video circuitry can display. In this way, no visual data is "simplified"; it's displayed, as the sRGB setting does.

- Gamma—2.0. This is a good baseline to work from, and unless images are printing darker or lighter than you see onscreen, you'll probably decide to keep the Gamma at 2.0. If your screen images don't even come close to output, try adjusting the Gamma anywhere from 1.9 to 2.2.

- White Point—Anywhere from 5500° to 6500° Kelvin should provide a neutral color cast in your images. Again, this is something you can come back and experiment with if your output is color casting toward excessively colder or warmer colors.

- Primaries—Again, Adobe RGB (1998) is the logical choice. You might notice that your images' midtones are a little more open when compared to the original file opened in an application other than Photoshop, but this can be corrected by adjusting the Gamma to a higher value.

Is this a lot of tweaking? Yes, but once you have your color accuracy down, you can, with confidence, edit images that display consistently across all applications. Do not forget to click the Save button in the RGB Setup dialog box and save this calibration work as a file to a safe place on your hard disk.

Figure 3.16 shows what both the Macintosh and Windows color settings should look like if you chose to accept Photoshop 5.0.2's settings in the Color Management utility.

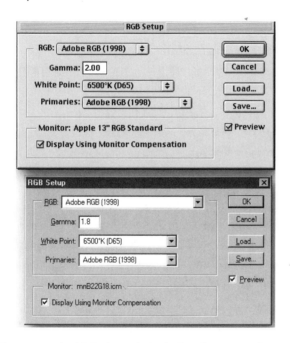

FIGURE 3.16   *These settings should closely match the display of images in other applications, and by choosing 3.0.5's color system, you have enabled profile embedding within saved images.*

ICC PROFILES

A lot of Photoshop 5.0.2's color-accuracy features revolve around the use of ICC profiles: You save RGB Setup parameters to an ICC file (the Windows extension is *.icm), you use ICC profiles when importing a PhotoCD image, and you can also elect to use ICC profiles when saving an RGB or CMYK image. The ICC standards define color space that can be expressed by a specific device. In theory, embedding ICC color profiles in an image can ensure color accuracy—what you see onscreen, for example, will look identical on someone else's monitor running the same ICC profile. The image will also print approximately to the same tones and colors when it's rendered to a high-resolution imagesetting device—if you've defined the correct profile to be embedded.

Ah, but if the designer's life were that simple! At present's best the universal implementation of ICC profiles is quite limited to bleeding-edge commercial printers. Unless you live in an urban hub, chances are that your local print shop will not be using the embedded information that's been tagged within an image you might send to them. Embedding an ICC profile adds to an image's overall size, and unless you're a whiz at pre-press, you are not going to use this feature correctly...and your printing results will be a disappointment.

Photoshop 5.0.2's File\Color Settings\Profile Setup is where you specify an ICC profile for an image that you open and save. By default, all Assumed Profiles are set to None, and for good reason. It keeps users with little or no experience with pre-press and the CMYK mode of images out of trouble! Do not touch the controls, as shown in Figure 3.17, unless you've spoken with your service bureau or commercial printer first and found out the exact specifications for the ICC profile to use (and save along with your image). If your work is entirely for onscreen presentations or for the Web, *absolutely do not* embed color profiles in images! Doing this increases file size, and some browsers and programs will not be able to read the color information correctly.

If you go ahead and start saving images with specific ICC profiles embedded in them, you're likely to see a warning box like that shown in Figure 3.18. Our advice is to click Don't Convert, let the image open, do not save the file, and reset your Profiles Setup to None for all types of images.

Photoshop does not change the data in a file that's opened and converted to the current screen color space, but it makes it very hard to edit an image when the picture is too light or the color-casting is off. Again, image color space and monitor color space are two different things, and you owe it to yourself to make sure that what you see onscreen is being saved to the same color space.

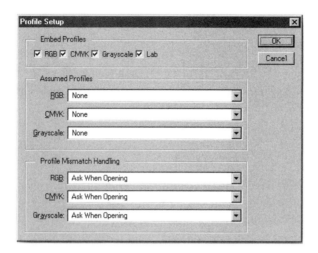

Figure 3.17 *The Profile Setup dialog box in Photoshop.*

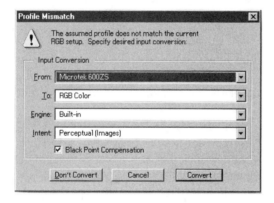

Figure 3.18 *Photoshop 5.0.2 handles profiles that do not match your color setup quite elegantly, but it is better not to have profiles set up for any type of image unless you know what you're doing with color profiles.*

To summarize, there are two things we'd like to stress to ensure that your adventures in image editing in Photoshop will contain consistent colors among other applications, systems, and other devices:

1. ICC profiles are a great idea whose proper implementation and wide acceptance have yet to come. ICC profiles, however, are extremely useful when opening a PhotoCD image, and this is covered in Chapter 2.

2. Gamma calibration, as the Adobe Gamma utility offers, is better than no calibration at all for your monitor. If your output more or less matches your screen, using the Gamma utility is like taking an aspirin when you don't have a headache. However, you should use the Adobe Gamma Control Panel if you feel that the tones in images you saved a few years ago don't look right today and that the age of your monitor has thrown the signal to brightness off.

PALETTES

Before discussing the options of each individual palette, the customizing of palette groups should be mentioned. You can tear a palette out of its group and combine palettes from different groups to create a custom group. For example, by default, the Navigator, Info, and Options palettes are one group. If you regularly use the painting tools, you would save screen space by combining the Brushes and Options palettes, then hiding the remaining palettes. Combining Brushes with Options is the author's recommendation, as you'll see in figures throughout this book.

Each palette has a drop-down menu icon located just below the Close (X) icon in Windows, and below the Zoom box on the Macintosh. In the drop-down menu, there are options specific to that palette.

Some palettes, Layers for example, have icons at the bottom for additional functions pertaining to that palette. In this book, when we recommend, say, creating a new layer, the quickest way to perform this is by clicking on the Create New Layer icon—you can easily discover what the icons mean if you leave ToolTips on and hover your cursor above an icon. You can also choose identical functions from the drop-down menu.

INFO PALETTE

A single click on the Eyedropper icons on this palette will bring out a selection of modes you can choose from, as you can see in Figure 3.19 (this figure was edited for illustration purposes; you can't really have two cursors on the same screen). A click on the + will give you a choice of measurement units for your cursor coordinates.

The First Color Readout and the Second Color Readout in the Info Palette Options set the modes for the top left and top right readouts in the Info palette, respectively. There are eight choices in each of the Mode fields. Three of the modes are:

- Actual Color—Displays values at the pointer's location in the current color mode of the image.

- Total Ink—Displays the total percentage of all CMYK ink based on the values set in the Separation Setup dialog box.

- Opacity—Displays the opacity of the current *layer* (not background) at the pointer's location.

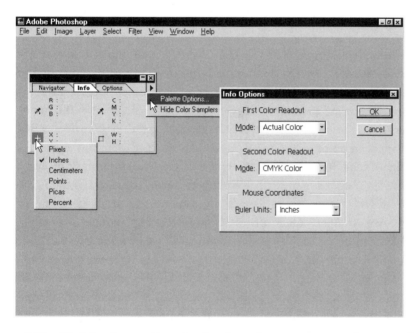

FIGURE 3.19   *The Info palette provides options for color readings, cursor position, distance specified using the Measure tool, and other handy statistics.*

The Info palette measures colors like a densitometer, provides measurements of a selection, the degree of a rotated layer, the exact position of the cursor, the results from the Measure tool, and much more. If your work relies a lot on precise measurements, you'll want to make full use of this palette. To quickly display the palette onscreen, press F8.

THE NEW COLOR SAMPLER TOOL AND THE INFO PALETTE

The Eyedropper tool in version 5 has some company on the toolbox; if you drag in the Eyedropper tool to reveal the drop down, you can choose the Color Sampler tool.

Suppose you want to pinpoint a color in an image, not to sample the color, but to see what the point's color values are, and what they will become when you apply changes to the area where the point is located in the image? For example, suppose you want to compare the RGB color of an area with the color of the same area when you apply the Hue/Saturation command to the entire image. Or suppose you want to compare the "before and after" tone of an area in an image when using the Levels command?

The solution is a simple one. You choose the Color Sampler tool, and you can click in up to four different areas in the image, leaving a color marker where you clicked. The Info palette will then extend and show a new field, with numbers 1 through 4, showing the color values underneath the markers in the image. The markers can be moved by the Color Sampler tool, and the Info palette will record the changes in color. When you make changes (or propose to make changes, while in a dialog box), the Info palette will change its bottom field to display the current color under a marker, followed by a forward slash, and to the right you'll see the proposed color change. Try placing a color marker or two in an image with the Info palette open. Then, press Ctrl(⌘)+L to display the Levels command. Change the midpoint slider's position, and you'll see how the Info palette reports changes for pixels beneath the color markers you placed in the image. In Figure 3.20, you can see the Color Selector tool and the Info palette in action. The figure does not show the Levels command, but the Levels command is being used on the image in this figure to change the midpoint in the image. Notice the before and after readings on the Info palette.

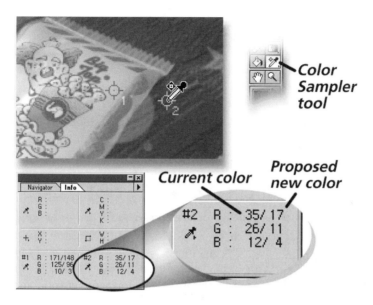

FIGURE 3.20   *The Info palette in version 5 now can record and save the values of pixels that have a Color Sampler tool marker placed on them.*

Perhaps the most useful implementation of the Color Sampler tool is in combination with the Color/Swatches palette. You can quickly and accurately define new colors based on the values shown on the Info palette by entering the numbers shown on the Info palette into the fields on the Color palette. You can then add these colors to the Swatches palette by clicking on an empty area of the Swatches palette.

The Color Sampler tool's markers are a persistent part of an image; they will stay where you placed them even after closing and then reopening a file. To remove color markers from an image, hold Alt(Opt), and then click on the marker(s).

OPTIONS PALETTE

The Options palette is where you can customize the use of all the tools on the toolbox, except the Hand and Type tools. Figure 3.21 shows the drop-down menu for all the tools: Reset Tool and Reset All Tools. Reset Tool will reset the brushes and options to the default of only the current tool. Reset All Tools will set every tool and option back to its factory default.

FIGURE 3.21   *All painting tools have the same options: Reset Tool and Reset All Tools.*

Let's take a look at tool and palette options.

RUBBER STAMP OPTIONS: USE ALL LAYERS, ALIGNED

The Use All Layers option is better described as Use All *visible* Layers. With Use All Layers checked, as shown in Figure 3.21, the Rubber Stamp clones from all layers with the uppermost layer in the image (shown on the Layers palette) being sampled first. When Use All Layers is unchecked, the Rubber Stamp samples only from the active layer. This is a useful feature, especially when there are many layers in your image.

A check in the Aligned box makes the sample point follow the Rubber Stamp on subsequent strokes. After the first stroke, if you move the cursor 2″ to the right, the sample point will also move 2″ to the right. With Aligned unchecked, the Rubber Stamp will sample from the original area until you set a new sample area.

MOVE OPTIONS: PIXEL DOUBLING, AUTO SELECT LAYER

When you move layer contents, the screen redraw is best described as jerky. To minimize this effect, you can choose Pixel Doubling as shown in Figure 3.22. To achieve this smoother movement, the layer contents become far less sharp in appearance during the move.

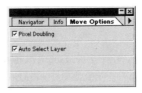

FIGURE 3.22   *Pixel Doubling and Auto Select Layer are available when the Move tool is active.*

Auto Select Layer is a new feature that enables you to click on a layer's contents and move it, regardless of which layer is currently active. In previous versions of Photoshop, you had to make the layer active before the Move tool could be used.

Brushes: New Brush, Load, Replace, and Save Brushes, Changing Brush Size

All the painting tools (third through sixth row on the toolbox) have the same drop-down menu options on the Brushes (*not* Options) palette, as shown in Figure 3.23. Any changes you make from this menu affect the brushes for all the painting tools.

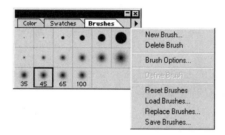

FIGURE 3.23   *The Brushes palette.*

New Brush allows you to design a brush tip (see Figure 3.24).

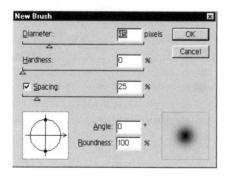

FIGURE 3.24   *In the New Brush dialog box you can configure a new brush for the Brushes palette.*

The diameter can be as small as 1 pixel and as large as 999 pixels. The range of Hardness is from the softest at 0% to the hardest at 100%. Spacing is the distance between brush marks in a stroke. For example, the Pencil with 100% spacing will place a mark each time the stroke moves 100% of the Pencil's current brush diameter. This effect and other Spacing settings are shown in Figure 3.25. If you prefer the smoothest spacing setting, uncheck the box to the left of Spacing. The last item in the New Brush dialog box is where you can design the shape and angle of a brush. You can drag on the anchor points to flatten the circle, and you can drag within the box to rotate the brush. The Angle and Roundness can also be entered manually. A preview of your new brush is shown in the lower right.

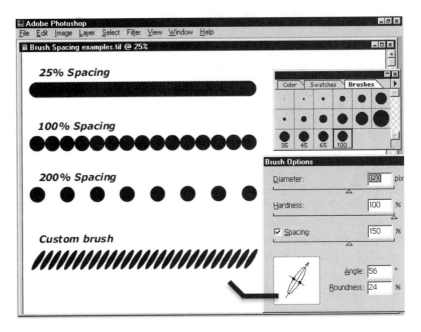

FIGURE 3.25 *Spacing and the shape and angle of a brush are performed in Brush Options.*

Delete Brush will delete the brush that is currently selected.

The Brush Options dialog box is identical to New Brush if the active brush is circular. Otherwise, a smaller box appears with Spacing and Anti-aliased as your options. Brush Options can also be chosen directly from a right-click on the brush.

Reset Brushes will return the brush selection to the default setting.

Load Brushes allows you to load from disk a premade set of brushes. In Photoshop's Brushes folder you will find three sets of brushes: Assorted, Shadows, and Square. Figure 3.26 shows the Brushes palette loaded with all three sets of brushes.

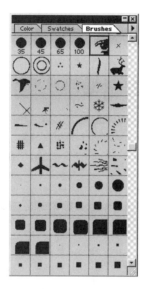

FIGURE 3.26   *A partial view of the Assorted, Shadows, and Square brush sets loaded in the Brushes palette.*

Define Brush is an interesting option you might want to choose. This option is how all the weird custom brushes were created. To create a custom brush, follow these steps:

CREATING A CUSTOM BRUSH

1. Create a new small image whose background is white. A 1″×1″ image at 72dpi in Grayscale mode is fine.

2. Make a squiggle with the Paintbrush tool.

3. With the Rectangular Marquee tool, select the squiggle.

4. Click on the Brushes palette's drop-down menu, and then choose Define Brush. The brush tip is added to your current set of tips at the end of the palette, and you can use it at any time now. Your only option for further modifying the custom brush tip is Spacing, and you can specify this in the Brush Options box, which is displayed when you double-click the custom tip.

HISTORY OPTIONS

History Options is located at the bottom of the History palette's drop-down menu, shown in Figure 3.27. In the Maximum History States field, you can enter any value between 1 and 100. In other words, Photoshop has 100 levels of undos! If you enter **14**, the History palette will remember the *last* 14 edits in your image. The higher the number you enter, the further back you can go in your session to remove an edit. Also, note that a higher number will use more system memory than a lower number.

FIGURE 3.27 *New in Photoshop 5 is up to 100 levels of Undo!*

To enable the History Brush tool to work, there must be a snapshot to read from. Photoshop can make a snapshot of your image as soon as the image is opened if you place a check in the Automatically Create First Snapshot box. Otherwise, you will need to click the Create New Snapshot icon at the bottom of the History palette.

Non-linear and linear history cause different effects on the History palette when you delete a History level. Say you have 14 edits in the History palette and drag the seventh edit to the Delete Current State icon. The Allow Non-linear History option allows the deletion of only the seventh history level. Linear history deletes the seventh level and all those proceeding it—first through the sixth.

TIP

You can delete non-essential History moves by dragging them into the trash icon if you've specified Non-Linear History. Say, for example, you have specified 14 as the maximum number of History States, and you're coming up on number 14. Before you make an editing move, scroll through the History list. Do you have a Rectangular Marquee, or several Deselects on the list? Dump them, you don't need them in your imaging work, and you pick up a few extra History States.

ACTIONS OPTIONS AND PLAYBACK OPTIONS

Accessible from the Actions drop-down menu in non-button mode, the Action Options allow you to edit the name, function key, and color of existing actions, as you can see in Figure 3.28. If you regularly use a specific action, you might want to assign it to a function key to save the time of scrolling through the Actions palette.

FIGURE 3.28   *You can edit an existing action's palette properties in Action Options.*

Playback Options control the performance of a running action (see Figure 3.29). Accelerated will run the action from start to finish. Step by Step will highlight the action in the Actions palette as it occurs. The Pause For field will highlight the action just like Step by Step, but will also add a pause between each step. The length of the pause can be anywhere between 1 and 60 seconds.

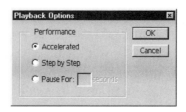

FIGURE 3.29 *The manner of a running action is set in the Playback Options dialog box.*

TIP

There are some actions you can perform using the Actions list to record them that can need user intervention. For example, suppose you want to batch feather a dozen images, but you want each image to have a different feathering amount. Before you play back your action, check the tiny menu icon to the right of the check-box, to the left of the action title. Each time you run the action now, the action will stop and display the Feather dialog box, in this example, waiting for you to type in a unique value.

Also, if you want to eliminate a step from an action you've programmed, uncheck the check-box to the left of the step before running the action. For example, if you've defined a Hue/Saturation shift as part of an action, but now want to use the action without changing Hue/Saturation, uncheck this title box, and the action, when run, will skip over this step.

LAYERS, CHANNELS, AND PATHS PALETTE OPTIONS

The choice in all of the Layers, Channels, and Paths Palette Options is the Thumbnail Size. The larger the thumbnail, the easier it is to recognize that layer's contents. The tradeoff is memory—the larger the thumbnail, the more memory is required. The author remembers when RAM was $65 per MB and as a result didn't have a lot of memory in his machine. While attempting to save a particularly large image, the error about being out of memory and scratch disk space appeared. The author selected None for the Thumbnail Size and freed up just enough memory to complete the save!

CHANNEL OPTIONS

The Channel Options box, as shown in Figure 3.30, is accessible from the Channel palette's drop-down menu (only if a channel is the current view) or when you double-click the title of a channel.

In the Channel Options dialog box, you can rename the channel to something more specific than Alpha *x*. The Color Indicates field allows you specify whether the selected area appears as white (Masked Areas) or black (Selected Areas). The author prefers Selected Areas because it is more natural to ignore white and notice black—like this page!

Spot Color (a color produced when printing a single ink) is used when working in CMYK mode. The color swatch at the bottom of the palette is where you choose the spot color. Generally, spot colors are used in addition to process color plates to visually emphasize an area. For example, a detergent box might be made of the four CMYK process colors, but there's a burst on the package that says "NEW!!!!" The client will most probably want the burst printed in a fluorescent spot color. What you do is create the "NEW!!!!" burst on a layer, painting only where the colored areas will go. You then Ctrl(⌘)+click on the layer to load it as a selection, save it to an alpha channel, and then specify in the Channel Options box that this alpha channel is to be used as a spot color. Then, when you delete the layer and convert the RGB image to CMYK and print separations, a fifth plate will kick out, and this will be the spot color plate.

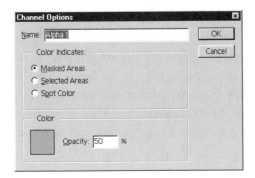

FIGURE 3.30   *Choosing to view a saved selection as white or black is performed in Channel Options.*

QUICK MASK OPTIONS (TOOLBOX)

Quick Mask Options, seen in Figure 3.31, is accessed by double-clicking on either the Edit in Standard Mode or the Edit in Quick Mask Mode icon in the toolbox.

The Color Indicates field allows you specify whether the selected area in Quick Mask mode is without color (Masked Areas) or contains color (Selected Areas). You can choose the color and opacity for the Quick Mask in the Color field. This Color feature is indispensable when, for example, you are using Quick Mask on a photo of a fire truck. The default red would be nearly impossible to see. From the color swatch, you can change the Quick Mask color to something that contrasts against red, such as cyan.

Like the Channel Options, the author recommends that Quick Mask color indicate Selected Areas, not Masked Areas. It's much easier to subtract and add from a small selected area in an image than to perform massive editing work on the areas that are not selected. We use this Color Indicates: Selected Areas several times in this book.

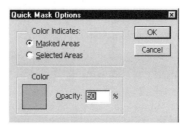

FIGURE 3.31 *In Quick Mask Options, you can set the color in Quick Mask to indicate Masked or Selected Areas.*

PERSONAL WORKING PREFERENCE

Photoshop is quite versatile—there are at least two ways to accomplish the same basic function. For example, to move from the Background layer to Layer 1, you can click on Layer 1 in the Layers palette or press Ctrl(⌘)+] (even Alt(Opt)+] performs the same function!). Finding your style of working in the Photoshop interface takes a little time and, to help you get started, let's discuss two styles.

The mousecentric user relies on clicks and double-clicks. Whenever a different tool is needed or a color adjustment dialog box must be called up, it's a click here, or two or three clicks there. This person is basically one handed. This is fine, but it slows progress.

The mouse and keyboard user takes advantage of Photoshop's keyboard shortcuts. Keyboard features include using the shortcut key to access items in the toolbox, the Spacebar to toggle to the Hand tool, keyboard (not keypad) number keys to set layer opacity or brush opacity, the [and] keys to select brush sizes, Ctrl(⌘) or Alt(Opt)+Spacebar for the Zoom tool, and so on. In effect, you can use two hands to speed the editing process.

SUMMARY

This chapter explores the many options and preferences Photoshop offers. The more comfortable you get in Photoshop, the more you will want to customize the environment, and your style of working will become *your* style. Now that you know how to make Photoshop more to your liking, adjusting the driver's seat so to speak, you will be more comfortable in your digital journeys.

In the next chapter, you will take your first ride with Photoshop and edit an image. You will find that Photoshop is both powerful and fun!

CHAPTER 4

THE PHOTOSHOP TEST-DRIVE

Remember when you were 14 and your folks let you back the car out of the garage? The trip was a little short, but it was exhilarating; you had very little idea what you were doing, but you were concentrating on the moment, the experience!

This chapter is a different sort of "test drive." Here, you get to try out many of the features in Photoshop, but you don't have to worry that you're doing anything right or wrong. The vehicle for this chapter is the Eye-Open.tif image, shown in Figure 4.1.

So what's wrong with this image that you can fix? There's not enough butter, there's only one shaker, the coffee doesn't have a lump of sugar, the clock's showing the wrong time—do you see now where the creative processes lie here? You'll take a crack at editing many different areas in the image, and through experience you'll become more familiar with Photoshop's tools.

FIGURE 4.1 *There are lots of things in this image that can get your creative motor running!*

THE MAGNETIC LASSO TOOL AND FLOATING SELECTIONS

New to Photoshop 5 is the Magnetic Lasso tool. This tool "guides" your cursor along edges of color contrast in an image, making quick work of selecting things. When you have something selected, it's a snap to make a copy of it, and move it within the image. This is precisely what you'll do with the butter in this image.

EDITING THE BUTTER

The success you'll have adding to the slab of butter has to do with the fact that the butter has a shape, but very little texture that you need to edit or align. Essentially, adding to the butter is as simple as extending the left end of it about an inch.

Here's how to use the Magnetic Lasso tool in combination with some of Photoshop's modifier keys to put more butter on the table:

CREATING A FLOATING SELECTION

1. Open the Eye-Open.tif image from the Chap04 folder of the Companion CD.

2. Press Ctrl(⌘)+the plus key until the image is at 300% viewing resolution.

3. Maximize the window. With Windows, use the Maximize/Restore button on the image window; on the Macintosh, use the Size box.

4. Hold down the Spacebar to toggle to the Hand tool, and then scroll the contents of the window until the butter is in the center of the screen.

5. Hold on the Lasso tool on the toolbox to reveal the tool flyout, and then choose the Magnetic Lasso tool.

6. Click on the top left edge of the butter, release the cursor, and then "glide" the cursor along the edge to the right of your first click point. As you can see in Figure 4.2, the Magnetic Lasso tool "knows" where the color edge exists, and follows it.

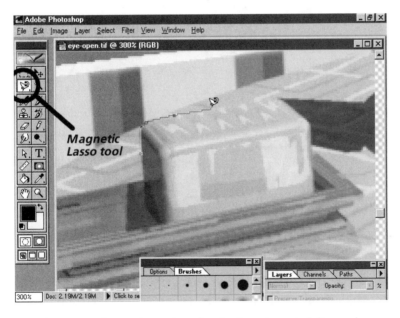

FIGURE 4.2 *The Magnetic Lasso tool recognizes color edges in an image and clings to them.*

7. "Slice off" about half the butter; create a selection like that shown in Figure 4.3. Click once at the beginning point of the selection to close it.

FIGURE 4.3 *Outline half the butter with the Magnetic Lasso tool. This is the selection you'll copy to extend the butter.*

8. Place the cursor inside the marquee selection. Hold Ctrl(⌘)+Alt(Opt) and then drag the contents of the selection to the left, as shown in Figure 4.4.

9. When you've moved the selection and it appears to line up with the rest of the butter, press Ctrl(⌘)+D to deselect the floating selection. The selection now becomes a permanent part of the image.

10. Press Ctrl(⌘)+Shift+S (File, Save As), and save the image as Eye-Open.tif in the TIFF file format to your hard disk. Keep the image open.

As you can see in Figure 4.5, everything appears to be normal with the butter, except that there are about three more servings of it. You'll continue rearranging the table in the next section.

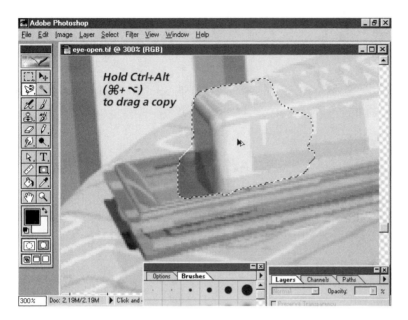

FIGURE 4.4 *Holding Ctrl(⌘)+Alt(Opt) creates a floating copy of the contents of the marquee selection.*

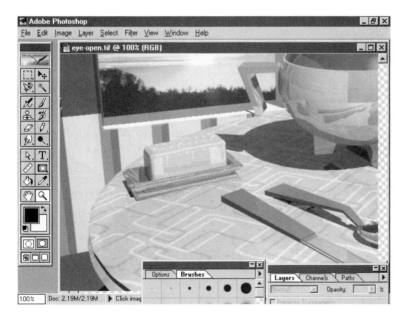

FIGURE 4.5 *It looks like butter, but it's not—it's Photoshop editing!*

THE LAYER VIA COPY COMMAND

One of the most powerful features of Photoshop 5 is its capability to isolate on their own layers the image areas you choose. The areas can then be manipulated independently of the rest of the image. It's only after you finish the composition that you might decide to merge the contents of a layer into the Background image.

COPYING THE SHAKER

You'll notice that whoever set the table wasn't a very thoughtful host; there's only one shaker and we can't tell whether it's salt or pepper. You'll fix this oversight shortly, by copying the shaker and then using a new Photoshop feature to label both shakers.

Here's how to place a duplicate of the shaker on the table:

DUPLICATING AN OBJECT WITH LAYER VIA COPY

1. Press Ctrl(⌘)+the minus key to zoom out to a 200% viewing resolution of the scene.

2. Hold down the Spacebar to toggle to the Hand tool, and then scroll your view until the shaker is in the center of the screen.

3. With the Magnetic Lasso tool, design a marquee outline around the shaker. Only the right side of the shaker will be visible in the finished image, so you do not have to be very careful as you select around the left edges.

4. Right-click (Macintosh: hold Ctrl and click), and then choose Layer Via Copy from the context menu, as shown in Figure 4.6. This puts a copy of the shaker on its own layer on top of the background.

5. With the Move tool, drag the copy shaker to the right of the original, so that the two shakers slightly overlap. Figure 4.7 shows this positioning.

6. Hide Layer 1 by clicking on the eye icon to the left of its title on the Layers palette. If the Layers palette isn't onscreen, press F7. Then, click on the Background layer title to make it the current editing layer.

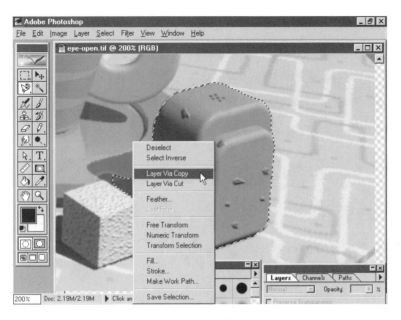

FIGURE 4.6 *The Layer Via Copy command makes a copy of a selection and places it on a new layer in the image.*

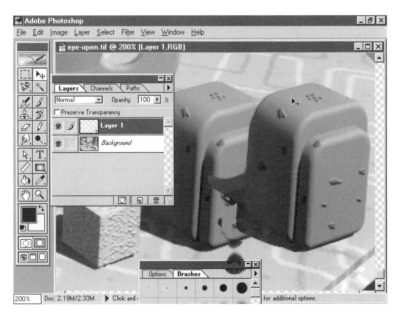

FIGURE 4.7 *The contents of a layer can be moved anywhere you like without disrupting other parts of the picture.*

7. With the Magnetic Lasso tool, design a selection around the right half of the original shaker, as in Figure 4.8.

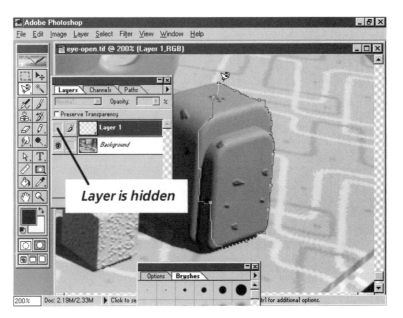

FIGURE 4.8 *Select the right half of the shaker. This selection will be used to delete the left half of the hidden shaker.*

8. Click on the Layer 1 title, click on the space where the eye icon was (to restore its visibility), and then press 5 on the keypad. This reduces the opacity of the layer's contents to 50%. Now you can clearly see the overlapping areas of the shakers.

9. Press Delete (Backspace). This removes the overlapping area of the copy shaker on Layer 1, as shown in Figure 4.9.

10. Press Ctrl($\mathcal{H}$)+D to deselect the marquee. Press 0 on the keypad to restore the contents of Layer 1 to 100% opacity.

11. Click on the Layer palette's flyout menu button, and choose Flatten Image from the menu.

12. Press Ctrl($\mathcal{H}$)+S; keep the file open.

FIGURE 4.9   *Delete the area of the copy shaker that the marquee selection encompasses.*

Now, one of the most irritating things on earth is to walk into a diner and see two identical shakers—unmarked. In the section that follows, you'll label the shakers, using Photoshop 5's new Layer Effects feature.

USING LAYER EFFECTS

Photoshop 5 comes with the following five effects that you can apply to anything you paint or copy to an effects layer:

- Drop Shadow
- Inner Shadow
- Outer Glow
- Inner Glow
- Bevel and Emboss

The effect you want for the shaker labels is sort of an engraved look, which is the opposite effect of the Bevel and Emboss Effects Layer. No problem; you simply invert the angle of the effect, and you've got instant engraving.

Here's how to use the Layer Effects to label the salt and pepper shakers:

USING THE BEVEL AND EMBOSS EFFECTS

1. On the Layers palette, click on the Create new Layer icon. This will be the Effects layer.

2. Right-click (Macintosh: hold Ctrl and click) on the Layer 1 title, and then choose Effects from the context menu.

3. Choose Bevel and Emboss from the drop-down list, and then check the Apply box to activate the controls for the effect.

You'll notice that the source of the light on the shakers is to their upper right. To make an engraving on the shakers, the angle for the effect must be pointing toward the lower left…

4. Click and hold on the flyout arrow to the right of the Angle field. Move the line in the proxy window to the lower left (about 7 o'clock), as shown in Figure 4.10.

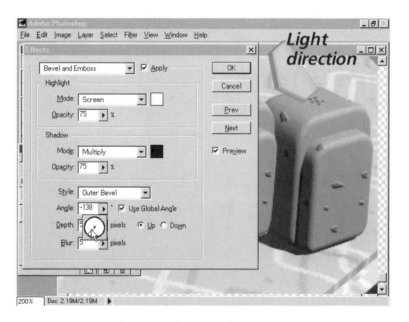

FIGURE 4.10 *Point the angle 180° in the opposite direction as the light source in the image.*

5. Click on OK to make this layer an Effects layer.

6. Press D and then press X to make the current foreground color white.

7. Choose the Paintbrush tool, choose the third tip from the left in the top row of the Brushes palette, and then draw the letter *P* on the leftmost shaker, as shown in Figure 4.11. Surprise! You're drawing in 3D!

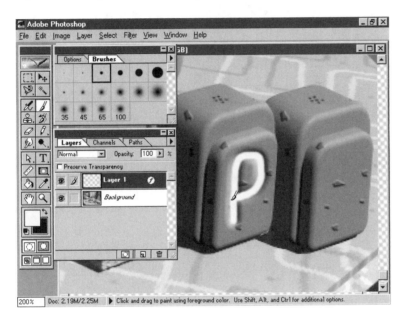

FIGURE 4.11 *Everything you paint onto the Effects layer will take on a recessed look.*

8. Paint an *S* on the other shaker, as in Figure 4.12.

9. Choose Flatten Image from the Layers menu flyout; press Ctrl(⌘)+S; keep the file open.

The letter f inside a circle on a layer indicates that the layer is an Effects layer. You can erase from the layer, apply paint, paste in an image—all the elements will take on the effect you've chosen for the layer.

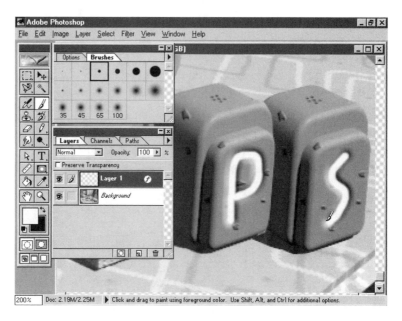

FIGURE 4.12 *By labeling the salt and pepper shakers, you take the risk out of pouring the wrong stuff on your food.*

CHANGING TIMES

Our next stop in the test-drive image is the clock on the wall. Wouldn't it be nice to make this breakfast a little later? To change the hour hand on the clock you must erase it and paint in a new one. Fortunately, the hands don't have much character; they're black triangles—easy enough to re-create.

Here's how to push 10 after 9 forward to 10 after 11:

CHANGING THE TIME ON THE CLOCK WITH QUICK MASK

1. Press Ctrl(⌘)+the plus key to zoom in to a 300% view of Eye-Open.tif. Hold down the Spacebar and scroll your view until you can see the clock in the picture.

2. With the Lasso tool, press and hold Alt(Opt) and then click a rough triangle around the hour hand. By holding Alt(Opt) you toggle the Lasso tool to the Polygon Lasso tool, shown in Figure 4.13.

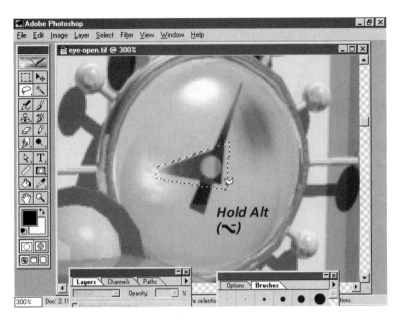

FIGURE 4.13 *Draw a selection marquee that encompasses the hour hand on the clock.*

3. Double-click on the Quick Mask mode icon toward the bottom of the toolbox. In the Quick Mask Options box, make sure that Color Indicates: Selected Areas, and then click on OK to close the Options box. You're in Quick Mask mode, and the selection marquee you created is now a color overlay in the image.

4. The cap where the hands are fastened to the clock's drive shaft should not be in the selection. With white as the foreground color, use the Paintbrush tool to paint over the cap, as shown in Figure 4.14. White removes Quick Mask, whereas Black applies Quick Mask.

5. Choose the Airbrush tool, click on the Standard Editing mode icon (to the left of the Quick Mask mode icon), and then press Alt(Opt)+click on the shade of blue that is close to the clock's hour hand. This samples the blue to use with the Airbrush tool.

6. Carefully brush inside the selection marquee until the hour hand vanishes. Figure 4.15 shows the clock at this stage of the process. Do not be concerned with the far side of the hour hand, as you'll paint in a new hand later to cover this area.

NOTE

Although this example doesn't require it, you can change the effect for a layer at any time. For example, you can make a Bevel and Emboss layer a Drop Shadow layer, simply by right-clicking (Macintosh: holding Ctrl and clicking) on the Effects layer title on the Layers palette, and then choosing Effects. Next, you disable the current effect by unchecking (clearing) the Apply box, and then you choose a different effect to apply.

FIGURE 4.14 *Remove the cap from the Quick Mask selection by painting over it with white.*

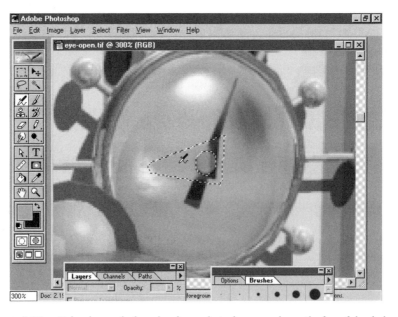

FIGURE 4.15 *Airbrush over the hour hand to make it the same color as the face of the clock.*

7. With the Lasso tool, hold Alt(Opt) and click a triangle shape that points toward the 11 o'clock position on the clock, as shown in Figure 4.16.

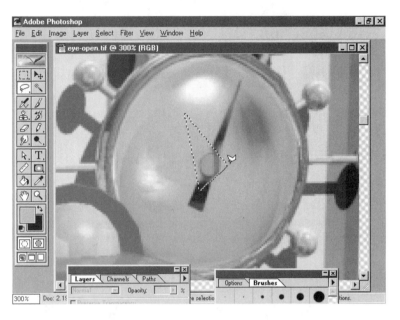

FIGURE 4.16 *Create a new hour hand outline for the face of the clock.*

8. Click on the Quick Mask mode icon; the marquee selection turns into a color overlay.

9. With the Paintbrush tool and white as the current foreground color, paint over the cap in the center of the clock to remove it from the selection, as shown in Figure 4.17.

10. Click on the Standard Editing mode icon, and then press Delete (Backspace). As you can see in Figure 4.18, the selection fills with background color (black).

11. Press Ctrl(⌘)+D to deselect the selection marquee, and then press Ctrl(⌘)+S; keep the file open.

Quick Mask is simply a different visual metaphor that Photoshop displays in an image to indicate a selected area or a masked area. Marquee selections and Quick Mask overlays are completely interchangeable. Hopefully, however, the preceding steps showed you the advantage of working with Quick Mask instead of trying to remove a circle from an active marquee selection.

FIGURE 4.17 *Remove the cap from the Quick Mask area.*

FIGURE 4.18 *Delete to background color to fill the selection marquee.*

Let's move on to the coffee cup and the lumps of sugar on the table. What can you do to creatively alter this part of the scene?

LAYER MASK MODE

Photoshop's Layer Mask mode gives the designer the opportunity to "erase" portions of an image on a layer, but the erasures aren't permanent. At any time, hidden areas can be exposed, and you can rework a layer's contents ad infinitum until you're happy with a specific arrangement.

COPYING AND MASKING A SUGAR CUBE

The Layer Mask feature is ideal for the next assignment—to dunk a lump of sugar in the coffee cup —because, naturally, only part of the sugar should be visible. You'll copy one of the sugar cubes to its own layer, and then put the Layer Mask feature to work.

ADDING SUGAR TO THE COFFEE

1. Press Ctrl(⌘)+the minus key to zoom out to 200% viewing resolution of the image.

2. Hold down the Spacebar and scroll your view until you can see the lumps of sugar.

3. Choose the Polygon Lasso tool from the Lasso tool flyout on the toolbox.

4. Click (don't drag) around the six corners of the sugar cube on the right, as shown in Figure 4.19. When you close the path at the beginning point, the selection becomes a marquee selection.

5. Right-click (Macintosh: hold Ctrl and click), and then choose Layer Via Copy from the context menu.

6. With the Move tool, drag the sugar cube upward to the center of the top lip of the coffee cup.

7. On the Layers palette, click on the Add layer mask icon, shown in Figure 4.20.

8. Press D (default colors), choose the Paintbrush tool, and then choose the fourth-from-left tip in the top row on the Brushes palette.

FIGURE 4.19 *For straight-edge selections, the Polygon Lasso tool is an ideal choice.*

FIGURE 4.20 *By clicking on the Add layer mask icon you switch to Layer Mask mode; now you can hide areas of the layer by applying black, and restore hidden areas by applying white.*

9. Brush over the bottom of the sugar cube, as shown in Figure 4.21. As you can see, the black foreground color hides areas you paint over. If you paint over too much of the cube, press X to switch foreground and background colors, and then stroke over the area you want to restore.

FIGURE 4.21 *Make the sugar cube look as though it is floating in the coffee.*

Note that in Figure 4.21, the Layers palette has an additional thumbnail icon to the right of the image thumbnail on the Layer 1 title. This is the Layer Mask thumbnail, which shows a miniature preview of areas where you've masked (painted) in the image.

10. When you've got the sugar looking partially submerged, it's time to actually delete the areas you've hidden on Layer 1. Click on the Layer Mask thumbnail on the Layers palette, and then drag it into the trash icon at the bottom of the palette. An attention box appears.

11. "Apply" means "delete those areas that are hidden"; "Discard" means "restore the areas I've hidden, and make no changes"; and "Cancel" means, "forget I dragged the thumbnail into the trash; let's continue." Click on Apply. The areas you've hidden are gone for good.

12. Choose Flatten Image from the Layers palette's flyout menu. Press Ctrl(⌘)+S; keep the file open.

WARMING UP THE COFFEE

There's a very simple trick you can use in Photoshop to make a brushstroke fade away to nothing; it's called the Fade option and it's located on the Options palette for all painting tools. In the following steps, you'll add some steam to the cup of coffee by painting with the Airbrush tool with Fade turned on.

ADDING STEAM EFFECTS WITH THE FADE OPTION

1. Double-click on the Hand tool. This reduces the viewing resolution of the image so that it fits entirely onscreen.

2. Press X so that white is the current foreground color.

3. Choose the Airbrush tool; on the Brushes palette, choose the 65-pixel tip.

4. On the Options palette, type **25** in the Fade field. This is a trial-and-error figure that happens to work in this example. (Calculating exact distances using the Fade option for any given size tip requires patience and a lot of math!)

5. Starting at the lip of the coffee cup, make a wiggly line upward until the Fade option has reduced the color to transparent, as shown in Figure 4.22.

6. Press Ctrl(⌘)+S; keep the file open.

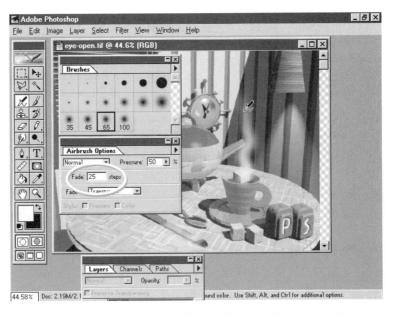

FIGURE 4.22 *Create semitransparent steam by using the Airbrush tool at partial pressure in combination with the Fade option.*

CLIPPING GROUPS

So far, we've taken a look at the way layers can display contents at partial opacity, as invisible (as with the Layer Mask), and as ordinary elements that you can move around, using the Move tool. But there is yet another property to be discovered, called clipping groups. Imagine that you've carved a stencil of a star out of a large, black piece of paper. Whatever is behind the star shows through as the contents of the star. Now imagine that there is no black paper; only the star exists, with its fill from whatever is behind it. This is what a clipping group does. The base layer is the "stencil," and whatever you place on top of the base layer is the fill for the stencil shape.

In the next section, you'll use a clipping group to recolor the coffee pot in the image.

SURFACING OVER THE COFFEE POT

If you didn't think the scene could possibly be more obnoxious in its 1950's style, you're in for a surprise. The gold bottom of the coffee pot is going to be replaced by a pattern of magenta and cream blobs. Clipping groups are the answer to the coffee pot makeover, and the best way to fully understand their power is through example…

CLIPPING GROUPS AND COFFEE POTS

1. Double-click on the Zoom tool to increase your viewing resolution to 100%. Resize the image window if necessary, and scroll your view until the coffee pot is in the center of the screen.

2. With the Magnetic Lasso tool, create a tight selection around the gold base of the coffee pot, as shown in Figure 4.23.

3. Right-click (Macintosh: hold Ctrl and click) and then choose Layer Via Copy from the context menu, as in Figure 4.24.

4. Open the Clown.tif image from the Chap04 folder on the Companion CD.

5. With the Move tool, drag the contents of Clown.tif into Eye-Open.tif, as shown in Figure 4.25. You can close Clown.tif at any time now.

6. Drag the clown texture so that it covers the base of the coffee pot.

7. On the Layers palette, press Alt(Opt) and click between the Layer 1 and Layer 2 titles. Your cursor changes to the shape shown in Figure 4.26, and the coffee pot base on Layer 1 is now a stencil through which you can see the clown texture.

FIGURE 4.23 *Let the Magnetic Lasso tool guide itself around the color edge of the coffee pot's base.*

FIGURE 4.24 *Copy the selection to its own layer.*

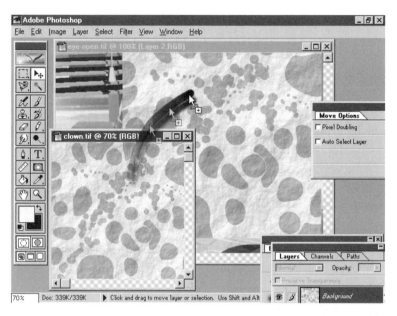

FIGURE 4.25   *Dragging the contents of one image window to another creates a new layer in the target image.*

FIGURE 4.26   *A clipping group hides everything except the contents of the base layer.*

8. Press Ctrl(⌘)+S; keep the file open.

A clipping group is a wonderful visualization tool for three reasons:

- You can change the shape of the base layer at any time,

- You can also change the contents of layers on top of the base layer.

- You can hide the base layer, thus hiding the entire clipping group, by unchecking the eye icon next to the base layer's title.

This means that if you want to go back to a shiny gold coffee pot bottom, click on the eye icon for Layer 1—all will return to normal.

Suppose, however, that "normal" isn't your cup of tea, and you want to take this clown texture a little farther toward looking realistic. You'll conclude your test drive in the following sections, with some new tools and techniques.

SHADING THE COFFEE POT

Simply put, the thing that's missing from the clown texture on the coffee pot is shading. The original gold finish had a little shadow on the left and a highlight toward the right. Both of these shading properties helped make the coffee pot base look dimensional and rounded. In contrast, the clown texture looks flat because, well…it is flat; there's no variation in tone across the surface of the coffee pot base.

Here's how to address this problem:

DIMENSIONALIZING A SURFACE

1. Click and hold on the Toning tools group on the toolbox; then, on the flyout, choose the Burn tool (the icon hand making an "okay" gesture).

2. On the Burn Options palette, choose Highlights, and leave the Exposure at its default of 50. Now, only highlight (light) areas will become more dense when you run the Burn tool over them. This is okay—the clown texture is mostly light.

3. Choose the 100-pixel tip on the Brushes palette, and then stroke over the left side of the clown texture in an arcing motion. In Figure 4.27, three or four passes have made the area significantly darker than the original areas.

FIGURE 4.27   *Add dimension to the coffee pot texture; shade the left side, using the Burn tool.*

4. Choose the Airbrush tool, choose the 65-pixel tip on the Brushes palette, and on the Options palette, type **0** in the Fade field. (Strokes will not fade now.)

5. Paint an arc once or twice through the right side of the texture. It's okay if the Airbrush strokes wipe out some of the texture, as in Figure 4.28 ; highlights on real objects tend to wipe out surface detail.

6. You're finished! The test drive has been a smashing success (okay, poor choice of words)! Save the image to your hard disk as Test Drive.psd, in Photoshop's native PSD file format. You can close the image at any time now.

Because the previous steps recommended that you keep the layers in the image, you must save it in Photoshop's PSD format, the only format that preserves layers, instead of flattening the image and saving it in the TIF, PICT, or some other common file format. By using this format, you can go back to the image and improvise some more. You might not want to eat here, but it's definitely a fun place to visit and edit, right?

In Figure 4.29, you can see the completed image. Somewhat of a transformation has taken place, eh?

FIGURE 4.28   *Use the Airbrush tool and white foreground color to simulate highlight areas on the textured coffee pot bottom.*

FIGURE 4.29   *Your test drive is complete, and you're ready now to travel the high roads to advanced Photoshop techniques.*

SUMMARY

Pure and simple, it's just plain fun to play with images, especially when there is no design goal in mind, as in this chapter. Along the way, however, you might have been intrigued by the way a certain tool works, and said to yourself, "Gosh, I'll bet I can use technique X on assignment Y, back at the office."

This chapter has been a sampler of some of Photoshop's more powerful features. As you proceed in this book, you'll find yourself building upon what you already know. Don't lose the investigative spirit, do what your instincts tell you, and you're way ahead in this digital editing game.

PART II

BASIC MAGIC USING PHOTOSHOP

CHAPTER 5

WORKING WITH NEW FEATURES

Photoshop 5 is a playground for those of us who are designers at heart. There are both new features and enhancements to existing ones. It seems as though the general graphics community's collective Wish List has been answered in version 5, and this chapter walks you through some of the most productive, exciting features.

WORKING WITH THE TYPE TOOL

There have been significant changes to the Type tool, not the least of which is the capability to preview text in an image before you commit to applying the text. Gone are the horizontal and vertical options from the Type tool dialog box; you now have vertical and horizontal tools and masking tools located on Photoshop's toolbox. Now, in addition to *autokerning* (intercharacter spacing), users can access *tracking* (how tight the kerning is), and Baseline shifting, in case you want to create a special "carnival-style" effect or simply need to bring a character up or down because the font you're using was poorly created.

This chapter includes a number of examples that show you how to leverage the power of the Type tool, using different types of graphical compositions. To be a little perverse, we'll begin with the Vertical Type tool.

USING THE VERTICAL TYPE TOOL AND DIALOG BOX

Suppose that the assignment you land is the title for the cover of "Gardening Monthly," a fictitious publication (the author hopes). The artwork has already been provided; Garden.tif is located in the Chap05 folder on the Companion CD. There's clearly room, as you'll soon see, to get creative with the use of text. The concept is to play the word "Gardening" off the word "Monthly," graphically. "Gardening" will be applied vertically as text, using a bold, tightly kerned font, whereas "Monthly" will run horizontally along the top of the cover—sleek, widely spaced, and in a lighter color than the word "Gardening."

You'll begin by creating the vertical "Gardening" text, and performing spacing and font sizing interactively:

WORKING WITH VERTICAL TEXT

1. Open the Garden.tif image from the Chap05 folder on the Companion CD. Type **33.3** in the Zoom Percentage field and then press Enter (Return). Position the document toward the top and left of the workspace, so that when you display the Type tool dialog box, you can see the target area for the text.

2. Drag on the Type tool flyout on the toolbox, and then choose the Vertical Type tool, the icon of the "T" with a down arrow beside it.

3. Click an insertion point in the upper-left corner of the Garden.tif image; the Type Tool dialog box displays. Drag the dialog box by its title bar so that you can see the left of the Garden.tif image.

4. Click the Align left icon, the leftmost of the alignment icons in the dialog box.

5. Click the Fit in window check box.

6. Choose a bold font from the Font drop-down list. Eras Black is used in this example, but you can also use Olive Antique Black, Futura, or Helvetica Black.

7. Click your cursor in the text field, and then type **GARDENING**. Highlight the entire word (by dragging from top to bottom), and then enter **75** in the Size field, with points chosen as the measurement from the drop-down list.

8. Click the lettering that appears in the Garden.tif window until the lettering is vertically centered in the blue area, as shown in Figure 5.1. Hmmmm. The text looks a little wimpy because the tracking is too loose, and the font size isn't as large as it could be.

FIGURE 5.1   *Drag in the image, outside the dialog box, to position the text.*

9. With the text in the text field highlighted, type **95** in the Size field, and then type **–85** in the Tracking field. As you can see in Figure 5.2, the text becomes more of a graphic within the composition, and is more visually striking.

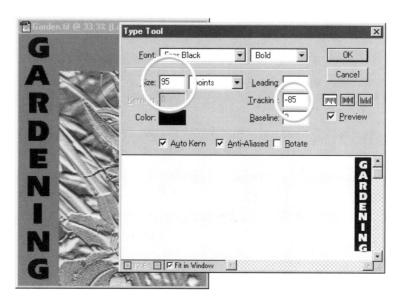

FIGURE 5.2 *Play with the Size and Tracking values for the font you've chosen to make it large and tightly spaced.*

The numbers recommended in step 9 work fine for Eras Black, but if you use a different typeface, it might not be large enough, or as tightly spaced as it could be. So don't follow these numbers to the letter (?); use your own eye to tell you when the right Size and Tracking have been reached.

10. Click the Color swatch to move to the Color Picker. Choose a light shade of blue, as shown in Figure 5.3. Then click on OK to return to the Type Tool dialog box.

11. Click on OK to exit the Type Tool dialog box.

12. Press Shift+Ctrl(⌘)+S (File, Save As), and then save the image to your hard disk as Garden.psd, in Photoshop's native file format. Leave the file open.

As you saw in this example, working with text in Photoshop 5 is now more like working with text in a vector drawing application, such as Illustrator. There's no more guesswork as to how many points in height a headline should be; if you see it fall off the page, you simply reduce the point size or tighten up the tracking.

FIGURE 5.3 *Choose a color that is of the same hue, but lighter than the blue area on the magazine cover.*

WORKING WITH THE HORIZONTAL TYPE TOOL

Unlike previous versions of Photoshop, in version 5 text is editable until you choose to render the text to bitmap format. To check this out, you will make a deliberate spelling blunder in the following steps, and then correct it.

Here's how to use the Type tool to finish designing the cover:

GETTING ACQUAINTED WITH THE TYPE TOOL OPTIONS

1. Drag on the face of the Vertical Type tool to expose the Type tool flyout on the toolbox, and then choose the (normal, nonvertical) Type tool.

2. Click an insertion point to the right of the "G" in "GARDENING"; the Type Tool dialog box appears, with the last entry you made in it still highlighted.

3. Place the text cursor at the end of the word GARDENING, and then backspace over the entire word. Alternatively, you can highlight the entire phrase, and then press Delete (Backspace).

4. Choose Times New Roman PS from the Font list (or Times New Roman or Palatino on the Macintosh if you don't have Adobe Type Manager installed).

5. Type **Munthly** in the text field and then highlight the text.

6. Type **90** in the Size field, and then type **500** in the Tracking field. Click on the color swatch and then choose white from the Color Picker. Click on OK to return to the Type Tool dialog box.

7. Drag on the text in the image window until it is centered, as shown in Figure 5.4.

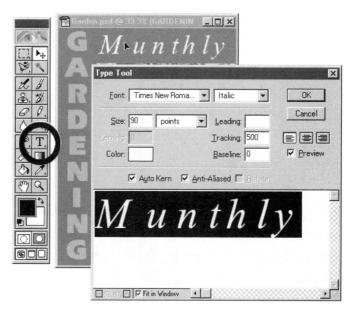

FIGURE 5.4 *Create a visual counterpoint to the style and size of the word "GARDENING," using horizontal text on the magazine cover.*

8. Click on OK to apply the text. You'll notice that each text element is located on its own layer on the Layers palette; the "T" on each layer title indicates that this is editable text.

9. Double-click on the "Munthly" layer title, as shown in Figure 5.5. Doing this displays the Type Tool dialog box, with the text entry for this layer displayed in the text field.

Double-click here

FIGURE 5.5 *Corrections to editable text can be made easily by double-clicking on their layer title.*

10. Highlight the character *u*, and then type **o**, as shown in Figure 5.6.

FIGURE 5.6 *Highlight the incorrect character and then type the correct one.*

11. You can flatten the image now by choosing Flatten Image from the Layers palette's flyout menu. The text will no longer be editable, but you'll be able to save the file in any number of bitmap formats. Or you can press Ctrl(⌘)+S, and have a copy of your work that you can change to "Weeds of the Week" or any other magazine headline weeks or months from now by retaining the PSD format for the file. You can close the file at any time now.

Fixing typographic errors is just one of the possibilities with the new Type tool features. Now you'll see how to mix fonts within a single phrase.

FOLKS AND BEACON: INSTALLING NEW FONTS

For the moment, close Photoshop and any other applications you have running. You're going to add two fonts to your system so that you can use them in a design assignment.

"Folks" is an extremely ornamental typeface created by the author that, used by itself, is visually overwhelming. As an *initial cap* (the first letter of a word), how-ever, Folks really perks up a phrase or slogan. "Beacon" is based on an anonymous shareware font the author stumbled upon years ago on a BBS. The font comple-ments Folks, and is decorative but less ornamental than Folks. Both of these fonts are Charityware, as explained in the FST-7.pdf document in the BOUTONS folder on the Companion CD.

To Load these fonts in Windows, if you have Adobe Type Manager installed, run Adobe Type Manager, choose the Add Fonts tab, and then use the directory con-trols to make a path to Boutons/Fonts on the Companion CD. If you don't use ATM, double-click the Control Panel in Win95. Double-click the Fonts folder, and then choose File, Install New Font. In the directory box, choose the path to Boutons/Fonts on the Companion CD, Ctrl+click on Folks and Beacon TT, and then click OK. Close the Fonts folder and then start Photoshop.

To load Folks and Beacon Type 1s or TrueType on the Macintosh, open the Boutons/Fonts window from the Companion CD, open the System Folder/Fonts folder, and then drag the fonts into the folder. Remember not to have any appli-cations running while you install typefaces.

Using Mixed Typefaces

In this section, you'll create a simple "Good Luck" image to send over the Web to a friend who's interviewing for a high-paying position. Now that you have Folks and Beacon installed, let's get going on a flashy, ornamental, classy design:

Creating a "Good Luck" Image

1. Press Ctrl(⌘)+N, and then in the New dialog box, type **5** (inches) in the Width field, type **3** (inches) in the Height field, type **72** (points per inch) in the Resolution field, choose RGB Color from the Mode drop-down list, and then make sure that Contents: White is selected. Click OK to create the new document.

2. Double-click the Gradient tool to choose it, and to display the Options box. Press Shift+G until the button on the toolbox is the Linear Gradient button. In the Options box, choose Spectrum from the Gradient drop-down list.

3. Drag horizontally within the new image window.

4. Click the Type tool, and then click an insertion point toward the upper left of the image. The Type Tool dialog box appears. Move it out of the way so that you can see the document window.

5. Insert your cursor behind the last letter in the text field, and then double-click to highlight the whole phrase. Press Delete (Backspace) to clear the phrase, and then type **GOOD**. Highlight the word.

6. Choose Folks from the Font list, type **75** in the Size field, and choose white from the Color Picker by first clicking on the Color swatch in the dialog box. Your screen should look like that shown in Figure 5.7.

7. Press Enter (Return), and then type **Luck**. Highlight the entire phrase and then click the center alignment button in the dialog box. Type **75** in the Leading field. This is called *dead leading* in the publishing trade, meaning "very tight Leading"; it only works well when you use a large font size. Your screen should now look like Figure 5.8.

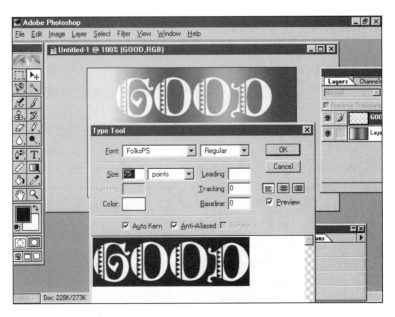

FIGURE 5.7   *Use Folks at 75 points to begin the text message in the image.*

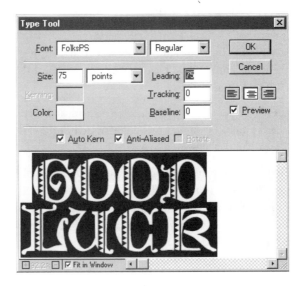

FIGURE 5.8   *To center-align a phrase, the phrase must be highlighted first.*

8. Highlight the "OOD" in "GOOD," and then choose Beacon from the Font drop-down list. Reduce the font Size to 65 points. Your screen should look like Figure 5.9 now.

FIGURE 5.9 *Highlight and then change the font used in the Type Tool dialog box.*

9. Highlight the "uck" in "Luck", and then specify Beacon as the Font, at 65 point Size.

10. Click OK to apply the text to a new layer in the image, as shown in Figure 5.10.

FIGURE 5.10 *In the Type Tool dialog box you can mix and match fonts, sizes, and even the tracking between individual characters.*

11. You don't need to save the file, because this is not a "High Art" example, and you can use the document in the following section as we continue to explore the Type tool. So keep the document open.

PHOTOSHOP'S TYPE MASK TOOL

For those designers who would prefer not to commit to a specific font color while creating a text composition, there is the Type Mask tool (and the Vertical Type Mask tool). These tools do not apply pixel coloring to areas in an image; instead, they create a marquee that can be repositioned and filled at any time.

Now you'll invert the "Good Luck" composition, make the background a solid color and make the text a gradient-filled one:

USING THE TYPE MASK TOOL

1. Choose Flatten Image from the Layers palette's menu flyout.

2. Press D (**d**efault colors), press Alt(Opt)+Delete (Backspace), and then press Ctrl(⌘)+D. Your document is entirely black now, with no text layers.

3. Drag on the face of the Type tool, and then choose the Type Mask tool (the letter "T" made of a dotted outline).

4. Click an insertion point toward the top right in the image window; the Type Tool dialog box appears.

5. For the sake of experimentation, backspace over "OOD" and then type **ood**, lowercase; then click OK, as shown in Figure 5.11.

6. Place your cursor inside any of the marquee lines, and then drag the selection to center it in the image window, as shown in Figure 5.12.

FIGURE 5.11 *Lowercase some of the text, and then click OK to create a marquee selection of the text you've entered.*

FIGURE 5.12 *You can drag a selection, but not the underlying contents, by clicking and dragging inside the selection.*

7. Choose the Linear Gradient tool, and then in the image window, drag straight down from top to bottom, as shown in Figure 5.13.

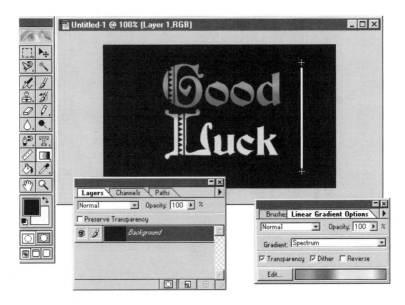

FIGURE 5.13   *The Type Mask tool has produced a floating selection. You shade only the selected regions of the composition when you apply the Linear Gradient tool.*

8. Press Ctrl(⌘)+D. The text is part of the Background layer and you cannot edit it. If you have a friend who needs good luck, save this composition as goodluck.jpg, in the JPEG format, to your hard disk, and email it to him or her. If not, you can close the file at any time without saving it.

Let's move from typography to some calligraphy, as you learn about the new Freeform Pen tool.

PHOTOSHOP'S FREEFORM PEN TOOL

You'll get a more detailed, hands-on explanation of the basic Pen tool in Chapter 6, "Selections, Paths, and Layers." For the moment, the author has decided to put the Freeform Pen tool into its own category; it's almost not a Pen tool at all, but instead, a very flexible tool for laying down vector paths that you can manipulate later, using the other Pen tools.

Whether you use a mouse or a digitizing tablet, the next assignment is bound to appeal to designers who are seeking a "wet look" in their illustrations. In the following section, you'll design the word "Wet," giving it a liquid look on the surface of some marble that's provided for you.

USING THE FREEFORM PEN TOOL FOR DESIGN WORK

One of the terrific things about using the Pen tools is that you're not locked into a marquee selection of anything until you've refined the path segments and loaded the path(s) as a selection. Unlike the "click and drag and then steer the path segment" use of the Pen tool, the Freeform Pen tool puts total expression at your fingertips. The Freeform Pen tool is "smart"; it *automatically* creates anchor points as you draw swoops and curves. Then you can elect to modify the anchor points—or not—by using the Convert Point and Direct Selection tools.

In the example coming up, you're going to draw loosely with the Freeform Pen tool the word "Wet." Then you'll slightly modify your drawing and load it as a selection. Finally, you'll use one of the new Layer Effects commands and a little paint to make the lettering look as though it's actually wet.

Here's how to work with the Freeform Pen tool:

WRITING WITH THE FREEFORM PEN TOOL

1. Open the Stone.tif image from the Chap05 folder of the Companion CD. Type **70** in the Zoom Percentage field and then press Enter (Return).

2. Drag on the face of the Pen tool on the toolbox, and then choose the Freeform Pen tool (the pen with the squiggly line).

3. Create an outline version of the character *W*, as shown in Figure 5.14. Create this character, as shown, toward the bottom left of the image window, because you have two more characters to create. Be sure to close the path by dragging to meet the first anchor point.

4. Draw the character *e* after the *W* shape, and don't forget to draw a subpath for the "inside" of the *e*. Then draw the letter *t* to the right of the *e*, as shown in Figure 5.15.

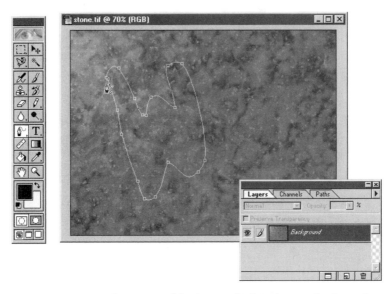

FIGURE 5.14 *Create an outline version of the character "W." Don't try too hard to make it as precise as a typeface; instead, let the character flow like a liquid.*

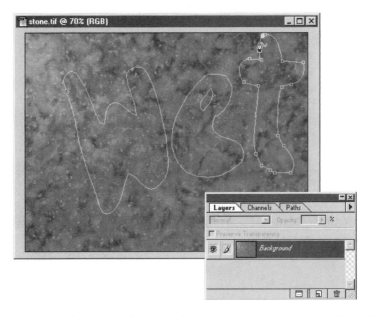

FIGURE 5.15 *Each character you draw is a subpath of a main path that is currently titled "Work Path" on the Paths palette.*

If you're like the author, the "Wet" text is not centered within the Stone.tif document. To fix this, keep on following these steps:

5. Drag on the face of the Freeform Pen tool on the toolbox, and then choose the Direct Selection tool (the white arrowhead icon).

6. Hold Shift+Alt(Opt) and then click on each subpath in "Wet" to select the entire subpath. Then move the selection to center it within the stone image, as shown in Figure 15.16.

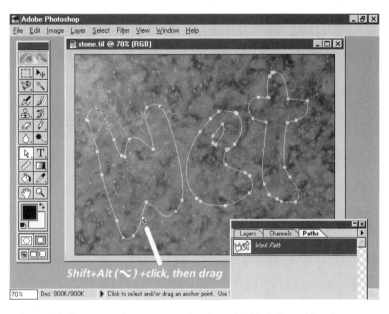

FIGURE 5.16   *Hold Alt(Opt) to select an entire subpath, and hold Shift to add to the current selection.*

7. On the Paths palette, click the Loads path as a selection icon at the bottom of the palette, and then click on an empty area of the palette to hide the Work Path. Right-click (Macintosh: hold Ctrl and click), and choose Layer Via Copy from the context menu, as shown in Figure 5.17.

8. Press Shift+Ctrl(⌘)+S, and save the file to your hard disk as Wet.psd in Photoshop's native file format. Keep the file open.

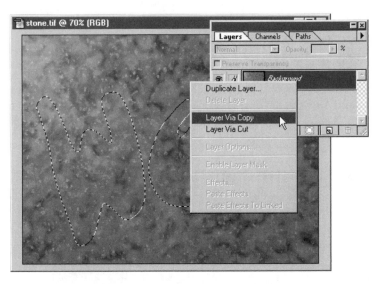

FIGURE 5.17 *Copy to a new layer the stone image that's within the marquee selection.*

Our next stop is to explore the Layer Effects command.

PILLOW EMBOSSING THE NEW LAYER

Another new feature in Photoshop 5 is the Layer Effects option. Anything you place on a layer can have a drop shadow, a glow, or a Pillow Emboss effect like the one you'll use in the steps that follow. All the commands under Layer, Effects are applied to the edge where opaque elements meet the transparent layer background. Also, anything you place on an Effects layer takes on the property assigned to that layer. A drop-shadow Effects layer, for example, will place a drop shadow beneath everything you paste or draw on that layer.

Here's how to make the lettering on the new layer look as though it's bumping outward from the image, as though it were some spilled liquid:

ADDING A PILLOW EMBOSS TO THE NEW LAYER'S ELEMENTS

1. Click the Layer 1 title on the Layers palette to make certain that this is the current editing layer.

2. Position the Wet.psd image to the upper right in the workspace, so that you'll be able to see part of the image as well as the Effects dialog box.

3. Choose Layer, Effects, and then choose Bevel and Emboss from the menu.

4. In the Style drop-down list toward the bottom of the dialog box, choose Pillow Emboss.

5. Type **14** in the Depth field, and then click the Blur fly-out button to reveal the slider.

6. Drag the slider to about 29, as shown in Figure 15.18, and then click OK to apply the Layer Effect.

NOTE

Sliders are hidden in Photoshop 5. Whenever you see a flyout button to the right of a text entry field, click on this button to reveal a slider you can manipulate instead of having to type values.

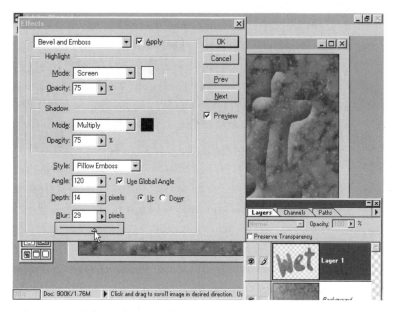

FIGURE 5.18 *Create a bulging collection of letters on the new layer by applying a moderate amount of Depth and Blur to the layer.*

7. Click the Create new layer icon at the bottom of the Layers palette. This is the current editing layer; by default, it is named Layer 2.

8. Choose the Paintbrush tool, press D, and then press X to make the current foreground color white. Zoom out to a 50% viewing resolution of the Wet.psd image, and then on the Brushes palette, choose the second-from-right tip in the second row.

9. On the Options palette, specify 65% Opacity for the Paintbrush tool.

10. Stroke broken lines inside the "Wet" text in areas where there are highlights, as shown in Figure 15.19. Wet objects frequently show *specular* (direct reflection) highlights, which is what you're simulating here.

11. Press Ctrl(⌘)+S. You can close the image at any time now.

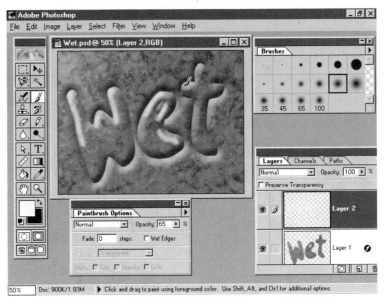

FIGURE 5.19 *Add specular highlights to light areas in the image, using the Paintbrush tool.*

Layers give you the creative freedom to redo and undo changes you've made to a composition (unless you've rendered the text), but there's another way you can work with a piece, creating variations to your (or your client's) heart's content. The following section takes a look at the practical uses for Photoshop's new History list.

PHOTOSHOP 5'S HISTORY LIST

Instead of offering multiple undos from a menu, Photoshop 5 has gone one step farther with the History list. The History list tracks everything you do in an image, and you can go back to a previous state for the image by simply clicking on a title on the History palette.

Open the History palette now, so that you can customize it for the examples that follow (choose Window, Show History).

Click on the flyout menu on the History palette, and then choose History Options. In the Maximum History States field, you're probably best off with the default of 20. This gives you 20 steps to undo things, which will be more than adequate for the example in this section. Leave the Automatically Create First Snapshot box checked. This means that, at any time, you can go back to the original image.

Finally, check the Allow Non-Linear History check box. By doing this, you can selectively remove superfluous edits (such as deselect) from the list, and keep the history of the image down to fewer than 20 moves. Click on OK to close the Options dialog box.

In the following section you'll see how to present a client with variations on a movie poster design through the use of the History palette.

TRACKING AND REFINING EMBELLISHMENTS USING THE HISTORY PALETTE

Suppose that you're handed a still from a motion picture about a tiny ocean liner that's shipwrecked, a film in which the passengers are saved by a lifeguard with a pool skimmer. Pretend also that your client is watching over your shoulder as you work, and that your client has an annoying trait of wanting to see variations on an image in split-second time.

In the steps that follow, you'll use the History palette in combination with Photoshop's editing tools to show the client sprocket holes in the image, two different ways. Gigantic.tif is the image to which you'll add a border, film sprocket holes, and stars to draw attention to the image.

USING THE HISTORY PALETTE TO PERFORM MULTIPLE EDITS

1. Open the Gigantic.tif image from the Chap05 folder on the Companion CD, type **50** in the Zoom Percentage field, and press Enter (Return). Drag the image window borders away from the image so that you can see some background, as shown in Figure 5.20. Black should be the current background color.

FIGURE 5.20 *Open the Gigantic.tif image, and then drag the image window borders away from the image.*

2. Choose Window, Show History (or press F9 if the History palette is grouped with the Actions palette, as recommended in Chapter 3).

3. Choose Image, Canvas Size, and then type **1000** (pixels) in the Width field, and type **600** in the Height field, and then click on OK. You'll note that Canvas Size is listed after Open on the History palette. Drag the image window border away from the image so that you can see the whole image.

4. With the Rectangular Marquee tool, drag a small rectangle the shape and size of a film sprocket in the upper right of the image, and then press Alt(Opt)+Delete (Backspace), as shown in Figure 5.21.

5. Press Ctrl(⌘)+D to deselect the marquee, and then drag a marquee around the white sprocket hole and some of the background black.

6. Choose Edit, Define Pattern, and then press Ctrl(⌘)+D to deselect the marquee.

FIGURE 5.21 *You've used 4 of 20 editing moves so far on the History list.*

7. Marquee select the entire left side of the black in the image, leaving a fraction of an inch between the selection and the framed image.

8. Right-click (Macintosh: hold Ctrl and click) and then choose Fill from the context menu. Choose Pattern from the drop-down list and then click on OK. As you can see in Figure 5.22, the spacing between the sprocket holes is too wide (and your client is the first to point this out to you). No problem; the History list will take care of it.

9. Drag the slider on the History palette up to Rectangular Marquee, as shown in Figure 5.23. The pattern fill is now gone from the image.

10. With the Rectangular Marquee tool, drag a tighter selection than you did in step 5, and then choose Edit, Define Pattern.

11. With the Rectangular Marquee tool, drag a selection along the left edge of the image, as you did in step 7.

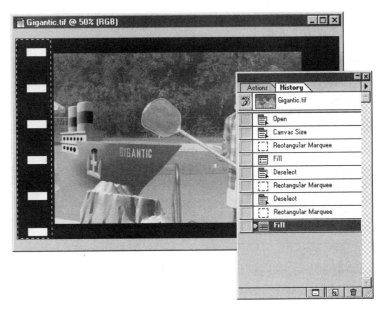

FIGURE 5.22 *Everything you've done within the image has been recorded by the History list. This means that you can undo the mistakes you've made.*

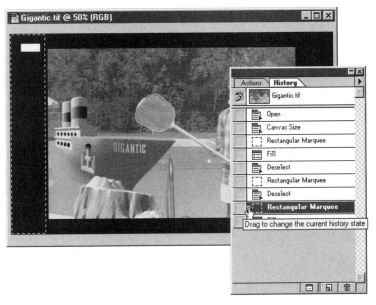

FIGURE 5.23 *Undo an editing move by dragging the History slider up to a previous move.*

12. Right-click (Macintosh: hold Ctrl and click), and then choose Fill from the context menu. Choose Pattern from the Use drop-down list, and then click on OK. This time it appears to be a success, as shown in Figure 5.24.

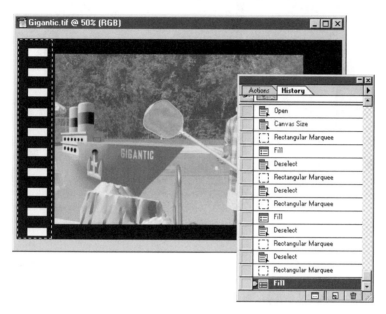

FIGURE 5.24 *A second try at spacing the sprocket holes by using the Define Pattern command is successful.*

13. Hold Ctrl(⌘) and Alt(Opt), place your cursor inside the selection, and then drag it to the right side of the image, as shown in Figure 5.25. This duplicates the sprocket holes, and counts as a move on the History palette.

14. Press Ctrl(⌘)+D to deselect the marquee.

15. Choose File, Save As, and then save the image to your hard disk in the TIFF file format, as Gigantic.tif. Keep the image open.

You'll note that as long as you keep the file open, the History list still contains the editing moves you've made since you opened the file. If you by chance should close the file and then reopen it, the History list will be cleared of all editing moves.

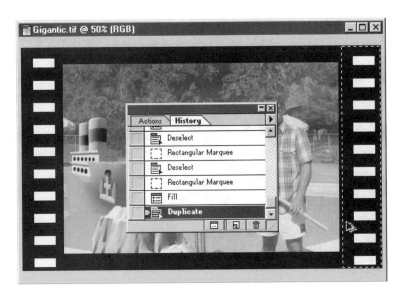

FIGURE 5.25 *Duplicate the element you need by pressing Ctrl(⌘)+Alt(Opt) and dragging inside the selection.*

SNAPSHOTS AND NEW VARIATIONS

Let's say for the moment that your client is happy with the design. The first thing you'll want to do is take a snapshot of the current state of the image. By doing this, you can always go back to it on the History list. Okay, let's get real and say the client has now changed his mind…possibly. He likes the design, but thinks it might look better with stars along the edges instead of film sprocket holes. Which leads us to the following steps:

TAKING SNAPSHOTS AND CONTINUING THE IMAGE'S HISTORY

1. Click on the Create new snapshot icon on the History palette, as shown in Figure 5.26. A thumbnail on a Snapshot 1 title appears at the top of the History list, and this is where the history of the image is now.

2. Click on the Canvas Size title on the History palette. Doing this takes you back in the image before you created a rectangular sprocket hole on the border.

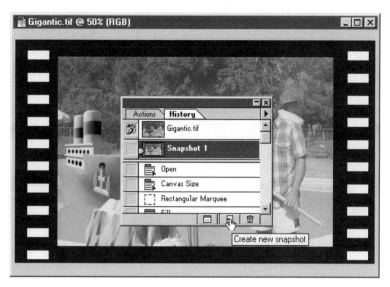

FIGURE 5.26 *Creating a snapshot of the image preserves all the edits you've performed to bring the image to its current state.*

3. With the Type tool, click in the upper-right part of the image, where you first created a sprocket hole. The Type Tool dialog box appears.

4. Press Shift and type **H** in the text field. Highlight the text, and then choose Zapf Dingbats from the Font list. A star appears in the text field. Type **65** in the Size (points) field, and then reposition the star in the Gigantic.tif document if necessary, as shown in Figure 5.27.

5. Choose Type, Render Layer from the main menu, as shown in Figure 5.28. The type can no longer be edited.

6. Click on the Layers palette's flyout menu button, and then choose Flatten Image.

7. You're getting pretty close to the maximum number of steps (20) the History list can hold. Let's delete unnecessary steps. Click on any Deselect title and drag it into the trash icon, as shown in Figure 5.29. Leave one Deselect title on the History palette, however, or a marquee will appear in the image. Similarly, you do not need all the Rectangular Marquee titles; drag them into the trash icon also.

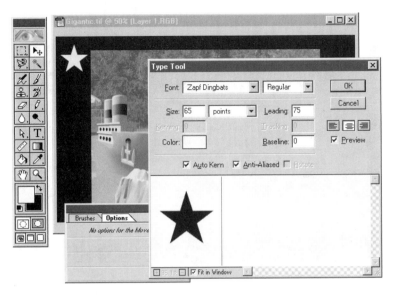

FIGURE 5.27 *Type a star in the Type Tool dialog box to add it to the composition.*

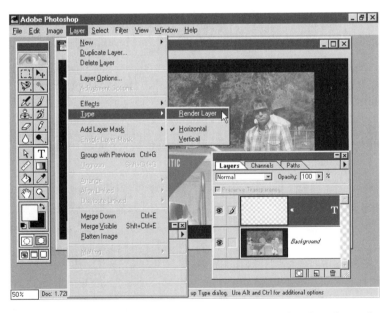

FIGURE 5.28 *Turn an editable symbol into an ordinary collection of pixels on the new layer.*

FIGURE 5.29   *Pare down the editing moves listed in the History list by dragging them into the trash icon.*

8. Drag a rectangular marquee selection around the star, with a little black space around it, and then choose Edit, Define Pattern. Press Ctrl(⌘)+D to deselect the marquee.

9. With the Rectangular Marquee tool, first drag a selection around the left edge of the image, and then hold Shift and drag a selection marquee around the right side of the image. Both marquee selections should be in the black; peek ahead at Figure 5.30 to see their locations.

10. Right-click (Macintosh: hold Ctrl and click), and then choose Fill from the context menu. Choose Pattern from the Use drop-down list, and click on OK. Your image should look like Figure 5.30 now.

11. Press Ctrl(⌘)+D, and then press Ctrl(⌘)+S. Keep the image open.

Pretty nifty, huh? You've gone from sprocket holes to stars without duplicating the image and without depending upon layers. Okay, you'll address a final, unreasonable request from the client in the following section.

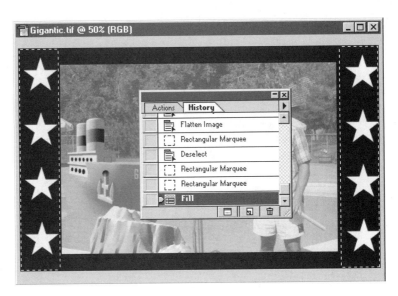

FIGURE 5.30 *Fill the marquee selections with the pattern you sampled.*

USING THE HISTORY BRUSH

The History Brush tool is a local undo tool. With it, you can back up to any progression of edits you've created. Let's suppose now that the creative client wants both sprocket holes *and* stars on the image; stars on the left and sprockets on the right. It's a lousy design concept but a perfect opportunity to show off the History Brush tool.

Here's how to take part of the image back to the snapshot you took earlier in this example:

LOCAL UNDOING WITH THE HISTORY BRUSH TOOL

1. Click on the bottom title on the History list. This makes the active state of the image the version that contains the stars along the edges.

2. Scroll up on the History list to the Snapshot 1 title. Do not click on it, but instead click in the column to the left of the title to make the History Brush tool appear. Any edits you make now, using the History Brush tool, will return the image to the snapshot state.

3. Click on the History Brush tool on the toolbox, and then choose the tip at the far right of the top row in the Brushes palette.

4. Stroke over the right side of the image, as shown in Figure 5.31. Keep stroking until all the sprockets have returned to the right side of the image.

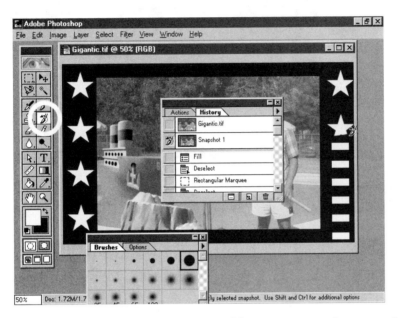

FIGURE 5.31 *The History Brush tool will cause an area of the image to revert to the state you select next to the title on the palette.*

5. Choose File, Save. You can close the image at any time now, but be forewarned that if you do, and then reopen the image, the History palette will be cleared.

In Figure 5.32 you can see the final image. It's been through five big-time edits, but you accomplished them without resorting to layers, and you did it in real-time to please the client.

New features are not limited to palettes and commands. In the following section, you'll experiment with the new Magnetic Lasso tool.

FIGURE 5.32   *Every picture can have a History, and unlike the times we live in, you can go back to any point in History in Photoshop 5.*

EXPLORING THE MAGNETIC TOOLS

The Magnetic Lasso tool and its sister, the Magnetic Pen tool, are both designed to be time savers when you're selecting elements in an image. Quite frequently, when there are different objects in an image, these objects have different colors. The Magnetic Lasso tool locates the edge of color differences in an image and then creates a selection edge that is fairly faithful to the color outline in the image.

There are three controls for the Magnetic tools on the Options palette:

- **Lasso/Pen Width.** This setting determines the tool's sensitivity to color changes as you guide it (the tool) along a path. If you have an image of foliage that contains different shades of green, for example, you'd want to increase the Width to the maximum of 40 to create a very precise edge.

- **Lasso/Pen Frequency.** This setting determines how complex the selection is—how many anchors are inserted automatically as your cursor changes directions along the path. This is a new feature for the Lasso tool, which historically has placed no anchor points you can back up to along the outline of a selection. When you feel that the Magnetic Lasso tool is veering off course, back up a little with the selection and then click an anchor point. You can then continue tracing the color edge of the element in the image.

- **Edge Contrast.** This setting determines how different neighboring colors must be in an image to have the Magnetic tool attracted to them. If you have an image with very different, sharp color transitions, you can specify a higher setting here; if colors in the image are similar, decrease the Edge Contrast percentage.

The Magnetic Lasso tool is used in the following section because it produces precise selections more easily than the Magnetic Pen tool, which tends to round off corners and simplify a path around the target shape.

USING MAGNETIC SELECTIONS IN YOUR EDITING WORK

Aren't fire hydrants boring in color? We realize that a garish color is important for fire hydrants, so that the Fire Department can quickly spot them in an emergency, but the same primary colors are often used: uninspired, uninspired!

In the following example, you'll use the Magnetic Lasso tool to define the edge of the top of a fire hydrant, and then you'll use an Adjustment layer to change the color of the selection within the image.

Here's how to spruce up the neighborhood, and find out how much easier it is to select clearly defined colors when you use the Magnetic Lasso tool:

USING THE MAGNETIC LASSO TOOL

1. Open the Hydrant.tif image from the Chap05 folder of the Companion CD. Double-click on the Zoom tool to move your view of the image to 100% (1:1). Maximize the image window and scroll until you can clearly see the top of the fire hydrant.

2. Choose the Magnetic Lasso tool from the Lasso tool flyout. It's the icon with the horseshoe magnet in its design.

3. On the Options palette, type **10** in the Lasso Width field (not a lot of sensitivity required), type **50** in the Frequency field (not a lot of automatically placed anchors in the image), and type **10** in the Edge Contrast field (not a lot of searching by the tool for the edge of color in the image).

4. Click on the top of the fire hydrant to begin the selection marquee. You're going to select only the red top of the hydrant.

5. Drag, but *do not click* the mouse button (this is commonly called "hovering") to guide the cursor along the right edge of the hydrant top; you're working clockwise. When the cursor appears to drift into unwanted background areas, backtrack the cursor to the last automatically inserted anchor point, and then click. Then release the cursor and continue guiding the selection along the edge of the hydrant top, as shown in Figure 5.33.

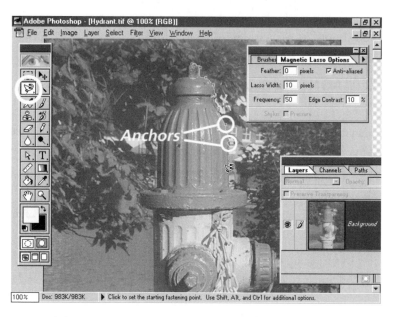

FIGURE 5.33 *Click on an anchor point when your selection is going off-course, and then release the mouse button and continue "hovering" along the edge of the hydrant top.*

6. Work clockwise around the edge of the hydrant top; when you arrive at the first point you clicked, a tiny circle will appear to the bottom right of your cursor, indicating that this is the point to click to close the selection. Click at the beginning point, and in a moment a marquee selection will appear, as shown in Figure 5.34. The selection is not perfectly precise, but it's good enough for the purposes of demonstration; you'll learn how to refine selections in the next chapter.

7. On the Layers palette, click on the flyout menu button and then choose New Adjustment Layer. The New Adjustment Layer dialog box appears.

FIGURE 5.34 *The selection marquee might not be as precise as you'd like it to be, but for coarse selec-tion work, you can't top this tool for speed.*

8. Choose Hue/Saturation from the Type drop-down list, as shown in Figure 5.35, and then click on OK.

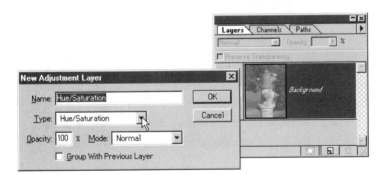

FIGURE 5.35 *An Adjustment layer can be used to change the color or tone of the background layer without creating a permanent change in the document.*

9. The Hue/Saturation dialog box appears, and the selection marquee disappears in the image. The area is still selected in the image; the Adjustment layer is going to modify this selected area through masking on the new layer. Drag the Hue slid-er to –57, as shown in Figure 5.36. The top of the fire hydrant is now a brilliant magenta.

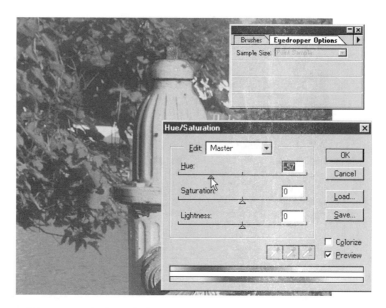

FIGURE 5.36 *You're only changing the unmasked areas on a layer when you use the Adjustment layers. You have not changed the base image at all.*

10. Click on OK to apply the Adjustment layer. If you'd like, you can use a white foreground color and the Paintbrush tool to change other red areas on the hydrant to magenta. Otherwise, you can close this file without saving it. Now you've seen how two features in Photoshop 5 work.

Many tasks seem to be automated in this new version of Photoshop, don't they? The truth is that Photoshop 5 is the easiest version to date for the beginner; it is so packed with automated features that Automate is now one of the menus under File. Let's explore the new Contact Sheet feature in the following section.

A CONTACT SHEET FOR QUICK BROWSING

Hard disks are cheaper than ever these days, and if you're like the author, you have multiple versions of the same image saved to hard disk because the space and the luxury are now available. The author has an entire folder of small 300-by-200-pixel images saved in JPEG format that he sends to other users across the Web, to see whether they'd like the full-sized version of the image.

Although many browsers are available for the Macintosh and Windows for quickly viewing a single file, wouldn't it be nice to view an entire collection of images at a glance? This is precisely what the Contact Sheet command does, and you'll gain hands-on experience with this feature in the next section.

CREATING YOUR OWN CONTACT SHEET

The Boutons folder on the Companion CD contains an excellent collection of fonts, textures, and full-size scenes. Although we've created an Acrobat document in the root of the folder that's a handy thumbnail gallery for the folder's contents, you might want to create your *own* contact sheet of, say, the first 30 textures in the Boutons/Textures folder.

It's a little silly to describe in steps what Photoshop does automatically, because the term "automation" suggests a hands-off atmosphere. We'll run through the process of creating a contact sheet from Photoshop, however, to show you what your options are and what is produced:

PRODUCING A CONTACT SHEET

1. Choose File, Automate, and then choose Contact Sheet.

2. In the Contact Sheet dialog box, specify the Width and Height of the Contact sheet. (8 by 10 inches is a good size for the contact sheet, as this is the coverage of most color inkjet printers on 8 1/2 by 11 inch paper.) You might want to run off a color copy of your contact sheet to show others.

3. Choose 72 pixels/inch as the Resolution of the contact sheet, and choose RGB Color as the Mode. This will produce a file that is 1.19 MB in saved file size. Today's inkjet printers can faithfully render images up to 300 pixels/inch, but this would dramatically increase the saved file size, and we're experimenting here, not trying to break any records! The 72 pixels/inch is monitor resolution, and will give you a fair idea of what the contact sheet images look like.

4. Click the Place Across First button. In the Western Hemisphere we tend to read from left to right, and because Photoshop will not produce captions beneath the images on the contact sheet, alphabetically left-to-right, top-to-bottom placement will prove more useful when you're looking for a specific image.

5. In the Layout area, leave the Columns at the default of 5, and the Rows at 6. This will produce a contact sheet with 30 images, all at a viewable size.

6. Click on the Choose button in the Source Directory field, as shown in Figure 5.37.

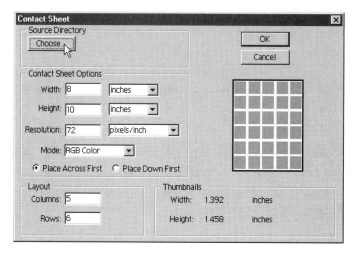

FIGURE 5.37 *Choose a folder from which you want Photoshop to create a contact sheet.*

7. In the directory box, choose the Boutons/Textures folder on the Companion CD, and then click on OK (Select), as shown in Figure 5.38.

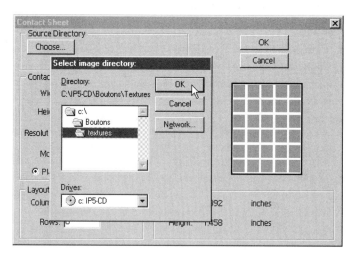

FIGURE 5.38 *Select a directory where the Contact Sheet command can find the images you want catalogued.*

8. Sit back for the ride! Photoshop automatically resizes and places thumbnails of the images in neat columns and rows.

9. Photoshop will build as many contact sheets as necessary to catalogue the folder you directed it to. Let's say you're comfortable with a single sheet of 30 images from the Boutons/Textures folder. When the last image has been placed, press Esc. The contact sheet process is halted, and you have a contact sheet on a single layer in the image file, as shown in Figure 5.39.

FIGURE 5.39 *A contact sheet is composed of thumbnail-sized versions of art that Photoshop finds in a specific directory.*

10. Choose Flatten Image from the Layer palette's flyout menu, and then save the file to your hard drive as My Contact Sheet.tif, in the TIFF file format. You can print the sheet now, or close the file at any time.

When you flatten a layer, the background is always white. This is good, because who wants an inkjet or other printer rendering a solid color background when all you're interested in is the art, and not depleting the ink cartridges?

Because Photoshop does nothing but resize artwork found in a specific folder, your contact sheet might not be as sharp as you'd like it to be. Before closing the file, you might want to pass your contact sheet once through the Unsharp Mask filter to make a crisper collection of images.

From PDF to PSD

The Adobe Acrobat format makes document fidelity and integrity 100 percent when viewed across operating platforms. The same Acrobat documents you'll find on the Companion CD can be viewed by using Acrobat Reader 3 for DOS, Windows, the Macintosh, and UNIX. But what if you don't own the entire suite of Acrobat tools, and you want to edit a specific page from an Acrobat document? You won't be able to edit text as text, but you can annotate, and create text as a graphic, and even replace elements if you use the new Multi-page PDF to PSD filter.

Creating a TIFF File from a PDF Page

Page 14 is a really nice one from the authors' FST-7.pdf document in the root of the Boutons folder on the Companion CD. It features a handful of thumbnail textures that, when clicked on in Acrobat Reader 3, will launch Photoshop and display the full-sized texture. But let's suppose that you *like* the thumbnails and have no interest in the full-sized textures.

In the following steps, you'll see how to create a bitmap copy of page 14 in the FST-7.pdf document, all within Photoshop:

Creating a Bitmap from an Acrobat Page

1. Choose File, Automate, and then choose Multi-Page PDF to PSD.

2. In the Convert Multi-Page PDF to PSD dialog box, click on Choose in the Source PDF field, and then choose the FST-7.pdf file from the Boutons folder on the Companion CD.

3. In the Page Range field, type **14** in both the From and To fields.

4. Leave the Output Options at their default of 72 pixels/inch, Anti-aliased, and RGB Color Mode. You need to do this because this is the color mode and resolution at which the document was created. You can specify a higher Resolution, but all Photoshop will do is *interpolate* (average) the visual data to a larger size, and you'll lose a little image focus.

5. Accept the default name of FST-7, click on the Choose button in the Destination field, and then pick a hard disk location for the file in the directory box.

6. Click on OK (Select). Photoshop creates a bitmap copy of page 14, displays it briefly onscreen, and then closes it and saves it as FST-70014.psd to the location you specified in the dialog box.

7. Choose File, Open, and then Open the FST-70014.psd image.

8. Choose Flatten Image from the Layers palette's flyout menu, and save the file to your hard disk as Page14.tif, in the TIFF file format. Now anyone with a computer who has even a fair image browser can view this page, shown in Figure 5.40, without the assistance of Acrobat Reader 3. You can also crop and edit the file, using any of Photoshop's features.

FIGURE 5.40   *Using the Multi-Page PDF to PSD command, you can turn a PDF page into a piece of artwork that can be edited in Photoshop.*

Automation isn't the only area where Photoshop has become more user friendly. Let's stroll into the next section where you'll find out about Photoshop Assistants that make Web work a snap.

THE RESIZE AND EXPORT TRANSPARENT IMAGE ASSISTANTS

If you're an experienced user of Photoshop, you might not have any use for the "wizards" included in the version 5 Help menu. Resizing an image, and exporting images with a transparent background for the Web do seem to be two of the

TIP

The link button is not a new feature, but you might be interested to know that if you click on the image at the top of Photoshop's toolbox, you can connect to Adobe's Photoshop site on the Web, if you have a connection open.

It is on this part of Adobe's site that you'll find the latest Photoshop news and updates.

tasks most in demand with users, however. If you're not sure how large an image should be for print or online, open the image in Photoshop, choose Help, Resize Image, and then work your way through the menus—questionnaire-style dialog boxes—until you have a copy of the original image in the workspace. It's that simple, and the Resize Image Assistant really requires no further discussion in this book.

If you want to create a GIF 89a or PNG image that has a transparent background, however, you do indeed have options that can be confusing. The following section walks along with the Export Transparent Image Assistant to show you how to make stunning, commercial Web graphics.

EXPORTING TO GIF 89A FORMAT

When folks speak of GIF 89a, they are referring to one of several GIF formats that CompuServe introduced to the online community years ago. GIF 89a simply has a unique property that until recently no one had discovered: the 89a format can contain a masking color that drops out any color you specify within the image, creating a transparency effect.

The assignment here is to export the Head.psd graphic to GIF 89a format for a client. The first thing you need to do is ask the client what the background color for the document is, because you can only drop out one specific value in GIF artwork. Let's suppose that the client tells you it's 50% black: B:128, R:128, and G:128. You now know everything you need to know about making choices in the Assistant (Wizard).

Here's how to take a piece of clip art from the Chap05 folder on the Companion CD and crank out a transparent GIF:

USING PHOTOSHOP'S GIF 89A HELPER TO CREATE A TRANSPARENT GIF

1. Open the Head.psd image from the Chap05 folder on the Companion CD.

2. Choose Help, Export Transparent Image.

3. In the first of several dialog boxes, click on the My image is on a transparent background button, and then click on Next, as shown in Figure 5.41.

4. In the next dialog box, which asks what the image will be used for, click on the Online button, and then click on Next.

5. In the next dialog box, which asks Which image format would you like?, click on GIF, and then click on Next.

6. The next dialog box informs you that the GIF format only supports 8 bits per pixel (256 colors), and that the following step will be to color-reduce a copy of your artwork. Click on Next.

7. In the Indexed Color dialog box, choose Exact from the Palette drop-down list. Head.psd contains only 170 colors, so the Options field is dimmed. If an image of your own contains more than 256 colors, the Options field will be active, and you should choose Diffusion Dithering, Best Color Matching, and check the Preserve Exact Colors check box. Click on Next after filling out this dialog box.

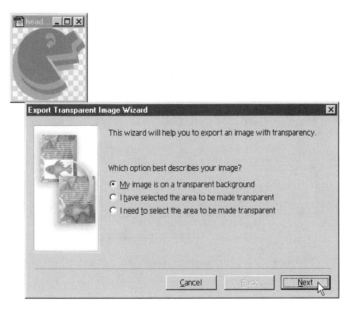

FIGURE 5.41 *If you need to export a transparent GIF image, it is always best to create the artwork on a transparent layer.*

8. In the GIF 89a Export Options box, click on the Transparency From drop-down list, and choose Export Wizard (Assistant) Selection. The Transparency Preview Color box becomes active, and you should now click in it, as shown in Figure 5.42, to go to the Color Picker.

9. Choose R:128, G:128, and B:128 in the Color Picker, and then click on OK to return to the dialog box.

10. Click on OK to display a directory box. Choose a file location for the image, name the image head.gif, and then click on Save.

11. Click on Finish in the last dialog box. You are left with an Export Wizard (Assistant) image in the workspace that you can close without saving. Keep the Head.psd image open.

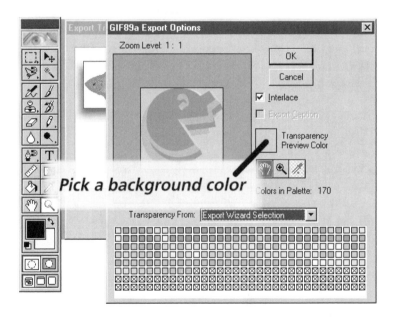

FIGURE 5.42 *By choosing the Export Wizard (Assistant) Selection, you can choose the color your client wants.*

EXPORTING TO PNG FORMAT

The PNG image format is still a little avant-garde; not all Web browsers support this file format, but it has the following two advantages over the GIF89a format:

- A PNG file uses lossless compression, so you are not limited to 256 colors for your work.

- A PNG file can contain an alpha channel selection, so it can display transparency when used as a Web page element, and the design can be transported to a layer when you're editing it in Photoshop.

The authors do not recommend PNG format images for Web work at this point, due to poor universal acceptance of the format. If a client insists, however, here are the steps to follow:

EXPORTING TO PNG FORMAT

1. Press Ctrl(⌘) and click on the Layer 1 title on the Layers palette to load the opaque areas of Head.psd as a marquee selection.

2. On the Channels palette, click on the Save selection as channel icon, as shown in Figure 5.43.

FIGURE 5.43 *Save the transparency information in the Head.psd image to an alpha channel.*

3. On the Layers palette, click on the Create new layer icon, and then drag the title to beneath Layer 1.

4. Click on the foreground color swatch, and then define 50 percent black for the foreground color (R:128, G:128, B:128). Click on OK to return to the workspace.

5. Press Ctrl(⌘)+A and then, with Layer 2 as the active layer, press Alt(Opt)+Delete (Backspace) to fill the layer with the transparency color your client insists on, as shown in Figure 5.44.

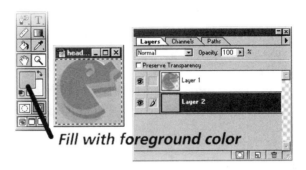

Fill with foreground color

FIGURE 5.44 *Add, to a new layer in the image, the background color that will be used on the Web page.*

6. Press Ctrl(⌘)+D to deselect the marquee, and then choose Flatten Image from the Layers palette's flyout menu.

7. Press Ctrl(⌘) and click on the Alpha channel title on the Channels palette to load the selection; then choose Help, Export Transparent Image.

8. In the first dialog box, choose the I have selected the area to be made transparent button, and then click on Next.

9. In the next dialog box, click on the Online button, and then click on Next.

10. In the next dialog box, click on the PNG button, and then click on Next.

11. In the Save As dialog box, name the file head.png, choose a location on your hard disk for the image, and then click on Save.

12. In the PNG Options box, accept the defaults by clicking on OK.

13. Click on Finish in the last dialog box, and then close the Wizard (Assistant) image in the workspace without saving it.

As you can see in Figure 5.45, the head graphic blends seamlessly into the background color defined for the page.

As long as we're up on the Web in this section, let's turn to a new link and art-protection feature in Photoshop 5.

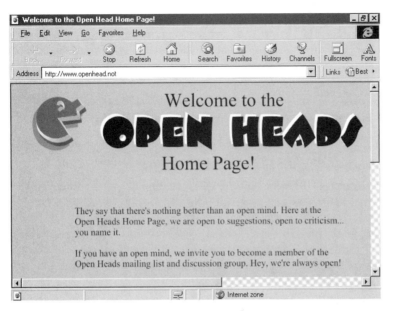

FIGURE 5.45 *Transparency images on the Web allow the designer of the page more freedom than images with a solid background color.*

FILE INFO'S COPYRIGHT AND URL

Photoshop has had a File Info box for several versions, but version 5 is the first to sport a Copyright & URL field. This means that you can protect your intellectual property on the Web to a certain degree, as well as provide a link to a site using this new feature. Let's explore what the Copyright & URL field is good for.

INFO FROM PHOTOSHOP USER TO PHOTOSHOP USER

Because Photoshop is such a widespread application, the chances are good that a JPEG file you have posted on a Web page will be downloaded and viewed by another Photoshop user. Photoshop 5 has the perfect "calling card" for images saved in JPEG, Photoshop's native PSD, and TIFF file formats.

Here's how to brand your images with a copyright notice and provide a link to an HTML page on the Web—your own page, or someone else's:

ADDING COPYRIGHTS AND URLs

1. Open any small image you like in Photoshop. The image should not have layers.

2. Choose File, File Info.

3. Press Ctrl(⌘)+6 to move to the Copyright & URL dialog box.

4. Check the Mark as Copyrighted check box, and then in the Copyright Notice field type **Copyright 1998 (*your name here*)**, or something similar.

5. In the Image URL field, type the URL you want people to be able to go to from within Photoshop when they read this dialog box. Figure 5.46 shows a sparse but typical entry in each of these fields.

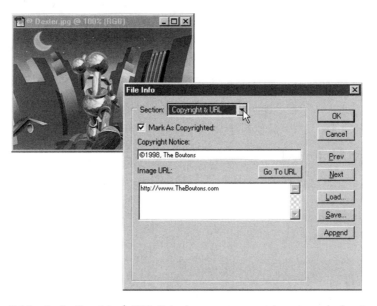

FIGURE 5.46   *In the Copyright & URL dialog box, create a copyright notice and a location on the Web for others to surf to.*

6. Save the image to JPEG, TIFF, or PSD format. You can close the image at any time.

The next time you or another Photoshop user opens the file, a copyright symbol will be displayed before the name of the file on the title bar, and if you (or they) choose File, File Info, Copyright & URL, and then click on the Go to URL button, the user's Web browser and an Internet connection will launch (if the machine is wired for the Web).

MORE PROTECTION FOR YOUR IMAGES

If you're interested in truly protecting your images, check out Filter, Digimarc on Photoshop's menu. This filter is a trial version of Digimarc's patented "noise branding" of images, that permanently embeds user information within an image, and resists vandalism of the file, cropping to remove information, or other methods for trying to appropriate a file. The fees for annual registration are quite reasonable, and if you click on Filter, Digimarc, Embed Watermark, and then click on Personalize and then Register, you'll connect to Digimarc's site on the Web and you can become a patron of this antipiracy technology.

NOTE

The Copyright & URL dialog box provides very little protection from piracy of images on the Web. The copyright notice will not appear in applications other than Photoshop, other Photoshop users can modify your copyright, and the mere act of resaving the image in an application other than Photo-shop removes the copyright and URL message embedded in the file.

AN IMPROVED ACTIONS LIST

Users of Photoshop 4 were delighted that finally Photoshop could record menu commands and execute them in batch mode to a whole directory of images. This feature is shown in Chapter 20, "Building Animations," but there's more good news about the Actions palette with version 5. Now you can create a selection marquee in an image, and the Actions palette will record it as a step that can be repeated later on other images. When you use the Lasso tool or the Rectangular or Elliptical Marquee tools as part of a procedure, Photoshop can replicate the selection relative to the upper-left corner of any other document, to produce a selection of the same size and shape.

CREATING A SOFT STAR MACRO

Okay—suppose you need several feathered, star shapes filled with a texture. The easiest way to do this with consistency is by programming the Actions palette to perform the chore; you do the steps once, and the Actions palette will repeat them.

Here's how to set up the Actions palette to create a soft-edged star shape in any image that is at least the same size or larger than the image you use during the programming of the palette:

CREATING A SOFT STAR ACTION

1. Press F9 if the Actions palette is not currently in the workspace.

2. Open any image you like from your hard disk, as long as it is at least 300 pixels wide by 300 pixels in height. In this example, one of the textures from the Boutons/Textures folder on the Companion CD is used.

3. Click on the Create new action icon at the bottom of the Actions palette (the turned-over page icon).

4. In the New Action dialog box, type **Softstar** in the Name field, as shown in Figure 5.47, and then click on Record. Now everything you do to the image, excluding painting and using paths, will be recorded.

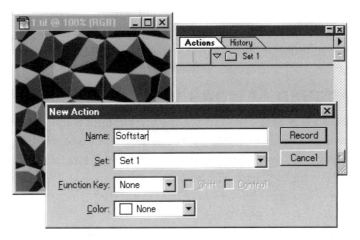

FIGURE 5.47 *Name the Action you will create, and then click on Record to begin the process.*

5. With the Lasso tool, draw a star shape in the image, as shown in Figure 5.48. Accuracy is not important; we're simply trying to show a process here.

6. Right-click (Macintosh: hold Ctrl and click), and then choose Feather from the context menu.

7. In the Feather Selection dialog box, type **5** in the pixels field, and then click on OK, as shown in Figure 5.49. Click on OK to apply the feathering.

8. Press D (**d**efault colors), and then press Shift+F7 to invert the selection.

9. Press Delete (Backspace), and then press Ctrl(⌘)+D to deselect the marquee.

10. Click on the Stop playing/recording button on the Actions palette, as shown in Figure 5.50.

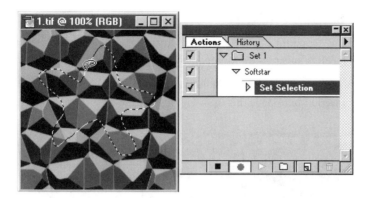

FIGURE 5.48 *Drag the shape of a star in the image window.*

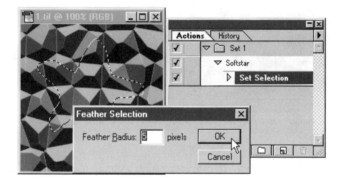

FIGURE 5.49 *Soften the selection edge by applying a 5-pixel feathering to it.*

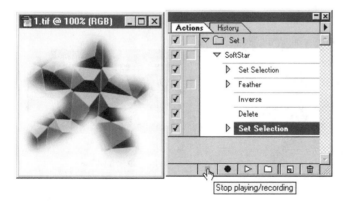

FIGURE 5.50 *Stop recording the Softstar Action after you've deselected the marquee.*

11. You've finished recording the custom Action.

Let's take the Action for a spin now with a different image. Load Bonbon.tif from the Boutons/Textures folder on the Companion CD.

12. Click on the Softstar title on the Actions palette, and then click on the Play current selection button, as shown in Figure 5.51.

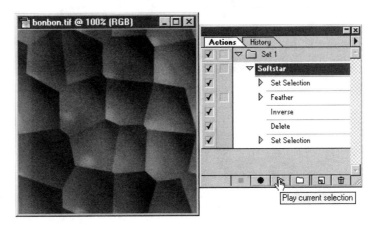

FIGURE 5.51 *You are launching the same editing moves you created in your own image, applied to a different image.*

13. Allow the Actions palette to run without intervening (don't touch the palette or any other commands with the cursor). The Actions palette will stop automatically when the last command in the Softstar action has been completed, as shown in Figure 5.52.

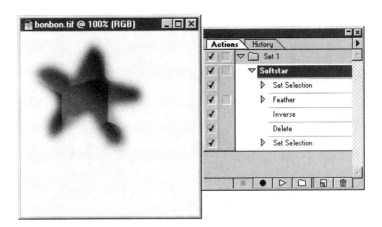

FIGURE 5.52 *The Softstar Action is a success! It created the same soft star shape, in the same location relative to the top left of the document.*

14. Close the file without saving.

You might want to add a Canvas Size command to the Softstar action, or actions of your own, if you want the images that are modified to be of the same size. But as you can clearly see, if you need a number of images framed with the same shape and same size, it couldn't be easier to do than with the Actions palette.

ALIGNING LINKED LAYERS

Photoshop 5 has gone one step beyond the Guides and Grids commands to bring us the Align Linked command. Let's suppose that you have a number of small elements on different layers that you want aligned to the left before you merge the layers. No problem; the Align Linked command is a one-stop time saver.

USING THE ALIGN LINKED COMMAND

In Photoshop, layers that are linked can have their opaque areas moved in tandem by using the Move tool. This is a great advantage over moving elements manually by the same amount in the same direction. The next logical step for Photoshop features would be a command that aligns elements on different layers to their respective tops, bottoms, lefts, rights, and so on, as PageMaker and Illustrator can do.

In the following steps, we say farewell to this new features chapter with a simple graphic whose layers need aligning. Here's how to align elements across layers, using the new Align Linked command:

ALIGNING LINKED LAYERS

1. Open the Goodbye.psd image from the Chap05 folder on the Companion CD. Double-click on the Zoom tool to move your view of the image to 100% resolution, and drag the image window border away from the image so that you can see the entire image.

2. Press F7 if the Layers palette is not currently onscreen.

TIP

To remove a component action from a list of commands, uncheck the check box to the far left of the Actions title before launching the Action.

If you want to stop a process, such as the Feather command, and specify a unique number in the pixels field, for example, click on the box to the right of the check boxes. This displays a miniature menu icon, and every time the Action gets to this part of the modifications, you will be prompted (through a dialog box that pops up) to enter a unique value. Not all commands offer a dialog box, so not all the components of a user-defined Action list will offer the menu check box.

3. Click on the check box closest to the "Good-" layer title, as shown in Figure 5.53. The "Good-" layer is now linked to the highlighted, active "Bye" layer.

4. Choose Layer, Align Linked, and then choose Top, as shown in Figure 5.54. The linked layer's contents will align to the top of the currently selected layer's contents.

5. As you can see in Figure 5.55, the lettering "Good-" moved downward to align to the top of the "Bye" lettering. You can close the file at any time without saving now.

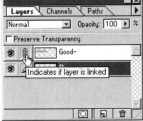

FIGURE 5.53 *Link the "Good-" layer to the "Bye" layer by clicking on the link check box.*

The Align Linked command works with more than two layers. You can, for example, have five or six layers of buttons that you want aligned to the left when you're building a Web page graphic. All you need to do is click on the linked check boxes for all the inactive layers and use the Align Linked command.

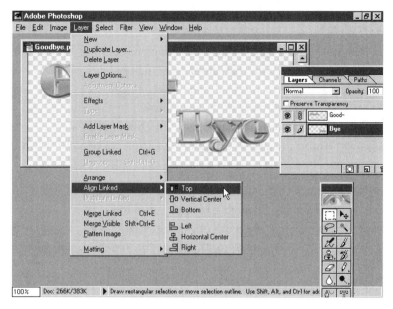

FIGURE 5.54 *When you're aligning them, the linked layers will always move to the chosen position relative to the currently active layer.*

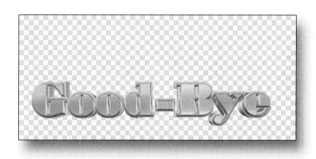

FIGURE 5.55 *The Layer, Align Linked command enables you to align to the center, top, or bottom of layers that you've linked.*

SUMMARY

Although Photoshop is a very strong production and pre-press application, there's a creative side to the program that simply gets richer and richer with every ensuing version. In addition to the traditional tools and features that are unique to Photoshop, we've covered many of the new features in this chapter, and you'll see more use of them—and others—throughout this book. Photoshop is clearly more than a bitmap editor; it excels at bringing your concepts to fruition, and is easier than ever to use effectively.

At least 50 percent of the features you will use as a designer in Photoshop lie in the creation of selections, through paths, marquee tools, layers, and alpha channels. You'll find some brush-up work for the experienced designer and some introductory work for the beginner in the next chapter, "Selections, Layers, and Paths."

CHAPTER 6

SELECTIONS, LAYERS, AND PATHS

If you were to ask most experienced Photoshop users what single property of Photoshop holds the greatest creative power, the answer would be, "selections." Fine: so why is this chapter getting into layers and paths, also?

Simply put, layers are a place you can put things you've selected, and paths are a way to define a precise selection. And oh, yes—channels are a part of the discussion in this chapter, too, for it is in channels that you can save the outlines of selections you've carefully worked on. You can select image areas in at least five different ways in Photoshop:

- By the selection tools such as the Lasso.

- With the Magic Wand tool.

- With the Quick Mask mode.

- With selections based on paths.

- By loading the contents of a layer or a channel as a selection.

You choose the method or a combination of methods that suits the type of selecting you're doing. This chapter shows you how to tap into the capabilities of selections as well as selection "sister" functions. And your adventures here are going to be *fun*, too!

THE ICONS MASTERPIECE

To help you better concentrate on the tasks at hand, an image for this chapter has been carefully, thoughtfully, and scientifically prepared for you (okay, I'm exaggerating a little). The Icons.tif file contains many different shapes, shown in Figure 6.1, each of which requires a different selection technique. The goal in this chapter is to select and manipulate objects, and that's it; there is no "passing grade" to concern yourself about, no finished piece of artwork you need to toil over.

FIGURE 6.1   *The Icons.tif image contains many shapes, each one requiring a different selection technique.*

HITCHING YOUR LASSO TO A STAR

The simplest object to select in the Icons.tif image is the star shape; its outline is composed of only straight lines. The best choice of selection tools, therefore, is the Polygon Lasso tool, one of the variants on the Lasso tool. In the steps that follow, you'll learn a shortcut for accessing the tool, and see how the tool works.

NOTE

This chapter is required reading if you want to complete complex assignments such as those in chapter 11. Without some selecting prowess, your adventures in Photoshop won't be as rewarding.

USING THE POLYGON LASSO TOOL TO SELECT A SIMPLE SHAPE

1. Open the Icons.tif image from the Chap06 folder on the Companion CD.

2. Type **200** in the zoom percentage box, and then press Enter (Return). Resize the image window to maximize your view, and then scroll until the star shape is in the center of your screen.

3. Choose the Lasso tool, hold Alt(Opt), and then click on the points along the edge of the star. Work clockwise; when you reach the first point, release the Alt(Opt) key. A marquee selection appears around the star shape, as shown in Figure 6.2. In its normal selection mode, the Lasso tool is used by dragging it around areas—not terribly precise. But when you hold Alt(Opt), the tool toggles to the Polygon Lasso tool and selections are made by clicking points, and not by dragging—marquee lines are automatically created between clicked points.

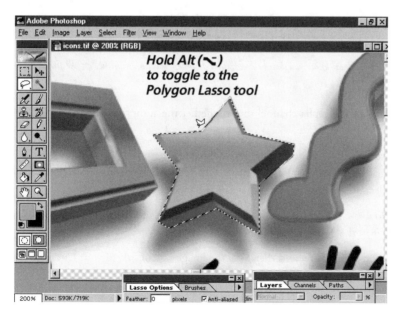

FIGURE 6.2 *Hold Alt(Opt) and then click points around the outline of the star shape.*

It would be a shame to accidentally deselect your hard work here, so you're now going to save the selection you created to an alpha channel…

4. Press F7 to display the Channels palette if it isn't already in the workspace. Click on the Channels tab in this grouped palette, and then click on the Save selection as channel icon at the bottom of the palette, as shown in Figure 6.3. The selection is now saved as a shape in a channel named Alpha 1. The selection can be reloaded at any time.

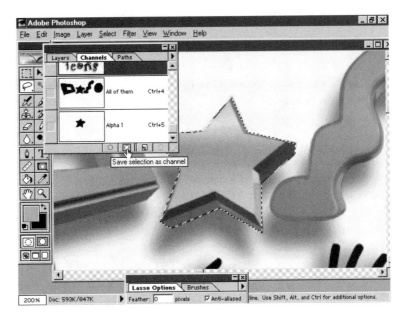

FIGURE 6.3 *If you know you'll need a carefully designed selection marquee in the future, save it to an alpha channel.*

Let's test out this alpha channel to see whether the author is telling the truth here (he is)…

5. Press Ctrl(⌘)+D to deselect the marquee in the image. Now, press Ctrl(⌘) and click on the Alpha 1 title on the Channels palette. You'll note that the saved selection reappears as a marquee in the image. Cool, huh?

6. Double-click on the Alpha 1 title, and then in the Channel Options box, type **star** in the Name field; then click on OK.

7. Choose File, Save, and then save the image as Icons.tif to your hard disk. Keep the image open.

Selecting a star is easy stuff, using the Lasso tool. What do you say to more of a challenge? How about selecting something that has a hole in its middle? Read on!

THE LASSO TOOL AND POLYGON LASSO TOOL MODES

You can use modifier keys to change the functionality of Photoshop's selection and painting tools. You've already tried one; holding Alt(Opt) toggles the Lasso tool to the Polygon Lasso tool. For the next assignment, you're going to use the Polygon Lasso tool and check out one of its extended functions, that of subtracting from an existing selection. Basically, you can't go wrong when adding or subtracting from a selection if you make a mental note of what the keyboard modifiers do:

NOTE

You may have noticed that there is an additional alpha channel in the Icons.tif image, called "all of them." This channel was created by the author so that you can experiment independently with all the shapes in the image before you have your selection skills down pat. Simply press Ctrl(⌘) and click on the channel name to load the marquee selections, as you did with the star selection.

- Holding Shift when using most of Photoshop's selection tools adds image area(s) to the existing active selection.

- Conversely, holding Alt(Opt) while using most selection tools subtracts image area(s)from an existing active selection within an image.

Let's use the Polygon Lasso tool now to create an accurate selection around the square shape at the left of Icons.tif.

SUBTRACTING FROM A SELECTION

1. Scroll your view over to the gold, square icon at far left in Icons.tif.

2. Drag on the Lasso tool button on the toolbox to reveal the button flyout, and then choose the Polygon Lasso tool.

3. Click on the outside corners of the shape, as shown in Figure 6.4. When you reach your first click point, click again to close the selection marquee.

You now need to remove the hole from the selection you've created...

4. Press and hold Alt(Opt), and then click on the inside corners of the square shape, as in Figure 6.5. Release the Alt(Opt) key, and you'll see that the hole has been neatly trimmed out of your original selection.

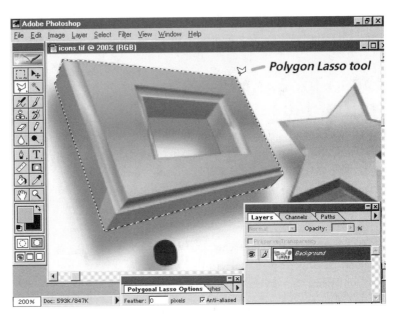

FIGURE 6.4   *The Polygon Lasso tool creates straight edges between points you click.*

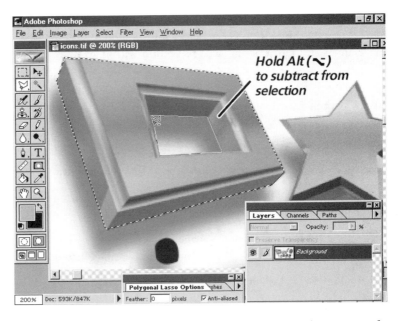

FIGURE 6.5   *Holding Alt(Opt) in combination with the Polygon Lasso tool removes areas from the current selection.*

There's another way in Photoshop to remove an area from a selection, and this method involves Quick Mask mode. Let's try it out...

5. Press and hold Shift while you use the Lasso Tool to make a circle around the inside hole of the shape, as shown in Figure 6.6. This action adds to the selection, effectively removing the hole marquee you created within the outside marquee.

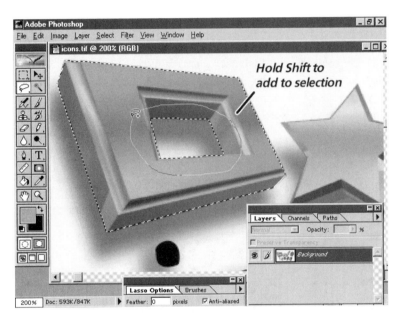

FIGURE 6.6   *Want to remove a hole? Hold Shift and then lasso the area.*

6. Double-click on the Quick Mask mode button, below and to the right of the color selection boxes on the toolbox, to display the Quick Mask Options dialog box. When you use Quick Mask mode, areas have a color overlay applied to them.

7. Click on the Color Indicates Selected Areas button, and then click on the Color Swatch to display the Color Picker, as in Figure 6.7.

8. Choose a deep blue color in the Color Picker and then click on OK to exit. This will make the color overlay quite obvious in the image. Click on OK to exit the Quick Mask Options box. You should still be in Quick Mask mode.

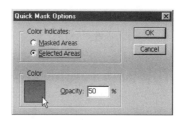

FIGURE 6.7   *The Quick Mask options box enables you to decide whether color overlay indicates masked (protected) areas or selected areas.*

9. With the Polygon Lasso tool, click points around the hole in the masked rectangle and close it to make a marquee selection. Press D (default colors) and then press Delete (Backspace). This deletes the Quick Mask that the marquee surrounds, as you can see in Figure 6.8. Black color adds Quick Mask, whereas applying white (as you've just done by deleting to white background color) removes Quick Mask.

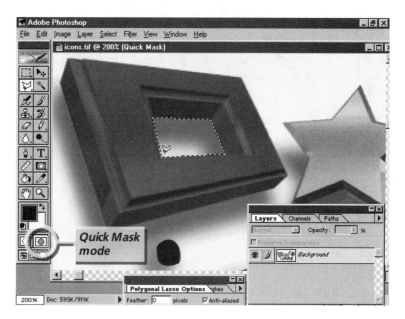

FIGURE 6.8   *Remove the color overlay inside the hole by pressing Delete (Backspace).*

10. Click on the Standard Editing mode icon, shown in Figure 6.9; the overlay vanishes, to be replaced by marquee lines that encompass areas fomerly covered with Quick Mask color overlay.

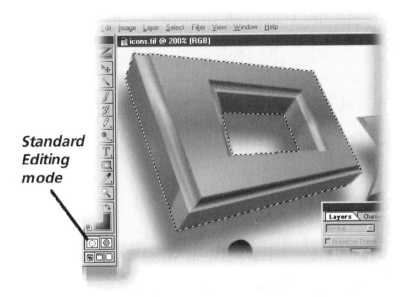

Standard Editing mode

FIGURE 6.9 *Quick Mask mode displays selected areas covered by a color overlay, whereas Standard Editing mode surrounds selected areas with marquee lines.*

11. Save the selection to an alpha channel by clicking on the Save selection as channel icon on the Channels palette. Double click on the channel title, and rename the channel **square**. Click on OK to exit the Channel Options box.

12. Press Ctrl(⌘)+S; keep the file open.

Having played with two simple, hard-edged shapes, it's time now to get a little more ambitious. In the following section, you'll tackle the circle shape in the Icons.tif image.

DEFINING A SELECTION WITH QUICK MASK

The convertibility of marquee selections to Quick Mask overlay and back has been demonstrated, but did you know that you can paint Quick Mask into an image to define new selection areas? This is a terrific feature for shapes whose edges are not straight lines, like the circle object in the composition of the previous figures.

In the following steps you'll use the Paintbrush tool in combination with Quick Mask mode to accurately select the circle shape.

TIP

Although the Icons image is only a practice image, you should be aware that as you save alpha channels in an image, you'll need more memory (RAM) to work with the image and that the size of the saved image file also increases. You should make it a regular practice in your own work to delete alpha channels you no longer need by dragging the unwanted alpha channel by its title into the trash icon on the Channels palette.

PAINTING A SELECTION WITH QUICK MASK

1. Press Ctrl(⌘)+the plus key to zoom in to a 300% viewing resolution of Icons.tif. Generally, when working with small shapes, a 200–400% viewing resolution is best for selecting things. Scroll over to the circle shape.

2. Choose the Paintbrush tool, and then press F5 if the Brushes palette isn't onscreen.

3. Click on the top row, fourth-column tip on the Brushes palette.

4. Click on the Quick Mask mode icon. Press D (default colors).

5. Paint a test stroke or two inside the circle to get a feel for the size of the brush tip.

6. Start painting along the inside edge of the circle shape, as shown in Figure 6.10. Don't bother with the interior of the shape; simply outline the inside edge.

FIGURE 6.10 *Define the inside of the edge of the circle by applying Quick Mask.*

7. Choose the Lasso tool, and then while holding Alt(Opt), click a shape that defines the inside of the circle. There will be overlapping areas where you've painted Quick Mask, as you can see in Figure 6.11.

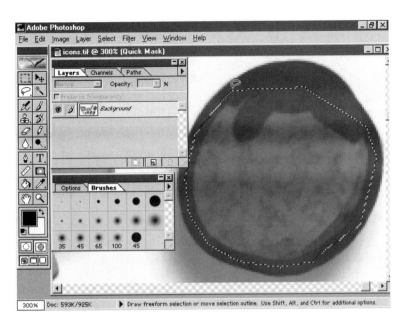

FIGURE 6.11 *Define the interior of the circle shape, using the Lasso tool in Polygon Lasso mode.*

8. Press Alt(Opt)+Delete (Backspace), and then press Ctrl(⌘)+D to deselect the marquee. You've applied black foreground color, effectively completing the masking work.

9. Click on the Standard Editing mode button, then on the Channels palette, and then click on the Save selection as channel icon. Double-click on the newly created channel title, name the alpha channel **circle**, and then click OK to close the Channel Options box. You'll be coming back to the circle shape later in this chapter, so saving your selection work is a must.

10. Press Ctrl(⌘)+S to save the file; keep the file open.

As we work with increasingly complex shapes in Photoshop, our tools must change. In the following section, you'll design a selection marquee around the squiggle, a totally freeform object. One of the best approaches to creating a selection around a freeform, organically shaped object is to create a path around the object with the Pen tool. Let's examine the components of a path, and the way paths work in Photoshop.

NOTE

You cannot save a selection while you're working in Quick Mask mode. You must have an active marquee selection in the image to save the selection.

USING PATHS TO CREATE SELECTIONS

If you're familiar with Adobe Illustrator, Macromedia Freehand, or CorelXARA, you're already acquainted with paths and the way they are designed. It'll be a breeze for you to apply your knowledge of vector paths to the sections that follow. But if you're new to vector graphics, you'll want to thoroughly familiarize yourself with the way Photoshop's family of Pen tools works because they are powerful tools that make selecting complex outlines child's play. See chapter 5 for the run-down on all of the new Pen group tools.

NOTE

Vector artwork is one of the two families of computer graphics. The type of graphics that Photoshop produces is called a bitmap graphic. Vector artwork depends on math algorithms to define shapes in space that are resolution independent, while bitmap graphics are a mesh, a quilt, or pixels.(For more information on bitmaps and vector graphics, see chapter 1.)

WHAT'S IN A PATH?

A *path* in Photoshop is a nonprinting guide you create. A path can have any shape and also can contain subpaths. *Subpaths* are closed paths within paths, such as the inside path of a donut (the hole).

The basic components of a path are *anchor points* and *path segments.* Path segments are automatically drawn between anchor points in Photoshop, and anchor points can have either a *cusp* (sharp) or smooth property when the path segments pass through them.

To change the shape of a path segment during the creation of the path or anytime afterward, you use various Pen-related tools to adjust the direction lines and direction points that emanate from anchor points. You "steer" a path segment by dragging on a direction point, and you change the overall shape of a path when you move an anchor point or two.

In Figure 6.12 you can see an open path with labels of each component. The steps that follow will refer to the components by name, so now's a good time to familiarize yourself with them.

There are seven tools on the Pen tool flyout. You should become familiar with at least three of them for most path construction; you'll use two of these tools—the Pen and the Direct Selection tools— to build an outline around the squiggle shape in Icons.tif:

- **The Pen tool.** Used for clicking anchor points and for dragging path segments to reshape them.

- **The Direct Selection tool.** Used for relocating anchor points and for changing the slope of path segments by manipulating direction points.

- **The Convert Point tool.** Changes the way a path segment passes through an anchor point. You drag on a direction point associated with an anchor point to make a smooth transition through the anchor; clicking on a smooth anchor changes it to a corner (cusp) anchor, whose associated path "breaks angle" as it passes through the anchor.

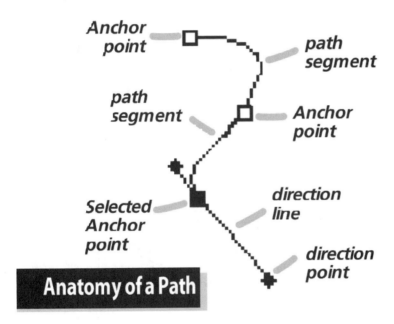

FIGURE 6.12 *A path in Photoshop consists of anchors, path segments, direction lines, and direction points.*

Because the squiggle shape consists of smooth lines only, you won't be using the Convert Point tool in the steps that follow. Figure 6.13 is a handy reference for what the basic drawing tools in Photoshop do.

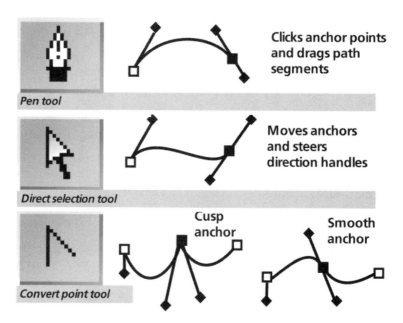

Figure 6.13 *There are three basic drawing and manipulating tools for paths in the Pen tool flyout.*

The best way to begin your experience with the Pen tool is at the beginning, so let's start creating a closed path around the squiggle shape in the image:

Creating a Complex, Closed Path

1. At the top of the squiggle shape, click, hold, and then drag the point to the right. You'll notice that the cursor is now a selection cursor, and it's holding a direction point. What you're doing is determining that the first anchor point has a smooth property.

2. Click and drag (moving clockwise) a second anchor point below and to the right of the first anchor, where the squiggle makes a turn in its outline. Don't release the cursor yet; instead, try to steer the path segment between the first and second anchors so that the path fits the curve of the squiggle's outline.

3. Repeat step 2 by moving down and to the left to an area of the squiggle outline where there is a bend. The tightest-fitting paths around image outlines are created by placing anchors at the *points of inflection* around the outline—those areas that display a sharp turn—as illustrated in Figure 6.14.

Chances are that the path isn't perfect so far; the path might be encroaching on the outline of the squiggle shape. To correct this, here's what to do:

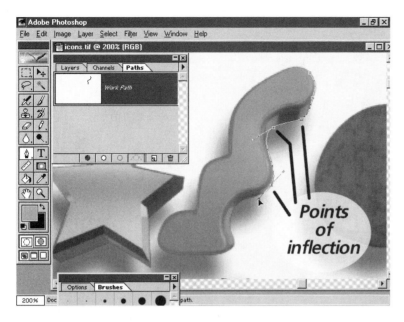

FIGURE 6.14 *Click and drag anchor points at the points of inflection around the squiggle shape.*

4. Press and hold Ctrl(⌘). This toggles the Pen tool to the Direct Selection tool.

5. Click on an anchor to expose the direction lines and direction points.

6. Drag on a direction point to steer the associated path segment closer to the outline of the squiggle shape, as shown in Figure 6.15.

7. Release Ctrl(⌘) and continue your path.

8. When you've reached the top of the squiggle, at your first anchor point, single click to close the path.

It doesn't matter if the path is not perfect. First, this is a practice chapter, and second, you'll learn shortly how to edit the outline you've created with the path…

9. If the Paths palette is not onscreen, press F7 and then click on the Paths tab.

10. Double-click on the Working Path title on the Paths palette, type **My path** in the name field, and then click on OK to close the dialog box. Naming a path makes it permanent; a working path can be accidentally overwritten by creating new paths.

11. Click on the Loads path as a selection icon at the bottom of the palette, and then click on an empty space on the palette, so that the selection marquee—not the path—is visible (see Figure 6.16).

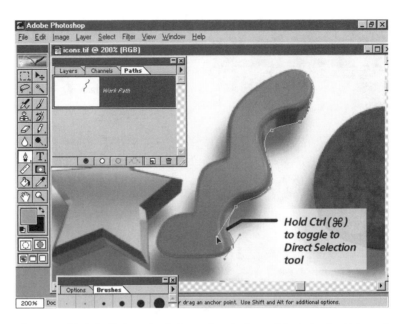

FIGURE 6.15 *Holding Ctrl(⌘) toggles the Pen tool to the Direct Selection tool, which can be used to move anchor points and to steer direction points, thus changing the slope of path segments.*

FIGURE 6.16 *Base a selection marquee on the geometry of the path you created by clicking on the Loads path as a selection icon.*

12. Click on the Quick Mask mode icon on the toolbox, and then press D and then X so that white is the current foreground color (white removes Quick Mask).

13. With the Paintbrush tool and the fourth-from-left tip in the top row on the Brushes palette, carefully trim around areas of the Quick Mask that should not be in the selection, as shown in Figure 6.17.

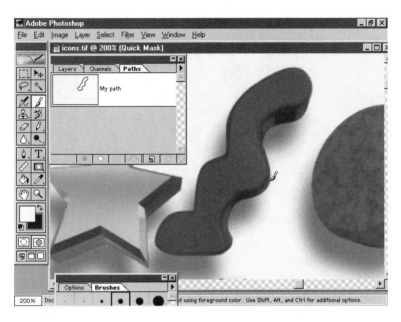

FIGURE 6.17 *Refine the selection you defined, using Quick Mask and the Paintbrush tool.*

14. When you've finished editing, click on the Standard Editing mode button; the Quick Mask then becomes a selection marquee.

15. Choose a selection tool (the Lasso tool is fine), and then right-click (Macintosh: hold Ctrl and click) inside the selection marquee. Choose Layer Via Copy from the context menu, as in Figure 6.18, and all of a sudden our discussions must turn from paths to layers!

16. Keep the file open; there's more fun in store.

Let's talk about layers for a moment before getting into the process of manipulating them.

NOTE

To delete a saved path, you can drag its title into the trash icon on the Paths palette, or press backspace twice. The first backspace removes the last-created path segment, and the second backspace deletes the remainder of the path.

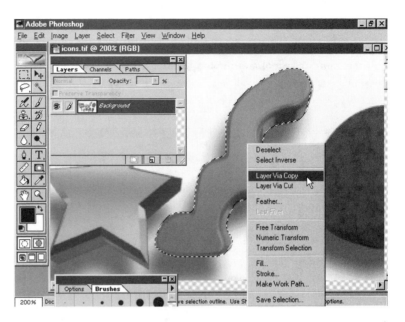

FIGURE 6.18 *You can copy or cut the contents of a selection marquee to a new layer, using the context menu commands.*

THE LOWDOWN ON LAYERS

If you're familiar with cel animation, layers will come very intuitively to you. In animation, cartoonists paint on a clear sheet of acetate and then photograph the acetate and its contents against a background. Something similar goes on with the squiggle, for example, that you've now copied to a new layer in the Icons.tif image. The copy of the squiggle shape does not belong to the background, as you can see from Figure 6.19; you can freely move it as you would a vector object without disturbing the rest of the composition.

It is only when you are happy with the location and appearance of an element on a layer that you'll want to flatten the image and make the layer's contents part of the background. Layers are a proprietary feature of Photoshop, and layered images can only be saved to Photoshop's PSD format (which is why you were not asked to save the image in the previous steps). To make a composition available to be saved in more common file formats such as TIFF, Targa, BMP, and PICT, you must flatten layered images.

In the next set of steps, you'll perform some fancy editing work with the squiggle copy—you'll make it look as though it's sticking through the gold rectangle shape at the far left in Icons.tif.

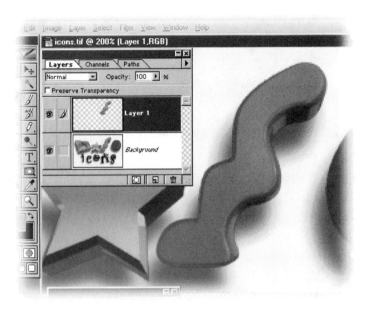

FIGURE 6.19   *The squiggle shape is now on its own layer—Layer 1—and can be moved independently of the other elements in the composition.*

Ready for your adventure with layer editing? Let's go:

CREATING A MULTILAYER COMPOSITION BY USING FLOATING SELECTIONS

1. Double-click on the Zoom tool to move your view of the Icons.tif image to 100% (1:1).

2. On the Layers palette, click on the Layer 1 title to make sure it's the current editing layer.

3. Choose the Move tool, and then drag in the window until the squiggle copy is directly above the gold rectangle, as in Figure 6.20.

To get the squiggle to stick through the hole in the gold rectangle, the squiggle needs to be longer. No problem; you'll divide the squiggle in two and reposition its lower portion …

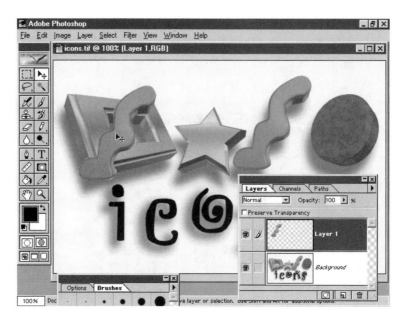

FIGURE 6.20 *The Move tool is the only tool that can be used to move the contents of a layer without having selected the contents.*

4. Zoom in to a 200% viewing resolution of the image (for precise editing work), and then choose the Lasso tool.

5. Make a selection marquee around the bottom of the squiggle, as shown in Figure 6.21.

6. Press and hold Ctrl(⌘) and then drag inside the selection, moving the selection's contents downward and slightly to the left, as illustrated in Figure 6.22. What you've created is a *floating* selection; it does not belong to the layer until you deselect it. You can release Ctrl(⌘) now and simply drag the piece around if you keep the cursor inside the floating selection's marquee.

7. Click outside the selection marquee after you've positioned the floating selection; it once again becomes part of the layer.

8. On the Layers palette, turn the opacity for the layer down to about 50%. Now you can clearly see which parts of the squiggle need to be deleted.

9. Click on the Layer Mask icon on the Layers palette. Like Quick Mask, Layer Mask mode hides areas on a layer you paint (or fill) with black, and reveals hidden areas when you paint or fill with white.

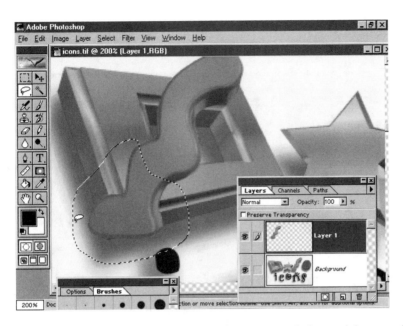

FIGURE 6.21 *You can make selection marquees around opaque areas of a layer and then move the contents of the selections.*

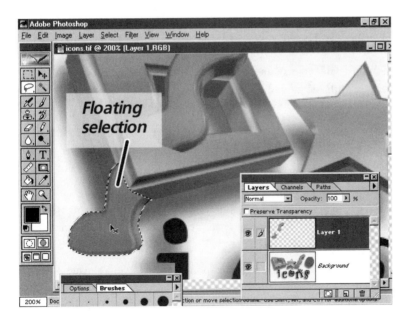

FIGURE 6.22 *Pressing Ctrl(⌘) and dragging inside a marquee selection on a layer makes the contents of the selection a floating selection.*

10. With the Polygon Lasso tool, encompass the top part of the squiggle areas that should be removed, as shown in Figure 6.23.

FIGURE 6.23 *Create a marquee selection around the area of the squiggle shape that should be removed.*

11. Press D (default colors), and then press Alt(Opt)+Delete (Backspace) to fill the marquee with foreground color (and hide the unwanted portion of the squiggle). Press Ctrl(⌘)+D to deselect the marquee now.

12. Choose the Paintbrush tool (for the sake of variety here), choose the third-from-smallest tip in the top row on the Brushes palette, and paint over the bottom portions of the squiggle, where it overlaps the gold rectangle. Figure 6.24 shows you where to paint.

13. Zoom out to 100% viewing resolution, drag the opacity slider to 100% on the Layers palette, and take a gander at your editing work. It should look something like Figure 6.25.

14. It's time to make permanent the temporary changes you've made on the layer. When you *apply* a layer mask, it *deletes* the areas you've hidden from a layer. Click on the Layer Mask thumbnail on the Layers palette, and then drag it into the trash icon. An attention box appears.

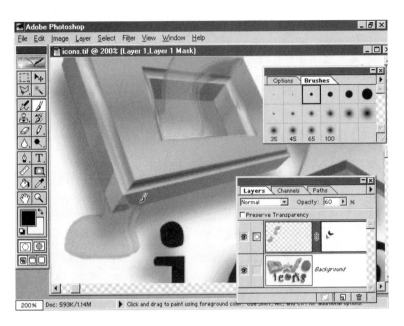

FIGURE 6.24 *Applying black color hides layer areas in Layer Mask mode.*

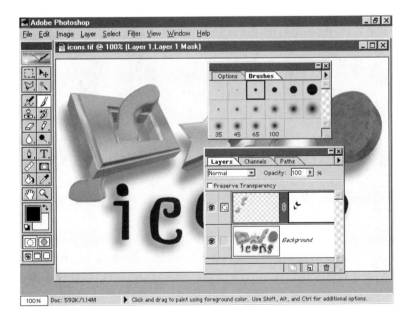

FIGURE 6.25 *Using the Layer Mask feature, you've created an optical illusion that looks completely realistic.*

You have three options in the attention box. *Apply* means that hidden areas on the layer will be deleted. *Discard* means that all the areas you've hidden will reappear (restoring everything) and all your work was for nothing. And *Cancel* means cancel— you return to your work with no changes on the layer.

15. Click on Apply. You're finished editing on the layer, and it's time to merge the layer with the Background image. Click on the Layers palette's menu flyout button, and choose Merge Visible from the menu, as shown in Figure 6.26.

    Merge Visible combines all layers in an image that are *currently visible* (that have the eye icon displayed next to their titles). Layers that are not visible (no eye icon) are not disturbed and can be made visible and then edited at any time.

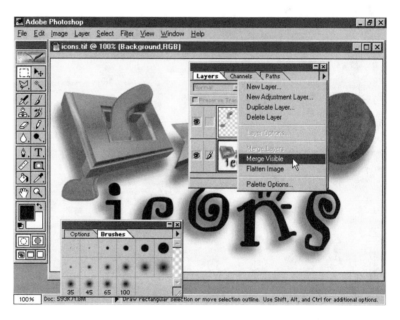

FIGURE 6.26 *Layers can be created, and layers can be merged back into a composition.*

16. Press Ctrl(⌘)+S; keep the file open.

Floating selections were only briefly covered in the previous section. It's time to explore a little more, and see what creative possibilities are held by floating selections.

SUBTRACTING FROM A FLOATING SELECTION

As mentioned earlier, a floating selection does not belong to a layer or to a background of an image. It's simply a floating entity that eventually must be merged with a layer so you can save the file. But as long as a floating selection is hovering about, you can do some interesting things with it, which the following steps explore.

REMOVING PARTS OF A FLOATING SELECTION

1. On the Channels palette, press Ctrl(⌘) and click on the Circle channel. This loads a marquee selection you saved earlier around the circle shape.

2. With a selection tool chosen, right-click (Macintosh: hold Ctrl and click) and then choose Layer Via Copy from the context menu. A new layer appears in the image; the thumbnail on the Layers palette is named Layer 1.

3. To be tidy, double-click on the Layer 1 title, type **Circle** in the Name field of the Layer Options dialog box, and then click on OK to close the box and rename the layer.

4. With the Rectangular Marquee tool, drag around the circle shape on the layer, as shown in Figure 6.27.

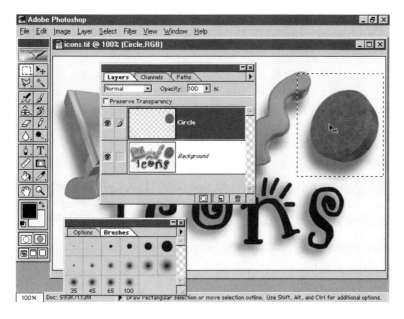

FIGURE 6.27 *Create a selection marquee around the opaque area on the Circle layer.*

5. Press and hold Ctrl(⌘) and drag within the selection marquee. The circle is now a floating selection, as you can see from Figure 6.28.

FIGURE 6.28 *Holding Ctrl(⌘) cuts the shape off the layer and makes it a floating selection.*

6. Press Ctrl(⌘)+the plus key to zoom in to a 200% viewing resolution of the image.

7. Press and hold Alt(Opt), and then with the Lasso tool trim away at the floating selection. As you can see in Figure 6.29, the areas you trim away simply vanish from existence—they are not hidden, they are not masked. Now that you can see the power of deleting from floating selections, do not accidentally remove portions of floating selections that you want to save—or you'll need to visit the History palette!

8. Drag the Circle layer into the trash icon on the Layers palette. You're left with the marquee outline of the floating selection. Press Ctrl(⌘)+D to deselect the marquee, and then press Ctrl(⌘)+S; keep the file open.

Clearly, the uses for removing portions of a floating selection are limited, but it's important in this chapter to cover *all* the selection features because it is you, the designer, who is inventive with features.

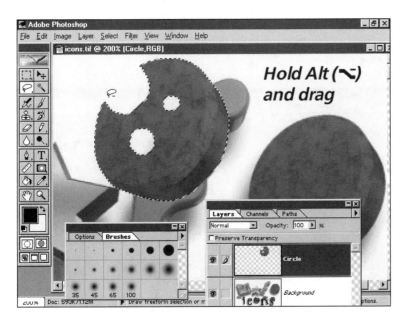

FIGURE 6.29 *Areas subtracted from floating selections are deleted.*

WORKING WITH CLIPPING GROUPS

There is yet another type of mask, called a *clipping group,* you can apply to shapes in a composition in Photoshop. A clipping group works when you have two layers in an image; the bottom layer is the "stencil," and all linked layers above the stencil can peek through the stencil. This is easier to see in the context of an example than it is to explain, however, so let's see how we can recolor the "icons" text in the image by using a clipping group.

SELECTING THE BASE FOR A CLIPPING GROUP

1. Double-click on the Magic Wand tool to choose it and to display the Options palette for the tool.

2. On the Options palette, type **1** in the Tolerance field, and check the Anti-aliasing box. Now you'll be able to select the lettering in the image without picking up the drop shadow behind the text.

3. Click on the first character, and then hold Shift and click on the other characters, as shown in Figure 6.30. By holding Shift while you click, you add to the current selection.

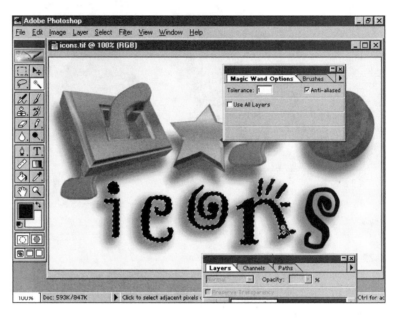

FIGURE 6.30 *By pressing the Shift key, you can define multiple selections.*

4. Choose Layer, New, Layer Via Copy from the main menu. We're doing this simply to show you where the command is on the menu—you're already familiar with the context menu!

5. Click on the Create new layer icon on the Layers palette. You should now have text on Layer 1 and an empty Layer 2 above Layer 1.

6. Choose the Linear Gradient tool, choose "Violet, Orange" from the Gradient drop-down list on the Options palette; then drag from top to bottom on Layer 2, as shown in Figure 6.31.

It's sort of difficult to see the text now, huh? Not for long…

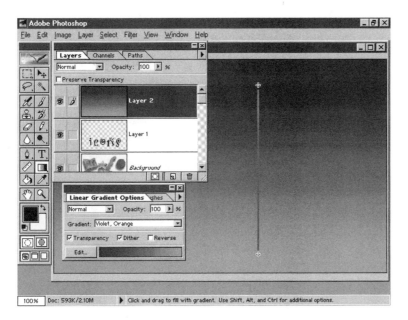

FIGURE 6.31   *Add a gradient to fill Layer 2.*

7. Press and hold Alt(Opt) and then click between the Layer 1 and Layer 2 titles on the Layers palette. Surprise! Now Layer 2 is "inside" the opaque text areas of Layer 1. You've created a clipping group. An easy visual reminder of this is that the base layer is underlined on the Layers palette, and affected layers above have their thumbnail images moved to the right on the Layers palette, as in Figure 6.32.

You can do anything you like with either the base layer or the layers on top of it. This means that you can move the text by using the Move tool, if you like, and the fill on Layer 2 will change to reflect its new relative position. You can also recolor the layers on top of the base layer, as follows...

8. Choose the Spectrum Gradient from the Options palette's drop-down list, and then drag vertically on Layer 2. Note that the fill for the text changes (although you can't see it in the black-and-white Figure 6.33).

9. Save the file to your hard drive as Icons.psd, in Photoshop's native file format. You can close the image at any time now.

FIGURE 6.32 *The base layer of the clipping group is the stencil, and layers above the base layer are the fill within the composition.*

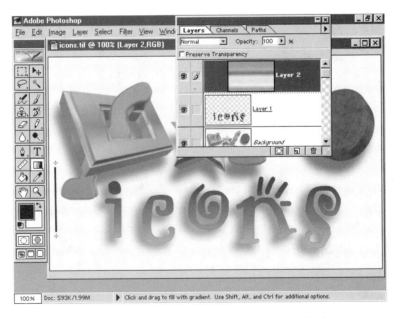

FIGURE 6.33 *Anything you apply or add to a clipping group is seen "through" the opaque areas of the base layer.*

To *remove* a clipping group property, you simply hold Alt(Opt) and click between the titles on the layers palette.

SUMMARY

The skills you've been introduced to in this chapter need to be refined on your own time but, hopefully, you can see the rewards of being able to work between selections, layers, and paths. Photoshop offers so many way to select things, you'll soon have your own personal work style.

Now that you've had a taste of working with selections and a trial image, let's move on to Chapter 7, "Retouching a Photograph," where you'll put together some of the pieces you've learned so far by retouching an image.

CHAPTER 7

RETOUCHING A PHOTOGRAPH

Often, the "perfect" photograph doesn't wait for you. Say, for example, that your senator is visiting town and you have exactly 30 seconds to take his picture before crowds of newspaper people and taxpayers intrude on the scene. So you frantically snap away, only to discover after the film is developed that in the best photo you have of the senator he's sticking his finger in his cheek! It's a sad fact of life the you don't always have the time to get your subject to pose properly.

What do you do? Do you call and ask him to come on over and pose again? Not likely. Your second best bet is to use Photoshop to correct the image, and that is what this chapter is all about: retouching an image…significantly.

ASSESSING THE COMPOSITIONAL DAMAGE

Let's take a look at the picture you have to work with. In Figure 7.1, you can see that Senator Dave is dressed properly, his facial expression is a good one, and there are two areas of the image that need retouching:

- His finger needs to be removed from his cheek.

- His left hand should not be in the figure at all.

FIGURE 7.1 *Photography performed without planning often leads to images with awkward, unexpected composition.*

The most difficult part of this retouching assignment will be to remove Senator Dave's finger from his cheek. Whatever will replace the finger must match the tone and texture of Dave's face. You'll work on this area first, in the following section.

USING THE PEN TOOL AND FLOATING SELECTIONS

Because the silhouette of Senator Dave's cheek is smooth and well-defined, the Pen tool is a natural for creating an edge in this area. After the area of his finger has been encompassed with a path, you need to decide how to restore this area.

Fortunately, the lighting is overcast in the picture, with no strong shadows. This means that Dave's face is mostly evenly illuminated. And this means that you can copy and flip Dave's right cheek area to serve as a replacement for part of his left cheek. In the steps that follow, you'll create the path, create a floating copy of Dave's right cheek, flip the floating selection, create a marquee from the path, and then use the Paste Into command to replace the area that contains the finger. When you use the Paste Into command, a new layer is created in the image; because it is in Layer Mask mode, you can reposition and change the tone of the pasted area so that it looks right.

Here's how to use a floating selection to replace the area of Dave's face that contains the finger:

REPLACING AREAS WITH FLOATING SELECTIONS

1. Open the Dave.tif image from the Chap07 folder on the Companion CD.

2. Zoom in to a 200% viewing resolution of the image, and scroll the window so that the offending finger is in the center of the screen.

3. With the Pen tool, carefully trace around the cheek outline, intersecting the finger, and then close the path so that it encompasses the finger tip as well as the dent Dave is making in his cheek, as shown in Figure 7.2.

4. Click on an empty area of the Paths palette to hide the work path.

5. With the Lasso tool, drag a selection area around Dave's right cheek, and then hold Ctrl(⌘)+Alt(Opt) and drag inside the selection so that the area is now a copy, a floating selection of the area you defined. Figure 7.3 shows the shape and location of the marquee selection.

6. Choose Edit, Transform, and then choose Flip Horizontal. The selection of Dave's right cheek now becomes a replacement for his left cheek, as shown in Figure 7.4.

7. Choose Edit, Cut. The floating selection is now on the clipboard.

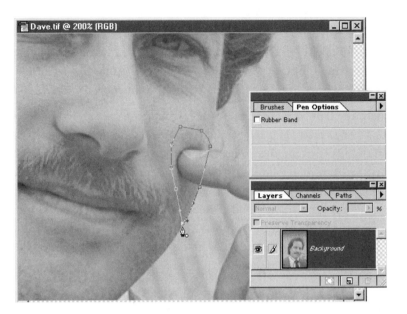

FIGURE 7.2 *The edge of the cheek is the most important area for the path's accuracy.*

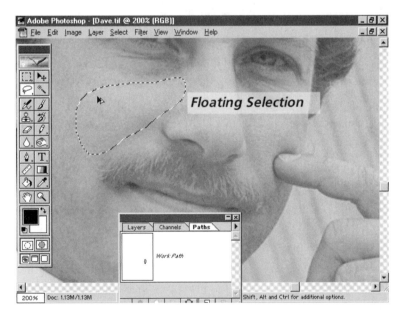

FIGURE 7.3 *Create a floating selection that you can use to replace areas inside the path you designed.*

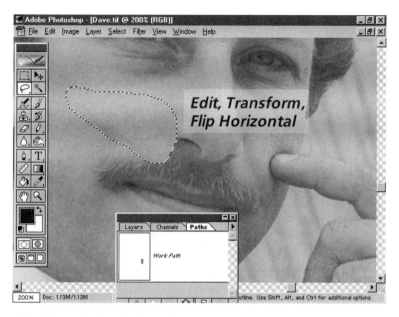

FIGURE 7.4 *Flip the floating selection horizontally.*

8. Click on the Work Path title on the Paths palette, and then click on the Loads path as a selection icon at the bottom of the palette. Click on an empty area of the palette to hide the path.

9. Choose Edit, Paste Into from the menu. As you can see in Figure 7.5, the paste from the clipboard is now masked on its own layer.

10. With the Move tool, drag the contents of Layer 1 around until there is a good continuity between the flesh and Dave's left cheek.

11. Press Ctrl(⌘)+L to display the Levels command.

12. Drag the midtone slider to about .86, as shown in Figure 7.6. The trick here is to make the contents of the Layer 1 consistent in tone with the original, surrounding areas. Do not worry about the hard edges of the selection; you'll soften them later. Right now, concentrate only on matching the skin tones on the two layers.

13. Click on OK to apply the change, and then choose Flatten Image from the Layers palette's flyout menu.

14. Choose File, Save As, and then save the image as Dave.tif to your hard disk. Keep the image open.

WARNING

Unlike previous versions of Photoshop, the Move tool cursor must be *over* the layer contents to move an element. Regardless of what layer is active, the Move tool will act *only* on the element it is positioned over.

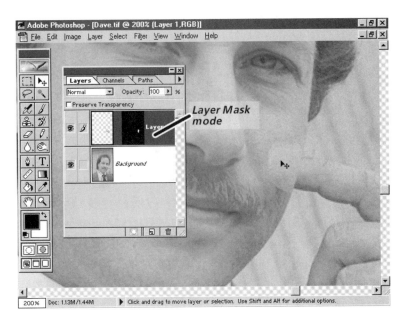

FIGURE 7.5   *The contents on the new layer are from the clipboard. The shape of the Layer Mask is defined from the marquee selection you loaded.*

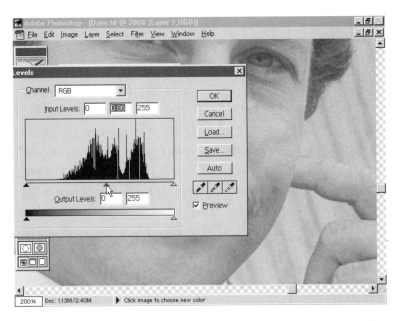

FIGURE 7.6   *Decrease the brightness in the midtones of the selection, using the midtone slider in the Levels command.*

Pasting a copy of the Senator's opposite cheek certainly has gone a long way toward restoring the left side of his face. Now, however, you need to remove from his cheek the hard edges caused by the selection's hard edges.

RETOUCHING WITH THE RUBBER STAMP TOOL

Skin color varies, depending on its location on one's face. There are the rosy tone of one's cheeks, a different color under the eyes, and occasionally, a five o'clock shadow dulls the appearance of skin. The selection you just created borders on all three types of skin areas in the image. To remove the hard selection edge, you must work very closely to the selection edge to sample areas with the Rubber Stamp tool. As you apply cloned samples, the variation in the skin tones will not be dramatic, and you'll have achieved your goal by using only a few well-placed strokes.

Here's how to remove the selection edge from Dave's face:

USING THE RUBBER STAMP TOOL AT PARTIAL OPACITY

1. Choose the Rubber Stamp tool, and then press 5 on the keypad. This reduces the tool's cloning power to 50% opacity. Choose the second-from-left tip in the second row on the Brushes palette.

2. Press Alt(Opt) and click a point above the hard-edge selection, about 1/4 screen inch away from the edge, to set the sampling point for the Rubber Stamp tool.

3. Make short strokes into the selection edge, as shown in Figure 7.7. It will take more than one stroke to cover the edge, because the tool is operating at partial opacity. What you're trying to achieve here is just enough cloning to cover the selection edge, but not so much that you replace the area you pasted (grafted) in. You do not want to eliminate the texture of the skin.

4. When the top edge has been made invisible, press Alt(Opt) and click another sample point outside the selection edge on the left, and then carefully clone in skin texture to hide the edge. Resample the source point for the tool frequently to avoid a cheek on Dave that's too even in consistency. Skin texture and color are never consistent across large—and sometimes even small—areas of the body.

5. When you're finished with the left edge, press Alt(Opt) and click a sample point in Dave's five o'clock shadow; then stroke upward once or twice across the bottom selection edge, as shown in Figure 7.8.

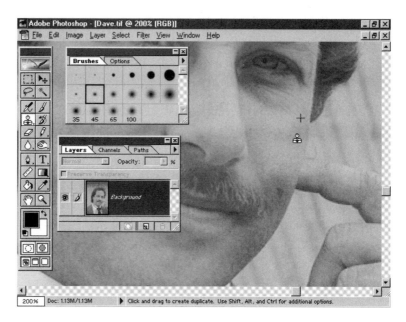

FIGURE 7.7 *Keep the source point and the target point for the Rubber Stamp tool close together as you clone over the edge.*

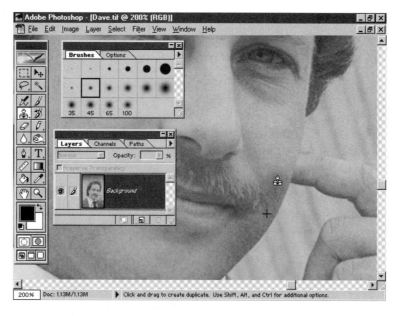

FIGURE 7.8 *Blend Dave's five o'clock shadow into the hard selection area.*

6. Press 0 (zero) to return the Rubber Stamp tool to 100% opacity. Press Ctrl(⌘)+S; keep the file open.

What you've performed is pretty amazing stuff. Senator Dave no longer has a finger in his cheek—it looks as though he has a finger *behind* his cheek, however. In the following section, you'll begin the process of cloning over Dave's hand with background image, an easy enough task if you keep the source point aligned to the pattern of the concrete in the background.

CHANGING A PATH TO MAKE A NEW SELECTION

The work path you created around Dave's cheek will serve another purpose after you've modified it somewhat. The path segment on the edge of the cheek should remain where it is, but the other sides should now fall outside the face, to encompass the rest of Dave's finger. You'll use this modified path to create a selection marquee you'll clone into to make the finger vanish.

Here's how to change the path and select a target area for cloning into the area described by the path:

CLONING ON THE OPPOSITE SIDE OF THE ORIGINAL PATH

1. Click and hold on the Pen tool to expose the Pen tool flyout, and then choose the Direct Selection tool (the white arrowhead). Click on the Work Path title on the Paths palette to make it visible.

2. With the exception of the path segment that lies on the edge of Dave's cheek, move the anchor points, one by one, out of Dave's face to encompass his finger, as shown in Figure 7.9.

3. Zoom out to 100% viewing resolution, click on the Loads path as a selection icon at the bottom of the Paths palette, and then click on an empty space on the palette to hide the path.

4. Choose the second from the right brush on the second row of the Brushes palette. Press Alt(Opt) and click with the Rubber Stamp tool on one of the diagonal lines of concrete in the background, and then brush the pattern into the area of Dave's finger, beginning your strokes where they align to the concrete pattern, as shown in Figure 7.10. You might need to define a new sample point as you fill in the selection marquee (you might run out of concrete pattern to the upper left of the image).

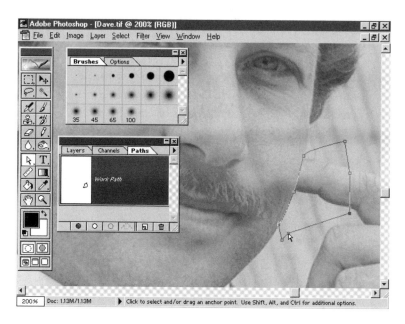

FIGURE 7.9 *Drag the anchor points to reshape the path to enclose the next area of the picture you will retouch.*

FIGURE 7.10 *Keep the area from which you sample consistent with the pattern of the area you clone into.*

5. When the interior of the selection marquee has been completely cloned into, press Ctrl(⌘)+D to deselect the marquee. Press Ctrl(⌘)+S; keep the file open.

As you'll note in the image now, Dave's hand crosses his shoulder. This means that an edge needs to be defined for his shoulder in the same way you defined the edge of Dave's cheek, and areas on both sides of the edge will need retouching.

CREATING A PATH TO DEFINE THE SHOULDER

Because Dave's hand intrudes on his shoulder, it is impossible to tell exactly where the edge of his jacket lies. If you examine his right shoulder, however, you can see that there is a definite slope downward. In the next set of steps you'll create a downward-sloping edge for the shoulder, and then encompass the part of Dave's hand that is in front of the concrete background.

Here's how to put the Pen tool to work again:

USING THE PEN TOOL TO CREATE A PATH

1. Drag the right side of the image window away from the image so that you can see some image window background. You'll be creating a path segment that is flush with this edge.

2. With the Pen tool, begin a path directly on Dave's shoulder, to the left of his hand.

3. Click and drag toward the middle of his shoulder, to create a second anchor and to steer the arc of the path slightly downward, to give a dip in the shoulder.

4. Click an anchor at the edge of the image, click another anchor on the edge at about the height of Dave's index finger, and then close the path, encompassing Dave's hand. Figure 7.11 shows the shape and location of the path.

5. On the Paths palette, click on the Loads path as a selection icon, and then click on an empty space on the palette to hide the path.

6. With the Rubber Stamp tool, press Alt(Opt) and click to sample one of the ridges on the concrete, and then stroke within the marquee to replace Dave's hand with concrete background. Make certain that your first stroke is on one of the concrete ridges. You may need to set a new sampling point once or twice to preserve the continuity of the diagonal concrete pattern, as in Figure 7.12.

7. Press Ctrl(⌘)+D to deselect the marquee. Press Ctrl(⌘)+S; keep the file open.

It's time now to twist the work path downward to encompass the rest of Dave's hand.

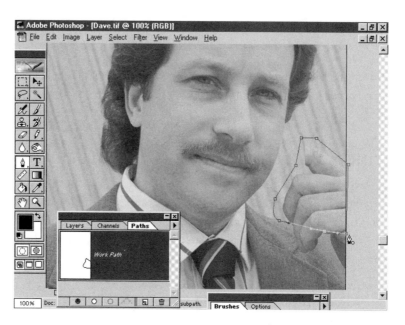

FIGURE 7.11 *Define the shoulder edge, and then complete the path to encompass Dave's hand.*

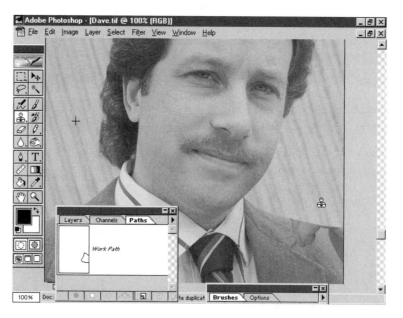

FIGURE 7.12 *Align the sample point to the target point; both cursors should start out on the grooves of the concrete.*

CLONING A PATTERN

Using the Rubber Stamp tool to remove the remainder of Senator Dave's hand will not be as simple as it might seem. True, you'll simply be cloning over fabric, but because the fabric has shading to it, you must select your source point for the Rubber Stamp tool carefully.

You'll begin the jacket portion of the assignment by moving the anchors in the work path to encompass what's left of Dave's hand:

INVISIBLE MENDING

1. Click on the Work Path title on the Paths palette to make it visible.

2. Choose the Direct Selection tool, and then drag anchor points, except those that define the shoulder, downward. Position them so that they encompass Dave's hand; keep the boundary tight around the hand, as shown in Figure 7.13.

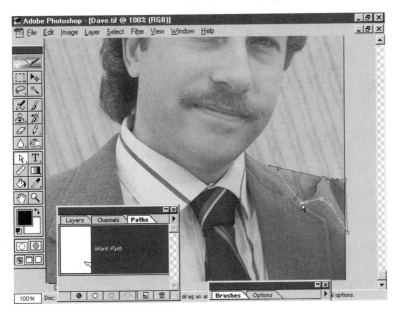

FIGURE 7.13 *Move the top anchor points to the bottom of the image so that they are a close fit to the remaining hand area.*

3. Zoom in to 200% viewing resolution, click on the Loads path as a selection icon at the bottom of the Paths palette, and then click on an empty space on the palette to hide the path.

4. With the Rubber Stamp tool, press Alt(Opt) and click on an area of light charcoal on Dave's jacket, and then begin cloning where his hand is, over similar tones of charcoal as shown in Figure 7.14. Use short strokes, and resample when you've moved into an area where cloning already exists. See the following Note on a new and possibly frustrating feature of the Rubber Stamp tool.

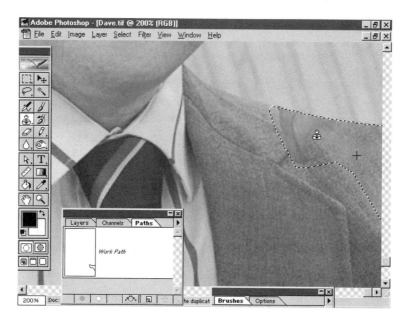

FIGURE 7.14 *Clone over similarly shaded areas of the jacket.*

NOTE

Photoshop does not allow you to clone, using samples of areas that have already been cloned, *using one continuous pass* of the Rubber Stamp tool. If you find yourself restoring areas instead of cloning over them, press Ctrl(⌘)+Z to Undo, and then take a new sample point in the cloned-in area by pressing Alt(Opt) and clicking. Then you can use this area as a sample.

5. Due to the light casting on Dave's jacket, there's a stretch of darker charcoal color to the left of the area you worked on. Press Alt(Opt) and click on a sample of the darker charcoal color, and then brush into Dave's hand areas.

You'll notice that points on the jacket's lapel are covered by Dave's fingers. This area is not an exceptionally difficult one to fix, but it requires a different technique, so...

6. Press Ctrl(⌘)+S; keep the file open.

There's only one area left on the jacket that needs to be corrected to complete the picture. In the following section, you'll see how to use the Rubber Stamp tool to restore the point on Dave's lapel.

THE TRICK IS TO EXTEND WHAT'S AVAILABLE

You'll notice that many areas of Dave's lapel have not been retouched; these areas converge on the point of the lapel, which is hidden by Dave's knuckles. Here's a revolutionary concept: why not clone the top lapel line, and then the bottom one, until the lines converge?

This is exactly what you'll do in the following steps:

RESTORING THE LAPEL WITH THE RUBBER STAMP TOOL

1. Zoom in to 300% viewing resolution, and center the lapel area onscreen.

2. Choose the Rubber Stamp tool, and then choose the second-from-left tip in the second row on the Brushes palette.

3. Press Alt(Opt) and click on the horizontal midpoint of the top lapel seam.

4. Start extending the lapel line by brushing directly over the seam, removing Dave's knuckles. Stop when the lapel line has been extended to where it would logically come to a point, as in Figure 7.15.

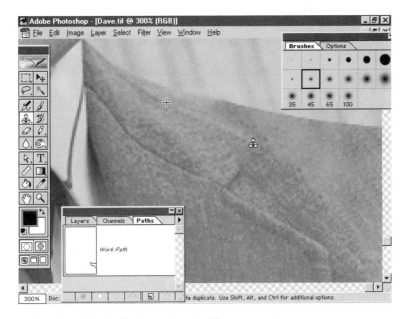

FIGURE 7.15 *Extend the lapel's edge to where it will come to a point.*

5. Press Alt(Opt) and click on the very bottom of the short, diagonal lapel line that points toward 2 o'clock.

6. Brush upward until the lapel line meets the lapel line you created in step 4, as in Figure 7.16.

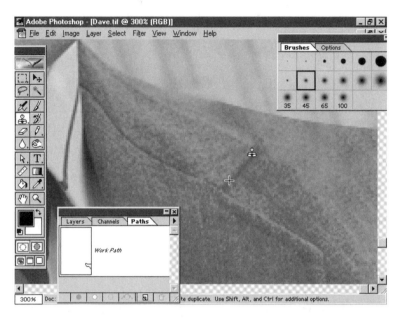

FIGURE 7.16 *Conclude the lapel line at the point where the previous lapel line you cloned in ends.*

7. You might need to apply a hit or two of cloned fabric to completely remove the fleshtones in this area.

8. You're finished! Press Ctrl(⌘)+S; keep the file open.

What you've achieved with Senator Dave's image is nothing short of a miracle. But you can still do two things to make the composition look even better and draw attention away from your editing work.

CROPPING THE IMAGE

Let's extend your relationship with the fictitious senator. Suppose that he likes what you've done with the image so much, he wants a campaign poster made from it. One of the first things you want to do is fix the cropping of the image; there is far too much background detail in the image, and cropping part of his left shoulder from the scene means less Photoshop fakery to dwell on in the finished image.

Here's how to crop the image so that the senator's face plays the predominant compositional role in the image:

CROPPING TO ENHANCE AN IMAGE

1. Zoom out to a 50% view of the image. With the Rectangular Marquee tool, drag a box around the image. The four sides of the box should be located as follows:

   - On the left, about 1/2 screen inch from Dave's hair.

   - On the top, about 1/2 screen inch from his hair. This makes Dave look taller, without the looming concrete ceiling in the picture.

   - On the right, about 1/2 screen inch from the right edge of the image. This allows a fraction of Dave's hair on his left side to remain in the image, and crops some of the shoulder restoration work you've done.

   - On the bottom, crop slightly above the bottom of the knot in the tie.

   Figure 7.17 shows the location of the crop box you should design.

FIGURE 7.17 *Crop closely so that the focus of the image is on the senator's face.*

2. Choose Image, Crop.

3. Press Ctrl(⌘)+S; keep the file open.

"SHARED ATTENTION" IN THE FINISHED IMAGE

Some bold text in boxes at the top and bottom of the image would accomplish two things:

- It would make clear to everyone who the guy in the picture is.

- It would provide another element to distract the viewer from the retouching work you've performed.

Adding bold text around a retouched image is sort of a cheap trick, but it's very effective. In Figure 7.18, you can see the original image and the finished image with some text. Who would know that these are the same photos?

FIGURE 7.18 *From photo-flub to poster boy, all the elements are now in the right place and proportion to present a professional campaign poster.*

If you'd like to add text to your finished image, you don't need a set of steps; instead, here are a few guidelines:

- Make your default background color white, and expand the Canvas Size of the image on top and bottom to add room for text blocks.

- Stick to a single font family. The author used Helvetica in different weights to create the lettering.

- If you feel you don't have the right weights of a font, use a vector drawing application such as Illustrator to create "smooshed" or extended text, and then import the text to Photoshop.

- Use patriotic colors for the text. In the United States, that would be red and blue. You also might want to run a banner of small stars between lines of text to overstate the message that this is a campaign poster.

SUMMARY

More than anything else, this chapter has taught you not to see the impossible, but instead to see the creative ways in which you can use Photoshop techniques to perform big-time cosmetic surgery on an image. You can use these same techniques to remove a person from a group picture, take a cigar out of someone's face—you name it. It's all in the art of defining selections and knowing where the source point should be for cloning.

You'll take a step beyond photo-retouching in Chapter 8, "Restoring Heirloom Photographs," where you'll learn how to restore an heirloom photo that's ostensibly beyond repair.

PART III

INTERMEDIATE MAGIC AND PHOTOSHOP

RESTORING HEIRLOOM PHOTOGRAPHS

"But it doesn't look like him," cried the customer as she stared at the hand-painted photo restoration of her grandfather. "And his eyes don't look identical!" The artist tried to explain how difficult it is to flawlessly retouch photographs, using dyes. The customer responded with, "And this is the only print I have!"

All but gone are the days when a photo retoucher actually paints on the damaged photograph. The traditional photo retoucher was not only an artist, but also a magician who needed to preserve the realistic look of a photograph when applying the paint. Fortunately, with today's pixel manipulating tools, you can repair precious photos with relative ease and to a much greater extent than you could with traditional retouching.

In this chapter, you will learn to restore three photographs. Each of these pictures, shown in Figure 8.1, has a problem common in old photos: faded color and contrast, fine cracks in the emulsion, and a liquid stain. Don't be daunted by the number of restoration problems—Photoshop has the power to make the job of repairing most of them very quick work! But before you begin the first project, let's examine some of the common defects found in the aged photograph.

FIGURE 8.1   *Old photographs have common problems that you will repair in this chapter.*

CONCERNS UNIQUE TO OLD PHOTOGRAPHS

Unlike today's photos that have a smooth and flat surface and a full tonal range, every decades-old photograph has faded and many have a textured or hand-painted surface. Each photo can have a unique flaw that you need to deal with. Foreknowledge and preplanning are of great value when you set out on your restoration adventures.

DIGITIZING A WARPED PHOTO

A once-popular way to display a photo was to glue it to a hard backing. Unfortunately, this backing material warps and becomes brittle over time, which makes the photograph very difficult to scan.

If the photo does not lie flat against the scanner's glass, the result can be an inferior scan (with parts of the image being out of focus, for example). Inexpensive scanners can leave a bluish cast where the material doesn't touch the glass, and can also distort the image. Depending on the condition of the photograph's mounting material, you might be able to gently apply enough pressure to flatten the picture. Be careful though! Breaking the heirloom photo in half is not the goal here!

A safer approach to bringing the warped photo into your computer is to have a quality photo lab create a copy negative of it, and then scan the negative, or to have a film-processing place put the image onto a PhotoCD. The author recommends the film scan over the Photo CD—it's much sharper. Transparency scanners are cheaper than ever; the average price for an excellent scanner is around $750.

SCANNING THE WRINKLED PHOTO

A wrinkled photo is much easier to scan than a warped photograph. A decent scanner will have no problem yielding good tonal values in and near the small creases. Often, though, you will need to place some weight on the scanner's lid to help flatten the image consistently across its surface. (This *Inside Adobe Photoshop 5* book is good for more than just reference.)

If the wrinkles are significant and the photographic paper is limp, there's a chance that elements in the photo won't line up correctly to each other. For example, a scan of a portrait with a severe wrinkle could show a mouth or nose that is not aligned on either side of the wrinkle. You must place the picture carefully on the scanner's *platen* (scanning surface), and then gradually apply pressure before scanning; otherwise, the scan will wind up with a distorted image.

SCANNING THE BLACK-AND-WHITE PHOTO IN COLOR

Most old black-and white-photographs develop a color cast, usually sepia or a yellowish tint. No matter how subtle the cast is, detail will be lost if the image is scanned in B&W mode. Your best bet is to scan in RGB mode and then decide what to do with the color—keep the tint, or convert it to grayscale (this is strictly a personal choice). Some people prefer to keep that "aged" look, as it retains the charm of the photo. Sepia tints (shown in Chapter 11, "Using Different Color Modes") are especially popular.

On the other hand, some photos develop a less-appealing color cast, such as green or magenta. If this is the case, you might want to consider converting the scan to grayscale (see Chapter 11) or remove the tint with the Curves command, as in this chapter's first restoration example.

KNOWING THE CHARACTERISTICS OF YOUR OUTPUT

Scan an old photograph and send it to a color printer, a color laser copier, a film recorder, a dye sublimation printer (a high-quality photographic printer), and any other output you might have access to (see Chapter 18, "Outputting Your Input," for details on outputting your image). Then compare each copy to the original under good lighting (the sun, for example), and notice, or better yet, write down the differences.

DOES THE RESOLUTION MATCH THE OUTPUT?

You can arrive at the right resolution for scanning by trial and error. One obvious sign that you need to cram more pixels into your images is the size of the pixels in the output. If you can see the pixels with the naked eye, you haven't sampled enough of the image with your scanner. You can see in Figure 8.2 the difference in quality between a photo scanned at only 36 ppi (pixels per inch) and the same photo scanned at 200 ppi.

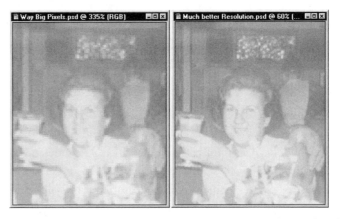

FIGURE 8.2 *The image on the right has a better resolution due to its higher number of pixels.*

Detail is lost when a photo is under-scanned. On the other hand, if your machine is chugging away with every edit you apply to the image, there are *too many* pixels in the image. For example, if you output to a dye-sublimation printer for a 5×7 print, a 5MB file is adequate. There is no need to work on (and wait for!) a 40MB file to print. Larger-than-necessary image files only slow down the printer spooling process, while image information that will never be printed is ignored by the printer.

DOES THE COLOR MATCH?

Something you want to look for when comparing the original print to the copy is *color saturation* (the intensity of the color). Does color saturation need to be reduced or increased? Does the color cast need to be shifted (perhaps by adding a little magenta to eliminate the green)? Does a color shift need to occur throughout the entire image, or do you simply need to correct a particular color?

After performing all the color and tonal corrections you can think of, the photo might still have a color problem. Adding to this dilemma is the fact that old photos are more sensitive than new ones to any color changes you apply. You will find that a little change goes a long way. The same color correction applied to a photo taken yesterday and to a decades-old photo would have a much greater effect on the older photo. This inconsistency is due the loss of color and contrast in the older photo.

HOW ARE DETAILS REPRODUCED?

Look closely at the details of the original photograph. A detail such as grain, for example, might not appear at all in the reproduced image or, on the other hand, the grain might be amplified. Texture can look greatly exaggerated and almost ruin a reproduction when a scanned, retouched image is printed. Notice areas in the finished print where you have used the Rubber Stamp tool in your retouching. Do the edges of the brush show as smudges, or are they too sharp? Sometimes what you don't see on your monitor shows up in the output.

Now that you have a better understanding of some of the issues involved in acquiring and printing old photographs, it's time to move on to your first project.

RESTORING THE FADED PHOTOGRAPH

Time has a way of fading just about everything, from checking accounts to hair color, and photographs are no exception. Years ago, archival photographic papers and acid-free storage materials were not available, and photographs faded and cracked very quickly. Today, with Photoshop, you can bring back most of the original condition of the photograph.

ADJUSTMENT LAYERS AND THE CURVES COMMAND

NOTE

An Adjustment layer is analogous to a color-correcting filter placed over the lens of a camera yet is more versatile. You can experiment with color and tonal adjustments in your image without permanently modifying the image or layers beneath the Adjustment layer.

The menu under Image, Adjust has commands you will use on a regular basis; most of these tonal adjustments are also featured in the Adjustment layer, as seen in Figure 8.3. You should become familiar with the Adjustment layers and consider using this feature regularly. Why? If you apply a correction with Curves and Hue/Saturation, for example, you can go back later and either apply further individual adjustments or totally delete one particular effect. It is also possible to turn off the visibility of the Adjustment layer as well as to erase portions of the layer to see the image without a specific correction you've made.

The most precise and powerful tonal correcting command is the Curves command. More robust than the similar Levels command, which provides adjustments of only three ranges (highlights, shadows, and midtones), Curves provides the capability to adjust any point along a 0–255 tonal scale and keep as many as 15 other values constant. Figure 8.4 shows where the tones fall on a diagonal line in the Curves dialog box. Also shown is the author's preferred and more precise view of the graph, with 10 sections instead of the default 4. To change the number of divisions, hold Alt(Opt) and click anywhere inside the graph.

You'll use the Adjustment layers and Curves command in the following steps to restore the color and vibrancy of a faded anniversary photograph.

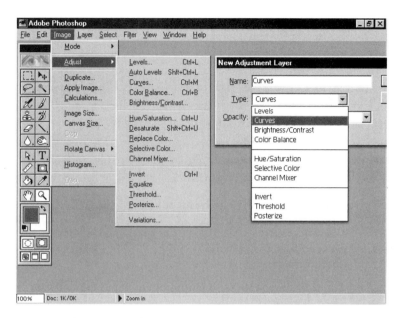

FIGURE 8.3 *An Adjustment layer features most of the Image, Adjust commands but is far more versatile than any single command.*

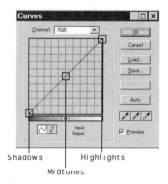

FIGURE 8.4 *The Curves dialog box and the default locations of the brightness values.*

USING A CURVES ADJUSTMENT LAYER TO RESTORE COLOR AND CONTRAST

1. Open cheers.tif from the Chap08 folder of the Companion CD. Type **33.33** in the Zoom Percentage field and then press Enter (Return). Notice the greenish cast. Notice also that there is no pure white or pure black in the image. Drag the title bar of the image to place the image toward the upper left of the workspace. The Curves command dialog box is fairly large; when it's displayed it must not obscure your view of the image.

2. On the Layers palette, hold down the Ctrl(⌘) key and click the Create new layer icon. The New Adjustment Layer dialog box appears.

3. In the Type field, click on the flyout menu button and choose Curves from the list. Click OK; the Curves dialog box appears.

4. Drag the Curves dialog box down and to the right to reveal as much of the cheers.tif image as possible.

5. Click the White eyedropper (lower right in the box), and then click the triangular object in the bottom center of the image, as shown in Figure 8.5. This creates a new white point.

6. Click the Black eyedropper and then click in the small dark area at the left edge of the photo, just below the man's elbow, as shown in Figure 8.5. A new black point is created in the image.

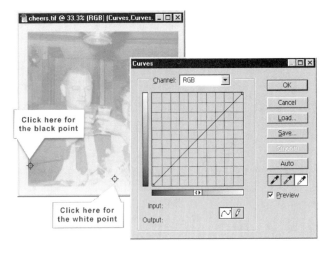

FIGURE 8.5 *Create new white and black points by using the Eyedropper tools in the Curves dialog box.*

7. In the Channel field, choose Green from the drop-down menu. Any adjustments you make now will add either green or magenta.

8. Place the cursor at the midpoint of the diagonal line, and then click and drag slightly down and to the right to add magenta in the middle values of the image. The Input value should read about 161 and the Output value about 123. These values can also be entered in the field boxes.

9. There is still unflattering green in the highlights of the image. While the Curves dialog box is still open, click and hold in the shadow area on the back of the woman's hand in the image, as shown in Figure 8.6. In the Curves graph, notice where a circle appears on the line. This is the tonal value for the area you've clicked in the image.

10. Click a point in the Curves graph where you saw the circle. Drag slightly to the lower right until the green in the highlights disappears or until the Input reads about 208 and the Output 199, as shown in Figure 8.6. Click OK to apply the changes.

> **NOTE**
>
> Any point you click the Curves graph can later be moved or deleted. To delete a point on the line, click and drag it completely off the graph.

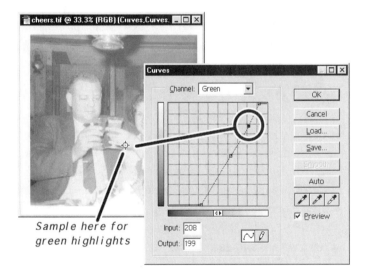

FIGURE 8.6   *Sample the tonal value for the hand, and drag that area of the curve to the Input and Output values shown.*

11. Click the Indicates layer visibility icon (the eye icon) to the left of the Curves layer on the Layers palette to turn off the effect of the Adjustment Layer and notice the significant change in the image so far! Click again to turn on the visibility of the Curves Adjustment Layer.

12. The cheers.tif image shows a bluish cast. This is easy enough to correct with an Adjustment layer—double-click directly on the Curves title on the Layers palette to make the Curves dialog box reappear.

13. Choose Blue from the Channel drop-down menu. Click the midpoint of the diagonal line to create an anchor, and then drag slightly down and to the right. Input should read about 140; Output, 127. Click OK.

14. Press Shift+Ctrl(⌘)+S (File, Save As) and save the image as Anniversary.PSD to your hard disk. Leave the image open.

You have just stripped away a greenish-yellow cast and restored the contrast to a 30-year-old photograph. Now, this photo shows what the title implies: a snapshot from an anniversary celebration (the 25th, to be exact). To strengthen this sentimental moment, you'll change part of the background, making it less distracting by removing the person at the right. This is best accomplished by using the Rubber Stamp tool on a new layer.

RUBBING OUT AN UNWANTED PERSON

The Rubber Stamp tool will be one of the Photoshop features you use the most if you do a lot of photo restorations. Therefore, you should become very familiar with the Rubber Stamp tool (a good place to start is Chapter 7, "Retouching a Photograph"). In Anniversary.PSD you will clone the wood paneling to the left of the woman to remove the person in the background. To provide more flexibility, the new wall section will be cloned onto a separate layer.

CLONING AN AREA WITH THE RUBBER STAMP TOOL

1. Click the Curves title in the Layers palette to make it the current layer if it isn't already, and then click the Create new layer icon at the bottom of the palette. This creates a new layer called Layer 1, and places it above the Curves layer.

2. Press Z (Zoom tool) and double-click over the person in the background.

3. Press S (Rubber Stamp tool) and choose the far right brush on the second row in the Brushes palette.

4. On the Options palette, check the Use All Layers checkbox. Now you can clone from the background layer onto the current layer.

5. Press Alt(Opt) and click the area of the wall shown in Figure 8.7; then click and drag to the right of the woman's head. Clone as much of the wall as you can, and include some non-wall areas.

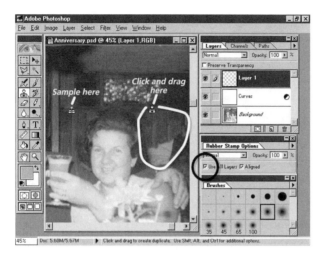

FIGURE 8.7 *Sample from the wall area at the left, and clone over the person in the background.*

6. Press Alt(Opt) and click at the middle of the bottom section of the window frame; then clone directly to the right, completing this section. Perform similar strokes on the vertical section of the window frame, as shown in Figure 8.8.

FIGURE 8.8 *Use existing areas of the window to create the missing areas.*

7. Continue cloning over the person in the background by reusing wall areas. As you get to the edge of the image, you will need to clone into the white border.

8. Choose the Rectangular Marquee tool and drag a rectangular selection in the white border to include any areas that you might have cloned into, as shown in Figure 8.9. Press the Delete (Backspace) key to remove the excess wall area.

FIGURE 8.9 *Create a rectangular selection in the white border around areas you cloned into the border.*

9. Press Ctrl(⌘)+D to deselect the marquee.

10. From the menu bar, choose Layer, Flatten Image. Double-click the Zoom tool to view the entire image at 100% viewing resolution.

11. PressCtrl (⌘)+S to save the image. Open the original Cheers.tif from the Companion CD. Bring the two images side-by-side, as in Figure 8.10, and notice the difference you made in the vintage photograph! You can close both images now at any time.

FIGURE 8.10 *Compare the "before and after" of your restoration and pat yourself on the back!*

Using only three features in Photoshop—Adjustments layers, Curves, and the Rubber Stamp tool—you dramatically improved the anniversary image. Now to move on to the second restoration, Family.tif. This is a studio portrait that has pencil marks, stains, and hundreds of small cracks throughout the image. The cracks are very easy to repair in this image, and you are already familiar with the Rubber Stamp, so let's get cracking!

REPAIRING THE CRACKED PHOTOGRAPH

As mentioned earlier, you should know the characteristics of your output before you sample your input. This is especially important with photo restorations because what might appear as an insignificant blemish can stand out like a sore thumb in the final print. Family.tif is a perfect example. The scratches and stains are far more pronounced in a dye-sublimation print than in the original. One reason for this is that old photographs have a lot of texture in which the minor flaws tend to get lost. But when those old photos are reproduced on today's flat papers, there is no texture to compete with and the insignificant becomes significant.

In this family portrait, you will quickly and easily eliminate the cracks with Photoshop's Dust & Scratches filter, and then remove any remaining imperfections with the Rubber Stamp tool.

USING THE DUST & SCRATCHES FILTER TO REMOVE BLEMISHES

When you are presented with a photo that contains hundreds of scratches or dust specks, you have two options:

- Spend a month using the Rubber Stamp tool.
- Use the Dust & Scratches filter.

The Dust & Scratches filter greatly reduces or eliminates the "noise" of scratches and dust. The Dust & Scratches dialog box offers two controls: the Radius slider and the Threshold slider. The Radius slider controls how far the filter will search for *noise* (random pixels) within a selected image area. The higher the number, though, the more blurry the image becomes, so use the smallest value that eliminates the noise. The Threshold slider determines the amount of tonal difference among pixels that will be affected.

Given how primitive photography was when this photo was taken, Family.tif has an interesting effect—the faces are in focus, yet the remaining areas have been softened. You'll work with this effect and determine how to best apply the Dust & Scratches filter.

SELECTIVELY APPLYING THE DUST & SCRATCHES FILTER

1. Open the Family.tif image from the Chap08 folder of the Companion CD.

2. Press M (Marquee tool) and then, starting in the lower-right corner of the photo, click and drag a selection that encompasses only the portrait, as shown in Figure 8.11. Photos of this era tend to have irregular edges and look more up to date if a clean edge crop is created.

FIGURE 8.11 *Drag a rectangular marquee to include only the photograph.*

3. From the menu, choose Image, Crop.

4. Type **50** in the Zoom percentage box, and press F once to change the view to Full Screen Mode with Menu Bar.

5. Choose the Lasso tool and drag a marquee loosely around the man's face. Hold down the Shift key and draw a marquee around the other two faces (look ahead to Figure 8.12).

6. Press Ctrl(⌘)+Shift+I to invert the selection. Because the Dust & Scratches filter tends to soften the image, you want to exclude the faces from this effect.

7. Press Ctrl(⌘)+Alt(Opt)+D for the Feather dialog box. Enter **10** in the pixels field and click OK. This will soften the edges of the selection to avoid sharp edges in the image when the filter is applied.

8. Choose Filter, Noise, Dust & Scratches. As Figure 8.12 shows, enter **1** in the Radius field and leave the Threshold at 0. Click OK.

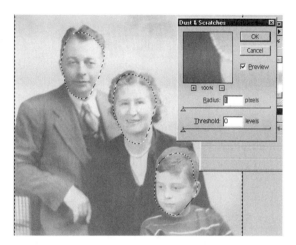

FIGURE 8.12   *Apply the best compromise between eliminating the scratches and retaining the sharpness of the image.*

9. Click Filter, Noise, Add Noise; enter **4** for the Amount, check Gaussian, and leave the Monochromatic box unchecked, as in Figure 8.13. This effectively re-creates the grain that was blurred in the previous step. Click OK.

FIGURE 8.13   *Use the Add Noise dialog box with these values to re-create grain.*

10. Press Ctrl(⌘)+D to deselect the marquee; then press Shift+Ctrl(Cmd)+S and save the image as Family.tif on your hard disk. Leave the image open.

You will find that some photographs look out of focus after the Dust & Scratches filter is applied, so be selective when dealing with unwanted photographic noise. This photo was ideal for correction by using the Dust & Scratches filter because the area you applied the filter to was already out of focus. Let's inspect this photo more closely for imperfections before calling it a wrap.

THE FINAL INSPECTION

As with all restorations, it is wise to give the image a final once-over so that you don't miss anything. In the next exercise you will use a fool-proof, step-by-step technique to scan through Family.tif. You'll notice some scratches, and a few stains and pencil marks that can be quickly removed by using the Rubber Stamp tool.

USING THE RUBBER STAMP TOOL FOR LAST-MINUTE FIXES

1. With the current view of Family.tif set at 200%, press S (Rubber Stamp tool) and choose the second brush on the second row in the Brushes palette.

2. Press the Tab key to hide all palettes and the toolbox. Press the Home key to view the upper-left area of the image.

3. Press Alt(Opt) and click near one of the three blemishes to sample that area, and then clone over the unwanted spot, as in Figure 8.14. Then remove the other two other unwanted areas.

FIGURE 8.14 *Remove the three spots in the upper-left area of the image.*

4. Press the Page Down key once and continue cloning out any cracks or marks. When you reach the bottom of the image, hold down the Spacebar to toggle to

the Hand tool, and drag the image by one screen's width to the left. Then use the Page Up key to continue sifting through the photo.

5. When you get to the bottom right of the image, you'll notice three lines caused by a pencil going through the boy's hands. Choose the sampling points very close to the damaged area. You might want to use the next-smallest brush tip (press the [key) in some of the areas.

6. Press Ctrl(⌘)+0 for a full-screen view, and then press Ctrl(⌘)+S to save your changes. Press Tab to restore the palettes to the workspace. You can close the image now.

In only two assignments, you've restored more than a hundred cracks and multiple blemishes. Photoshop is an extremely powerful tool and the more you know what it is capable of, the quicker you can work.

You might have noticed that we left the color and contrast as is in the Family.tif image. Again, this is a personal preference. You can experiment with the Curves command and decide for yourself whether to apply any corrections. Be sure to use the Adjustment layers, because it never changes the original image. You can change or discard the Adjustment layer at anytime.

In the next project, you'll repair a very old photograph that has been severely stained by a liquid.

REMOVING A STAIN FROM A PHOTOGRAPH

The author will always remember the day his wife found her baby picture in the damp basement. She was extremely upset to find this photo stained with mold and, unfortunately, the year was "BP"—Before Photoshop. Perhaps you have one or more priceless pictures that are in need of the stain-removing power of Photoshop.

As with anything that needs repair, examining the object is the first step. Find out exactly what is wrong with an image, and then get the necessary tools for the job.

NOTE

As in word processing programs, the Home, End, Page Up, and Page Down keys can be used to navigate within a Photoshop document. This feature is especially useful when you want to "comb through" the entire image.

- Home takes you to the upper-left corner.
- End takes you to the bottom-left corner.
- Pressing Page Up a number of times takes you eventually to the top of the image window.
- Pressing Page Down a number of times takes you eventually to the bottom of the image window.

These are handy shortcuts when your workspace is too congested to feature the Navigation palette.

ASSESSING THE DAMAGE

Say that your car leaks oil, so you take it to a mechanic. He determines that the car needs a new head gasket and gives you two options: replace the gasket or install a new engine. Both have the same result, but which would you choose?

The power of Photoshop enables you to reach the same result using more than one method. You should always try to find the quickest, easiest process to achieve your creative goal. In the next exercise you will examine dad-son.tif and determine the best course of action to repair it.

DETERMINING THE QUICKEST METHOD OF REPAIR

1. Open the dad-son.tif image from the Chap08 folder on the Companion CD. Notice that the stain covers half the photo, so it's not something that you can simply crop out. But areas you can lose are the wavy border and the large amount of the space at the top of the image.

2. Press M (Rectangular Marquee tool) and drag a selection around the two people, as shown in Figure 8.15. (This figure was edited to help indicate where to create the marquee.) Choose Image, Crop from the menu. You've just reduced the stained area by almost half and created a stronger focus on the subject by losing the extraneous elements.

FIGURE 8.15   *Select the subject of the photograph with the Marquee tool.*

3. On the Channels palette, click the Blue channel. The stain appears very dark in this channel because the image is predominantly yellow and because blue makes little contribution to the color composite image. Blue, on the color wheel, is the color opposite of yellow. Unlike our example, some stains are located exclusively in one channel; in such cases it is very easy to reduce or eliminate the stains by using the Curves command to lighten that area.

4. Click the Green channel, then the Red channel, and notice that the offending area is dark here also. Because the stain is not limited to only one channel, we'll look for another method to repair this area. Click the RGB channel to return to the composite view.

At this point, you can proceed in either of the following ways:

- Work with all three RGB colors (in essence, replace the engine, as in the leaking oil analogy).

- Lose all the colors by going to grayscale mode and work with one channel. This option speeds things up and does not leave you cursing at your computer.

In this case, we'll choose to proceed with the latter option.

5. From the menu, choose Image, Mode, Lab Color. Click the Lightness channel title on the Channels palette. Next, choose Image, Mode, Grayscale and click OK in the confirmation box. This is the most accurate way to convert a color image to grayscale; it is covered in detail in Chapter 11, "Using Different Color Modes."

6. Save the image as Dad-N-son.tif on your hard disk, and keep the file open.

You just determined the nonessential area of the photograph and cropped it out. You also discovered that the discoloration affected all color channels. By cropping and converting the image to one channel, you've shaved hours off the time involved in bringing this photo back to its original condition. The remaining work involves adjusting the tonal values in the stained area to resemble those in the unaffected portion of the photograph.

REMOVING THE STAIN

You've reduced the image to gray values only. This procedure is well worth duplicating in some of your own restorations where color is not a concern—you can always re-create an "old-fashioned" tint after you're finished, if you want to. A few adjustments to the tonal curve in the offending area virtually erase it, as you'll see in the following steps.

ADJUSTING THE TONAL CURVE TO BLOT OUT THE STAIN

1. Drag the document to the left side of the screen, and resize the window to be slightly larger than the image. You'll need to see the entire image while working with a large dialog box.

2. Press L (Lasso tool) and create a marquee that encompasses the entire stain. Be sure to follow the line that goes through the fence and the man's arm, as shown in Figure 8.16.

FIGURE 8.16 *Carefully follow the shape of the stain with the Lasso tool.*

3. Press Ctrl(⌘)+H to hide the marquee. It's much easier to see the effect of a correction when the marquee is not visible.

4. Press Ctrl(⌘)+M for the Curves dialog box. Feel free to drag the dialog box to the right if it obstructs your view of the image.

5. Click once inside the box with the two arrows, located just below the graph, to change the direction of any adjustments made on the curve. The grayscale curve, by default, functions in the opposite direction of the RGB mode that you worked with earlier. It's easier to understand Curves if the graph is plotted in the same way.

6. Click at the midpoint of the diagonal line and drag slightly to the upper left until the Input reads about 114 and the Output 139. This significantly lightens the midtones and brings them closer to the other areas in the image.

7. Now for the highlights in the image. Click another point midway between the first point and the upper right of the curve's line. Drag this point upward and to the left until the highlights in the stain match the rest of the image (Input about 174 and Output 219). For help with this location, peek ahead to Figure 8.16.

8. The shadows need to be made darker now. Click a point between the bottom left of the curve and the first point you made. The graph should look similar to that in Figure 8.17.

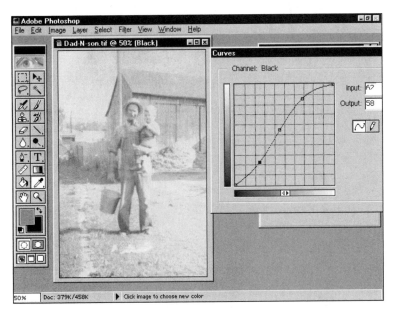

FIGURE 8.17 *Set the Curves dialog box as shown, and the stain virtually disappears.*

9. Click OK to apply the corrections. Press Ctrl(⌘)+D to deselect the hidden selection.

10. Press Ctrl(⌘)+S to save your changes, and leave the image open.

Converting the image to grayscale and applying some tonal corrections quickly and effectively brought the image much closer to its original state. To complete this restoration, you'll blend the edges of the once-stained section with the surrounding area, and replace any missing elements.

APPLYING THE FINISHING TOUCHES WITH THE RUBBER STAMP TOOL

1. Press Ctrl(⌘)+Spacebar and double-click in the upper-left area of the image to zoom to a 100% magnification. Drag the right edge of the image window to include the boy in this view.

2. Press S (Rubber Stamp tool) and choose the third brush on the second row of the Brushes palette.

3. The area you sample from by pressing Alt(Opt) and clicking is up to your designer's eye, as long as it blends well along the border of the stain. Clone out the line that forms the border of the stained area, and remove the white blotch on the fence. Refer to Figure 8.18 for the locations of the most obviously flawed areas.

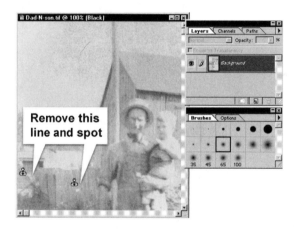

FIGURE 8.18 *Clone out the line and the small white area.*

4. Press the Page Down key and continue the cloning process. Proceed with caution when you use the Rubber Stamp tool on the man and boy. Any time you edit a person, it must look believable, and any lines in clothing or skin must line up. There are many crooked fences and trees in the world, but not a lot of crooked people. (Well, you know what I mean!)

5. Choose the second brush from the right on the second row of the Brushes palette, and clone the grass over the damaged area just below the man's feet. Sample from numerous points around the white area as you work inward.

6. Press the End key to move the view to the bottom right of the image, and continue using the Rubber Stamp tool to remove the line created at the border of the stain. Also repair the damaged area in the grass. Figure 8.19 is a visual of this step.

7. Press Ctrl(⌘)+0 to return to the full image view. Press Ctrl(⌘)+S to save your changes. You can close the image at any time.

TIP

When you use the Rubber Stamp tool to repair a large area, avoid creating a pattern; otherwise, you'll end up with a blob that says, "The attempt to fix this area was a failure." The easiest way to avoid the pattern look is to sample from many areas at regular intervals in your work.

FIGURE 8.19 *Finish repairing the line created from the stain and remove the damaged area in the grass.*

FIGURE 8.20 *Got a stain? No problem! Get it out with Photoshop!*

SUMMARY

You now have a better understanding of how to restore photographs that have faded, developed cracks, and been discolored by a liquid. Now might be a good time to go through your own photo collection and perform some Photoshop magic!

Photoshop's wizardry is not limited to altering the existing image. Photoshop is certainly the tool of choice to help bring into existence the image that resides only within your mind—one of the most frequent quotes regarding Photoshop is "Your imagination is your only limitation." Let's move on to the next chapter where you will create a surrealistic scene and take a look at the thoughts that went into the design.

CHAPTER 9

CREATING SURREALISTIC IMAGES

One of the most popular images many new Photoshop users create is one in which the heads of two (or more) people are switched. This kind of manipulation guarantees a loud reaction from the viewer for two reasons: the viewer knows what the people actually look like and the subject matter has been altered to an impossible situation.

Rene' Magritte, one of the greatest surrealist painters, regularly depicted objects from everyday life and placed them in a way that subverts rational order. His methods included juxtaposing common objects (for example, a locomotive appearing from a fireplace), manipulating the scale of objects (filling a room with a giant apple), and placing objects in incongruous settings (an afternoon downpour consisting not of water, but of men wearing bowler hats and long coats).

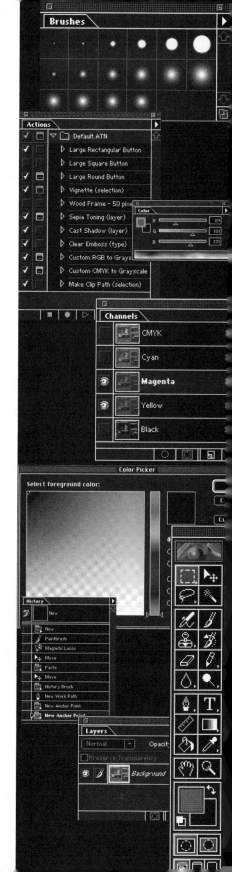

Additionally, the surrealist M.C. Escher often played with perspective in his art. One of his most famous pen-and-ink sketches shows a room with mannequins walking on the ceiling, on the walls, and on the floor. The structure of the room is not a normal one: from the perspective of each of the mannequins, "up" is up, and down is down. It is the audience, and not the mannequins in the image, who are disoriented!

Granted, artfully creating reality in an impossible setting takes imagination, but it can be easy to render the concept with Photoshop as your tool. In this chapter, you will composite an image of a park with an everyday object—a building. The *perspective* of the building is not the same as that of the park image, however; the perspectives in the two images are per-pendicular to one another. The result is surrealistic, and the journey to the finished piece contains concepts and techniques you can use in your own imaging. But before we begin working on this chapter's assignment, let's look at how this image was conceived.

STOCK PHOTOGRAPHY AND THIS CHAPTER'S IMAGE

If Magritte wanted a train, he painted a train. If you want a train for use in Photoshop, generally you need to photograph a train and then bring it into Photoshop—a process that can be time-consuming. You can speed up your work by having a stock of your own photographs. That way, if you need a particular subject, you will already have it.

Chapter 2, "Getting Stock Images," shows you various ways to bring your images into your computer. When you've accumulated hundreds or thousands of images, you'll need some help organizing them. The author uses ImageAXS™ by Digital Arts and Sciences. You can see in Figure 9.1 that when you choose the keyword *Buildings*, for example, ImageAXS™ sorts through the current database and calls up all images containing that keyword.

Half of the author's ideas for images are realized while scanning through his database of photographs. For this chapter's image, The Park, shown in Figure 9.2, in which two people are sitting on a bench, seems to have surrealistic potential. Here are two people relaxing on a park bench, both looking toward the water's edge. Now, we've all seen the effect of *one* person looking straight up—everyone else looks up! So, here is an opportunity to place something in the water area that the viewer will look at, and something out of the ordinary will do quite nicely. It's time to go back to ImageAXS.

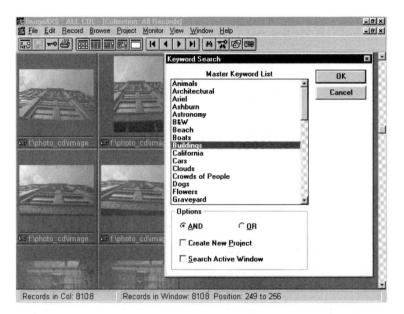

FIGURE 9.1 *If you use an image database program such as ImageAXS, you can quickly locate items by using keywords.*

FIGURE 9.2 *A couple on a park bench makes up the first image for this chapter's assignment.*

After scanning through hundreds of images to find an element that would work with the park setting, one shot of a building showed promise. The camera's angle made the building appear almost flattened and horizontal, like a road, as you can see in Figure 9.3. Part of the building's name appears at the bottom of the photo, ideally located to make the couple look as though they are reading the words.

Now that we've touched on databasing images and the reasons these two photographs were chosen, let's move on to combining the building and the park setting.

FIGURE 9.3 *A towering building with visually strong lines is the second element for The Park.*

COMPOSITING TWO IMAGES TO CREATE A SURREALISTIC IMAGE

In your imaging adventures, you might have an idea that looks perfect in your mind, but the finished product is, well, less than perfect. One way to see whether your idea has potential is to create a rough draft of the image. Take just a few minutes to whip it together, giving no attention to details, and decide whether the idea is worth investing your time in.

USING LAYER OPACITY TO VISUALIZE A COMPOSITE

The feature of adjusting a layer's opacity is not just for allowing an element to be transparent in the final image. Reducing the opacity is extremely useful for positioning elements relative to another layer's contents and for allowing you to visualize how two or more layers will look after they are combined.

For this chapter's image, it's a very short process to check whether the two images will combine to create a strong surrealistic image. In the following set of steps, you will do a quick rough draft by reducing a layer's opacity.

PERFORMING A ROUGH DRAFT, USING LAYER OPACITY

1. Open the building.tif and thepark.tif images from the Chap09 folder on the Companion CD.

2. With thepark.tif as the current foreground image, type **25** in the Zoom Percentage box located at the left in the Status bar (Macintosh: at the bottom left of the document window). Press Enter (Return) to move the view of thepark.tif image to 25%. Size the document window to fit around the image.

3. Click on the title bar of the building.tif image to make it the active document, and move it to a 25% view also, using the same procedure as in step 2.

4. Drag the two images so that thepark.tif is in the upper part of your screen and building.tif is toward the bottom.

5. With building.tif active, hold down the Shift key and drag the Background layer title on the Layers palette onto thepark.tif image, as shown in Figure 9.4. This creates a copy of the building image on a new layer in thepark.tif.Holding the Shift key down forces the layer to be centered in the target image.

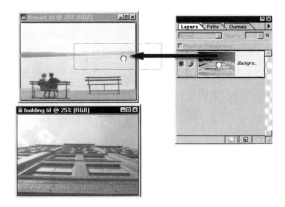

FIGURE 9.4 *Hold down the Shift key to center the layer in the target image.*

You might have noticed that no specific tool was used to drag this layer title. In Photoshop 5, any tool can be active when you drag a layer title into another document.

6. Double-click on the Background layer on the Layers palette and click OK in the Make Layer dialog box. The background layer can now be edited like a standard layer.

7. Click and drag the Layer 1 title beneath the Layer 0 title. You should now see the park image again.

8. Click on the Layer 0 title to make it active for editing. Press V (Move tool) and then press 5 (on the keyboard, not the keypad) to reduce the layer's opacity to 50%.

9. Click on the Layer 1 title. Type **50** in the Zoom Percentage box and press Enter (Return).

10. Press the Tab key to hide all palettes.

Now that you can see the composited image, notice that the letters on the building are in the grass area. After the building layer is moved so that the text is in the water area, you can get a better idea how visually strong this image can be.

11. With the Move tool, drag the building layer upward and slightly to the left until the "TT" is centered between the benches and is just above the sidewalk, as in Figure 9.5.

FIGURE 9.5 *Drag the building layer upward until the "TT" is in the water area.*

The rough draft shows you three things: the composite of these two images is visually strong enough to complete it, the bench on the right is more of a distraction than a supportive element, and the building is slightly crooked.

12. Choose File, Save As, name the image **The Park.PSD**, and save it to your hard disk. Leave the document open.

13. Close the building.tif image.

Testing ideas with quick renderings should be part of your imaging practice. Seeing your idea onscreen gives you more information about that image and can give you ideas for other images, too. Jerry Uelsmann, a master of surrealistic photography, said that he realizes 99 percent of his final images in the darkroom, not in the camera. Photoshop is the digital equivalent of the darkroom, and setting time aside for experimentation can be very rewarding.

Now that your experiment has shown The Park to be a potentially strong image, you will work with the The Park.psd elements to complete the composition. The first step is to remove the water and sky areas on Layer 0, using the Layer Mask.

USING MULTIPLE TOOLS TO APPLY A LAYER MASK

A Layer Mask is what the name implies—for any layer except the background layer, you can paint on a mask and totally or partially hide that layer's contents. You can change your edits at any time until you apply or discard the mask.

The best method for applying a fill to a layer mask depends on the image you are working on. Sometimes filling a selected area is best; at other times, only the Pencil tool will provide the best masking effect. Speed and accuracy is your goal, and situations can call for using more than one tool to apply layer mask. In The Park image, you will use a Fill shortcut, the Pencil tool, and the Paintbrush tool to erase the water, sky, and land in Layer 0.

PAINTING ON A LAYER MASK

1. Press the Tab key to show the palettes. Double-click on the Layer 0 title and type **Couple** in the name field in the Layer Options box. Click OK.

2. Press **0** (zero) on the keyboard to return the Couple layer opacity to 100%.

3. Click the Add layer mask icon located at the bottom of the Layers palette. A thumbnail of the layer mask appears to the right of the Couple thumbnail.

4. Type **25** in the zoom percentage box and press Enter (Return).

5. Choose the Rectangular Marquee tool and select approximately the upper two-thirds of the image, not including the man's head, as shown in Figure 9.6.

6. With black as the foreground color, press Alt(Opt)+Backspace (Delete) to fill the selected area with black on the layer mask, as in Figure 9.7.

7. Press Ctrl(⌘)+D to deselect the area you just filled.

8. Choose the Pencil tool and click on the 35-pixel width tip on the Brushes palette. Type 200 in the Zoom percentage box and press Enter (Return).

9. Hold down the spacebar to toggle to the Hand tool, and drag inside the image window to move your view to the left edge and down to the woman. Press the Tab key to hide any palettes that might be obstructing your view of the document.

10. Use the Pencil in the water area to apply mask. You will only be able to paint in the larger areas because of the large brush size.

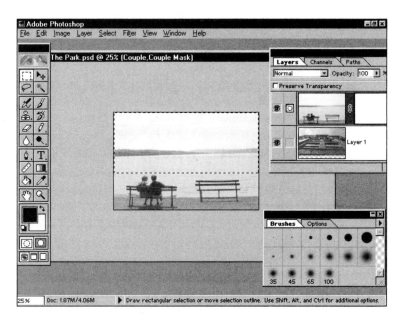

FIGURE 9.6 *Select the entire area above the man's head.*

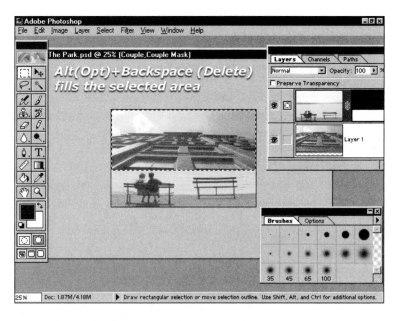

FIGURE 9.7 *Filling a selected area is a quick way to apply layer mask to a large area.*

Do not apply the Pencil at the edge of any areas that border the water, such as the sidewalk or bench. The Pencil tool has a hard edge and will leave a very rough line. If you accidentally paint outside the water area, press X to make the foreground color white, and then paint the area you need to retain (or you can press Ctrl(⌘)+Z to undo the last edit).

11. Press F5 to show the Brushes palette, and choose the third brush from the right on the top row. Apply layer mask in the areas you were unable to cover with the larger brush. Your image should look similar to Figure 9.8.

NOTE

If you are familiar with the Magic Wand tool, you might be wondering why it wasn't used to select the water areas. The author did experiment with the Magic Wand's various tolerances and found that no setting worked perfectly. The highlights from the sun on the benches and on people's arms are too close to the tonal values found in the water.

FIGURE 9.8 *Use the Pencil to paint layer mask through most of the water area.*

12. Hold down the Spacebar to toggle to the Hand tool, and drag the image to the left. Continue applying layer mask (as you did in step 7) to the remaining water areas until you reach the right side of the image. Remember to remove the bench on the right, because it is more of a distraction than a visual support. Remove only the sections of the bench that are in the water area.

13. Press **B** (Paintbrush) and select the third brush from the left on the top row of the Brushes palette. Continue adding layer mask to finish removing the water areas. Toggle to the Hand tool (hold down the Spacebar) to move your view of the image.

14. Move your view to 50%. Your image should look like Figure 9.10.

FIGURE 9.9 *Take the time to remove any remaining pixels from the water area.*

FIGURE 9.10 *After you've used three tools to apply layer mask, your image should look similar to this.*

15. Press Tab to show the palettes, and then drag the Couple layer mask thumbnail to the Trash icon at the bottom of the Layers palette. Click Apply in the confirmation box. Press Ctrl(⌘)+S to save your changes. Leave the document open.

Now that you've removed the water, sky, and land areas, it's time to finish editing this layer. The bench on the right, or more precisely, the *half*-bench on the right needs to be removed. No tool can do this job better than the Rubber Stamp tool.

REMOVING THE BENCH WITH THE RUBBER STAMP TOOL

For work involving photorealistic editing, you may get more mileage from the Rubber Stamp tool than from any other tool. Possibly because there's no traditional art tool like it, or because it appears easy to use, the Rubber Stamp seems to be the most famous of Photoshop's painting tools. Like all painting tools, both real and virtual, it takes practice and an understanding of the Rubber Stamp tool's features to use it correctly.

In the next set of steps, you'll remove the remaining parts of the bench, but only after an intentional goof-up. It is through this mistake that you will see the *mis*-use of the Rubber Stamp.

THE CORRECT AND INCORRECT USE OF THE RUBBER STAMP

1. Type **200** in the Zoom percentage box, press Enter (Return), and then press the End key to move the view to the bottom left area of The Park image. Pan the image to the left just enough to center the remaining bench elements, and drag the document window away from the image so that you can see the entire bench.

2. Click to place a check inside the Preserve Transparency box on the Layers palette for the Couple layer. As you clone over the parts of the bench nearest the edge of the layer contents (above the sidewalk area), preserving transparency will prevent your work from spilling onto the building.

3. Choose the Rubber Stamp tool from the toolbox. Press the Tab key to hide all palettes, press F5 to show only the Brushes palette, and drag it to the upper right of the screen.

4. Choose the far-right brush on the top row on the Brushes palette.

5. Press Alt(Opt) and click on a grass area directly below the right leg of the bench to set the sample point. Click on the bottom of the leg and drag left to clone over the shadow of the bench. Perform this drag in one stroke.

TIP

There are many straight lines around the bench the people are sitting on, and along the sidewalk. Take advantage of a feature of the Paintbrush tool and make it do the work for you. This is how: click once at the beginning of the line; then hold down the Shift key and click at the end of the line. The Paintbrush tool will apply layer mask in a straight line between the two points you clicked.

Also, edges of the layer mask can "make or break" your image. Leave no signs that say, "This image has been manipulated," like those you can see in Figure 9.9. Be very careful to apply the Paintbrush so that the edge of the mask area does not contain any pixels from the water area (use a smaller brush tip, if necessary). Details like these *are* tedious but are also very important to the success of your finished masterpiece.

Notice the pattern of the shades of grass you created in that stroke of the Rubber Stamp. Figure 9.11 shows the patterns relative to where the sampling point was made. There are two causes for the pattern: the brush tip is too hard and the sampling point was too close to the brush stroke.

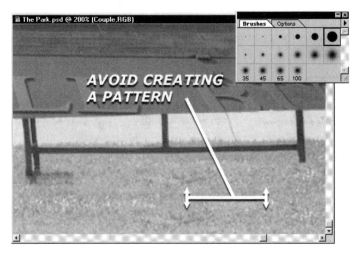

FIGURE 9.11 *Avoid creating a pattern in areas that should not have a pattern.*

6. Press Ctrl(⌘)+Z to undo the last edit.

7. Now for the correct technique. Choose the second-from-right tip on the second row on the Brushes palette. Press Alt(Opt) and click on any area below the left half of the bench and drag, starting as you did in step 5 but stopping about one-third the distance to the left, as shown in Figure 9.12.

8. Click another sample point at the far right of the grass area and continue the motion only about another one-third the distance.

9. Click one more sample point anywhere at the right, and finish cloning over the shadow.

10. Choose the second-from-left brush on the second row and, using the same technique you used in steps 7 and 8, remove the bench's horizontal support. Your image should look similar to Figure 9.13.

11. Use the same brush tip to clone over the legs of the bench. Be careful to keep the grass's edge consistent.

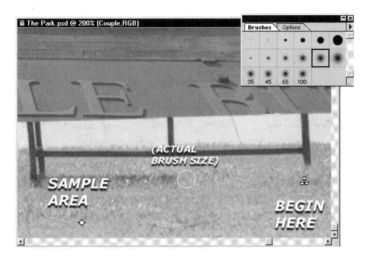

FIGURE 9.12 *Use a softer brush tip and sample an area far from where you want to clone.*

FIGURE 9.13 *Change brush tip sizes and change sample point to seamlessly remove the bench in the grass area.*

12. Type **50** in the Zoom percentage box, and then press Enter (Return). Press Ctrl(⌘)+S to save the changes, and leave the image open.

Now that you've successfully removed the bench, it's time to edit the layer containing the building. You'll be using Layer Transform commands to make the building appear more "natural" in its current location.

USING GUIDES AND ROTATING A LAYER

If you are familiar with desktop publishing programs, such as PageMaker and Quark, then you are aware of the usefulness of guides. When guides were added in Photoshop 4, many people wondered, "Who needs them in an image editing program?" Now most of those people are probably wondering how they got along without guides!

In The Park image, the building is slightly rotated in a clockwise direction. This happened because the photographer (the author) lost his balance while looking straight up through the camera. Crooked buildings are no match for Photoshop's power. In the steps to follow, you'll use guides to help level the building faster than Bob Vila can say, "Hi, I'm Bob Vila!"

USING GUIDES TO HELP POSITION A LAYER

1. Press F7 to display the Layers palette, and double-click on the Layer 1 title. Type **Building** in the Name field and click OK.

2. Press the Tab key to hide all currently visible palettes.

3. Press F once to change the view to the Full screen mode with menu bar.

4. Press Ctrl(⌘)+R to show the rulers; then press V (Move tool) and click and drag a rule out from the horizontal ruler and down to the upper-left corner of the building, as shown in Figure 9.14.

5. From the menu bar, choose Edit, Transform, Rotate.

6. Place the cursor anywhere outside the image area, click and drag in a counter-clockwise direction until the top of the building is parallel with the guide, as shown in Figure 9.15.

7. Press Enter (Return) to apply the rotation.

8. With the Move tool, drag the guide back into the ruler. Press Ctrl(⌘)+R to hide the rulers, and then press Ctrl(⌘)+; (semicolon) to hide the guide.

9. Save your changes; then press Ctrl(⌘)+S and leave the image open.

NOTE

Any tool can drag a guide out from the rulers, but only the Move tool can reposition a guide.

In a surrealistic image, such as The Park, a skewed building would not seem out of place. But aligning the building is an artistic decision made so as to not overwhelm the image with effects. There are no rights or wrongs in artistic decisions—they're your personal touch.

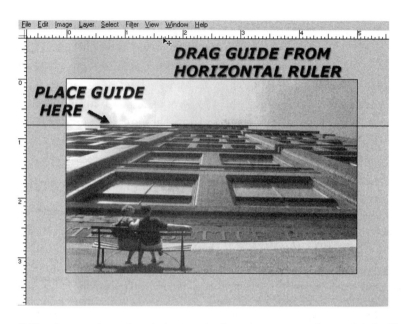

FIGURE 9.14 *Drag a rule out from the horizontal ruler and position it at the top of the building.*

FIGURE 9.15 *Rotate the Building layer so that the top of the building is parallel with the guide.*

The building element is visually very strong; it looms over the couple, demanding too much attention, and the balance of the image is weighing too heavily on the building. If the image were real and you were able to view The Park from either side, the building would appear to lean at about a 30° angle. The image would be more visually startling and the composition would be more balanced with the building lying flat, or parallel to the ground. The effect you'll use to make the building appear as level as a desert road is the Layer Distort command.

DISTORTING AN OBJECT TO ACHIEVE PERSPECTIVE

Located under the Edit, Transform menu, the Distort command surrounds the active layer with six anchors. Each of the corner anchors can be moved independently of the other anchors, enabling you to shape the layer in different ways. In contrast, when you move a corner anchor with the Perspective command, three other anchors will move in relation to the anchor you're moving.

Before proceeding to the next example, where you'll distort the Building layer, look at Figure 9.16 for a few examples of what the Distort command can do to a layer.

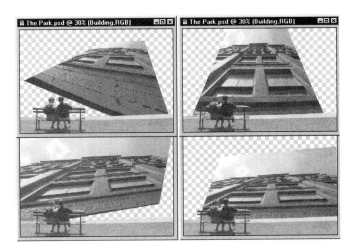

FIGURE 9.16 *"Distort" is an appropriate name for this command!*

CHANGING THE SHAPE OF A LAYER WITH THE DISTORT COMMAND

1. With The Park image open and the Building layer active, press Ctrl(⌘)+T (Free Transform). A bounding box with six anchors now surrounds the layer.

2. Place the cursor inside the box area and right-click (Macintosh: hold Ctrl and click). When the Transform menu appears, choose Distort, as shown in Figure 9.17.

FIGURE 9.17   *The Free Transform context menu.*

3. Click and drag the middle top anchor to about halfway down the image. The building becomes "squashed" but convincingly looks as though it is lying flat.

4. Use the right-arrow key to nudge the layer if the rotation in the previous set of steps moved the edge of the layer contents into the image window.

5. Use the up-arrow key to nudge the Building layer until you see the black area of the building appear at the left of the sidewalk. Refer to Figure 9.18 for the placement of the layer.

FIGURE 9.18   *Use the arrow keys to move the Building layer by one pixel per keystroke.*

The reason for showing this black area is an artistic decision to create more of a visual separation between the building and the sidewalk.

6. Double-click inside the bounding box to apply the transformation.

7. Press Ctrl(⌘)+S to save the changes. Leave the image open.

In just a few quick exercises you've changed a peaceful setting into an image that challenges our perception of reality. Just one more area requires editing—the sky.

There are many different ways to complete the sky area, and arriving at the "correct" method is an artistic decision. A new sky can be created by using the Gradient tool, a sky from a different photograph could be imported, or a sky could be created in a program like Painter and imported into the image. Any method will work, but if it is only the building that presents the surrealism in the image, the sky needs to be undistorted and should also match the lighting conditions of the couple on the Couple layer. The new sky should follow some clues already present in The Park image: It's a very bright day, as indicated by the deep shadows cast by the couple, and the sky is ever-so-slightly hazy, as seen at the left half of the building. Unless you are extremely ambitious or already have the "perfect" sky, the ideal sky is the one already there—it just needs to be stretched a little!

MANIPULATING THE SKY AREA

Perhaps you've thought of another alternative for perfecting the sky area—cropping the image. That is certainly an option, but wouldn't it be valuable to learn how to increase the expanse of a sunny sky (especially if you are a meteorologist)?

With the same command you used for decreasing the height of the building (Layer Transform), you can expand the sky area. This time, though, you need to select the sky area so that the building is not changed. Here's how:

EXPANDING THE SKY AREA WITH THE LAYER TRANSFORM COMMAND

1. Press W (Magic Wand) and then press Enter (Return) to bring up the Magic Wand Options palette.

2. Type **29** in the Tolerance field.

3. Click on the right half of the sky area.

4. Hold down the Shift key and click in the middle of the sky area. The Shift key adds a selected area to the current selection.

5. Hold down the Shift key and click on the left half of the sky area.

Depending on exactly where you clicked, you might have a few areas that are not selected yet. Continue this Shift+click method in unselected areas to add to the current selection until all the sky area is within the marquee. The Magic Wand's tolerance could be increased to avoid the Shift+clicks, but through trial and error, the author found that higher values made the selection overlap onto the building.

6. Press Ctrl(⌘)+Shift+J. This key combination cuts the selected area from the current layer and pastes the contents onto a new layer.

7. Press F7 to show the Layers palette. Click and drag Layer 1 below the Building layer. Your Layers palette should look like Figure 9.19 (but with smaller thumbnails). Press F7 again to hide the palette.

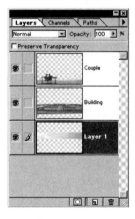

FIGURE 9.19 *Move the new layer containing the sky area below the Building layer.*

8. Press Ctrl(⌘)+T to activate the Layer Transform command.

9. Drag the top middle anchor straight up to the top of the image. Drag the bottom center anchor straight down and only enough to cover, with sky area, any visible transparent areas.

10. Drag the top middle anchor upward again to stretch the sky into any transparent area created from the previous step, as shown in Figure 9.20.

FIGURE 9.20 *Stretch the sky area to fill the section above the building.*

11. Press Enter (Return) to apply the transformation.

12. Press Ctrl(⌘)+S to save your work. Keep The Park open.

Any of the Layer Transform commands come with a price: quality loss. How noticeable the drop in image quality is depends on the resolution of the image, the subject matter being transformed, and the number of times the effect is applied. If you zoom in to about a 300% view of the right side of the sky area, you can see "stretch marks." The sky area was manipulated two times, and this is not a high-resolution image. But that's okay; the visual content of the sky is vague compared to the rest of the composition. It would be good, though, to perform a *little* plastic surgery on the stretch marks, just in case someone *does* zoom in on the sky area!

In the next set of steps you will finish The Park image by eliminating the unwanted effects of the layer transformations, and you will make the sky more vibrant.

RESTORING AND ENHANCING THE SKY

1. Press F two times to return to Standard Screen Mode.

2. Choose Window, Show Status bar (on the Macintosh, the status line is already at the bottom of the image). Type **300** in the Zoom percentage box, and then press Enter (Return).

3. Press the End key, and then press the Page Up key enough times to see the upper-right area of the image.

4. Choose Filter, Blur, Gaussian Blur.

5. Drag the Radius slider all the way to the left, as shown in Figure 9.21. This is the minimum setting—a good place to begin when you're determining the best setting. Slowly drag the slider to the right, stopping about every .5 pixels, and notice the effect of the Gaussian Blur. Stop increasing the Radius when the blotches from the transformations are gone (about 2.6 Pixels), as shown in Figure 9.22.

FIGURE 9.21 *Begin at the minimum Radius setting for the Gaussian Blur.*

FIGURE 9.22 *Use the lowest Radius setting to completely blur the blotches.*

6. Click OK to apply the Gaussian Blur.

7. Press Ctrl(⌘)+0 (zero) to move the view to fit on screen.

8. Press Ctrl(⌘)+U to display the Hue/Saturation dialog box. Drag the box to the bottom of the screen so that you can see the sky area.

9. Drag the Saturation slider to +40. This setting increases the saturation of the blue in the sky to equal the saturation of the green in the grass area, thus visually balancing the two areas. Click OK.

10. Choose Layer, Flatten Image to combine all three layers onto the Background layer. Your image should look like Figure 9.23.

11. Press Ctrl(⌘)+S to save the changes. You can close the image at any time now.

FIGURE 9.23 *Photoshop has more than enough tools to help you create a surrealistic scene.*

Lots of special effects or many visually stunning objects are not prerequisites for a successful surrealistic image. Miës van der Rohe, the famous architect, said, "Less is more." Although Photoshop puts more tools at your disposal than any other imaging program, don't go overboard and lose the concept of your image in a sea of effects.

If you come from a background other than photography, you will also find Photoshop very useful for your imaging needs. In the next chapter you'll learn how to bring your physical artwork into Photoshop and apply digital tools to express the best of the two media.

CHAPTER 10

WORKING WITH MIXED MEDIA

Although many skilled professionals depend on Photoshop for pre-press color correction and for photographic image retouching, there is a creative side to Photoshop, with bounds limited only by the user's imagination and ability to bring source material other than digital images into the application.

In this chapter, you'll experiment with the transformation of a traditional art form—a pen-and-ink cartoon—to see how different types of digital elements can be incorporated into a Photoshop composition.

CREATING A DIGITAL CARTOON

Artists from many traditional disciplines come to Photoshop as the gateway to creative expression for new media—the Web, *Director!* movies, interactive titles, and desktop publishing—to name but a few. The author has found through discussion lists that a frequently asked question is, "How do I make a digital cartoon?" Today, many comic books have turned to glossy, high-quality stock, and the content creators have made the move to the digital equivalents of Bristol board, brushes, pens, and permanent inks. The sections that follow describe an easy migration path to Photoshop cartooning from the physical drafting table.

SCANNING A PHYSICAL PEN AND INK DRAWING

Regardless of how good a digitizing tablet is, it's been my experience that nothing compares stylistically to a scan of a physically drawn cartoon or other type of line drawing. The expression of the lines, the way the ink takes to the paper, and other characteristics over which the artist has direct control, can be successfully digitized to produce a more human quality in the art.

Your adventure in porting a physical cartoon begins, then, with scanning a drawing.

As mentioned throughout this book, your final output of a design should be taken into account before you place one pixel in a document window. The digital sampling, the *acquisition phase*, requires that a sufficient amount of physical area on a piece of paper exists to enable you to work with the piece in its digital state. Too few samples can result in a harsh, unaesthetic digital design that cannot be manipulated successfully in Photoshop, whereas oversampling a physical cartoon can create a needlessly large file that is unwieldy to work with on a system with modest resources.

As a rule of thumb, if the cartoon you want to scan is about half the size of a sheet of 8 1/2" by 11" paper—6" by 4", let's say—then you should scan at 1:1 size at 150 pixels/inch in grayscale mode. Grayscale is the preferred mode because cartoons should not be colored in…this is what Photoshop is used for! Such a sampled image will result in a file of about 600 KB, in case your scanner measures scanned images in file size instead of dimensions.

In Figure 10.1, you can see the TWAIN interface for the author's UMAX S-12 flatbed scanner, with a physical cartoon sample showing in the preview window. If you have your system configured to use a scanner, we'll walk through some of the settings you'll want to use for your own work. If you're working in Windows 95 or NT, you can take advantage of Photoshop's 32-bit TWAIN drivers. In either case, the command in Photoshop to activate the scanner interface is File, Import; options unique to your scanner can be found under this menu.

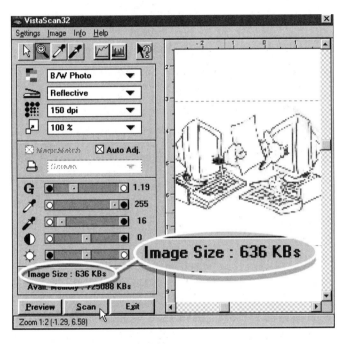

FIGURE 10.1 *The TWAIN interface for the UMAX S-12 flatbed scanner. About 600 KB is a good sampling file size for a half-sheet of artwork.*

Although this chapter works with a specific cartoon piece, you can use the following steps on your own artwork in future scanning adventures:

SCANNING A DRAWING INTO PHOTOSHOP

1. Make certain that your artwork contains only ink lines. If you did a pencil sketch first, to rough in the cartoon, use a kneaded eraser to thoroughly erase the pencil marks. The scanner should "see" only the ink lines.

2. Make certain that the paper is perfectly aligned to the scanner's imaging surface (platen). Photoshop offers no easy way to remove skewing from a crooked scan.

3. In Photoshop, with the scanner turned on and configured properly, choose File, Import, and then choose Select TWAIN_32 Source (or Select TWAIN Source, if your system doesn't support 32-bit scanning). On the Macintosh, choose File, Import, and then choose Twain Select.

4. A list appears of all the available TWAIN sources installed on your machine. Choose the one that corresponds to your scanner, and then click on Select.

5. Choose File, Import, TWAIN_32 (or TWAIN). On the Macintosh, choose File, Import, and then choose Twain Acquire. In a moment, the TWAIN interface for your scanner appears as a large dialog box in Photoshop.

Depending on the manufacturer, different terms that generally mean the same thing are used in the interface. The following scanner settings are the ones the author used, with parenthetical remarks for equivalent terms for your own scanner…

6. Click on Preview (where offered; some scanners immediately offer a preview).

7. Drag the crop box in the preview to encompass only the artwork. There is no sense in scanning empty space.

8. Choose the color mode from the drop-down list in the interface. Figure 10.1 shows the color mode as B/W Photo. This is actually the grayscale color mode, and your own scanner will probably offer this option.

9. Choose the type of artwork, if that option is available. Opaque artwork is considered to be *Reflective* art, whereas slides, overheads, and other transparent material are called *Transparent* art.

10. Set the scaling of the acquired image to 100%, and then choose 150 pixels per inch (sometimes called samples/inch or dots/inch) as the Resolution of the scan.

11. If on-board color and contrast controls are offered, you might want to tweak these settings before scanning.

12. Click on Scan (or OK). In a few moments, the TWAIN interface will be replaced by the image you've scanned in Photoshop. Some TWAIN interfaces must be closed manually after a scanning session; close the interface, you're finished.

13. Save the image as Xchange1.tif in the TIFF file format to your hard disk. Keep the image open.

Figure 10.2 shows the scan of the cartoon image. Note that because all the pencil marks weren't thoroughly erased, this image shouldn't be used without some filtering. This sloppy scan was done deliberately to show you two different methods for setting up a cartoon for coloring in Photoshop.

FIGURE 10.2 *Pencil marks are almost impossible to clean up in Photoshop. Try to remove them thoroughly before scanning.*

PREPARING A CLEAN SCAN FOR COLORING

Before we show a method for cleaning up a pencil-marked scan, let's assume that you followed the preceding steps and now have a clean image to work with. Clean.tif is in the Chap10 folder on the Companion CD, and the following steps show you how to make the interiors of the black lines transparent (ideal for coloring) instead of white:

USING CHANNELS TO SEPARATE TONES

1. Open the Clean.tif image from the Chap10 folder on the Companion CD.

2. Press F7 if the Channels palette is not currently onscreen.

3. On the Channels palette, drag the Black channel title into the Create new channel icon at the bottom of the palette. A Black copy is created within the image, as shown in Figure 10.3.

FIGURE 10.3 *Create an alpha channel that contains the same visual information as the Black channel.*

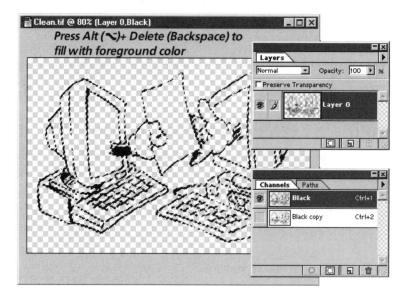

FIGURE 10.4 *Fill the marquee selection on Layer 0 with foreground color.*

4. On the Layers palette, double-click on the Background title to display the Make Layer dialog box. Accept the default name of Layer 0 and click on OK to close the box. The Background is now a layer in the image.

5. Press Ctrl(⌘)+A and then press Delete (Backspace). Press Ctrl(⌘)+D to dese-lect the marquee. You have nothing but transparency on Layer 0 now.

6. On the Channels palette, press Ctrl(⌘) and click on the Black copy title to load colored areas as a selection marquee.

7. Press D (default colors), and then press Alt(Opt)+Delete (Backspace) to fill the selection marquee with foreground black, as shown in Figure 10.4. Press Ctrl(⌘)+D to deselect the marquee in the image.

8. You can now add layers to the image for applying colors and other elements. Save the image as Xchange1.psd to your hard disk.

As mentioned earlier, a less-than-clean scan of a cartoon can be filtered by using another Adobe product called Streamline. Streamline converts bitmap informa-tion to vector, Encapsulated PostScript (EPS) data. In the process, shades of gray (such as pencil marks) are eliminated, and what you're left with is a vector image that Photoshop can import as a bitmap to any size.

PREPPING ARTWORK FOR STREAMLINE

There's a file on the Companion CD called Xchange.eps. It was created by tak-ing the "dirty" scan of the cartoon, auto-tracing it to vector format, and then doing some minor tweaking for line thickness and white areas that should appear in the finished image.

If you own Streamline, there's an artistic technique for making certain that the application traces *empty* shapes (shapes with no fill). In Figure 10.5 you can see two simple cartoons. The upper cartoon ball is made of closed lines, whereas the one at the bottom has breaks along the pen lines. Streamline treats these images in two entirely different ways. With closed shapes, Streamline progressively over-lays closed shapes of alternating colors to reconstruct the bitmap cartoon. With the broken line version of the art, Streamline creates closed paths that leave the "interior" of the design empty. This broken line method of drawing might seem unusual to the traditional designer, but if you practice it a little, the reward will be that you'll have to fuss far less with the resulting EPS file.

If you own Streamline and would like to try out its tracing prowess, here are the steps for cleaning up and converting Xchange1.tif:

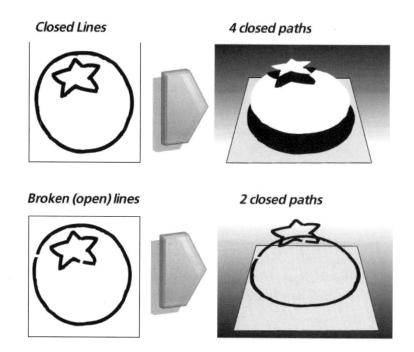

FIGURE 10.5 *If you create breaks in the outline of your artwork, Streamline will generate fewer paths, and also will generate shapes filled with transparency that you can later fill in Photoshop.*

USING ADOBE STREAMLINE TO CLEAN UP ARTWORK

1. Open Streamline, choose File, Open, and then open the XChange1.tif image from the Chap10 folder on the Companion CD.

2. With the Rectangular selection tool, drag a marquee around the design. Then hold Ctrl(⌘), choose the Lasso tool, and marquee select around the marks at the bottom right edge of the paper, shown in Figure 10.6, where the artist was trying out pens. The marks will not be included in the conversion process.

3. Choose File, Convert. In seconds, Streamline displays the traced artwork as vector art, as shown in Figure 10.7. Notice that all the smudges and pencil marks have vanished. Vectors can either represent a path or the absence of a path—Streamline does not trace around vague tones along a much stronger line.

4. Choose File, Save Art, and then choose Illustrator EPS from the Save As Type drop-down list in the Save As dialog box. Name the file **Xchange.eps** and save it to your hard disk. You can close Streamline at any time now.

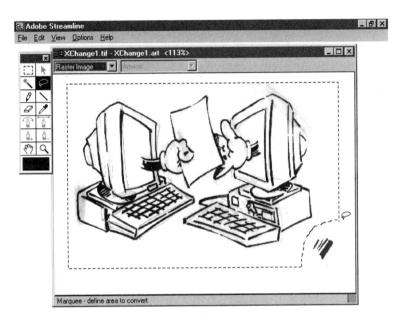

FIGURE 10.6 *Use Streamline's selection tools to define the area you want the program to autotrace.*

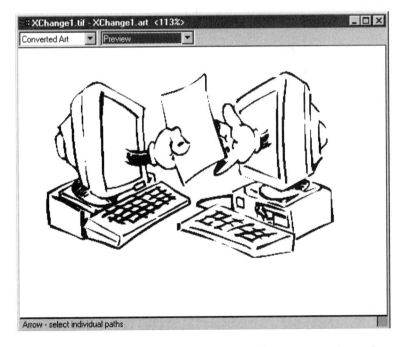

FIGURE 10.7 *Streamline converts the strongest lines in a scanned image to vector lines and curves.*

Having gone through this process with an additional program, the cartoon can now be scaled to any size in Photoshop with no loss of visual content. Vectors are resolution-independent (until you make a bitmap copy from the art).

Although Streamline costs a few bucks, and you need to perform a few steps in it to convert and clean up artwork, it's really worth the investment if you have a lot of line drawings you want to enhance in Photoshop. In the next section, you'll import the Xchange.eps image to Photoshop and get to work filling the empty spaces in the illustration.

IMPORTING AN EPS FILE

Photoshop calls the process of converting vector data to bitmap format *rasterizing*. This is done without much user intervention, except for specification of the size at which the bitmap version of the vector art is to appear. In the next set of steps, you'll import the Xchange.eps file, specify a comfortable working size for the image, and then see how certain areas are translated to white, while others are transparent.

Here's how to bring the cartoon into Photoshop:

IMPORTING VECTOR DATA

1. In Photoshop, choose File, Open, and then choose the Xchange.eps image from the Chap10 folder on the Companion CD.

2. In the Rasterize Generic EPS Format dialog box, type **325** in the Height field (the Width field changes accordingly), specify pixels as the unit of measurement, choose 72 pixels/inch Resolution, and choose RGB Color Mode, as shown in Figure 10.8. Click on OK to launch the conversion process.

As you can see in Figure 10.9, some of the areas of the image are filled with white, whereas other areas are filled with transparency. This occurs because some closed lines and many broken lines were used to create the cartoon.

3. Choose Image, Canvas Size, and then type **7.5** in the Width, inches field, type **5** in the Height, inches field, and then click on OK. EPS imports are cropped to the nearest opaque element in the image, and this cropping is too tight to work in.

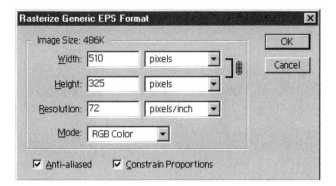

FIGURE 10.8 *510 by 325 is a comfortable size in which to work on the cartoon, even at monitor resolutions of 640×480.*

FIGURE 10.9 *Depending on the way the artwork was constructed, there will be black lines and perhaps a few white fills in the illustration.*

4. Save the image as **XChange.psd** in Photoshop's native file format to hard disk. Keep the image open.

Now that you have a good working copy of the cartoon, it's time to begin filling the empty spaces in the image.

NOTE

If you have a cartoon that requires reworking after Streamline has converted it, you might want to invest in Adobe Illustrator. Illustrator can open the EPS image, and you can alter paths, create compound paths (so that the center of objects is transparent), and perform other tasks. The Illustrator file can then be imported to Photoshop in exactly the same way as a Streamline EPS file.

SELECTING AND COLORING ON A UNIQUE LAYER

It stands to reason that if you can see clear through to the transparency grid in much of the image, you can also add to the composition a layer reserved for coloring. In this way, there are no original artwork lines to disturb; the process is very much like traditional animation, in which acetate layers were stacked and colored on.

Here's how to begin the fleshing-out procedure, beginning with a new image layer and one of the cartoon hands in the image:

COLORING ON AN INDEPENDENT LAYER

1. On the Layers palette, click on the Create new layer icon, and then drag the layer title beneath the Layer 1 (the artwork) layer.

2. Double-click on the Layer 2 title, and then name the layer **Fill**; click on OK to close the Layer Options box.

3. Zoom in to a 200% viewing resolution of the image, and then scroll until the left hand in the image is centered onscreen.

4. With the Polygon Lasso tool, click points directly in the center of the line that makes up the hand, as shown in Figure 10.10. Close the selection by clicking on the original point where you began the marquee.

5. Press D and then press X; then choose the Airbrush tool. Choose the 35-pixel tip on the Brushes palette; this will easily cover the selection area in a few strokes.

6. Stroke into the selection marquee until the area is covered with foreground white, and then click on the foreground color swatch to bring up the Color Picker.

7. Choose a pale violet color; H: 254, S:22, and B: 94 is a good selection. Click on OK to close the Color Picker.

8. Click (but don't drag) once or twice on the cartoon hand's palm and thumb, as shown in Figure 10.11. This adds subtle shading to the hand to make it appear more three dimensional.

FIGURE 10.10   *You're creating a selection marquee that you will fill with foreground color.*

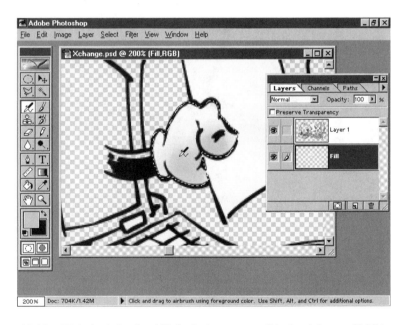

FIGURE 10.11   *With the Airbrush, add light shading to areas of the hand that would fall in shadow.*

9. Repeat steps 4–8 to fill and shade the *right* hand in the image.

10. Press Ctrl(⌘)+S; keep the file open.

The thumb of the left hand you colored in the previous steps should be casting a shadow on the piece of paper it's holding. To add this shadow, you must change layers and apply color in Multiply mode to leave the black lines on this layer untouched. Here's how to create the shadow effect:

APPLYING COLOR IN MULTIPLY MODE

1. Click on the Layer 1 title to make it the current editing layer.

2. With the Lasso tool, drag a triangular notch shape below the thumb of the cartoon hand (peek ahead at Figure 10.12 for the shape and location).

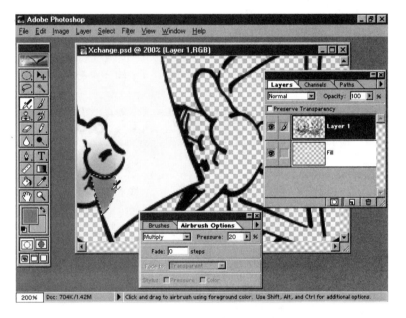

FIGURE 10.12 *Multiply mode at low pressure is the key to coloring on the layer that contains the artwork.*

3. Click on the foreground color swatch and define a neutral, medium shade of gray. Click on OK to exit the Color Picker.

4. Double-click on the Airbrush tool to choose it and to display the Options palette.

5. Choose Multiply mode from the drop-down list, and then drag the Pressure slider to about 20.

6. Stroke once (or twice, tops) in the selection. As you can see in Figure 10.12, the shadow does not interfere with the lines on the layer. Multiply mode only increases density in areas; it does not smear or otherwise alter dense lines that are already there.

7. Press Ctrl(⌘)+D to deselect the marquee. Press Ctrl(⌘)+S; keep the file open.

Because hands—cartoon or not—have character, and because these cartoon hands are such a focal point in the composition, the next section covers a technique with which you add shading upon shading to emphasize the roundness of the hands.

SHADING WITH THE PAINTBRUSH TOOL

What you're creating in this chapter is a cartoon that sort of transcends "normal" cartooning. The shading you are applying is soft and realistic, and contrasts nicely with the crude outlines of the shapes. Somewhere along the line, however, you need to unify the fancy shading with the crude line drawing, and this is best accomplished by shading with the Paintbrush tool. You'll use a color similar to the airbrushed shading on the hands, but the hard edge of the Paintbrush tool will remind the audience of the hard outlines everywhere in the drawing.

Here's how to add a few strokes to the composition to bring out the roundness of the cartoon hands and to tie the composition together visually:

APPLYING A SHADOW WITH THE PAINTBRUSH TOOL

1. On the Layers palette, click on the Fill title. With the Paintbrush tool, hold Alt(Opt) and then click on the shaded area of either of the hands. This toggles the tool to the Eyedropper, and you now have a sample of the pale violet as your foreground color.

2. Click on the foreground color swatch, and then drag the circle in the color field slightly down and to the right. A good color for the shading is H: 254, S:29, and B: 87. Click on OK to exit the Color Picker.

3. Choose the third-from-left tip in the top row on the Brushes palette.

4. In the shaded area of the left hand make a brisk, curved stroke similar in shape to the bottom curve of the hand. Do the same thing with the right hand, as shown in Figure 10.13.

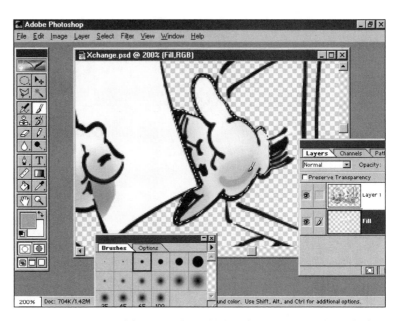

FIGURE 10.13 *Make a single, definitive stroke in the shaded areas to suggest deeper shading and to make the composition's color a little more cartoonish in tone.*

5. Press Ctrl(⌘)+S; keep the file open.

It's time now to color in the monitor, the keyboard, and the computer. Fortunately, as we all know, personal computers are a shade of *beige*, so we won't have to get *too* creative in choosing colors in the next section!

APPLYING AUTHENTIC LIGHTING EFFECTS

There should be a source of lighting suggested in the composition. Say, for example, that the light is directly in front of the scene; this means that there will be light fall-off toward the back of the scene. This also means that the front faces of the computer equipment will have a little brighter tone than the faces toward the back of the scene.

To quickly accomplish a gradual fall-off of light on the monitors and other equipment, you'll use the Linear Gradient tool in combination with two slightly different shades of beige. Because cartoons are notoriously a parody of real life, technically accurate shading in the cartoon is not a big concern. It's more important to keep the colors "moving" on the surfaces of shapes, thus breaking up any static compositional quality in the image and inviting the audience to look where the colors lead the eye.

Here's how to shade the monitor in the left of the scene:

APPLYING SHADING WITH THE LINEAR GRADIENT TOOL

1. Click on the foreground color swatch on the toolbox. In the Color Picker, choose a light beige; H:31, S:13, and B: 99% is good. Click on OK to close the Color Picker.

2. Click on the background color swatch. In the Color Picker, choose a beige that is slightly deeper than your selection in step 1. H:34, S:19, and B: 83% is good. Click on OK to close the Color Picker.

3. With the Polygon Lasso tool, click points around the monitor on the left (look ahead to Figure 10.14). Close the selection by clicking once on the first point you clicked.

4. Double-click on the Linear Gradient tool on the toolbox to display the Options palette. Make sure that the gradient style is Foreground to Background (you select from the drop-down list).

5. Drag, starting on the left edge of the monitor, and then release when the cursor is in the screen area, as shown in Figure 10.14.

6. One at a time, select the other areas of the monitor and apply the same left-to-right dragging motion with the Linear Gradient tool within each selection. When you've completed a selection, press Ctrl(⌘)+D to deselect the marquee.

7. When the monitor looks similar to the one shown in Figure 10.15, press Ctrl(⌘)+S; keep the file open.

So far, you've used color and a few of Photoshop's paint application tools, but this in and of itself does not constitute a "mixed media" composition. In the next section you'll fill the screen on the cartoon monitor with what is typically expected onscreen—an application running.

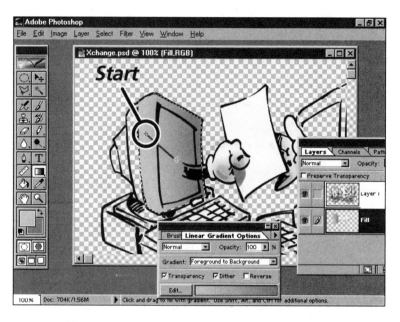

FIGURE 10.14 *Add a gradual fall-off of light to the monitor by dragging the Linear Gradient tool within the selection marquee.*

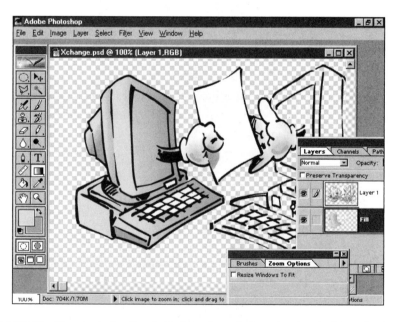

FIGURE 10.15 *Keep the shading "moving" within the static shapes by using the Linear Gradient tool.*

USING SCREEN CAPTURES IN THE SCENE

You can use any screen capture you like in the composition, but two screen captures are provided for you on the Companion CD: XL.tif, and Word.tif. The author chose to capture these screens because they are very busy; at the small size on the cartoon monitors, they will intimate an application without actually depicting one (which would spoil the focal point of the scene). Think of the screen captures as embellishments, and not as the stars of the composition.

In the following steps you'll add the Word.tif image to the monitor at the left of the scene, and then use the Free Transform's Distort mode to make the image conform to the angle of the monitor's screen.

USING THE DISTORT MODE TO CORRECT PERSPECTIVE

1. Open the Word.tif image from the Chap10 folder on the Companion CD. This image, which was captured at 640×480 video resolution, is far too large to work with comfortably in the cartoon.

2. Choose Image, Image Size, and then type **300** in the Width field of the Pixel Dimensions area; then click on OK. Some blurring of the image is the natural result, but you'll sharpen the image after applying the Distort transformation.

3. With the Move tool, drag the Word image into the XChange.psd image, as shown in Figure 10.16. A new layer, Layer 2, is added to the Xchange image. Close the Word.tif image at any time now.

4. On the Layers palette, drag the Layer 2 title to beneath the Layer 1 title if it's not already there.

5. Press Ctrl(⌘)+T to display the Free Transform bounding box around the screen capture element, and then right-click (Macintosh: Ctrl+click) and choose Distort from the context menu.

6. Drag each corner of the Word image's bounding box to conform to the corners of the monitor screen, as shown in Figure 10.17. When the image is positioned correctly, double-click inside the image to finalize your edit (or press Enter/Return).

7. Press Ctrl(⌘)+S; keep the file open.

NOTE

If you'd like to use screen captures of your own, the process is quite simple:

- *On the Macintosh*: Prepare what you want the screen to look like, and then press ⌘+Ctrl+Shift+3. This sends whatever is on your screen to the clipboard; you can then paste the image into a Photoshop document to save it as a TIFF or PICT file.

- *In Windows*: Press PrintScreen to send a copy of the screen to the clipboard. Open a new document in Photoshop, paste in the image, and save it as a TIFF or BMP file.

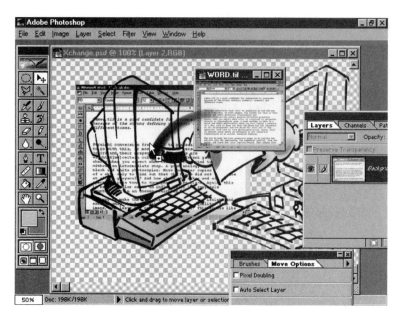

FIGURE 10.16 *Drag the Word.tif image into the XChange image with the Move tool to make a copy of it on a unique layer.*

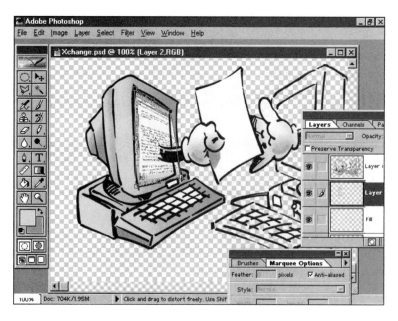

FIGURE 10.17 *Match up the corners of the Free Transform's Distort bounding box with the corners of the monitor's screen.*

The monitor at the right has not been colored. You'll use the same beiges for the monitor itself, and you need to save those colors now on the Swatches palette. Then you'll use other colors to shade the monitor screen.

Here's a brief set of steps for saving the beige colors to the Swatches palette:

SAVING A COLOR TO THE SWATCHES PALETTE

1. Press F6 if the Color/Swatches palette isn't currently onscreen.

2. Hover your cursor around the empty space to the right of the last swatch on the Swatches palette. The cursor will change to a paint bucket icon.

3. Click on the empty space to add the current foreground color, as shown in Figure 10.18.

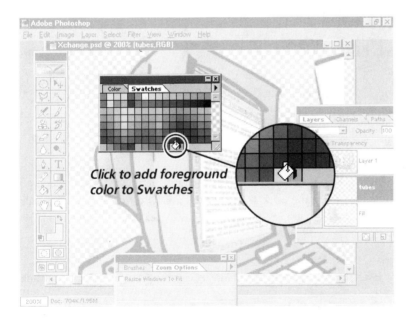

FIGURE 10.18 *Save the colors you've defined to the Swatches palette.*

4. Press X (switch foreground/background colors), and then repeat steps 2 and 3 to add the second beige color to the Swatches palette.

The colors you add to the Swatches palette can be loaded onto the foreground/background colors on the toolbox at any time by clicking on the swatch on the Swatches palette. Also, the colors you add to the Swatches palette will remain there from session to Photoshop session until you choose Reset Swatches, the top command on the Swatches palette's flyout menu.

Now, you're free to start defining other colors for the toolbox.

ADDING A TINT TO THE MONITOR

The following procedures belong to the "cartoon psychology" of coloring. Monitors do not have a greenish cast. In fact, if your monitor displays this, it's time for a new monitor! In the cartoon realm, however, a greenish cast on the monitor will make it stand out in the composition, and we sort of accept this because television sets through the years have cast colors anywhere from green to blue.

Here's how to add a tint to the monitor's screen:

CASTING CALL

1. Click on the foreground swatch on the toolbox; then, in the Color Picker, choose white. Click on OK to close the Color Picker.

2. Click on the background color swatch on the toolbox, and then choose a pale bluish-green from the Color Picker. H: 164, S: 60%, and B: 85% works well here. Click on OK to close the Color Picker.

3. Double-click on the Layer 2 title on the Layers palette, and in the Layer Options dialog box, name the layer **Tubes**. Click on OK to finalize the name change. You'll be working with several layers in this scene, and the better you label the layers, the easier it will be to locate them later.

4. Press Ctrl(⌘) and click on the Tubes layer title. This loads the opaque areas on the layer, the Word screen, as a marquee selection. You can now paint inside the selection.

5. Choose the Radial Gradient tool from the toolbox, and on the Options palette, make sure that the Gradient style in the drop-down list is Foreground to Background. Choose Multiply as the application mode.

6. Drag diagonally from the upper left to the bottom right of the selection, as shown in Figure 10.19. This adds a greenish cast to the monitor screen, with a highlight of white where you began dragging. Press Ctrl(⌘)+D to deselect the marquee.

7. Press Ctrl(⌘)+S; keep the file open.

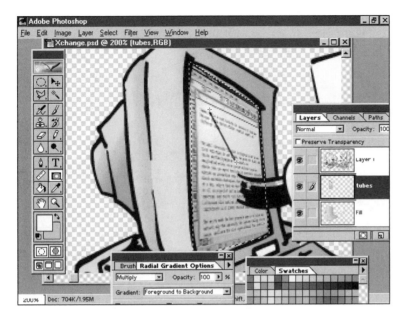

FIGURE 10.19 *Multiply mode only darkens areas with dense colors. Colors such as white (foreground color) have no effect on the underlying image.*

From our point of view, the monitor should be casting a slight shadow on the tube; the tube is slightly inside of the front mount of monitors. In this exaggerated cartoon, the monitor is way inside the front mount!

Here's how to add shading on the screen to make the lighting correct in the scene:

SHADING WITH THE PAINTBRUSH TOOL

1. With the Polygon Lasso tool, click an upside-down "L" shape that frames the inside edge of the left and top sides of the monitor screen (peek ahead to Figure 10.20 to see the shape and location).

2. Press X so that the greenish-blue is the current foreground color.

3. Choose the Paintbrush tool, choose the 35-pixel tip on the Brushes palette, and on the Options palette choose Multiply mode.

4. Stroke once or twice inside the selection marquee, as shown in Figure 10.20. Press Ctrl(⌘)+H to hide the selection marquee if the marquee visually interferes with your work.

5. Press Ctrl(⌘)+D to deselect the marquee, and then press Ctrl(⌘)+S; keep the file open.

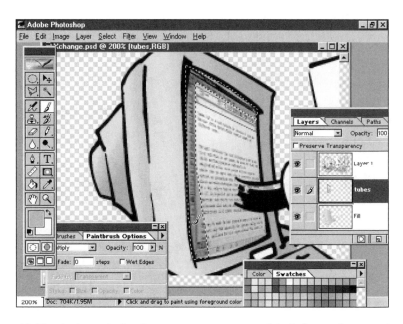

FIGURE 10.20 *Stroke inside the selection marquee to create a subtle shadow on the monitor's screen.*

CREATING A HIGHLIGHT THAT FADES

You'll notice that although the cartoon arm is mostly black (thus covering layer colors beneath it), a highlight, which consists of transparent space, was drawn on the arm. You are going to add white to part of the arm's highlight to allow it to gently fade into the monitor.

Here's how to perform a little cartoon retouching:

ADDING A HIGHLIGHT

1. With the Polygon Lasso tool, create a selection around the highlight area of the arm.

2. Press X so that white is the current foreground color.

3. Choose the Airbrush tool; on the Options palette, choose Normal painting mode and about 70% Pressure.

4. On the Brushes palette, choose the 35-pixel tip.

5. Click, don't drag, once or twice toward the right of the selection, as shown in Figure 10.21. Now the highlight appears to be fading into the monitor screen, and the illusion is complete.

FIGURE 10.21 *Fade the arm into the monitor screen by applying white only to the right side of the selection marquee.*

6. Press Ctrl(⌘)+S; keep the file open.

Before proceeding, there's ample room in the illustration for some "independent study" work you should perform. So far, you've learned the following skills:

- How to shade areas using the Airbrush tool
- How to add shadows by using Multiply mode at partial opacity on the drawing layer
- How to use the Linear Gradient tool to shade the chassis of the computer
- How to add a monitor screen to the composition
- How to save colors you'll need later to the Swatches palette
- How to shade the screen

Now would be a good time to complete the computer on the right, using these same techniques. Get inventive, get creative, add shadows where you think there ought to be shadows, and use the XL.tif image in the Chap10 folder on the Companion CD to add a screen to the second computer.

USING THE LAYER MASK TO REMOVE UNWANTED AREAS

When you're finished touching up the screen on the right, there will be a problem that needs to be solved. Unlike the hand at left, which extends out of the screen, the hand at right is situated mostly within the screen. This means that the monitor screen of the Excel spreadsheet will encroach on the hand, as it is on a layer on top of the hand shading.

As a first step in solving the problem, distort the screen on the right monitor, and then choose Merge Down from the Layers palette's flyout menu. This puts both monitor screens on the same layer (and makes them easier to identify later).

Here's how to use the Layer Mask feature in Photoshop to erase areas of the Excel spreadsheet that should not fill the right hand:

EDITING WITH THE LAYER MASK

1. Click on the Tubes layer title on the layers palette to make it the current editing layer.

2. Click on the Layer Mask mode icon at the bottom of the palette. A second thumbnail image appears on the Tubes title; it's highlighted, which means that you're going to be painting a mask, not applying color to the layer. The color swatches automatically change to foreground black and background white on the toolbox.

3. Choose the Paintbrush tool, choose Normal Painting mode on the Options palette, and choose the third tip in the top of the Brushes palette.

4. Paint away the areas of the screen that are intruding on the hand and arm, as illustrated in Figure 10.22.

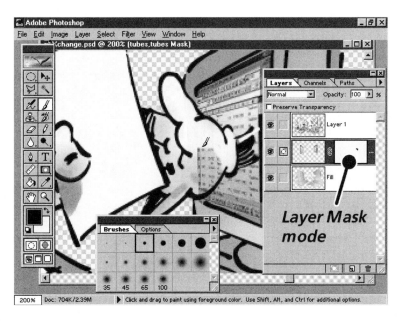

FIGURE 10.22 *Using Layer Mask mode, hide the areas that should not appear in the finished image.*

5. When you're finished, click on the Layer Mask thumbnail on the Layers palette, and then drag it into the trash icon. In the attention box that pops up, click on Apply to delete the areas you've hidden with the Paintbrush.

6. Press Ctrl(⌘)+S; keep the file open.

If your composition looks like the one in Figure 10.23, you're in good shape, and you can continue to flesh it out.

Creating a floor is the next task, and it's easy to accomplish when you use a stock image of flooring that seamlessly tiles.

FIGURE 10.23 *Everything looks nice and dimensional now, but we're sort of missing a floor and a background, no?*

USING A SEAMLESS, PATTERNED TILE TO CREATE PERSPECTIVE

In Chapter 17, "Special Effects and Photoshop," you'll learn how to create a seamless tiling texture that can be used to fill an area of any dimensions. For now, you'll use a seamless floor pattern that the author created for the cartoon scene.

Because this scene has depth, simply adding a pattern of wood floor to the image is not enough—the wood must be in perspective, larger toward the "front" of the image than the background.

Here's how to add a floor to the image and put this element in perspective:

APPLYING A REPEATING TILE TO CREATE DIMENSION

1. Open the Plank.tif image from the Chap10 folder of the Companion CD.

2. Press Ctrl(⌘)+A to select the entire image.

3. Choose Edit, Define Pattern, as in Figure 10.24.

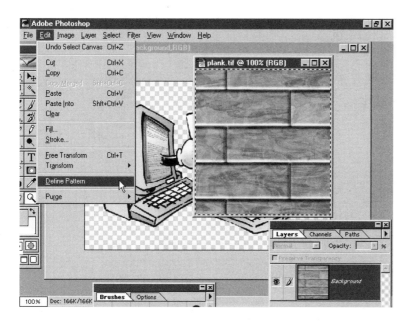

FIGURE 10.24 *Define a seamless tiling pattern to use as the floor element in the scene.*

4. Close the Plank.tif image without saving.

5. Click on the Fill layer on the Layers palette, and then click on the Create new layer icon. Drag the new layer title beneath the Fill layer title.

6. Choose Edit, Fill, and then choose Pattern from the Use: drop-down list; then click on OK. Your image should look like that in Figure 10.25 now.

7. Press Ctrl(⌘)+T, and then right-click (Macintosh: hold Ctrl and click) and choose Distort from the context menu.

8. Drag the image window borders away from the image so that you have plenty of room to drag the bottom pair of Distort bounding box handles.

9. Drag the two top handles straight down (one at a time) until they are approximately at the vertical center of the image.

10. One at a time, drag the bottom handles away from the center of the image, so that your screen looks something like Figure 10.26.

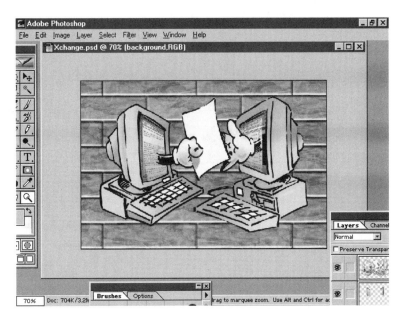

FIGURE 10.25 *Fill a new layer with the wood plank texture.*

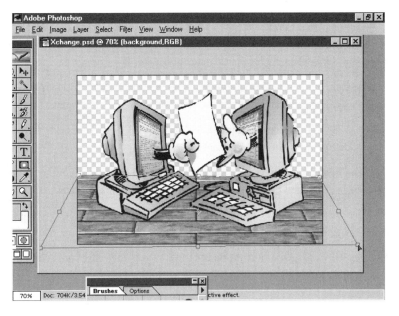

FIGURE 10.26 *Create a perspective shape for the floor, using the Distort command's bounding box handles.*

11. Double-click inside the bounding box to finalize the distortion.

12. Press Ctrl(⌘)+S; keep the file open.

One last element needs to be added to the composition, and this is an easy one. In the following section, you'll create a back wall.

HIGHLIGHTING THE CENTER OF THE PIECE

As mentioned earlier, some of the most successful compositions lead the viewer's eye from place to place in the composition. It's the next best thing to actually animating a piece! This composition seems to say, "There is a document, and two computers are sharing it." Notice that the piece of paper in the composition is actually the first place one would look; then the eye travels to the hands, and then to the computers.

Next, to emphasize the paper as the "hero" of the piece, you'll add a gradient fill that is bright near the center of the image and falls off to black at the edges. This will ensure that the visual interest of the piece is followed in a logical order by the audience.

HIGHLIGHTING A FOCAL POINT

1. Double-click on the Layer 2 (the wooden floor layer) title on the Layers palette, and then name the layer **Background** in the Layer Options box. Click on OK to close the box and change the name of the layer.

2. Click on the Create new layer icon, and then drag the layer title to the bottom of the palette. This is the layer you'll work on next.

3. Click on the foreground color swatch on the toolbox, and then define a dull mustard color in the Color Picker. H: 47, S: 100%, and B: 98% is good. Click on OK to exit the Color Picker.

4. Click on the background color swatch; then, in the Color Picker, define black. Click on OK to exit the Color Picker.

5. Choose the Radial Gradient tool from the toolbox, make sure that the setting on the Options palette is Foreground to Background and that the mode is Normal.

6. Drag from the center of the piece of paper to slightly inside the top of the image, as shown in Figure 10.27.

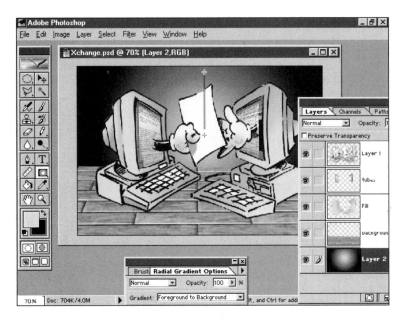

FIGURE 10.27 *Create a "burst" effect to draw the viewer's attention to the center of the image.*

7. You're finished! Press Ctrl(⌘)+S; and you can close the image at any time now.

SUMMARY

We've walked through the process by which you can transform your physical art-work to digital media and perform additional conversions to different digital media types. You've also learned how this data can be manipulated to reach a cartoon that expresses the best of different mixed media. Although the image used in this chapter is lighthearted and fanciful in content, you can choose any sort of theme, and express your graphical ideas with a complement of tools from both the digital and traditional worlds of Art.

In Chapter 11, "Using Different Color Modes," we take a look at the different color modes in which you can work, and offer some tips and techniques for making an image as interesting as possible regardless of how many colors are in the image.

USING DIFFERENT COLOR MODES

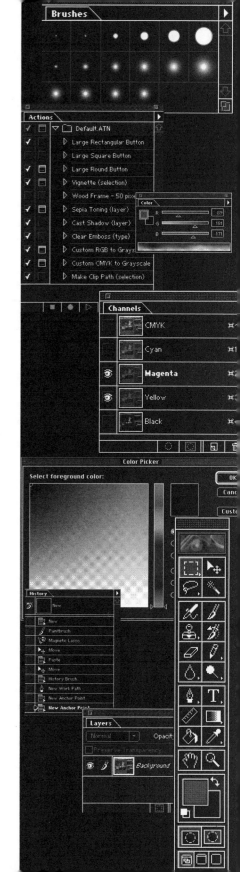

The world is in color. We see the world in color, but color printing is not always in the budget, nor is color printing always appropriate! The good news is that there are many alternatives to color printing, printing limited colors can sometimes fit the bill, and there are a number of creative things you can do with grayscale images and images in other modes.

This chapter explores the use of color modes other than RGB; indexed color, duotones, and creatively filtered grayscale images can all express what's in your creative mind. You'll take a look in this chapter at the best way to convert color pictures to other color spaces (modes), how to hand-tint a black-and-white image so that it looks as though it's in color, and how to achieve "period" looks for an image by using Photoshop's features.

CREATING THE BEST GRAYSCALE IMAGE

Photoshop's Image, Mode menu makes it very easy to convert an image from one color space to another. Straight conversion between color modes often leads to loss of original image information, however. This is okay because there's obviously less visual information in a grayscale image, for example, than an RGB color image. Performing color reduction is an art, however, and you are the person responsible for telling Photoshop exactly what visual information to discard when you convert color modes.

Color spaces as we use them on a computer might be visualized as a group of concentric circles, with each more color-capable mode embracing a less capable one. In Figure 11.1, you can see the most common color modes you'll work with in Photoshop. Note that LAB color is a *superset*—it encompasses all others—when it comes to color capability.

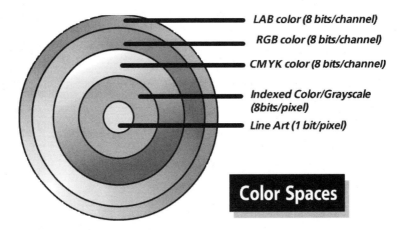

LAB color (8 bits/channel)
RGB color (8 bits/channel)
CMYK color (8 bits/channel)
Indexed Color/Grayscale (8bits/pixel)
Line Art (1 bit/pixel)

Color Spaces

FIGURE 11.1 *More capable color modes can encompass less capable ones. But if you need to go from a larger to a smaller color space, color reduction (loss) must be performed.*

The LAB color model (also called *CIELAB*) was created as an international color-specification standard set by the Commission Internationale d'Eclairage (CIE). Instead of using red, green, and blue like the RGB color model, or the hue, saturation, and brightness of HSB models, *LAB color* is built around the qualities of lightness and chroma. In a LAB image, the L channel contains all the information

"INFORMATION EXCHANGE" *(Top)* In Chapter 10, "Working with Mixed Media," you see how a humble pen-and-ink graphic is digitized and brought into Photoshop for some grafting of other photographic and digital elements, and a coat of paint or two. **"AQUAVOX"** *(Bottom)* In Chapter 20, "Building Animations," you take a look at the animation "pipeline" that Photoshop plugs into. Flo' is used to create still images, then the images are batch-processed in Photoshop. Finally, you use animation compilers for both Windows and the Macintosh to create AVI and QuickTime digital films.

"Park Wow"

You can't always take the "perfect" picture, but by using Photoshop 5 with the right stock images, you *can* create the perfect image. In Chapter 13, "Creating a 'Perfect' Image," you walk through the steps necessary for converting the blah photo at upper left into the eye-catcher at bottom right.

"DAD AND SON"

As shown in Chapter 8, "Restoring Heirloom Photographs," the upper right photo appears to be stained beyond repair. Using Photoshop's tone and color commands, however, you learn how to make this image come alive, as shown in the lower left photo.

"Eye Opener"

This image was created using Macromedia Extreme 3D and Caligari trueSpace. The surface textures were painted using Fractal Design Painter, and the image was tweaked a little using Photoshop and CorelXARA 2. The composition was assembled in Photoshop 5. In Chapter 4, "The Photoshop Test-Drive," you get hands-on experience creating dramatic changes in the image, using Photoshop's new and traditional features.

"DAD AND SON"

As shown in Chapter 8, "Restoring Heirloom Photographs," the upper right photo appears to be stained beyond repair. Using Photoshop's tone and color commands, however, you learn how to make this image come alive, as shown in the lower left photo.

In Chapter 11, "Using Different Color Modes," the color image at top left is transformed into a Duotone *(middle right)*, and a rotogravure-style image *(bottom)*. See how the RGB color model can be changed in an image to reflect other visual qualities, and see how to produce the best grayscale image from a color photo.

"A Big Hand for the Little Girl"

This image is implausible in nature, but photographically accurate. In Chapter 14, "Making Things Appear Small," you get hands-on experience using the techniques and tricks of the digital imaging trade to re-create this picture. Then you can make *anything* small—except your reputation as a graphics professional!

"EYE OPENER"

This image was created using Macromedia Extreme 3D and Caligari trueSpace. The surface textures were painted using Fractal Design Painter, and the image was tweaked a little using Photoshop and CorelXARA 2. The composition was assembled in Photoshop 5. In Chapter 4, "The Photoshop Test-Drive," you get hands-on experience creating dramatic changes in the image, using Photoshop's new and traditional features.

"TROPICAFÉ"

Sometimes an image is beyond correction, using Photoshop tools alone. When this happens, check out Chapter 15, "Working Between Applications." In this chapter, you use a vector drawing application to re-create the can label, and then bring the artwork into Photoshop as a bitmap image. When you work between applications, *anything* is possible!

Re-Elect

Senator
Dave
Brian is his middle name

In Chapter 7, "Retouching a Photograph," we take you through all the steps necessary to retouch Senator Dave's finger from his cheek and his hand from his jacket, and then add a snappy banner to the top and bottom of the photograph to distract the viewer from your handiwork!

ALIENS IN PLAID

The movie is fake, but the retouching steps are very real! In Chapter 12, "Creating a Photorealistic Fantasy," you merge a model of an alien with a photographic background and put a Hollywood-quality bug zapper in the hands of a man in black who was originally photographed holding a water pistol. Before your very eyes it all comes together into a photorealistic fantasy scene.

"Bronze Boy"

In Chapter 17, "Special Effects and Photoshop," you learn how to remove a human from his clothes, which is indeed special because in real life it's usually done the other way around! Catch the secrets to accurately defining selections, retouching, and other advanced techniques.

"ANNIVERSARY"

The worn-out looking image at top right is a challenge for you to restore, but you can bring back the moment—and the life to the image—by using Photoshop's commands and tools. The techniques are described in Chapter 8, "Restoring Heirloom Photographs." As you can see in the bottom left photo, using Photoshop, you can even remove the waiter from the background!

"Flamingo"

This image was originally taken without the consent of the gentleman in the picture. What do you do when you need to use an image but don't have a model release? You replace a face! In Chapter 17, "Special Effects and Photoshop," you learn how to put a different puss on a person. Get acquainted with working on layers and using the Hue/Saturation command to significantly change an image.

"DESKTOP"

You'll find choosing the right filter for the right image to be a breeze after reading Chapter 16, "Creatively Working with Filters." Learn how to change the visual emphasis in an image, how to make a boring image more attractive, and how to filter part of an image to produce innovative, creative work.

"THE PARK"

In Chapter 9, "Creating Surrealistic Images," you uncover the compositional secrets that the pros use to build attention-getting images, while you have fun with reality. Make your audience look both at and into an image you've designed, using Photoshop steps and some thought-provoking conceptual work.

The common button has a long, time-honored tradition of keeping two pieces of garment together. More elegant than a zipper, the button (from the French "bouton") comes in thousands of different styles today, any one bound to complement a shirt, a coat, or other apparel.
Buttons can be of any shape or size as long as the button hole corresponds.
Round, oval, triangular, (Con't. on page 87)

All About Buttons

"BUTTONS"

This layout didn't require a camera to compose. Instead, buttons were directly scanned using a flatbed scanner. In Chapter 2, "Getting Stock Images," you'll learn the different acquisition methods—from PhotoCD to digital camera—to get real world scenes into digitized format.

"Glossary"

If you think this *page* looks crowded, wait until you check out the Companion CD-ROM! The publisher and the authors have packed this CD-ROM with high-resolution scenes, 200 seamless tiling textures, demos of exciting new applications, a 250+ page online glossary…and more!

about the luminance in the image, the A channel stores information about hues from green to magenta, and the B channel holds information about hues from blue to yellow.

LAB color is of particular interest to designers because it effectively isolates tonal information (the Lightness channel) from color information, unlike the structure of other color models.

In the following section you'll convert the color image Cameo.tif to an accurate grayscale representation.

From RGB Color to Grayscale

Many soft images with subtle pastel colors do not lend themselves to conversion to grayscale; there is simply too much lightness information that falls in the same zones. The trick to successful color-to-grayscale conversion is to first choose an image that has strong geometric elements. The Cameo.tif image you'll use in this section works well because there is good contrast between the model's face, the background, the blouse, and the hat. In Figure 11.2 (and in the color section of this book) you can see the Cameo.tif image.

Straight conversion from color to grayscale through Photoshop's Modes command is not the way to go with this, or most images. The reason for this is that colors and their grayscale counterparts are *weighted*—certain colors produce different grayscale shades than you expect when color is converted to grayscale without an intermediate step. A good analogy is that of a black-and-white photocopier. Have you ever copied a picture of a sky, only to find that the blues did not reproduce at all in grayscale? And how about the other end of the spectrum; reds tend to turn photocopies black. Again, this is because color casts an influence on its grayscale counterparts in an uneven, weighted fashion.

NOTE

For designers, one of the advantages of the LAB model (compared to the RGB color model) is that it is device independent. For example, the same values of LAB's color components can be used to describe both printed color and colored light emanating from a monitor. A need has always existed in the world to be able to specify color in a way that can be used by devices of all kinds. The LAB color model is a way to accurately specify color to anyone in the world, for use with any kind of output, display device, or material. Its use is similar to the widely accepted use of PANTONE swatches to specify exactly the color of ink you want a printer to use.

The way to make the best grayscale image is to isolate and extract only the luminosity, the quality of light, from the image, and leave the color aspects behind. This sounds like a complex procedure, but fortunately we have computers these days with Photoshop.

FIGURE 11.2 *Cameo.tif is a good candidate for conversion to grayscale because of the strong defining geometric elements and different tones.*

Here's how to create the most eye-pleasing grayscale version of the Cameo.tif image:

CONVERTING COLOR TO GRAYSCALE THROUGH LAB

1. Open the Cameo.tif image from the Chap11 folder of the Companion CD.

2. Press F7 if the Channels palette isn't currently onscreen.

3. Choose Image, Mode, and then choose LAB Color. You will not notice a color difference in the image because LAB color mode *encompasses* RGB color mode.

4. Click on the Lightness channel title on the Channels palette, as shown in Figure 11.3. This channel represents the visual content of the Cameo.tif image, without color.

FIGURE 11.3 *The Lightness channel in LAB color represents tonal information in the image, not influenced by color. The color quality of the image is isolated in the a and the b channels.*

5. Choose Image, Mode, and then choose Grayscale. An attention box pops up asking whether you want to discard the other channels. You do; click on OK.

6. Save the grayscale image to your hard disk as Cameo.tif. Keep the file open.

If you have any doubts about the superiority of going to LAB color over a straight conversion from color to grayscale, check out the two images in Figure 11.4. The image on the left was converted to grayscale by choosing LAB's Lightness channel. For the one on the right, we simply choose Image, Mode, Grayscale. As you can see, the image on the right is duller and darker than the LAB-converted image.

Now that we have a grayscale copy of Cameo.tif, it's time to get creative with it. Your printing budget might not allow full color, but how about a duotone of the image?

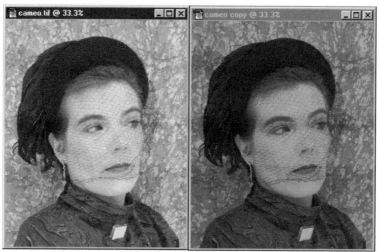

Lightness channel

**Straight conversion
from color to grayscale**

FIGURE 11.4 *The Lightness channel is more representative of the visual content of the image than the color image converted to grayscale.*

DUOTONES: COMPLEMENTARY COLOR PLATES

Black-and-white printing costs significantly less when your design is envisioned or edited to grayscale mode. At times, however, you might have a few cents left over in a budget, and although the money still won't get you process color printing, the cash can be used to create a Duotone image of your work.

A Duotone is considered to be a color mode in Photoshop, as are Grayscale, RGB, and other color models. Because a Duotone is actually a print specification, and not really a mode of color you'd work with directly in Photoshop, your RGB monitor might not display an image in Duotone mode with absolute fidelity, compared to the printed result.

In commercial printing, there is a certain "gap" in the reproduction of brightnesses in a digital image to the medium of paper. Because there is a limitation to how much a single application of pigment to a surface can cover in a single pass, you might not see the rich tonal variations in a print of your grayscale work. The sad reality in digital press work is that a single pass of black cannot achieve the simulation of 256 shades of black.

One of the creative solutions the commercial printing industry discovered is the application of a second, colored ink to a black-and-white print to accentuate the tones that might be too faint to recognize with the first pass of black ink. The result of this process is called a Duotone. The effect is a subtle tinting of an image to fill in areas of the image. Do not expect a posterized print or a sepiatone from the process of Duotoning, however—these are entirely different processes (covered later in the book), which are much less subtle than a Duotone.

Here are the steps to follow to create a Duotone version of the grayscale Cameo image:

ROLLING YOUR OWN DUOTONE

1. Choose Image, Mode, and then choose Duotone. The Duotone Options box appears. Don't be intimidated by the steps to follow; everything will fall into place and you'll have a handsome sepia-and-black Duotone shortly.

2. Choose Duotone from the drop-down list. Below Ink 1 (black), there appears Ink 2 with a blank color box.

3. Click on the color box, as shown in Figure 11.5. This displays the Custom Colors dialog box next to Ink 2, where you can pick inks from many different color specification collections.

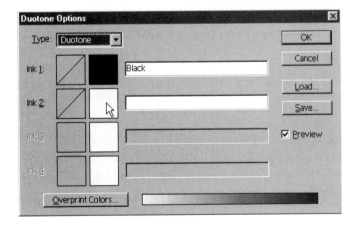

FIGURE 11.5 *The color box for Ink 2 leads to a number of different ink specifications you can use.*

4. Suppose, for example, that your Duotone masterpiece will be printed to uncoated stock paper. Choose PANTONE Uncoated from the Book drop-down list.

5. You'll pick a warm brown for the second color in this Duotone. You can either browse the color strip, as shown in Figure 11.6, or type on the keypad the color number you want. You'd use the keypad method only if you have a physical swatch book handy with the numbers in it, or if your client has the number of the ink for you. To get on with this example, type **126** on the keypad to scoot to PANTONE color 126, the brown you'll use.

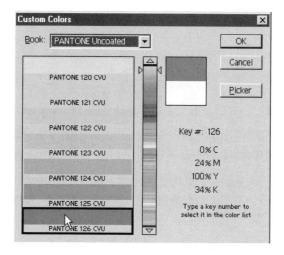

FIGURE 11.6 *You can pick an ink from several different collections of color-matching standards in the Custom Colors dialog box.*

6. Click on OK to confirm your Ink 2 choice and return to the Duotone dialog box.

Now, there need to be opposing distribution curves for the application of the two inks, or you'll wind up with a blobby mess instead of a handsome Duotone. A *distribution curve* plots the amount of ink versus the brightness in the image. To see browns in the midtones of the Cameo.tif image, you must knock down the Ink 1, the black plate, in the midtones area...

7. Click on the distribution curve (the box with the diagonal line) to the left of the black color swatch in the Duotones Options box. The Duotone Curve dialog box appears.

8. Click in the center of the curve and drag left and down, as shown in Figure 11.7. This lessens some of the application of ink in the midtones of the image, ink that you'll add with PANTONE 126.

Reduce midtones for black plate

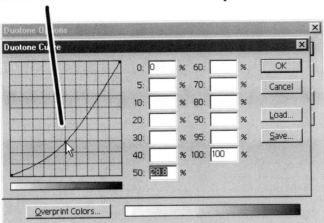

FIGURE 11.7 *Create a space in the midtones of the Ink 1 printing plate, that'll be filled with the second ink color.*

10. Drag the midpoint on the curve up and to the left, as in Figure 11.8. What you've done is specify that the midtones in the photograph will display predominant brown tones. Click on OK to return to the Duotones Options box.

11. As you can see in Figure 11.9, the curves for the black and the PANTONE inks complement each other. You will get shades of both brown and black in the highlights and shadow areas of the image, but the midtone regions, those regions that contain much visual information in photos, will be predominantly brown.

12. Click on OK in the Duotone Options box to return to the image and the workspace. As you'll see onscreen, with that second color mixed in the cameo image is richer-looking than a grayscale image. Again, it's not a vintage sepiatone image, but it will print with clarity and visual interest to uncoated paper.

13. Save the file as Cameo.eps in the Photoshop EPS format. Choose TIFF (8 bits/pixel) as the Preview option. This allows the EPS file to be placed with more precision than a 1 bit/pixel preview image. Choose ASCII encoding, as this is the most portable format for EPS images; UNIX, Windows, and Macintosh machines can all read ASCII-encoded data. The EPS format allows the file to be saved in Duotone format, to be placed in a desktop publishing document, or to be printed directly from Photoshop. You can close the file at any time.

TIP

If you like the look of your Duotone image but have no intention of sending the file to a commercial press house, you can still print a personal copy to an inkjet printer. Copy the file, and then choose Image, Mode, RGB Color. The file then becomes a standard bitmap image that contains the same colors as the Duotone but can be printed from Photoshop and many other graphics applications.

Increase midtones for color plate

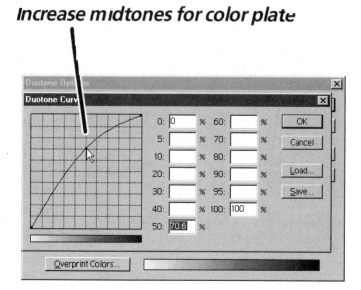

FIGURE 11.8 *Create a distribution curve for the second ink that will show up predominantly in the midtones.*

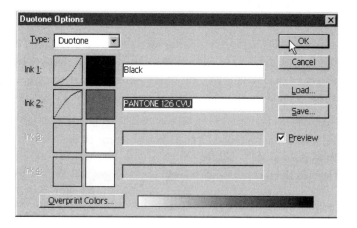

FIGURE 11.9 *The curves for the inks yield to one another. Browns will predominate in the midtones, whereas the highlights and shadows will contain a combination of black and brown.*

Let's suppose for a moment that you're not printing this Cameo image at all, but instead want to feature it on a Web page. Chances are you'll want the sepia effect to be much more pronounced. In the following sections you'll see two different approaches to "aging" a photograph.

CREATING A SEPIATONE EFFECT

Traditionally, sepiatone photos have been accomplished in the following ways:

- Natural aging of the photo fades the emulsion from black-and-white to brown-and-off-white.

- You can buy a chemical, called sepia toner, at a photographic supply store and use it to replace the black in a photo with warm browns.

Photoshop is very good at replacing colors, too! In the brief set of steps that follow, you'll see how to create a sepiatone image from the grayscale Cameo.tif you saved earlier to hard disk:

CREATING A SEPIATONE FOR PRINT OUTPUT

1. Open the Cameo.tif image you saved to hard disk.

2. Choose Image, Mode, and then choose RGB Color.

3. Press Ctrl(⌘)+U to display the Hue/Saturation command.

4. Click on the Colorize check box, and then drag the Hue Slider to about 40 degrees, the segment of the color spectrum where brown is located. Leave the Saturation slider at its default of 25, as shown in Figure 11.10, and then click on OK.

5. Save the image as Sepia1.tif to your hard disk. You can close the file at any time now. And check out the color plate section in this book for the results.

NOTE

Photoshop 5 ships with a number of preset Duotones, tritones (one black and two color inks), and quadtones (one black and three passes of color). If you'd like to use these presets instead of creating your own, click on the Load button in the Duotone Options dialog box, and then search for Photoshop/Duotones/Duotone on your hard disk.

FIGURE 11.10   *The Colorize feature in the Hue/Saturation command creates a monotone version of an image tinted with any hue you define.*

Let's suppose that your sepiatone work is not destined to be printed at all, but instead you'd like a nice vintage graphic on a Web page. Let's further suppose that you want to save the image in GIF 89a format.

The GIF 89a file format is limited to 256 unique colors. Coincidentally, grayscale images also are limited to 256 possible brightnesses. If you want to create a sepiatone image that's ready to be saved for Web use, follow these steps:

CREATING A SEPIATONE FOR WEB OUTPUT

1. Open the Cameo.tif image from your hard disk.

2. Choose Image, Mode, Indexed Color. Then choose Image, Mode, Color Table. The color table for the image appears in a dialog box.

3. Drag your cursor diagonally from the first upper-left color swatch to the last lower-right one, to highlight all the color swatches, as in Figure 11.11.

4. Choose a deep brown color from the Color Picker; Figure 11.12 shows a recommended color setting. Click on OK.

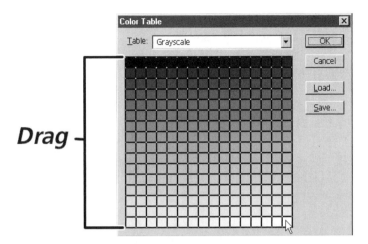

FIGURE 11.11 *Select all the color swatches by dragging diagonally.*

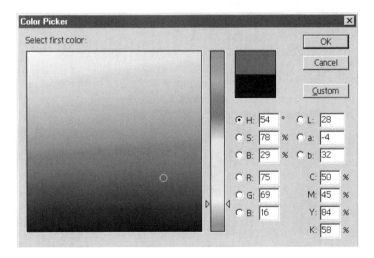

FIGURE 11.12 *Choose the first color in the spectrum for recoloring the image.*

5. The Color Picker appears again, with the statement "Select last color" at the top of the palette. Choose a pale cream color; the settings in Figure 11.13 work well. Click on OK to return to the Color Table dialog box.

6. Click on OK to reassign the shades in the image. As you can see in Figure 11.14, the Channels palette displays but a single channel, called Index. This means that the image can be exported as a GIF image without further color reduction; the GIF image format is Indexed color.

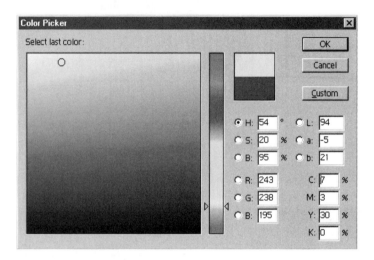

FIGURE 11.13 *Choose the last color in the spectrum to recolor the grayscale image.*

FIGURE 11.14 *An eye-pleasing sepiatone version of the grayscale image can be created by changing the color spectrum in Indexed color mode.*

7. Choose File, Export, and then choose GIF 89a.

8. Click on OK to accept the default settings in the GIF 89a Export Options box, and then save the image to hard disk as Cameo.gif. You now have a copy of the image that can be used on an HTML page, and that can be viewed by anyone who drags the image file into Netscape Navigator or MS-Internet Explorer.

9. Choose File, Revert, and then click on the Revert button in the attention box. The Cameo.tif image becomes grayscale again. Keep the image open.

The sepiatone look is fun, but suppose that your printing budget is limited to black-and-white—the following sections take us back to ways to enhance grayscale images.

FILTERING GRAYSCALE IMAGES

As exciting as color photography and imaging is, black-and-white photography still has a place in the world of media. You may need to produce black-and-white work when preparing a newsletter, flyer, or other promotion. There's both a photographic purism and an economy to be had with the black-and-white medium.

The human eye is attracted subliminally to a color image over a grayscale one, often for the wrong reasons. The eye is attracted to bright pastels and saturated colors, and often overlooks poor composition in a color image. When you look at a grayscale image that contains no distracting color information, you are forced to analyze the image solely on its visual content. The special effects you'll work with in this chapter are particularly effective when applied to an image that contains only visual detail, without the distracting element of color.

A GRAYSCALE FILTER SAMPLER

Photoshop's filters work as artistic enhancements in grayscale images for the following reasons:

- Shifting the focal point in a color photo by adding a special effect is almost impossible to do. The eye is drawn primarily to an interesting color area and registers an effect as a secondary consideration.

- Blending a special effect into a grayscale image is much easier to do than blending it into a color image. Because there are no hues, you don't have to worry about matching saturation and hue values between special and not-so-special areas of the image.

In the steps that follow, you'll use Photoshop's Chalk and Charcoal filter on a selected area of the Cameo.tif image. The filtered area will make a smooth transition to original image areas, and the entire composition will look like a finely detailed artistic piece, with emphasis on the model's face.

Here's how to make the image more visually striking, while keeping to the spirit of the photo:

SELECTIVELY APPLYING A FILTER

1. With the Lasso tool, drag a marquee selection around the model's face in Cameo.tif, as shown in Figure 11.15. Make this a "relaxed" selection; do not define the marquee too tightly around the model's face, as you'll be feathering the selection shortly.

FIGURE 11.15 *Create a moderately loose marquee selection around the model's face, using the Lasso tool.*

2. Right-click (Macintosh: hold Ctrl and click), and then choose Feather from the context menu. Enter **16** in the Pixels field and then click on OK to apply a wide amount of feathering.

3. Press Shift+F7. This inverts the selection marquee so that everything except the model's face is selected.

4. Choose Filter, Sketch, and then choose Chalk & Charcoal.

5. Drag the Charcoal Area slider to 4 (less Charcoal in the filtered effect), drag the Chalk Area to 8 (more Chalk in the filtered effect), and leave the Stroke Pressure at its default of 1, as shown in Figure 11.16. You will now be applying more of the Chalk effect than the Charcoal effect, for a soft look. Click on OK to apply the filter.

FIGURE 11.16 *Emphasize the soft chalk effect by increasing its value in the Chalk & Charcoal filter.*

6. Press Ctrl(⌘)+D to deselect the marquee. Your image should look something like Figure 11.17. Save the image to disk as Sketch.tif.

You've created a grayscale image that is far more interesting than the original thanks to the selective application of a filter. Let's get a little more ambitious now, and see whether we can re-create a rotogravure effect.

FIGURE 11.17 *By feathering the selection, you've created a gradual transition in the image between filtered and original areas.*

AN HOMAGE TO TRADITIONAL PHOTOGRAPHIC REPRODUCTIONS

Before there was photolithograpy and the screening of images, photographs were reproduced by hand onto press plates. This method, called rotogravure, had a very characteristic look because a lot of cross-hatching and broken horizontal lines were used in the execution of the image.

Photoshop ships with 20 patterns in Adobe Illustrator format that can be scaled to any size and used as repeating patterns in an image, each of which can help you create a rotogravure effect. What happens when you subtract a pattern from a continuous-tone image? You get a picture that looks remarkably like a traditional rotogravure!

Here's how to make the Cameo.tif image look as though it was reproduced generations ago:

CREATING A VINTAGE LITHOGRAPH

1. Open the Cameo.tif image from your hard disk.

2. Press and hold Alt(Opt) and then click on the Document Sizes box on the status line (Macintosh: on the lower-left corner of the image window). The Document Sizes box tells you that the image is about 12" wide at 72 pixels/inch. This means that the pattern you'll apply to the image should repeat more than about four times or so, and gives you an idea to what dimensions the Illustrator pattern should be converted to bitmap format (*rasterized*).

3. Choose File, Open, and then choose Waves.ai from the Photoshop5/Patterns folder on your hard disk. This file and others shipped with Photoshop 5. The Rasterize Generic EPS format dialog box appears.

4. Type **3** in the width (inches) field; the Height field automatically scales up. Type **72** in the Resolution field, choose Grayscale from the Mode drop-down, as shown in Figure 11.18. Now click on OK to create a bitmap version of the Illustrator file in the workspace. The pattern will tile about four times across the width of the image.

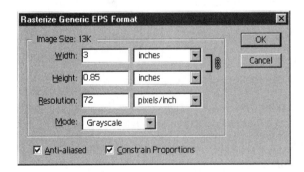

FIGURE 11.18 *Specify a size for the Illustrator file that will tile a few times in the image.*

5. Click on OK; in a moment, the Waves.ai image appears in the workspace.

6. Press Ctrl($\mathcal{H}$)+A to select all of the pattern, and then choose Define Pattern, as shown in Figure 11.19.

FIGURE 11.19 *You are defining a pattern that you will apply to an alpha channel in the Cameo.tif image.*

7. Close the Waves.ai image without saving it; then, on the Channels palette, click on the Create new channel icon. Alpha 1 appears as a title below the Black channel on the Channels palette's list. Double-click on the Alpha 1 channel title and click Selected Areas in the Color Indicates field, then click OK.

8. Choose Edit, Fill, choose Pattern from the Use: drop-down list, and then click on OK. The Waves pattern fills the alpha channel.

9. Press Ctrl(⌘) and click on the Alpha 1 title on the Channels palette to load the colored areas as a marquee selection, as shown in Figure 11.20.

10. Press Ctrl(⌘)+1 to return to the grayscale view of the image within the window, shown in Figure 11.21.

11. Position the Cameo.tif image in the workspace at the top left corner. You'll be displaying the Levels command in the next step, and you'll want a clear view of both the image and the dialog box.

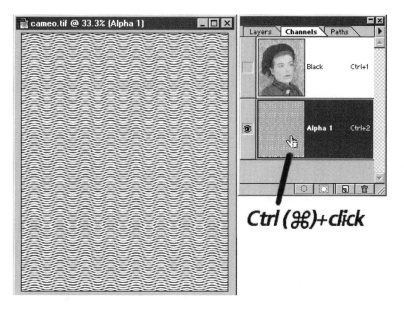

FIGURE 11.20 *Press Ctrl(⌘) and click on a channel title to load the contents of the channel as a selection.*

12. Press Ctrl(⌘)+L. Drag the midpoint slider to the left until the Input Levels middle field reads about 2.8. Then drag the black point Output Levels slider to the right until the left field reads about 90. As you can see from Figure 11.22, a pattern is being mixed with the image; the selected areas of the image are being lightened, and some image detail is being lost.

TIP

Press Ctrl(⌘)+H to hide the marquee lines. Doing this does not remove the marquee; it simply hides the "marching ants" in the image so that you can concentrate on the editing at hand.

13. Click on OK to apply the tonal changes. Press Ctrl(⌘)+D to deselect the marquee, and drag the Alpha 1 title on the Channels palette into the trash icon (you're finished with it).

14. Save the image as Gravure.tif to your hard disk; keep the image open for a moment.

If you'd like to add a framing effect to the image at this point, to further reinforce the idea that this is a vintage photo, the steps are quite simple:

FIGURE 11.21 *The selected areas of the image will be faded to produce a rotogravure look.*

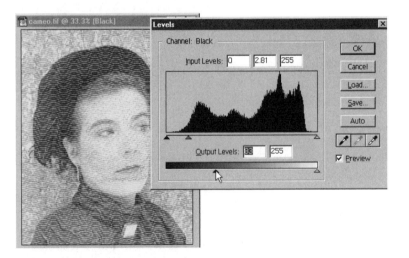

FIGURE 11.22 *Lightening only the selected areas in the image gives the picture a rotogravure feeling.*

FRAMING THE ROTOGRAVURE

1. With the Elliptical Marquee tool, drag an oval around the model's face, hat, and part of her blouse.

2. Right-click (Macintosh: hold Ctrl and click) and choose Feather from the context menu. Type **16** in the pixels field and then click on OK to apply the feathering.

3. Press Ctrl(⌘)+Shift+I (which is the same as Shift+F7) to invert the selection marquee.

4. Figure 11.23 shows what happens when you press D (default colors) and then press Delete (Backspace). Now press Ctrl(⌘)+D, and you have a very nice cameo image.

FIGURE 11.23 *Feathering and deleting areas outside the oval produces a soft framing effect.*

5. Save the image; you can close it at any time now.

So far, we've covered how to make a color image into a grayscale image, a Duotone, a sepiatone, and a rotogravure-style image. Let's turn the (color) tables now, and see how to colorize a grayscale image.

GETTING TINTS FROM AN IMAGE

Before color photography, a common practice was for photo-finishers to hire talented artists who applied watercolor washes to grayscale images to make them appear more lifelike. The practice has faded, but the charming look of a hand-tinted image has not necessarily gone away, not when you use Photoshop.

The best place to gather a collection of natural fleshtones and other colors is from an actual color photograph. Photoshop provides a quick, easy way to automatically sample colors from an image. By sampling and saving a number of unique colors from an RGB image, you can apply the saved colors to an image that has only grayscale values, thereby performing the digital equivalent of hand-tinting an image.

NOTE

The 122 default colors on the Swatches palette are only one of several collections of colors you can display; PANTONE, TRU-MATCH, and other digital color-matching systems can be loaded by clicking on the Swatches palette flyout and choosing Replace Swatches. If you direct the Load dialog box to the Photoshop\palettes folder on your hard disk, you will see the different palettes you can choose from.

Theoretically, the Swatches palette in Photoshop can hold an infinite number of color samples, limited only by your system resources.

When you want to sample only a few colors from an image, you might choose to "hand pick" them by sampling a photo or illustration and then adding (*appending*) the colors to Photoshop's default color swatches. This is done by choosing the Eyedropper tool, clicking in the image, and then clicking at the end of the current Swatches palette to add the color. Clearly, this process can become tedious. If you want a large sampling of colors, however, don't despair; the next section shows you how to auto-load colors from an image.

Right now, let's walk through the process of saving a color collection to the Swatches palette, so that you can reuse the colors in other images:

SAVING A CUSTOM INDEXED PALETTE

1. Open the Cameo.tif image from the Chap11 folder on the Companion CD.

2. Press F6 if the Swatches palette is not currently onscreen. Then click on the Swatches tab.

3. Choose Image, Mode, and then choose Indexed Color. Figure 11.24 shows the dialog box that appears. Choose the Adaptive Palette, leave the other settings at their default, and then click on OK.

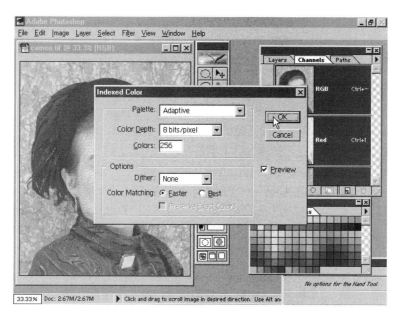

FIGURE 11.24 *The Adaptive palette method of indexing colors favors the most commonly occurring colors in the image.*

You'll notice that the Swatches palette has changed to reflect the colors in the Indexed color image. The palette displays only 122 of the 256 colors you've reduced this image to, however. To get the rest of the colors to display on the palette, do this...

4. Choose Image, Mode, and then choose Color Table. The Color Table dialog box appears, and all 256 indexed colors you've defined are visible.

5. Click on Save, and then name the file Cameo.act (Macintosh users do not need the "act" file extension), and then save the color palette to Photoshop's Palettes directory on your hard disk, as illustrated in Figure 11.25.

6. Click on the menu flyout on the Swatches palette, and then choose Load Swatches. From the directory box, choose your Palettes folder, choose Cameo.act, and then click on Load (Open).

7. Expand the Swatches palette so that you can see all the colors.

8. Close Cameo.tif without saving it, and then load Cameo.tif (the grayscale version) from your hard disk.

9. Choose Image, Mode, and then choose RGB Color. This doesn't change the visual information in the image, but it does allow color to be added now.

TIP

If you intend to spend a lot of time hand-tinting photographs, you might want to increase the saturation on the tinting layer to make the colors less subtle. To do this, press Ctrl(⌘)+U, and then increase the Saturation by moving the slider to a higher number in the Hue/Saturation command.

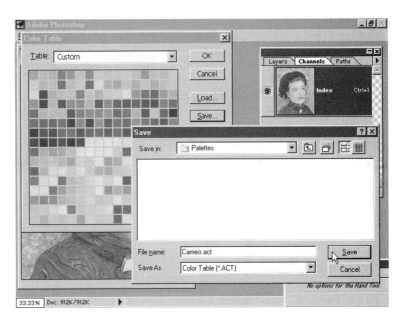

FIGURE 11.25 *Save the Color Table to your Palettes folder. You can then load the palette into your Swatches palette.*

10. On the Layers palette, click on the Create new layer icon. Layer 1 appears as a title on the Layers palette, and is the current editing layer.

11. Choose Color from the drop-down modes list on the Layers palette.

12. Choose the Paintbrush tool, choose the 65-pixel tip from the Brushes palette, select a fleshtone from the Swatches palette, and begin painting, as shown in Figure 11.26. Color mode treats the colors you apply to Layer 1 as a semitransparent tint.

13. That's it! You can complete as much or as little of the image as you like; better still, get out a grayscale image of your own and apply the Swatches colors to it. This Cameo.act palette contains some of the best fleshtones you'd want to use in tinting a grayscale picture of a relative or friend.

This chapter has concentrated on different color modes and how to make a limited color space look its best, using a picture of a model extensively to illustrate different techniques. In the next section, you will learn a trick that can be used with color or monochrome images, using it to stylize a still life image and in the process make it more attention-getting.

FIGURE 11.26 *Color mode registers only the hue and saturation of the foreground color, in combination with the underlying brightness values, to display the composite color in an image.*

EMBOSSING USING COLOR CHANNEL INFORMATION

First, the reason for using a picture of flowers in the next set of steps if that the technique you'll learn is completely unflattering when applied to a picture of a human. The effect we're seeking here is of a color, 3D embossed look. To accomplish this, you'll copy and blur a channel in the image to be used as the Lighting Effects filter's Texture Channel function. The look can be used on any still life image of your own; the simpler the composition is, the better the effect will show through.

Here's how to create a 3D embossed look:

CREATING AN EMBOSSED EFFECT VIA CHANNELS

1. Open the IMG0083.psd image from the Chap11 folder on the Companion CD.

2. On the Channels palette, drag the Green channel title into the Create new channel icon, as shown in Figure 11.27). This creates an alpha channel copy of the Green channel, and it is the current editing channel.

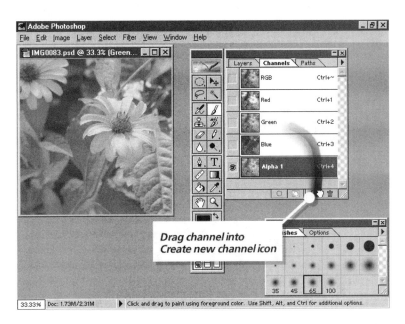

FIGURE 11.27 *Copy the Green channel by dragging the title into the Create new channel icon.*

3. Choose Filter, Blur, and then choose Gaussian Blur.

By blurring the Alpha 1 channel, you'll make more pronounced "bumps" in the image when the Lighting Effects filter is applied.

4. Drag the slider to about 2.3 in the Gaussian Blur dialog box, as shown in Figure 11.28; then click on OK to apply the filter. Click on the RGB channel to make it active for editing.

5. Choose Filter, Render, and then choose Lighting Effects.

6. Choose Directional from the Light Type drop-down list, and then drag the source point for the light toward the proxy image until the exposure of the proxy image is about the same as the image in the workspace.

7. Choose Alpha 1 from the Texture Channel drop-down list, and then drag the Height slider to about 28. When the dialog box looks like that shown in Figure 11.29, click on OK to apply the filter.

8. Save your work as Emboss.tif to your hard disk. You can close the image at any time now.

FIGURE 11.28 *"Less is more" when blurring the Alpha channel. You want to apply a subtle amount of blurring to achieve the best effect in the Lighting Effects filter.*

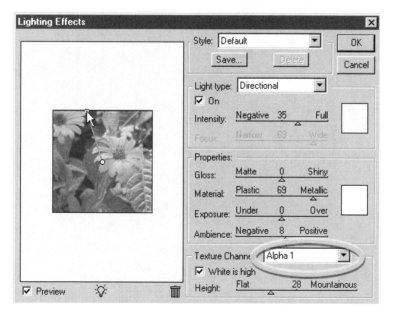

FIGURE 11.29 *The Alpha 1 channel adds soft yet pronounced relief to the image.*

As mentioned earlier, this embossing technique can be used on either color or black-and-white images. In Figure 11.30, you can see the completed image. It's stylized, but you have to admit that the visual content is recognizable, and that there is something innately interesting about a "stamped" image.

SUMMARY

Hopefully, this chapter has demonstrated that regardless of the color mode in which you have to work, there's always something artistic you can do to enhance the finished product. Whether you work in color or in black-and-white, this chapter provides a small sampling of the creative possibilities that lie ahead when you understand how to work with—and leverage the power of—Photoshop's capability to display image data in different modes.

FIGURE 11.30 *Explore the different ways you can use Photoshop's features to add visual interest without detracting from visual content.*

Special effects is our next stop. In Chapter 12, "Creating a Photorealistic Fantasy," you will see how some photographic elements and some synthetic ones can be combined to make a visually compelling fantasy image.

CHAPTER 12

CREATING A PHOTOREALISTIC FANTASY

If you think about big box office attractions these days, science fiction films top the bill, and also top the budgets for special effects. This author harbored the notion of creating a sci-fi extravaganza a while back, too. The tale was of aliens who live on earth and blend into society, with but one faux pas— they dress in tacky suits that look more appropriate for a family reunion than a stroll down Fifth Avenue.

Aliens in Plaid *was the intended title of the author's film, but unfortunately Hollywood pulled off the idea with the movie* Men in Black *before the author had a chance to do little more than a few production sketches. The good news, however, is that the author now has the time to take you through the steps needed to created a science fiction poster for the film. You'll see how to meld aliens with men in black suits, add out-of-this-world weapons, and convincingly blend all the fiction with photographic reality.*

WHAT ELEMENTS ARE NEEDED FOR THE COMPOSITION?

In Figure 12.1, you can see the finished poster for the *Aliens in Plaid* movie. The first step in re-creating the poster is to take a look at what digital and photographic elements are needed: an alien, a space laser, a photograph of a man in a suit, and a cityscape.

FIGURE 12.1 *The composition is a blend of photographic and computer-generated elements.*

Now, don't worry; all the elements needed to create this poster are on the Companion CD, but if you own a modeling application, we'll briskly walk through the steps needed to build the alien and also the laser pistol our actor is holding.

SIZING-UP THE PHOTOGRAPHIC IMAGE

For readers who are not familiar with modeling applications, here's a brief explanation of what they do. A three-dimensional wireframe is designed for objects that are then surfaced with materials of the user's choice. As long as the models exist in this wireframe state, they are *resolution-independent* (they can be of any dimensions). But to make the surfaced wireframe models useful in a 2D program such as Photoshop, the modeling program needs to render the models to bitmap format—which of course is two-dimensional and *resolution-dependent* (contains a finite number of pixels).

How large you should render the bitmap files of the alien and the laser pistol depends on how large you want these images to appear when they are combined with the photo of the actor. The quickest way to find the dimensions of the base image (the photo of the actor) is to open the base image and then press Alt(Opt) and click and hold on the Document Sizes space on Photoshop's status line (Macintosh: at the bottom of the image window). In Figure 12.2, you can see that the first image you'll work with in this chapter (Gary-K.tif), measures 1036 pixels in height. This means that if you intend to model an alien of human height for the poster, you should define 1036 pixels as the rendered height for the alien. Notice also in Figure 12.2 that there is some headroom between the top of the actor and the top edge of the image window. If you're modeling an alien, you will need to add similar headroom to the rendered image to make the alien and the guy the same size.

**Alt (Opt)+
hold here**

Width: 700 pixels (2.333 inches)
Height: 1036 pixels (3.453 inches)
Channels: 4 (RGB Color)
Resolution: 300 pixels/inch

FIGURE 12.2 *The Document Sizes space in Photoshop quickly tells you the dimensions, color mode, and resolution of the current image.*

Here's the recipe for creating an alien dressed in positively hideous plaid: use Fractal Design Poser to create the multiarmed torso, export the body as a 3D Metafile to Macromedia Extreme 3D or another modeling program, and then replace the human head with one a little more in keeping with the sci-fi poster. In Figure 12.3, you can see what the alien looks like in Extreme 3D; the bounding box is the rendering window for the model and as you can see, it's 1036 pixels in height, the same as the Gary-K.tif image you'll use shortly.

Head Modeled in E3D

1036 Pixels height

Body from Poser 2

FIGURE 12.3 *Scale the rendered image from your modeling program to the same height as the photograph you'll use.*

Another handy property of most modeling programs is that they generate an alpha channel in the rendered image, so selecting around the foreground sphere, cylinder, or alien is a snap. In Figure 12.4, you can see the Photoshop document that is used in this chapter for the background of the actor. Henry Shtunq, our alien in plaid, is on a separate layer from the background of the city; this makes moving and color-correcting the alien or the city easy to do.

Many of the details in the Gary-K.tif image are correct for the composition: the secret service suit, the cool shades, and the actor's attitude all contribute to making a pleasing contrast to the goofy alien in plaid. The water pistol he's holding as a prop has *got* to be replaced, however! Again, a modeling application is used to make an appropriate science fiction weapon, but the size to which the modeled laser pistol needs to be rendered is not easy to guess.

FIGURE 12.4 *Keeping multielement compositions as multilayer documents makes repositioning and editing selected elements much easier.*

In the very short tutorial that follows, you'll use a new feature in Photoshop 5, the Measure tool, to see what dimensions are ideal for a replacement weapon for the actor.

MEASURING IMAGE SPACE WITH THE NEW MEASURE TOOL

1. Open the Gary-K.tif image from the Chap12 folder on the Companion CD. Type **50** in the zoom field box and then press Enter (Return) to zoom to a comfortable view for measuring the space for the laser pistol replacement. Drag the image window edges away from the window if necessary.

2. Press F8 to display the Info palette. Click on the plus sign to the left of the XY coordinate field on the palette, and choose pixels from the flyout menu.

3. Press u (Measure tool), and then drag a horizontal line from behind the water pistol in the image close to the right edge of the image, as shown in Figure 12.5. The replacement laser pistol can certainly be larger than that wimpy water pistol the actor is holding! As you can see, the replacement pistol can be about 312 pixels wide, as it fits within the frame of an image window.

4. Take this number back to a modeling program, create a laser pistol at the same angle as the actor is holding his water pistol, and render it to approximately 312 pixels in width. In Figure 12.6, you can see the laser pistol that is used in this chapter. Note that the width

NOTE

A key element to making a fantasy composition believable is to keep the lighting on elements consistent. You'll notice as you begin to work with this chapter's images that everything is lit from the upper right. When you're adding computer art to photographic images, you first need to see where the lighting is in the photograph (because you can't change it); then you can light your computer-generated scenes to match the photo.

of the rendering window is 360 pixels, a little more than the 312 figure we measured in step 3. The additional pixels are simply "padding" around the model, because the author doesn't believe in excessive cropping (you might accidentally crop an area that you need!).

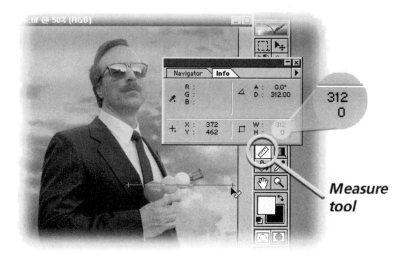

FIGURE 12.5 *To measure the space you have available, click with the Measure tool on the point of the image where you want to begin measuring and then drag to the point where you want to end measuring.*

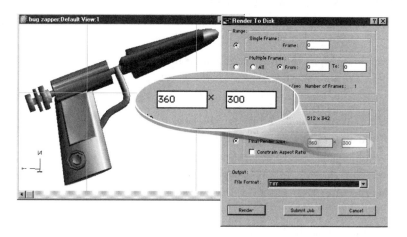

FIGURE 12.6 *Plan to add a little empty space around your model to the number you measured in Photoshop.*

5. Keep Gary-K.tif open. You'll be editing the image shortly. You can close your modeling program at any time after you've rendered the pistol.

To transport the actor to the Shtunq.psd image, you'll need to carefully trim around his silhouette before copying the image. Fortunately, the cloud background in the Gary-K. image contains colors not found on the actor, so Photoshop 5's new selection tools can make quick work of the task at hand.

SELECTING SILHOUETTES

If you take a careful look at the outline of the actor in the Gary-K.tif image, you'll note that in some areas there is a clear contrast between, for example, his jacket and the surrounding sky. In other areas, particularly where there are highlights (in his hair and near his shirt color), there is no clear definition between profile and areas outside his profile. This means that you must use a *combination* of techniques—and different tools— to isolate foreground actor from background sky.

USING THE MAGNETIC LASSO TOOL

Although the water pistol is not used in the finished composition, we'll keep it in the picture for a while as a practice area for one of Photoshop's new selection tools.

The Magnetic Lasso tool is ideal for separating the actor from the sky background. You're going to delete the sky background to leave only the actor in the image. In the following set of steps, you'll use the Magnetic Lasso tool to trim away sky areas with edges that are clearly defined.

REMOVING AREAS FROM A LAYER BY USING THE MAGNETIC LASSO TOOL

1. Double-click on the Background layer title on the Layers palette (press F7 if the palette isn't onscreen). This displays the Make Layer dialog box.

2. Type **Gary K.** in the Name field, and then click on OK. Now areas you delete in the image will turn transparent and will not default to the current background color.

3. Drag on the Lasso tool button, and then choose the Magnetic Lasso tool. Double-click on the button now to display the Options palette for the tool.

4. Click twice in the Lasso Width field to highlight the number, and then type **5**. The Lasso Width is sort of like a tolerance setting for the tool. Areas that are five pixels away from wherever you drag with the tool will be considered for a contrasting edge in the image that the path you draw will adhere to. This tight tolerance will produce clean edges.

5. Click twice in the Frequency field, and then type **20**. The frequency determines how often control points are automatically inserted along the path you drag. In previous versions of Photoshop, you had to click to insert a corner point along a selection path.

6. Click twice in the Edge Contrast field, and then type **10**. This is a fairly narrow setting; pixels must display no more than a 10 percent color difference before the Magnetic Lasso tool will "see" an edge in the image.

7. Press Ctrl(⌘)+ the plus key several times until the zoom percentage box reads 200%. Maximize the image in the workspace (Windows: use the Maximize/Restore button; Macintosh: use the Size box in the lower-right corner of the image window).

8. Press and hold the Spacebar to toggle to the Hand tool, and then scroll your view in the window until you see the water pistol and the actor's necktie.

9. Click an initial point on the edge of the water pistol, release the mouse button, and then drag the cursor along the edge of the water pistol in the direction away from his hand until you reach the actor's jacket. Follow the contour of the pistol and *do not* click as you move; simply drag (hover) the cursor and it will snap to the edges in the image.

10. When you reach the top of the visible portion of the actor's jacket, move the cursor around a large chunk of sky, and then close the selection path by returning to your original click point. You'll notice that the cursor will display a small circle which indicates that you are going to close the selection. Click once, and then wait for the marquee selection to appear.

11. Press Delete (Backspace), and Photoshop's transparency grid replaces your view of the sky area you deleted, as shown in Figure 12.7. Press Ctrl(⌘)+D to deselect the marquee.

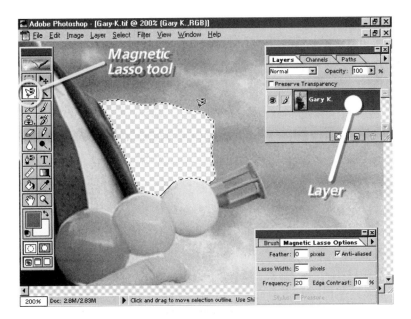

FIGURE 12.7 *Guide the Magnetic Lasso tool along the edge of the actor, complete the selection outside the actor, and then press Delete (Backspace).*

12. Press Ctrl(⌘)+Shift+S and save the image as Gary.psd in Photoshop format. Keep the image open in Photoshop.

The Magnetic Lasso tool can be used for much—but not all—of the selection work that lies ahead. In certain areas of the actor the colors fall too close to those of the sky. To work quickly and with precision, you can use the Magnetic Lasso tool in combination with Photoshop's Quick Mask to edit the selection made by the Magnetic Lasso tool.

USING A COMBINATION EDITING TECHNIQUE

If any fringe is in the trimmed image of the actor, it will become obvious that he's been pasted into the Shtunq.psd document, and that will spoil the fantasy aspect of the finished image. As mentioned earlier, the Magnetic Lasso tool can be used effectively in areas of high color contrast, but it falls short of its intended purpose in areas of low color contrast, such as the actor's white shirt collar. However, if we use the Magnetic Lasso tool in addition to using the Quick Mask mode, we'll be able to create a much more refined selection. The Quick Mask mode enables us to edit a color overlay with any of Photoshop's selection or painting tools, as you'll soon see.

USING QUICK MASK MODE TO MASK AREAS WITH LOW COLOR CONTRAST

1. Press Ctrl(⌘)+the plus key twice to zoom into 400% viewing resolution.

2. Hold down the Spacebar and drag in the document window until you can clearly see the actor's shirt collar and the knot in his tie.

3. Choose the Magnetic Lasso tool, click at the point where the shirt collar meets the tie knot, and then move the cursor upward along the edge of the collar. It's okay to move past the shirt collar and include part of the actor's neck as you're defining this edge.

4. Move the cursor outside the actor to encompass some of the sky background, and then close the selection by single-clicking at the beginning point of the selection.

5. Double-click on the Quick Mask mode icon on the toolbox. In the Options dialog box, click on the Color Indicates Selected Areas button, and then click on the Color swatch. In the Color Picker, choose a dark blue, click on OK to exit the Color Picker, and then click on OK to exit the Options dialog box. The area you defined with the Magnetic Lasso tool is now a deep blue tint.

6. Press D and then press X to make the current foreground color white.

7. Choose the Paintbrush tool, and on the Brushes palette choose the second-to-smallest tip on the top row.

8. Stroke inside the shirt collar, wherever there is blue Quick Mask tint. White foreground color removes Quick Mask, while black applies Quick Mask (see Figure 12.8).

9. When you've refined the edge of the selection so that the actor's shirt collar and neck are completely outside the Quick Mask, click on the Standard Editing mode icon, to the left of the Quick Mask icon on the toolbox. The mask becomes a marquee selection again.

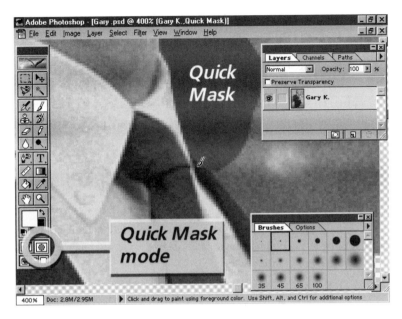

FIGURE 12.8 *Carefully remove areas of Quick Mask from image areas that you want to save.*

10. Press Delete (Backspace), and then press Ctrl(⌘)+D to deselect the marquee selection.

11. Press Ctrl(⌘)+S; keep the file open.

It's time for a little independent study in this assignment. You've moved from one area of the image to another, with unedited areas in-between. Take a moment to trim away the sky areas between the actor's left arm and the shirt collar; the shoulder of the actor can be cleanly defined by using the current settings for the Magnetic Lasso tool. After that, scroll the document window upward and trim away the sky that borders the left side of the actor's face. Stop when you reach the sunglasses, and read on.

USING PATHS TO DEFINE HARD EDGES

You're working counterclockwise around the silhouette of the actor. The next stop, after you've trimmed around the left side of the actor's face, is the edge of the sunglasses. The Magnetic Lasso tool is unacceptable for defining the edge of the sunglasses because the rim of the glasses consists of too few pixels for the Magnetic Lasso tool to "find" a color edge.

If you've read and worked through the examples in Chapter 6, "Selections, Layers, and Paths" (or if you're an experienced Photoshop user), you now have the experience to use the Pen tool to define the edge of the sunglasses. Here's how to draw the edge and remove the bordering sky areas:

USING THE PEN TOOL TO SELECT NARROW PATHS

1. Choose the Pen tool from the toolbox, and then click a point where the sunglasses touch the actor's cheek.

2. Click a point about 3/4" up on the edge of the glasses and then drag upward and toward the actor to make the path segment between the two anchor points conform to the edge of the sunglasses.

3. Repeat step 2; the third anchor point you define should be about half the distance up on the edge of the sunglasses.

4. Click a point on the farthest point to the right on the top of the sunglasses, and then click two more points to negotiate the sharp corner of the sunglasses.

5. Click, and then drag a point where the sunglasses meet the actor's hairline. You've finished defining the edge; now click a few points to encompass the sky and close the path at the origin point, as shown in Figure 12.9.

6. If you've made any mistakes along the path's edge, press and hold Ctrl(⌘) to toggle the Pen tool to the Direct Selection tool, and then reposition any anchor points. If any of the path segments intrude upon the sunglasses, hold down Ctrl(⌘), click on an anchor point to expose the direction handles for the path, and then bend the path segment by steering the direction handle.

7. Press F7 if the grouped Layers palette is not onscreen, and then click on the Paths tab.

8. Click on the Loads path as a selection icon, and then click on a blank area of the palette to hide the path. Now you should see only a selection marquee.

9. Press Delete (Backspace) and then press Ctrl(⌘)+D to remove the selection marquee. Drag the Work Path title on the Paths palette into the trash icon.

10. Press Ctrl(⌘)+S; keep the file open.

The next section addresses a manual selection technique for removing sky areas that surround the actor's hair.

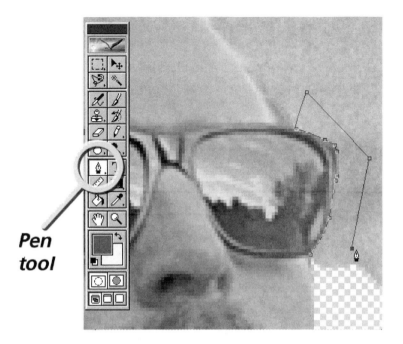

Pen
tool

FIGURE 12.9 *Define the edge of the sunglasses, using the Pen tool.*

CREATING COMPLEX SELECTIONS IN LAYER MASK MODE

Photoshop 5 offers a number of safeguards against editing mistakes; the History list is only one of them. Layer Mask mode, described in previous chapters, is an erasing state for an image; this state can be undone and redone ad infinitum, until you're happy with the selections you've hidden. It is only when you click the Apply button that the Layer Mask removes image areas.

The Layer Mask, used in combination with a small-tipped Paintbrush tool, is ideal for use around the actor's hair. Hair in a photograph is diffuse around the edges, particularly when there's a mild breeze outdoors, and a few strands of hair are blown about. It is recommended that you do not use ultimate care and hours of time neatly picking around the actor's hair. Don't bother with individual strands; simply mask over them. Toward the end of this chapter you'll paint in strands of hair to avoid the

WARNING

It's important to remember that as long as a path is visible, pressing the Delete (Backspace) key affects the path and not a selection marquee made from a path. Therefore, if you do not hide a path before you press Delete (Backspace), you'll delete the path itself, and not the contents of the marquee selection.

infamous "helmet hairdo" frequently seen in amateurish-looking advertisements in which compositing has transported a couple to the beach, and so on.

The next set of steps take you through both the Layer Mask feature and a way to customize the transparency grid to get a better view of what you're editing:

USING THE LAYER MASK TO CREATE COMPLEX SELECTIONS

1. Hold down the Spacebar and drag downward in the image window until you have a good view of the actor's left temple.

2. On the Layers palette click on the Add Layer Mask icon. The image is now in Layer Masking mode.

3. Press D (default colors) and then, with the Paintbrush tool, stroke along the outside edge of the actor's hair, as in Figure 12.10. Because you are using a small brush tip, you'll want to make several strokes way outside the hair edge to create a wide path that can be selected later with a less precise selection tool.

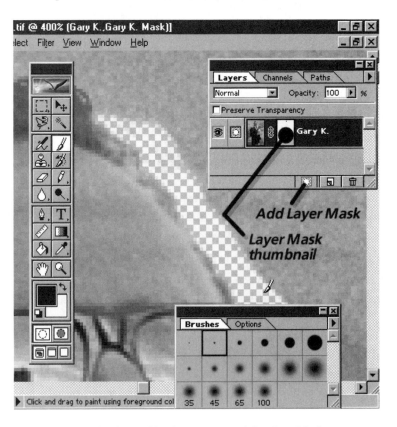

FIGURE 12.10 *Use a small, soft-tipped brush to erase around the edges of the hair.*

You might notice a problem now that needs to be resolved. By default, Photoshop's transparency grid is light-gray and white checks. Both of these colors are too close to the tones in the actor's hair to make for accurate editing around the edges. Let's change the color of the transparency grid to a deep, solid color that will contrast against the actor's hair...

4. Press Ctrl(⌘)+K to display Photoshop's Preferences, and then press Ctrl(⌘)+4 to go to the Transparency & Gamut preferences.

5. Click on the white swatch, then, in the Color Picker, choose a deep blue. Click on OK to exit the Color Picker.

6. Click on the light-gray swatch; then, in the Color Picker, choose a deep blue. Click on OK to exit the Color Picker (see Figure 12.11).

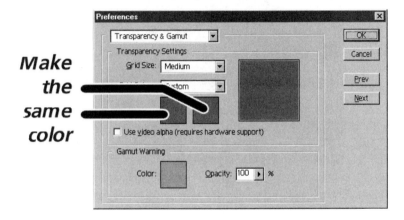

FIGURE 12.11   *Make the transparency grid a solid, dark color so that you can better see the edges of the actor's hair.*

7. Click on OK in the Preferences box to return to the document. Now, everywhere you paint transparency the deep blue will appear, making it very easy to spot fringing problems.

8. Continue painting along the outside edge of the hair, adjusting your view by holding down the Spacebar and scrolling the document (see Figure 12.12).

9. When you've completed the masking and arrived at the right side of the actor's shirt collar, it's time to finalize your editing. Click on the Layer Mask thumbnail, and then drag it into the trash icon at the bottom right of the Layers palette. An attention box appears.

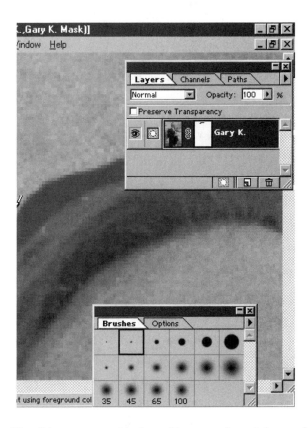

FIGURE 12.12 *The solid transparency grid color enables you to edit precisely around the actor's hair.*

10. Click on Apply in the attention box to permanently remove the areas you've hidden while you worked in Layer Mask mode. The image is no longer in Layer Mask mode.

11. Press Ctrl(⌘)+S; keep the file open.

You've now learned four techniques for isolating the actor in the image:

- Use the Magnetic Lasso tool along areas of strong color contrast.

- Use the Magnetic Lasso tool in combination with Quick Mask when areas do not have sufficient contrast for the tool to accurately select around them.

- Use the Pen tool to define paths that are too narrow for the Magnetic Lasso tool.

- Use the Layer Mask feature with a small brush tip for trimming around the diffuse edges of hair.

In Figure 12.13, you can see the process continuing; the sky around the actor's right shoulder is trimmed away with the Magnetic Lasso tool.

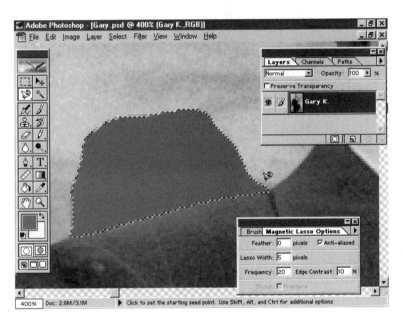

FIGURE 12.13 *Use the Magnetic Lasso tool to trim away areas that display strong contrast.*

The rest of the image displays good contrast, and you can use the Magnetic Lasso tool to easily trim away the remaining outside edges of the image. When you've completed a wide path outline that separates the actor from the sky, use the regular (not the Magnetic) Lasso tool to encompass areas of the sky, and then press Delete (Backspace) to remove them. When you're finished, you should have an image that looks like Figure 12.14—the actor alone, surrounded by the deep blue transparency grid.

FIGURE 12.14 *You've successfully removed the actor from his environment.*

You haven't finished finessing the actor yet. You'll note that on the occasion of the photographic session, the actor decided that formal pants were not important (the author promised that this was to be a "waist-up" photo). Unfortunately, this decision leaves us with two options:

- Cropping the image to above the waist, which would crop out part of his left hand (not such a good option), or

- Painting in some pants that match his suit.

In the following section you'll use the second option and put a pair of formal pants over the actor's Hawaiian shorts. Let's break out the Freeform Pen tool and get to work.

PAINTING OVER ITEMS THAT DON'T MATCH YOUR NEW IMAGE

One of the factors that makes photo-retouching of this image an easy task is that the actor is wearing a dark suit. This means that there is very little image detail toward the bottom of his jacket, and that formal pants can be "faked" into the image with a little solid foreground color.

PAINTING AN IMAGE SELECTION

The first thing you want to do before painting a single brush stroke into the image is to define the color you're going to use. This is accomplished easily with the Eyedropper tool. In Figure 12.15, you can see that the author has clicked on the bottom of the jacket; the Info palette tells us that the color is almost absolute black.

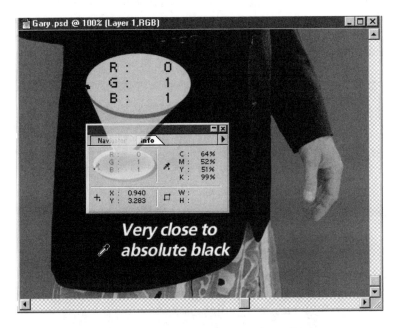

FIGURE 12.15 *Sample a foreground color from the jacket, a color you'll use to paint in pants.*

Do this now with the image onscreen, so that you can define the shape of the pants and do the editing work needed to replace the Hawaiian trunks:

USING THE FREEFORM PEN TOOL TO CREATE A PATH

1. Press Ctrl(⌘)+ the minus key three times to zoom out to a 100% (1:1) view of Gary.psd.

2. Hold down the Spacebar and drag upward in the image window so that you can see the actor's shorts.

3. Drag on the Pen tool on the toolbox to reveal the tool flyout; choose the Freeform Pen tool.

   The Freeform Pen tool is unlike the Pen tool in that you create paths by dragging, not by clicking anchor points.

4. Create a closed path like the one shown in Figure 12.16. The front of the actor's pants should be fairly straight and inside the loose Hawaiian trunks. The back side of the pants should scoop inside the jacket's tails. It is perfectly all right to have the path go into the jacket, as the overall color of the jacket is nearly identical to the foreground color you've defined.

FIGURE 12.16 *Draw a freeform path that is the silhouette of the pants you'll paint on the actor.*

5. On the Paths palette, click on the Loads path as a selection icon, and then click on a blank area of the palette to hide the path.

6. Choose the Airbrush tool, and then paint the interior of the selection marquee.

7. Press Shift+F7 to invert the selection. The area you painted is protected from change, and outside areas, such as the remainder of the Hawaiian shorts, can now be edited.

8. Double-click on the Eraser tool to select it and to display the Options palette. Choose Paintbrush from the drop-down list on the Eraser Options palette. On the Brushes palette, choose the second-from-right, top tip.

9. Carefully erase the areas where there are still portions of the Hawaiian shorts, as shown in Figure 12.17. Press Ctrl(⌘)+D when you're finished.

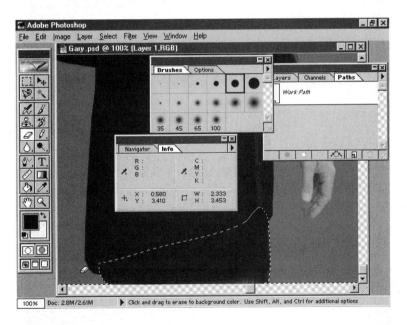

FIGURE 12.17   *Erase the areas of Hawaiian shorts.*

10. Press Ctrl(⌘)+S; keep the file open.

Okay; we have a very serious man in black holding a water pistol now, and you can guess what needs to be edited next!

EDITING-IN A PROP

The entire water pistol does not have to be deleted from the Gary.psd image. Only areas that show outside the modeled laser pistol need to be erased, or else cloned in with areas of the actor's shirt and jacket. In the following section, you'll add the contents of Zapper.psd (or an image of your own design) to that of the actor.

"SLEEK" DOESN'T COVER "CLUNKY"

The choice of water pistols for the actor was a poor one; if the author had been planning, he'd have recommended a sleeker water pistol for the actor to brandish. The spheres of this water pistol will not be covered by the sleek, elegant, modeled laser pistol. Additionally, the spheres of the water pistol hide some of the actor's jacket. If you think this mistake was deliberate, you're right! There would be no tutorial steps if everything went perfectly!

Here's how to copy the laser pistol into the Gary.psd image and begin the editing procedure:

USING THE MOVE TOOL TO COMPOSITE AN IMAGE

1. Open the Zapper.psd image from the Chap12 folder on the Companion CD, or open the image of the pistol you created in a modeling application.

2. With the Move tool, drag from the Zapper image window to the Gary.psd image window, as shown in Figure 12.18. This makes a copy of the pistol in the Gary image on its own layer.

3. Zoom in to a 200% view of the Gary.psd image, close the Zapper.psd image without saving it, and then with the Move tool, position the Bug Zapper Layer in the image so that the pistol lies directly on top of the water pistol.

4. Click on the Gary K. title on the Layers palette to make it the current editing layer.

5. Choose the Rubber Stamp tool. On the Brushes palette, choose the third-from-left, top tip.

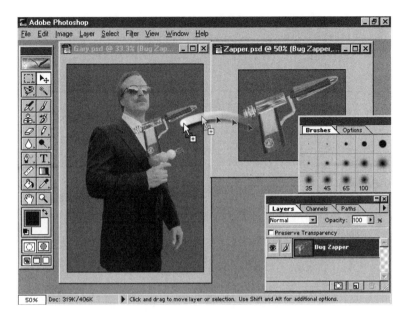

FIGURE 12.18   *Drag and drop the pistol into the Gary.psd image.*

6. Press Alt(Opt) and click a sampling point on the far edge of the actor's tie, as in Figure 12.19; then begin stroking the Gary K. layer, downward, at the point where the red sphere on the water pistol obscures your view of the tie. Continue across with the tool until you've filled the red sphere with tie pattern.

7. Press Alt(Opt) and click a sample point above the pistol, where the actor's jacket casts a shadow on his shirt.

8. Drag the tool downward to cover the orange sphere. Take care to align the clone point and the sample point so that the edge of the jacket you're cloning in is straight.

9. Press Ctrl(⌘)+S; keep the file open.

It's time now to fit the pistol into the actor's hand (instead of leaving it *on top of* his hand). To do this, you'll use Layer Mask mode again.

FIGURE 12.19 *Remove parts of the water pistol by cloning in from the necktie.*

MASKING OUT UNWANTED AREAS

The actor's hand must cover the grip of the laser pistol, which means that you have to erase part of the Bug Zapper layer. This chore is not as simple as it might seem, however—exactly where must the erasure end when you can't clearly see the actor's hand? The trick to accomplishing the following editing maneuver is to use both the hiding and exposing capabilities of Layer Mask mode. Remember: White restores hidden areas and black hides layer areas.

Here's how to place the bug zapper in the actor's hand:

ERASING AND EXPOSING WITH THE LAYER MASK

1. Hold down the Spacebar and drag up in the image window so that you can clearly see the laser pistol.

2. Choose the Paintbrush tool, and then choose the middle tip in the top row on the Brushes palette.

3. Click on the Bug Zapper title on the Layers palette to make it the current editing layer. Then click on the Add Layer Mask icon on the palette.

4. Press D (default colors), and then begin painting away at the handle of the laser pistol, as shown in Figure 12.20. It is okay to hide more of the handle than is necessary, to expose the actor's hand. As long as you can see the edge of the hand, you can restore the areas of the pistol that will appear in the finished image.

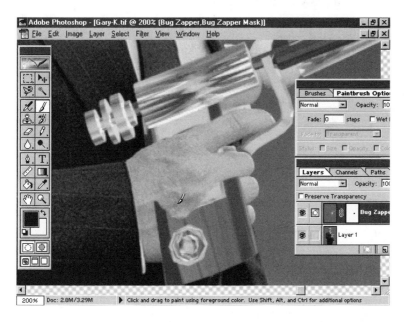

FIGURE 12.20 *Applying black foreground color hides areas on a layer while in Layer Mask mode.*

5. When all of the pistol handle has been removed from the actor's hand, press X (switch foreground/background colors), and then choose the second-from-left tip in the top row on the Brushes palette.

6. Paint carefully around the outside edge of the hand. As you can see in Figure 12.21, applying white restores areas of the pistol that were hidden by black foreground color.

7. Press Ctrl(⌘)+S; keep the file open.

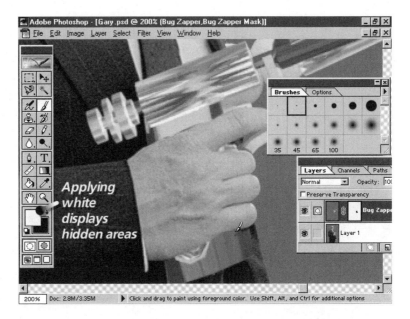

FIGURE 12.21 *Carefully restore the areas of the pistol that you want exposed on the Layer Masked layer.*

Now that you have a pretty good visualization of the way the laser pistol fits in the actor's hand, it's time to go back to the Gary K. layer in the image and remove the rest of the water pistol.

DEFINING A SELECTION

Part of the water pistol on the Gary K. layer needs jacket cloned into it, and other areas simply need to be deleted. *Defining* these areas accurately is more important than the techniques you'll use. By properly setting up selections, you'll make it impossible for anyone to detect that the actor was ever holding anything other than this oversized bug zapper.

Here's how to conclude the editing work in the Gary.psd image:

EDITING INTO NEW SELECTION AREAS

1. Click on the Gary K. layer title on the Layers palette to make it the current editing layer.

2. Choose the Pen tool, and then create a path similar to the one shown in Figure 12.22. Follow the curve of the finger, leave yourself enough room to work on the outside edge, and then close the path inside the shirt area.

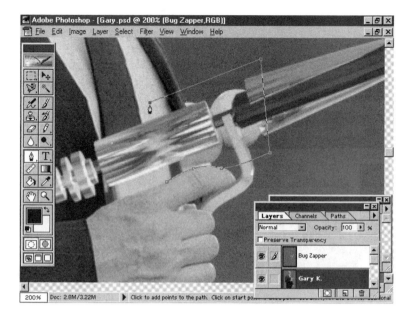

FIGURE 12.22 *Use the Pen tool to define the area that will be edited.*

3. Click on the Loads path as a selection icon on the Paths palette, and then click on an empty area of the palette to hide the path.

4. Choose the Rubber Stamp tool, choose the second-from-left tip in the top row of the Brushes palette, and then press Alt(Opt) and click a sample point on the outside edge of the jacket.

5. Drag downward in the image to clone over the orange water pistol sphere that remains between the laser pistol and the actor's trigger finger, as in Figure 12.23.

6. Press Ctrl(⌘)+D to deselect the selection marquee, and then choose the Pen tool.

7. Draw a path that encompasses the visible portions of the water pistol, as in Figure 12.24.

8. Click on the Loads path as a selection icon on the Paths palette; then click on an empty area of the palette list to hide the path.

9. Press Delete (Backspace) and then press Ctrl(⌘)+D to deselect the selection marquee.

10. Press Ctrl(⌘)+S; keep the file open.

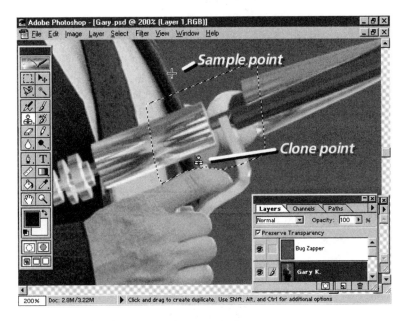

FIGURE 12.23 *Copy the jacket area into the water pistol area.*

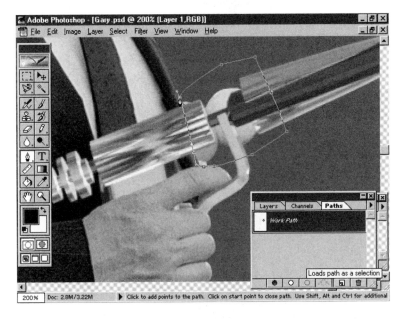

FIGURE 12.24 *Click and drag a path around the remaining area of the water pistol.*

There's a small detail missing from the Gary.psd image now that you'll fix in the next section of this chapter. To make it look as though the laser pistol is actually in the actor's hand, a shadow needs to be cast onto the handle of the pistol. You'll correct this by using tools you're already familiar with.

USING PARTIAL OPACITY PAINT

To make totally convincing shadows in images, you need to accomplish the following two things:

- The shadow needs to be of partial opacity, because shadows almost never totally obscure surfaces in the real world. There's too much ambient light to cast a 100 percent opaque shadow.

- The shadow needs to be approximately the same shape as the object casting the shadow.

If we take a look at the Gary K. image, the actor's pinkie finger should be casting a slight shadow on the butt of the laser pistol (the lighting in the image is from the upper right). Here are the steps you need to create the shadow effect:

CREATING A SHADOW

1. Choose the Magnetic Lasso tool, and then click a point at the tip of the actor's pinkie finger.

2. Move the cursor along the bottom edge of the pinkie finger, up into the hand, and then close the path with a single click at the origin point, as in Figure 12.25.

3. Click inside the selection marquee, and then drag down and to the right by about 1/2 screen inches. You're moving the marquee, not the image contents of the marquee.

4. Choose the Paintbrush tool, and then on the Options palette, drag the Opacity slider down to about 30%.

5. Choose a large Brushes palette tip, and then stroke once or twice inside the marquee selection, as shown in Figure 12.26. Do not stroke more than twice; if you do the selection area will become opaque, spoiling the illusion.

6. Press Ctrl(⌘)+D to deselect the marquee.

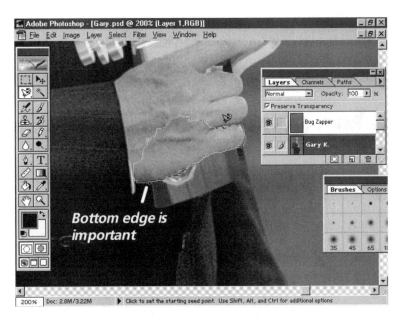

FIGURE 12.25 *Create a path that resembles the actor's pinkie finger along the bottom edge.*

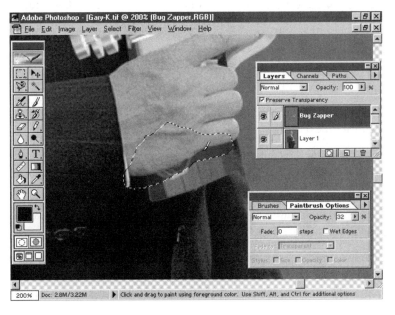

FIGURE 12.26 *Fill the selection marquee with black foreground color at partial opacity to create the shadow.*

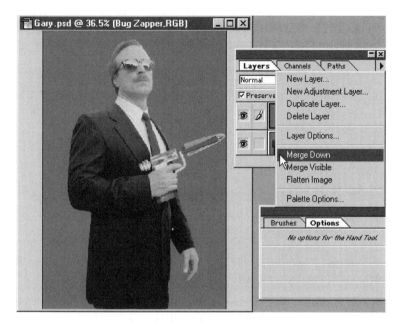

FIGURE 12.27   *Merge the Bug Zapper layer with the Gary K. layer to make a seamless composition.*

7. Click on the Layers palette's flyout button, and then choose Merge Down from the list (see Figure 12.27).

8. Press Ctrl(⌘)+S; keep the file open.

The most difficult part of this composition—the realistic part—has now been accomplished. In the following section, you'll unite the actor with the alien in the composition.

CREATING THE FANTASY COMPOSITION

All well-composed designs consist of a background element that is subordinate to the foreground elements. As we get into the conclusion of this assignment, you'll notice that the city layer in the Shtunq.psd image is way too attractive, and way too busy to allow the actor and the alien to dominate the scene. This can be corrected in a fantasy sort of way by adjusting the hue and saturation of the city scene. The city will still look like a photo of a city, but it will have a layer of abstractness.

COPYING THE ACTOR AND ARRANGING THE SCENE

The author goofed on the pose of the alien; originally, I'd wanted one of the alien's three arms to be hugging the actor, but the alien's left arm is poised way too high to accomplish this. It's in the wrong position to even be on the actor's shoulder. No problem; you'll remove the arm from the scene after copying and positioning the actor into the Shtunq.psd image.

Here's how to compose the scene:

COMPOSING YOUR SCENE

1. Open the Shtunq.psd image from the Chap12 folder on the Companion CD (or use your own image here).

2. Click on the Henry Shtunq layer on the Layers palette to make it the current layer.

3. Click on the title bar of the Gary.psd image, type **25** in the zoom percentage box, and then press Enter (Return). Resize the image window so that there is no background to Gary.psd and you can clearly see both images in the workspace.

4. With the Move tool, drag the Gary.psd image into the Shtunq.psd image, as shown in Figure 12.28.

5. Position the actor so that he is in front of the alien, covering only the alien's left shoulder.

6. Click on the Henry Shtunq layer title on the Layers palette, and then with the Lasso tool drag a marquee around the left arm of the alien.

7. Press Delete (Backspace) and then press Ctrl(⌘)+D to deselect the marquee.

8. Save the composition as Shtunq.psd to your hard disk. Leave the image open. (You can close Gary.psd at any time now.)

The focal point of this composition should be the faces of the actor and the alien, with secondary importance given to the laser pistol. At present, the composition looks like visual confetti because of the busyness of the buildings on the city layer. You'll correct this next.

FIGURE 12.28   *Copy the actor into the Shtunq image by dragging and dropping with the Move tool.*

DEEMPHASIZING A BACKGROUND

As mentioned earlier, we can stylize the background of the composition to better highlight the main attraction without removing all the photographic qualities of the city. Follow these steps to make a harmonious blend between background and foreground:

STYLIZING A CITYSCAPE

1. Click on the City layer title on the Layers palette.

2. Press Ctrl(⌘)+U to display the Hue/Saturation dialog box.

3. Drag the Saturation slider to **–100**, as in Figure 12.29. This removes all the color from the City layer.

4. Click on OK to apply the effect.

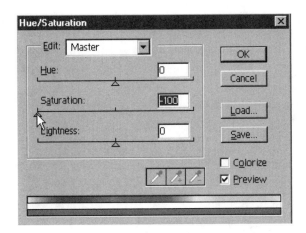

FIGURE 12.29 *Lowering the saturation in an image reduces it to grayscale.*

5. On the Layers palette, click on the Create new layer icon. The new layer, titled Layer 1, appears on top of the City layer.

6. Double-click on the Layer 1 title on the Layers palette. In the Layer Options box, type **Multiply** in the Name field, choose Multiply from the mode drop-down list, and then click on OK to exit the box.

7. Click on the background color swatch on the toolbox and then, using the color field circle and the hue slider, pick a pale cream. Click on OK to exit the Color Picker.

8. Choose the Linear Gradient tool from the toolbox; on the Options palette choose Foreground to Background from the drop-down list.

9. Hold Shift (constrains the tool to 45° increments) and then drag from the top of the image to the bottom, as shown in Figure 12.30. Because the layer is in Multiply mode, the black foreground color wipes out much of the visual detail at the top of the image; as the fill makes the transition to pale cream at the bottom, we can see more detail of the underlying city layer.

10. Press Ctrl(⌘)+S; keep the file open.

The composition looks pretty dramatic now, with a happy blend of fantasy and reality in the scene. In the following section, you'll pay attention to the finishing details.

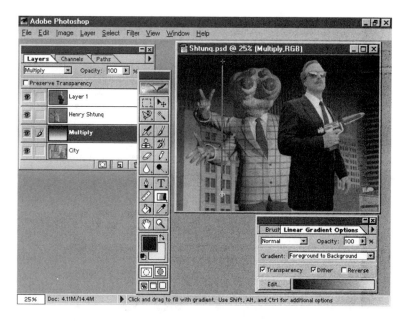

FIGURE 12.30   *Create a linear gradient fill to diminish the city detail toward the top of the composition.*

FINESSING THE FANTASY

It would be a shame to call it quits at this point, especially since there probably is still some fringe around the actor. The dark background will indeed display any sky background that was not thoroughly deleted around the actor. Also, some loose strands of hair would make a nice, believable touch for the actor. Finally, the film poster needs a title (and the author needs a chance to show off the new Type tool features!).

THE LAYER MASK AND FRINGED HAIR

Of all the areas around the actor, the place where you most probably will find fringing is around the edge of the hair. Hair, even in high-resolution images, is only one or two pixels wide, and even the most careful masking work is bound to leave a background pixel or two. This is why it's always a good idea to perform your masking on an image to separate the background, move the elements to a new background, and then check again for fringing.

Here's how to make certain that the actor blends into his new surroundings:

REMOVING FRINGING

1. Zoom in to a 200% view of the Shtunq image, and scroll your view to see the top of the actor's head. Click on the Gary K. layer on the Layers palette.

2. Click on the Add layer mask icon at the bottom of the Layers palette.

3. Choose the Paintbrush tool, choose the second-from-left tip in the top row, and then on the Options palette, double-click in the Opacity field and type **100**.

4. Carefully stroke over any areas along the edge of the hair that appear sky blue, as in Figure 12.31.

FIGURE 12.31 *Use Layer Mask mode to perform last-minute, detailed corrections to the composition.*

5. When you've looked at the entire silhouette of the actor, and you're certain that you've removed all fringing, click on the Layer Mask thumbnail on the Layers palette, and drag it into the trash icon. When the attention box pops up, click on Apply to make your changes permanent.

6. Press Ctrl(⌘)+S; keep the file open.

Although the sky is completely gone from the edges of the actor's profile, so are some of the nuances that make a photograph look photographic. A hard edge around the actor's suit and sunglasses is believable, but hard-edged hair? In the following section, you'll paint in strands of hair to make a more natural-looking composition.

FINISHING THE ACTOR'S HAIR

The following steps belong to the "less is more" category of image retouching. You want to continue some of the strands of hair that have been deleted from the image, while leaving other areas alone. Strands of hair tend to blow away unevenly when there's a breeze.

Here's how to make the actor's hairdo look perfectly natural:

ADDING STRANDS OF HAIR

1. Choose the Paintbrush tool, and then choose the smallest tip on the Brushes palette.

2. Hold down Alt(Opt) and click on an area of hair close to where you will be painting. Doing this toggles to the Eyedropper tool; you've now sampled a foreground color for painting.

3. Make a brisk stroke that begins and ends at the edge of the actor's hair; you're painting an arc, as you can see from Figure 12.32.

4. Repeat steps 2 and 3 about five more times in different locations around the actor's hair.

5. Chances are that one or two of the strands will look too sharp, contrasted against the rest of the hair. In this event, choose the Blur tool, choose the smallest tip from the Brushes palette, run it once or twice over the strand of hair you painted.

6. Press Ctrl(⌘)+S; keep the file open.

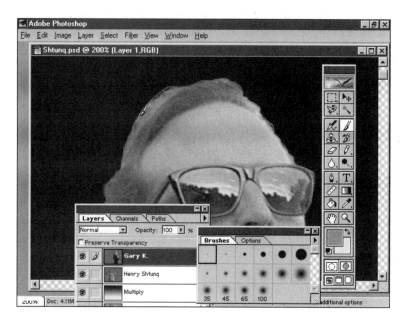

FIGURE 12.32 *Create arcs of color that begin and end at the edge of the actor's hair.*

SIZING AND ADDING TEXT

Photoshop 5's Type tool has improved dramatically. You can now see text in an image before you leave the Type Tool dialog box, and you can leave the Type Tool dialog box to position text before you click on OK.

Here's how to finish the poster with a catchy title:

ADDING TYPE TO YOUR IMAGE

1. Type **25** in the zoom percentage box and then press Enter (Return). Manually resize the window edges until the Shtunq.psd image takes up as little space as possible while you can still see the whole image.

2. Position the image in the upper left of the workspace. The Type Tool dialog box is large, and you want a clear view of both the dialog box and the image as you work.

3. Choose the Type tool and then click an insertion point in the image. The Type tool dialog box appears.

4. Choose a futuristic font from the Font drop-down list. The author used a shareware font, Steel Wool, but you can use Stop, Avant Garde, or Futura in this example.

5. In the Size field, type **125**. How can you know in advance the size of the type? You can't; this is the trial-and-error part of the assignment. The font size depends on the specific typeface you use because fonts are created to different relative sizes, and the difference becomes more obvious at large sizes.

6. Click on the Color swatch, and then choose white in the Color Picker. Click on OK to exit the Color Picker.

7. Type **ALIENS IN PLAID** in the text field. Click on the Fit in Window check box so that you can see the whole phrase, and highlight it if necessary (see Figure 12.33). The type immediately appears in the image window.

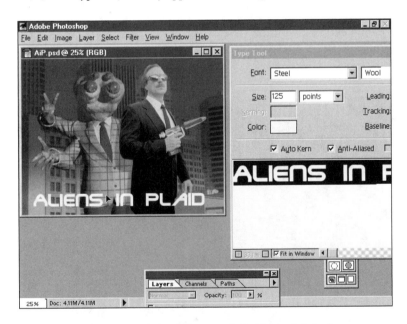

FIGURE 12.33 *Type appears in an image before you exit the Type tool dialog box.*

8. Highlight the entire phrase in the text field, and then drag the type in the image to center it. If the type is too wide, type a smaller size value in the Type tool dialog box.

9. When the type appears to fit within the image, click on OK in the dialog box to finalize the type.

10. Press Ctrl(⌘)+Alt(Opt)+S to save a copy of your work. Choose a directory where you want to save the copy, and then choose the TIFF format from the Save As drop-down list. Windows users can also check the Use Lower Case Extension option to make the file name easier to read in a folder window. Click on Save. You now have a copy of your work saved to hard disk and can share it with people who might not use Photoshop.

11. Press Ctrl(⌘)+S to save your work one last time. You can close the image at any time now; we're finished!

From start to finish, this fantasy composition has proved to be a challenge, but you succeeded because you followed a "recipe" for its creation (see Figure 12.34). With techniques you now know, you can create a composition featuring an alien or an elephant; the outcome will be rewarding because you understand how elements fit together.

FIGURE 12.34 *The final fantasy composition.*

SUMMARY

The following four key elements make a fantasy composition come alive:

- Proper emphasis on the foreground and background elements
- Accurate selection around those elements you combine in the composition
- A few fantasy elements
- A few photographic elements

When you perfect your personal talent by creating accurate selections, all the rest of the work comes easily. Get creative with the steps you've learned in this chapter, and start spinning off variations on this composition's theme.

Now that you have created your first photorealistic fantasy image, it's time to move on and create the *perfect* image. What is a "perfect" image? Is it in the eye of the beholder? Can you influence the perfection by retouching? The answers and more are coming up in the following chapter.

CHAPTER 13

CREATING A "PERFECT" IMAGE

Often, when we speak of a "perfect image," we mean that all the elements are in proper proportion, the colors stimulate the eye, and on some level we are emotionally provoked by such an image. Unfortunately, unless you have a camera hung around your neck 24 hours a day, and have an endless supply of film, the "perfect" picture might elude you. The sun could suddenly go behind a cloud, a stranger could walk in front of your camera...a million and one things can spoil that once-in-a-lifetime photo.

One of the most common problems with images is the sky—it's overcast and hazy, but the composition of the image is an award winner. On occasions like these, you can turn to Photoshop to turn a humdrum image into an eye-catcher through a little sky-grafting.

INTRODUCING "PARK BLAH"

The Parkblah.psd image in the Chap13 folder on the Companion CD has a lot of good things going for it. As you can see in Figure 13.1, there's a perfectly enchanting gazebo on the edge of a small pond that is lined by graceful weeping willows.

FIGURE 13.1 *A "perfect" picture is an inspired blend of color and composition.*

You'd never know, however, that Parkblah.psd was taken on a warm, breezy summer day. The sky simply leaves the viewer cold because it's a solid sheet of institutional blue! Regardless of the image you'll use to replace the sky, the very first thing you need to do is to accurately define the sky area, which is not difficult because of the consistency of its tone.

USING THE COLOR RANGE COMMAND TO SELECT THE SKY

The Color Range command is sort of like a global Magic Wand tool. It selects given areas, but it does so by color similarity throughout the selected area in the image. Now problem #1 is that the color of other elements in the image, such as the dome roof on the gazebo, are affected by the color of the sky. Objects always reflect the color of the light that is cast on them. In this case, the blue of the sky casts along the fringe of the trees and onto the gazebo. Ordinarily, it would be difficult to select only the sky from an image like this, because the color of the sky is part of the coloration of many of the other elements in the scene—the gazebo, the rocks, the railings, and the water. The solution? Create a selection by applying Quick Mask over only the top portion of the image, and *then* allow the Color Range command to do its thing within the selection.

In the following steps you'll isolate the sky from colors in the image that are similar in tone. Then you'll use the Color Range command to define areas around the trees. You'll then save the selection you've created to a channel where you'll fine tune the selection.

Here's how to define the sky area in Parkblah.psd:

USING SELECTION TOOLS, PATH TOOLS, AND QUICK MASK MODE

1. Open the Parkblah.psd image from the Chap13 folder on the Companion CD. Type **50** in the Zoom Percentage field and then press Enter (Return). Drag the window border away from the image so that you can select edge-to-edge within the document.

2. Double-click on the Quick Mask Mode icon toward the bottom of the toolbox. Click on the Color Indicates: Selected Areas button, and then click on OK to return to the workspace. The image is in Quick Mask mode now, and areas where you apply Quick Mask will become selected areas.

3. With the Rectangular Marquee tool, drag a marquee around the sky in the image, beginning at the top edge of the image and ending a little below the treetops. Press D (default colors), and then press Alt(Opt)+Delete (Backspace), as shown in Figure 13.2, to fill the marquee selection with Quick Mask overlay.

4. Drag a rectangle around the lamppost at the right of the image, and then press Delete, as shown in Figure 13.3. The light on the lamppost is too close in color to the sky, and you do not want it selected when you use the Color Range command.

5. The dome on the gazebo, too, is very close in color to the sky. Type **300** in the Zoom Percentage field, and then press Enter (Return). Scroll the image window so that you have a clear view of the gazebo dome.

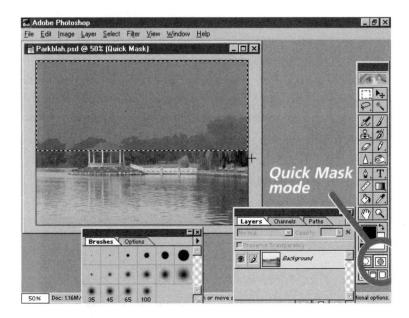

FIGURE 13.2 *Fill the selection with foreground color to apply the Quick Mask overlay "tint." Soon this tint will be converted to a selection marquee.*

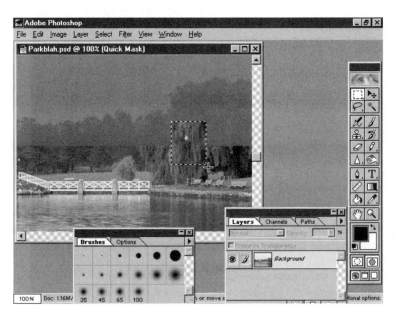

FIGURE 13.3 *Remove the Quick Mask tint from elements that are close in color to the sky.*

6. With the Pen tool, click an anchor point at the left of the dome where it meets the trees. Then click and drag a second anchor a little farther to the right on the edge of the gazebo dome, and then click and drag a third point where the dome meets the trees on the right of the image. Chances are that the path segments do not align perfectly with the edge of the dome; if this is the case, hold down Ctrl(⌘) to toggle to the Direct Selection tool, and move the anchors or steer the direction points associated with the anchor points so that the path segments line up with the edge of the dome, As shown in Figure 13.4.

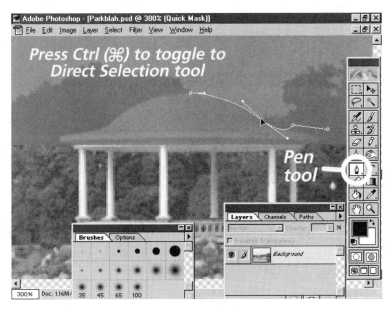

FIGURE 13.4 *Create an accurate edge to the gazebo's dome, using the Pen tool and the Direct Selection tool.*

7. After you've cleared the trees with your path, click down from the last point on the right, click across to the left, and then click up on the first anchor point to close the path.

8. Click on the Loads path as a selection icon at the bottom of the Paths palette, and then click on an empty space on the palette to hide the Work Path.

9. Press Delete (Backspace). As you can see in Figure 13.5, the dome of the gazebo is not covered now by the Quick Mask tint; therefore, it will not become part of the marquee selection you are defining.

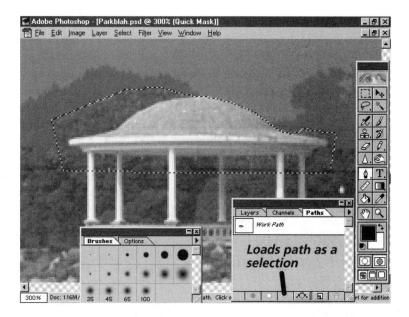

FIGURE 13.5 *Clear away unwanted Quick Mask by pressing Delete (Backspace) with the marquee selection loaded.*

10. Press Ctrl(⌘)+D to deselect the marquee. On the Paths palette, double-click on the Work Path title, and in the Save Path dialog box, name the path **Dome**. You'll be using this path later, and don't want to accidentally delete it. Click on OK to return to the image.

11. Click on the Standard Editing Mode icon, to the left of the Quick Mask icon. Doing this turns all the Quick Masked areas into a selection marquee.

12. Choose Select, Color Range.

13. In the Color Range dialog box, click the Eyedropper tool in the sky in the Parkblah.psd image, and then drag the Fuzziness slider to about 133 for a nice, tight selection of the sky and treetops, as shown in Figure 13.6. Do not be concerned that the gazebo's dome appears to be included in the selection (the white areas in the Color Range preview box). This is a case in which the preview is not entirely accurate. The active selection marquee in the image does *not* include the dome, which means that the Color Range command is prohibited from including the dome in the final selection it creates. Click on OK to make the selection.

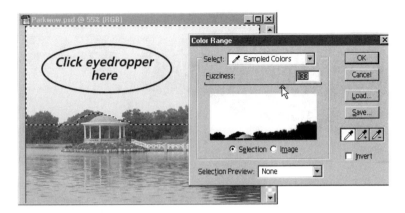

FIGURE 13.6 *Drag the Fuzziness slider to the right until the sky is white and the treetops are black.*

14. On the Channels palette, click on the Save selection as channel icon.

If the sky is white in the thumbnail icon of the Alpha 1 channel, and the rest of the image is black, press Ctrl(⌘)+D to deselect the marquee, double-click on the Alpha 1 title, and then choose the Color Indicates: Selected Areas button and click on OK.

15. Press Ctrl(⌘)+D to deselect the marquee, and then save the composition as Parkwow.psd, in Photoshop's native file format, to your hard disk. Keep the image open.

Now it's time for a little clean-up work on the Alpha 1 channel, which doesn't really merit a set of detailed steps. Click on the Alpha 1 channel to move your view to this channel, double-click on the Zoom tool to move your viewing resolution to 100% (1:1). Then, with the Eraser tool set to Paintbrush and using the tip to the far right of the top row, erase some of the black areas beneath the edge of the treetops, as shown in Figure 13.7. The Color Range command is good, but not perfect, at color-edge detection.

Now that you have an accurate selection of the sky, it's time to introduce a replacement sky to the composition.

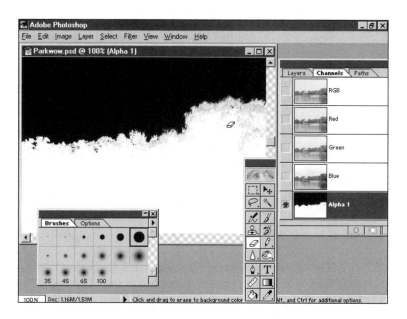

FIGURE 13.7 *Erase the black and off-white areas near the edge of the treetop selection in the alpha channel.*

ADDING A NEW SKY TO THE IMAGE

The authors have the proud distinction of living in an area with more cloudy skies than any other city in the United States. (Yes, it is cloudier and rainier here than in Seattle!) In Central New York we get a blue sky once in a blue moon, but basically it's clouds and haze day-in-and-day-out. The silver lining, so to speak, is that we *are* treated to some of the most fantastic clouds and sunsets you can imagine. We take lots of pictures of these clouds, and are pleased to share some of them with you in the Boutons/Scenes folder on the Companion CD.

We chose one particularly breathtaking sunset from our archives, Skydark.psd, that you will use in the following steps to replace the hazy, monochromatic sky in Parkwow.psd. The overall coloration Skydark is not a good match with Parkwow.psd, but in later steps you'll use Photoshop's Color Balance command to make a harmonious match between the two images. The next set of steps details how to get Skydark into the Parkwow area of the sky while maintaining the delicate outline of the treetops—all done *without* fringing around the trees (a *most* difficult assignment).

REPLACING THE SKY BY USING LAYERS AND SAVED SELECTIONS

1. Open the Skydark.psd image from the Chap13 folder on the Companion CD. Move it out of the way of Parkwow.psd, and make sure that you have a clear view of the Layers palette.

2. With Skydark.psd in the foreground in the workspace, drag its title from the Layers palette into the Parkwow image, as shown in Figure 13.8. This makes a copy of Skydark on a new layer in the Parkwow image.

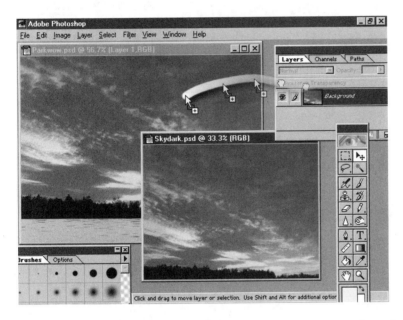

FIGURE 13.8   *To copy a layer to a different image window, you can drag its Layers palette title into the window.*

3. Press **5** on the keyboard (not the keypad) to reduce the opacity of the current layer—the Skydark layer—to 50%. Now you can see both layers.

4. With the Move tool, drag on the layer until the treetops of the Skydark image are a little below the sky area on the Background layer (Parkwow image), as shown in Figure 13.9.

5. Press 0 (zero) on the keyboard to restore the top layer to 100% opacity.

6. On the Channels palette, press Ctrl(⌘) and click on the Alpha 1 title to load the channel's contents as a selection marquee, as shown in Figure 13.10.

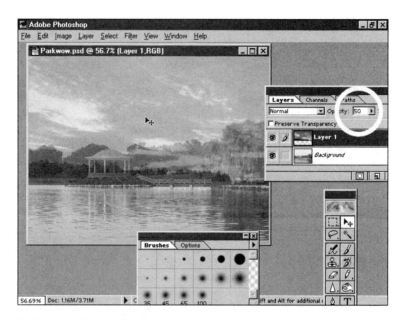

FIGURE 13.9 *Drag the partially opaque layer so that most of the dramatic sunset can be seen in the sky area of the Background layer.*

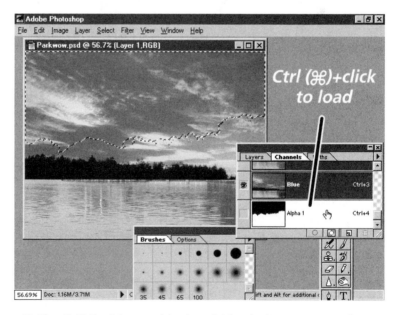

FIGURE 13.10 *Ctrl(⌘)+click on an alpha channel title to load its contents as a selection.*

You may expect that we're going to ask you to invert the selection in the next step so that the selected area becomes the bottom part of Skydark—the part of the image you don't need. You will be asked to invert the selection in a later step, but right now is a good time to modify the selection to avoid the dreaded fringing you commonly see in amateur Photoshop work.

7. Choose Select, Modify, and then choose Expand. In the Expand Selection dialog box, shown in Figure 13.11, type **2** in the pixels field, and then click on OK. What you're doing here is expanding the saved selection ever so slightly so that the new sky trims away the hazy blue fringing around the treetops on the Background layer.

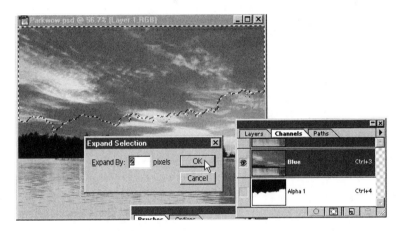

FIGURE 13.11 *Expand the selection you saved so that the area of the new sky slightly overlaps the treetops on the Background layer.*

8. Press Ctrl(⌘)+Alt(Opt)+D (Select, Feather). Then, in the Feather Selection dialog box, type **1** in the pixels field, as shown in Figure 13.12, and click on OK. By feathering the selection edge you've given Photoshop permission to soften the selection edge, which allows Photoshop to create a naturalistic transition between the selection on the layer and the Background image.

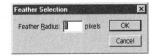

FIGURE 13.12 *Feather the selection edge by one pixel to soften the transition between the new sky and the treetops.*

9. Press Shift+F7 to invert the selection, and then press Delete (Backspace), to produce an image like that shown in Figure 13.13. Press Ctrl(⌘)+D to deselect the marquee.

FIGURE 13.13 *Delete the area of the sky image on Layer 1 that you do not want in the composition.*

Because the entire selection edge was feathered, the edge of the gazebo dome was feathered too. Right now it looks as though the sky has eaten into the dome. To restore the crisp, hard edge of the roof line, you need to delete the Skydark pixels that overlap onto the roof. This problem is easily corrected in the next two steps, using the path that you saved at the beginning of the chapter.

10. Zoom in to about 200% on the gazebo dome. On the Paths palette, click on the Dome path, and then click on the Loads path as selection icon. Click on an empty space on the Paths palette to hide the path.

11. Press Delete. As shown in Figure 13.14, the gazebo dome now has a sharp edge against the new sky. Press Ctrl(⌘)+D to deselect the marquee.

12. Press Ctrl(⌘)+S; keep the file open.

Most, but not all, of the treetops look perfectly integrated with the sky on Layer 1. In the next section you'll see how to correct some of the treetops.

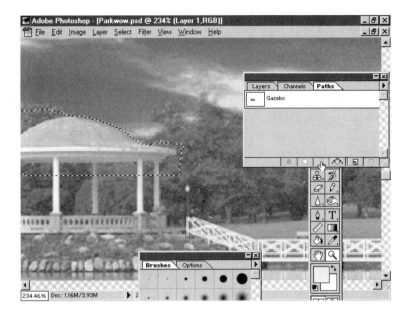

Figure 13.14 *Sharpen the feathered edge around the dome by loading the saved path and deleting the Skydark image area that overlaps the dome.*

Using the Sharpen Tool to Enhance Focus

Sometimes, solutions lead to problems. Although the expansion and feathering of the sky on Layer 1 took care of the hazy blue pixels at the edge of the trees on the Background layer, some fuzziness was introduced by the feathering of the selection.

Again, most of the trees blend in quite nicely with the new sky. Your mission in the steps to follow is to sharpen the edge of the most out-of-focus treetops in the image.

Adding Contrast to Part of an Image

1. Zoom to a 200% viewing resolution of the image, and maximize the image window.

2. Drag on the Toning tools flyout on the toolbox, and then choose the Sharpen tool. Although it's not shown in this book's figures, you might want to press Caps Lock to toggle the Sharpen tool cursor to a precision cursor.

3. On the Brushes palette, choose the far-right tip in the second row, and on the Options palette, set the Pressure to 20 and check the Use All Layers check box. The Sharpen tool will now sharpen "between layers," using image sources from both Layer 1 and the Background layer.

4. About 3 screen inches to the right of the dome, the treetops look a little fuzzy. Stroke over the edge of the trees in this area once, twice tops, as shown in Figure 13.15. *Do not* apply the Sharpen tool more than twice in the same area, or the area will begin to look as though lint was left on the image's negative.

FIGURE 13.15 *Apply the Sharpen tool to isolated areas of the image where the fuzziness of the tree-top edges looks phony.*

5. Press Ctrl(⌘)+S; keep the file open.

It's time for some color correction now, to be applied to both the Background image as well as the Skydark layer.

USING THE COLOR BALANCE COMMAND

In this composition the sky is too cold to support the gazebo, the lake, and the trees. You need to warm up the layer by moving blue tones to yellow, and green tones toward magenta. You will be surprised at how much color, particularly a warm orange, will appear on the layer after a few simple adjustments.

Here's how to use the Color Balance on the sky layer:

CORRECTING THE COLOR CAST

1. Press Ctrl(⌘)+B (Image, Adjust, Color Balance).

2. With the Midtones button selected, drag the Yellow/Blue slider to about –19.

3. Drag the Magenta/Green slider to about –8, as shown in Figure 13.16. You've done much to improve the warmth of the layer now, and more cloud detail should be apparent.

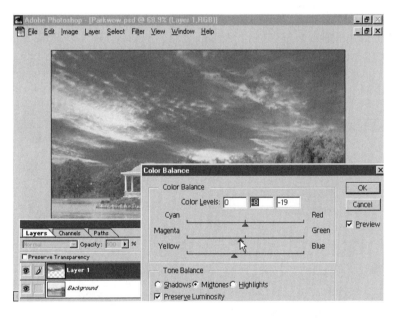

FIGURE 13.16 *Remove some of the green and blue color cast from the sky image, and watch it warm up.*

4. Click on the Shadows button in the Color Balance dialog box, and use your own artist's eye to see whether moving the sliders contributes, or pushes the overall warmth of the sky image too far. The author did not touch a thing in the Shadows region of the image, but this is a personal, artistic choice.

5. Click on the Highlights button, and experiment with the sliders. Again, the author did not feel it was necessary to adjust the color cast of the highlights in the image.

6. Click on OK to apply the changes.

You might notice now that although the colors in the sky are glorious, when contrasted against the foliage in the image, the sky dominates and makes the trees look washed out. Here's how to correct the cold color cast of the Background layer...

7. Click on the Background layer title on the Layers palette to make it the current editing layer.

8. Press Ctrl(⌘)+B, and then drag the Color Balance dialog box out of the way so you can see the trees.

9. With Midtones chosen, drag the Yellow/Blue slider to about −18, drag the Magenta/Green slider to about +18, and then drag the Cyan/Red slider to about +5, as shown in Figure 13.17. Although you can experiment with the Highlights and Shadows in the Color Balance dialog box, the author felt that Midtones corrections were enough to bring out the green, some density, and some warmth in the Background image.

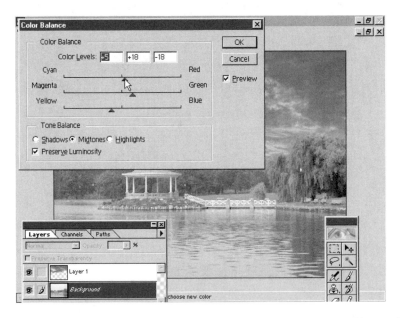

FIGURE 13.17 *Add some warmth and some green to the midtones of the Background layer, to better integrate this part of the image with the cloudy sunset.*

10. Press Ctrl(⌘)+S; keep the file open.

Can you see what looks patently fake in this image right now? It's not the color. It's the reality that the lake is reflecting the bridge and the gazebo, but not the dramatic sky! In the following section, you'll select the water in the lake to prepare it for sunset enhancement.

USING QUICK MASK TO CREATE A REALISTIC REFLECTION

You're faced with a bit of a dilemma when editing the water in Parkwow. You will place an upside-down copy of Skydark.psd in the water, but you don't want the Skydark image to overpower or totally cover up the water. Your goal is to place the sky's reflection into the water and still be able to see the gentle waves in the water as well as the existing natural reflections of the trees, gazebo, and bridge.

First things first. You need to define a rough outline of the lake, and to do this, you'll use the Paintbrush tool in Quick Mask mode:

DEFINING AN AREA THROUGH QUICK MASKING

1. Zoom in to about a 200% viewing resolution of the lake area.

2. Choose the Paintbrush tool, press D (default colors), and then choose the second-from-right tip in the top row on the Brushes palette.

3. Click on the Quick Mask mode icon on the toolbox.

4. Beginning at the right of the image, stroke along the edge of the lake, as shown in Figure 13.18. If you make a mistake and mask into the shore, press X and then stroke over the area; then press X again to make black the current foreground color.

5. Hold down the Spacebar to toggle to the Hand tool, and then drag right in the window to expose more of the unmasked image.

6. Continue painting along the edge of the lake until you hit the left edge of the image. Notice that in Figure 13.19 there's a little concave area of the lake that is not masked. This is okay; the brush tip is too large to paint into this area, and this tiny area will not feature a reflection of the sky in the finished composition.

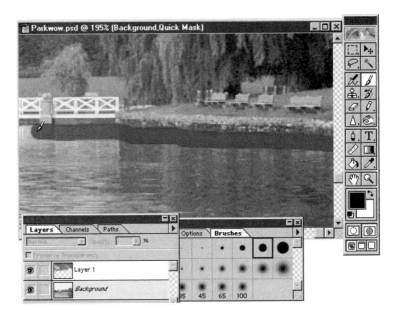

Figure 13.18 *Stroke along the inside edge of the lake to apply Quick Mask.*

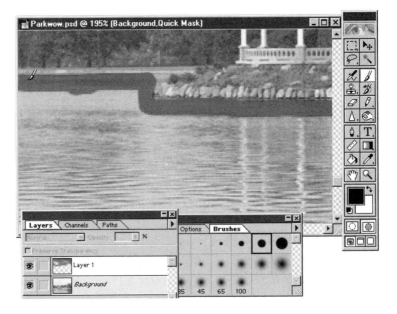

Figure 13.19 *Keep stroking along the inside edge of the lake area; ignore the shallow bend at the left of the image.*

7. At the left edge of the image, stroke straight down until you hit the bottom of the image. Then stroke right until you have made a wide Quick Mask selection along the bottom edge of the image.

8. At the right, bottom of the image, carefully stroke along the edge of the image until you arrive at the beginning point of your Quick Masking work.

9. Double-click on the Hand tool to move your view of the image so that you can see it in its entirety.

10. With the Lasso tool, hold Alt(Opt), and then click within the Quick Mask, creating a path that lies along the middle of the Quick Mask, as shown in Figure 13.20.

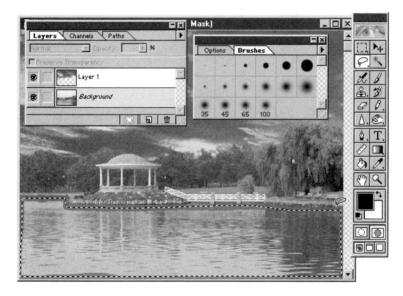

FIGURE 13.20   *Create a selection marquee whose edge lies inside the Quick Mask path you created.*

11. Press Alt(Opt)+Delete (Backspace), and then press Ctrl(⌘)+D to deselect the marquee.

12. Click on the Standard Editing mode button on the toolbox (to the left of the Quick Mask button), and then on the Channels palette, click on the Save selection as channel icon, as shown in Figure 13.21.

13. Press Ctrl(⌘)+D. Press Ctrl(⌘)+S; keep the file open.

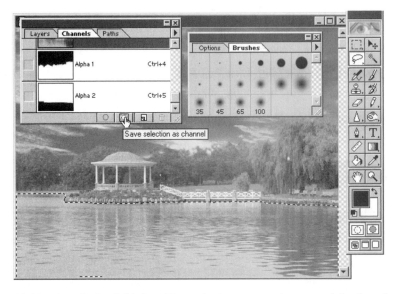

FIGURE 13.21 *Save the Quick Mask and Lasso selection you created to a new alpha channel.*

Your next stop in this editing odyssey is to add a magnificent sky reflection to the lake, without overshadowing the existing reflections.

ROTATING, COPYING, AND POSITIONING THE SKY

It's time for a return appearance of Skydark.psd, except this time you're going to flip the image to make it appear as though it's a reflection in the lake.

Here's how to add the reflection to the water in the image:

ADDING A REFLECTION OF THE SKY

1. Open the Skydark.psd image from the Chap13 folder on the Companion CD.

2. Choose Image, Rotate Canvas, and then choose Flip Vertical, as shown in Figure 13.22.

3. Reduce the window size of Skydark.psd, and get the Layers palette and Parkwow.psd in clear view.

4. With Skydark.psd as the foreground image in the workspace, drag the Background title from the Layers palette into Parkwow.psd, as shown in Figure 13.23.

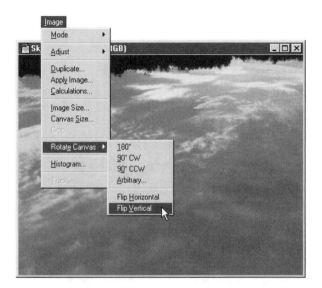

FIGURE 13.22 *Flip the image upside down to represent a reflection in the image.*

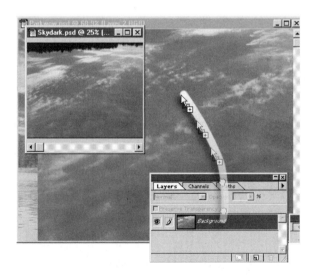

FIGURE 13.23 *Copy the upside-down image into the Parkwow.psd image window by dragging its title into the window.*

5. Close Skydark.psd without saving it.

6. Type **5** on the keyboard to decrease the opacity of the new layer in Parkwow.psd to 50%.

7. With the Move tool, move the image so that the (upside-down) treetops on the layer fall above the lake's outline, as shown in Figure 13.24.

FIGURE 13.24 *Drag the contents of Layer 2 upward until the tops of the trees are away from the lake's edge.*

8. Press 0 (zero) on the keyboard to restore Layer 2 to 100% opacity. Press Ctrl(⌘)+S; keep the file open.

It's time (late afternoon, by the looks of the image) to integrate the reflection with the rest of the composition.

ALPHA SELECTING AND LAYER MASKING THE LAKE

You'll now delete the part of Layer 2 that is obscuring the rest of the image, and also decrease the opacity of Layer 2 so that some of the Background layer can show through (making the lake look more like a lake and not a mirror!).

Here's how to edit Layer 2 into the composition:

COMPOSING THE LAKE REFLECTION

1. Double-click on the Hand tool to zoom your view of the image out so that you can see all of it onscreen.

2. On the Channels palette, press Ctrl(⌘) and click on the Alpha 2 title to load the selection you created of the lake.

3. Press Ctrl(⌘)+Shift+I (or Shift+F7, they're the same shortcuts) to invert the selection marquee, and then press Delete. As you can see in Figure 13.25, the gazebo, the bridge, the trees and sky are now visible, and the lake is perfectly mirror-like and a little surreal.

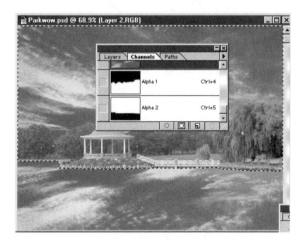

FIGURE 13.25   *Invert the loaded selection, and then delete the areas that are covering the trees, sky, and the gazebo.*

4. Press Ctrl(⌘)+D, and then on the Layers palette, drag the Opacity slider down to about 60%, as shown in Figure 13.26. *Now,* we're seeing a lake!

The effects of the reflection Layer 2 looks pretty good now, but what if you decrease the artificial reflection to 0% opacity closest to shore to allow the real reflection of the gazebo and the bridge to show through? This can be accomplished easily, using the Layer Mask feature in combination with the Linear Gradient tool...

5. Click on the Add layer mask icon at the bottom of the Layers palette. Layer 2 is now in Layer Mask Mode.

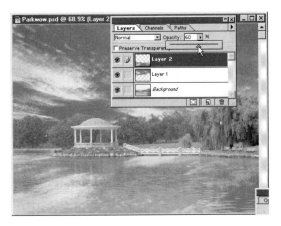

FIGURE 13.26 *Decrease the Opacity of the layer to allow some of the background lake to show through.*

6. Double-click on the Linear Gradient tool on the toolbox to choose the tool and to bring up the Options palette.

7. Choose Foreground to Background from the Gradient drop-down list on the palette.

8. Click, and then drag the Gradient tool straight down from slightly below the lake's top edge to about 1/4 screen inch from the bottom of the image, as shown in Figure 13.27. If you hold Shift while you drag, you'll constrain the Linear Gradient tool to 45° increments, one of which is exactly downward.

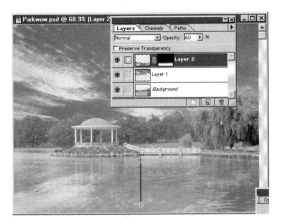

FIGURE 13.27 *Drag downward in the image to fully mask the layer at top, and fully expose the layer at the bottom.*

9. If you like what you see, click on the Layer Mask thumbnail on the Layer 2 title on the Layers palette, and then drag it into the trash icon. In the attention box that appears, click on Apply to make your changes to this layer permanent. If you want to try again, or experiment with a different gradient type, press Ctrl(⌘)+Z to remove the gradient you applied, and go back to step 8.

10. Press Ctrl(⌘)+S; keep the file open.

It is the author's opinion that this Layer 2 "reflection" doesn't need any color correction. What you *can* do, however, to make all of the water warmer and more inviting, is to change the color balance of the lake on the background layer. You've already got a saved selection of the lake in an alpha channel, so why not?

WARMING THE WATERS: CHANGING THE COLOR CAST IN A LAKE SCENE

Although you're free to use the Color Balance command in any way you like in the next set of steps, the author can tell you right now which colors need to be emphasized to make the lake look more tropical. By adding some cyan and green to the selected area of the lake on the Background layer, you'll make the water appear more inviting and also neutralize some of the cold color cast on Layer 2.

COLOR-CORRECTING FOR THE LAKE

1. Click on the Background layer title on the Layers palette to make it the current editing layer.

2. On the Channels palette, press Ctrl(⌘) and click on the Alpha 2 title to load the colored areas as a marquee selection.

3. Press Ctrl(⌘)+B, and with the Midtones button chosen, drag the Magenta/Green slider to about +30, and then drag the Cyan/Red slider to about −18, as shown in Figure 13.28.

4. Press Ctrl(⌘)+D. Press Ctrl(⌘)+S; keep the file open.

You're almost there! Although you've performed color corrections to individual components of the image, it's time to make a *global* color change to the image to bring all the individual components and their colors into a common, harmonious, and believable color scheme.

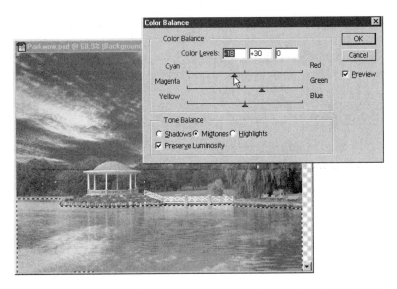

FIGURE 13.28   *Cyan and green will make the waters beneath Layer 2 (the reflection layer) look warmer and more inviting.*

USING THE VARIATIONS COMMAND TO CORRECT COLOR CAST

The Variations command is sort of like a collection of colored gels through which you can see what an image would look like if a specific color were used to tint the image. It's been emphasized throughout this book that the midtones in a photo are where most of the visual information is located, and this composite image is no exception. In the steps that follow, you'll tint, ever so slightly, the midtones in a flattened version of Parkwow.psd, to bring out contrast and make the warmth of the image a little more realistic (the trees are a little too green for the sunset lighting conditions).

Let's push the colors of the image as a whole a little bit more toward magenta, and move it a little farther away from green:

COLOR-CORRECTING THE ENTIRE IMAGE

1. (Optional) If you want to experiment with the individual layers in this image in the future—putting in different sky images, for example, or making different color-correction choices—choose Image, Duplicate, accept the default file name in the Duplicate Image dialog box by clicking on OK, and then close Parkwow.psd.

2. On the Layers palette, choose Flatten Image from the flyout menu.

3. Save the image as Parkwow.tif in the TIFF file format.

4. Choose Image, Adjust, and then choose Variations.

The seven images in the main field of the Variations box are arranged in a "color circle." Each variation has its color opposite 180° across from it. As you'll see, magenta is the color opposite of green, and you want just a little less green in the overall image, so...

5. Click on the Midtones button, drag the slider all the way to Fine, and then click on the More Magenta thumbnail in the dialog box, as shown in Figure 13.29. What Figure 13.29 *doesn't* show (because this is a black-and-white book) are the Original and Current Pick thumbnails next to each other at the top of the dialog box. You'll see onscreen that the Current Pick is more realistic in its colors, so click on OK to apply this color change.

6. Press Ctrl($\mathcal{H}$)+S. Take a look at your work; open Parkblah.psd from the Companion CD again and compare it to Parkwow.tif. Pretty impressive work you've done, eh? You can close the images at any time now.

Throughout this chapter, you've been asked to shift an area's color one way, and then shift another area another way, and finally, to put a mild magenta cast over the entire image. Isn't there some redundancy involved? Haven't you backtracked, and couldn't you have saved a few color-correcting steps? The answer is no, because the changes you've made are *progressive* changes—changes that you've applied to other changes. The color changes could not have been made in one step, nor could they be restored to their original state by applying further changes. The only way you have to go back to the original colors, or any of the intermediate color stages is to use the History palette's Allow Non-Linear History option.

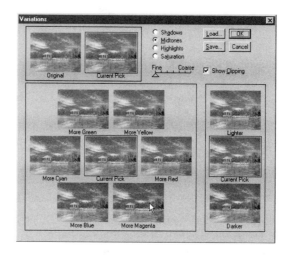

FIGURE 13.29 *Remove a little green and replace it with magenta in the midtones to make the image look more realistic.*

In Figure 13.30 (and in the color section of this book), you can see the finished image. It's a pretty "perfect" image now, isn't it?

FIGURE 13.30 *When a picture that's lacking a certain something meets Photoshop and the right resource material, the result can be a perfect image.*

SUMMARY

The author has used the term "perfect" in quotation marks several times in this chapter, to

- Annoy the very capable and diligent copy editors of this book, and…

- Make it a little more apparent that the word *perfect* can only be used in a relative sense in this world.

Can Parkblah.psd become "perfect" by using an image *other* than Skydark.psd? Of course it can; you can photograph any number of dramatic skies that play a visual counterpoint to the humble, gentle, yet enchanted elements in Parkblah.psd. The real trick to creating the perfect image is to realize what it is you want to visually communicate, supply the missing elements in the photograph you want to make perfect, and use the techniques in this chapter to disguise your handiwork. The editing in Parkwow.tif should go unnoticed by the viewing audience; they should only gaze at the beauty you helped created within the composition. The very best Photoshop work is invisible.

In Chapter 14, "Making Things Appear Small," you'll use your invisible grafting talents from this chapter, and apply your skills to making a "perfectly" plausible scene of a guy holding a 12" girl in the palm of his hand.

PART IV

EXTENDED USES FOR PHOTOSHOP

CHAPTER 14

MAKING THINGS APPEAR SMALL

Quick! Of the options listed below, which one would be the most sensible if asked the question, "Why would you want to make people 12" tall?

- *The world food supply would increase proportionately.*

- *Car pools could fit about 150 people in a single auto, thus reducing traffic and air pollution.*

- *There's something intrinsically funny about a picture of a full-sized person holding another person in the palm of his hand.*

All three answers are correct, but hopefully you've already guessed what this is leading up to. That's right. In this chapter, you will learn how to create the image shown in Figure 14.1.

FIGURE 14.1   *Hold me, squeeze me, but don't drop me!*

Imagine the design opportunities that lie ahead after you've mastered the knack of making people small! Spokespeople can climb under the hood of a car; they can tell an audience that everything in a store is reduced; you name it.

But before you run off with your camera to get the stock photography for this illusion, let's examine what you should do to *prepare* photographic conditions, so that the time you spend editing in Photoshop is well-spent.

SCALE, CAMERA ANGLE, AND LIGHTING

In Figure 14.2, you can see the images you'll use in this chapter to produce the palm-sized girl. Notice that both images are viewed in Photoshop at 33%, and you have a pretty good idea that the tinygal.tif image's contents (the girl) will fit nicely in the bighand.tif image.

When you set out to take your pictures, keep in mind the field size of the subject through the viewfinder. Scaling the minuscule person in Photoshop *after* the picture has been taken makes no sense when:

- It's easier to back away from the person when you're photographing him or her.

- By resizing the image of the person who is to be tiny in the composite image, you will degrade the quality of the image, which most certainly will need sharpening.

FIGURE 14.2   *Plan your photography so that both elements scale correctly at 1:1 size.*

Get it right through the viewfinder; let the big person in the picture take up most of the frame, and then take the picture of the small person from a distance. That is the way this chapter's example images were taken; much of the background of tinygal.tif was cropped out to conserve file size.

Scale is only one factor to keep in mind. Camera angle is equally important. You'll notice that both bighand.tif and tinygal.tif were taken with the people perpendicular to the viewing plane of the camera. It's a natural faux pas to take all images at your natural height standing up. For the tinygal.tif image, the author had to get on his knees to make the woman's attitude toward the camera a flat one. If the author had stood, the camera angle would have captured the crown of her head, and something phony would appear when the two images were composited.

TIP

When you plan to composite pictures, always take them from the same horizon line, even if you have to change your own height to take the picture.

Finally, matching the lighting between the two images is critical to maintaining visual credibility when the pictures are melded. The author has to confess here that, lighting-wise, tinygal.tif is a good match, yet not a perfect one, for the big-hand.tif image. You'll notice that the woman's face is brilliantly illuminated because the surrounding shrubbery didn't shade it, but that nothing in big-hand.tif is brilliantly illuminated—for a very simple reason. During our photographic session, the clouds came out when bighand.tif was taken. Generally, try to pick either an overcast day or a day without a cloud in the sky when you take the two pictures you want to composite. Take them within moments of each other, and make sure that the sun or other source of illumination is in the same place, shining in the same direction in both pictures.

Actually, the brilliant tinygal.tif image works out okay in this chapter's composition because it attracts attention to the tiny gal, setting her off against the sea of leaves in the background and the flatly illuminated big guy. The brilliant face becomes a contrapuntal element that helps direct the viewer's eye through the scene and helps balance the composition. The author doesn't recommend that you make this "fortunate" mistake in your own work, but as you'll see, the illusion of a tiny woman in the palm of a big guy's hand is sustained.

SEPARATING THE WOMAN FROM THE BACKGROUND

Obviously, the tiny gal needs to be separated from her surroundings to be able to be placed in the bighand.tif image. Shortly, you'll open the tinygal.tif file and work with it, but before proceeding, let's take a look at the the tools you'll be working with in Photoshop.

The edge of the tiny gal is composed of several different focuses. Her shirt is very clearly defined against the background. The edge of her pants is less clearly defined because her jeans are of brushed cotton. Also, her arms are not as clearly defined along the edges because flesh absorbs ambient light from the surroundings and tends to blend into background areas when photographed.

Therefore, our course of action is to use a *number* of selection tools to isolate the tiny gal from the background.

SETTING UP THE IMAGE AS A LAYER AND WORKING WITH TRANSPARENCY OPTIONS

The easiest way to separate the girl from the background is to convert the image to a single-layer image; then the areas you remove around her will become transparent. Additionally, the *transparency grid*—the checkerboard that appears wherever there is transparency in an image—is unsuitable for your editing work. Too many areas are close in tone to the gray-and-white transparency grid, but this is okay; you'll customize the grid in the next few steps.

You'll begin this surreal composition by setting up the tinygal.tif image for editing:

LAYER AND TRANSPARENCY GRID EDITING

1. Open the tinygal.tif image from the CHAP14 folder on the Companion CD. The zoom size is unimportant at this point.

2. Press F7 to display the Layers palette, and then double-click the title "Background."

3. In the Make Layer dialog box, simply click OK. The background is now a layer, surrounded by transparency. Save the file to your hard disk as tinygal.psd, in Photoshop's native format, as shown in Figure 14.3.

NOTE

The figures in this chapter might appear a little odd when displaying transparency information. Although the color recommended here is a good choice, it reproduces poorly in a black-and-white book. So wherever you see very light areas in the following figures, imagine that this is the color of the transparency grid. Don't be put off or confused by the apparent lightness of the grid as it appears in this book.

FIGURE 14.3 *Turn the ordinary TIFF image file into a layer file.*

4. Press Ctrl(⌘)+K, and then press Ctrl(⌘)+4 to display the Transparency & Gamut dialog box.

5. Click the white color swatch; then, in the Color Picker, choose H:282, S:38%, and B:100%. Click OK to return to the Preferences dialog box.

6. Click the gray color swatch; then, in the Color Picker, choose H:282, S:38%, and B:100%. Click OK to return to the Preferences dialog box. The Preferences box should look something like Figure 14.4 now.

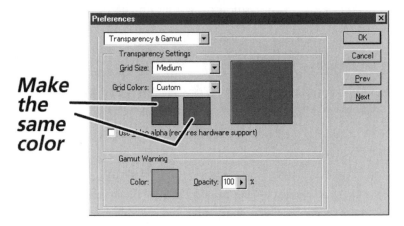

FIGURE 14.4   *Create a solid color for the transparency grid.*

7. Click OK to return to the workspace; keep the file open.

There's a reason you were asked to pick a solid, medium purple for the transparency grid in the preceding steps. Because this color is not to be found in the tinygal.psd image, it will be easy to see the edge you'll create around the girl.

BEGINNING THE SILHOUETTING WORK

Here's the strategy you'll use for trimming away all areas of the image that do not contain the girl. First, you'll work clockwise around the girl's silhouette, starting with the right side of her hair. Although the hair's edge is very well defined in this image (fortunately, there wasn't a breeze when the photo was taken!), you will want to use a small brush tip and zoom in to about 400% viewing resolution to perform your work. The "lane" you create at the outside edge of the girl's hair will be a narrow one that you'll broaden outward later, using the Polygon Lasso tool.

You will be working in Layer Mask mode to create the outline around the girl. If you make any mistakes, press X to make the current foreground color white, and then paint over the mistake to restore this image area.

All set to go?

LAYER MASKING ALONG THE HAIR'S EDGE

1. Type **400** in the Zoom Percentage box and then press Enter (Return).

2. Hold down the Spacebar to toggle to the Hand tool, and then drag in the image window until you can see the girl's hair to the right of the image.

3. Press B (Paintbrush tool), and then on the Brushes palette, choose the second-from-left, top tip.

4. On the Layers palette, click the Add layer mask icon at the bottom of the palette.

5. Press D (default colors). Beginning at the part in the girl's hair, stroke outside the hair, following the curve downward, until your image looks like Figure 14.5.

FIGURE 14.5 *Apply black color to "erase" the outside edge of the girl's hair to transparency.*

6. If necessary, hold down the Spacebar to move your view down and to the right.

7. Continue stroking until you reach the girl's earring.

8. Choose the Polygon Lasso tool, and then click within the transparency (the medium purple that's showing) all the way from the earring to the top of her head. Then click points far away from the girl's hair to encompass a large area of unwanted background image.

9. Close the polygon selection by clicking the first point you clicked near the earring, as shown in Figure 14.6.

FIGURE 14.6 *Encompass a substantial part of the image that you will not use in the composition.*

10. Press Alt(Opt)+Delete (Backspace) and then press Ctrl(⌘)+D to deselect the marquee.

11. Press B (Paintbrush tool) and then paint around the edge of the earring. Stop when you've begun to paint around the top of the girl's collar.

12. Repeat steps 8–10 so that more of the background is hidden. At this point, you should save, but do keep the file open.

Now, we're down to some very well-defined areas of the image—areas in the girl's blouse. And this calls for another editing strategy: using the Pen tool to define selections.

USING THE PEN TOOL TO SELECT THE EDGE OF A BLOUSE

If you're not familiar with the Pen tool, the Direct Selection tool, and the Convert Point tools, it is recommended that you put a bookmark right here, and work through Chapter 6, "Selections, Layers, and Paths." The following steps are not demanding of your skills, but you will want to define a path that falls precisely on the edge of the girl's collar and sleeve.

Here's how to handle selections on edges of well-defined areas in photos:

CREATING A PATH ON THE EDGE OF THE BLOUSE

1. Choose the Pen tool from the toolbox, and then press Tab to clear the palettes and toolbox from the screen.

2. Hold down the Spacebar and drag in the image window so that you have a clear view of the girl's shirt collar and sleeve.

3. Click an anchor point at the edge of the collar, a little inside of where you exposed transparency in the previous steps.

4. Click and drag a second point on the collar, dragging the direction handle for the second anchor to steer the path segment so that it conforms to the edge of the collar. You can use as many anchors and short path segments as you like in this example; you're striving for an accurate selection, and the folds and turns in the cloth will necessitate many anchors and path segments.

5. Continue downward until you're at the bottom edge of the screen.

6. Click an anchor to the far right of the screen, and then click an anchor straight up so that it is horizontally a little above your first anchor point.

7. Close the path by clicking the first anchor point, as shown in Figure 14.7.

FIGURE 14.7   *Create an accurate selection on the left side, and then encompass areas that will be removed on the right side.*

8. Press F7. This displays only the Layers grouped palette. Click the Paths tab.

9. Click the Loads path as a selection icon, and then click an empty space on the palette to hide the path.

10. Press Alt(Opt)+Delete(Backspace). You've removed another hunk of the background and added more to your silhouette work, as shown in Figure 14.8.

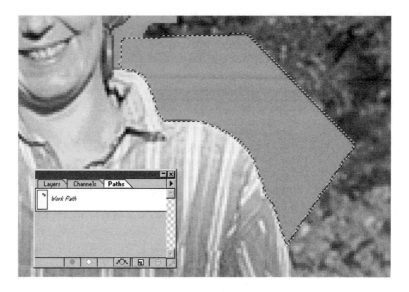

FIGURE 14.8   *Fill the selection area with foreground black to hide it.*

11. Press Ctrl(⌘)+D to deselect the marquee, press Ctrl(⌘)+S, and keep the file open.

Don't put that Pen tool away yet! In fact, press Tab now to display the toolbox because in the next section of this chapter you'll be using more than one tool in the Pen tool group to define the inside of the girl's arm.

USING THE PEN AND CONVERT POINT TOOLS

The Pen tool produces only smooth anchors when you draw with it. This means that path segments that pass through the anchor have continuity—the angle doesn't change. This presents somewhat of a challenge in the steps that follow because the area you'll work on next, the inside of the arm on the right of the image, has some concave areas whose anchor points begin a new direction for path segments. Not to worry; this is what the Convert Point tool is for—for changing the anchor angle through which path segments pass.

Although the steps in this chapter don't include explicit instructions for attaining the best view for your editing work, here are a few tips:

- You might want to stay zoomed in to 400% throughout this assignment. To make it easier to move clockwise around the larger-than-screen image, press F8 to display the Navigator palette, and then drag your way around in the Proxy preview window after you've completed a section on editing.

- Palettes pile up and eventually clog your view of the image window. If you're going to be working with, say, the Pen tool for a while (hint: you are), there's no reason for the palettes or the toolbox to be onscreen. Press the Tab key to hide all the palettes and the toolbox; press Tab again to restore them.

- Maximize your view of the image in the file window. Windows users should click the Maximize/Restore icon on the title bar, and Macintosh users should drag on the Size box to fill the screen with the image.

- The standard icon cursors are wonderful for telling you at a glance which tool you're using, but occasionally their size can get in the way of your editing view. Press the Caps Lock key to switch standard icon cursors to the precision crosshairs in this event. And *do not* type anything until you've pressed Caps Lock again, OR yOU mIGHT BE IN fOR A sURPRISE.

The figures also illustrate these tips.

Now that you have all the tips, let's tackle the inside of the arm area:

USING A COMBINATION OF VECTOR TOOLS TO CREATE A SELECTION

1. Hold down the Spacebar, and then drag in the window until the inside of the girl's arm and pant leg are centered onscreen.

2. With the Pen tool, click an anchor point where the girl's hand meets her pant leg. You're going to build this path in a counterclockwise direction.

3. Click and drag a second anchor point where there is a bend in the outline of the girl's arm. Drag the direction handle that is under your cursor right now to steer the path segment between the first and second anchor points so that the path segment is aligned to the edge of the inside of the girl's arm.

4. Continue clicking and dragging new anchor points, moving counterclockwise and eventually downward on the edge of the pants as you've drawn path segments at the edge of the sleeve and the blouse.

5. When a sharp dip is apparent on the edge of the pant leg, click and drag an anchor point, and then stop.

6. Choose the Convert Point tool from the Pen tool flyout on the toolbox.

7. Drag upward on the bottom direction handle, and then release the cursor. What you've done is to redefine the property of the anchor point. The following path segment can now be drawn at a discontinuous angle to the path segment that precedes it, as illustrated in Figure 14.9.

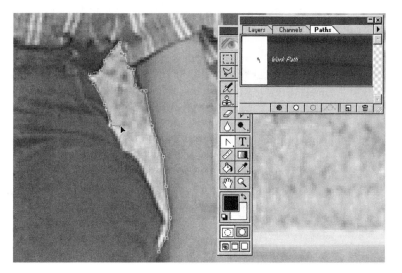

FIGURE 14.9 *Create an anchor point with a sharp angle-change property, using the Convert Point tool.*

8. Go get the Pen tool from the Pen tool flyout, click the anchor point you edited in step 7, and then click and drag another anchor point along the edge of the girl's pant leg. If the edited anchor point sends the path segment off course, hold Ctrl(⌘) to toggle to the Direct Selection tool, click the anchor to expose the direction handles, and then click on the bottom direction handle to steer the path segment to conform to the pant leg's edge.

9. Click the last anchor point you drew, and then click and drag another anchor below the previous one.

10. Close the path by clicking once on the first anchor point you drew. At this point, if there are any misplaced anchors, use the Direct Selection tool to move them. And if any path segments aren't directly on the edge of the selection area, click the anchor point with the Direct Selection tool to expose the direction handles, and then drag on a handle to steer the path to align with the edge of the selection.

11. Click the Loads path as selection icon at the bottom of the Paths palette, and then click an empty area of the palette to hide the path.

12. Press Alt(Opt)+Delete (Backspace); the area will be replaced with transparency, as shown in Figure 14.10.

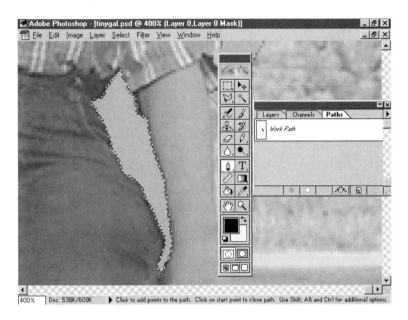

FIGURE 14.10   *Define a selection from the path you created, and then remove the area.*

13. Press Ctrl(⌘)+D to deselect the marquee. Press Ctrl(⌘)+S; keep the file open.

The outside edge of the girl's arm needs to be masked now; for this, you'll turn back to the Paintbrush tool.

FURTHER TRIMMING AWAY AT THE IMAGE

As mentioned earlier, human skin does not always provide a clear edge against a background when photographed. Too much ambient light often casts into the skin, and hair on skin further tends to blur the edge of an exposed arm, leg, or torso.

In the steps that follow, you'll paint away at the edge of the girl's arm down to her hand. The hand will require a different technique for masking, so let's get to the task at hand now:

Masking the Edge of the Arm

1. Choose the Paintbrush tool, and then carefully paint a line along the outside edge of the girl's arm, as shown in Figure 14.11. You can paint along the edge right down to the girl's pinkie finger, and stop there.

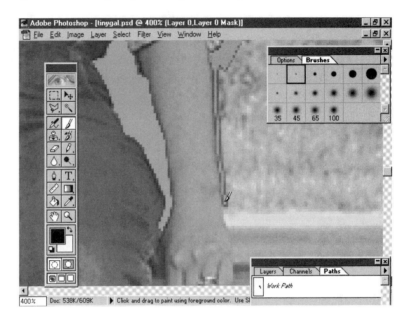

Figure 14.11   *Use the Paintbrush tool to create a soft edge along the skin on the girl's arm.*

2. Press Ctrl(⌘)+S; keep the file open.

Using the Pen Tool on Hands

When it comes to defining an accurate selection in this image, the hands are perhaps the most intricate part. They are relatively small (they are made up of very few pixels). And you need to create both convex and concave areas along the hand's edge.

Here's how to perform the edge work on the girl's left hand:

MAKING A SELECTION AROUND THE HAND

1. Type **500** in the Zoom Percentage box and then press Enter (Return).

2. With the Pen tool, click an anchor point about half a screen inch below the girl's index finger, midway between her thigh and her index finger. You're going to be working counterclockwise to make the path.

3. Click (don't drag) an anchor point to the right of the first anchor, making this second anchor horizontally parallel to the first anchor point and about one screen inch to the right of the girl's pinkie finger.

4. Click a third point within the transparency you created with the Paintbrush tool in the previous example. Sneak a peek at Figure 14.12 to see the location of these points you've clicked.

5. Click and then drag downward on the edge of the pinkie finger. Use as many anchor points as you need to reach the tip of the girl's fingernail.

6. As you draw the path around the girl's hand, you will need to create sharp direction-change anchors. Instead of stopping to get the Convert Point tool at every concave area of the edge of her fingers, simply click and drag anchors, and then go back to these points later. Hold Alt(Opt) as you click an anchor with the wrong direction property (doing this toggles to the Convert Point tool), click and hold on the direction handle that appears, and then steer the path segment associated with the anchor point so that it falls directly on the edge of the girl's fingers.

7. When you've reached the top of the girl's index finger, click a point, and then click (don't drag) another point at the edge of her pants. Click a point below the previous anchor, and then close the path by clicking the first point you created. Figure 14.12 shows the location and shape of the path.

8. On the Paths palette, click the Loads path as a selection icon, and then click an empty area of the palette to hide the path.

9. Press Alt(Opt)+Delete (Backspace). Press Ctrl(⌘)+D to deselect the marquee.

10. Press Ctrl(⌘)+S; keep the file open.

TIP

If you're comfortable memorizing keyboard modifiers, you don't need the toolbox onscreen to access the Pen tool, the Direct Selection tool, and the Convert Point tool. With the Pen tool chosen, here's what you can do:

- Hold Ctrl(⌘) to toggle to the Direct Selection tool.
- Hold Alt(Opt) to toggle to the Convert Point tool.

You might find that remembering these shortcuts helps you work faster because you won't need to constantly select different tools.

It's time for a little independent study here. With the Polygon Lasso tool, click in the transparent regions you've exposed, create a marquee selection that encompasses the background but not the girl, and then press Alt(Opt)+Delete (Backspace) to remove large areas of the background. Always remember to press Ctrl(⌘)+D afterward, because an active marquee selection can accidentally be moved, and then there's the possibility of deleting areas you do not want deleted.

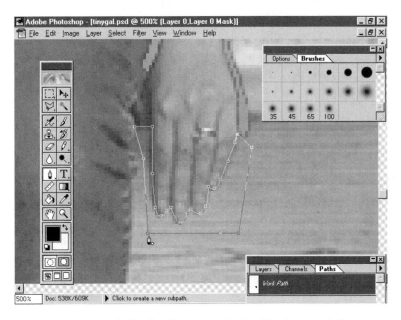

FIGURE 14.12 *Create a path that describes the outside edge of the fingers and also encompasses some unwanted background areas.*

EDITING THE PANTS AND THE SHOES

You'll notice that both of the girl's thumbs are hidden by the fence she's sitting on. This is okay. You do not need to have these areas to work with in the final composition; the missing areas will look as though they are hidden by the hand in the bighand.tif image.

Your next stop is the girl's pant leg and shoes. For this work, you will use the Paintbrush tool, with the same tip size you've used all along:

MASKING SOFT-EDGED AREAS WITH THE PAINTBRUSH TOOL

1. With the Paintbrush tool, start painting over areas between the girl's thigh and hand.

2. Paint an edge down the outside of the pant leg. Take your time on this one; as you can see in Figure 14.13, the background and the pants begin to take on the same tone as you proceed downward in the photograph.

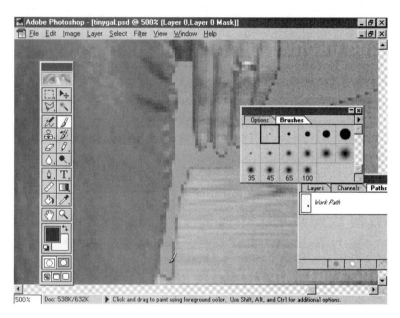

FIGURE 14.13   *Carefully paint masking along the outside edge of the pant leg.*

3. Hold down the Spacebar to toggle to the Hand tool, and then drag upward to reveal more pant leg area to be masked. Release the Spacebar.

4. Zoom out to 400% viewing resolution, and then paint strokes similar to those shown in Figure 14.14. Do not attempt to paint over the triangle formed by the angle of the shoes. Because the Paintbrush tool uses anti-aliasing (softening around the edges), you cannot be certain that you'll completely mask large areas by using such a small brush.

5. With the Polygon Lasso tool, click points around the triangle of background, and then press Alt(Opt)+Delete (Backspace), as shown in Figure 14.15.

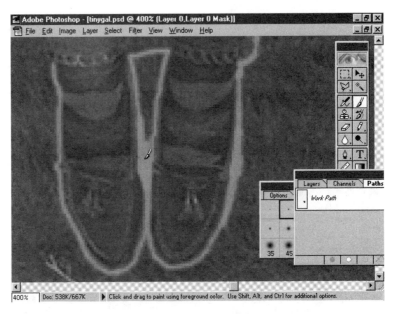

FIGURE 14.14 *Use a stroke of a single width to define the edges of the shoes.*

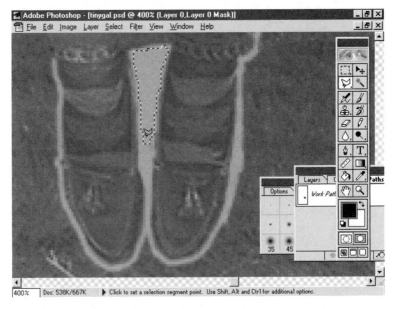

FIGURE 14.15 *Use the Polygon Lasso tool to remove large areas of the background.*

6. With the Paintbrush tool, mask the area of the girl's legs up to her knees. Now, because the edge where her knees meet forms a concave angle, you need to go a little farther into the knee area than you might want, press X to make white the foreground color, and then restore the areas you want saved in the image. Don't forget to press X when you're finished so that black is again the current foreground color.

7. Press Ctrl(⌘)+S; keep the file open.

ROUGH MASKING AROUND THE PANTS AND THE OTHER HAND

The left side of the image needs a lot of "coarse" masking work. Before you start using the Pen tool to make precise selections in the hand area, you must first use the Paintbrush tool to define the edge of the leg and the area around the girl's right hand.

CONTINUING THE MASKING EDGE

1. Hold down the Spacebar and drag to the right and up so that you can see the girl's pant leg and her right hand.

2. With the Paintbrush tool, continue following the edge of the pant leg until you reach the area where the pant leg meets the hand.

3. Stroke downward, about 1/4 screen inch from the girl's index finger, and then stop.

4. With the Polygon Lasso tool, trace within the transparency; when you reach the hand area, move farther away from the hand, and encompass unwanted background areas. Close the selection marquee at the point where you started.

5. Press Alt(Opt)+Delete (Backspace) to mask this area, as shown in Figure 14.16. Press Ctrl(⌘)+D to deselect the marquee.

6. Press Ctrl(⌘)+S; keep the file open.

It's worth mentioning here that all this time, the image is (and has been) in Layer Mask mode, and anything you've done that you didn't mean to do can be restored. Simply make white the current foreground color, and paint away at areas you might want to restore. Nothing has been permanently deleted from the image yet.

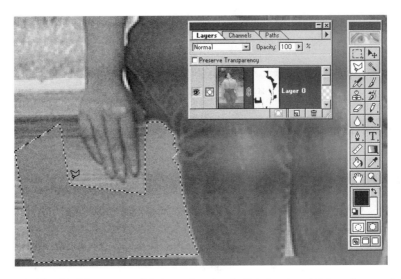

Figure 14.16 *Mask large areas of the image by using the Paintbrush and Polygon Lasso tools to define the selection.*

Masking Around the Other Hand

There are no steps in this section that detail how to mask around the girl's other hand. The technique you use is identical to the one you used to mask around the first hand. In Figure 14.17, you can see that the Pen tool has been used to define the finger edges, and a large outside perimeter has been defined to encompass the background.

After you've closed the path—that's right—click the Loads path as selection icon on the Paths palette, hide the path by clicking an empty palette space, and then press Alt(Opt)+Delete (Backspace). Be sure to deselect the marquee when you've finished this maneuver.

Deleting Around the Outside of the Arm

Again, the steps to follow might seem familiar. The outside edge of the girl's arm needs masking, and this presents yet another perfect opportunity to define the arm's edge and to remove unwanted background areas.

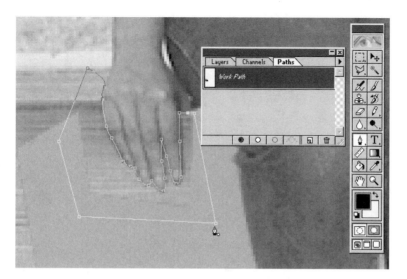

FIGURE 14.17   *Create an edge around the fingers, using the Pen and associated Pen tools, and make the interior of the path enclose a large area of background.*

Here's how to mask around the area from the girl's hand to her sleeve:

AND YET MORE MASKING!

1. Hold down the Spacebar, and then drag downward in the image window so that you have a clear view of the girl's right arm, plus some of the masking you performed around her hand.

2. With the Paintbrush tool, stroke along the outside edge of the arm, beginning in a masked area and moving upward to her shirt sleeve, as shown in Figure 14.18.

3. With the Polygon Lasso tool, click points within the transparency you created in step 2, and then close the selection marquee to encompass a large area of background.

4. Press Alt(Opt)+Delete (Backspace), and then press Ctrl(⌘)+D to deselect the marquee.

5. Press Ctrl(⌘)+S; keep the file open.

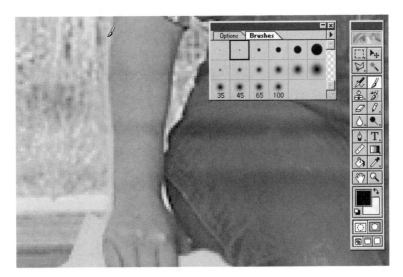

FIGURE 14.18 *Continue the masking edge you've created, up to the shirt sleeve.*

TWO TOOLS: ONE SELECTION GOAL

In the following steps, you'll remove an area between the girl's wrist and her pants. The area is quite small, and you can create a freehand selection with the Lasso tool to mark this region. Also, the inside of the girl's arm—the area whose far side is her waist—must also be selected and masked. To do this, you'll use the Pen tool exactly as you did earlier with the opposing "inside" area in the image.

It should come as no surprise that as bilaterally symmetrical human beings, we have the same, mirrored areas in photographs, which naturally would require the same selection techniques. Hey, this would make a pretty good Tip, huh?

Let's begin with the small crescent at the girl's wrist that needs to be deleted, and then move on to larger areas:

USING THE LASSO AND THE PEN TOOL TO DEFINE AREAS

1. Type **600** in the Zoom Percentage field, and then press Enter (Return).

2. Scroll the window so that you can see the girl's wrist.

3. Drag on the Lasso tool icon on the toolbox and then choose the (regular) Lasso tool.

4. Create a selection marquee that encompasses the area of background you want to mask, as shown in Figure 14.19. If you don't get it perfect on the first try, press Ctrl(⌘)+D to deselect the marquee, and try again.

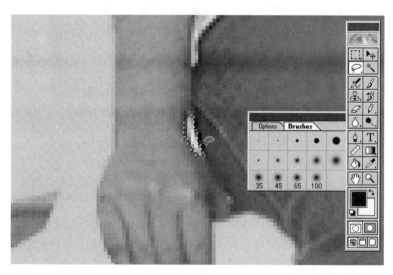

FIGURE 14.19   *Use the Lasso tool in its freehand mode to select the area that needs masking.*

5. Press Alt(Opt)+Delete (Backspace), and then press Ctrl(⌘)D.

6. Zoom out to 400% viewing resolution. Scroll your view so that you can see the inside of the girl's arm.

7. With the Pen tool, click and drag anchors that fall on the edge of the inside of the girl's arm and outside her pants. Use the Direct Selection and Convert Point tools when necessary to increase the accuracy of the path along the edge of this image area.

8. Click the Loads path as a selection icon, as shown in Figure 14.20.

9. Click an empty area of the Paths palette to hide the work path, and then press Alt(Opt)+Delete (Backspace).

10. Press Ctrl(⌘)+D; press Ctrl(⌘)+S; keep the file open.

You're into the home stretch now! Only the sleeve, the shirt collar, and the other side of the girl's hair remain to be defined.

TIP

Most of Photoshop's tools, including the Polygon Lasso tool, will automatically pan the image window when you drag your cursor off the image window's edge. This might lead to some initial disorientation, but it also means that you can encompass far larger areas of the superfluous background in this assignment than you can view at one time.

If you lose the original click point for the Polygon Lasso tool, double-click anywhere in the image, and the selection will close. Then you might want to zoom out to make sure that your selection does not include anything you want to remain in the image.

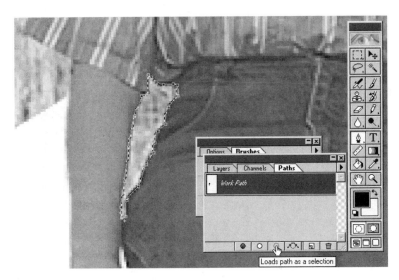

FIGURE 14.20 *Turn the path you created into a selection marquee.*

FAMILIAR TOOLS, IDENTICAL TECHNIQUES

This section, like one of the earlier ones, does not contain any steps. You're already comfortable with the Pen tool through hands-on practice, and it is the tool you'll use to select around the edge of the girl's sleeve.

As you can see in Figure 14.21, the edge of the sleeve has been defined, using the Pen tool, and the area the path encloses contains more unwanted background.

Create a path similar to that shown, click the Loads path as a selection button, and then press Alt(Opt)+Delete (Backspace). Press Ctrl(⌘)+D to deselect the marquee selection.

USING THE PAINTBRUSH TOOL TO FINISH THE MASKING

You might have noticed that in certain areas within the tinygal.psd image, you get equivalently sharp results whether you use the Paintbrush tool or the Pen tool to define a selection area. This happens because the tiny gal is composed of a relatively small number of pixels, and along wide stretches of edge area, such as the pants and the blouse, you can't make severe mistakes with your masking work.

FIGURE 14.21   *A clearly defined edge calls for the use of the Pen tool.*

In the steps that follow, you'll complete your clockwise masking efforts, beginning at your starting place; the top of the girl's hair. Here's how to finish the edge work:

USING THE PAINTBRUSH TOOL TO MASK OTHER AREAS

1. Hold down the Spacebar and drag down and to the right so that you can see the top of the sleeve, the shoulder, and part of the girl's hair.

2. With the Paintbrush tool, take your time and make continuous strokes that mark the outside edge of first the sleeve, then the shoulder, and then the collar of the girl's shirt.

3. Continue upward along the hair edge until you run out of room in the image window, as shown in Figure 14.22.

4. Hold down the Spacebar and drag downward so that you can see the top of the girl's head. Complete the masking by arriving at your original location in the image.

5. With the Polygon Lasso tool, click points along the transparency, click around some background areas, and close the selection; then press Alt(Opt)+Delete (Backspace) to make the selection transparent.

6. Press Ctrl(⌘)+D, press Ctrl(⌘)+S, and keep the file open.

FIGURE 14.22 *Keep the Paintbrush tool to outside of the edge of the girl. Press Tab to switch to a precision cursor if the Paintbrush icon is interfering with your view.*

You've done it! You now have all the edge work done in the tinygal.psd image. Your image should look something like Figure 14.23 now.

You don't need the author's advice on what to do next. The image still contains large areas of unwanted background. To remove these areas quickly, zoom out to a resolution where you can see the image full-frame, and then use the Polygon Lasso tool to select the unwanted shards. You then press Alt(Opt)+Delete (Backspace), press Ctrl(⌘)+D to deselect the marquee, and then move on to another area until all you can see in the image is the girl surrounded by medium purple.

To make the masking a permanent deletion from the image, click the Layer Mask thumbnail on the Layers palette, drag it into the trash icon on the palette, and then click Apply in the attention box that appears onscreen.

After you've done this work, it would be a good idea to turn the transparency grid back to its default colors. To do this, press Ctrl(⌘)+K, press Ctrl(⌘)+4, and then in the Grid Colors drop-down list, choose Light. Click on OK to return to the workspace.

FIGURE 14.23   *Right up to the edge of the tiny gal, you've created transparent areas.*

GIVING THE GIRL A BIG HAND

You've completed phase one of the composition; the image of the tiny gal is now ready to be placed in the bighand.tif image. The remainder of the chapter focuses on how to position the gal on the big guy's hand, how to check for tiny imperfections in your masking work on the gal when she's in different surroundings, and how to apply shadows to the scene. And oh, yes, it will definitely help the illusion if the big guy's thumb rests over, not under, the tiny gal's leg.

Moving and Positioning the Tiny Gal

To add the tiny gal to the bighand.tif image is as simple as drag and drop. What is not so simple is aligning the gal so that she looks as though she's actually resting in the palm of the big guy. In the next set of steps follow, you'll move a copy of the tiny gal to the bighand.tif image, and the bighand image will become the focal point of the remainder of this assignment:

Here's how to begin this photographic illusion:

Copying and Moving Elements Between Document Windows

1. Type **33** in the Zoom Percentage box and then press Enter (Return).

2. Move the tinygal.psd image to the upper left of the workspace.

3. Open the bighand.tif image from the Chap14 folder of the Companion CD, and then type **33** in the Zoom Percentage box and press Enter (Return).

4. Move the bighand image to the right of the tinygal image.

5. Press V (Move tool), and then click inside the tinygal document window. With one definitive drag, pull the image into the bighand.tif document, as shown in Figure 14.24. A new layer is added to the bighand.tif document.

Figure 14.24 *Drag a copy of the tiny gal you masked into the bighand document window.*

6. Save and close tinygal.psd, maximize bighand.tif onscreen at 100% viewing resolution, and then save the image to your hard disk as big-hand.psd, in Photoshop's native format.

7. With the Move tool, position the girl on Layer 1 so that she appears to be resting in the big palm, with her hands on the finger and thumb knuckle of the big hand, as shown in Figure 14.25.

TIP

An alternative method for copying a layer to a different image window is to drag the title on the Layers palette into the host window.

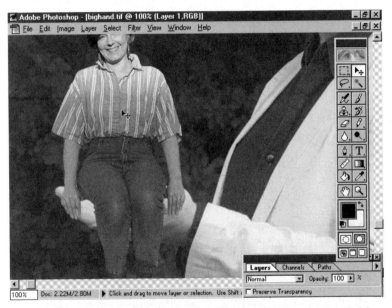

FIGURE 14.25 *Position the tiny gal so that she appears to be resting comfortably in the big guy's palm.*

8. Press Ctrl(⌘)+S; keep the file open.

It's on now to some fancy masking work, as you apparently place the big guy's thumb over the tiny gal's leg.

THUMBS UP

To make the big hand's thumb appear to be over the tiny gal's leg, some of the gal's leg must be masked and eventually discarded. Make sure right now that the tiny gal is situated where you want her; the masking work to come will become misaligned if you change your mind about the girl's position.

To discern where the edge of the thumb is, you must "over-mask," extending the masking of the girl's leg farther than is necessary. You'll then switch to white foreground color, and paint back the leg, right to the edge of the thumb.

Here's how to add dimension to the composition:

MASKING THE LEG ON TOP OF THE THUMB

1. Zoom to 200% viewing resolution, and then scroll the window so that the girl's leg and the guy's thumb are centered onscreen. You'll need the Layers palette and the Brushes palette onscreen; arrange them so that they do not interfere with your view of the composition.

2. Click the Add layer mask icon at the bottom of the Layers palette. Layer 1, the layer containing the girl, is now in mask mode.

3. Choose the Paintbrush tool, and choose the fourth tip from the left in the top row.

4. Start painting on the right side of the girl's leg. Continue masking until you can see all the big guy's thumb, as shown in Figure 14.26.

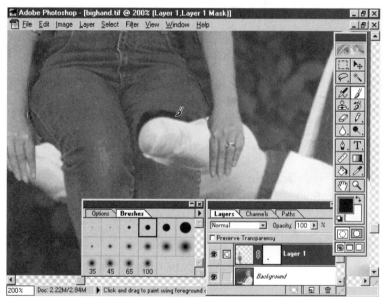

FIGURE 14.26 *Reveal the thumb by masking over the tiny gal's leg.*

5. When you've got the thumb completely uncovered, zoom into a 300% viewing resolution, centered on the thumb.

6. Choose the third from left, top row tip from the Brushes palette, and then press X so that white is the current foreground color. White will restore areas you've hidden.

7. Take your time, and brush carefully around the outside edge of the thumb, as shown in Figure 14.27.

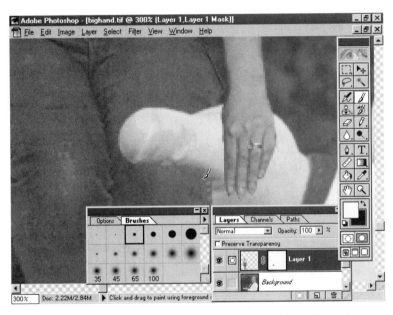

FIGURE 14.27 *Restore the areas of the girl's pants around the thumb by applying white.*

8. When your editing is complete, click on the Layer Mask thumbnail and drag it into the trash. In the attention box that pops up, click Apply to make your changes permanent.

9. Press Ctrl(⌘)+S; keep the file open.

Shadows are next on the agenda. Let's see how you can further integrate the tiny gal with the big guy.

CREATING A THUMB SHADOW

The thumb in the image rests on the gal's jeans, or so it appears. With the light casting from the upper right of the scene, this means that there should be a shadow the shape and size of the big guy's thumb, below the thumb, casting on her pants. Shadows usually have some ambient color to them, but light casting on blue jeans is generally a neutral color. Therefore, in the following steps you'll use black to create the shadow.

PAINTING A SHADOW INTO THE SCENE

1. On the Layers palette, click on the menu flyout button, and choose New Layer.

2. In the New Layer dialog box, type **Thumb shadow** in the Name field, choose Multiply from the Mode drop-down list, and then click on OK. The new Thumb shadow layer is on top of Layer 1, which contains the girl.

3. Very carefully paint a shadow of the thumb, as shown in Figure 14.28. If you go into the thumb or big hand at any point, use the Eraser tool to correct the problem. Take your time with this one; you're quite literally *painting* something, not retouching it!

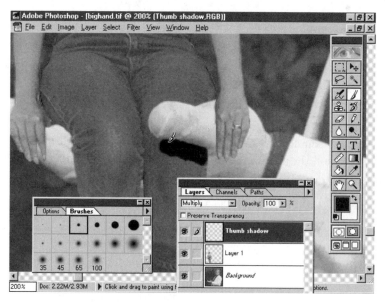

FIGURE 14.28 *Create a shadow by using black foreground color on the new layer you created.*

Shadows should not be 100 percent opaque; they aren't in real life and they aren't in this chapter. This is why you were asked to paint the shadow on a new layer—so that you can decrease its opacity without messing up the rest of the composition.

4. On the Layers palette, click the Opacity flyout button, and then drag the opacity slider to about 40%, as shown in Figure 14.29.

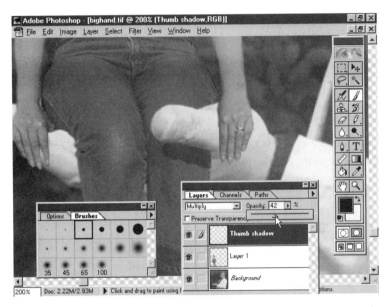

FIGURE 14.29 *Reduce the opacity of the shadow so that the audience can see some pants detail through it.*

5. Press Ctrl(⌘)+S; keep the file open.

There are three more areas to be shaded in this composition, and they all can reside on the same layer. In the following section you'll add a new layer, sample a shading color for "flesh against flesh," and truly make the girl look as though she's happy that she's in a giant's palm.

SAMPLING AND APPLYING A SHADING COLOR

As opposed to the flat black you used to shade the girl's pants, the area next to her hands is the big guy's hand—and her hands should not cast a shadow consisting of black.

Where do we look for this special color that is indicative of an element casting a shadow on flesh? It's simple; you find the deepest shaded portion of the big guy's hand, sample it, and then paint with the sample.

Here's how to use the Eyedropper tool in combination with the Paintbrush tool to add a shadow beneath the girl's hand:

SAMPLING AND SHADING

1. Click the Background layer title on the Layers palette. When you do this, the next layer created will be directly above the current layer, which is exactly where you want this new shadow layer to be.

2. Click the Layers palette's menu flyout button, and then choose New Layer.

3. In the New Layer dialog box, type **Other Shadows** in the Name field, choose Multiply from the Mode drop-down list, and then click OK. "Other Shadows" is now the current editing layer.

4. Choose the Paintbrush tool, and then press Alt(Opt) and click over the most shaded area of the big guy's hand—the bottom of his hand, which is farthest from the light source. This is your new shadow-painting color.

5. Paint around the left and bottom of the girl's hand, as shown in Figure 14.30. Because the Other Shadows layer is beneath the girl layer, you need not be awfully careful about painting around the edge of the girl's hand. Her hand hides brush strokes behind it.

6. Paint between the girl's knees. Logically, her legs would be casting a shadow on the guy's finger.

7. Scroll over to the big guy's index fingertip, and then paint another shadow to the left of the girl's leg, as shown in Figure 14.31. Take care to keep your brush strokes inside the silhouette of the guy's finger; otherwise, you'll add shading to the background of the composition.

8. Finally, apply a stroke or two between the girl's fingers on the left of the image.

9. Drag the Opacity slider for the Other Shadows layer down to about 70%, or until you feel the shadows are visible without being overly intense.

10. Press Ctrl(⌘)+S; keep the file open.

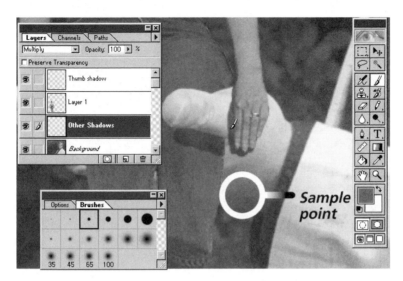

FIGURE 14.30 *Sample a fleshtone color that's good for shading, and then paint with it along the bottom and left edge of the girl's hand.*

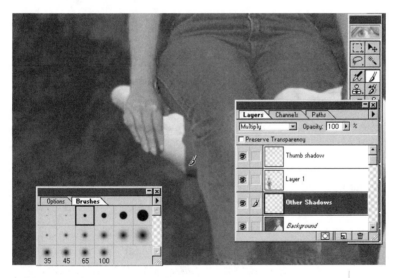

FIGURE 14.31 *To keep overall shading consistent, you must add a shadow casting from the girl's leg onto the big index finger.*

It's clean-up time next. You'll probably notice that a pixel or two along the edge of the girl does not blend into the background. This is to be expected; anti-aliased brush tips produce clean edges but do not always eliminate lone pixels whose color is wrong when composited against a new background.

LAYER MASKING FOR TOUCH-UP WORK

You return to the Layer Mask feature in Photoshop to tie up any loose ends on the girl layer. After all your hard work, it would spoil the illusion if there were any fringing around the girl, a sure sign that "Photoshop's been here." The big secret to creating fantasy compositions that look real lies in the detail work: Photoshop's work is *supposed* to be invisible to the viewing audience.

You'll clean up the edge work around the girl in the following brief set of steps:

PERFORMING EXTREMELY SMALL EDITS

1. Click the Layer 1 title on the Layers palette to make it the current editing layer.

2. Zoom in to a 300% viewing resolution of the image, and then scroll the image so that you can see the girl's left arm, center screen.

3. Click the Layer Mask icon on the Layers palette, choose the Paintbrush tool, and choose the second-from-left tip in the top row on the Brushes palette.

4. Press D (**d**efault colors) to ensure that the current foreground color is black (which hides areas you paint over in this mode).

5. Press Caps Lock to toggle the Paintbrush tool cursor to the precision cursor. The screen figures don't show this because the precision cursor is almost impossible to see in this black-and-white book.

6. Start looking for any fringing on the girl's edge. When you see some, stroke over it, as shown in Figure 14.32.

7. Hold down the Spacebar to toggle to the Hand tool, and then drag the image to other areas after you've cleaned up a specific area. Paint over any fringing you see.

8. When you're finished, drag the Layer Mask thumbnail into the trash icon at the bottom of the Layers palette. Click Apply in the attention box that pops up.

9. Press Ctrl(⌘)+S; keep the file open.

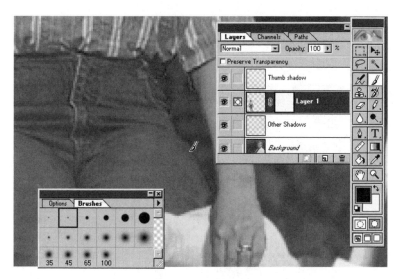

FIGURE 14.32   *Hide, by painting over them, areas that visually separate the girl from the hand she's perched on.*

A QUESTION OF LENS FOCUS

The more nit-picky you are with this composition, the more startling it will look in its photo-reality. If you look carefully at the background layer and the girl on Layer 1, you'll notice a slight difference in image focus. The girl is sharper than the guy (*all* girls seem to be sharper than guys), and this minor difference in focus does not help integrate the composition.

You know what you're going to do? You will blur the girl—ever so slightly—to make her match the focus of the big guy in the background.

Here's how to make a more harmonious blend in the picture:

USING THE GAUSSIAN BLUR FILTER TO CORRECT FOCUS

1. Choose Filter, Blur, and then choose Gaussian Blur.

2. Drag the slider to 0.3 pixels in the dialog box, or if you can't get that precise amount by using the slider, type **0.3** in the pixels field, as shown in Figure 14.33. The Gaussian Blur filter goes down as far as

TIP

The problem of images having two different focuses lies in the quality of the lens, the f-stop used in taking the images, and the distance between the elements and the camera. The author suggests that, in your own "making people small" adventures, you invest in a moderately expensive lens and find lighting conditions that allow you to take the images at f8 or greater. And there's really nothing you can do about the relative distance of the subject to the camera except crop through the viewfinder; this will make the film grain the same size in both images.

0.1 pixels. The author arrived at 0.3 through trial and error. If you were to work with larger images, this amount probably would not work. Click OK to apply the blur.

FIGURE 14.33 *Lose a minute amount of image focus by blurring the layer. The edges blend into the background layer.*

3. Press Ctrl(⌘)+S; keep the file open.

As you can see in Figure 14.34, there is perfect focus continuity between the girl and the big hand.

FIGURE 14.34 *When the elements in a composition have the same focus, the audience tends to believe in the visual story you present!*

COLOR CASTING AND CORRECTION

One last nit-picky detail—a simple but important one—and then you'll have yourself an outstanding piece of imaging. Did you ever notice that people's skin looks different indoors than it does outdoors? This happens because outdoors there's a huge tent of blue sky that reflects blue onto people's skin, only to be perceived by the viewer as a bluish cast on the person they're viewing. Indoors, with incandescent light around, people's skin takes on a warmer tone.

So what's the tone of this composition? Actually, it's faintly green, because the big guy is surrounded by green trees. This, in contrast to the girl, who is illuminated by the sun "in the clear"—away from foliage—makes her complexion a little too rosy. The way to correct this is to use the Hue/Saturation command to slightly cast the girl toward green.

This is a really simple set of steps; here goes:

USING THE HUE/SATURATION COMMAND TO CORRECT COLOR CASTS

1. Press Ctrl(„)+U to display the Hue/Saturation command.

2. Drag the Hue slider to about +4, as shown in Figure 14.35. You do not need much Hue shift to make the girl look more as though she, too, was photographed against greenery.

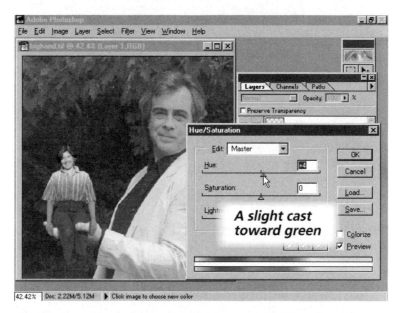

FIGURE 14.35 *Change the color cast on the girl layer to match the fleshtones on the Background layer.*

3. Click OK to apply the change.

4. Press Ctrl(⌘)+S.

5. (Optional) You might want to save a flattened copy of your work in a file format that is accessible to most users. To do this, press Ctrl(⌘)+Alt(Opt)+S. Choose a destination for the file, click the TIFF format from the Save As (Macintosh: Format) drop-down list, and then click Save.

6. You can close the file at any time now.

Admittedly, the creation of smaller than (or larger than) life compositions lies mostly in how adeptly you define selections. The rest of the procedures are partially manual and part Photoshop automation. The next time you need a visually striking image to sell something, or simply to add to a very strange family album, think small.

SUMMARY

There are two key elements to making a successful "small" composition: getting the images to be composited correctly, and knowing how to use Photoshop's selection tools, perhaps the core of Photoshop's strength as an image editor. If you diligently worked through the steps in this chapter, you have a great many variations at your disposal for performing unusual or invisible editing work. Transport people to a sunny beach when they were photographed in the middle of winter; add a missing relative to a family reunion picture. You name it and you can do it; you've learned the techniques.

Chapter 15 transports you to the inter-world creative place called "Working Between Applications." When you can't find the quickest, best graphics solution entirely within Photoshop (which is usually unlikely), use a helper application to make your Photoshop work come alive. Get some product designs handy for your continuing adventures.

WORKING BETWEEN APPLICATIONS

The world of publishing is a vast ocean of applications, output devices, typefaces, and other electronic and physical elements. Although Photoshop today plays a pivotal role in getting the goods to press (or to the Web), it is unrealistic to expect Photoshop to do everything as well as, say, a "sister" application, such as Adobe Illustrator.

The real tricks to accomplishing any assignment that comes your way are as follows:

- Knowing when Photoshop is not the best choice for an element of an assignment

- Knowing which application can provide the support Photoshop needs to complete the assignment

This chapter's assignment is a challenging one; it involves a label on a can in a photograph, a label so crooked that the client says, "No way!". If there's no budget or time to take a better picture, you'll see on the following pages how a vector drawing application and Photoshop together can make things right.

COMPLETE REPLACEMENT AS A RETOUCHING METHOD

Professionally, you might never come across an image with as glaring a flaw as the one in Figure 15.1. The crooked label is an exaggeration of what could go wrong if there weren't enough glue on the back of a label. If you can correct something as grossly wrong as the can label in this assignment, you'll breeze through similar minor corrections.

FIGURE 15.1 *What seems like an insurmountable photographic problem can be corrected if you know which tools to use.*

Because a digitized image is a bitmap, rotating the label on the coffee can would make the focus of the label less sharp, and the point of this picture is to sell a specific coffee brand. A fuzzy label simply won't do. No, what needs to be done in this picture is to completely remove the label from the can, re-create the logo in an illustration (vector), program, and then merge the hand-created logo with the can in the image. By using an illustration program, you will be able to rotate the label without losing any focus or clarity.

USING THE PEN TOOL TO DEFINE THE COFFEE CAN

To completely remove the label on the coffee can, you'll paint over it, using a gradient fill because there is uneven lighting on the can. You'll notice that the brown of the can is brighter on the right side than on the left.

To create the most accurate selection of the can, you'll use the Pen tool in the following steps to define the edge of the can.

DEFINING THE COFFEE CAN'S EDGE

1. Open the Tropcafe.tif image from the Chap15 folder on the Companion CD.

2. Double-click on the Zoom tool to move your view of the Tropcafe.tif image to 100%, and then maximize the image window.

3. With the Hand tool, drag in the image so that the top of the coffee can is in clear view.

4. Choose the Pen tool. You'll be working counterclockwise around the edge of the can to define it.

5. Click an anchor point on the top right edge of the brown can, not the metal lip of the can.

6. About 1 screen inch to the left of the first anchor point, click and drag a second anchor point on the edge between the metal lip and the brown of the can. Your cursor is now holding a direction point. Drag on the direction point to steer the path segment between the first and second anchors so that it conforms to the edge between the can and the lip of the can.

7. Click and drag another anchor point on the edge of the metal lip and the brown can itself, to the left of the previous anchor point, as shown in Figure 15.2.

FIGURE 15.2 *Define the edge of the coffee can by clicking+dragging with the Pen tool.*

8. Click and drag a point on the left, top edge of the brown can. Hold Alt(Opt) to toggle to the Convert Point tool, and then drag the leftmost direction point down so that the direction line connected to the direction point is flush with the left edge of the can.

9. Click on the last anchor point you created, hold down the Spacebar to toggle to the Hand tool, and then drag upward on the image to scroll to the bottom of the can. Release the Spacebar; now the Pen tool is again active.

10. Click an anchor point where the bottom visible edge of the can meets the coffee beans. You've created a path segment now that defines the left edge of the can.

11. Click and drag along the coffee bean edges, as shown in Figure 15.3. When you are faced with a sharp, concave area among the edge of the beans, hold Alt(Opt) to toggle to the Convert Point tool, and then drag on a direction point to make the property of the anchor point a sharp connection between path segments. Then hold Ctrl(⌘) to toggle to the Direct Selection tool, and drag the direction point to steer the associated path segment to meet the edge of the coffee beans. Don't forget to click once on the last anchor point before you continue with the Pen tool, to keep the path a single, continuous path composed of segments between anchors.

12. Click (don't drag) an anchor at the bottom right of the can, as shown in Figure 15.4. When you've done that, hold Alt(Opt) and then drag upward by about a screen inch to make the direction point flush with the right side of the can.

FIGURE 15.3   *Use the keyboard modifier keys to switch between the Pen tool, the Convert Point tool, and the Direct Selection tool as you work on the bottom edge.*

FIGURE 15.4   *Stop dragging anchor points, and simply click on the bottom right of the can.*

13. Click on the anchor point with the Pen tool. Hold down the Spacebar, and then drag downward in the image until you can see the first anchor point you clicked.

14. Click on the first anchor point to close the path.

15. On the Paths palette (press F7 if it isn't currently onscreen), double-click on the Work Path title to display the Save Path dialog box.

16. Name the path **Can path**, and then click on OK. The path is now saved; it cannot be overwritten.

17. Press Shift+Ctrl(⌘)+S and save the image as Tropcafe.tif, in the TIFF file format, to your hard disk. Keep the image open. Double-click on the Hand tool to move your viewing resolution so that you can see the entire image.

Next, you're going to sample two original colors on the can, colors you'll use in the following section to create a blank can.

FILLING IN THE COFFEE CAN

The artistic success with which you paint over the coffee can depends entirely on how precisely you defined the can's edge. Take a moment, and zoom around the edge of the can to make sure that anchor points are precisely placed. If they're not, use the Direct Selection tool to move anchors, and steer direction points to modify the path-segment curve between anchor points.

In the steps that follow, you'll load the path you created as a selection, sample colors on the can, replace the can with a gradient fill, and save the selection to a channel for later use.

PAINTING OVER THE CAN

1. Choose the Eyedropper tool, and then click on a light area of the can.

2. Click on the Switch foreground/background colors icon on the toolbox so that the color you sampled is the current background color.

3. Click on a darker area of brown toward the left of the can. Figure 15.5 shows two good areas from which to sample.

FIGURE 15.5 *Sample a light and a dark color from the can, using the Eyedropper tool.*

4. On the Paths palette, click on the Loads path as a selection icon, as shown in Figure 15.6, and then click on an empty area of the palette to hide the path, to display the selection marquee only.

FIGURE 15.6 *Load the path you created as a selection marquee in the image.*

5. Click on the Layers tab on the palette, and then click on the Create new layer icon. Layer 1 is created; it is the current editing layer.

6. Double-click on the Gradient tool on the toolbox. This activates the tool and displays the Options palette. Drag on the face of the tool on the toolbox and choose the Linear tool if it is not the current tool.

7. On the Options palette, choose Foreground to Background from the Gradient drop-down list.

8. Drag the Gradient tool from an 8 o'clock position on the left of the can to a 3 o'clock position on the right of the can, as shown in Figure 15.7.

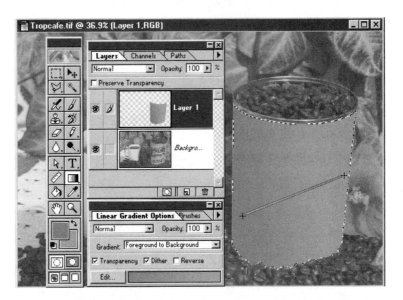

FIGURE 15.7 *Simulate the lighting effect on the can, using the Linear Gradient tool and colors sampled from the original image.*

9. On the Channels palette, click on the Save selection as channel icon, shown in Figure 15.8. Press Ctrl(⌘)+D to deselect the marquee.

If you see a black Alpha 1 channel with a white silhouette of the can, instead of a white channel with a black can, double-click on the Alpha 1 title on the Channels palette. In the Channel Options box, choose Color Indicates: Selected Areas, and then click on OK. The color scheme of the alpha channel will become inverted and you can proceed.

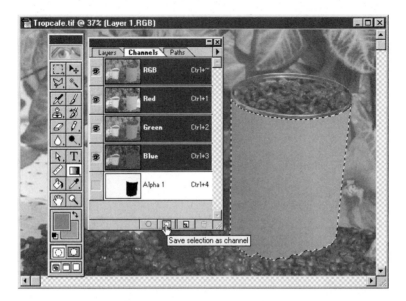

FIGURE 15.8 *Save the selection you've created to an alpha channel.*

10. Choose File Save As, and save the image as Tropcafe.psd, in Photoshop's native PSD format. Keep the image open.

You're not going to use the selection you saved to a channel; instead, you are going to modify it so that it serves as a selection for shading the top lip of the can.

CREATING A DROP-SHADOW TEMPLATE

The alpha channel you saved describes the top lip of the can as well as its other sides. What you're interested in at this point is creating a subtle drop-shadow cast by the metal rim of the can onto the can's brown surface, as this shadow is apparent in the original photo. By selectively trimming away at the saved alpha channel, using a duplicate path you move downward, you'll arrive at a near perfect channel template for loading and then shading in the image.

Here's how to perform some shading:

Moving a Path to Trim a Channel

1. Click on the Alpha 1 title on the Channels palette. This moves you to a view of the saved selection.

2. On the Paths palette, drag the Can path title into the Creates new path icon at the bottom of the palette. You now have a new duplicate path titled Can path copy, and it's the current selected path.

3. Choose the Direct Selection tool, hold Alt(Opt) and click on the path to select the entire path, and then use the keyboard nudge keys about four times to nudge the path down, as shown in Figure 15.9.

FIGURE 15.9 *Nudge the copy of the path you created downward by using the arrow keyboard keys.*

4. On the Paths palette, click on the Loads path as a selection icon, and then press D (default colors) so that your current background color is white. Click on an empty part of the palette to hide the path.

5. Press Delete (Backspace), so that you are left with a sliver of the can selection, as shown in Figure 15.10.

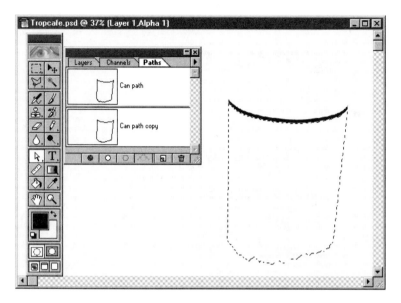

FIGURE 15.10   *The sliver you are creating will serve as a template for shading the can.*

Now, your erasure of the bottom of the can isn't perfect because you nudged the path straight downward, and the can in the image is at an angle. You need to remove some of the black areas you don't want in the alpha channel next...

6. Press Ctrl(⌘)+D, choose the Eraser tool, and on the Options palette, choose Block from the drop-down list.

7. Run your cursor over the shards to the left of the can selection's top, as shown in Figure 15.11. This should be all the work required to create a clean template for the drop shadow.

8. Press Ctrl(⌘) and click on the Alpha 1 title to load it as a selection marquee.

9. Press Ctrl(⌘)+~ (tilde) to move your view to the color composite of the Tropcafe.psd image, and then double-click on the Zoom tool to bring your viewing resolution of this image to 100%.

10. Scroll the image so that the marquee selection is centered onscreen, and then choose the Burn tool from the toning tools flyout on the toolbox. The Burn tool looks like a tiny hand giving the "okay" sign.

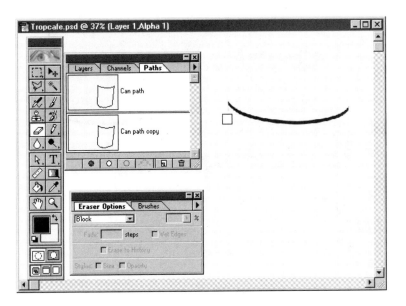

FIGURE 15.11 *Erase the superfluous edge in the alpha channel silhouette of the can.*

11. On the Options palette, choose Highlights from the drop-down list, and leave the Exposure at 50%.

12. Choose the 65-pixel brush tip from the Brushes palette.

13. Make sure that Layer 1 is the current editing layer, and then stroke inside the marquee once or twice to burn in the color, making the selected area appear to be a shadow cast by the rim of the can, as shown in Figure 15.12.

14. Press Ctrl(⌘)+D to deselect the marquee, and then press Ctrl(⌘)+S; keep the file open.

You're taking a pretty close look at this can as you re-create it, and you should notice a glaring flaw along its outline by now. The label was so poorly affixed to the can that the bottom-right corner popped up and intrudes on part of the flower at the right of the can. You'll fix this in lightning time in the next section.

FIGURE 15.12   *Use the Burn tool to decrease the exposure of the highlights in the marquee-selected area.*

CLONING OVER A COFFEE CAN EDGE

The area we are looking at in this section lies outside the Can path (the original, not the copy). To make it easy to keep the can's edge clean while cloning over part of the flower, you'll load the Can path, and then invert the selection so that the can is masked but the rest of the image (including the flower) is available for editing.

Here's how to use the Rubber Stamp tool to clear the remaining portion of the can label from the image:

RETOUCHING AN ELEMENT ACROSS LAYERS

1. Choose the Rubber Stamp tool, type **200** in the Zoom Percentage field, and then press Enter (Return). Scroll the image so that you can see where the label intrudes upon the flower.

2. On the Layers palette, click on the Background title, as this is where the piece of label and flower are located in the document.

3. On the Brushes palette, choose the second-from-left tip in the second row.

4. On the Paths palette, click on the Can path title, and then click on the Loads path as a selection icon at the bottom of the palette. Click on an empty area of the palette now to hide the path.

5. Press Ctrl(⌘)+Shift+I to invert the selection.

6. Press Alt(Opt) and click on the edge of the flower, very close to the can; then stroke over the label area right up to the marquee edge.

7. Press Alt(Opt) and click on an area of the flower that's not too close to the remaining can label, and then stroke over the remaining part of the can label, as shown in Figure 15.13.

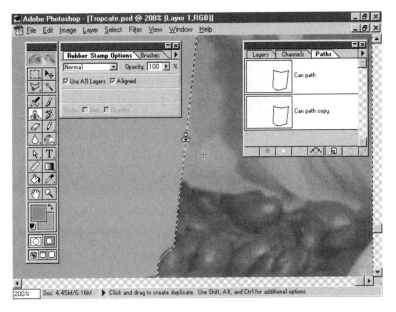

FIGURE 15.13 *Clone over the label with sampled areas of the flower.*

8. Press Ctrl(⌘)+D. Press Ctrl(⌘)+S; keep the file open.

Next, you're going to do some reconstruction work on a little film grain and some focus problems.

ADDING PHOTOREALISTIC TOUCHES

Two problems exist in the composition at the moment:

- The edge of the can is a little too sharp where it meets the coffee beans.

- The can you've re-created on Layer 1 has absolutely no film grain, unlike the rest of the picture.

In the following steps, you'll soften the focus across layers so that the edge of the beans blends a little more into the bottom of the can, and then you'll add noise to the can to simulate film grain.

Here's how it goes:

ENHANCING THE ART PORTION OF THE COMPOSITION

1. Zoom to a 200% viewing resolution of the bottom of the can, where it meets the coffee beans.

2. Choose the Blur tool from the Focus tools flyout on the toolbox. The cursor's shaped like a teardrop.

3. On the Options palette, check the Use all layers check box. This means you'll be blurring areas of the background layer into Layer 1; both layers will be affected. Set the Pressure for the Blur tool to 20 on the Options palette.

4. Choose the third-from-left tip in the second row on the Brushes palette.

5. Stroke over the edge of the beans, as shown in Figure 15.14. You should not have to stroke an edge more than twice to make the focus correct for the image. Also, you might want to switch to a precise cursor for this fine editing work by pressing Caps Lock. (Don't forget to turn off Caps Lock when you're finished, especially if you have word processing work to do!)

6. When you've finished softening the edge, click on the Channels tab on the palette onscreen.

7. Drag the Alpha 1 channel title into the trash icon.

8. Click on the Paths tab, click on the Can path title, and then click on the Loads path as a selection icon. Click on an empty area of the palette to hide the path.

9. On the Channels palette, click on the Save Selection as channel icon. Press Ctrl(⌘)+D to deselect the marquee.

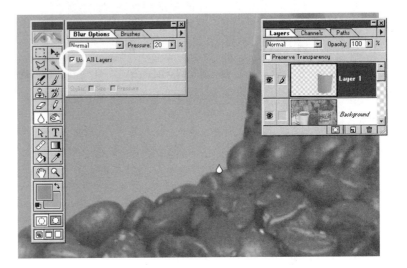

FIGURE 15.14 *Blur the edges of the beans slightly to make the coffee can edge have a focus consistent with the rest of the image.*

10. On the Layers palette, click on the menu flyout, and then choose Flatten Image.

The reason you're flattening the image is that shortly you'll apply noise to only the coffee can you painted. If the coffee can were still on a Layer, the preview box for the Noise filter would not show both the background and Layer 1; instead, it would show only the current editing layer. And you'd have no preview comparison for the amount of noise to add to the selection.

11. Press Ctrl(⌘) and click on the Alpha 1 channel on the Channels layer to load the selection you saved of the can silhouette.

12. Choose Filter, Noise, and then choose Add Noise.

13. In the Add Noise dialog box, drag in the preview window until you can see half the can and half the background of the image.

14. Increase the Amount of noise to 5 (which should make the preview window "noisily consistent"), and choose Gaussian as the distribution of the noise, as shown in Figure 15.15. Gaussian Noise tends to leave "clumps" of noise in an image, most faithfully reproducing the grain in the emulsion of photographic film.

15. Click on OK, press Ctrl(⌘)+D to deselect the marquee, and then press Ctrl(⌘)+S. Keep the image open.

FIGURE 15.15   *Use a small amount of Gaussian noise to make the can label consistent with the rest of the image.*

You've gone about as far as you can in Photoshop. Although the 3D Transform's cylinder mode could bend a logo to conform to the curvature of the can, it would reassign pixels in the logo artwork, and the result would be fuzzier text than you or the client would like. Nope, our next trip is to a vector drawing application to re-create the logo. First, however, you'll make a copy of only the area you need to trace over in the vector application.

A BRIEF THINGY ON EPS, ILLUSTRATOR FILES, AND RESOLUTION

The game plan is this: In the following steps you'll crop a copy of the image you've worked on to include only the can. By doing this, you are not burdening the vector drawing application with the entire image held in memory.

NOTE

The authors anticipate that some readers might not own a vector drawing application such as Illustrator, Macromedia FreeHand, CorelXARA, or CorelDRAW (the predominant players in vector drawing tools). You can work through this chapter without owning a drawing app because an EPS file of the can label has been created, to proper orientation and size, and you can load this file into Photoshop from the Companion CD. The authors hope you can get your hands on a vector drawing application for a brief while, however, because this chapter is all about working between applications, as you'll soon see.

The Macintosh steps for label construction is covered first in this chapter. However, Windows users will want to read what is documented here on EPS formats. Before getting into your first adventure with Illustrator and Extensis VectorTools for the Macintosh, a general overview of the transport mechanism between vector art and the bitmap world of Photoshop is in order.

If you read Chapter 1, "Getting Acquainted with Computer Graphics and Terms," you realize that vector graphics and bitmap graphics belong to two entirely different computer graphics camps. There is a portal between these graphics worlds, however, the de facto one being the *E*ncapsulated *P*ost*S*cript (EPS), type of file. There are two types of EPS files:

- The *interpreted* EPS file, which contains vector information and can be opened and edited in vector drawing applications such as Illustrator, CorelDRAW, and CorelXARA.

- The *placeable* EPS file, which Photoshop and Illustrator are capable of writing, but incapable of reopening, because the EPS information is strictly printer code. Placeable EPS images typically contain a low-resolution image header, so you have a good idea where to place them in, for example, a Quark or PageMaker document. When the document is printed the printer is fed this EPS information, and it appears in the printed document. The placeable EPS file cannot be interpreted by Photoshop or vector drawing packages as artwork, however, and we dismiss this type of EPS file in our work in this chapter.

An Illustrator file (for Windows users, a file with the AI extension) is a special type of EPS file. It contains interpreted information like the first type of EPS file mentioned above, but it can also contain additional graphics information such as the number of blend steps, position on a page, and so on. It is accurate to say that an "AI" file is a type of EPS file, but it's inaccurate to say that all EPS files are Illustrator files. This is because EPS files might be lacking certain graphics definitions, which is a result of the EPS files being written by non-Illustrator vector applications such as CorelXARA and FreeHand.

The key thing that makes it easy for a vector program to write an EPS file that scales perfectly to a target photograph is that EPS files contain information on the width and height of a design. This means that Photoshop can read this width and height, you provide the resolution information, and before you know it, you have a bitmap copy of a logo that is accurately scaled and can be placed on a layer in the Photoshop composition.

You'll prepare the target image before you launch into can label design. In Figure 15.16 you can see a copy of the Tropcafe.psd image being cropped. To do this, choose Image, Duplicate, and then name the file Tropicafe can.tif., and click on OK. Then take the Rectangular Marquee tool, drag a marquee around the can, and choose Image, Crop. Save the file to your hard disk in the TIFF format, and then you can close Photoshop.

FIGURE 15.16 *Crop a copy of the composite to use as a template in the vector drawing application.*

Because all vector programs are not created equal across platforms, our first excursion into logo replacement designs will be on the Macintosh. In the next section you'll use Illustrator (or FreeHand) and a demo version of Extensis VectorTools 2.0 for the Macintosh to design a label for the can, and then distort it so that it conforms to the curvature of the coffee can in Tropcafe.psd.

INSTALLING VECTORTOOLS ON THE MACINTOSH

The people at Extensis have outdone themselves with the creation of VectorTools 2.0. This version offers not only a screen's worth of shortcut icons for much-used features such as the Pathfinder commands and Arrange menu commands, but there are tools that Illustrator and FreeHand simply don't have. And without certain tools, you would not be able to create a can label that curves around a can.

The special version of VectorTools 2.0 on the Companion CD is fully functional. You can create designs and implement shortcuts with the demo version, but you can only use VectorTools for 30 days. So if you have no intention of working through the following examples within the next week or so, we recommend that you put off installing VectorTools right now, so that you'll have the full 30 days later to appreciate this marvelous suite.

Here's how to install VectorTools:

INSTALLING VECTORTOOLS

1. Close all running applications.

2. With the Companion CD in the CD-ROM player, double-click on the Extensis icon on the Desktop.

3. In the Extensis window, double-click on the Product Installers icon.

4. In the Product Installers window, double-click on the VectorTools 2.0 icon.

5. In the VectorTools 2.0 window, double-click on the VectorTools 2.0.1 Installer icon, as shown in Figure 15.17.

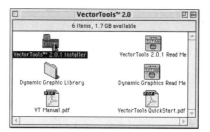

FIGURE 15.17   *The VectorTools Installer is fairly deeply nested, but it's worth the trip!*

6. Click on Continue, click on Accept, and then click on Continue again, as the opening screens progress.

7. Pull down the Easy Install box, and choose Custom Install, choose the host application (Illustrator 6 or 7, or FreeHand 5.5 or 7), and then click on the Select Folder button.

8. Either create a new folder (recommended) or choose from an existing folder on your hard disk for installation, and then click on Select.

9. Click on Install. The Install countdown box appears.

10. The Installation was successful if a box appears. Click on Quit.

11. Launch Illustrator or FreeHand. You'll see how to use Illustrator in the following section; the FreeHand commands are the same as the Illustrator ones described there.

You're all set to get down to business now. In the following section, you'll import the Tropicafe can image and work with layers and VectorTools.

PLACING THE IMAGE AND THE LABEL

Troplabl.eps has been provided for you in the Examples folder, Chap15 on the Companion CD. This design was originally used to print the label on the photo, but if you'd like to flex your creative prowess and design a label of your own in the steps that follow, go right ahead.

You'll note a distinguishing characteristic of the Troplabl.eps image that you will want to add to your design, should you decide to create a better logo. (Hint: it's not difficult!) The Troplabl.eps file has a hairline border that runs .3 inches outside the label itself. This is a guideline; you do not want to distort the label so that it fits over the can edge-to-edge. Labels on cans need some breathing room so that you can read the label at a glance without being distracted by severely angled text on a cylindrical can. If you design the logo yourself, add this "padding" to the design; working with VectorTools' VectorShape module will be much easier if you do.

Here's how to get a label to conform to the curve of the coffee can in the image:

USING ILLUSTRATOR AND VECTORTOOLS

1. Press ⌘+O, choose the Tropicafe can.tif image from your hard disk, and then press Open.

2. Choose Window, Show Layers.

3. Double-click on the Layer 1 title, and then in the Layer Options box, type **Photo** in the Name field. Click on OK to return to the workspace.

4. Uncheck the editability icon (the pencil) next to the Photo title on the Layers palette. The photograph is locked now and you can't accidentally move it.

5. Click on the Layers palette's flyout button, and then choose New Layer. Name the layer **Tropicafe logo**, and then click on OK, as shown in Figure 15.18. This is now the current editing layer.

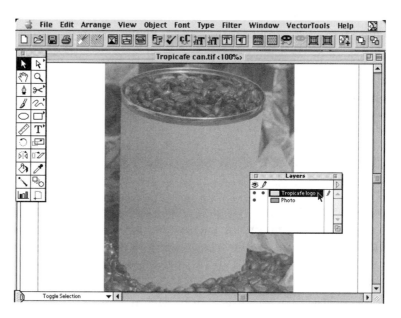

FIGURE 15.18 *Lock the image on a layer, and then create a new layer upon which to design.*

6. This step can go in either of two directions. If you want to design your own logo, hide the Photo layer (click on the dot beneath the eye icon), and then design away without the distraction of the image. If you want to use Troplabl.eps as the logo, press ⌘+O, and then select it from the Chap15 folder on the Companion CD. Press ⌘+A to Select All, press ⌘+C to copy, and then press ⌘+W to close the file without saving.

7. Press ⌘+V to paste the logo into the document, and then click outside the logo to deselect it.

8. With the Selection tool, drag the logo until it is over the image (users who designed their own logo should restore the visibility of the Photo layer at this point). Note in Figure 15.19 that the Troplabl logo has that outline mentioned earlier, and that all the objects that make up the logo are grouped. So, independent designers, make sure that your logo is grouped, with a stroke but no fill outline outside the label.

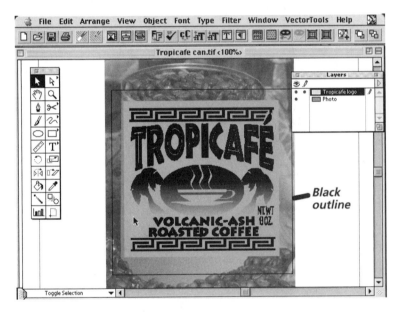

FIGURE 15.19 *Whether you create the art or copy it, make sure that the art is grouped (⌘+G), and that you have a border outside the design.*

9. Choose VectorTools from the menu, and then choose Show VectorShape.

10. Click on the logo with the Selection tool, and then click on the Cylinder icon on the VectorShape palette.

11. Check the Copy check box because the VectorShape palette creates progressive changes to a selected group of objects. If your first try at creating an arcing label fails, you can delete the copy and still have the original on the Tropicafe logo layer.

12. Experiment with the Height, Diameter, and—most important—with the Interpolation sliders, shown in Figure 15.20, until the preview window more or less shows the distortion you want for the artwork. The interpolation slider controls how far down you peer at the transformed artwork. Then, click on Apply; a copy of the original logo is bent to conform to a cylindrical shape.

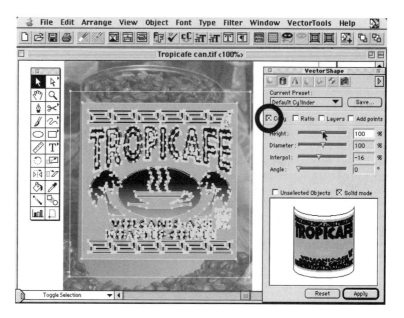

FIGURE 15.20 *Experiment with the amount of distortion you want to apply to the label.*

13. If the label looks as though it's affixed to the can, you've succeeded, and should deselect the distorted label and then delete the original from the layer. If you didn't quite make the label bend the way it should, delete the transformed label, select the original label, and try a different setting on the VectorShape palette.

14. Close the VectorShape palette, and then with the Rotate tool, rotate the label ever so slightly clockwise to conform to the angle of the can, as shown in Figure 15.21. You might want to scale the artwork, too, if the outline edges don't meet the edges of the can.

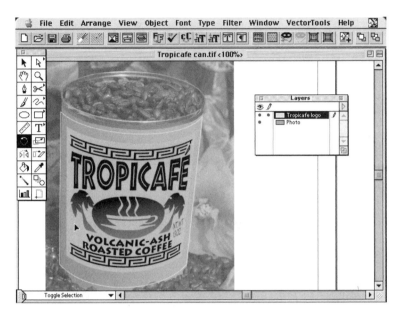

Figure 15.21   *Rotate the label so that the outline within the group of shapes lines up with the left and right edges of the can.*

15. Save the document as Tropicafe logo.ai.

16. Click on the Photo layer, click on the menu flyout button, and then choose the command Delete "Photo". Users of Illustrator 7 can simply drag the Photo layer title into the trash icon. If your screen looks like Figure 15.22, you're in business, and should save the file one last time before closing Illustrator.

Macintosh users don't need to worry about file extensions or whether an Illustrator file or an EPS file is best for saving. The author used an extension in the previous screen figures so that Windows users would know what's going on with the format of file used in this assignment.

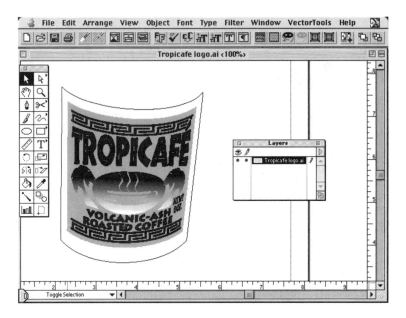

FIGURE 15.22 *Delete the bitmap image from the file, and then save the artwork only as an Illustrator file.*

USING WINDOWS PROGRAMS TO BEND THE LABEL

Although Windows users of CorelDRAW or CorelXARA can import the Troplabl.eps image on the Companion CD, the author has included a CMX file of the label in the Chap15 folder, which those of you with CorelDRAW 5 and later versions, and CorelXARA 1.5 and later versions can use in the following example.

NOTE

If you own neither CorelDRAW nor XARA, you can use the tropbent.eps file in the Chap15 folder to complete this chapter's assignment.

Bending stuff, more accurately called "enveloping" or "moulding" a selected group of objects, is a feature built into CorelDRAW and CorelXARA. You do not need a plug-in application to achieve the same effects Macintosh users get with VectorTools.

If you do own either of these programs, here are the steps needed to create a distorted label, as shown in XARA, with equivalent commands listed for CorelDRAW:

Distorting the Can Label in CorelXARA

1. In XARA, press Ctrl+O, and then choose the Tropicafe can.tif image from your hard disk. In a moment, the image appears on Layer 1. In CorelDRAW, you must choose to File, Import the image, and it, too, will appear on Layer 1.

2. Lock the Layer, and if you intend to design your own logo, hide the layer now. In XARA, the Layers palette is displayed by clicking on the Layer Gallery button on the toolbox; in CorelDRAW, the Layers roll-up can be found under the Layout menu.

3. In both programs, create a new layer and make it the current editing layer.

4. If you're not into designing your own logo, in XARA, press Ctrl+Shift+I to import the Troplabl.cmx file from the Chap15 folder on the CD, as shown in Figure 15.23. Similarly, import the Troplabl.cmx file into CorelDRAW on its own layer. If you want to design your own logo, do not import the file, and hide the layer that contains the photo.

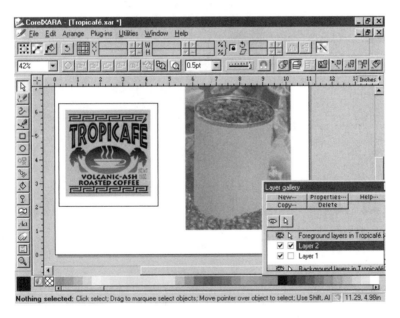

Figure 15.23 *Make sure that the photo is on a locked layer and your logo design is on a new, unlocked layer.*

5. With either the CD's logo or your own on Layer 2, unhide the image on Layer 1.

6. In XARA, choose the logo, group it (Ctrl+A, and then Ctrl+G), and then choose the Mould tool. In DRAW, choose Effects, Envelope roll-up.

7. In XARA, click on the Banner envelope button, as shown in Figure 15.24. The left and right sides of the mould are straight lines and the top and bottom are curved (by a little too much, but you'll correct this). In DRAW, click on Add New, marquee select the middle envelope nodes along the horizontal plane and delete them, and then do the same with the vertical middle nodes. Double-click on the left envelope edge to display the Nodes roll-up, and choose the To Line button. Then do the same with the right envelope dotted line.

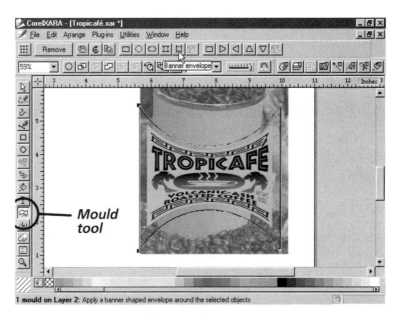

FIGURE 15.24 *Create an envelope around the selected logo. Make certain that the left and right sides are straight, and the top and bottom are curved.*

8. With the Mould tool or the Selector tool, in both programs, align the four corners of the outline box of the logo design to the corners of the coffee can. Then drag on the control handles of the four nodes to mold the shape of the logo so that it conforms to the can, as shown in Figure 15.25. Then, if you're using DRAW, click on the Apply button on the envelope roll-up.

9. In both programs, delete the layer that contains the photo, as shown in Figure 15.26, and then choose File, Export.

FIGURE 15.25 *Mold the outline of the envelope to create an arcing cylinder shape that conforms to the geometry of the coffee can.*

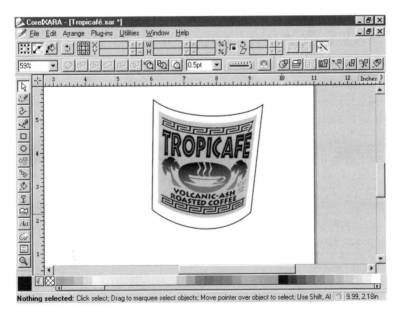

FIGURE 15.26 *Do not export the photo! Delete it before you export the distorted can label.*

10. In the Export box, choose Adobe Illustrator (*.ai, *.eps) as the format you want to export to, and choose a location and name for the file. In DRAW, choose Illustrator 3.0 as the Format, click the Export Text as curves button, and then click on OK. In XARA, press Ctrl+Shift+E, choose Adobe Illustrator as the export format, name the file, and then click on the Export button.

11. You're finished. Save the file in its native format to hard disk and then exit the vector drawing program.

Okay, one way or another you now have an EPS file of the can's label. It's time to move back to Photoshop and import your work.

PHOTOSHOP'S GOT YOUR DIMENSIONS

As mentioned earlier in this chapter, Encapsulated PostScript (and PostScript) is a page description language that tells any output device—a laser printer, a dye-sublimation printer, even your monitor—the specifics of an EPS or PS file. This means that in addition to a description of the colors and geometry used in the logo file, the *dimensions* of the design are also explicitly described to Photoshop or Illustrator, when it's imported.

IMPORTING, COPYING, AND ALIGNING THE LOGO

If you haven't checked out the size and resolution of Tropcafe.psd, now would be a good time to do so. If you reopen the file now in Photoshop, and then choose Image, Image Size, you will see that the image is 10.12 inches wide by 6.827 inches high, and has a resolution of 150 pixels per inch. The resolution is a key factor when you import the logo design. The height and width will be correct, because PostScript technology includes the design's dimensions in a PostScript file, but as a vector design, the logo is resolution-independent. Therefore, you need to tell Photoshop what the resolution of the imported file should be.

In the steps that follow, you'll convert the logo to bitmap format at the correct resolution, add it to the Tropcafe.psd document, and then position it so that it fits nicely on the can.

OPENING AND POSITIONING A VECTOR GRAPHIC

1. With Tropcafe.psd open at about 25% viewing resolution, choose File, Open, and then choose either the file you created in the vector drawing program, or the tropbent.eps file in the Chap15 folder on the Companion CD.

2. The Rasterize Generic EPS Format dialog box opens. As you can see in Figure 15.27, Photoshop read the image Width and Height correctly, as measured in Inches (you could verify this by measuring the artwork in your drawing application), but the resolution will be the last resolution you've specified in this box, so it's most likely incorrect for this assignment. Type **150** in the Resolution field, choose RGB Color from the Mode drop-down menu, and then click on OK.

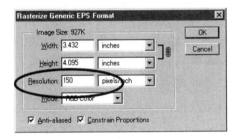

FIGURE 15.27 *Make sure that the Width and Height units are inches, and then type 150 in the Resolution field, the same resolution as Tropcafe.psd.*

3. In a moment, tropbent.eps (or whatever you named your file) will appear in the workspace. With the Move tool, drag the label from its image window into the Tropcafe.psd file, as shown in Figure 15.28. There is a new Layer 1 in the Tropcafe.psd image now.

4. Close the tropbent.eps file without saving it.

5. Zoom in to a 100% view of the Tropcafe.psd image, and maximize the window. Hold down the Spacebar and drag in the image window until you can see the top of the coffee can.

6. With the Move tool, drag the contents of Layer 1 around to position the guides, the outline you created around the logo, so that the left and right edges meet the left and right of the coffee can, and there's about 1/4 screen inch of space between the top of the outline and the top of the can, as shown in Figure 15.29.

FIGURE 15.28   *To copy the EPS label, drag it into the Tropcafe document, using the Move tool.*

FIGURE 15.29   *Position the label on top of the can in the image.*

7. With the Eraser tool set to Block mode, erase the outline on Layer 1, as shown in Figure 15.30. Pan the window around so that you can erase the whole outline.

FIGURE 15.30 *Using the Eraser tool, remove the outline you designed around the label.*

8. Press Ctrl(⌘)+S; keep the file open.

If you looked carefully at the original label in the image, you'd have seen the edge of the label at the top of the can (because paper labels have depth, although not a lot). It is this subtle detail you'll re-create next.

CREATING A FAKE LABEL EDGE

The Pen tool will be your tool of choice for accurately defining the top edge of the label. Paths in Photoshop do not need to be closed paths, and an open path you design will be stroked to produce the illusion that the label you have on Layer 1 is *on top* of the surface of the can.

Here's how to enhance the dimension of the label:

STROKING A PATH

1. Scroll to the top of the can in the image.

2. Make sure that the two saved paths aren't selected by clicking on an empty area of the Paths palette.

3. With the Pen tool, click and drag a line that defines the top edge of the can label, as shown in Figure 15.31.

FIGURE 15.31 *Use the Pen tool to draw a path that is on the edge of the top of the label.*

4. Click on the foreground color swatch, and then in the Color Picker, choose a very light brown. H:31, S:36%, and B: 100% is a good color. Click on OK to exit the Color Picker.

5. Choose the Paintbrush tool; then, on the Options palette, choose the smallest tip in the top row.

6. Click on the Work Path on the Paths palette, and then click on the Strokes path with foreground color icon at the bottom of the palette, as shown in Figure 15.32.

FIGURE 15.32   *Stroke the path you created to illustrate a top edge of the can label.*

7. Click on an empty space on the Paths palette to hide the Work Path so that you can see what you've created, as shown in Figure 15.33.

FIGURE 15.33   *The label fits better into the image now that it has a top edge.*

8. Press Ctrl(⌘)+S; keep the file open.

Your restoration work has been excellent so far. What is needed now to further integrate the artwork portion of the photo is to add some noise to the label, and a subtle highlight to the can, an element that was not in the original image.

ADDING NOISE AND A HIGHLIGHT

The label, like the shading on the can, needs a little noise to make it appear as though photographic grain exists within it. This is a simple step. What is not so simple is adding a highlight to the can, which will require several steps. The highlight should be faint enough to be believable, but strong enough to tie the can visually into the rest of the picture.

Here's how to add two touches of photorealism to the composition:

ADDING PHOTOREALISTIC ELEMENTS

1. Choose Filter, Noise, Add Noise.

2. In the Add Noise dialog box, type **5**, and click on the Gaussian Distribution button, as shown in Figure 15.34. These are the same settings you applied earlier to the can.

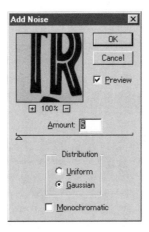

FIGURE 15.34 *Add the same amount of noise to the label as you did to the can.*

3. Click on OK to apply the noise, and then double-click on the Hand tool to zoom the image out so that you can see it in its entirety.

4. On the Paths palette, click on the Can path title, and then click on the Loads path as a selection icon at the bottom of the palette, as shown in Figure 15.35.

FIGURE 15.35   *Create a selection in the image of the can.*

5. On the Channels palette, click on the Save selection as channel icon, and then press Ctrl(⌘)+D to deselect the selection. You should now have a black can silhouette against white in the new Alpha 1 channel. If this is not the case, double-click on the Alpha 1 channel, choose the Color Indicates: Selected Areas button, and then click on OK to close the Channel Options box.

6. With the Polygon Lasso tool create a marquee, as shown in Figure 15.36. This area will be used as a template for creating a highlight on the can.

7. Press Ctrl(⌘)+Shift+I to invert the selection. Press D (default colors), and then press Delete (Backspace). This removes everything outside the marquee; you're left with a vertical wedge in the Alpha 1 channel. Press Ctrl(⌘)+D to deselect the marquee.

8. Choose the Blur tool (the teardrop-shaped icon) from the Focus tools flyout on the toolbox. On the Options palette, type **90** in the Pressure field, and then press Enter (Return). On the Brushes palette, choose the 100-pixel brush tip.

9. Stroke the left and right edges of the vertical shape, as shown in Figure 15.37. This blurs the left and right edges of the can; when you create the can highlight, it will gradually fade into the rest of the can and there will be no hard edges.

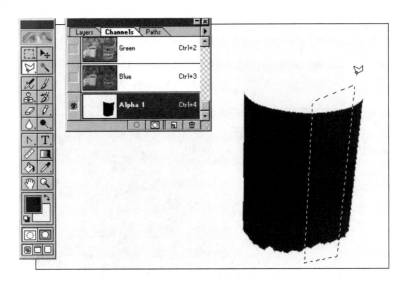

FIGURE 15.36 *You only need a vertical portion of the saved selection to use as a template for the can's highlight in the image.*

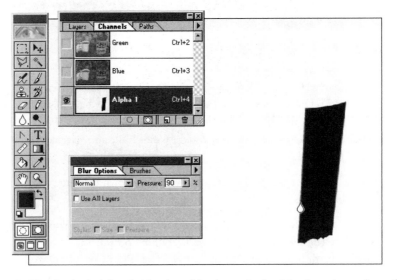

FIGURE 15.37 *Stroke the left and right edges of the element in the alpha channel to make a soft transition between black (selected) and white (masked).*

10. On the Layers palette, drag the Opacity slider for Layer 1 (the label), down to about 80%. Doing this reduces the density of the black on the label. You'll notice that nothing in the image is 100% black, and by reducing the opacity, the label integrates better with the photographic elements in the image.

11. On the Layers palette, click on the menu flyout and then choose Flatten image.

12. On the Channels palette, press Ctrl(⌘) and click on the Alpha 1 title to load the selection.

13. Choose the Dodge tool from the Toning tools flyout on the toolbox. On the Options palette, choose Shadows from the drop-down list, and set the Exposure to about 60%.

14. On the Brushes palette, choose the 100-pixel tip, and then stroke once—two times tops—downward within the selection marquee, as shown in Figure 15.38.

FIGURE 15.38 *Stroke the densest parts of the selection to make it lighter, simulating a subtle highlight on the can.*

15. Press Ctrl(⌘)+D to deselect the marquee. Press Ctrl(⌘)+S; keep the file open.

As long as the can has been embellished, why not add a touch of steam to the coffee cup to make the overall image look more appetizing:

ADDING STEAM TO THE CUP

1. With the Dodge tool and its current settings, stroke around the coffee in the cup about three times.

2. Stroke a wavy line coming out of the cup and heading toward the coffee can, to visually lead the eye toward the product. You might need to stroke over the same area more than once to make the steam visible, but don't let it become too obvious or pronounced. The steam in Figure 15.39 is about right.

FIGURE 15.39 *Stroke the top of the coffee in the cup, and then make a stroke or two away and above the cup to simulate steam.*

3. You're finished! If you'd like to, drag the alpha channel into the trash icon, drag the paths you've created into the trash icon, and then save the image as Tropicafe.tif, in the TIFF format, to your hard disk. By doing this, you enable clients who don't own Photoshop to view and print your masterpiece.

As you can see in Figure 15.40, you now have a professionally retouched image that is worthy of being printed in a magazine or other media. And your success in this assignment is all due to knowing when to call on a helper application for Photoshop.

FIGURE 15.40 *You've taken this image from amateurish to professional looking by using both Photoshop and a vector drawing application.*

SUMMARY

Photoshop is very friendly and responsive when it comes to working with files that were not generated in Photoshop. A vector drawing application complements Photoshop, and you should seriously consider adding one to your arsenal of graphics tools. You'll work faster and with more precision when you know which tools to use on an assignment, and how these tools work.

Equally important in your Photoshop education is knowing when to use (and when *not* to use) a specific filter. Come along to Chapter 16, "Creatively Working with Filters," where you'll see you how to mate the right image with a filter that will enhance it.

CHAPTER 16

CREATIVELY WORKING WITH FILTERS

Photoshop 5 ships with 98 plug-in filters.

This chapter makes no attempt to show you screen figures of every one of them.

A filter is only as good as the purpose it serves, and commands in Photoshop that can be considered a filter aren't always on the Filter menu. This chapter takes you through the integration process, the way a filter fits into your design pipeline, so it is you who have complete control over the outcome of a piece you've enhanced by using a filter. Use plug-ins on the right occasion, and always, always do something in addition to filtering when you work on an image. Put something of yourself into the design; the filter will be the artistic icing on the cake.

Creating a Woodworking Home Page with the Help of Filters

Let's suppose that the fictitious Woodwork Lover's Organization wants you to design some background wallpaper and a few snazzy buttons for their official Web site. The background wallpaper should *suggest* wood instead of depicting it, so this means you need to use Photoshop's features to design the background. The same is true of the navigation buttons for the site; the buttons should be artwork and not a scan of a wooden button. Let's first see how to accomplish the background in Photoshop; after that, we'll take a look at how to create the navigation buttons.

Using the Gradient Editor

There was a time in Photoshop (version 3) when you needed a third-party plug-in filter to create blends that consisted of more than two colors. Versions 4 and 5 of Photoshop changed that with the advent of the Gradient Editor (which can be considered a plug-in). If you have the right stock image of natural texture, you can quickly sample colors to create a complex blend that looks like wood, stone, or metal.

Here's how to use Photoshop's Gradient Editor to create a custom blend that looks like wood grain:

Sampling Colors with the Gradient Editor

1. Launch Photoshop and then open the wood.tif image from the Chap16 folder on the Companion CD. This is the image from which you'll sample some wood tones.

2. Double-click on the Linear Gradient tool to select it and to display the Options palette.

3. Click on Edit on the Options palette, and then move the Gradient Editor so that you have a clear view of both the Editor and the wood.tif image.

4. Click on New; type **wood** in the name field, and then click on OK to close the dialog box.

5. Click on the left color marker on the gradient strip, and then click in the wood.tif image with the Eyedropper tool, as shown in Figure 16.1. This selects the color marker and adds the color you sampled to the gradient strip.

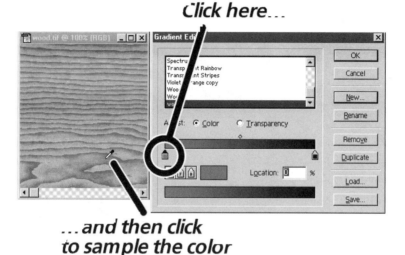

FIGURE 16.1   *Select a color marker and then use the Eyedropper tool to reassign the color of the marker on the strip.*

6. Click directly to the right of the first color marker to add a new color marker to the strip.

7. Click on a different shade of brown in the wood.tif image. The new marker now takes on the color you clicked on.

8. Repeat steps 6 and 7 another three times so that you have a collection of different colored wood tones, as shown in Figure 16.2.

   You need to sample only about five colors from the wood.tif image. To fill the rest of the gradient strip, you can *duplicate* color markers…

9. Hold Alt(Opt) and then drag on one of the color markers to put it to the right of the other markers. Doing this duplicates a color marker.

10. Repeat step 9 about 15 times to fill the gradient strip with alternating colors, as shown in Figure 16.3.

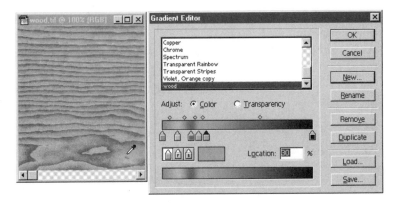

FIGURE 16.2 *Sample different areas of the wood.tif image to make different tones on the gradient strip.*

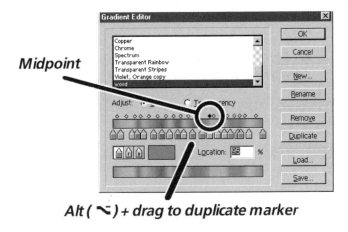

FIGURE 16.3 *Create a pattern of alternating tones by duplicating color markers.*

11. Click on OK to return to the workspace. You can close wood.tif at any time now.

You now have the stock ingredient—a palette of sample colors—for the recipe of making synthetic wood. You'll put the blend you created to work in the following section.

FILTERING THE CUSTOM BLEND

Although the gradient you designed in the preceding section is intricate and shares many visual qualities of actual wood, a linear or other type of gradient will simply produce a pattern, not necessarily one that looks like wood. To simulate wood, you need to filter a sample of the linear gradient a few times.

Here's how to turn a complex blend into a piece of background artwork:

DISTORTING A LINEAR GRADIENT TO CREATE A SEAMLESS TEXTURE

1. Press Ctrl(⌘)+N, name the new image **My-wood.tif**, type **300** in the Width field, type **200** in the Height field, type **72** in the Resolution field, and choose RGB Color from the Mode drop-down list. Click on OK to create the new image.

   You'll be creating a seamless tiling texture, using these steps. The dimensions can be anything you like, but it is recommended that you keep the size small because tiling background textures on the WWW download quickly when they are small.

2. Choose the Linear Gradient tool from the toolbox, hold Shift, and then drag from top to bottom in the new image window, as in Figure 16.4.

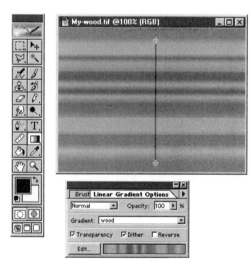

TIP

There are three locations from which you can sample colors for a gradient, from within the workspace:

- Any open image window. You can sample from either a current image window or one that is in the background in the workspace. An eyedropper tool becomes your cursor whenever you "step outside" of the Editor.

- By clicking on the foreground/background color swatches on the toolbox.

- From the color strip on the Color palette. You can display the Color palette by pressing F6, even when you are in the Gradient Editor dialog box.

FIGURE 16.4   *Apply the Linear Gradient in combination with the custom blend you created.*

3. Choose Filter, Distort, and then choose Wave. Wave is an ideal filter for simulating wood because it bends image areas to look like the grain in wood.

4. Use the settings in Figure 16.5 to create a wavy blend in the image. Make certain that you've clicked the Wrap Around button before clicking on OK.

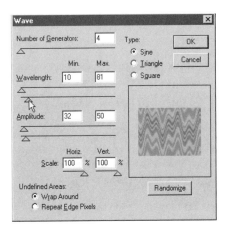

FIGURE 16.5 *Make waves out of the striations in the image to create a woodlike image.*

Although the Wrap Around option takes care of the vertical aspect of the image—vertically, it will tile seamlessly—the horizontal aspect of the image probably will not tile seamlessly. This is because of the number of wave generators used and the overall width of the image. Not to worry; we'll fix this shortly…

5. Choose Filter, Other, and then choose Offset. Type **100** in both the Horizontal and Vertical fields, click the Wrap Around button (see Figure 16.6), and then click on OK. The Offset filter shows you how an image will look when it's tiled.

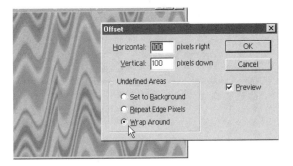

FIGURE 16.6 *Use the Offset filter to turn an image "inside out." The edges of the image are now toward the image's center.*

As you'll probably note in your My-wood image, there is a hard vertical edge where the pattern doesn't align perfectly. No problem; you'll use the Smudge tool to make the edge disappear…

6. Choose the Smudge tool, choose the second-to-right tip in the second row of the Brushes palette, and then drag in the image to smooth out the hard vertical line, as shown in Figure 16.7. It does not matter if your editing work produces perfect "rings" in the image. You'll be applying another filter shortly that will obscure any flaws in your editing.

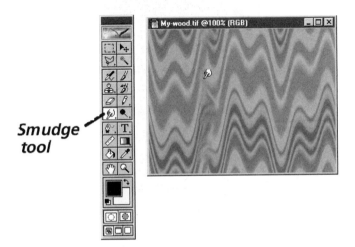

Smudge tool

FIGURE 16.7 *The Smudge tool treats image areas as though they are wet paint. Use the tool to remove the hard edge in the image.*

7. Choose Filter, Distort, and then choose Ocean Ripple (see Figure 16.8). Click on OK to apply the default settings for this filter. Ocean Ripple creates irregular creases and bumps in the image to make it look more like natural wood.

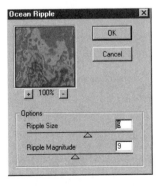

FIGURE 16.8 *The Ocean Ripple filter helps give the pattern a more organic feel.*

The Ocean Ripple filter should not overwhelm your composition. You need to fade the effect to allow some of the Wave filter's effects to show through...

8. Press Ctrl(⌘)+Shift+F to display the Fade dialog box. Drag the Opacity slider to about 50%, as in Figure 16.9, and then click on OK.

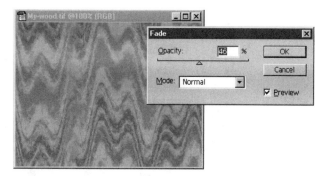

FIGURE 16.9 *The Fade command blends the filtered image with the image before the filter was applied.*

9. Press Ctrl(⌘)+S; keep the file open.

NOTE

The Fade command is not limited to filters. You can press Ctrl(⌘)+Shift+F and fade Levels, Hue/Saturation, and other commands after you apply them.

It's time to add a little surface texture to the wood illustration. The Lighting Effects filter is perfect for the task.

LIGHTING EFFECTS AND THE TEXTURE CHANNEL

In addition to simulating light in a scene, Photoshop's Lighting Effects filter can create bumps in an image, called Texture Channel effects. You can base the bumps on information in an alpha channel, or use any of the color channels to create steep or shallow bumps.

In the next set of steps, you'll add a mild amount of bumpiness to the My-wood.tif image, and then lighten and decrease the contrast in the image, so that black text can be used over the background on the Web site.

Here's how to finish the wood background for the client:

USING LIGHTING EFFECTS TO CREATE TEXTURES

1. Choose Filter, Render, and then choose Lighting Effects. The Lighting Effects dialog box appears in the workspace.

2. Choose Directional from the Light type drop-down list, drag the Material slider to zero (midway between Metallic and Plastic), and then choose Green from the Texture Channel drop-down list. Green is a good color channel to produce bumps, because it contains a moderate amount of tonal information for the predominantly brown My-wood image (green and red produce brown in the additive RGB color model).

3. Drag the light direction point in the proxy window to slightly above and outside the proxy window. Drag the Height slider to about 8 to produce subtle bumps in the image. Figure 16.10 shows the image and these settings. The exposure of the image can be defined by the distance from the light target and the light direction point; try to make the exposure the same in the proxy window as it is in the My-wood.tif image window.

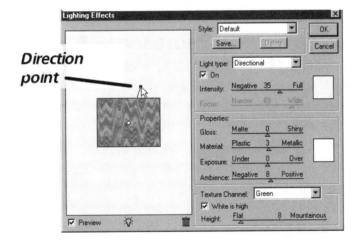

FIGURE 16.10 *The Lighting Effects filter can apply a texture to your image.*

4. Click on OK to apply the Lighting Effects texture.

5. Use the Image, Duplicate command at this point if you'd like to save your textured wood, as is. Work on the copy of the My-wood image from here on.

6. Press Ctrl(⌘)+L to display the Levels command box. Type **2.08** in the middle Input Levels field. This increases the brightness of the midtones in the image. Type **24** in the left Output Levels field. This increases the brightness of the black tones in the image. Click on OK to apply the changes.

7. Choose File, Save As, and then choose JPEG from the Save As drop-down list.

8. In the JPEG Options box, drag the Quality slider to 7, click on the Baseline Optimized button, and then click on OK.

9. You're finished! Save the original My-wood.tif image one last time, and close it. You can close the JPEG copy of the file also. And don't take any wooden nickels from your client.

When it comes to using JPEG images on the WWW, it is best to choose a compression standard that is commonly accepted. Some Web browsers cannot read a Progressive JPEG (although both MS-Explorer 4 and Netscape Navigator 4 can), so the option to choose to make the image the most widely available on the Web is Baseline Optimized.

CREATING BUTTONS IN PHOTOSHOP

Navigation buttons on Web pages should be small; anywhere from 10 pixels to 30 pixels in width is acceptable. We're going to work a little larger than this in the following sections, however, so that you can better see the effects you create with some of Photoshop's new features.

First things first: you need to design a template in an alpha channel that will serve as the button shape. Here's how to use Photoshop's Guides to create a handsome wooden button template:

CREATING A BUTTON TEMPLATE

1. Press Ctrl(⌘)+N, type **200** in both the Height and Width fields of the New dialog box, type **72** in the Resolution field, choose RGB Color from the Mode drop-down list, and then click on OK.

2. Press Ctrl(⌘)+the plus key to zoom your view to 200% resolution.

3. Press F7 if the Layers palette is not currently onscreen. Click on the Channels tab, and then click on the Create new channel icon at the bottom of the palette. Alpha 1 appears as the title on the palette; this channel is your current editing channel. Click on the menu flyout on the Channels palette, choose Channel Options, and then make certain Color Indicates: Selected Areas is chosen. Click on OK to exit the Options box.

4. Press Ctrl(⌘)+R to display rulers on the top and left of the image window. Drag a vertical guide to the center of the image from the vertical ruler, and then drag a horizontal guide from the horizontal ruler so that you have a crosshair in the center of the image window.

5. Press Ctrl(⌘)+Shift+; (semicolon) to enable Snap to Guides. Drag the *origin box* (the box at the vertex of the horizontal and vertical rulers) to the point where the horizontal and vertical guides meet. This is the starting point for the button template.

6. Press and hold Shift+Alt(Opt) while, with the Elliptical Marquee tool, you drag away from the center point of the guidelines until your cursor is at about the 40-point mark on the rulers. You're creating a button 80 pixels in diameter (a pixel is approximately equal to a point).

7. Press D (default colors), and then press Alt(Opt)+Delete (Backspace). Press Ctrl(⌘)+D to deselect the selection marquee. You now have a dot, 80 pixels in diameter, in the document window.

8. Hold Shift+Alt(Opt) and then, starting at the zero point, drag a circle that is slightly smaller than the 80-pixel circle. Press Delete (Backspace), and then press Ctrl(⌘)+D. You have a donut shape now.

9. Hold Shift+Alt(Opt) and then, starting at the zero point, drag a circle that fits inside the donut. Press Alt(Opt)+Delete (Backspace), and then press Ctrl(⌘)+D to deselect the selection marquee. You should now have a template that looks like Figure 16.11.

10. Choose Flatten Image from the Layers palette's menu flyout. Choose File, Save and save the composition as Button.psd, in Photoshop's native file format. Choose View, Clear Guides, and then press Ctrl(⌘)+R to hide the rulers. Keep the document open.

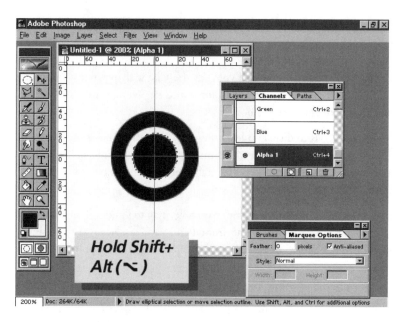

FIGURE 16.11 *Create a collection of concentric circles to make an elegant button template.*

Next you'll apply a fill to the button, and then explore the Layer Effects feature in Photoshop 5.

DIMENSIONALIZING THE BUTTON

For a button to stand out on a Web page, it should look three-dimensional. Your button already has shape, but there are two additional properties you must build into the button:

1. The surface texture—what the button is made of

2. The third dimension for the button—its depth, and the way this depth reacts to lighting

Adding surface texture is not a chore; you'll simply use the custom blend—wood—you created earlier in the Gradient Editor. The big trick is deciding on the right filter to make the button look 3D. Here's how to address both issues:

CREATING A PHOTOREALISTIC BUTTON

1. On the Layers palette, click on the Create new layer icon. You're working on Layer 1 now.

2. On the Channels palette, press Ctrl(⌘) and click on the Alpha 1 title to load the template as a selection marquee.

3. With the Linear Gradient tool, with the "wood" gradient defined on the Options palette, drag from the top to the bottom of the selection marquee, as shown in Figure 16.12. Press Ctrl(⌘)+D to deselect the marquee now.

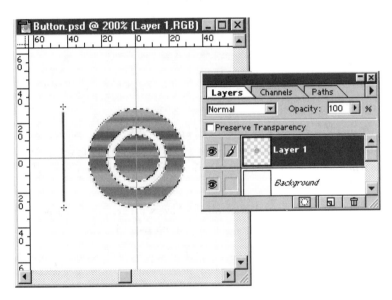

FIGURE 16.12 *Create a complex fill for the button by using the Linear Gradient fill in combination with your custom blend.*

4. Choose Layer, Effects, and then choose Bevel and Emboss.

5. From the Style drop-down list, choose Inner Bevel. Hold on the Angle flyout button to expose the direction proxy box, and then drag the proxy line in the box to the upper left, as shown in Figure 16.13. This will make the button look as though it is lit from the upper left.

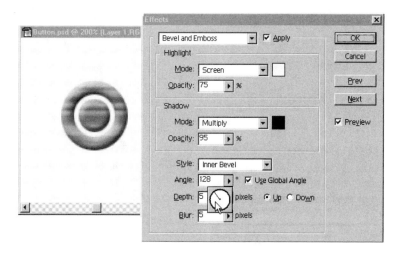

FIGURE 16.13 *Create lighting, shading, and a sense of a third dimension by using the Layer Effects command.*

6. Click on OK to apply the Inner Bevel effect to the contents of the layer. You'll notice that an *f* in a circle appears on the layer title on the Layers palette. This is a reminder that anything you paint in the future on this layer will take on the Inner Bevel effect.

7. Click on the Background layer on the Layers palette, and then click on the Create new layer icon. Layer 2 is now beneath Layer 1.

8. Choose the Elliptical Marquee tool, hold Shift, and then, beginning at the upper left of the button, drag down and to the right until you have a selection marquee of similar size to the shape of the button.

9. Drag inside the marquee so that it is positioned slightly to the right and bottom of the button. Press Alt(Opt)+Delete (Backspace) to fill the button with foreground color, as shown in Figure 16.14; then press Ctrl(⌘)+D to deselect the marquee.

10. Drag the Opacity slider for Layer 2 to about 50%.

11. Choose Filter, Blur, and then choose Gaussian Blur.

12. In the Gaussian Blur dialog box, type **3** in the pixels field, and then click on OK to blur the circle.

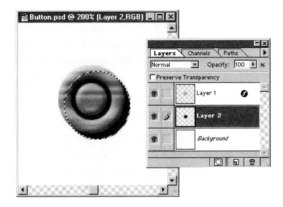

FIGURE 16.14 *Create a drop shadow for the button by filling a circle on a layer below the button.*

13. Press Ctrl(⌘)+S; keep the file open.

The only thing left to do now is add a background so that the button will blend into the background of the Web page.

TILING THE TEXTURE

When a design is intricate enough, like the wood background you created, visitors to Web sites tend not to notice the rectangular bounding box around buttons, as long as the texture in the background is the same as that in the background for the document. See Chapter 19 for more information on this technique.

Here's how to finish the button for the Web page:

ADDING A BACKGROUND BY DEFINING A PATTERN

1. Open the Wood.jpg image you saved earlier. Press Ctrl(⌘)+A to select all, and then choose Edit, Define Pattern. You can close the wood.jpg image now.

2. Click on the Background layer title on the Layers palette, and then press Ctrl(⌘)+A.

3. Make sure that the Elliptical Marquee tool is still chosen, right-click (Macintosh: hold Ctrl and click), and then choose Fill from the context menu.

4. Choose Pattern from the Use: drop-down list, and then click on OK. Press Ctrl(⌘)+D to deselect the marquee. Figure 16.15 shows the finished product.

5. With the Rectangular Marquee tool, carefully drag a selection marquee that is tight around the button and shadow, but does not crop any of the foreground elements out of the selection.

6. Choose Image, Crop.

7. Press Ctrl+Alt(⌘+Opt)+S, and save a copy of your work to JPEG format, as Button.jpg. Use Baseline Optimized compression; click on OK to save the copy.

8. Save the Button.psd image one last time, and then close it.

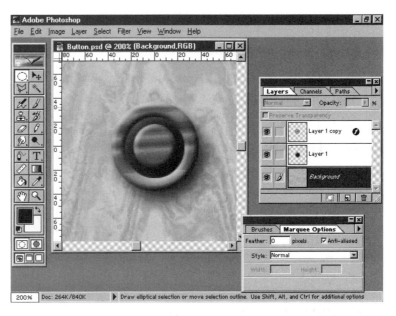

FIGURE 16.15 *Add the same background as the one you'll use on the Web page by using the Fill, Use:Pattern command.*

Figure 16.16 shows what a little HTML code and the work you've designed looks like on the Web. If you'd like to reproduce this piece and you already own a good HTML editor, the Woodwork.psd file—the wooden lettering—is in the Chap16 folder on the Companion CD.

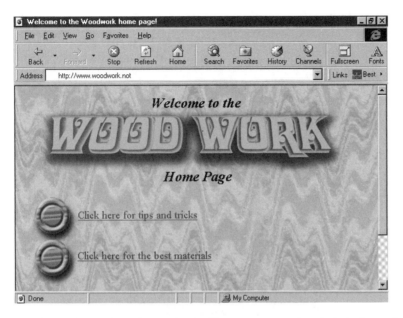

FIGURE 16.16 *With the right gradient and a few filters, you can reproduce the look of natural elements.*

CREATING FRACTAL TERRAIN

The look of aerial photography is another popular look on Web page backgrounds. You can simulate land masses or simply a close-up view of dirt, using a few undocumented tricks, and a filter or two in Photoshop.

THE RENDER CLOUDS FILTER

The Render Clouds filter produces procedural noise, which is a fancy way of saying that it produces a good simulation of clouds and smoke. Procedural textures are usually mathematically written in one of two ways: so that the texture terminates (it produces a tiling pattern when applied to large areas), or the texture never terminates (it continues to produce unique areas regardless of image size). Photoshop's Clouds filter is a terminating procedural texture; it repeats every 256 pixels.

We can use this little-known fact to our advantage in constructing a background for any type of Web site. Let's begin this assignment with the correct-sized canvas, the Clouds filter, and by saving a copy of the clouds effect to be blended into the composition later.

SETTING UP A TILING CLOUDS PICTURE

1. Press Ctrl(⌘)+N. In the New dialog box, type **256** in both the Height and Width fields, type **72** in the Resolution field, and then choose RGB Color from the Mode drop-down list, all options shown in Figure 16.17. Click OK to create the new document window.

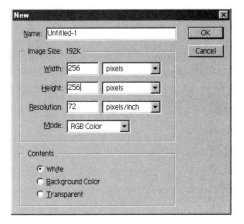

FIGURE 16.17 *Create a new image that is the same size as the repeating quality of the Clouds filter.*

2. Press D (default colors), choose Filter, Render, and then choose Clouds. Figure 16.18 shows the clouds image that is rendered to the document, using the default foreground and background colors.

3. You might not like the clouds image; Photoshop generates thousands of different cloud designs each time you use the filter. Press Ctrl(⌘)+F to reapply the filter until you see a clouds design you like.

4. Press Ctrl(⌘)+A, and then press Ctrl(⌘)+C.

5. On the Channels palette, click on the Create new channel icon, and then press Ctrl(⌘)+V to paste a copy of the clouds pattern into the channel. Press Ctrl(⌘)+D to deselect the marquee. Choose Flatten Image from the Layers palette's menu flyout.

FIGURE 16.18 *The Clouds filter produces a procedural texture with colors that are the current fore-ground/background colors.*

6. Press Ctrl(⌘)+S, and name the image Land.tif; keep the file open.

It's time to play a little with the image, using Photoshop's modes commands.

FROM RGB COLOR TO INDEXED

For several versions of Photoshop, users have had the ability to map indexed color images to different spectrums of color by changing the color look-up table. And for several versions, users have wondered *why* they'd want to do this! By selectively replacing colors in an indexed color version of the Land.tif image, you will be able to simulate land masses.

Here's the procedure for remapping colors in the image:

REMAPPING A COLOR TABLE

1. Choose Image, Mode, and then choose Indexed Color.

2. Accept the defaults in the Indexed Color dialog box by clicking on OK.

3. Choose Image, Mode, and then choose Color Table.

4. Starting at the first color, drag across and down so that the top five rows are highlighted, as illustrated in Figure 16.19. This action sends Photoshop a signal that you want to remap the first five rows in the image's color table.

5. The Color Picker appears with the command "Select first color" at top. Define a pale cream color, using the color field and the hue slider, as shown in Figure 16.20.

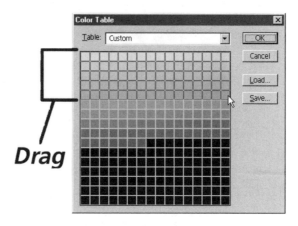

Drag

FIGURE 16.19 *In an image's Color Table, you can select any color or group of colors that you want to reassign.*

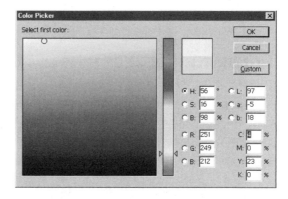

FIGURE 16.20 *Choose the beginning color for the group of colors you want to change.*

6. Click on OK. Photoshop then displays the Color Picker with the command "Select last color" at the top, as you can see in Figure 16.21. Choose a dark brown, using the color field and hue slider, and then click on OK.

7. In the Color Table dialog box, drag to select the next six rows of color swatches. Follow steps 5–6 to reassign the colors.

8. Finally, in the Color Table dialog box, drag to select the bottom rows of color swatches. Follow steps 5–6 to reassign the colors. The Color Table should look like Figure 16.22 now (except yours will be in color!).

FIGURE 16.21   *Select the last color in the group of selected colors you want to change.*

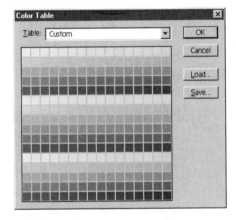

FIGURE 16.22   *Bands of color gradations will create land masses in the clouds image.*

9. Click on OK. The Land.tif image will look similar to Figure 16.23. It will not look identical, because the cloud pattern the author used is probably not the same as the one you used.

10. Choose Image, Mode, and then choose RGB Color. Choose Filter, Render, and then choose Lighting Effects.

11. In the Lighting Effects dialog box, choose Directional from the Light Type drop-down list, position the direction point in the proxy window so that the light direction line points at about one o'clock. Drag the direction point toward the proxy window so that the overall exposure of the proxy image is the same as that in your image.

FIGURE 16.23 *Altering an indexed image's color table can produce hard edges in the image, with gentle gradations of color.*

12. In the Texture Channel drop-down list, choose alpha 1, and then drag the Height slider to about 60, as shown in Figure 16.24. Click on OK to apply texture to your land masses.

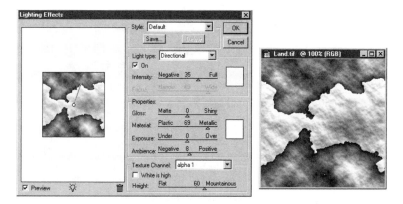

FIGURE 16.24 *Use the Lighting Effect's Texture Channel to add a cloudy texture to the image.*

13. Press Ctrl(⌘)+S; keep the file open.

You've completed the assignment. You might want to save a copy of the Land.tif image as a JPEG image now and use it as a seamless tiling background for a Web page. In any event, you should at least test out the seamless tiling property of your creation by either using the Offset command, or by defining the image as a pattern and filling a full-screen image window.

There are plenty of ways to take flat artwork and make it look 3D in Photoshop. In the following section, we take a look at a new feature, the 3D Transform filter.

3D TRANSFORM AND PRODUCT VISUALIZATION

Imagine a method for mapping a 2D surface onto a 3D object, right within Photoshop. You could turn rectangles into cubes and circles into spheres. Okay, stop imagining—Photoshop 5 provides these services! With the right artwork and a few careful steps, you'll soon be turning the label for a box of cereal into a 3D scene.

PREPARING THE ART FOR 3D TRANSFORM

The 3D Transform filter only draws cube wireframes to which you match your target artwork in one way; there's a left facet, a right, and a top facet to the distortion wireframe. Therefore, if you want to put the label on the front of a box, as you'll do in the following steps, you'd best create the artwork with plenty of empty space around it, and position the label toward either the lower left or lower right of the image window. In Figure 16.25, you can see our fictitious product, Harvest Pride, as it is positioned in the Pride.tif document. If you'd like to use your own design in the steps that follow, position your artwork similarly in an image window.

FIGURE 16.25 *Position the artwork in the image window so that it will line up with a left or right facet of a cube you'll design with the 3D Transform filter.*

The results of the 3D Transform filter are realistic, but they by no means complete a scene. The following sections show you how to embellish upon the filter's effect to create an entire tabletop scene for the cereal.

Here's how to begin the assignment:

CREATING A 3D SHAPE

1. Open the Pride.tif image from the Chap16 folder of the Companion CD (or use your own image here).

2. Choose Filter, Render, and then choose 3D Transform.

3. Click on the cube button and then drag from upper left to lower right in the image, so that the right facet of the cube is more or less over the package design, as in Figure 16.26.

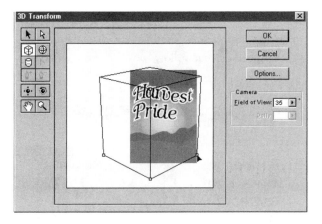

FIGURE 16.26   *Create the cube wireframe so that it's right face lies over the illustration of the cereal box.*

4. If the right face is not directly over the illustration, choose the Selection tool, the upper-left tool on the toolbox, and then drag the wireframe so that the vertex between its left and right faces lies on the left edge of the illustration.

5. With the Direct Selection tool (the upper-right tool on the toolbox), drag the bottom-left anchor on the wireframe toward the vertex. This makes the box shallower. Then drag the rightmost bottom anchor toward the bottom-right corner of the illustration (see Figure 16.27). You might need to go back to the left bottom anchor one more time to make the box shallow...like a cereal box.

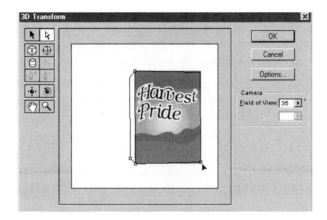

FIGURE 16.27 *Drag the right face anchor points so that the right face of the wireframe conforms to the shape of the cereal illustration.*

6. When the right face basically conforms to the illustration's shape, it's time to move and rotate the selection. Click on the Trackball tool, shown in Figure 16.28 and drag down and to the right so that you have a three-quarters view of the box. Then, with the Move tool, drag the box to the left, so that you have a clear view of it in the proxy window. The 3D Transform filter makes a copy of whatever is in an image window, so you now have an undistorted illustration and the 3D box onscreen.

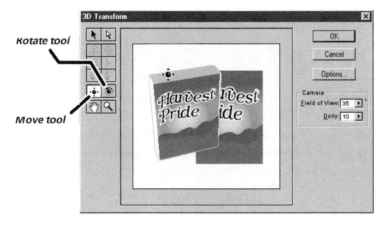

FIGURE 16.28 *Give the illustration dimension by using 3D Tranform's Trackball tool.*

7. Click on OK to apply the 3D Transform.

8. With the Polygon Lasso tool, click on the six corners of the box in the image window, and then close the selection by clicking a single time on the first click point.

9. Right-click (Macintosh: hold Ctrl and click), and then choose Layer Via Cut from the context menu.

10. Drag the Background layer on the Layers palette into the trash icon on the palette.

11. Save your work as Pride.psd in Photoshop's native file format. Keep the file open.

Well, the 2D illustration definitely looks like a 3D cereal box now, except that it's floating in space. Now you'll use Photoshop's features to contextualize the cereal box—you'll put it in a simple yet attractive surrounding.

ADDING A TABLE TOP

A wood table top would complement the natural theme of the 3D cereal box. In the steps to follow, you'll use a stock image of some wood in combination with Photoshop's Free Transform feature to create a table top.

USING THE FREE TRANSFORM'S DISTORT MODE TO CREATE PERSPECTIVE

1. Open the Oak.tif image from the Chap16 folder of the Companion CD.

2. On the Layers palette, drag the Background title into the Pride.psd image window. This makes a copy of the wood in the Pride image.

3. Drag the Layer 2 title and drop it on the Layer 1 title on the Layers palette to put the wood beneath the cereal box.

4. Drag the image window away from the Pride.psd image so that you can see background color. You'll need some extra space to manipulate the Free Transform's Distort control handles.

5. Press Ctrl(⌘)+T to display the Free Transform bounding box, and then right-click (Macintosh: hold Ctrl and click) and choose Distort from the Context menu, as shown in Figure 16.29.

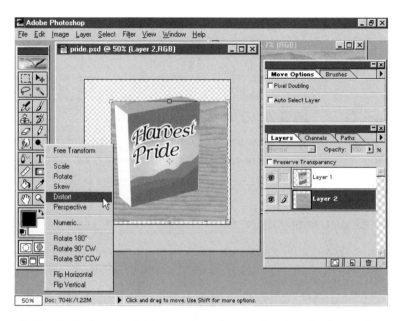

FIGURE 16.29 *In Free Transform's Distort mode, each corner of the bounding box can be moved independently, without moving the other corners.*

6. Drag the bounding box handles so that an irregular shape is created, as shown in Figure 16.30. You've created a table top in perspective, with one corner sticking out on the right of the composition.

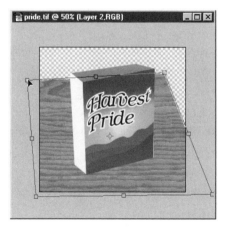

FIGURE 16.30 *Distort the wood selection so that it shares the same perspective as the cereal box.*

7. When the wood looks appropriately distorted, double-click inside the bounding box to finalize the effect—or press Enter(Return).

8. Press Ctrl(⌘)+S; keep the file open.

ADDING SHADING AND A BACKGROUND

Now to dress up the design a little more. In the steps to follow, you'll add a background tone to the composition, and add a shadow to the cereal box.

Here's how to work across layers to flesh out the design:

ADDING SHADING TO THE DESIGN

1. Click on the Create new layer icon on the Layers palette, and then drag Layer 3 to the bottom of the palette. Layer 3 is the current editing layer.

2. Drag on the face of the Gradient tool, and then choose the Radial Gradient from the toolbox flyout (second from the left).

3. On the Options palette, choose Foreground to Background from the drop-down list.

4. Press D and then press X so that white is the current foreground color.

5. Starting at the upper-right corner of the box, drag a line like that shown in Figure 16.31. You've created a "sunrise" sort of effect for the composition, intimating the time of day most people eat cereal.

6. Click on the Layer 2 title on the Layers palette to make it the current editing layer, and then click on the Create new layer icon. There's a new layer now between the wood and the cereal box.

7. With the Polygon Lasso tool, click points behind and to the left of the box to make an oblong shape, shown in Figure 16.32. Press D and then press Alt(Opt)+Delete (Backspace) to fill the shape with foreground black. Press Ctrl(⌘)+D to deselect the marquee.

8. Drag the Opacity slider on the Layers palette to about 50%. This allows some wood grain to show through the shadow you created.

9. Press Ctrl(⌘)+S; keep the file open.

Start point

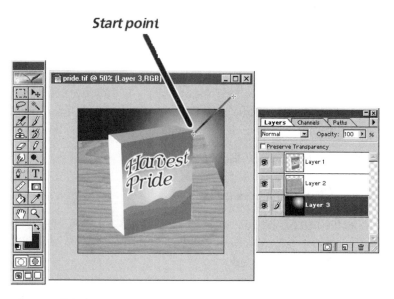

FIGURE 16.31 *Fill the bottom layer with a gradient that moves the audience's eye toward the package design.*

The left side of the cereal box looks a little sparse. Usually, it would be covered with nutrition information, a list of ingredients, and those bonus points no one ever seems to clip out. You'll address this oversight in the following section.

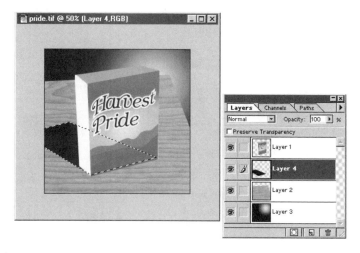

FIGURE 16.32 *Create a shadow "behind" the cereal box.*

Adding "Business" to the Box

When the ingredients of cereal are printed on the box, the shape of the text's bounding box is rectangular. From our viewpoint of the box, however, the left panel is a parallelogram. In the next set of steps, you'll create *greeking* (dummy text) for the side of the box, and then use the Free Transform Distort mode again to match the sides of the panel you create with the panel on the box.

Here's how to finish the composition:

Adding a Side Panel to a Cereal Box

1. Click on the Layer 1 title (the cereal box) on the Layers palette, and then click on the Create new layer icon at the bottom of the palette. A Layer 5 title appears; this is where you'll design the side panel for the box.

2. With the Rectangular Marquee tool, drag a shape that's about the same size as the box's left panel. Press X, and then press Alt(Opt)+Delete (Backspace) to fill the rectangular selection with white. Press Ctrl(⌘)+D to deselect the marquee.

3. Press X, choose the Paintbrush tool, choose the second-to-smallest tip on the Brushes palette, and then make some straight-line doodles on the panel you've created. In Figure 16.33, you can see the author's version of the side panel greeking.

4. Press Ctrl(⌘)+T, and then right-click (Macintosh: hold Ctrl and click), and choose Distort from the context menu.

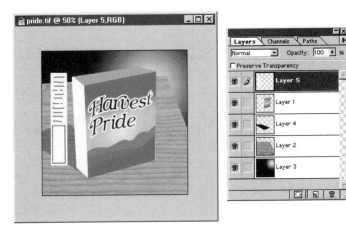

Figure 16.33 *Simulate the look of very small text by painting squiggly lines across the panel you created.*

5. Line up the four corners of the panel with the four corners of the panel on the box, as shown in Figure 16.34.

FIGURE 16.34 *Match the angle of perspective on the side panel of the box by lining up the Distort bounding box at each corner.*

6. Press Enter (Return) or double-click inside the Distort bounding box to finalize the change you've made.

7. Press Ctrl(⌘)+S. You're finished. The design should look like Figure 16.35, and you can close the image at any time now.

FIGURE 16.35 *Using layers, Free Transform's Distort mode, and the 3D Transform filter, you can create a complete scene.*

You've seen only one use for the 3D Transform filter so far. What do you say to a little text-bending adventure now?

WORKING WITH 3D TRANSFORM'S SPHERE SHAPE

One of the most common tasks to designs, and one of the most difficult to execute, is the subtle bending of text to create a typographical design element. In the following section you'll see how to transform text in a different way than you transformed the cereal box.

CREATING ARCING TEXT

One of the best ways to attract attention to a headline or other phrase in a design is to bow, to arc, the type. The 3D Transform tool makes this a practically effortless task, and the following steps take you through the procedure:

THE 3D SPHERICAL TRANSFORM

1. Open the Birthday.psd image from the Chap16 folder on the Companion CD. This image has black text on the "Happy Birthday!" layer, with a background image of a cupcake with a candle.

2. Click on the Happy Birthday! Layer to make it the current editing layer, choose Filter, Render, and then choose 3D Transform.

3. Choose the Sphere tool, and then drag a circle around the Happy Birthday! text. Use the Selection tool to center the circle around the text if necessary.

4. With the Trackball tool, push upward until the text looks like that shown in Figure 16.36. Click on OK to apply the effect.

The text is the wrong color to be read against the cupcake image, but it was done this way so that you could better see the text in the 3D Transform preview window. You can't really see white text on a layer in the 3D Transform window. This can be easily changed, and we also need to remove an "artifact" of the 3D Transform process from the image. You'll note that the 3D Transform also rendered part of the back of the sphere image into the design, and you don't want it there...

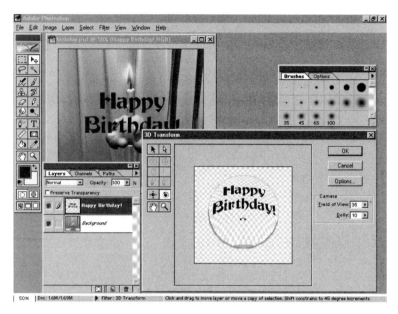

FIGURE 16.36 *The sphere tool treats text and other design shapes as though they were on the skin of a balloon.*

5. On the Layers palette, check the Preserve Transparency check box.

6. Choose the Paintbrush tool, choose the last tip on the top row on the Brushes palette, and make the current foreground color white.

7. Paint over the black text with white. As you can see in Figure 16.37, the paint goes only where there are opaque areas on the layer.

8. Uncheck the Preserve Transparency check box, and then with the Lasso tool drag a marquee around the crescent in the image. Press Delete (Backspace), and then press Ctrl(⌘)+D to deselect the marquee.

9. You're finished! Save the image as Birthday.psd to your hard disk. You can close the image at any time now.

The Sphere mode of the 3D Transform tool opens up dozens of design possibilities for text. You can make text swoop and curve and embrace other design elements in your composition.

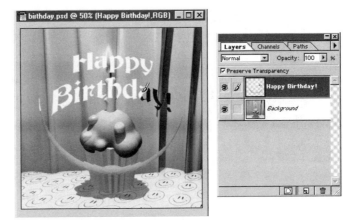

FIGURE 16.37 *Use the Preserve Transparency option to create your own frisket for recoloring the text.*

GOING WITH THE FLOW; FILTERS THAT COMPLEMENT GEOMETRY

Next you'll take a look at a handful of the "Gallery Effects" filters that Photoshop ships with. These are powerful filters that might not offer the creative latitude of the filters covered so far, but with the right image you can indeed produce outstanding work.

The key to the following sections is, "pick the right image for a filter." Some images do not lend themselves to all plug-in filters. In essence, you should "go with the flow." In other words, if you have an image with a geometric composition that is hard and well-defined, use a filter that accentuates this property. And if you have an image with a content that is soft, choose a filter that brings out soft qualities.

STYLIZING THE DESK SCENE

Changing the focal point of interest in an image is easy to do with filters. You can leave areas unfiltered, and then play with the brightness and contrast in the scene to direct the audience anywhere you like. The next assignment works with the Desk.tif image on the Companion CD. As you can see in Figure 16.38, the lamp dominates the composition due to its color and relative size. Suppose, however, that you want to make the yo-yo the focal attraction of the composition. How would you do this, using filters? Follow these steps!

FIGURE 16.38   *In this image, the lamp is clearly the focal point.*

SHIFTING VISUAL EMPHASIS BY USING FILTERS

1. Open the Desk.tif image from the Chap16 folder of the Companion CD. And bear with the figures that follow; Desk.tif is a color piece that can only be appreciated on your screen!

2. With the Rectangular Marquee tool, drag around the yo-yo in the image, and then right-click (Macintosh: hold Ctrl and click) and choose Layer Via Copy from the menu.

3. Hide the new layer (click on the eye icon) and click on the Background layer to make it the current editing layer.

4. Choose Filter, Artistic, and then choose Cutout.

5. Drag the No. of Levels slider to 3. This control posterizes the original image, and 3 simplifies all the colors in Desk.tif.

6. Drag the Edge Simplicity slider to 2. This makes the lines in the image simple; finer details are ignored.

7. Leave Edge Fidelity at its default of 2. This creates a more distorted representation of the scene, which as you can see from Figure 16.39 is now more stylized, and diminished in visual importance.

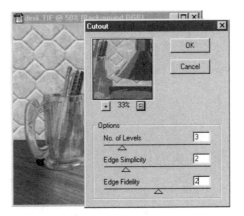

FIGURE 16.39 *Use the Cutout filter to stylize the Background layer areas.*

8. Click on OK to apply the filter.

9. Press Ctrl(⌘)+U to display the Hue/Saturation command.

10. Click on the Colorize check box, and then drag the Hue slider to about 259. This gives a purplish tone to the image. Click on OK to apply the command.

11. Unhide the yo-yo on Layer 1, make it the current editing layer, and then choose Layer, Effects, Drop Shadow.

12. Type **28** in the Distance field, type **28** in the Blur field, and then click on OK. These settings produce the fat but subtle drop shadow shown in Figure 16.40.

FIGURE 16.40 *Use Layer Effects to further distance the highlighted yo-yo from its background.*

13. You're finished! You've succeeded at emphasizing the yo-yo in the image despite the other dominating elements. Save your work as Yo-Yo.psd in Photoshop's native file format.

Now you'll try a different approach and create an "unfinished symphony" from the Desk.tif image.

USING TWO FILTERS AND TWO LAYERS

The American painter Gilbert Stuart is perhaps best remembered for his unfinished rendering of George Washington. Although Stuart and his daughter created several versions of this piece, the version with the unpainted, roughed-out corner has become an icon among masterpieces.

In the steps that follow, you will create this classic look by using different filters and a spare copy of the Desk image on a layer.

CREATING AN UNFINISHED MASTERPIECE

1. Open the Desk.tif image from the Chap16 folder on the Companion CD.

2. On the Layers palette, drag the Background title into the Create new layer icon. This duplicates the layer, and the Background copy is now the current editing layer.

3. Choose Filter, Stylize, Find Edges. There are no options for this filter; it's immediately applied (see Figure 16.41). Notice that the Find Edges filter works best with images that contain clearly defined geometry, such as this one.

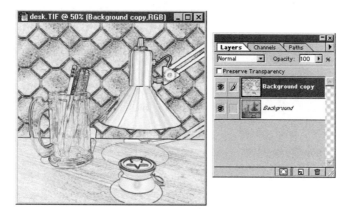

FIGURE 16.41 *The Find Edges filter removes the fill from areas and traces an edge where there is color contrast.*

4. Choose the Eraser tool, and on the Options palette, choose Paintbrush from the drop-down list.

5. Click on an empty area of the Brushes palette. The New Brush dialog box appears.

6. Type **45** in the Diameter field, make sure that Hardness is set to 100%, and then click on OK. You have a new, large, hard-edged brush tip on the palette.

7. Using diagonal strokes, start erasing the Background copy layer, from top to bottom. Leave individual strokes showing and do not completely erase the layer. Stop when the image looks something like Figure 16.42.

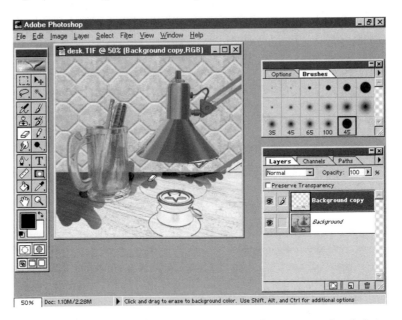

FIGURE 16.42 *By erasing most of the Find Edges layer, you make it appear as though the image is an unfinished painting, with pencil lines showing.*

The Background image is too intricate to contrast effectively against the Find Edges layer. In the following steps, you'll simplify the Background layer...

8. Click on the Background title on the Layers palette, choose Filter, Artistic, and then choose Poster Edges.

9. Drag the Edge Thickness slider to 4. This makes the edges drawn into the image thicker.

10. Drag the Edge Intensity slider to 7. This makes the edges rendered into the image quite apparent.

11. Leave the Posterization slider at its default of 2. This slider controls the number of unique colors the filter will reproduce in the image. Click on OK to apply the filter.

12. Click on the Background copy layer, and then press Ctrl(⌘)+U.

13. In the Hue/Saturation command, drag the Saturation slider to –100 to remove all the color, and then click on OK. There is sufficient contrast between the posterized color image and the "pencil sketch" Find Edges layer, as shown in Figure 16.43.

FIGURE 16.43 *Two versions of the same image blend harmoniously because the right filters were used.*

14. Choose File, Save As, and then save the image to your hard disk as Sketch.psd in Photoshop's native file format. You can close the image at any time.

So far, you haven't had to prepare an image before applying a filter because the images you've used required no special enhancement prior to the application of a specific filter. To round out your exploration of creative filter uses, let's take a look now at the author's favorite filter, the Watercolor filter.

USING THE WATERCOLOR FILTER

The Watercolor filter is perhaps the most sophisticated of all the plug-in filters because it actually renders images that look like fine, traditional watercolors, complete with washes and blotches on the surface.

The best sort of images to use with the Watercolor filter are scenes of nature. Why? Because watercolor and nature studies have historically gone hand in hand. Your audience will expect the visual content of your synthetic watercolor to be of a nature scene.

Applying the Watercolor filter to a photographic nature scene without first tuning the image would, however, produce an ugly watercolor. The Watercolor filter tends to create dark areas; overall, it diminishes the intensity of color in an image. Therefore, you must first increase the color and lighten the overall image before applying the filter.

Here's how to create "instant hotel room art," using the Watercolor filter:

CREATING WATERCOLOR SCENES (PRICE DOES NOT INCLUDE FRAME)

1. Open the Fall.tif image from the Chap16 folder on the Companion CD.

2. Press Ctrl(⌘)+L to display the Levels command.

3. Type **1.45** in the middle Input field and then click on OK. This washes out the midtones in the image, but that's okay; the Watercolor filter will render deep shades into most of the areas you've lightened.

4. Press Ctrl(⌘)+U to display the Hue/Saturation command.

5. Drag the Saturation slider to about +30 and then click on OK. The fall scene is brighter than you'd expect in an image, but the Watercolor filter will dull the image somewhat.

6. Choose Filter, Artistic, and then choose Watercolor.

7. Drag the Brush Detail slider to 14. This control adds more detail to the filtered image.

8. Drag the Shadow Intensity slider to 0. This eliminates some, but not all of a "blocking in" effect traditionally seen when physical watercolors dry unevenly.

9. Drag the Texture slider to 2. This controls the amount of artistic license the filter takes with the original image. When the dialog box looks like the one in Figure 16.44, click on OK.

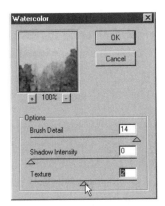

FIGURE 16.44   *Use these settings to make a fairly detailed watercolor version of the original image.*

10. You're finished. As you can see in Figure 16.45 (even though it's in black-and-white), the translation of the scene to a different medium, photography to watercolor, results in more visual interest than was originally in the scene.

FIGURE 16.45   *Photoshop trick #1,003: A visually boring photograph can be made to look more interesting by filtering it!*

11. Unless you need something to hang over your sofa, you do not need to save Fall.tif at this point. You can close the image, without saving, at any time now.

The Watercolor filter also works well on photographs of people. You might not be able to *recognize* the people after filtering the image, but the more character a face has, the more visual interest is drawn out through the use of the Watercolor filter.

Summary

We've walked through several examples of how to use a filter as a step in the creative process. With few exceptions, a plug-in filter will not make an image better looking, any more than dressing up as an artist will make someone a better artist.

We move from filter effects to special effects in Chapter 17, "Special Effects and Photoshop." Come see how the tricks you see in Hollywood can be achieved right on your personal computer.

CHAPTER 17

SPECIAL EFFECTS AND PHOTOSHOP

Special effects belong to these two categories:

- *You're completely unaware that a special effect has been used.*

- *A special effect is obvious, but it's so realistically executed that the audience suspends disbelief.*

This chapter is going to take you through both types of special effects—a convincing illusion, as well as a piece of retouching that's completely invisible to the viewer.

You'll see shortly how to create an invisible man, and later in the chapter, you'll use one person's face to retouch a different person's face. If this sounds like fun, it is, and it's all part of the professional designer's bag of tricks.

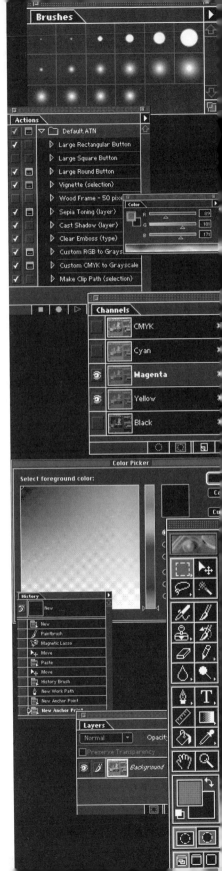

Removing Someone from Their Clothing (with Their Permission)

In the author's opinion, far too many instances of Photoshop work have produced images of famous people with their clothing removed. So why not remove the person from the clothing, leaving only the *clothing* behind??? It's a neat visual trick to create an "invisible man," and the first section in this chapter walks you through the steps needed to create the illusion.

Start with an Image that Contains Motion

The image you'll use in this invisible man section was carefully planned to make the actor's body look as though he's in motion. If you have your model simply stand and pose, the invisible man illusion isn't nearly as convincing because it looks as though you simply stuffed a suit with newspapers or something. No, by the time you finish with it, the BigWalk.tif image will look as though a leisure shirt and jeans are strolling down a sidewalk on their own.

The base image for your invisible man adventure can be seen in Figure 17.1. Note the movement, and also the nice folds on both the shirt and the pants. Equally important are the actor's surroundings; leafy vegetation and concrete will make it easy to clone these areas into the actor.

Removing an Area by Cloning Over It

The actor's head area will be easy to remove by cloning in trees. Filling in the shirt where the actor's neck is will be more challenging. Let's tackle first things first, though. In the steps that follow, you'll use the Rubber Stamp tool to remove most of the actor's head. You'll tackle to the shirt collar area later.

FIGURE 17.1 *Plan your special effects image carefully so that image editing becomes an inspired task instead of a chore!*

LOSING YOUR HEAD IN YOUR WORK

1. Open the Bigwalk.tif image from the Chap17 folder on the Companion CD.

2. Zoom into the head of the actor, to a 200% viewing resolution.

3. Choose the Rubber Stamp tool, choose the third tip from the left in the second row on the Brushes palette.

4. Press Alt(Opt) and click on an area of greenery in the image, not too close to the actor's head. This sets the sample point for the Rubber Stamp tool.

5. Brush across the top of the actor's head, as shown in Figure 17.2.

FIGURE 17.2   *Replace the top of the actor's head with surrounding greenery.*

6. Press Alt(Opt), click in a different green area of the background, and continue to remove the actor's head. It is important that the areas you replace do not all look the same; this is why altering your sample point for the Rubber Stamp tool at regular intervals is key. Remember, these green areas will be visible in the finished image.

7. When you've reached the top of the actor's shirt collar, choose File, Save As, and then save the image as Bigwalk.tif to your hard disk. Keep the file open.

It's time to replace the actor's neck with color that suggests the inside of an empty shirt.

USING THE PEN AND AIRBRUSH TOOLS

For hard-edged selections such as the edge of the actor's shirt collar, the Pen tool is ideal for isolating the areas you want to paint into. If you look at the shading on the shirt, you'll notice some hard color transitions and some soft ones. We need to presume that this invisible man's shirt would be hanging on his shoulders, and that there will not be many creases inside it. Therefore, smooth transitions of shading are necessary to create the inside of the shirt. The Airbrush tool is used in the following steps because it leaves no brush marks, but only smooth transitions of different colors you specify.

Here's how to fill in the inside of the shirt collar:

REMOVING THE NECKLINE

1. Zoom in to a 400% viewing resolution of the actor's neck (what's left of it).

2. With the Pen tool, drag anchors that match the outline of the actor's fleshtones along the neck and inside collar of the shirt, as in Figure 17.3.

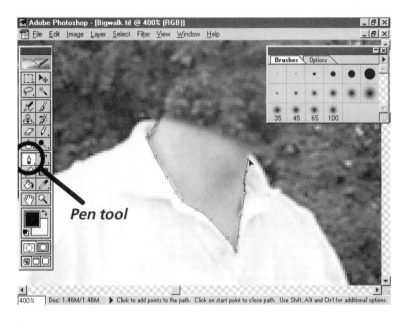

FIGURE 17.3   *Define a path that lies on the edge of the actor's shirt collar.*

3. Close the path along the top of the collar. You do not need to be precise, as you'll refine the collar line later.

4. On the Paths palette, click on the Loads path as a selection icon, and then click on an empty area of the palette to hide the path.

5. Choose the Airbrush tool, choose the 35-pixel tip on the Brushes palette, and then press Alt(Opt) and click on a white area of the actor's shirt. This color will be the base layer for the inside of the shirt.

6. Cover the entire interior of the marquee selection, and then press Alt(Opt) and click on a shaded area near the actor's collar to sample this color.

7. Paint in the right side of the marquee selection, as shown in Figure 17.4. You're adding shading as it would be cast from the front of the shirt to inside the shirt.

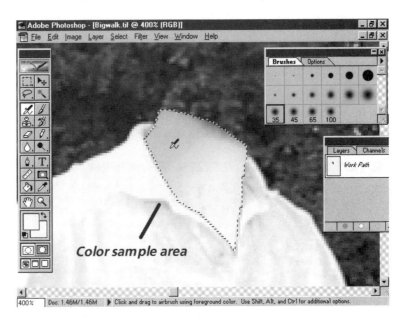

FIGURE 17.4   *Add gentle shading, using the Airbrush tool.*

8. Press Ctrl(⌘)+D to deselect the marquee.

9. Press Ctrl(⌘)+S; keep the file open.

Let's address the top of the actor's shirt now.

THE "RHYTHM" OF THE TOOLS

Before too long, you will notice that you'll adopt a certain natural rhythm when you work on this assignment. There's sort of a "one-two" step: first you define an area with the Pen tool, and then you clone into it with the Rubber Stamp tool.

This is exactly what's needed now to create the top edge of the actor's collar. Here's how to complete this area:

RING AROUND THE COLLAR

1. With the Pen tool, create an arc that connects the left side of the collar with the right side. Close the path to the outside top of the collar, as in Figure 17.5.

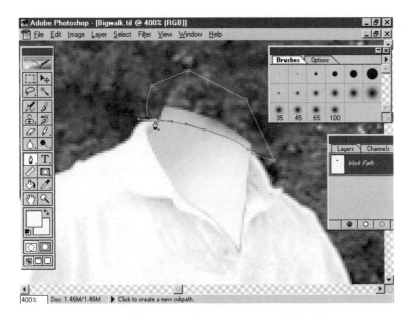

FIGURE 17.5 *Define an edge of the collar that is consistent with the areas still in the picture.*

2. On the Paths palette, click on the Loads path as selection icon, and then click on an empty area of the palette to hide the work path.

3. With the Rubber Stamp tool, press Alt(Opt) and click on an area of greenery that is not too close to the marquee selection; then stroke along the bottom edge of the selection until you have a clean, continuous top to the collar.

4. Press Ctrl(⌘)+D to deselect the marquee. Press Ctrl(⌘)+S; keep the file open.

You'll notice that some areas at the edge of the collar's front might not blend in with your airbrush work. The following section corrects this.

USING THE SMUDGE TOOL

The Smudge tool is terrific for "faking" image areas of which you are uncertain. Using the Smudge tool, which treats pixels like wet paint, you can reconcile different, hard-edged areas quite nicely.

Currently, two areas need a little work: the top left of the collar, and the middle right, where there are some folds in the collar. Let's see how the Smudge tool can fix both problem areas:

SMUDGING IMAGE AREAS

1. Choose the Smudge tool; in version 5 of Photoshop, this tool has been relocated to the Focus tools flyout on the toolbox.

2. Choose the tip at the far left of the second row on the Brushes palette, and on the Options palette, make sure that the Pressure is set to 50%.

3. Drag from the left edge of the collar into the airbrush work you performed earlier, as shown in Figure 17.6. It only takes about three or four strokes to blend the two areas together. Drag *from* the collar edge *into* the airbrush area.

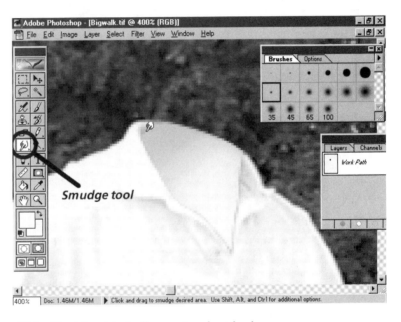

FIGURE 17.6 *Blend the original collar areas into the airbrush area.*

4. On the right side of the collar, drag the Smudge tool from the shaded areas of the folds into the airbrush areas, as in Figure 17.7. You've created continuity with the collar—continuity not originally in the image!

5. Press Ctrl(⌘)+S; keep the file open.

What is missing from the picture now is the inside seam of the collar. Naturally, this was hidden by the actor's neck, but you'll paint in a convincing seam in the following section.

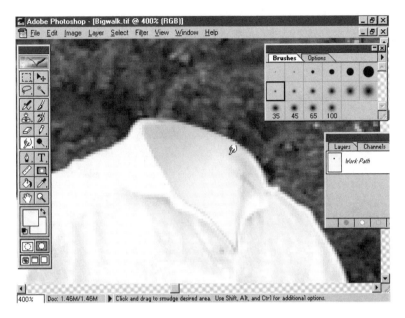

FIGURE 17.7 *Extend the shading of the folds in the collar; drag the Smudge tool from the original areas into the airbrush area.*

STROKING A SEAM PATH

Even if you use a digitizing tablet, it is very difficult to create clean, even arcs by using painting tools. This is why Photoshop provides paths that can be used as guides for painting. In the next set of steps, you'll create an open path and then stroke it with foreground color to simulate the seam in the shirt collar.

USING THE PATH'S STROKE FUNCTION

1. With the Pen tool, drag an arc that is about 1/2 screen inch inside the shirt collar. Peek ahead to Figure 17.8 for the shape and location of the path.

2. With the Eyedropper tool, choose a shaded area of the actor's shirt. This is now the current foreground color.

3. Choose the Paintbrush tool, choose second-from-left tip in the top row, and then click on the Strokes path with foreground color icon at the bottom of the Paths palette. Figure 17.8 shows this process.

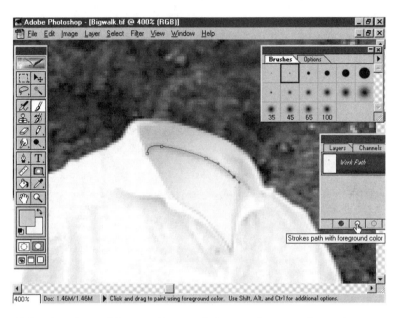

FIGURE 17.8 *Smooth, graceful arcs can be painted when you choose to stroke a path.*

4. Click on an empty area of the Paths palette to hide the path and see your work.

As long as you're working on the collar, what do you say to suggesting a manufacturer's tag inside the collar?

5. With the Lasso tool, press and hold Alt(Opt) and then click four corners in the middle of the collar, slightly above the seam you created, as shown in Figure 17.9.

FIGURE 17.9 *Define a rectangle that can be used as a template for a manufacturer's tag.*

6. Right-click (Macintosh: hold Ctrl and click) and then choose Stroke from the context menu.

7. In the Stroke dialog box, specify 1 pixel at the Center location of the marquee selection; then click on OK to apply the stroke.

8. Press Ctrl(⌘)+D to deselect the marquee; press Ctrl(⌘)+S; keep the file open.

WARNING

If you choose to stroke a path, but no painting tool is selected, the path will be stroked by the Pencil tool with a tip one pixel in diameter.

There is actually no point in embellishing the manufacturer's tag beyond this simple rectangle. The resolution of the image is not sufficient to try to work a name or logo into this small rectangle; you'll note that the jeans and the belt the actor is wearing do not sport detailed lettering either.

In Figure 17.10 you can see the first phase of the illusion completed. Now the guy sort of looks like the author's college roommate.

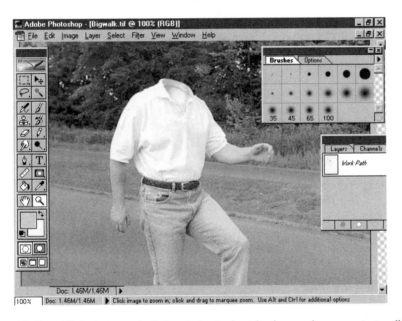

FIGURE 17.10 *A little cloning and a little painting in the right places produces a convincing illusion.*

ALIGNING SAMPLE POINTS AND ERASING ARMS

One of the benefits to having taken this picture on a walkway is that you have several reference points for aligning the Rubber Stamp tool to its target. For example, the actor's right arm is encroaching on an area where the grass meets the sidewalk. Erasing the arm then becomes more a matter of precisely defining the sample point than one of raw skill.

Here's how to make the actor vanish a little more:

Cloning in Additional Background Scenery

1. Zoom out to a 300% viewing resolution. Scroll the window so that the actor's right arm is centered onscreen.

2. Choose the Rubber Stamp tool and the second brush from the left on the second row on the Brushes palette. Alt(Opt)+click directly on the edge where the grass meets the sidewalk.

3. Click on the area where you think the road meets the grass behind the actor's wrist, more or less in the area shown in Figure 17.11. You've aligned the sample and the target points, and now you can freely clone away the actor's arm.

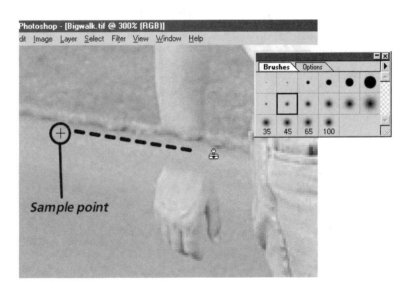

Figure 17.11   *Make the Rubber Stamp tool align with the edge between the grass and the side-walk. Cloning over other areas now becomes simple.*

4. Before you reach the actor's elbow, stop. Get out the Pen tool and define a tight selection edge where his forearm meets the shirt sleeve. Close the path outside the elbow area to encompass the rest of the actor's arm, as shown in Figure 17.12.

5. Click on the Loads path as a selection icon at the bottom of the Paths palette, and then click on an empty area of the palette to hide the work path.

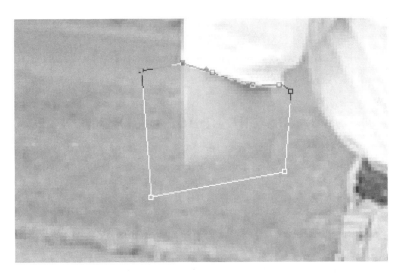

FIGURE 17.12 *Draw a path around the remaining area to be cloned over. Make sure that the edge of the shirt sleeve has the most accurate path segment.*

6. With the Rubber Stamp tool, press Alt(Opt) and click on an area of grass not too close to the marquee selection.

7. Stroke over the selection area, as shown in Figure 17.13.

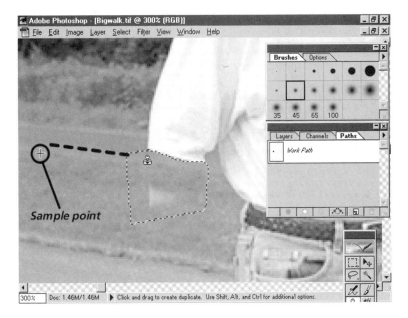

FIGURE 17.13 *Keep the sample and target points for the Rubber Stamp tool going in the same diagonal direction as the sidewalk in the image.*

8. Press Ctrl(⌘)+S; keep the file open.

It's time to continue the assignment; you'll tackle the actor's left arm in the following section.

SHOWING THE INSIDE OF THE SLEEVE

If you look carefully at the previous example's retouching steps, you noticed that the sleeve was directed away from the viewer, which made it simple to select up to the edge and erase the arm.

If you look carefully at the actor's left arm, however, you can see a problem that needs to be addressed. The shirt sleeve points ever-so-slightly toward the viewer; therefore, to make a convincing "empty" sleeve, you must use a technique similar to that of removing the actor's head.

Here's how to "retouch out" the actor's left arm:

BEARING ARMS

1. With the Pen tool, create a closed path similar to that shown in Figure 17.14. Note that a sliver of the actor's arm falls outside the path. This is intentional; this area will be replaced by an "inside" view of the sleeve.

2. Click on the Load path as a selection icon at the bottom of the Paths palette, and then click on an empty area of the palette to hide the path.

3. With the Rubber Stamp tool, use the road as a guide for the sample point; press Alt(Opt) and click on the very edge of the back road.

4. Click on the actor's elbow, where you believe it is covering the edge between the back road and the grass. Drag freely within the selection now to clone over the left arm, as shown in Figure 17.15.

5. Press Ctrl(⌘)+D to deselect the marquee. Zoom in to a 400% view of the shirt sleeve.

FIGURE 17.14 *Create a path that encompasses the left arm; do not completely encompass the elbow area.*

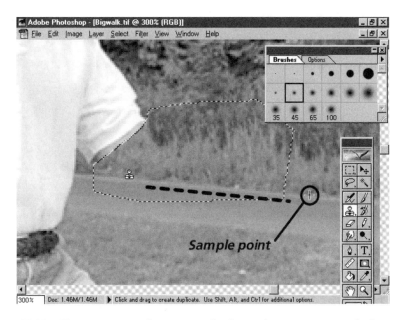

FIGURE 17.15 *Keep your source and target points for cloning along a common visual reference point, and your work will always be undetected.*

6. With the Pen tool, create a slightly oval shape that hits both the edge of the uncloned arm area and the edge of the shirt sleeve. Figure 17.16 shows this area clearly.

FIGURE 17.16   *Create a shape that will serve as the end of the shirt sleeve.*

7. Click on the Loads path as a selection icon on the Paths palette, and then click on an empty space on the palette to hide the work path.

8. With the Airbrush tool, press Alt(Opt) and click over a white area of the shirt to sample the color; then fill in the marquee selection.

9. Press Alt(Opt) and click on a shaded area of the shirt. On the Options palette for the Airbrush tool, choose Multiply mode.

10. Click, don't drag, once or twice at the left side of the selection marquee. As you can see in Figure 17.17, you've successfully shaded the "inside" of the shirt sleeve.

11. Press Ctrl(⌘)+D to deselect the marquee. Press Ctrl(⌘)+S; keep the file open.

Progress update: if your image looks like Figure 17.18 at this point, you're doing magnificently! This guy is looking less and less substantial as time goes by, huh?

Your editing work has been splendid in this example, and now it's time to take it a little further. It would indeed make a startling illusion if all the scene contained were the jeans and the shirt, sans sneakers, breezing along the sidewalk. In the following sections you'll take off the guy's sneakers.

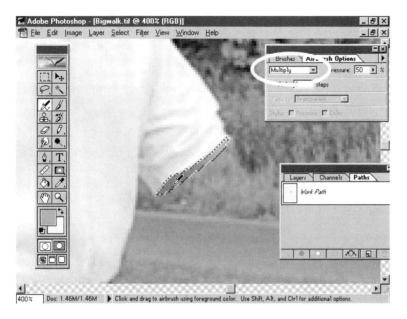

FIGURE 17.17 *Less is more. Use only use one or two "hits" of the Airbrush tool to complete the shading inside the sleeve.*

FIGURE 17.18 *A head and two arms down, and two sneakers to go!*

JEANS ARE EITHER TOO LONG OR TOO SHORT

Even if you think you're the perfect size for a pair of jeans, the length always seems to be "hip-wader time," or you have two extra inches to catch your heels on. The actor was no exception to this rule, and he creatively hung the tongues of the sneakers out to catch the additional material.

This poses a problem of sorts in removing the sneakers because some of the pant cuff is hidden by the sneaker. We'll address this minor difficulty in the steps that follow:

CLONING OVER THE LEFT SNEAKER

1. Zoom out to a 300% viewing resolution of the scene; center the actor's left sneaker (his left, your right) onscreen.

2. With the Pen tool, define a path that encompasses the foot, with the top of the path neatly trimming off the tongue of the sneaker, as shown in Figure 17.19.

NOTE

When you pay less than $40 for informal footwear, they are called "sneakers." When you pay more, you're entitled to call them "running shoes."

FIGURE 17.19   *Keep the top line of the path consistent with the pant cuff; ignore the tongue of the sneaker intruding on the cuff.*

3. Click on the Loads path as a selection icon at the bottom of the Paths palette, and then click on an empty area of the palette to hide the path.

4. With the Rubber Stamp tool, press Alt(Opt) and click on part of the sidewalk; then paint over the sneaker in the selection marquee, as shown in Figure 17.20.

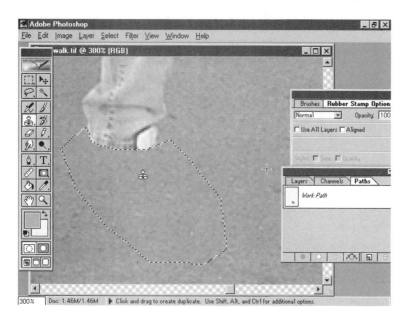

FIGURE 17.20 *Clone over the sneaker area with pavement area.*

5. Press Ctrl(⌘)+D to deselect the marquee.

6. With the Pen tool, define an area directly to the left of the sneaker tongue, and a little larger than the sneaker tongue. This area, shown in Figure 17.21, will be the replacement piece for the tongue.

7. Click on the Loads path as a selection icon on the Paths palette, and then click on an empty space on the palette to hide the path.

8. With the Move tool, hold Ctrl(⌘)+Alt(Opt) and then drag a copy of the contents of the marquee selection to cover the sneaker tongue, as shown in Figure 17.22.

9. When the copy is in the correct position, press Ctrl(⌘)+D to drop the copy, thus replacing the sneaker tongue area.

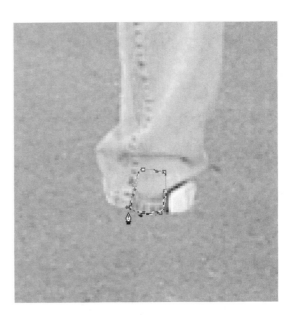

FIGURE 17.21 *Create a path around a portion of the pant leg that can be used to replace the sneaker tongue area.*

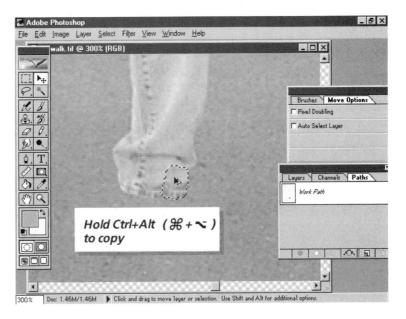

FIGURE 17.22 *With the Move tool and other selection tools, Ctrl(⌘)+Alt(Opt) drags a copy of the contents of the selection.*

10. Press Ctrl(⌘)+S; keep the file open.

When cloth has folds in it, it is difficult to tell whether a piece you've copied "belongs" to the weave of the fabric. This is true of the copying work you performed in the previous example. Is that front piece of the cuff absolutely correct? Nope, but no one will question it.

Erasing the Other Sneaker

The selection and cloning techniques for removing the remaining sneaker are essentially the same as the steps you've used so far in this section. You'll use a different method, however, to finish the cuff of the pant leg after the superfluous sneaker has been cloned out.

Here's how to finish editing the invisible man:

Completing the Editing Work

1. Scroll the image window until the remaining sneaker is in the center of the screen.

2. With the Pen tool, create a closed path that encompasses the sneaker, paying extra attention to keeping the line on the edge of the pant cuff consistent. As you can see in Figure 17.23, some of the sneaker's tongue will be outside the path.

Figure 17.23 *Allow the top of the path to cross the tongue of the sneaker.*

3. Click on the Loads path as a selection icon at the bottom of the Paths palette; click on an empty space on the palette to hide the path.

4. With the Rubber Stamp tool, press Alt(Opt) and click on part of the road; then brush into the selection to clone over the sneaker, As shown in Figure 17.24.

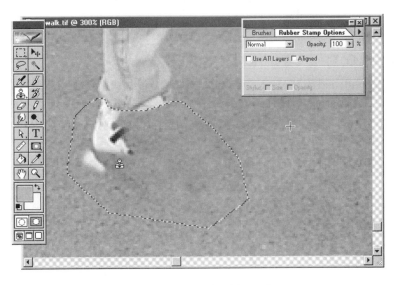

FIGURE 17.24 *Replace the sneaker area with samples of the road.*

5. Press Ctrl(⌘)+D to deselect the marquee.

6. Choose the Paintbrush tool, choose the second-from-left tip in the second row of the Brushes palette, and then on the Options palette choose Multiply from the modes drop-down list.

7. Hold Alt(Opt) to toggle to the Eyedropper tool, and then click on an area of the faded blue jeans. This sets the current foreground color.

8. Carefully stroke over the tongue of the sneaker that remains in the image. One or two strokes should do the trick in Multiply mode. Figure 17.25 shows the end of this process.

9. You're finished! Press Ctrl(⌘)+S; keep the file open.

Oddly, although the day the picture was taken was a nice day, there were no shadows. This is okay; in the following section you'll add a shadow of the clothes to the scene, heightening the reality of this fantastic image.

FIGURE 17.25 *Multiply mode increases the density of the chosen foreground color, effectively shading in the white part of the sneaker.*

MAKING AND IMPORTING SHADOWS

Probably the toughest challenge you'll face when you're retouching images is that of reconstructing a shadow. This is part guesswork, part artistry, and part trial and error. To help you conclude your edit of the invisible man, the author has provided a shadow for you to copy into the Bigwalk.tif image. Here's how that shadow was created, in case you'd like to try your hand at shadow making in the future:

1. The Bigwalk.tif image was exported to Adobe Illustrator. It was locked on a layer, and a new layer for the shadow was created.

2. The figure was traced and then skewed, using the Shear tool to create an angular, flattened look.

3. The shadow was then saved as an Illustrator EPS file and brought into Photoshop so that it could be converted to bitmap format. Because the size of the shadow is in proportion to the clothes casting the shadow, no resizing was necessary.

Is the shadow totally accurate? Probably not, but it contains the right shape and details to make the audience suspend disbelief. Don't overwork when you create a shadow; if it looks right, it'll work.

Here's how to add a shadow of the strutting clothes to the sidewalk:

Adding a Shadow to the Scene

1. Open the Shadow.tif image from the Chap17 folder on the Companion CD.

2. With the Move tool, drag the image into the Bigwalk.tif image, as shown in Figure 17.26. You can close the Shadow.tif image at any time now.

FIGURE 17.26 *Copy the shadow image to the Bigwalk.tif image by using the Move tool.*

3. When you use the Move tool to copy images across windows, a new layer is created in the target image. This is good news, because the shadow needs repositioning. Reduce your viewing resolution of the Bigwalk image to 50%. Press 5 on the numeric keypad to make the current (shadow) layer 50% opaque. Now you can see both the shadow and the underlying layer of the clothes.

4. With the Move tool, drag the shadow so that it is slightly behind the clothes in the image, as shown in Figure 17.27. You'll note that some of the shadow encroaches on the leg of the pants; this is okay, as you'll remove these areas shortly.

FIGURE 17.27 *Because the lighting in the scene comes from the upper right, the shadow needs to go below and to the left of the clothes.*

5. Click on the Layer Mask mode button on the Layers palette.

6. Choose the Paintbrush tool; on the Options palette, make sure that the mode is Normal and 100% opacity, and on the Brushes palette, choose the third tip from the left in the top row.

7. Zoom to 200% viewing resolution, and center the area to be worked on, the legs, onscreen.

8. Brush inside the legs to hide the shadow layer areas, as shown in Figure 17.28. Wherever a shadow is crossing the legs, paint over it.

9. When you've removed the shadow from the interior of the legs, drag the Layer Mask thumbnail into the trash icon on the Layers palette. In the resulting attention box, click on Apply to delete those areas you've hidden with the mask.

10. Choose Multiply mode for the shadow layer on the Layers palette. This drops out the white in the shadow layer image.

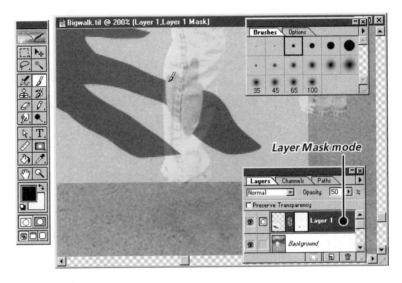

Figure 17.28   *Apply Layer Mask to hide those portions of the shadow that overlap the pant legs.*

11. Play a little with the opacity of this layer. The author has found that about 40% opacity makes a nice shadow that allows details of the road to show through, as an actual shadow would.

12. On the Layers palette, click on the menu flyout button, and then choose Flatten Image.

13. Press Ctrl(⌘)+S. You're finished! You can close the image at any time now.

Figure 17.29 shows the finished image. It sort of lends a new meaning to the phrase "work-out clothes"!

Okay, the "illusion that looks real" part of this chapter has drawn to a close. Now it's time to address the very real need in design to change the look of a person without anyone ever noticing. Virtual plastic surgery lies ahead!

FIGURE 17.29 *"Gary, if you don't wash those clothes soon, they're going to get up and walk away by themselves!"*

HOW TO REPLACE A FACE

Suppose that you took a "once in a lifetime" photograph like the one the author took for this section—an image of a Canadian Mounted policeman guarding a flamingo sanctuary. (Okay, so I played with the image a little!) And suppose that the image has commercial possibilities, but oops—you did not get a signed release from the model (the policeman in this case).

Figure 17.30 shows the image you'll work with in this chapter. Now, the author does indeed have the rights to publish the picture of the officer's face, but we're pretending here that he—and you—did not. The equation's quite simple: if you have no model release, you can't use the likeness of the subject.

FIGURE 17.30   *If you're photographing people for profit, or even for fun, be sure to have them sign a model release.*

All right, we've dwelt on the legal issue enough; the focus of this section is on how to change a person's face.

GETTING THE SIZING AND LIGHTING RIGHT

The replacement face for the officer is provided for you; it's Stand-in.tif, and it's in the Chap17 folder of the Companion CD. This picture was taken with the same upper-right lighting as the photo of the Canadian Mountie, and the actor was asked to don a serious expression, similar to that of the officer. What cannot be determined through the lens is the exact size of the replacement face. This is something that needs to be measured in Photoshop, and then you need to scale the replacement face accordingly.

Here's how to get the ball rolling and perform some preliminary calculations:

USING THE MEASURE TOOL

1. Press F8 if the Info palette is not already onscreen. Click on the XY field crosshair (toward the bottom left of the Info palette), and choose Pixels from the flyout list. Now, everything you measure with the Measure tool is expressed in pixels on the Info palette.

2. Open the Flamingo.tif image from the Chap17 folder on the Companion CD. Double-click on the Zoom tool to make the viewing resolution of the image 100% (1:1).

3. Size the image window so that you see only the face of the officer. You'll need to leave room onscreen to display the stand-in's image.

4. Open the Stand-in.tif image from the Chap17 folder of the Companion CD.

5. Position both images so that you have a clear view of the faces. Make the Flamingo.tif image the current foreground image.

6. Choose the Measure tool, and then drag from the officer's chin to the bridge of his nose. As you can see in Figure 17.31, the distance is approximately 123 pixels.

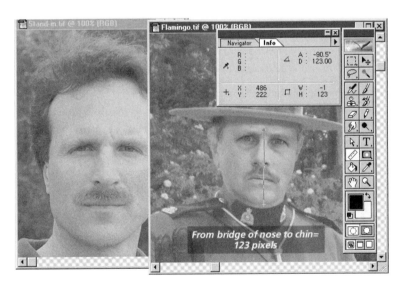

FIGURE 17.31   *Measure the length of the area you will replace.*

7. Click in the Stand-in.tif image, and then with the Measure tool, drag from the actor's chin to the bridge of his nose. In Figure 17.32, you can see that the distance—about 189 pixels—is larger than that in the officer's face. The size to which you must scale the Stand-in.tif image is 65%; 123 divided by 189 equals 65.

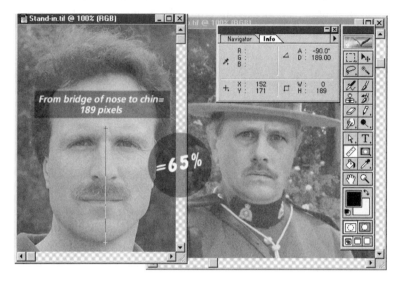

FIGURE 17.32 *Set up a proportion between the two measurements to give you a percentage by which the replacement image must be scaled.*

8. With Stand-in.tif in the foreground, choose Image, Image Size.

9. Click to place a check in the Resample Image box. In the Pixel Dimensions area, choose percent from the drop-down list; then, in the Width field, type **65**. The Height measurement will change accordingly. Click on OK to apply the size change. Figure 17.33 shows the resized image.

10. Save the image as Stand-in.tif to your hard disk, and save the other image as Flamingo.tif to your hard disk. Keep both images open.

You might notice that the replacement image is good, but not quite perfect now. The officer in the flamingo picture has his head tilted ever so slightly. In the next section, you'll correct this in the Stand-in.tif image, and start the replacement work.

FIGURE 17.33   *Change the size of the replacement image to match the size you measured for the face in the original image.*

ROTATING AN IMAGE

The Stand-in image needs to be rotated, but by how much? Generally, a degree of rotation is more than we perceive it to be. If you were to guess that the replacement image needs 5 degrees of rotation, this would be far too much. The best course of action here is to practice trial and error; start with a small amount of rotation and if it's not right, you can undo it by using the History list.

Here's how to tilt the actor's head and begin the retouching work:

TURNING HEADS

1. With the Stand-in.tif image in the foreground, choose Image, Rotate Canvas, and then choose Arbitrary. The Rotate Canvas box pops up.

2. Type **2** in the Angle field, click on the CW (clockwise) button, as shown in Figure 17.34, and then click on OK to apply the rotation.

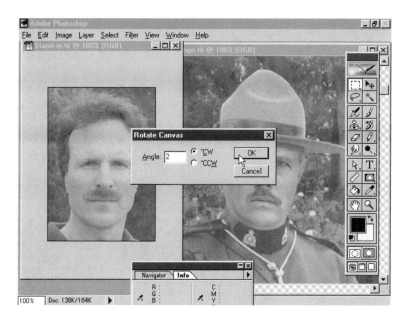

FIGURE 17.34 *Choose a small amount of rotation to begin with.*

3. The amount of rotation you applied looks right, and you're ready to proceed. With the Flamingo.tif image in the foreground, press F7 to display the Layers palette, and then click on the Create new layer icon. You'll be performing this retouching work with the "safety net" of working on a layer.

4. Choose the Rubber Stamp tool, choose the fourth tip from the left in the second row on the Brushes palette, and make sure that you have a good, clear view of both the images now.

5. Press Alt(Opt) and click on the center of the actor's chin in Stand-in.tif to set the sampling point.

6. Click on the title of the flamingo.tif image to make it the current editing window, and then start dragging upward, beginning directly in the center of the officer's chin, as shown in Figure 17.35.

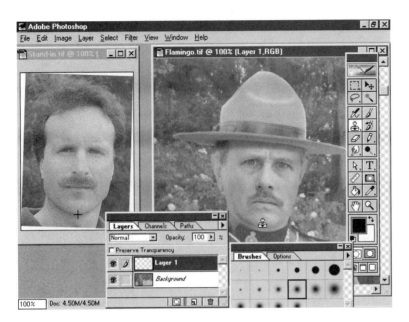

FIGURE 17.35   *Synchronize the sample and target areas between the two images.*

7. Work upward, keeping inside the officer's face. And enjoy what you're doing; this is funny stuff! In Figure 17.36, you can see the retouching completed up to the officer's eyes.

8. Complete the editing by cloning over the eyes. If your image looks like that in Figure 17.37, you're in fine shape.

9. Save the image as Flamingo.psd, in Photoshop's native file format, to your hard disk. You can close Stand-in.tif at any time, but keep the flamingo image open.

Pretty neat and effective work, isn't it? And it's all because you took the time to measure the two images. But wait, there's still something amiss in the image. Read on!

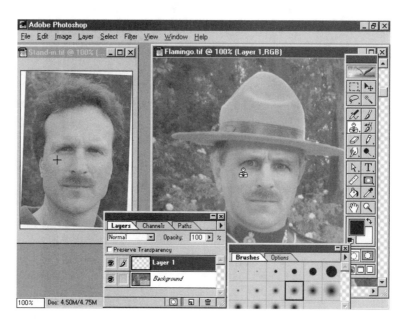

FIGURE 17.36 *Keep the Rubber Stamp tool close to the officer's features. Do not wander into the hairline, the edge of the face, or the ears, as these areas will not line up correctly.*

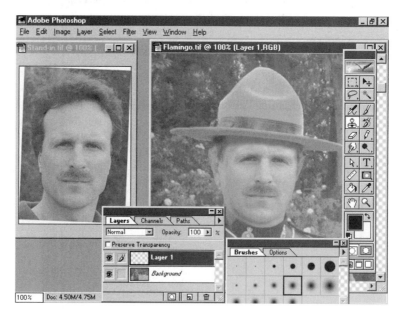

FIGURE 17.37 *In reality, it is not this easy to become a Mounted Policeman.*

MATCHING SKIN TONES

There is an additional reason you were asked to work on a layer in the flamingos image, beyond the "safety net" maneuver. Onscreen, the officer's skin is paler than that of the actor you cloned in (you can't tell in this black-and-white book!).

This is a very simple thing to correct, as you'll see in the following steps:

USING THE HUE/SATURATION COMMAND

1. Position the Flamingo image in the far right of your screen.

2. Press Ctrl(⌘)+U to display the Hue/Saturation command.

3. Drag the saturation slider down to about –20, as shown in Figure 17.38, or until the fleshtones on Layer 1 look about the same as the fleshtones on the Background layer.

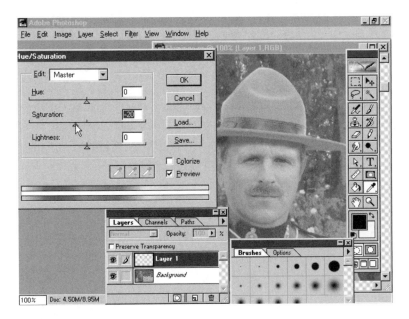

FIGURE 17.38   *Reduce the saturation until there is no apparent difference between the fleshtones on each layer.*

4. Click on OK to apply the change.

5. Zoom out to full-screen view to better see your work; press Ctrl(⌘)+S. You can close the image at any time now.

Actually, the author's opinion is that the replacement face looks more natural than the officer's face! In Figure 17.39, you can see the finished image.

FIGURE 17.39 *Who would suspect that the face of the officer was cloned in from a different image?*

There's a subliminal trick going on in the image that helps sustain the editing work you performed. The scene itself is so ridiculous that the audience's attention is distracted from the face of the officer. Misdirection is a powerful imaging tool!

SUMMARY

Special effects are what you make them. If your goal is to change an image without drawing attention to the change, you now know some of the steps. And if you want to create a set of clothes strolling down the street, you know those secrets, too.

Regardless of how skilled you become with Photoshop, the images you create need to have a life beyond the monitor. Chapter 18, "Outputting Your Input," takes you through the ins and outs of outputting your work.

PART V

PUBLISHING AND BEYOND

CHAPTER 18

OUTPUTTING YOUR INPUT

It seems that all the buzz in the graphics community revolves around producing compelling graphics for the World Wide Web. Web work may be where the excitement lies for many, but the vast majority of graphic artists' work is still destined for output to physical media. The creation and embellishment of advertisements, billboards, newspapers, magazines, packaging, photography, and tee shirts are just a few areas in which artists are asked day in and day out to apply their creativity. Even if your work is exclusively centered around electronic publishing, it is likely that you or your client will also want to print your work to paper or other physical media.

For all the novelty, speed, and ease of publishing offered by the World Wide Web, the classic art form of creating an imprint on a physical surface still remains the primary vehicle of popular communications today. Unless every client you have owns a personal computer, or your monitor has an infinitely long

cable—and neither situation is likely—the need for a hard copy of your Photoshop work is a continuing one. This chapter is an excursion to the routes you can take to achieve the best-looking output from your creative input. From ink on paper, to 35mm film, to color separations, physical output requires that specific translations, and sometimes accommodations, be made to a copy of your original work. Rule number one in publishing is to decide on the output device *before* you compose your image. Let's take a look at the WYSIFO—What You See Is Faithfully Output—considerations that go into making a traditional rendering of your designs, using state-of-the-art equipment.

THE MANY ROUTES TO PHYSICAL OUTPUT

Although some proprietary printing methods are available to computer graphics artists, the milieu of output options can be narrowed to a handful of basic categories. The following options are covered in this book:

- **Home or small office personal printing**. Typically, black-and-white laser or color inkjet printers that print to paper are the output equipment.

- **Service bureau printing**. Depending on the size and specialty of a service bureau, you can order anything from dye sublimation prints to 35mm and larger format film recorded slides of your Photoshop images.

- **Commercial printing**. Of all the categories of output media, commercial printing of color separations offers the highest-resolution work. It is also one of the least familiar processes to many graphics designers.

- **Electronic publishing**. Preparation of your work is necessary to optimize it for onscreen display, but electronic publishing—in-house presentations or work on the Web—is a medium that does not use traditional printing color spaces or image resolution. Chapters 19, "Creating Graphics for the Web," and 20, "Building Animations," are devoted to electronic publishing techniques and specifications.

In Figure 18.1 you can see the areas of output most commonly used today.

Publishing—the art of outputting your input—is a dynamic education, one that changes in its technology almost daily. The *scope* of the topic of output cannot possibly be documented in this chapter. This chapter covers some of the basic stumbling blocks to—and solutions for—accurately representing your work in a physical medium. As a Photoshop designer or artist, you should become familiar with the many kinds of output for digital work.

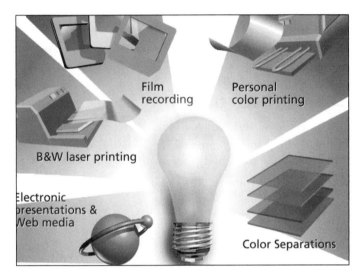

FIGURE 18.1 *When you need to publish a graphical thought, you have many options for the media used. Choose the one that best suits your audience.*

PERSONAL PRINTING

In 1998, the small office and home market for personal printing can be divided into two distinct categories: black-and-white laser printing and color printing. As designers, we might immediately conclude that color and black-and-white output are completely different methods of artistic expression, but there is also a *technical* aspect that separates color output from black-and-white.

Inkjet and other types of color printers output a finished product only; that is, output from personal color printers can be used to produce short, low-budget print runs. The color produced is nowhere near equal to that produced by a printing press in terms of quality, color accuracy, or longevity (inkjet inks fade with time), although scores of different inkjet papers are available for different types of physical output. Regardless of the personal color printer's limitations, the output just may fit the bill when you are faced with a limited budget and color quality is not of paramount inportance.

On the other hand, high-resolution black-and-white personal laser prints can serve as both hard copy proofs of your work *and* as camera-ready prints. Because the capability of a black-and-white laser printer is extensible, this chapter looks first at personal color output, and then at where black-and-white printing can lead.

PERSONAL COLOR PRINTERS

Much has been said in trade magazines and computer publications about "affordable" color printing from the desktop. Today, a color printer that costs less than $300 puts color printing well within the reach of anyone purchasing her first computer system. Personal color printing is an exciting concept, but "affordable" shouldn't become synonymous with "professional," if you're serious about your craft. The personal color printer is on the verge of becoming a mature market, but at present its output pales in comparison to the product of a color printing press or a photographic print. Personal color printers can't be used for color-critical work.

ADVANTAGES AND DISADVANTAGES OF PERSONAL COLOR PRINTERS

If you compare color output to the same image onscreen, or in high-quality printing or film-recorded slides, the magnitude of difference in image quality and accurate color reproduction is similar to comparing a Polaroid snapshot to an 8×10-inch transparency. Personal color printers have much smaller color *gamuts* (the range of colors they can reproduce) than a monitor, film, or printing press. Typically, there is a significant drop-off in a specific hue within the printable range of colors. A personal color printer might, for example, print rich violets and blues, but subtle turquoises would color cast to green, and golds would turn to orange. How do you correct a particular fall-off in the color spectrum? Sometimes, you can correct the color balance of a print from the printer's proprietary print driver controls (but not by using Photoshop's print options), but most of the time, a noticeable color cast in a printed image *cannot* be totally corrected unless you cast the source image in the opposite direction as the color cast in the image.

If you cannot print the colors you see on your monitor to a personal color printer, the workaround is to balance the color of a *copy* of a specific file. Rule number two in digital imaging is that when the end product is a printed piece, the colors in the *printed* piece are all that matter. This means that the colors you see on the monitor might look grossly inaccurate, but if the file looks correct when it's printed, it is the file or the monitor, and not the color printer, that displays "wrong" colors. This might seem a strange philosophy, particularly when color-management systems come with almost every graphics product, and Photoshop itself has a handsome set of calibration controls. If a color print looks wrong, however, and you can't significantly change the printer's color options, it is the *file information* that must be changed to attain the printed colors you envision. And this is always best done with a *copy* of your work, in case you decide in the future to render a design to several different output devices, all of which will certainly have different color gamuts.

Personal color printing should be seen by the serious professional designer as both person-ally gratifying and as a means for transporting a rough idea of the finished product to anywhere you can mail or otherwise send a piece of paper. Despite the color inaccuracy of personal color printers, they are simply nice to have around for a quick hard copy, a greeting card, or for other final product purposes. Additionally, many manufacturers of media for color printers offer acetate, label stock, business card stock, and even small swatches of fabric. The media becomes part of the art form with color printers and carefully chosen paper, film, or cloth stock. For the artistic purist, these options take you far from the image you see onscreen, but there is a definite cottage industry possibility for the combination of creative talent, Photoshop, and a color printer.

There are two things you should do to ensure the best output when your finished design is to be rendered to a personal color printer:

- Print all your images in RGB color mode from Photoshop. Although most personal color printers use a combination of cyan, magenta, yellow, and frequently black, there is color mode conversion circuitry in these printers, which are designed to internally convert RGB images to CMYK. Check your documentation for specific printer instructions, but most of the time, inkjet printers require RGB color input.

- Gather a representative sampling of your imaging work, use Photoshop's Eyedropper tool to create color samples of about 100 different colors in your images, and then paint these colors as swatches into a new image document. Print this document to your color printer, and then compare the swatches to the colors you see onscreen.

  The color swatches that are not even remotely similar to the colors you see onscreen are "problem colors" for your printer. These are colors you should avoid using when your final output involves this specific printer; you should use Photoshop's Color Range command to select these areas in copies of the original files, and change the colors to ones that will print accurately.

As color-capable beings, we tend to be forgiving when it comes to evaluating either a poor design done in color, or color accuracy. "Some color is better than none" might be the best observation regarding color printing that is within the financial reach of most designers and many clients. But simply because the quality of a piece printed on a personal color printer can't be considered to be equal to that printed on a four-color press, *doesn't* mean that professional-quality output can't be personally generated.

Professional quality *black-and-white* desktop output is within the reach of almost everyone. Black-and-white output is a stable, mature medium in the computer graphics community. The following sections concentrate on printing specifics and the techniques you can use with Photoshop to produce high-quality professional black-and-white output from your desktop.

BLACK-AND-WHITE OUTPUT: PERSONAL AND PROFESSIONAL

Computer and printing technologies have advanced in recent years to the point at which a black-and-white laser proof can legitimately serve as a camera-ready piece of artwork. The physical line screens and halftone dots used in traditional printing can now be simulated with laser printers and digital imagesetters to provide quality printed copies of your work to suit design, publication, presentation, and "send one to your mom" needs.

All digital imaging hardware must convert color information to whole, quantized amounts of pigment (called *dots*). Different kinds of dots are used; the two primary types are halftone and non-halftone dots. The type of dot used can significantly impact whether you can have your work commercially printed. Let's take a look at the physiology of electronic dot-making, and examine the methods by which every rendered image can look as faithful to your onscreen display as possible.

USING A PRINTER COMMAND LANGUAGE (PCL) PRINTER

The technology that drives Hewlett-Packard's LaserJets, the *Printer Command Language* (PCL), was quickly adopted by the business community and became an industry standard that other manufacturers emulated. PCL-based printers are noted for their speed and the rich blacks they produce.

Grayscale images, however, have a gamut much wider than a laser printer can express with its limited palette of available tones. Laser printers can place a dot of colored toner (usually black) on a surface (usually white paper). The gamut of color for laser printer output is exactly 2—black and white—with no percentages of black in between. PCL-based printers simulate the appearance of continuous tones in an image by using a technique similar to what commercial printing presses use to create tones. Both use dots arranged on a page in such a way that your eye integrates the dots and your brain "sees" them as a continuous, tonal image. In Figure 18.2, Pushpin.tif is a grayscale image in Photoshop, and Laserprint.tif is a file that was created by scanning a laser copy of the same image.

FIGURE 18.2 *Laser printers can only render a single color to a page, and therefore must use halftones to simulate grayscale images.*

Because *Inside Adobe Photoshop 5* is itself printed, we've exaggerated the examples in the figures in this chapter. The scans of the printed artwork were acquired at 35 pixels/inch, about one-fourth the sampling rate required to produce a medium-quality print.

How faithfully a laser copy represents the original image depends on three factors:

- How accurately the printer places dots on a page
- The organization or pattern of the dots on the page
- The resolution of the printer (size of the dots, as expressed in dots per inch)

Laser printers that use the PCL technology have a resolution of either 300 dpi or 600 dpi. Although 300–600 dpi is an adequate resolution for producing a business letter or a chart, you might be disappointed by the limitations of these resolutions when you're trying to reproduce a Photoshop masterpiece. The human eye easily perceives the dot patterns in a grayscale image that has been printed at 300–600 dpi. A laser printed image must meet or exceed 1,200 dots per inch before a viewer's eye focuses on its composition and tonality, and not the toner dots that make up the image.

Disadvantages of PCL Printers

PCL printers are more than suitable if you're printing correspondence, an invoice, or a simple graphic to show to a client. The drawback to PCL printers is that they fail to interpret tonal information that directly corresponds to the pattern of a printing press. Faithful copying of the way a printing press places dots of ink requires more information, processing power, and precision than the PCL technology and the printer's controller circuitry are designed to handle.

If you have a 300–600 dpi PCL printer hooked up to your computer, and you want to print a grayscale picture from Photoshop, there aren't any options you can choose to increase the quality and accuracy of the printed piece. Because a PCL printer cannot accurately arrange dots into traditional line patterns, Photoshop's Screen options in the Page Setup dialog box are, by default, dimmed. You can uncheck the Use Printer Defaults box and enter a (line) Frequency and Angle of your choice, but this will not improve the quality of a PCL print. A stylized version of your work will appear, but your work cannot print more accurately than the printer's language can understand.

ERROR DIFFUSION PRINTING

Error diffusion, as the name implies, uses a mathematical formula similar to Photoshop's Indexed Color Mode Dither Option to soften the harsh areas of contrast when an image goes from a high color capability to a much lower color capability—black toner on white paper. Unfortunately, error diffusion is not a Photoshop option. Adobe Systems is trying to encourage users to follow the professional route with imaging, and error diffusion printing is often met with gentle smiles and occasional laughter when mentioned in publication circles.

Error diffusion printing using a PCL-based printer requires a proprietary *printer driver*. A printer driver is a software program on your computer that takes information from an application and converts the information to machine code that a printer can understand. Windows 95 natively supports error diffusion dithering for non-PostScript printers (Print, Setup, Properties, Graphics, in Photoshop and other applications). Windows NT, as of this writing, does not support diffusion dithering in the Properties box under Page Setup. If you have Photoshop and a 300 dpi PCL printer and are not using Windows 95, think about investing in an error diffusion printer driver. The error diffusion printer driver intercepts the information an application sends to your system and instructs the printer to follow its own instructions rather than the instructions in the default printer drivers that were installed when you installed your printer. Figure 18.3 shows an error diffusion print placed next to a PCL print.

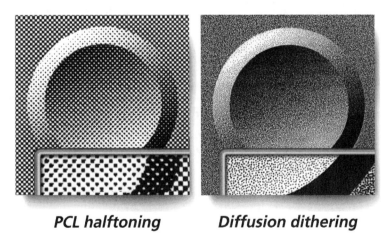

PCL halftoning   **Diffusion dithering**

FIGURE 18.3 *Error diffusion printing creates an unorganized arrangement of toner dots, which can be more visually appealing than PCL prints.*

The most notable disadvantage to error diffusion printing is imprecision. Error diffusion takes into account the inability of the printer to represent original image areas as different tonal values. As a result, dots of toner are spread in a random fashion on the page; denser areas receive more toner, and lighter areas receive less. There is no organization of dots in an error diffusion print, which makes it unsuitable for commercial camera-ready artwork. If you are not concerned with producing camera-ready artwork, error diffusion printing creates a smooth, eye-pleasing image from a printer that has limited resolution.

POSTSCRIPT PRINTERS

PostScript personal printers aren't news to Macintosh users; one of the first high-quality printing specifications for the personal computer came along with the Macintosh operating system years ago. Compared to a PCL laser printer, PostScript printers are a little slower, even with Level II PostScript, but their results are astoundingly faithful to original imagery. The method PostScript printers use to organize and place toner dots is almost identical to output of physical screens used by commercial printers.

Unlike PCL, Adobe System's PostScript descriptor language is a complete, complex programming language that was designed to be platform- and device-independent. Imagesetters, laser printers, film recorders, fax machines, and equipment that hasn't even been invented yet can all "read" a PostScript-standard file or image if their manufacturers outfitted them with PostScript interpreters. Therefore, one of the benefits of PostScript printing is a consistent standard of quality. You can rest assured that your image will reproduce as accurately as possible when it's translated from pixels to dots.

Because PostScript printing technology can simulate the screen patterns of traditional printing presses, hard copy can serve as camera-ready artwork. If you think about this, how would any of the images you've created in the assignments in this book be reproduced? As recently as the 1980s, a computer screen would have to be imaged by a film recorder, the resulting photographic negative then printed, a physical line screen dropped over it, and finally the image copied again to a photographic press plate. Generations of image quality are recaptured with the advent of the digital halftone, and Adobe's PostScript technology provides the means to create dots from printers and imagesetters that can faithfully hold up to traditional methods of imaging.

WHAT GOES INTO THAT DOT ON A PAGE

We might all be familiar with the general process by which laser printers and even imagesetters work. These machines lay down a pattern of dots on paper or film. What is not so obvious, however, is the *organization* of the dots, the shape, and frequency of the dots lined up into different angles, camera-ready to go. The following sections take you through halftoning, and calculating the right number of densities (shades of black) you'll need to achieve that perfect print.

EXAMINING A DIGITAL HALFTONE IMAGE

Continuous-tone images such as photographs have a gamut (a color or tonal breadth) so close to that of the human eye's perception, that *banding* (the demarcation of solid color values between transitional shades) is not seen. In other words, the tones in an image are *continuous*, without a beginning or end to a shade's component colors. A Photoshop gradient fill is a good visual example of a design element that displays continuous tone characteristics. In contrast, you can clearly see where the chocolate ends and the vanilla begins in Neapolitan ice cream; as long as the ice cream is kept frozen, it does not display continuous tone characteristics.

As described earlier in this chapter, the color gamut of black-and-white printed material is limited to foreground color and background color; to express the brightness values in a grayscale image, dots of different sizes are arranged in a precise pattern to correspond exactly to the values they represent in the original image. Figure 18.4 shows a PostScript printed image with the PCL print next to it. As you can see, the dots in the PostScript copy are of different sizes and are consistent in their shape. The quality is not only good enough to give to coworkers or clients, but also is invaluable in commercial printing.

Figure 18.5 gives you a better idea of how the PostScript dots correspond to their tonal equivalents in a digital image. As you can see, areas that are roughly 50 percent black in the original are represented in the PostScript print by halftone cells that occupy half the "white space." Each dot you see is a *digital halftone cell* within an invisible grid that contains all the halftone dots.

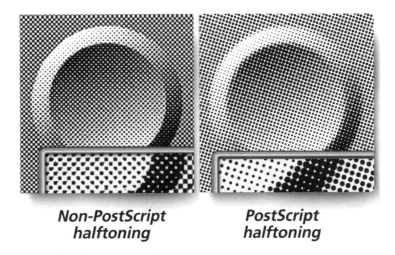

**Non-PostScript
halftoning**

**PostScript
halftoning**

FIGURE 18.4 *Most laser printers can produce halftones, but PostScript creates photographic halftones of publication quality.*

Original image

**PostScript
halftoning**

FIGURE 18.5 *PostScript halftone dots represent equivalent, continuous tones by their size, as arranged in a pattern.*

Try a little experiment: hold this book about four feet in front of you and look at the halftone example in the last figure. Try the same thing with the PCL and error diffusion figures. You'll see that the consistency of the dot shapes, size, and organization (called *line screens*) is such that your mind easily interprets what you see as an image of a button. This is the primary difference between halftone screening and other technologies. The organization of dots that compose a halftone image, and how to optimize your Photoshop designs so that they will print their best, are discussed next.

UNDERSTANDING THE HALFTONE CELL, RESOLUTION, AND OTHER FACTORS

Printer resolution and onscreen resolution are measured differently and have different capabilities for expressing tones and colors. *Resolution* plays an important role in printed image quality; you define resolution in PostScript printing not in dots per inch, but in *lines per inch* (of halftone dots). Halftone frequency and resolution are used to evaluate a printed image for aesthetic reasons and for commercial printing purposes.

To get a better idea of the way halftone printing works, imagine a grid that covers the area on the printed page where you want an image. This grid, or *line screen*, is composed of *cells*. Each cell in the line screen is composed of a small grid of toner dots that collectively make up the larger dot. The number of slots in the halftone cell's grid that are filled with toner determines the density of the individual halftone cell. The more filled grids in the halftone cell, the darker the cell, and the larger the digital halftone dot. The size of a single PostScript halftone dot has a direct relation to the *shade*, or degree of density, in the original image. Figure 18.6 is a representation of this halftone screen with halftone dots placed inside. The percentages of coverage at the bottom of the figure correspond to the size of the halftone dot in the cell. You can see the relationship in this figure between the traditional, physical halftone screen, the digital halftone, and a continuous-tone source image that has the same halftone values. Arranged in a line and viewed from a distance, halftone dots convey the feeling of continuous tones in a grayscale image.

Halftone dots on an invisible grid are not the only factor that determines good printed output. Other important factors are line angles, and the number of spaces on a line that are available for the halftone dots.

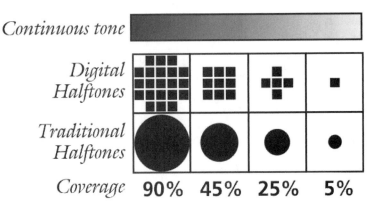

FIGURE 18.6 *A digital halftone is today's equivalent of a halftone screen applied to continuous-tone photographs.*

LINE ANGLES

The halftone dots must be arranged on the page in lines that collectively form the *line screen*. The angle at which the lines are positioned is called the *line angle*.

In nature, continuous-tone images contain many right angles; examples are the sides of buildings and the stripes in someone's shirt. For this reason, setting a halftone line angle at zero or 90 degrees is not a good idea. You should specify a halftone line-screen angle that's *oblique* to the elements in a digital image—45 degrees works in most cases. Line-screen patterns that closely resemble the patterns in images *resonate* visually, creating unwanted *moiré* patterns. Figure 18.7 illustrates the way different-sized halftone dots are arranged in a 45 degree angle screen.

Photoshop and many other applications offer a default line angle of 45 degrees for halftone dots. In Photoshop, you have the option of adjusting this angle, but you would only need to do this if you had photographed an image containing strong diagonal stripes.

To define specific halftone screens for printing, use Photoshop's File, Page Setup, Screen command to display the Halftone Screen dialog box shown in Figure 18.8. Although the same Halftone Screen options appear when a PostScript printer or a PCL printer is defined as the Specific Printer, the shape and frequency of dots are not rendered as true halftones with a non-Postscript (PCL) printer. To achieve a true digital halftone effect, you must use a PostScript-capable output device. If you check the Use Printer's Default Screen check box in the Halftone Screen dialog box, the options for screens is dimmed. Generally, when outputting to a non-Postscript printer, it's best to allow the printer to render using its own internal screening process.

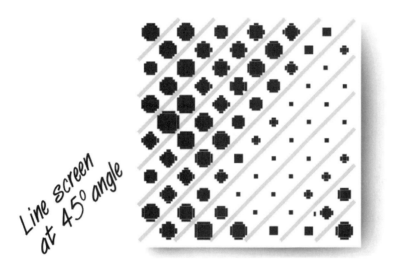

FIGURE 18.7   *Lines of halftone dots arranged at an angle help prevent unwanted patterning in the printed design.*

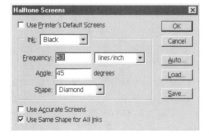

FIGURE 18.8   *Photoshop's Halftone Screen dialog box options are useful for PostScript output only.*

The options in Photoshop's Halftone Screen dialog box include Frequency and (dot) Shape, in addition to halftone Angle.

TIP

The Use Accurate Screens option in the Halftone Screens dialog box refers to an Adobe technology designed for high-end PostScript Level 2 printers and printers with Emerald controllers. PostScript Level 2 interpreters are installed in some of the newer PostScript printers, and they produce better and faster halftone prints than the older PostScript standard.

Accurate Screen technology is usually found on imagesetters and not on personal laser printers, but it's worth checking your printer's documentation to see whether it supports PostScript Level 2 and Accurate Screens. If it does, be sure to check this box so that you can benefit from this feature. If you're not sure whether your printer supports Accurate Screens, check the box anyway. If your printer doesn't support Accurate Screens, the information will be ignored.

Halftone screen *frequency* is another option to specify when you print from Photoshop. The frequency of lines per inch used when printing halftone dots has a direct correlation with *the number of unique tones* you can simulate in a print. There's a simple way, using your eyes and a little math, to achieve the best line frequency for a grayscale image.

LINE FREQUENCY

The default setting for a 300 dpi laser printer is usually about 45 to 60 lines per inch; for 600 dpi printers, it is about 85 lines per inch. The actual lines-per-inch capability of any given printer is determined by the manufacturer. The basic truth about medium- to low-resolution laser printer output is that when you *increase* lines per inch, you *decrease* the number of grayscale values you're simulating on the printed page. There is a direct correlation.

Two factors govern the maximum number of tonal values that laser printing can simulate: the resolution of the digital image, expressed in pixels per inch, and the number of densities that can portray the gray shades in the printed image.

THE TIMES TWO RULE

An accurate halftone print of a grayscale image should have a lines-per-inch value no less than half the pixels-per-inch value of the original file. For example, many of the example images on the Companion CD have a resolution of 150 pixels per inch. To print these image with any sense of aesthetic value, the halftone screen should be no less (or more) than 75 lpi.

To calculate the optimal resolution for printing a digital image, use this mathematical formula:

Printer Line Frequency (in lpi) $\times$ 2 = Image Resolution (in pixels/inch)

If you print an image with a resolution of more than two times the current line screen defined for a printer, you are creating a productivity bottleneck. You simply cannot squeeze more visual detail out of an image than the printer is capable of producing. Excess image information is spooled to the printer and then discarded at printing time, creating an unnecessary waste of time before you receive your hard copy. You have two alternatives if your image contains a higher resolution than your printer is capable of outputting:

- Choose Image, Image Size, check the Resample Image check box, and then enter a resolution in the Resolution field. The resolution you enter should be less than two times the Frequency of the Halftone Screen in the Halftone Screen dialog box in the Page Setup command.

  By using this option you physically change the arrangement of pixels to create a new resolution image. If you choose this option for printing, remember to save the resulting image file to a different file name. The Resample Image check box usually should remain unchecked to prevent inadvertent distortion of images you work with in the future.

- If you have no particular image dimensions in mind for your laser copy, you can also choose Image, Image Size, and then reduce the Resolution to less than two times the Halftone Screen Frequency value with the Resample Image box *unchecked*. Unlike most Windows and Macintosh applications, Photoshop does *not* offer sizing options from the Print command dialog box; before you print, image dimensions should be checked to make sure that the image will fit on the page. Because image resolution is inversely proportional to image dimensions, this approach does not change any visual content within the image; after you've printed the piece, resolution can be restored to the file's original resolution.

TIP

Keep this rule in mind when you specify image dimensions and resolution for a copy of an image you want printed. When you create an image, "shooting for the stars" is good practice. If you're particularly proud of some work you've done in Photoshop at 300 pixels/inch, save it this way. You might get to print it at a high resolution some day. But then make a copy of it, keeping in mind the resolution of your present target printer. You can use Photoshop's Image, Image Size command, or the Resize Image Wizard (Assistant) to specify a lower resolution for an image.

When you print from Photoshop the active document is printed in the center of the page. A useful feature in Photoshop is the image preview box, which can be displayed at any time (before you print) by clicking on the Document Sizes box to the right of the Zoom percentage field. As you can see in Figure 18.9, the image Oceanside.tif falls outside the currently defined print page in Photoshop. The white area of the page preview box is the live area of the printed page, and the box with the "x" inside it is the document. In its current orientation, this image needs to be resized so that the entire "x" is visible in the image preview box; otherwise, the print will be clipped on the left and right sides. If you want the image placed on the page in some other position, you'll have to import the image into a DTP program, such as PageMaker, and then print from there.

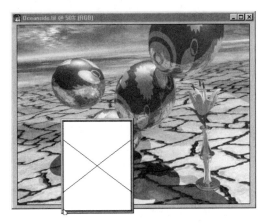

FIGURE 18.9 *The pop-up image size box will tell you whether the image is too large to print to the currently defined page size.*

In addition to the image preview box, Photoshop alerts the user prior to printing if an image is too large to print to the currently defined page size. In Figure 18.10 you can see the warning that appeared when the author attempted to print the Oceanside image.

FIGURE 18.10 *Photoshop alerts you when an image resolution and dimensions are too large for the currently defined page size.*

If this happens to you, you have three alternatives, besides letting the printer crop your work:

- Using the File, Page Setup command, rotate the printable page (with images, where possible) so that the widest side for the image falls within the new printable page orientation. To do this, click on either the Portrait or Landscape button in the Page Setup's Orientation field.

- Choose Image, Image Size from the menu, check the Constrain Proportions check box, check the Resample Image check box in the Image Size dialog box, and then enter smaller values in the Height and Width boxes of the Print Size field to create a smaller image. Click on OK and then print your image. This is *not* a recommended course of action, because it changes image quality, as described earlier.

- Choose Image, Image Size, and with the Resample Image box *un*checked, increase the pixels/inch amount in the Resolution field. This will decrease the physical dimensions of the image.

Even though no change to file content is made when you increase image resolution in the Image Size dialog box while the Resample Image check box is unchecked, Photoshop sees this as a change in the file. Photoshop will flag you if you've respecified an image's dimensions/resolution before you close the image.

The reason Photoshop asks about dimensions/resolution is that image resolution is a property specific to some, but not all file formats, and applications that can import images often use resolution information to determine the dimensions of an image placed within a document. In the Tagged Image File format (TIF, or TIFF), for example, image resolution information is stored in the header of the file. A 2" by 2" image with a resolution of 150 pixels/inch will usually import as 2" by 2" to an application such as PageMaker. If you were to increase the dimension of this file in Photoshop while the Resample Image check box was unchecked, the resolution of the image would decrease, and although the *content* of the image would not change, it would be imported to certain other applications as a dimensionally larger file that might not print at its best. The reason that output would look poor is that the file would cover a larger area, with fewer pixels per inch.

You're not quite ready to print from Photoshop yet. You hold some of the keys to printing the correct image resolution, but you still don't know how to achieve a balance between Halftone Screen Frequency and the number of unique shades your printer can handle. The Times Two Rule is only half the equation for printing a grayscale image from a laser printer.

As mentioned earlier, you have some flexibility in determining the lines-per-inch value when you use a PostScript printer. You can adjust the coarseness of the lines (the space between them) by specifying a lower line frequency, but depending on your printer's resolution (measured in dpi), you may not get a very good-looking print. The print may look blocked in or muddy and lack refinement. This is why you need to determine *how many unique tones* in a grayscale image can be represented by halftone lines.

The Number of Tones in a Grayscale Image

An 8-bit grayscale image can contain up to 256 unique tones. A laser printer has a definite threshold for expressing all the grayscale information; this may become painfully obvious when you print to a low-resolution printer. Occasionally, you'll need to strike a balance between line frequency and the number of shades the halftone dots can represent. The balance is expressed as this mathematical equation:

Printer Resolution (in dpi)/Printer Line Frequency (in lpi)= n (squared) = shades of gray

You'll "plug and play" with this equation shortly to see how faithfully a printer can represent the tonal values in a grayscale image.

Using Calculations to Determine Image Quality

Suppose that you have an image with a resolution of 150 pixels/inch, such as the one used earlier as an example. You know from the first equation that the setting for the halftone screen's lines-per-inch frequency should be half the image's pixel-per-inch resolution, or 75 lines per inch. The following calculation is for a 300 dpi printer:

300(dpi)/75(lpi)= 4, then

4^2 = 16 shades of gray

Pretty pathetic, right? When a 256-shades-of-gray image is reproduced at 75 lpi on a 300 dpi printer, all the tonal information is reduced to 16 shades! This is unacceptable for the serious imaging-type person.

To be fair, a 75 lpi halftone screen is way too high a value for a 300 dpi printer. Most manufacturers recommend a value between 45 and 60. The line screen frequency you should use with a printer, then, is really a question of aesthetics. The fewer lines per inch used to express the halftone patterns, the more shades they simulate, but the more visible the lines are in the image. A line screen frequency of *less* than 45 per inch is apparent on a printed page to the extent that the line pattern overwhelms the composition of the printed image.

HIGHER-RESOLUTION PRINTERS

To get a reasonable facsimile of your digital image, a personal printer capable of 600 to 1,800 dpi is more in keeping with hard-copy proofing needs. Many professional black-and-white publications, in fact, can be sent to press from a camera-ready 1,800 dpi laser print. Several add-in cards are available now that can step a 600 dpi printer's resolution up to 1,200 dpi PostScript output (which produces virtually the same results as an 1,800 dpi printer), and Lexmark, LaserMaster, NewGen and others make fairly affordable, high-resolution laser printers that can produce good camera-ready copy. So don't compromise the quality of your printed piece; instead, improve the capability of your output device. The following equation shows the gamut of grayscale a 1,200 dpi PostScript printer can simulate with a halftone line screen of 85 lpi:

$$1,200 (\text{dpi}) / 85 (\text{lpi}) = 14.12$$

$$14.2^2 = 199.37$$

Not bad! Of the 256 possible shades in a grayscale image, 199 can be represented at 1,200 dpi with an 85 lpi line screen.

But what happens when you use these settings for a grayscale image that contains *more* than 200 shades? You do lose some control over the finer visual details in the image, and you leave the extra shades to chance; sharp banding can occur in the image when not enough tones are allocated to the print. And if your print is to serve as camera-ready art for commercial printing, you run the risk of a final, ink-on-paper print that has harsh areas with contrast where you least expect them because you gave the machine more visual information than it could handle.

Consider an alternative to letting a machine dictate the quality of your finished print. Although you can't change the screen, you *can* reduce the number of tones in a *copy* of the image, with such subtlety and finesse that viewers will never notice that anything's missing. To reduce the number of tones in your image to match the printer-imposed limit, you first must determine how many shades are in your image, and then use Photoshop's Levels feature to eliminate as many shades of gray as necessary. In the following section, you'll see how to calculate the number of tones in an image.

THE PHOTOSHOP METHOD OF COUNTING COLORS

Photoshop can be used to determine the number of unique shades in a grayscale image. The approach you must take is not straightforward, however, and you should definitely have a copy of the image saved under a different name before you try this. When you convert an RGB image to Indexed mode, the Indexed Color dialog box's Colors field, beneath the Color Depth drop-down list, reports the number of colors in an image. If Photoshop does not offer the Exact Palette and the Other Color Depth, it means that the image contains more than 256 colors.

To make the best use of the Indexed Color mode's report of the unique colors in an image, you should first convert a color image to Grayscale mode, and then convert it back to RGB Color mode to determine the unique number of tones in the image. Use the techniques in Chapter 11, "Using Different Color Modes," to convert a copy of your color work to LAB mode, and then save the Lightness channel as the Grayscale mode image you want to use for printing.

In the following example, you use the Toaster.tif image in the CHAP18 folder on the Companion CD to have Photoshop calculate the unique tones in the image. This image was originally a color image, converted to Grayscale mode. Let's see how many unique tones the image contains.

CALCULATING UNIQUE GRAYSCALE TONES

1. Open the Toaster.tif image from the CHAP18 folder on the Companion CD.

2. Choose Image, Mode, and then choose RGB Color from the menu.

3. Choose, Image, Mode, Indexed Color from the menu. As you can see in Figure 18.11, Photoshop has calculated that an exact match of unique values can be made and saved to a custom color palette consisting of 213 colors.

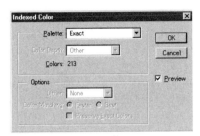

FIGURE 18.11   *When an image contains fewer than 256 unique colors or tones, Photoshop calculates an Exact palette containing only those colors.*

4. Click on Cancel and then choose File, Revert. Click on Revert in the attention box that pops up, and then save the image to your hard disk as Toaster.tif.

As discussed in the previous section, at 1,200 dpi and using an 85-line-per-inch screen, you can faithfully output 199 unique tones. To print the Toaster image successfully, 14 of the unique tones (213 –199) in the image must go!

But which ones? This is where you should pick up the telephone and learn the specifics of the commercial press used to output the image. Your printer (the human, not the machine!) knows the capability and limitations of printing from a plate made from your camera-ready image, using their printing presses. In fact, as you'll see in the next section, you might want to reduce the tonal information in an image to *less* than what your laser printer can handle, to create an image that can be successfully transferred to the ink-on-paper medium.

INK IS DIFFERENT FROM TONER

A print press and a laser printer are two different *physical* ways of rendering a halftone image. Halftone dots of ink on paper soak into the medium, whereas laser toner dots rest on top of the paper. Experienced commercial printers will often tell you to avoid shades that approach absolute white and absolute black in the camera-ready print you give them. The reason for this is that although a halftone screen printed from a laser is capable of fusing a 100 percent dense, black area *onto* a page, print press inks soak *into* a page and spread. Depending on the paper, the ink, the presses, and the line screen used, a digital halftone containing halftones that represent the extreme ends of possible brightness values won't "hold." For example, an area that screens at, say, a 90 percent or 95 percent density might completely saturate the corresponding printed area with ink.

When a screen doesn't "hold" on the press, the darkest areas become black and bleed together, creating a puddle that eventually dries to create a misrepresented area of your original design.

Design misrepresentation can also occur in light and white areas. A no-coverage area on a laser copy sent to a commercial press sometimes results in an image area that contains a "hot spot," caused by an absence of halftone ink dots in the image. Zero percent and one percent densities in an image, expressed as ink halftone dots, create an unwanted border—called *banding*—in the image. Think about this one for a moment. The one-percent dots have to *start* someplace, don't they? The idea is to cover even totally white areas in the original image with at least a one-percent density of halftone dots.

DECREASING CONTRAST IN THE LASER COPY

To handle image tonal extremes, go back to your original digital image and make a *copy* of it for modification. Then, in the copy, reduce the contrast of the image so that there are no absolute blacks or whites. Although the modified image will look flat and dull on the monitor, the image will snap up when printed from a plate made from your laser hard copy. Again, the "correct" rendition of your image, when paper is the final output, is the paper, and not what you see on the monitor.

For the purposes of this Toaster example, let's suppose that after your talk with the commercial printer, you learn that the press doesn't handle halftone percentages of less than 12 percent density. The solution is to change the distribution of tones in the image so that the first 12 percent (the very light tones) are reassigned to darker values. This shifts the tonal range of the image into a printable range of tonality. Don't think of it as degrading your work, but instead as optimizing the image for display in a different medium.

The first thing to do is calculate which tones in the image are located in the upper 12 percent of the image. A brightness gamut that ranges from 0 to 255 doesn't correspond directly to a density percentage that ranges from 0 percent to 100 percent, so we need to use the following equation:

$$256 - [\text{Halftone Density (in percent)} \times 2.56] = \text{Brightness Value}$$

Now to plug the 12 percent minimum density value for the print press into the equation:

$$12 (\text{percent}) \times 2.56 = 30.72$$

$$256 - 30.72 = 225.28$$

The solution, then, is to bring the output level for an image's upper range down to 225.

Similarly, if the commercial printer tells you that 90 percent black is *the densest* halftone dot the press can render, you should apply the same rule, as follows:

$$90 (\text{percent}) \times 2.56 = 230.40$$

$$256 - 230.40 = 25.60$$

In this case, you'd enter **26** in the left Output Level field in the Levels command dialog box.

In the following steps, you perform tonal reduction to the Toaster.tif image to optimize it for a camera-ready print that will reproduce accurately from a commercial press.

DECREASING IMAGE CONTRAST FOR PRINT PRESSES

1. Open the Toaster image you saved earlier to your hard disk.

2. Press Ctrl(⌘)+L to display the Levels command.

3. Enter **225** in the right Output Levels box.

4. Enter **26** in the left Output Levels box, as shown in Figure 18.12.

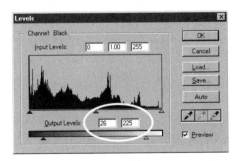

FIGURE 18.12 *Decrease the Output Levels for the image to reduce extreme blacks and white for black-and-white output.*

5. Click on OK to apply the tone changes, press Ctrl(⌘)+Shift+S (File, Save As), and then save the file as Output.tif to your hard disk.

If you perform the steps outlined in the previous section for converting the Grayscale mode image to RGB, and then check out the potential Indexed color palette for this image, you'll discover that the Output.tif image now contains 172 unique tones. This is within a 1,200 dpi printer's tonal gamut at 85 lpi, so you can successfully print this image, and it can serve as an optimized, camera-ready print for commercial printing in this example.

After you finish printing, you can free up hard drive space by deleting the copy of the Toaster image or any images of your own that you've optimized for camera-ready printing. After you degrade an image by reducing the tones, you can never retrieve the pixel information that's been simplified for printing purposes. That's why you should always specify digital image dimensions and resolutions for printing from a *copy* of your work.

WARNING

If your commercial printer specifies only a high *or* a low-density threshold, *don't* use Levels to redistribute both the bottom and top tonal extreme in the target image. Photoshop recalculates and redistributes *all* the pixels in an image when you make a change in a specific brightness area. Photoshop's capability to redistribute the scheme of tonal values so that they look smooth can wreck your chances of an optimal print if you specify an Output Level that the commercial printer has *not* specified!

PHOTOSHOP'S PRINTING OPTIONS

To bring our output discussion back to the application you'll most likely use for output, the following sections describe how Photoshop's output options are used for rendering images to paper. When you believe that you're all set to press Ctrl(⌘)Shift+P to access Page Setup, the following sections walk you through the options you'll encounter.

USING THE PAGE SETUP DIALOG BOX

When you choose Page Setup from the File menu, the Page Setup dialog box appears. Figure 18.13 shows this dialog box. The Page Setup screen always looks the same, regardless of which printer driver you have loaded on your system.

In this dialog box, you have the option to print from the default printer (the one currently defined for your system), or you can choose another printer from the Printer Name drop-down list, a list of all printer drivers currently installed on your system. Usually, most of the many buttons and check boxes in this dialog box can be left at their default settings. The next few sections explain these settings so that you'll know which settings to change when you have a special application or printing need. For the following examples, the authors have chosen an Epson Stylus Color printer driver. If your own printer is a black-and-white laser printer or a different output device, some of the options might not be available to you.

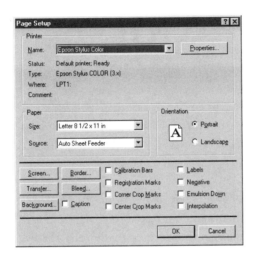

FIGURE 18.13   *The Page Setup dialog box.*

SCREENS

Like commercial printing presses, personal color printers use three colors (cyan, magenta, and yellow) or four colors (cyan, magenta, yellow, and black) to produce the colors in your image. These pigments can be in the form of wax, ink, toner, or dye. Printers that use four colors usually produce better results than three-color printers because pigments contain many impurities, and blacks in an image need a reinforcing pass of black pigment from the printer so that darker areas in the printed image will not display a greenish color cast.

The screen angles for each color the printer uses are defined at angles that do not cause resonating lines relative to each other. The use of different screen angles greatly reduces the chance that the cyan, magenta, yellow, and black pigments will build a moiré pattern into your printed image when they are printed to the same page in successive passes. A *moiré* pattern is the result of screen lines (lines composed of halftone cells) overlapping at regular intervals within the image.

When you click on the Screens button in the Page Setup dialog box, the Halftone Screens dialog box shown in Figure 18.14 is displayed. Notice that the Use Printer's Default Screens check box is selected. Unless you're attempting to achieve a special effect with your color print or are very familiar with the specifications for your machine, this is a good option to leave checked.

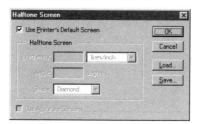

FIGURE 18.14   *Unless you understand the screen specifications for a specific output device, allow Photoshop to render to the device's internal screen settings.*

Personal color printer manufacturers have built the optimal screen angles right into the machine—there's really no need to change them. When you enable this option, all other options are dimmed, and you can't change the Halftone Screen settings.

BORDER

Click on this button to access a dialog box that enables you to place a black border around the edges of your image. You can specify the width of the border in inches, points, or millimeters, but you can't choose a color other than black.

BLEED

If you intend to physically crop the printed image, you can have Photoshop insert crop marks in the image to guide the person who runs the paper cutter. You can specify how far into the image the crop marks appear by entering a value in the Width field in the Bleed dialog box.

BACKGROUND

If your image doesn't fill the page, and you want color around your image, you can choose a color here. A click on the Background button displays Photoshop's Color Picker, or the color picker you've chosen in Photoshop's Preferences.

Because choosing a background color for output really eats up the costly ink, wax, or toner the printer uses, and increases print time dramatically, you should not choose this option frivolously.

TRANSFER

Transfer functions are designed to compensate for a miscalibrated imagesetter. These functions are *not* used with the typical personal color printer; they should be used only when you create black-and-white camera-ready art. Click on the Transfer button to display the Transfer Functions dialog box, where you can adjust the values used to compensate for dot gain. *Dot gain* is the growth in the size of halftone dots that occurs when the ink used to print an image on a printing press expands as it's absorbed into the paper. Imagesetters compensate for dot gain by reducing the size of the halftone dots they put on the film from which the press plates are made. The information needed to determine the values you enter in the Transfer Functions dialog box and the File, Color Settings, CMYK Setup dialog box (using the Dot Gain drop-down list and percentage field) *must* come from the commercial printer. Only the commercial printer knows what the appropriate value is for the paper, ink, and press your image will be printed on. If all this sounds complicated, it is. It is far better to insist that an imagesetter be properly calibrated than to "guesstimate" the Transfer Function curve.

CAPTION AND LABELS CHECK BOXES

Check the Caption check box if you've already made a caption entry in the Caption field of the File, File Info dialog box. The caption will be printed in nine-point Helvetica in the margin of your printout. Put a check in the Labels check box if you want the file name and channel name printed on the image in nine-point Helvetica. The size and typeface for these options cannot be changed. You might want to enable the Caption and Labels check boxes if you're sending a hard copy proof to a service bureau or other organization that handles massive numbers of images from different clients.

REGISTRATION MARKS

When you print color separations for spot color, process color, or duotones, check this box to place bullseyes in the margin around the image to enable the commercial printer to align the printing plates. Registration marks are not used for printing a composite image to a personal color printer; only a single page is printed.

CALIBRATION BARS

Enabling this feature causes a gradient-filled rectangle to be printed in the margin of the page. This is used by commercial printers to check that their press, or printer, is producing the proper density of color. The 10 percent part of the calibration bar, for example, actually should be 10 percent when the commercial printer measures it with a device called a *densitometer*. Densitometers are precision instruments designed to measure the tonal values in printed material. If you are printing CMYK separations, the Calibration Bar feature adds a progressive color bar. Progressive proofs are used at commercial printers to check the alignment and density values of the C, M, Y, and K values of pigments as they are applied in combination on the printed page. To see an example of a calibration bar in action, take apart a cereal box or other printed package. Calibration bars usually are printed on the inside flaps as a method for proofing a production run as it comes off the presses.

CORNER AND CENTER CROP MARKS CHECK BOXES

If your image does not fill the page and will be trimmed physically to the edges of the image, you can specify that Corner or Center crop marks be printed. To print both kinds of crop marks, check both boxes.

NEGATIVE AND EMULSION DOWN CHECK BOXES

You use these options when you print film to make printing plates. Check with your printer to determine how these options should be set for the printing press that will be used. *Don't* guess or make an assumption based on something you might have heard or read, or you might go to the expense of producing film that is unusable. When you are printing a complete, finished image on paper, these check boxes always should be left *unchecked*.

INTERPOLATION CHECK BOX

This option applies only to some PostScript Level 2 printers. If you are printing a low-resolution image, a check in this check box instructs the printer to increase (sample up) the resolution of the image. The advantage to using this option is that interpolation reduces a low-resolution image's tendency to produce stair-step, aliased edges. The disadvantage is that overall image quality is reduced, and the focus of the image will not be as clear as it is on the monitor. If you feel that interpolation of the image is necessary for final output, choose Image, Image Size in Photoshop and then increase the Print Size dimensions or resolution with the Resample Image box checked. In Photoshop, you have the opportunity to see what the effect of the interpolation will be; when the printer does it, you pay for a print with which you might be dissatisfied.

USING THE PRINT COMMAND FROM THE FILE MENU

After you have set all the Page Setup options, it's time to actually print the image, using Photoshop's File, Print (Ctrl(⌘)+P) command. This dialog box usually looks the same, no matter what kind of printer you are printing to. The important settings are Print Quality, PostScript (or Printer, when the printer's a PCL model) Color Management, and Encoding (only available with PostScript printer drivers). Print Quality should be set to the highest level your printer is capable of producing. The color mode chosen in the Space field should match the color mode of the printer. As noted earlier, most personal color printers expect RGB input and not CMYK.

PRINTING TO DIFFERENT COLOR MODES

Photoshop is capable of printing a color image to a black-and-white printer, and although the authors recommend grayscale mode images as the best visual data to send to a black-and-white printer, there will be times when your intended final output is to color separations, not as a single image that represents a mono-chrome copy of your original color piece. If you have a PostScript printer driver defined as your intended output device, Photoshop's Print dialog box looks a little different than when a non-PostScript printer is defined. Only with PostScript output do you have a complete set of output options. As you can see in Figure 18.15, the bottom of the Print dialog box has a Space field that contains many different monitor, broadcast, and specific grayscale gamma settings, all tailored to try to match your monitor's display to printed material.

These Space options appear in the Print dialog box for all kinds of printers when the image you're printing is a color image, but only Grayscale, Grayscale - Gamma 1.8, and Grayscale Gamma - 2.2 are displayed if you're printing a grayscale image. These options are convenient for default printing to a personal black-and-white laser printer.

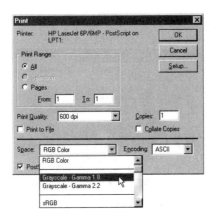

FIGURE 18.15 *Photoshop enables you to send to the printer information organized in different color spaces.*

CHOOSING RGB

A black-and-white printer doesn't understand color information; its only concern is the way black toner is distributed. When RGB is chosen in the Space field and you have a grayscale image saved to RGB color mode, Photoshop sends all color information in the file to the printer. The printer discards most of the information, processing only what it thinks is pertinent to printing the image as black dots of toner on the page. When you print a color image to a black-and-white printer the results are never optimal, and the process is slow because the printer must figure out which information to discard and which to keep, based on a pre-established set of rules programmed by the printer manufacturer. A similar printer "bottleneck" is created when you try to print an image with a resolution higher than that of the printer.

CHOOSING GRAYSCALE

If you choose Grayscale from the Space field, Photoshop gives you two gamma options to produce the print. Photoshop makes an internal copy of your color image and converts it to Grayscale, using its normal method for converting color images to Grayscale mode. Although this is a better course of action than choosing RGB information to send to the printer, Photoshop's Grayscale mode conversion methods are *not* the best way to produce a grayscale image. See Chapter 11 for information on accurate RGB-to-grayscale conversions. The best quality laser prints are produced from images that start with good tonal separation of image areas, have been manually converted to the appropriate grayscale image type, and in which the grayscale image has been adjusted to bring it in line with the capability of the printer.

Additionally, you can choose File, Color Settings, and then Grayscale Setup to preview what a color image will look like when it's sent to a black-and-white printer. Again, it's best to send grayscale information to a black-and-white printer.

CHOOSING SEPARATIONS

When you want color separations, you must first convert a copy of your work to CMYK mode (Image, Mode, CMYK color), and then choose Separations from the Space drop-down list to begin the separation printing process. The authors do not advise that users without an extensive background in color printing create their own separations, however. The sections that follow contain information on separations and what the best conversion procedures are.

When you print to a personal color printer, you are unlikely to need to print to CMYK or to convert the image you wish to print. Most affordable inkjet color printers insist upon using their own internal conversion circuitry to read image data in RGB mode to print CMYK inks.

It should be noted here that PostScript Level 2 color printers actually prefer to take LAB Color data. You'll get crisp colors and a better image if you send a LAB color mode image to these types of printers. PostScript Level 1 printers (found in older personal printers and imagesetters) do not handle LAB color gracefully.

ENCODING OPTIONS

An additional field—Encoding—sometimes appears at the bottom right of the Print dialog box, depending on the printer driver you are using. When Encoding is an option, the print should be set to ASCII for greatest compatibility when printing over a network. Binary is the option of choice if your printer supports binary mode and your printer is attached to your computer. Binary prints about twice as fast as ASCII. JPEG encoding is useful when you want to print very quickly and are willing to put up with the information loss associated with JPEG compression.

TIP

If you want to print only part of an image, use the Rectangular Marquee tool to select the area you want to print. All the pixels within the marquee must be opaque. Press Ctrl (⌘)+P; then, in the Print dialog box, choose Selection in the Print Range field, and click on OK.

Finally, the Print to File option should *not* be checked if you expect a hard-copy version of your work to come out of your printer. Later in this chapter we discuss Print to File options as a strategy for getting your work to a service bureau.

After you decide on all the settings on this dialog box, click on OK and wait for your image to come out of the printer. You might have to be patient; large, photorealistic images, printed at high-quality settings, can take a long time to print.

INCREASING PRINT QUALITY, DECREASING ARTIST INVOLVEMENT

You've seen in this chapter what you can do by yourself with a high-resolution laser printer and Photoshop methods that optimize an image for the best reproduction. As you gain experience with imaging, however, you'll find that you are spending equal amounts of time at your com-puter and at the commercial printer. You'll become familiar with the special requirements of a specific printing press and learn to trust the people who render your work as ink on the printed page.

This is also the time when you might consider abandoning the "home brew" halftone from your laser printer and letting the commercial printer render your computer file directly to an imagesetting device. Imagesetters don't depend on toner dots to render halftones; rather, imagesetters produce film positives and negatives from digital files. The film produced by an imagesetter can be made into printing press plates. Some imagesetters skip the film step altogether and instead create a printing plate directly from your digital file.

Many of the formulas and techniques you've learned in this chapter also apply to work that is sent to an imagesetter. If you are producing images that will be part of a color printing run, there are additional Photoshop features you can take advantage of to ensure great work. If you are ready to take the plunge into other types of output, the next sections are for you.

PRE-PRESS AND THE SERVICE BUREAU

Most people don't have a commercial printing press hooked directly into their computer. They need to establish a link between the ethereal nature of digital images and such physical, tangible things as press plates and ink on paper. Your allies in bridging the gap between your artistic input and physical output are the pre-press service bureau and the commercial printer.

A service bureau prepares and transforms your file into a form and a format that can be used to produce physical output. Service bureaus use expensive, complex equipment—imagesetters, film recorders, high-resolution color printers, and proofing devices are all the tools of high-quality output trade. The output from these devices might be all you need, as in the case of color laser prints or slides, to make your image come alive. On the other hand, to bring your images to the world, you might need to have film *separations* made, which any commercial printer can then use to make printing plates. If color printing from a commercial press is your goal, you'll need the services of a pre-press service bureau's image-setter as the intermediate step to the printing press.

Service bureaus and commercial printers are not always two separate businesses; sometimes you find them under one roof. And even when they are separate businesses, the services they offer might overlap. Both a commercial printer and a service bureau might own imagesetters, digital color printers, and proofing devices. The difference between service bureaus and commercial printers is that the commercial printer makes printing plates from negatives and mass produces your work on high-speed presses that apply ink to paper. Regardless of whether your service bureau and commercial printer are at the same location, the roles that both firms play, and their knowledge of a specialized craft, are vital to successfully producing beautiful printed copies of your work.

How Pre-Press Savvy Do You Need to Be?

As a computer imagist, your first responsibility is to devote your skills, talents, and time toward producing outstanding work. Like artists who seek mentors to help them refine their skills, you need to send your creations to people who are experts in their line of work. Although your level of involvement in producing a finished, printed copy of your imaging work is a limited one in some respects, you should understand a *few* things about the printing process. There are things you can do with a digital file before you send it to the service bureau or commercial printer that will make your business partner's work go more smoothly, and you'll be happier with the completed image.

Although you certainly don't need to acquire all the skills and knowledge that these folks have, you *do* need to know how to deliver digital copies of your color and grayscale work to them so that they can successfully transform your digital image into a physical image. You also need to know what kinds of services they provide, what to expect when you engage their services, and how their equipment affects many of your most basic design decisions.

If you're reading this chapter in sequence, you already have begun the process of learning what you need to know to be able to make the service bureau and the commercial printers your partners. PostScript technology, the way halftone cells and screening work, and the relationship between resolution and file dimensions are all as important to the production of commercially printed output as they are to personal printed output.

STRATEGIES FOR GETTING YOUR WORK OUT THE DOOR

To increase the distribution of your work in a high-quality medium, you need to give a commercial printer a copy of your digital image file. Up to this point we've provided one of two ways to accomplish this goal—by creating an in-house camera-ready hard copy of your work. But because not all commercial printers are computer-equipped, and partly because prop-erly preparing photographic images for reproduction on a printing press always has been highly specialized work, the service bureau was born. The service that the staff at a pre-press service bureau performs is to take your files and prep them for printing. Preparing your files for printing entails, at the very least, the use of an imagesetter or film recorder that renders digital files to film. After your image is on film, any printer can make the printing plates for the press.

So the real trick to producing high-quality output is how you go about bundling your work and getting it to the service bureau in a format they can render to camera-ready format. The following sections discuss the special processing and saving you'll need to perform on copies of your Photoshop files.

WORKING WITH CMYK IMAGES

If the intended output for your Photoshop work is a four-color printing press, you'll need to send your images to the service bureau in CMYK (Cyan, Magenta,

Yellow, Black) color mode. This color model uses four color channels to produce the colors that can be printed on a printing press. The gamut of colors is smaller than that available in RGB mode; our eyes can see a wider gamut of color than can be reproduced by using subtractive, reflective color pigments.

When the three process colors (cyan, magenta, and yellow) are mixed, they produce other colors. When the colors are mixed in equal proportions, black *should* be produced. Impurities in ink pigments usually make it impossible for perfect black (absorption of all light) to be achieved, however. To circumvent this problem an additional black color plate is used to apply black ink. Usually, a black separation plate is made from the weighted average of the three other color plates used to produce CMYK process color images.

Because the monitor you use to display your work uses a combination of additive red, green, and blue colors, you can never truly see onscreen what a CMYK color image looks like. For this reason, and because the extra channel the CMYK model uses creates much larger files, most image editing should be done by using the RGB color model. When editing is completed, convert a *copy* of the image to the CMYK model. Image quality is lost when you convert the same file from RGB to CMYK and back several times; always keep an RGB copy, and only convert duplicates to CMYK.

Using the Gamut Warning Feature

When you're working in RGB mode, it's easy to specify colors that can't be faithfully reproduced in the CMYK model. These colors are said to be *out of gamut.* Happily, Photoshop provides you with several ways to identify and correct out-of-gamut colors, the easiest being Photoshop's Gamut Warning feature, found on the View menu.

In the following steps, Photoshop's Gamut Warning is used to identify any colors in the Flowers.tif image that can't be converted faithfully to a CMYK color formulation.

Displaying Out-of-Gamut Colors

1. Open the Flowers.tif image from the CHAP18 folder of the Companion CD.

2. Double-click on the Hand tool to make the image display at a viewing resolution that is full screen without window scroll bars.

3. Press Ctrl(⌘)+Shift+Y (View, Gamut Warning). Suddenly, as shown in Figure 18.16, the brighter flowers in the image have spots of flat color all over them. These specks mark the colors that are out of gamut.

Gamut warning overlay color

FIGURE 18.16 *Photoshop displays a Gamut Warning overlay in the image window to indicate which areas of the image cannot be printed to CMYK inks.*

You set the color used to mark out-of-gamut colors by choosing Preferences, Transparency & Gamut. Depending on the colors in the image, you might want to choose a Gamut Warning color that contrasts against the original image information. White was chosen for the Flowers.tif image because white is not found within the image.

To correct out-of-gamut colors in the image, you need to change the highlighted areas to similar colors that are CMYK-legal. The Sponge tool can be used effectively to bring colors back into gamut in isolated image areas; the Gamut Warning colors provide an in-place marker in the image for only those areas that require color changing.

BRINGING COLORS BACK INTO GAMUT

1. Choose the Sponge tool from the Toning tools flyout on the toolbox.

2. On the Options palette, choose Desaturate from the drop-down list. A 50% Pressure setting is good for this example.

3. On the Brushes palette, choose the 35-pixel diameter tip.

4. Carefully drag back and forth over an area that displays the Gamut Warning color (see fig 18.17). A second application of the Sponge tool might be necessary in some areas that display the most concentration of the Gamut Warning color.

FIGURE 18.17 *Use the Sponge tool in its Desaturate setting to remove some of the out-of-gamut colors from the image.*

5. Press Ctrl(⌘)+Shift+S (File, Save As) and save the image to your hard disk as Flowers.tif.

Many times, as in this example, images that are fairly bursting with color cannot be successfully printed to CMYK because of the *saturation* of colors—the purity and strength of a hue as compared to other hues present in certain colors. Although the Sponge tool does a remarkable feat reducing the amount of saturation in local areas within the image, it also makes the areas look visually duller. This can be corrected to a certain extent after the image has been converted to CMYK mode, as discussed in the following section.

CONVERTING RGB IMAGES TO CMYK

Converting an RGB image to CMYK is simple to do. Choose CMYK Color from the Image, Mode menu. You should not click on the menu option without first ensuring that your monitor is correctly calibrated, however. Calibration is important because Photoshop uses the RGB values it finds in your image and builds equivalency tables that convert RGB colors to the appropriate CMYK formulations. If your monitor is not calibrated properly, you won't get what you expect when your image rolls off the presses. Before you proceed, be sure to see Chapter 3, "Customizing Photoshop 5," for tips and steps to using Photoshop's calibration features.

The only person who can tell you what the particulars of a CMYK separation should be is the commercial printer on whose presses this particular image will be printed. All the Photoshop fussing with an image depends on the kinds of paper, ink, and printing press that are used. The choices you make in the File, Color Settings, CMYK Setup dialog box require you to know which method—GCR or UCR—the printer plans to use, and what the settings for each should be. GCR *(Gray Component Removal)* and UCR *(Undercolor Removal)* are strategies that printers use to reduce the amount of process colors used in areas that are neutral or black, and then replace them with black ink. This is done to prevent muddiness and to prevent more ink from being applied in one area than can be absorbed by the paper. In the File, Color Settings, CMYK Setup dialog box, there is a huge laundry list of different kinds of ink specifications for coated and uncoated paper. Additionally, Photoshop compensates for the percentage of *expected dot gain*—the amount of spread a dot of ink will take on when applied and absorbed into the paper fibers in this dialog box.

Never guess about these settings, and don't waste your time and money converting RGB images to CMYK and then printing separations unless you have thoroughly discussed these settings with the commercial printer.

If you're certain that Photoshop's File, Color Settings have been defined correctly, choose Image, Mode, and then choose CMYK Color to convert the Flowers.tif image to printing color mode. To enhance the image's colors at this point, you might choose to use the Levels command to increase the contrast slightly in the image. Doing this assigns more neutral, tonal image information to areas in the image that lack contrast, and reinforces the presence of underlying colors. This action does change original image content, but if your goal is to create the best hard copy of a digital file, the appearance of the printed copy is what matters (and not a copy of the file as you see it on your monitor).

PRINTING COLOR SEPARATIONS

When you have a properly-made CMYK image before you, you can print color separations if you know exactly which printer settings to make. (These settings were described in the personal color printing section earlier in this chapter.) To make a perfect CMYK file, you need to have long conversations with your commercial printer. To print color separations, you need to know everything there is to know about the printer that will be used to create the separations. Most likely, if you are going to the expense of printing the image to a commercial color printing press, you will need better resolution than you can get from any personal printer you own. You need the services of an imagesetter. Imagesetters have resolutions that span the range from 1,200 dpi to more than 3,000 dpi, and can cost up to $500,000.

If you are having a service bureau print the separations to paper or film, give them the CMYK file and let them set it up for their imagesetter. Make sure that they know who the commercial printer for this project is, and encourage them to discuss the assignment with the commercial printer if they have any questions. You are expected to supply at least the following standard information about the commercial printer's requirements:

- Whether the image should be negative or positive

- Whether the image should be imaged emulsion up or down

- The optimal screen frequency for the printing press, the paper, and the inks that will be used

- The shape of halftone dots that should be used, and the screen angles for the plates that the commercial printer finds works best with the printing press

- The expected dot gain on the press

If, by chance, you have a PostScript printer that you want to use to create the color separations, you would make these settings—along with settings for crop marks, registration marks, and calibration bars—for your printer in the Page Setup dialog box, as discussed earlier in this chapter. Because you probably will be printing to paper and not to photographic film, leave the Negative and Emulsion Down option *un*checked. Then exit the Page Setup box. You then choose Print from the File menu and enter the necessary print-quality value. Click on Separations from the Space drop-down list, click on OK, and four black-and-white prints will come tumbling out of your printer. The printer can use these paper print separations as camera-ready separations from which to make the printing plates.

WARNING

If you change any of these prepress settings, including the Adobe Gamma settings in the system Control Panel, after you've converted an image to CMYK, you will have to throw out the image and create a new one from a saved RGB copy of the image. *You should never convert an RGB image to CMYK and then convert it back.* You will lose a great deal of color information because the CMYK color gamut is smaller than the RGB color gamut. After the color information has been converted to CMYK, it can't be returned to its original RGB values, and you are stuck with CMYK colors.

Always make a copy of an RGB image and convert the copy to CMYK. Then, if you have to make adjustments, you still have the original RGB image from which a new CMYK file can be created.

DECIDING WHETHER TO DO YOUR OWN COLOR SEPARATIONS

You now know that Photoshop has the *capability* to generate color separations from an image. This means that the cyan, magenta, yellow, and black plates a commercial printer runs on a press can be made from laser camera-ready art you can provide. But the fact that Photoshop gives you the tools to generate the separations *doesn't* mean that you necessarily want to—or *should*—do this.

In addition to being the application of choice for artists on both the Macintosh and Windows platforms, Photoshop is a magnificent tool for commercial printing houses to use in their work. Many copies of this program are used in production departments, service bureaus, and advertising agencies because the *other* half of creating digital artwork is *printing* an image. And Photoshop has features to do both.

But color printing is a science, and as such, it is best left to professionals. For this reason we recommend that artists and designers *not* use the bulk of Photoshop's color pre-press features. Let the people who know best about the medium of *publishing* handle your work. You might go through two or three commercial printers or service bureaus before you settle on one that you can work with, who understands the style or look you want to convey in an image. You will learn much by working with a good pre-press service bureau or printer, but why do what someone else is already doing well? (Unless you want to switch careers?)

A good commercial printer or service bureau that is wise in the ways of Adobe Photoshop can guide you and your work through the world of process printing. And only they know the best line screens, ink coverage, dot-gain settings, and emulsion placement needed to yield optimal results with the presses and the papers used to bring your work to life.

When you know how the assignment will be completed after it leaves your hands, you can plan your work (file size, color capability, resolution, and so on) in a way that ensures the best possible finished output.

PRINT TO FILE OPTIONS

Occasionally, you will want to pack off your work for a service bureau or commercial printer as a "pre-digested" *Print to File* document. The advantage to printing an image to file is that all the recipients of this document have to do is load the file to a specific output device, and you can receive the work. Because you specify the printer settings and other options exactly as you would to a local printing device hooked up to your machine, you eliminate the guesswork—and the possibility of errors introduced by the party performing the rendering work. The receiving party doesn't even need to have Photoshop installed on the machine that drives the imagesetter.

The disadvantage to sending a Print to File document to a service is that they cannot tweak the piece, should there be any errors in dot-gain, image cropping or sizing, or other aspects of the image as sent to a printer.

In general, we advise against using Photoshop's Print dialog box's Print to File option as a means for transporting a design to a service bureau or commercial printer. The file will typically be larger than a TIFF equivalent of the same digital information, and Print to File documents require that you use the specific print driver used by the service bureau's imagesetter, or you're out of luck. If you have a compelling corporate or personal reason to choose the Print to File option, please run through the following checklist before delivering the document to the service that will render the file:

- **Do you have the exact printer driver installed on your system that the service bureau or commercial printer uses?** Often, a service bureau will gladly copy its printer driver to a floppy disk for you to install, free of charge. This prevents headaches and ensures that the file is written in a way the service bureau's imagesetter will understand.

- **Do you know what type of encoding the service bureau uses?** If not, play it safe and encode the Print to File to ASCII encoding. ACSII is a universally understood printer language, and although it's slower and produces larger files than the Binary option in the Print dialog box, Macintosh, DOS, Windows, and UNIX machines can understand print commands as ASCII.

- **Are you certain that the file information is correct?** Print to File documents cannot be changed, except by a handful of individuals who can hack a PostScript file.

You might save spooling time at a service bureau by printing to file, but in many cases this option causes more headaches than you can imagine.

Printing to PDF or EPS

Because PostScript is platform- and device-independent, there have been numerous implementations of PostScript in different printers, and different interpreters for applications created that take advantage of this page description language. Unfortunately, this also leaves in question the "standard" for a specific design rendered to PostScript; often, a PostScript file will fail to render because of an *illegal operator* (a function that describes part of the PostScript code to the output device).

There are two way to output a Photoshop piece to PostScript—to essentially print the design to file—that minimize possible PostScript errors and make your experience with the service bureau a hassle-free one.

When you print to file using a PostScript printer driver, you are locked into the specifics of the output device. It is almost as though you were printing by proxy. The Encapsulated PostScript (EPS) format, however, is also a PostScript page description of a file's contents; this file format can be placed in a container document for output. For example, you can place an EPS file in a PageMaker document and have the service bureau render a high-resolution imagesetter copy of the file. The benefit to writing a file to EPS format is that you have some control over the way the file is written.

In Figure 18.18 you can see Photoshop's EPS Options dialog box. Here you can specify (or not specify) the screen angle or transfer function for the image, potentially eliminating errors that cannot be changed when you use a simple Print to File output procedure for the file. Additionally, you can include PostScript Color Management as part of the file. When you save to EPS format, you have your choice of encoding schemes (hint: always use ASCII), and the opportunity to write a low-resolution image for placement only if you decide this image should be part of a larger document.

The EPS format is "genuine" PostScript, and many different color and line screen properties of the design can be edited after the file has been written if you place the EPS file in a host document.

In the past two years, many imaging professionals have turned to Adobe's Acrobat document format as a means for "cleaning up" PostScript files that do not output correctly to imagesetters. An EPS file written from Photoshop or another program can also be converted to Acrobat format. Additionally, Photoshop 5 can save image files to Acrobat PDF format. Ask your commercial printer whether he can use an Acrobat document for final output to color printing. The Acrobat PDF file format is basically a goof-proof way of sending your commercial printer a document that will output accurately.

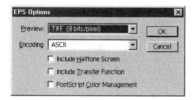

FIGURE 18.18   *Saving a file to the Encapsulated PostScript format enables you to print to file without including device-specific characteristics in the file.*

THE FILM RECORDER

As you've discovered throughout this book, there is a close, strong relationship between bitmap graphics and traditional photographic images. *Bitmapped images* portray graphical information as light and dark areas of continuous tones that our eyes recognize as a picture. The photosensitive grain of film and photographic paper also portray images as a wash of continuous tones. Many of the images you've worked with in this book, and many of the elements that comprise your own assignments, are traditional, photochemically based photographs that have been digitized.

Remarkable news for the digital imagist is that the conversion of photographic information to digital information is a two-way street. A device called a *film recorder* can take any image you've created or enhanced in Photoshop and faithfully render it to the familiar, aesthetically pleasing, and eminently practical medium of color film, as a film negative or transparency. You can find high-resolution film recorders at a special kind of service bureau, commonly called a *slide imaging service bureau*, or *imaging center*. Learning how to work with this type of service bureau should be high on your list of priorities because there is no greater satisfaction for the professional designer or hobbyist than to hold in your hands a photograph of your Photoshop work.

In this section, you'll see how to prepare a digital image in Photoshop to produce the best results on photographic film.

FORMATS OF FILM RECORDER OUTPUT

The most common film recorder found at an imaging center is one that renders digital images to 35mm film. Slides are the mainstay of business presentations today, whereas a photographer gets more mileage from a 35mm negative. Each of these needs is accommodated through the use of the same film recorder. Larger-format output film recorders are also found in specialty imaging centers that handle 4 × 5-inch or 8 × 10-inch film. The 4 × 5-inch formats can be used to produce high-quality, poster-sized prints for quality color publishing and for the television industry. The 8 × 10 format is most commonly used to produce high-quality overhead transparencies for corporate and educational presentations. This format is also used to produce wall-size enlargements for trade shows, for motion picture industry special effects work, and to meet the demanding requirements of very high-end, color-critical publishing.

TRANSFERRING A PHOTOSHOP IMAGE TO FILM

Before you start packing up images to take advantage of the digital-to-film experience, you need to explore some of the finer points of working with film and the imaging center. To ensure that your Photoshop-to-film work looks every byte as good as it does on your monitor, you need to understand the special requirements a film recorder has for the data it writes—preferred file formats, data types, aspect ratios, monitor settings, and the size of your file. These are universal considerations, regardless of the type of film recorder output you need. The following sections show you how each of these digital issues can affect your work, pleasantly or otherwise, by focusing on the most popular product of a slide imaging center: the 35mm slide.

YOUR MONITOR'S SETUP

Both your monitor and a film recorder use an RGB color model. When you save a Photoshop file in a 24-bit RGB file format, such as TIFF or Targa, every color used in the file has been described in terms of its red, green, and blue values. The film recorder reads these values to determine how to expose the film. If your monitor is properly calibrated, the colors you see onscreen will be represented accurately on the slide. If your monitor is *not* properly calibrated, you might get orange instead of gold, and purple where you wanted blue, in the finished piece of film.

Color-matching is a sport to be engaged in by every individual who cares about accurate output, but it's also a game in which you can never declare a decisive "win." A monitor, a television set, film, press ink on paper, the *same* ink on *different* paper, and different printing technologies—inkjet, thermal wax, dye sublimation—all display color differently because they use different physical materials and different technologies to express color. One technology might not be able to express a color that another technology can express. Fortunately, *film* can express a wide range of colors. If you used a properly calibrated monitor to edit your image, the colors you see onscreen can be accurately rendered to film.

Matching your monitor's gamma to an individual film recorder's CRT—the *cathode ray tube*, the central imaging element in a film recorder—involves an element of trial and error. Ask your service bureau what the gamma of their film recorder is, and set your monitor to match their figure. The gamma of a film recorder's CRT will most likely fall somewhere between 1.7 and 2.1. After calibrating your monitor to match the imaging center's gamma, save the calibration settings in Photoshop's Adobe Gamma utility and send the center an image to process as a test image. See Chapter 3 for information about calibrating your monitor, setting gamma, and saving custom settings. If the slide comes back too brilliant or too dull, reduce or increase your gamma by a few tenths of a point and try again. When you find the magic gamma figure, save this setting so that you can reuse it when you create images that will be rendered to film by the *same* film recorder at the *same* service bureau.

The gamma setting that produces the best results with the imaging center's film recorder may change over time. Gamma is a somewhat elusive factor—as monitors and CRTs age, their light-producing phosphors dim, and gamma values change. The changes in gamma caused by aging phosphors happen gradually, and you may not notice that changes are occurring. It's a good idea to take a critical look at your output for signs that you and the service bureau are drifting out of synchrony. If you find that your images are coming out a tad brighter or duller than they used to, it's time to make adjustments to your gamma settings.

SENDING THE RIGHT SIZE FILE

Determining the proper file size to send to a service bureau for slide-making is not as straightforward a process as determining resolution for print presses. Printing to paper and film imaging are different processes and different media. Measurements for image files rendered by film recorders are expressed in storage units (kilobytes and megabytes), not in pixels per inch. The ultimate quality of a film recorder's output is based on how much information the film recorder can handle *and* how much information you've given it to work with.

When service bureaus describe their services, they'll sometimes say that they do 2-KB (2,000-line), 4-KB (4,000-line), or 8-KB (8,000-line) imaging. These terms refer to the size of the *pixel grid* the film recorder can render. When a file is imaged at 2 KB, the "2 KB" describes a pixel grid 2,048 pixels wide by 2,048 pixels high. A 4 KB image is a pixel grid of 4,096 by 4,096. A 24-bit RGB file that is 2,048 pixels wide by 1,365 pixels high (2:3 ratio) produces an 8 MB file. A grayscale image of the same size is only 2.67 MB. A 24-bit RGB file imaged to 4 KB and in a 2:3 ratio would be 4,086 pixels wide by 2,731 pixels high and would occupy 32 MB, whereas its grayscale counterpart would occupy only 10.7 MB.

Service bureaus usually base a large portion of their imaging fees on the size of the file you bring to them because the larger the file, the harder it is to handle. Large files also take up large amounts of the bureau's hard disk space and take longer to image than smaller files. Files under 5 MB are fairly inexpensive to image (usually under $20), but you should expect substantially higher imaging costs for 20–30 MB files.

HOW LARGE IS LARGE ENOUGH?

So how large *should* your file be? There is no hard and fast rule. It depends on what you want to do with the slide, how detailed the slide is, and how critical an eye your viewing audience has. Slides have nice juicy colors; when slides are projected, the difference between a "low-resolution" slide and a "high-resolution" slide is often difficult to see because of the typically low quality of the projection equipment and the screen. If you look at both slides, side-by-side, through a loupe, on a good day, in a good mood—you might see a significant difference.

Most service bureaus are willing to run a test slide or two for you or provide you with samples of slides imaged from different-sized files. Experiment with different sizes of files to find the size that suits your needs, your patience, and your pocketbook. Although Zip disks have become the standard means of transporting large media, time is still money to a service bureau. Large files take longer to process—and you are charged for that time.

The fundamental question of how large your image should be boils down to your definition of *acceptable*—a relative term, but for 35mm slides we place it at somewhere between 1.13 MB and 4.5 MB. Ask your service bureau to show you slides they've made from files of different sizes so that you get the scope of the meaning of "acceptable."

USING THE PROPER ASPECT RATIO?

Aspect ratio is the height-to-width proportion of an image. If you want your image to fill the entire frame of the film to which it's rendered, your image must have the same aspect ratio as that of the film. The aspect ratio of 35mm film is 2:3; 4 × 5 and 8 × 10-inch film share the same 4:5 aspect ratio. If you anticipate sending an image to a film recorder, you should plan your composition so that the ratio of the image's height to width will match that of the film format to which you'll render the image.

One of the things that sends technicians at a service bureau up the wall is a file that doesn't have the proper aspect ratio. Regardless of how artistically inclined the bureau's staff is, you probably won't be happy if the bureau adjusts your image to fit the aspect ratio. When your image doesn't fill the frame, the service bureau has a decision to make—to crop or not to crop. If they crop the image, they are forced to make an artistic decision that was *your* responsibility to make as a designer.

ACHIEVING THE PROPER ASPECT RATIO

You don't have to be a math wizard, or even own a pocket calculator, to ensure that your work has the proper aspect ratio. Let Photoshop do the math for you, and then use your eye to decide whether to crop or to place a background around the image to make the overall image dimensions correspond to the aspect ratio of the film.

The following steps show you how to "trick" Photoshop into figuring out the dimensions your image has to have to achieve the proper aspect ratio for imaging to 35mm film.

DETERMINING AN IMAGE'S ASPECT RATIO

1. Press Ctrl(⌘)+N to display the New dialog box.

2. Click on the units drop-down list for Width, and choose Inches; do the same with the Height drop-down list.

3. Click on the Mode drop-down list and choose Grayscale. Any mode can be used here, but Grayscale uses one-third the system resources of RGB mode images.

4. In the Width field, type **3**; in the Height field, type **2**; in the Resolution field, type **72**, and then click on OK to open the new document.

   If you're sending work for large-format output (4 × 5 or 8 × 10-inch), put **5** in the Height field and 4 in the Width field. These two formats share the same 4:5 aspect ratio. Traditionally, 35mm work is imaged in landscape mode and larger formats are imaged in portrait mode.

5. Open the Pastime.tif file from the CHAP18 folder on the Companion CD.

6. Choose Image, Image Size; change the units to inches (if not already set that way).

7. With the Resample Image box unchecked, type **3** in the Width field. The image Resolution will change, and as shown in Figure 18.19, the new Height for the image is displayed as 2.737 inches.

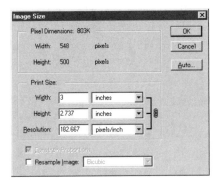

FIGURE 18.19 *Constrain the proportions of the Print Size boxes to arrive at the aspect ratio of the target image.*

The Height value of 2.737 means that the Pastime.tif image has an aspect ratio of 2.737 to 3, which is not the desired 2:3 aspect ratio for full-frame rendering to a 35mm film recorder.

8. Hold Alt(Opt) and click on the Reset button (which is the Cancel button when Alt(Opt) is not held). Write (on paper) the original Width and Height values (7.611, 6.944), and then click on Cancel.

   You pressed Cancel because you *do not* want to change the image size of Pastime.tif yet. Keep the image open.

When the Constrain Proportion box is checked in the Image Size dialog box, changing one dimension changes the other automatically to a value that retains the image's *current* aspect ratio (proportions). By setting the value to 3 in the width box, you can quickly determine whether the image can be scaled to a 2:3 proportion. In this example, the height is greater than 2, which indicates that it is not a 2:3 proportioned image. To bring this image into a 2:3 ratio without altering the design, you have to crop the image or add to it. But you might not want to crop one of your finished images *or* build more image information around one aspect of the image's borders. A good alternative, which is also image-enhancing, is to increase the size of the background canvas to create a border around the image, bringing the overall image into the proper aspect ratio.

Here's how to flesh out the image's proportions to make it suitable for a film recorder.

CALCULATING AN ASPECT RATIO

1. Click on Untitled-1's title bar (the 2"×3" blank image) to make it the current document in Photoshop.

2. Choose Image, Image Size. Type **7.25** in the Height field. 7.25" is slightly larger than Pastime.tif's 6.9" original height, but you'll want a background on all sides of the image, not simply the height aspect of the picture. After you type in the new Height, the Width field in the dialog box displays 10.875". Write these numbers down.

3. Click on Cancel, and then close Untitled-1 without saving it. Pastime.tif is now the current image in Photoshop.

4. Press I (Eyedropper tool) and click on a dark sky area in the image. The current foreground color in Photoshop is now dark blue.

5. Press X (Switch Foreground/Background colors).

6. Choose Image, Canvas Size; choose inches from the Width drop-down list, and then type **10.875** in the Width field. Choose inches for the Height field, type **7.25** in the field, as shown in Figure 18.20, and then click on OK.

7. Press Ctrl(⌘)+Shift+S (File, Save As), and then save the image to hard disk in the TIFF file format. As you can see in Figure 18.21, you now have a centered image with a border in a color that complements the image; it can be sent to a service bureau for film recording.

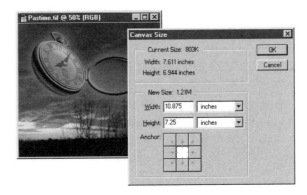

FIGURE 18.20 *Changing the size of the canvas brings the image to the proper aspect ratio.*

FIGURE 18.21 *Pastime.tif now has the proper aspect ratio for a slide—and also looks good.*

An image's size and the way it's positioned on the canvas are design decisions you make for each image—but the math for obtaining the proper aspect ratio is always the same.

MAKING 35MM NEGATIVES

If you plan to have a large, high-quality photographic print made from the negative, the first consideration you need to address is file size. You'll want to send a larger file than you normally send for a slide. Just as you need a large-format negative to make a really large print in traditional photography, with digital photography, larger files go hand-in-hand with larger prints because they contain more information.

As with a slide, there is no hard and fast rule for what size file makes an "acceptable" print. Kodak states that photofinishers should not make prints larger than 8 inches by 10 inches from the standard version of a Kodak PhotoCD file, a special digital format whose multiple resolutions include an 18 MB file. We believe that Kodak's definition of what an acceptable print looks like is a little overestimated, and that you will find a print made with a much smaller file to be "acceptable." Again, as with the slides, file size is a matter in which you have to find your own level of comfort, as you find the balance between file size and quality of the output.

If your commercial printer is not a computer "guru," and you plan to give him or her the negative for traditional pre-press production and placement into a printed document, produce your negative from a larger file.

Whether it's for the printing press or for you, tell the service bureau *why* you want a negative made. If the service bureau is aware of the specific purpose for the negative, they can make tiny adjustments to the film recorder's settings and "tweak" the negative so that it is optimized for photographic printing or print press printing.

In the previous section on slide preparation, you increased the canvas size of an image to a 2:3 proportion and made that additional canvas a dark color. Dark borders on slides are good because they keep the audience's attention on the image information, and spare viewers from the brilliant light of the projector as it passes through clear areas in the slide. But on prints and negatives, the tradition is to use white borders instead of dark ones. White is the border color most people expect on a print. And if the image is to be cropped, white usually makes the "live area"—the image area—easier to crop.

TIP

If you have a film recorder attached to your machine, and you're imaging your file from Photoshop, you could have Photoshop insert a background color for you. This option is available by choosing File, Page Setup and then clicking on the Background button in the lower-left corner of the Page Setup dialog box. Choose a color for the background in the color picker and click on OK. This doesn't change the image—just the way it prints. If you use this option, you can't preview the image to see how it looks before you image the file—this method leaves more to chance than adjusting the canvas size does.

NOTE

For more information on PhotoCD technology, check out Chapter 2, "Getting Stock Images."

Converting a Portrait Design to a Landscape Slide

Most film recorders are set up for landscape imaging, which satisfies the needs of most. Before you save your file to disk to send to the service bureau, you might want to turn your image on its side to get the whole image in frame and avoid excessive cropping.

Photoshop makes this easy for you to do, although the process is not so easy on your system's resources. Rotating images is processor-intensive. It's a Photoshop effect, similar to the Perspective or Distort command, in that the Rotate Canvas command tells Photoshop to recalculate the color values for every selected pixel in the image. Before you use the Rotate Canvas command, be sure that you've flattened the image and eliminated any unnecessary channels and paths. You should also close any other images you have open and make sure that you aren't running any other applications, such as word processors or screen savers, in the background. To rotate the image from portrait to landscape, click on the Image menu, choose Rotate Canvas, and then click on 90° CW or 90° CCW.

Summary

Regardless of the route you take to get your images out of the computer and onto media you can pass around, the key to successful images is the quality of the rendered image. Use monitor calibration up to a certain point, and then depend upon the principles you've learned in this chapter and your artistic eye to evaluate what makes the best image rendered to physical media.

In Chapter 19, "Creating Graphics for the Web," we move our attention to "new media" and the art of expressing one's concepts on the World Wide Web. You'll see how to be creative while at the same time keeping file sizes small for quick download.

CHAPTER 19

CREATING GRAPHICS FOR THE WEB

Sites compete for attention on the Web in the same way that magazine ads or billboards fight for your attention. One of the best tactics for getting your message noticed is to take your unique concept through Photoshop's arsenal of special-effects tools.

This chapter takes you through the concept, the tools, and the process by which a Web page is created. Heavy emphasis is given to designing an attractive, eye-catching background for the page, making the headline leap out at you, making the best thumbnail images for display on the page, and providing navigation buttons for the visitor to the site. The hardest part will be to make all these elements work together, but fortunately, you have this chapter as a guide and Photoshop as a tool.

THE CLIENT: THE TEXTURES HOME PAGE

The scenario for this chapter's assignment is that a fictitious client who does nothing but create attractive textures comes to you, wanting you to create a textures home page. Conceptually, then, it would be a good idea to feature a few of those textures on the Web page, and also to let the background of the page be a seamless, tiling texture.

You'll begin by building a background texture.

THE STAINED GLASS FILTER

Photoshop's Stained Glass filter works like this: you pick the image that you want reduced to shards of colored glass, and the foreground color becomes the leading between the glass pieces. What happens, though, when your image is entirely white? You wind up with black leading against white, and the effect looks like a mosaic, perfect as a base image for the texture you're going to create. To conserve bandwidth, however, this background texture should be small in size and repeat across the Web page without anyone detecting seams. With a little manual work, you can correct the stained glass piece so that it tiles seamlessly.

Here's how to create a stained glass piece, offset it, remove nontiling areas, and paint in lines to make the texture tile properly:

USING THE STAINED GLASS FILTER TO CREATE AN IMAGE TILE

1. Press Ctrl(⌘)+N and in the New image dialog box, type **300** in both the Width and Height fields, type **72** in the Resolution field, choose RGB color from the drop-down list, and then click on OK. Although 300 is a little large for a seamless tiling Web texture, you'll "work big" in this example to better see what's going on, and then reduce the image later.

2. Press D (default colors), and then choose Filter, Texture, Stained Glass.

3. Type **12** in the Cell size field. The cell size values have nothing to do with pixel size of the cells; it's a relative value. The number 12 works here; it's a number that the author arrived at through trial and error.

4. Drag the Border Thickness to 4. This will make the leading approximately four pixels wide. *Approximately* is the key word here; the leading can be three or five pixels wide, depending on the direction of the leading in the image.

5. Leave the Light Intensity at its default of 3. Light Intensity, which affects the color of the cells of stained glass, is not a relevant feature here because the cells in this exercise have no colors. If your filter dialog box looks like that in Figure 19.1, click on OK to apply the filter.

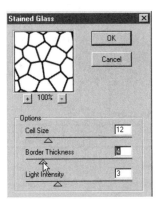

FIGURE 19.1 *These are the settings you should use to produce the texture for the Web background image.*

6. Choose Filter, Other, and then choose Offset.

7. In the Offset dialog box, type **150** in both fields, and then click on the Wrap Around option, as shown in Figure 19.2. As you can see, the stained glass pattern does not tile seamlessly at all—but you'll fix this. Click OK to apply the Offset.

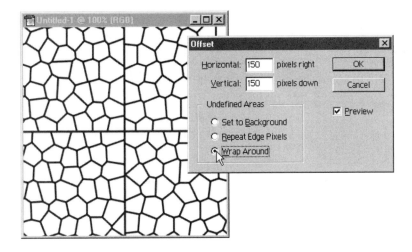

FIGURE 19.2 *Use the Offset command to see how the edges of an image tile, or fail to tile.*

8. Zoom to 200% viewing resolution of the image. Choose the Eraser tool, and on the Options palette, choose Block as the shape of the eraser.

9. Erase those hard vertical and horizontal lines that run through the center of the image. To make it easier to connect the cells, you might want to erase some of the leading, too, as shown in Figure 19.3.

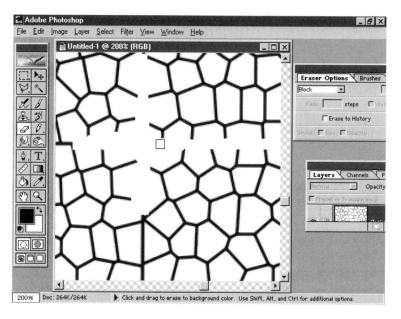

FIGURE 19.3 *Erase the areas in the image where the cells do not align properly with one another.*

10. On the Pencil tool flyout on the toolbox, choose the Line tool. On the Options palette, type **3** in the Weight field, and check the Anti-aliased box.

Although the Border Thickness in the Stained Glass dialog box was set to 4, we recommend that you use a 3-pixel–wide Line tool here. It simply looks of a consistent weight with the rest of the leading, and the value was chosen by experimenting with different weights for the tool.

11. Connect the cells, as shown in Figure 19.4.

12. When your image looks similar to that in Figure 19.5, choose File, Save, and save the image to hard disk as Cell.psd, in Photoshop's native format. Keep the file open.

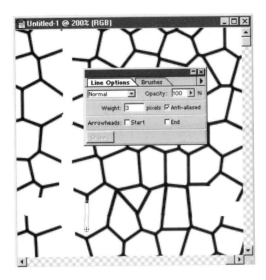

FIGURE 19.4   *Create straight lines that either connect the cells or extend lines that already exist in the image to make continuous cells in the image.*

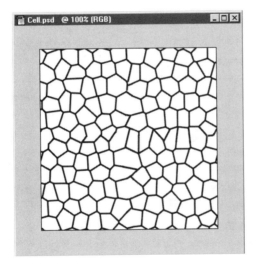

FIGURE 19.5   *You've created a seamless tiling pattern from the stained glass image.*

The Cell.psd image will now serve as a template for creating the tiling background image itself. We need to do a little more modification work on it first, as you'll see in the following section.

BLURRING THE WORK AND EDITING THE EFFECT

The stained glass design will serve as a texture map in the Lighting Effects filter. Now, the softer the image is in focus, the more pronounced the bumpy texture will become (which is the effect you want). If you blur the image, however, the *edges* of the design will not be perfectly blurred. No problem. In the steps that follow, you'll offset the image after blurring it, and then use the Smudge tool for some minor clean-up work:

CREATING AN OUT-OF-FOCUS LIGHTING EFFECTS TEMPLATE

1. Press F7 if the Channels palette isn't currently onscreen, and then click on the Channels tab.

2. Drag the Blue channel title into the Create new channel icon at the bottom of the palette. As you can see in Figure 19.6, Blue copy (Alpha 1) is the name of the new channel in the image. You're doing this because shortly you'll fill the RGB channel with a color, thus wiping out the intricate stained glass design.

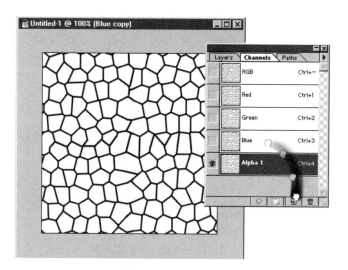

FIGURE 19.6 *Save the design by copying it to a channel.*

3. Choose Filter, Blur, and then choose Gaussian blur.

4. Drag the slider to 2 pixels, as shown in Figure 19.7, and then click on OK to apply this moderate amount of blurring.

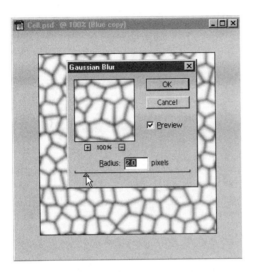

FIGURE 19.7 *Slightly blur the stained glass design to have the Lighting Effects filter make the texture more pronounced.*

5. Choose Filter, Other, and then choose Offset.

6. In the Offset dialog box, type **150** in both the Horizontal and Vertical fields, make sure that Wrap Around is checked, as shown in Figure 19.8, and then click on OK. You will notice a subtle disruption of the smooth, soft cells where the design has been turned inside out.

7. Zoom in to a 200% viewing resolution of the image.

8. Choose the Smudge tool, and then on the Brushes palette, choose the tip at the far left of the second row. On the Options palette, the default Pressure of 50 is good.

9. Smudge over any harsh edges in the image, as shown in Figure 19.9.

10. Press Ctrl(⌘)+S; keep the file open.

You're all set now to make the stained glass design work for you in building an eye-catching tiling pattern.

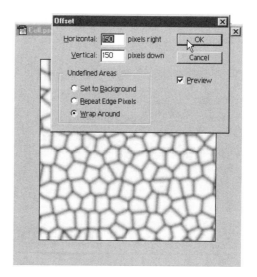

Figure 19.8 *Use the Offset filter to reveal inconsistencies in the tiling pattern.*

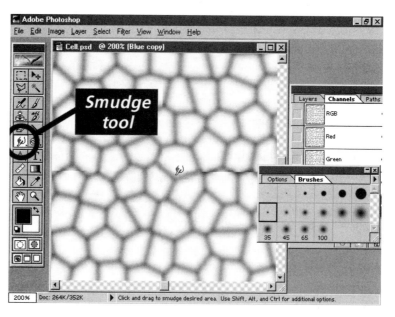

Figure 19.9 *The Smudge tool, with a small tip, removes hard edges from the design.*

THE LIGHTING EFFECTS FILTER AND TONE/COLOR EDITING

One of the things that separates the amateurs from the pros building Web sites out there is that the pro knows when to give up part of a design for the good of the page. Background graphics are supposed to be subtle, so that visitors can read the foreground message. In the following steps, you'll use the Lighting Effects' Texture Channel option to produce a visually striking texture—that you'll then tone way down so it serves its purpose on the Web site.

Here's how to create the textured image and then use the Levels and Hue/Saturation commands to "lighten up" the design:

CREATING A SUBTLE WEB BACKGROUND IMAGE

1. Press Ctrl(⌘)+tilde (~) to move your view to the RGB composite channel of Cell.psd.

2. Click on the foreground color swatch on the toolbox; then, in the Color Picker, choose a lavender. (H:271, S:35%, and B:98% is a good color.) Click on OK to return to the workspace.

3. Press Ctrl(⌘)+A (Select, All), and then press Alt(Opt)+Delete (Backspace) to fill the RGB channel with the color. Press Ctrl(⌘)+D to deselect the marquee now.

4. Choose Filter, Render, and then choose Lighting Effects.

5. Choose Directional from the Light Type drop-down list, and then move the source point in the proxy window closer to the image so that the proxy window image is about the same brightness as the original image.

6. Choose Alpha 1 from the Texture Channel drop-down list, and then drag the Height slider to about 6, as in Figure 19.10.

7. Click on OK to apply the filter, and then press Ctrl(⌘)+L to display the Levels command.

8. Drag the midtone slider to the left so that the middle Input Levels field reads around 1.9. Then drag the black point Output Levels slider to the right until the left field reads 133. As you can see in Figure 19.11, reassigning much brighter tones to the image really knocks the design into the category of pastel, which is exactly what you need in a WWW image background. Click on OK to apply the change.

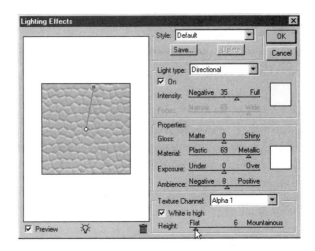

FIGURE 19.10 *Create a mildly bumpy texture, using the stained glass design in combination with the Lighting Effects filter.*

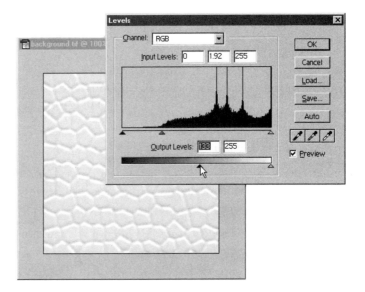

FIGURE 19.11 *Increase the black and midtones in the image to arrive at a washed-out version of the graphic.*

Reducing the amount of black in the image also made the graphic less colorful. Here's how to restore some of the color, while keeping the tones light...

9. Press Ctrl(⌘)+U to display the Hue/Saturation dialog box, and then drag the Saturation slider to about +54, as shown in Figure 19.12. Click on OK, drag the Alpha 1 title on the Channels palette into the trash icon, and then save the file as Background.tif in the TIFF file format to your hard disk. Keep the image open.

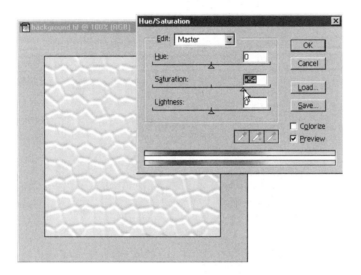

FIGURE 19.12 *Increase the saturation of the colors without changing their brightness.*

Okay, it's time to accept a little input from your fictitious client: they want navigation buttons on the left of the page, without a background texture. This might require a little more work and a little inventiveness. The following section shows you how a tiling pattern can feature an empty space on the left.

CREATING A LOPSIDED, HORIZONTAL PATTERN

The trick to leaving some room at the left of the Web page is to make graphic that's wide tiling but not awfully deep. The left side will repeat its empty pattern, and the right side will feature the texture you created. To accomplish this, you'll resize the graphic, define it as a pattern for a larger canvas, and then add an empty space and a snazzy border to separate the buttons from the main page on the Web site.

Here's how to resize, pattern tile, and edit the graphic:

CREATING AN ASYMMETRIC TILING PATTERN

1. With Background.tif, choose Image, Image Size, and then choose percent from the Width drop-down list. Type **50** in the Width field, as shown in Figure 19.13, and then click on OK to resize the graphic to 150 pixels on a side.

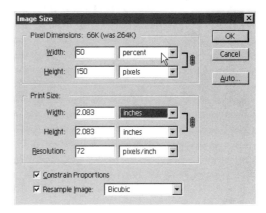

FIGURE 19.13 *Decrease the size of the pattern by 50 percent.*

2. Press Ctrl(⌘)+N, and then in the New dialog box, type **800** in the Width field and type **150** in the Height field, as shown in Figure 19.14.

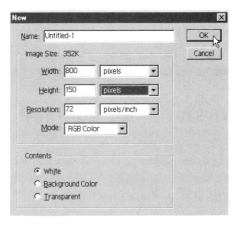

FIGURE 19.14 *These are the final dimensions for the horizontal tiling piece you'll create.*

Okay, break time. Why 800-by-150 pixels? Because you can presume that most people visiting the site in 1998 are running 800-by-600 video resolution. The 150 pixels represents the height of Background.tif. When you "pour" a pattern into this new image, the tiling will be preserved vertically...

3. Click on OK to create the new image.

4. With the Background.tif image in the foreground, press Ctrl(⌘)+A (Select, All), and then choose Edit, Define Pattern.

5. Click on the Untitled-1 image to make it the current foreground image in Photoshop, and then choose Edit, Fill.

6. In the Fill dialog box, choose Pattern from the Use: drop-down list, as shown in Figure 19.15. Click on OK to apply the pattern to the new image.

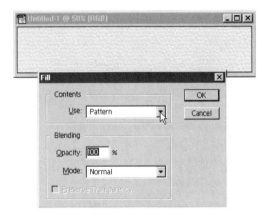

FIGURE 19.15 *Fill the new image with the pattern tile you created.*

7. Double-click on the Zoom tool to move your view of the untitled image to 100%. Scroll to the left of the document.

8. With the Rectangular Marquee tool, hold Shift, and then drag from the top left to the bottom, moving right. Press Alt(Opt)+Delete (Backspace) to fill the selection marquee with the pale lavender you selected earlier, as shown in Figure 19.16. Press Ctrl(⌘)+D now to deselect the marquee.

9. Save the image as Background tile.tif, in the TIFF file format, to your hard disk. Keep the file open.

A little more definition is needed between the solid color and the pattern. In the next section, you'll see how to use Photoshop's Gradient tool and Gradient Editor to create tubing.

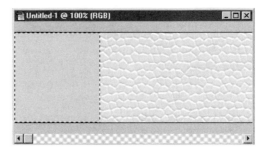

FIGURE 19.16 *The entire image is a tiling pattern. Create a break in the pattern at far left by filling it with foreground color.*

CREATING A CUSTOM GRADIENT

A "tube" or piping sort of effect in the image is not difficult to achieve. If you think about what a small, narrow, vertical tube would look like in the image, it would be a specific color with a highlight running through the center. Photoshop's Gradient Editor can be used to create a blend that makes this same transition between "tone, lighter tone, and then original tone again."

In the following steps, you'll mix a custom gradient blend and then apply it to the image, using the Linear Gradient tool:

CREATING TUBING, USING THE GRADIENT EDITOR

1. Click on the Linear Gradient tool; then, on the Options palette, click on Edit.

2. In the Gradient Editor, click on New, and then type **3D** in the Name field. Click on OK to return to the Gradient Editor.

3. Click on the far-left color marker to select it, and then click on the color swatch to go to the Color Picker.

4. Choose a deep purple from the Color Picker (H:274, S:79%, and B:26% is good), and then click on OK to return to the Gradient Editor.

5. Click on the far-right color marker, and then click on the color swatch to display the Color Picker.

6. Choose a pale purple color (H:274, S:20%, and B:97% is good), and then click on OK to exit the Color Picker.

7. Drag the pale purple color marker to the center of the gradient strip.

8. Click on the deep purple color marker, hold Alt(Opt), and then drag a copy of the color marker to the far right of the gradient strip.

9. Drag the midpoint markers on the top of the gradient strip toward the pale purple color marker in the center, as shown in Figure 19.17. Congratulations! You've created a "tube" gradient.

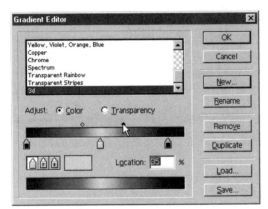

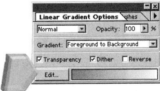

FIGURE 19.17 *Create a custom gradient by manipulating the position of the color markers and the midpoint markers.*

10. Click on OK to exit the Gradient Editor; then, with the Rectangular Marquee tool, select the area where the solid color meets the pattern in Background tile.tif. The selection should go from top to bottom and be about 12 pixels wide.

11. Choose the Linear Gradient tool, hold Shift, and then drag from the left of the selection to the right. See Figure 19.18. Okay—this is a very short distance. If you don't get the effect you want on the first try, repeat the step.

12. Press Ctrl(⌘)+D to deselect the marquee, and then press Ctrl(⌘)+S; keep the file open.

Now that you've completed the background tile image, it's time to create a workspace featuring the tiling background. You can use this workspace to design and proportion other elements for the Web page.

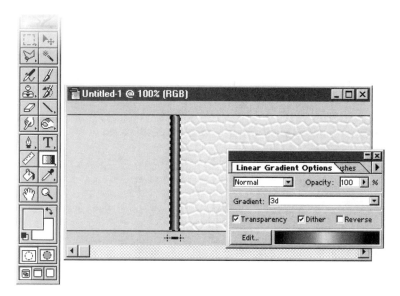

FIGURE 19.18 *Drag from left to right to apply the "tubing" gradient fill you created.*

SIZING UP AND CREATING A WORKSPACE

Obviously, a full-page graphic is not the way to go with Web pages; a full-screen graphic would take an eternity to download and you'd surely lose your audience's attention during the wait! But because you need to visualize how the small components of the Web page work together, we recommend that you create a full-scale "mock-up" of the page, and then play around with the way the elements come together.

How large should your design be? Although many designers use 800-by-600 video resolution and higher, there is still a large audience out there that uses 640×480 screen resolution. Because it is best to "play to the cheap seats" to ensure that everyone receives your message, the following steps show you how to set up a template that addresses the 640-by-480 crowd.

CREATING A TEMPLATE FOR WEB PAGE DESIGN WORK

1. Press Ctrl(⌘)+N, and then type **800** in the Width field and **600** in the Height field. Type **72** in the Resolution field, and then click on OK to create the new image window.

2. Save the new image as workspace.tif to your hard disk.

3. With the Background tile.tif image in the foreground, press Ctrl(⌘)+A (Select, All), and then choose Edit, Define Pattern. Press Ctrl(⌘)+D to deselect the marquee.

4. Choose File, Save As, and then save the Background tile.tif image as back.jpg in the JPEG file format. Choose Baseline Optimized in the Format Options field, and drag the quality slider to 5. Click on OK to save the file. You can close Back.jpg now.

5. With workspace.tif in the workspace, choose Edit, Fill, and then choose Pattern from the Use: drop-down list. When you have the image filled, as shown in Figure 19.19, you can close the Background tile.tif image at any time.

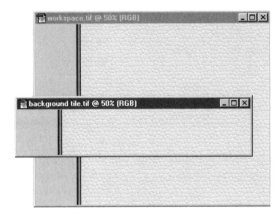

FIGURE 19.19 *Fill an 800-by-600 pixel image with the background tile to see what the audience will see at either 800×600 or 640×480 viewing resolution.*

Simply because a visitor might be running 640-by-480 monitor resolution does not mean that you have a whole 640×480 canvas with which to design the Web page. There are scroll bars and button bars on the most popular browsers, and they eat into the screen real estate. In Figure 19.20 you can see the interface of MS-Internet Explorer. The "live" space you have to work with is 620 pixels wide by 326 pixels high. Let's drag some guides out in the document to make page composition more simple...

6. Press Ctrl(⌘)+R to display rulers around the document. You need pixels here, so if the rulers are displaying inches or centimeters, press F8 to display the Info palette, click on the crosshairs next to the XY field, and then choose pixels from the flyout list.

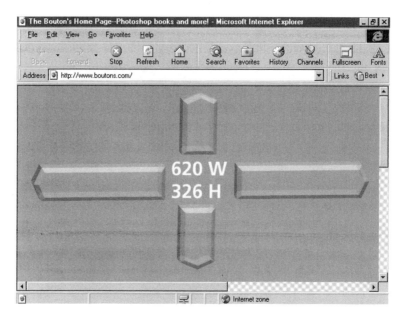

FIGURE 19.20 *Interface elements steal from the room in which you have to design the Web page.*

7. Drag a vertical guide from the vertical ruler to about 620, and then drag a horizontal guide from the horizontal ruler to about 326, as shown in Figure 19.21. The interior of the guides and the image border represent the space you have to work with for the 640×480 audience.

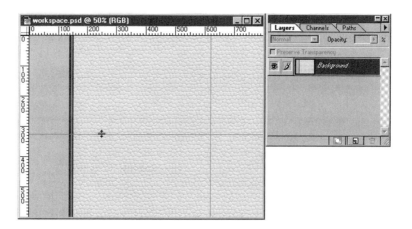

FIGURE 19.21 *Drag guides to the outer limit you've determined for the Web page's elements.*

8. Press Ctrl(⌘)+S; keep the file open.

It's time now to add a headline to the page. You'll play with the Type tool and Layer Effects next.

ADDING TEXT WITH THE TYPE TOOL

In the next set of steps, you'll add the phrase "Welcome to the Textures Home Page" to the top of the Web page. To add a little visual punch, the word "Textures" has been rendered for you, using Adobe Dimensions, a handy sidekick to Photoshop and anyone interested in building Web elements. This leaves you with the rest of the text to create.

Your choice of typefaces should be influenced by what special effects, if any, you intend to apply to the text. For example, the author's version of this assignment uses a font called Ad Lib, which is clean and legible and isn't difficult to read when displayed at a large size with an emboss effect applied. If you don't own Ad Lib, you can substitute a heavy weight of Helvetica and follow along with these steps:

BUILDING A HEADLINE, USING THE TYPE TOOL

1. Zoom in to a 100% viewing resolution of the Workspace document. Maximize your view of the document and position it so that the top of the image window meets Photoshop's menu. You'll want to see both the Type tool dialog box and the type you'll be creating in the document.

2. Click an insertion point with the Type tool in the image window. The Type Tool dialog box appears. Move it so that you can see the top of the image window.

3. Click on the Color swatch and pick a deep mustard color in the Color Picker (H:52, S:100%, B:59% is good). Click on OK to exit the Color Picker.

4. In the Font drop-down list, choose Ad Lib (or another clean, sans serif font).

5. In the text field, type **Welcome to the**.

6. In the Size field, type **45**, and then move your cursor outside the Type Tool box and move the type to make sure that it fits between the 3D tubing and the far-right guide. If it doesn't fit, decrease the font Size. When the document looks something like Figure 19.22, click on OK to enter the text.

7. Choose Layer, Effects, and then choose Bevel and Emboss.

8. In the Style field, choose Pillow Emboss, click on the Angle flyout button to reveal the direction box, and then drag the direction line so that it points to about 4 o'clock, as in Figure 19.23.

FIGURE 19.22 *Choose a font size that will make the phrase fit between the tubing and the guide to the right of the page.*

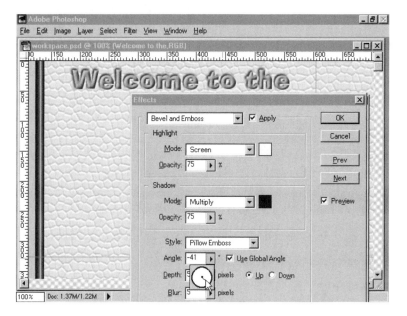

FIGURE 19.23 *The angle indicates the direction in which the shading should go in the Pillow Emboss effect. The highlights will be located in 180° in the opposite direction (10 o'clock).*

9. Click on OK to apply the Pillow Emboss Effect.

10. Press Ctrl(⌘)+S; keep the file open.

It's time now to add the second element to the composition—the 3D text provided for you on the Companion CD. In the following section you'll add the 3D text and then add a drop-shadow to it.

ADDING AN EFFECT TO AN IMPORTED OBJECT

When you work with Layer Effects, it doesn't make any difference whether you paint a stroke on the layer or import a piece of a graphic. The outline of the opaque areas on the layer will always display the effect you've chosen.

To make the Web page look dimensional, you'll import the 3D text and then use a different Layer Effect—Drop Shadow.

ADDING AN ELEMENT TO AN EFFECTS LAYER

1. Open the Textures.psd image from the Chap19 folder of the Companion CD.

2. With the Move tool, drag the image into the Workspace image, as shown in Figure 19.24.

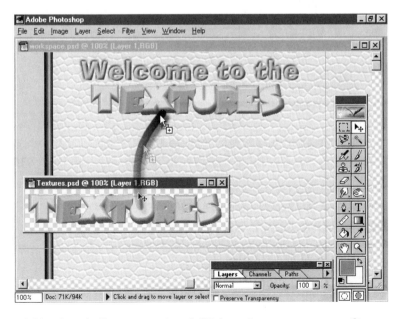

FIGURE 19.24 *Drag the Textures image into the Workspace image to create a copy of it on a new layer.*

3. Choose Layer, Effects, and then choose Drop Shadow.

4. Uncheck the Global Angle check box. This check box is used to "synch" the angle of all the Effects layers; in this instance, you do not want the drop shadow at the same angle as the Pillow Emboss text.

5. Type **120** in the Angle field, type **10** in the Blur field, and then when your onscreen preview looks like Figure 19.25, click on OK to apply the effect.

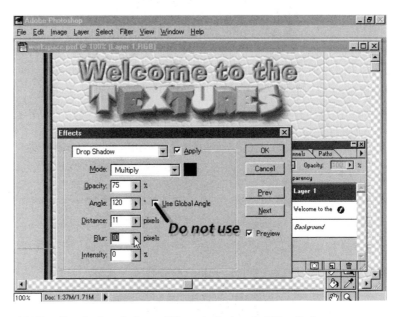

FIGURE 19.25 *Give the drop shadow a different angle than the Pillow Emboss text.*

6. Choose the Type tool and then click an insertion point below the 3D textures element.

7. Type **Home Page** in the text field, click on the color swatch, and in the Color Picker, choose the color you used for the "Welcome to the" text (H:52, S:100%, B:59% works well). Click on OK to exit the Color Picker.

8. Move the text on its layer in the image until the entire phrase is centered.

9. Click on OK to apply the text.

10. Choose Layer, Effects, and then choose Bevel and Emboss. Choose Pillow Emboss from the Style drop-down list. The angle for the text should be the same as the last time you used this effect. Photoshop "remembers" settings within the same Photoshop session. Click on OK to apply the effect.

11. It's time to conserve memory space by merging the layers together. Uncheck the eye icon for the Background layer, and click on any of the layer titles (except Background); then click on the menu flyout button on the Layers palette and choose Merge Visible, as in Figure 19.26.

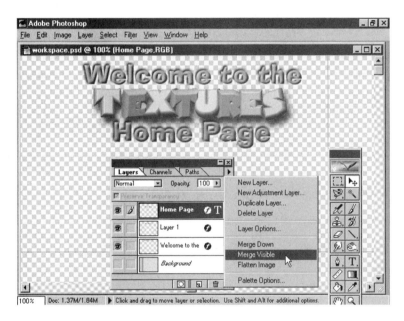

FIGURE 19.26 *When you finish composing elements across layers, you can condense the layers to a single layer.*

12. Click on the space that contained the eye icon (to the left of the Background title) to make the Background layer visible again.

13. Press Ctrl(⌘)+S; keep the file open.

You've got the background taken care of, as well as the headline. Now it's on to adding graphics to the page.

WARNING

When you merge layers that contain live text and effects, these properties go away. The resulting single layer contains only elements that cannot be edited. Make sure that your spelling is correct before you choose to make this move!

SIZING GRAPHICS AND THE ACTIONS LIST

An "eyeball" estimate will tell you that there's not a lot of room for graphics on this page, but if you reduce original artwork, there's room on this page for about three images of a nice size. In the following section, you'll program the Actions list to shrink, sharpen, and add an edge and a drop shadow to three candidates for this Web page. The Actions list makes it easy to repeat editing moves, so if you get the first image right, the other two will be a snap.

MEASURING AVAILABLE SPACE

You'll use Photoshop's Measure tool to measure both the vertical and horizontal space in which the images will fit on this page. Remember that the measurements should be on the "lean" side because HTML documents do not allow you to perfectly align and space individual graphics; there's always some padding around elements.

Here's how to decide on the final size for the graphics you'll use on the Web page:

USING THE MEASURE TOOL TO SIZE UP WORKING SPACE

1. Press F8 to display the Info palette.

2. Choose the Measure tool, and then drag from about 1/2 screen inch short of the tubing to about 1/2 screen inch short of the right guide. As you can see in Figure 19.27, the available width for images is about 410 pixels. When you divide this number by 3, you see that the maximum width of any of the three images cannot exceed 137 pixels. Less would be better here, so that there's some space between the pictures. Let's make that maximum width 126 pixels to allow 10 pixels of padding between the images.

3. Drag the Measure tool from about 1/2 screen inch below the headline text to 1/2 screen inch short of the horizontal guide. As you can see in Figure 19.28, you have about 126 pixels maximum height for the artwork. Therefore, the maximum size of the three images you'll place on the page should be about 126 pixels in both width and height.

4. You're finished with the Measure tool. Keep the file open, and remember the number 126; you'll be using it in the Actions script you'll program.

FIGURE 19.27   *Measure the width of the space on the page, divide by 3, and then allow for some padding between images.*

FIGURE 19.28   *Measure the maximum height for the images you'll place on the Web page.*

PROGRAMMING THE ACTIONS PALETTE

The Actions palette has been improved in version 5, so there are a lot more things you can automate. As described earlier, you will resize the graphics provided for you on the Companion CD (or use your own graphics), and then create a framing look for the images so that they appear to "sink into" the background in much the same way that the pillow emboss text appears to recede into the background.

Here's how to create an Action list of commands that will make a graphic fit on the Web page. Later, you'll apply the Action you've programmed to the other two images.

CREATING A CUSTOM ACTIONS LIST

1. Open the Boca.tif image from the Chap19 folder on the Companion CD.

2. Choose Window, Show Actions.

3. On the Actions menu flyout, choose New Action.

4. Type **Cropping** in the Name field, as shown in Figure 19.29, and then click on Record. Everything you do now will become part of an Actions script called Cropping.

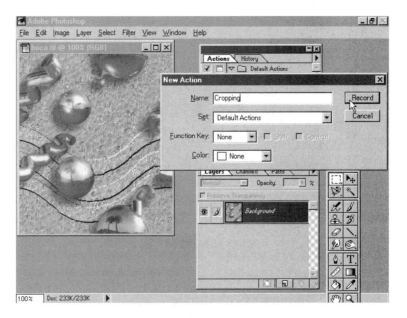

FIGURE 19.29 *Name the Actions script and then start recording.*

5. Choose Image, Image Size, and then type **126** in the Height (in pixels) field, as shown in Figure 19.30. The Width field will automatically decrease proportionately. Click on OK to resize the graphic.

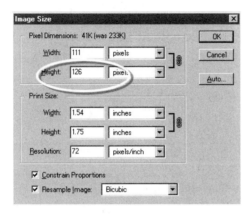

FIGURE 19.30 *Resize the graphic so that it will fit comfortably with the other two on the bottom of the Web page.*

6. Choose Filter, Sharpen, and then choose Unsharp Mask.

7. Drag the Amount slider to about 39%. The Amount of Unsharp Mask determines the percentage of the effect from 1 to 500; you're using a mild amount here.

8. Type **.9** (pixels) in the Radius field. This setting determines the depth of pixels that will be affected at color edges. If you specify a high value, more of the pixels surrounding the color-edge pixels are sharpened. If you specify a low value, only the edges are sharpened. Values can be from .1 to 250, so you're only sharpening the edges in the image here.

9. Type **1** in the Threshold field. The threshold defines the required range of contrast between neighboring pixels before sharpening is applied to an edge. Values can range from 0 to 255. A lower value, such as 1, produces a pronounced sharpening effect. If the Unsharp Mask dialog box looks like Figure 19.31, click on OK to apply the effect.

10. With the Move tool selected, press the up-arrow key on the keyboard twice, and then press the keyboard's left-arrow key twice. This turns the Background image into a layer, and you've offset the image to create a frame on the right and bottom sides, as in Figure 19.32.

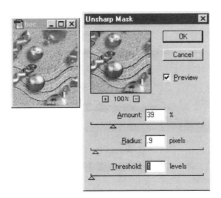

FIGURE 19.31 *Unsharp Mask can apply a strong but subtle amount of sharpening to an image.*

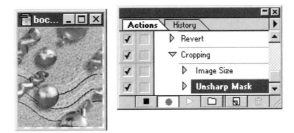

FIGURE 19.32 *Move the image by using the keyboard arrow "nudge" keys to create a frame on the right and bottom sides.*

11. Choose Layer, Effects, and then choose Inner Shadow.

12. In the Inner Shadow dialog box, choose Angle: 132°, and Distance: 8 pixels, as shown in Figure 19.33. Click on OK to apply the Inner Shadow.

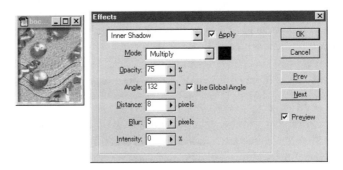

FIGURE 19.33 *You can create a shadow box effect, using the Inner Shadow.*

13. Choose Flatten Image from the Layers palette's menu flyout, and then choose File, Save As.

14. Choose JPEG from the Save As drop down list, and save the image to hard disk as Boca.jpg.

15. In the JPEG Options box, choose 7 for the quality (see Figure 19.34), and choose Baseline Optimized as the Format Option. Click on OK to save the file.

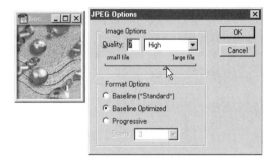

FIGURE 19.34   *Choose High Quality and Baseline Optimized for saving the JPEG image.*

16. Click on the Stop recording button, as shown in Figure 19.35. Your Actions script is complete now and can be applied to the two other images.

17. You can close the Boca.jpg file at any time now.

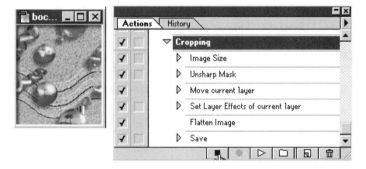

FIGURE 19.35   *When your "recipe" of Actions is concluded, click on the Stop recording button. The script is then saved.*

Now that you have the routine saved as an Actions script, it's time to apply the script to the two other images:

RUNNING AN ACTIONS SCRIPT

1. Open the fastfood.tif image from the Chap19 folder on the Companion CD.

2. Click on the Cropping title on the Actions palette, and then click on the Play button, as shown in Figure 19.36. The same actions you applied to the Boca image are now applied to the fastfood image, and it, too, is saved in JPEG format. Click on Stop once the script has been run.

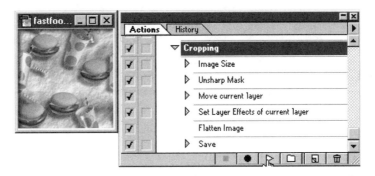

FIGURE 19.36 *The long string of modifications you performed to the Boca image have now been applied to the fastfood image.*

3. Close the fastfood.jpg image, and open the glasbrik.tif image from the Chap19 folder of the Companion CD.

4. Click on the Play button; in moments, you will have a glasbrik.jpg image in the workspace. You can close the file at any time now.

Suppose that your client, Mr. Texture, drops by and wants to see the progress of your work. The following section shows how to build a lightning-fast mock-up of the Web page.

PREVIEWING THE APPEARANCE OF THE WEB PAGE

Because the assembly of an HTML page requires that separate elements be combined, there's only one way at this point to show the client your work without writing HTML code. You'll place the images you batch-processed on layers on the Workspace image. Here's how:

BUILDING A PREVIEW HTML PAGE

1. Open the workspace.psd image, and then open the Boca.jpg image you created in the previous steps.

2. With the Move tool, drag the Boca image into the workspace.psd image. Then position the image to the left at the bottom of the page, within the guidelines. You can close Boca.jpg at any time now.

3. Repeat steps 1–2 with the glasbrik and then the fastfood JPEG images. Position them equally spaced and aligned vertically, as shown in Figure 19.37.

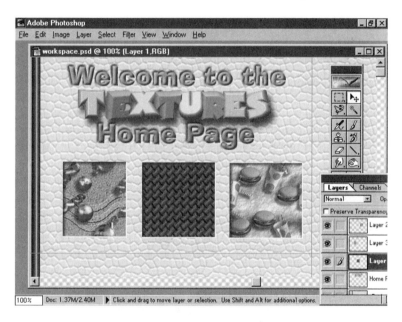

FIGURE 19.37   *Adding the JPEG images to the Workspace image helps you and your client visualize the finished page.*

4. Press Ctrl(⌘)+S; keep the file open.

The page is coming together nicely; it's a good-looking site. You're still missing navigation buttons, however. To correct this oversight, you'll measure the space you can use on the page, and then use Photoshop's effects to make a 3D button.

MEASURING SPACE AND CREATING NAVIGATION BUTTONS

As you may recall, the solid color to the left of the tubing effect is where the client wants the navigation buttons. For the sake of consistency, you'll use one button design and then, when the HTML page is created, you'll reference this single button file as many times as the client needs it on the page.

First things first—you'll see in the following steps how large a button you can create:

DEFINING THE SPACE ALLOWED FOR NAVIGATION BUTTONS

1. Scroll over to the far left of the Workspace document.

2. Press F8 if the Info palette isn't already onscreen.

3. With the Measure tool, drag a horizontal line within the solid-color part of the page, starting and ending about 1/2 screen inches inside the border, as shown in Figure 19.38. The Info palette tells you that a button can fit comfortably on the left of the page if it's 83 pixels wide.

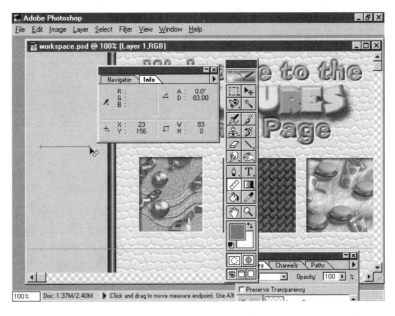

FIGURE 19.38 *Measure the width of the solid area on the Web page to decide how wide navigation buttons can be.*

It only smells expensive.

"TIMELESS"

In Chapter 22, "Creating Reflections and Shadows," you'll see how to turn a dull surface into a shiny, reflective one. Learn the tricks for evaluating perspective in reflections, and how a *mirror plane* in an image treats reflections. See how to use Photoshop's Free Transform feature and other tools to accomplish a seemingly impossible feat of image retouching.

"TUDOR GUY"

Does the bottom image look like an ordinary photograph? It *should*, because the depth of field in the image displays the foreground branches and background house as out of focus. The guy in the scene was never standing in front of the house, however! In Chapter 21, "Simulating Depth of Field in an Image," you learn how to combine images and then selectively blur layers to arrive at an image that *looks* as though it was taken with a camera, using a medium aperture.

"KITCHEN"

In Chapter 21 you work with both photographic and digital media to create this image. "Simulating Depth of Field in an Image" is both the name of the chapter and the technique you'll learn, using step-by-step instructions, to bring three different images together. See how depth of field is as important to an image's reality as perspective, shading, and other photographic aspects.

"Ball 1" and "Ball 2"

In Chapter 22, "Creating Reflections and Shadows," the creation of artificial shadows is emphasized. How should a shadow fall in a scene, depending on the lighting of the scene? What happens to a shadow when it is cast on both the ground and a background perpendicular to the ground? These questions and more are answered in hands-on tutorials that deal with manually creating realistic shadows in a scene.

"WINE BOTTLE AND GLASS"

Creating shadows is not as simple as it might seem, when the objects casting the shadows are partially transparent and tinted. In Chapter 22, "Creating Reflections and Shadows," you become familiar with using Andromeda Software's Shadow filter to automatically create shadows that contain transparency. You'll also learn a technique that adds a color tint to the shadow, so that the composition looks professional and authentic.

"SMIRK"

Chapter 22 discussions of shadow creation include the use of Alien Skin's Eye Candy Perspective Shadow filter. See how this filter can render a cast shadow, like the one shown in this illustration, onto any active layer in an image file. A demo version of the Perspective Shadow filter is on the *Limited Edition* CD-ROM; you'll learn the ins and outs of working with this filter before you purchase it!

"GIGANTIC"

Chapter 5, "Working with New Features," includes information about working with an image to which you need to add a border for a client. The only problem is that the client is indecisive (IOW, wishy-washy!), and you need to present to him with *a number* of variations of the border. No problem; learn to take command of Photoshop 5's History palette to undo and redo the border until your client appears to be happy!

"Inside Adobe Photoshop 3"

You won't find a specific tutorial in this book on how this image was created—we simply wanted to show new readers the cover, designed by the author, of the first cross-platform book we wrote on Photoshop 3 (circa 1995). All the special effects in this image were created using Photoshop 3, so it's reasonable to expect that you can out-accomplish the author by reading through *this* book!

"CHROME"

The spheres were added to the picture using a modeling program, and the shadows were created using techniques found in Chapter 22, but the "Chrome" illustration was created *manually*, using the techniques found in Chapter 24, "Making Your Own Chrome Lettering." Learn the secrets to painting a hyper-realistic piece that looks reflective, using Photoshop's new tools and features.

"Park Bench"

Okay—which way is up? It all depends on your perspective! Learn in Chapter 23, "Playing with Perspective," how to create different points of view within an image, all relative to the person in the image—not to the audience. It's fantastic, photorealistic fun, and easy to accomplish using the steps in this chapter.

"DEXTER TAKES A WALK"

In Chapter 25, "The Author's Favorite Third-Party Plug-Ins," you see how to complete a scene by generating a realistic sky, using the Four Seasons filter, one of many filters featured in this chapter. Want a gorgeous sunset? Need a convincing picture of a sunny day? How about a night-time scene with a full moon? Learn how to complete the upper half of any image—digital or photographic—using the Four Seasons plug-in.

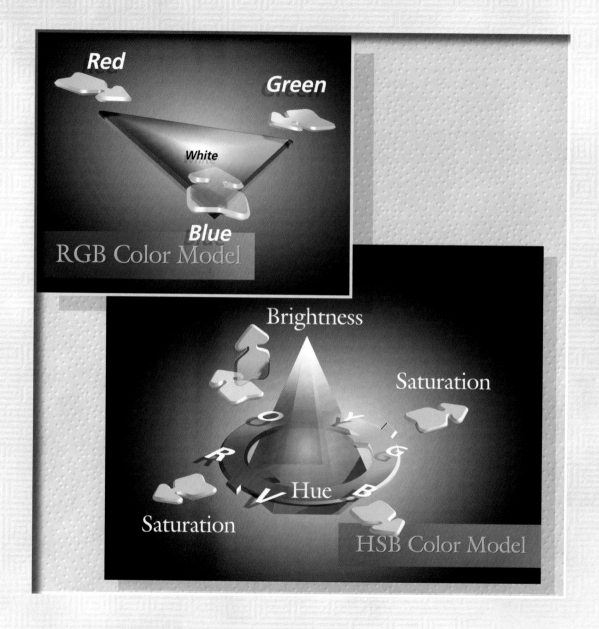

Illustrated here are the RGB and HSB color models, which are commonly used in Photoshop during image editing stages. A color model describes a *color space*—the number of different colors a color model can hold. As you can see from these illustrations, different components at the extremes of these color spaces converge or travel outward to make up the specific color you're looking for. In Chapter 11, "Using Different Color Modes," we walk through the conversion of one color space to another, to create fascinating images using different color spaces.

In Chapter 25, "The Author's Favorite Third-Party Plug-Ins," you're treated to work with demo versions of XAOS|tools Paint Alchemy and Terrazzo plug-ins. In this illustration you can see only three of the many different textures you can create and then modify in Photoshop and other applications. You'll see how to work with these plug-ins to create amazing textures (many of which can be found on the *Limited Edition* CD-ROM), and get hands-on experience with the many features in the XAOS|tools bundle.

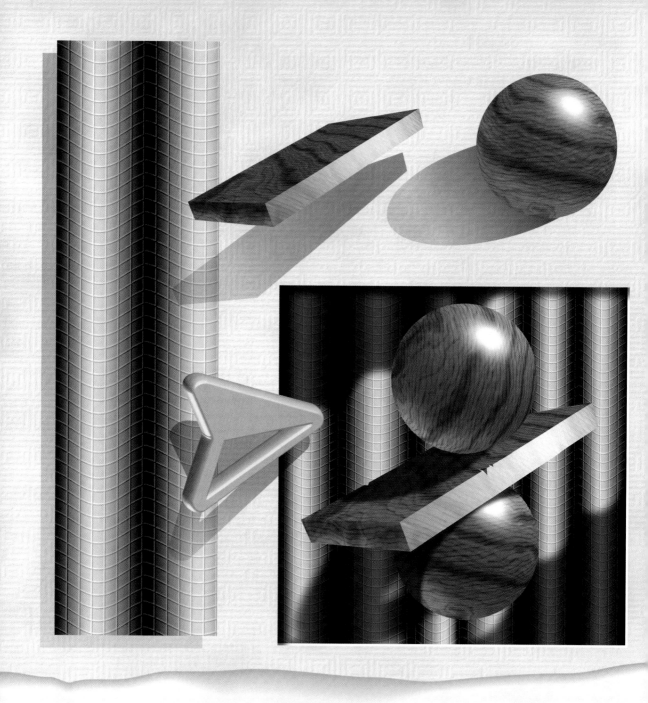

"DIVISION"

The image's surfaces look realistic, the shadows look properly placed, and the background and shading support the composition. But "Division" was created entirely within the computer—using sample textures provided on the Companion CD-ROM—and by using Andromeda Software's 3-D filter and some manual work in Photoshop. Learn how to create a scene that's abstract in approach but realistic in content in Chapter 25, "The Author's Favorite Third-Party Plug-Ins."

"HONEY, I FOUND THE LEAK"

In Chapter 25, "The Author's Favorite Third-Party Plug-Ins," you work with a fully functional copy of Extensis Mask Pro to mask areas as fine as a human hair in the image of the plumber. You then combine the plumber image with an image of a sink, color balance the scene, and add shadows (as you learn to do in Chapter 22, "Creating Reflections and Shadows"). It's all in the name of pure fun, but you'll discover that the power of Mask Pro and Photoshop's native tools is very serious.

The *Limited Edition* CD-ROM is packed with more textures, fonts, clip objects, and stock photography images than you'll find on the Companion CD-ROM—and that's a *lot*! To discover all the useful resource files that the Boutons have created on the *Limited Edition* CD-ROM, use Adobe Acrobat Reader 3 (included on the Companion CD-ROM), and peruse the FST-8.pdf document in the Boutons folder.

4. Press Ctrl(⌘)+N to open the New document dialog box.

5. In the Width field, type **83** (pixels); in the Height field, type **44** (pixels) (to make the button rectangular); type **72** in the Resolution field, click on the Transparent button in the contents field, and then click on OK to create the new document. This is a layer document, so you can apply Layer Effects without having to convert the document first.

6. Fill the image with a medium purple (H:280, S:73%, and B: 94% is good).

7. Choose Layer, Effects, and then choose Bevel and Emboss.

8. Choose Inner Bevel from the Style drop-down list. Type **120** in the Angle field. This will make the highlight on the button toward 10 o'clock, which is consistent with the lighting on the rest of the elements for the page.

9. Click on the Depth flyout button, and then drag the slider to 10. When the dialog box looks like Figure 19.39, click on OK to create the button.

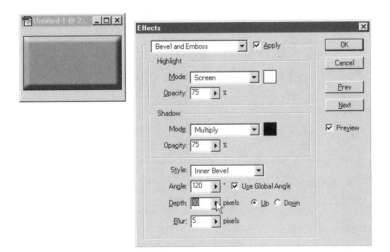

FIGURE 19.39   *Create a 3D button in the Layer Effects dialog box.*

10. Choose Flatten image from the Layers palette's flyout menu, and then save the image as Button.jpg. In the JPEG Options box, choose Baseline Optimized. You can go a little crude on the quality, as there is not much image detail on the button. Choose 3 or 4 as the Quality setting, and then click on OK to save the button image.

11. You can close the Button.jpg image at any time now. Keep the workspace.psd document open.

There's only one element that has yet to become a JPEG version for placement in the HTML document, and that is the headline. Let's get to it, and get paid for this assignment!

FLATTENING AND CROPPING A COPY OF YOUR WORK

There is no way you would want to ruin your workspace.psd file by cropping out the headline elements. Instead, in the following steps, you'll work with a copy of workspace.psd.

Here's how to crop and export the last of the elements needed for the Textures Home Page:

CONDENSING THE TEXT ELEMENTS TO A SINGLE LAYER

NOTE

These are the three format options for JPEG exports from Photoshop:

- **Baseline Standard**. The least compact of the JPEG options. Although your file will download to a visitor's machine slower than it has to, Baseline Standard JPEG can be read by almost every WWW browser.

- **Baseline Optimized**. Can be read by most WWW browsers. Baseline Optimized offers higher compression and better color than Baseline Standard.

- **Progressive**. Displays the image gradually as it is downloaded from a Web browser, using a series of scans to show increasingly detailed versions of the entire image until all the data has finished downloading.

1. Choose Image, Duplicate. Accept the default name for the duplicate image in the Duplicate Image dialog box by clicking on OK. You can close workspace.psd at any time now.

2. Hide the images at the bottom of the page by unchecking their eye icons on the Layers palette.

3. With the Rectangular Marquee tool, drag a box around the headline in the image, as shown in Figure 19.40.

4. Choose Image, Crop.

5. Choose Flatten Image from the Layers palette's flyout menu. An attention box appears, asking whether you want to discard hidden layers.

6. Click on OK. Your image should now look like that shown in Figure 19.41.

7. Choose File, Save As, and then save the image as Textures.jpg in the JPEG file format. In the JPEG Options box, choose Quality of 6, and choose Baseline Optimized as the Format Option. Click on OK to save the file.

8. You can close Textures.jpg and quit Photoshop at any time now.

FIGURE 19.40   *Crop as tightly as possible with the Rectangular Marquee tool to encompass only the headline, with a minimum of background texture showing.*

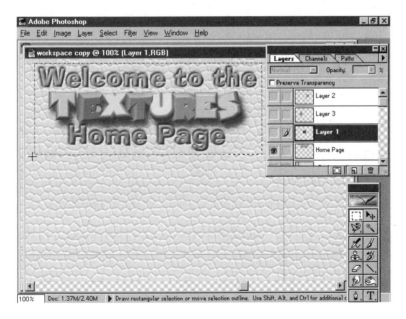

FIGURE 19.41   *The final element for the Web site has now been cropped and flattened.*

It is beyond the scope of this book to teach you how to write HTML to make all the elements fit together. Using the graphics you've designed in this chapter, however, a completed document called Textures.html has been created for you. Textures.html is located in the Chap19/HTML folder on the Companion CD. To view this document, drag the Textures.html folder into your WWW browser. If you like, you can examine the way the document was built by viewing the Textures.html document in a text editor. Also, you can substitute your own JPEG images for those provided in the HTML folder. Copy the folder to your desktop, delete the JPEG images, copy your own to the folder, and then load the HTML document in your browser to see how your work fits together. As you can see in Figure 19.42, there really aren't any surprises. Except for the text the author added above the buttons, the document looks pretty much the same in HTML format as it does as your workspace.psd image.

FIGURE 19.42 *The completed HTML document.*

SUMMARY

If you work with a partner who's a whiz at HTML, you'll impress her (or him) with what you've learned in this chapter, and your partnership is well on the way to commanding greater fees. If you work as a lone designer, you might want to invest in a program such as Adobe PageMill that makes HTML coding as simple as drag and drop. In any event, you've seen in this chapter what a difference a carefully designed page can make with respect to attractiveness and attention-getting powers. Perform variations on the elements, and you can design scores of exciting, original-looking work.

Chapter 20, "Building Animations," takes you one step beyond graphics and Photoshop, and into animation. Photoshop is the workspace, and with a helper application or two, you'll be producing animations in no time.

BUILDING ANIMATIONS

Several applications for both Windows and the Macintosh can produce Video for Windows and QuickTime movies. Often, however, animation programs are not able to provide that "something special" you want in the animation—a title, perhaps, or a new background.

The good news is that you don't need an expensive video editing software suite to produce totally professional, edited movies for the personal computer. This chapter takes you through the process of producing a QuickTime or Video for Windows digital film, using some software you already own and the shareware versions of animation compilers—programs that assemble still frames—provided on the Companion CD.

EXAMINING THE ANIMATION PIPELINE

Although QuickTime and Microsoft's Video for Windows are different technologies, they essentially do the same thing: they play back a highly compressed sequence of still images (and usually sound) that were compiled using special mathematical procedures, not unlike the way JPEG images are compressed.

This chapter takes you through concept-to-completion of a movie, as illustrated in Figure 20.1.

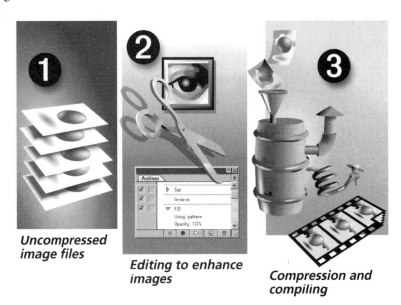

Uncompressed
image files

Editing to enhance
images

Compression and
compiling

FIGURE 20.1 *The three phases of animation are creating a sequence of stills, batch-editing them in Photoshop, and finally compiling the frames into an animation.*

The following three phases of animation are discussed in this chapter:

- Creating a sequence of stills
- Batch-editing them in Photoshop
- Compiling the frames into an animation

CREATING STILL IMAGES

Where does one begin creating an animation? Well, you *could* paint progressively moving designs on image backgrounds, all images being the same dimensions—but this would be tedious, and the artistic merit of such an animation would be suspect at best. Today, most programs with animation capability *also* offer the option to write uncompressed still frames that are autonumbered, making it easy for the user, and an animation compiler, to properly sequence the collection of images.

In this chapter, you not only will work with still images on the Companion CD, but also have an opportunity to work with a limited demo version of the Valis Group's Flo', a program that enables you to move, scale, and distort selected areas of a still image to produce an animation.

CREATING SEQUENTIAL STILL FRAMES BY USING THIRD-PARTY ANIMATION TOOLS

You will see in this chapter how Photoshop's Actions palette can batch process still frames to create an enhanced overall production. If you have any of the following products, you might want to create a simple animation that does not have a background:

- **Macromedia Extreme 3D.** Set the background color of the animation to a color not found in the foreground objects. Alternatively, you can specify that the rendered still frames are in TIFF or the Macintosh PICT format and should contain an alpha channel. Alpha channels are additional information channels in an image; they can mark areas as being transparent, opaque, or partially transparent. The point here is that you will need a way to separate the foreground action from the background; a solid color can work as well as an alpha channel because Photoshop's Color Range command can create a selection you can save to an alpha channel.

- **The Valis Group's Flo'** A sequence of animated stills can be generated from Flo', the stills include an alpha channel that makes the separation of foreground elements from an empty background effortless when you use Photoshop. Flo' will write the stills to a number of file formats, all of which Photoshop can work with.

- **Fractal Design Poser 2.** You can create your own stills if you set the Poser document's background color to one that is not found in the foreground figures or props.

- **trueSpace, Lightwave, and 3D Studio MAX.** Because all three can also write sequential still frames, and can contain alpha channels, a specific background color is not important.

- **Fractal Design Painter 3.** This and later versions can write still frames with a single image-masking channel. Additionally, this program can decompile an existing animation. If you have already created an animation and you want to enhance it, use Painter to write sequential, numbered still frames.

Other programs also can generate a sequence of still files. Again, the Companion CD contains still frames for you to use when you reach the *second* phase of the animation pipeline.

BATCH EDITING IN PHOTOSHOP

Chapter 19, "Creating Graphics for the Web," took a nod at Photoshop's Actions list, but the capability to program this script-style list goes beyond mere cropping and sharpening images. You can move objects between layers, change layers, add fills, create and save selections, and more.

NOTE

Several years ago, using PIXAR Typestry, I created an animation that contained no background. At some point during the ensuing years I lost the source file with the animation tracks, and had only the AVI file to work with. The inspiration for this chapter's examples came to me a few months ago, when I wanted to enhance the file.

It was easy enough to decompile the animation, but here's a very important tip for designers who want to get into animation.

In the examples that follow, you use uncompressed frames, and a fancy Actions list script you program yourself, to add different backgrounds to the still images.

COMPRESSING AND COMPILING FRAMES INTO ANIMATION

After the sequential frames have been edited in Photoshop, you need an animation compiler to distill the images into a seamless movie. To be honest, if animation is to be your career, you might be better off buying Adobe Premiere or Macromedia Director to serve as both a video editing suite and a compiling engine for your still frames. But we all seem to have budgets. Photoshop is terrific at batch-processing edits to frames, and the Companion CD has two full-featured shareware animation compilers: MainActor for Windows, and MooVer for the Macintosh.

FILE FORMATS AND COMPILER COMPATIBILITY

The source files that dump into the shareware compilers on the Companion CD must be in a specific format. MainActor for Windows accepts files in BMP, PCX, GIF, and JPEG formats; MooVer for the Macintosh requires 16-bit PICT files (no alpha channels).

Although offering platform-specific instructions for a platform-specific procedure in this chapter is not a problem, resource files on the Companion CD were created in both BMP and PICT format, on the assumption that you do not own the commercial version of Flo'—the application shown in this chapter. Therefore:

- Photoshop's Actions list will not change the file extension or the format of files you edit from the CD. The CD's file names are in 8.3 format—even the Macintosh files—because of the cross-platform compatibility issue involved in mastering a hybrid CD.

- Photoshop will not create a copy of a file on the Macintosh that has, for example, a BMP extension even though the file's format is PICT. This could become very confusing in the future when you want to clean up your hard disk!

- The edited files can be imported directly into the compiling shareware without the need to run a separate Photoshop Actions list command to convert file formats.

If you *do* own Flo', when you get to the file-naming steps, feel free to name the files anything you like—specifically, you can use long file names if you're running Windows 95, Windows NT, or the Mac OS, and Macintosh users need not add a three-character extension to a file.

TIP

Instead of allowing the animation package to compile a finished product, write an uncompressed animation to sequentially numbered files. To make a video play back at a reasonable speed, every compiler uses lossy compression on the still frames, and you will never retrieve the original quality of the source material. Get a large hard disk, get a box of Iomega Zip disks, get a CD burner, and organize these uncompressed files for the future. Not only will you find that editing the frames is easier (as shown in this chapter), but you can create different variations on an animation by reusing the original uncompressed still frames. For example, you can have a character strutting down the street in a crowded city, or change your mind and use Photoshop to change the city to a cow pasture. You will have many returns (movies) for the price of rendering still animation files once—and investing in some large media in which to archive them!

ANIMATING WITH FLO' AND TRANSPARENCY MASKS

When you add the feature of alpha channels, your animation adventures (and the results) take a serious professional upswing.

Unlike the commercial version of Flo', the demo version of Flo' (included on the Companion CD) does not accept alpha channel information and therefore cannot reproduce the examples in this chapter. But you can gain experience with all the tools and even write a QuickTime or AVI movie from the trial version— and then you'll have a good excuse to *buy* the commercial version!

Flo' imports a single still image, and then you use vector drawing tools to select areas. The selected area can then be stretched, moved, rotated—nearly anything you can do with a vector drawing, except that the effects are happening with bitmap images. And there are no telltale seams between selected, distorted areas and original image areas.

Although Flo' might appear to be similar to HSC Software's "Goo" product, Flo' precedes Goo by several years and is a very capable, very serious image editing stand-alone program with results that are of professional quality. On the Macintosh, Flo' has versions specifically designed for creating multilayer imaging (MetaFlo') and compositing film work (MovieFlo'), both with Web animation capability. This section shows you how the "standard" Flo', available in both Macintosh and Windows versions, can be used.

The *interpolation* quality—the way Flo' evaluates pixel colors when areas are stretched or shrunk—is on a par with Photoshop's Free Transform function, which is top-notch. Please feel free to install and experiment with Flo'. The following sections describe the features found in both the demo and commercial versions, and show you how to use the commercial version to write still frames that contain an alpha channel.

EDITING THE BOOMBOX IMAGE FOR ANIMATION PURPOSES

The trick to compositing a boombox, a shadow, and a background is to make the shadow partially opaque, so that some of the background visual comes through. This produces a wonderful, believable animation, even with the silly contortions the boombox goes through.

To build an alpha channel that "tells" another application (such as Flo') that "the boombox is 100 percent opaque, but the shadow is only 40 percent opaque," you need to work with layers in Photoshop, and then save the opacity of the layers' contents to a single alpha channel before flattening the image. In the following steps, some of the work has been done for you: Aquavox.psd, in the Examples/CHAP20 folder on the Companion CD, contains the boombox floating in an image window of 100 percent transparency. Also in this file is a cast shadow of 100 percent opacity; this opacity needs to be decreased to allow some of the background image to show through. Then you can save this file as a Targa (Windows) or PICT (Macintosh) file that the retail version of Flo' can read in and work with.

Here's how—in Photoshop—to define an alpha channel that contains different amounts of transparency:

CREATING A SEMITRANSPARENT SHADOW

1. Open the Aquavox.psd image from the Examples/CHAP20 folder on the CD. With the Lasso tool, select the shadow, and then hold Ctrl(⌘) and drag the interior of the selection a fraction of an inch to make it a floating selection, as shown in Figure 20.2.

FIGURE 20.2   *Float the selection of the shadow by lassoing it and then holding Ctrl(⌘) and dragging it a fraction of an inch.*

NOTE

The Aquaback.tif image can be seen in these figures but is not used until later, and you shouldn't load it right now. It's simply onscreen to give you an idea of the background used in this animation sequence.

2. Right-click (Macintosh: hold Ctrl and click), and then choose Layer Via Cut from the context menu. The shadow is now on Layer 1, above the Aquavox layer.

3. Drag the Layer 1 title on the Layers palette to beneath the Aquavox title.

4. Drag the Opacity slider on the Layers palette to about 40% to make the shadow semitransparent, as shown in Figure 20.3.

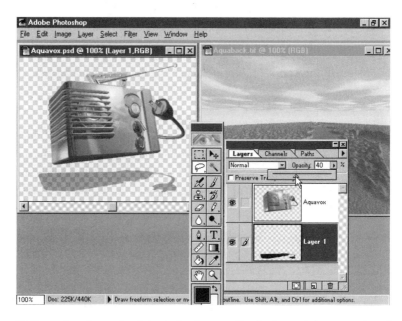

FIGURE 20.3 *Reduce the opacity of the shadow layer to allow background elements to show through when the animation is compiled.*

5. Choose Merge Visible from the Layers palette's flyout menu. The single layer is now labeled Layer 1 on the Layers palette.

6. Press Ctrl(⌘) and click the Layer title on the Layers palette to load the non-transparent areas of the layer as a marquee selection. Note in Figure 20.4 that no "marching ants" surround the shadow portion of this single layer. The reason is that areas of less than 50 percent opacity are selected, but Photoshop doesn't mark them with marquee selection lines.

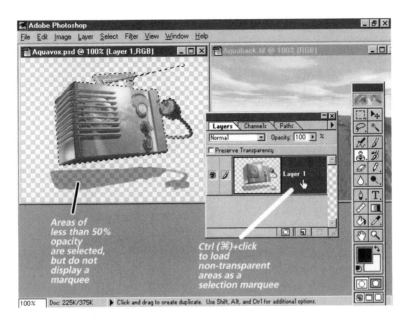

FIGURE 20.4   *When you press Ctrl(⌘) and click a layer title, all nontransparent areas are loaded, even if no marquee lines appear.*

7. Click the Channels tab, and then click the Save selection as channel button. Then press Ctrl(⌘)+D to deselect.

Flo' uses white to indicate selections, and you cannot change this option for images imported into Flo', so...

8. Click the Alpha 1 title on the Channels palette. If channel Alpha 1 looks like a white boombox silhouette with a faint, light shadow like the figure at right, proceed to step 10, and everything is okay. But if Alpha 1 channel looks like the image at left in Figure 20.5, deselect the marquee and press Ctrl(⌘)+I to invert the color scheme in this channel.

9. Press Ctrl(⌘)+~(tilde) to return to the color composite view of the image. On the Layers palette, click the Create new layer icon, and then drag the Layer 2 title beneath the layer with the boombox and shadow.

10. With black as the current foreground color, press Ctrl(⌘)+A, and then press Alt(Opt)+Delete (Backspace). Press Ctrl(⌘)+D to deselect now. Next, you're going to flatten this image and apparently ruin the semitransparent boombox shadow. This is not true; the selection information for the shadow is saved in the

TIP

Break time—for two seconds. On the left side of Figure 20.5 you can see the result of step #7, using my configuration for channel selections. I used Color Indicates: Selected areas—this can be specified by double-clicking any saved alpha channel to display the Channel Options dialog box. Photoshop's default setting is Color Indicates: Masked Areas, the option needed for the steps to follow.

Alpha 1 channel, and you're adding black to the background so that when the alpha channel is read into Flo', partially selected areas of black will represent the shadow. Additionally, by creating a black background, you ensure that fringing around the boombox when it is composited into the Aquaback.tif image will be practically invisible.

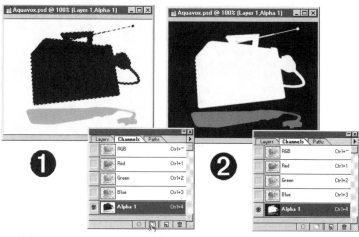

Click to save marquee selection

**Press Ctrl (⌘)+D,
the press Ctrl (⌘)+I**

FIGURE 20.5 *You can configure Photoshop to save selections as color or as white areas, but Flo' reads alpha information as "white=selection."*

11. Choose Flatten Image from the Layers palette's menu flyout, and press Ctrl(⌘)+Shift+S (File, Save As). Save the file as Aquavox.tga.Then Windows users should choose the Targa format, and check the 32 bits/pixel option in the Options box, as in Figure 20.6. Macintosh users should save the image in the PICT format and choose 32 bits/pixel as the save option. The two file formats are not the same, but both now contain an alpha channel that separates the boombox and shadow from the background of the image.

12. Close Photoshop. It's time to animate the boombox in Flo'.

FIGURE 20.6   *Both PICT and Targa files can contain a single additional channel of information that programs read-as-selection areas.*

GOING WITH THE FLO'

This section shows you how to work with the commercial version of Flo'. If you don't own the full working version, read on anyway to discover some of the advanced features of the program. When it's time to batch process the Flo' still images, use the files from the Companion CD.

You will work with the Aquavox.tga (or Aquavox.pict) image you saved in Photoshop to create keyframes. A *keyframe* is simply a still image in an animation sequence—an image that marks a dramatically different arrangement of objects when compared to the previous keyframe. A keyframe is sort of an anchor. For example, an animation of a door closing has two keyframes: one of the door open and another of the door closed. Flo' enables you to create keyframes, and then the application automatically calculates the frames that should go between the keyframes to complete a smooth, transitional sequence.

NOTE

You will have fun experimenting with the two sample images in the demo version of Flo', and I recommend that this application be part of every advanced designer's toolkit. But if your toolkit isn't fully stocked yet, all the still images created by the steps that follow are located in the Examples/Chap20/Aquavox folder, so that you can complete the tutorial in Photoshop after this excursion into working with alpha channels and the commercial version of Flo'.

Now would be a good time to copy all the still files to your hard disk. Select the Aquavox folder from the drive window of the Companion CD, and drag the folder onto your desktop or other hard disk location to copy it.

The following steps can be used with the boombox image to create a 42-frame animation in which each frame contains a modified alpha channel that reflects the distortions performed on the boombox.

ANIMATING THE BOOMBOX

1. Flo' opens to a new document window that has no contents. You are supposed to place an image in the window and then work with it. With images that contain alpha channels, however, you must choose File, Accept Alpha Channel, and *then* choose File, Place; *then* pick the boombox file, as shown in Figure 20.7.

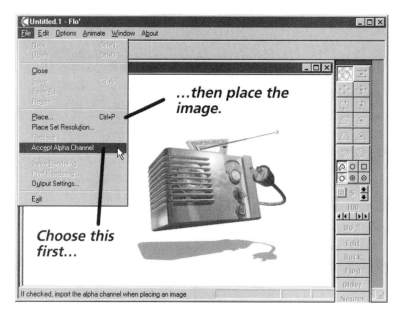

FIGURE 20.7 *Flo' doesn't know whether you want all information imported as an image, or whether an alpha channel should mask selected areas. Choose Accept Alpha Channel before importing an image that contains an alpha channel.*

In Figure 20.8, the basic controls you work with on an image are labeled. The controls in the left column apply changes to an entire image, whereas the buttons on the right are used to apply changes only to an area you define with a drawing tool cursor. As you can see, these functions are similar to Photoshop's Free Transform, but they can be applied to an isolated, user-defined area of the image, achieving an effect that resembles working with a finger painting that's wet.

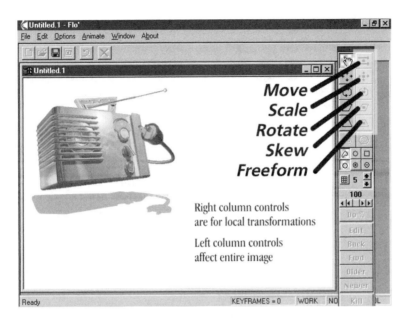

FIGURE 20.8 *Flo's right column controls offer different distortions you apply to a defined area, and a defined maximum extent of the effect within the image.*

Although this book stresses that a good design begins with a concept, the only concept the author can offer here is to create a twisting, bloating boombox with dimensions that are a result of the music it's playing. Silly? Yes, but this gives you a place to start twisting the image and creating keyframes.

2. Click the Scale tool in the right column, and then draw a circle around the speaker. A circle appears when you approach the beginning point of the path you drew. (This circle is similar to the miniature circle that appears when you're using Photoshop's Pen tool cursor to close a path at the beginning point.)

If you're not into freeform drawing, you can also choose circle and square modes for defining the area to be scaled, as shown in Figure 20.9.

After the path has been closed, a number of interface elements appear around the path. *Don't touch any element yet.* Wait until you understand what they do. In Figure 20.10 you can see callouts for a rotation handle—using this handle, you can rotate the bounding box for the Scale distortion before you scale the area. Also, if you click the outer path, nodes appear and you can reshape the extent of the Scale effect. This means that you can confine the scaling of the boombox speaker to a limited area within the image. The "X" is the center point of the Scale distortion effect; if you move it, the effect will occur relative to the new center location.

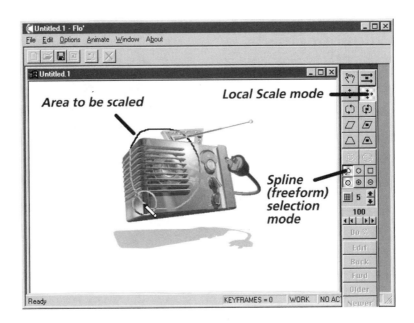

FIGURE 20.9 *Draw a path around the area you want to change in the image.*

3. Drag on any of the bounding box handles, away from the center (see Figure 20.10). Then release the cursor to apply the Scale Distortion effect.

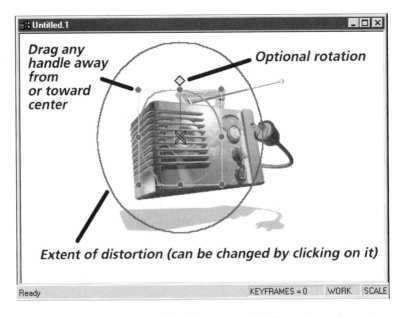

FIGURE 20.10 *Flo' offers many options for enhancing a simple effect, such as scaling an image area.*

4. Try out the Move tool by drawing a path around the top half of the boombox, and then dragging the center point slightly downward. After that, double-click Back to bring the image back to its unedited state.

5. Click the Rotate tool, draw a circle around the power cord, drag the center point to the center of the boombox, and then drag the Rotate cursor's arrowhead slightly to the left. This makes the power cord appear to wiggle in the finished animation.

6. You can click Back, Fwd, Older, and Newer to see a distortion you have made. If you think you can improve upon it, click the Edit button; the path and the extent of distortion path appear, and you can modify any of the settings you have made in the image.

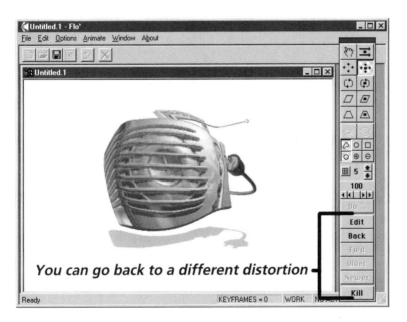

FIGURE 20.11 *Options to go back, remove, or move forward in a number of different distortions are available at the bottom of the toolbox.*

7. When you have made about six distortions (experiment with all the tools—there's no "right" way to complete this assignment), it's time to make the boombox into a sequential number of still frames. Find the frame at which you want the animation to begin—click on the Older, Newer, Back, or Fwd buttons—and then choose Animate, Start Keyframe, as in Figure 20.12.

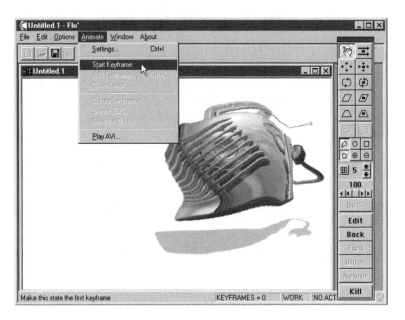

FIGURE 20.12 *The Start Keyframe command defines the first frame in an animation sequence.*

NOTE

In Figure 20.11 you can see the effect of scaling the path you drew around the boombox speaker. Do not be concerned about pixelation—the coarseness of the display in the image window. Flo' works in preview mode, and only when you choose to render to still image or animation does Flo' precisely calculate and interpolate pixels to create smooth distortions.

Notice also in Figure 20.11 that the bottom toolbox buttons are turned on. You have many options for going back to a previous distortion or removing a distortion by clicking these buttons. This is the way keyframes for the animation are defined; by "collecting" different poses and then specifying them as individual keyframes.

8. Click Back, Newer, or whichever distortion keyframe you think should be next, and then choose Animate, Add Keyframe. The dialog box that appears is slightly different in Windows than it is on the Macintosh, but essentially, you use it to determine the number of frames that should go between the first keyframe and the present one. Place the Frame Difference setting at 7 frames, and then click OK to return to the workspace.

9. Repeat step 8 five times, to create 35 frames of animation. Close the animation with the first keyframe, so that the animation will loop. Both Macintosh and Windows video players have a looping option for continuous playback of short segments of animation like this.

10. Click the Fwd and Back controls on the toolbox until you arrive at the first keyframe. Then choose Animate, Close Loop. In the dialog box, choose 7 as the Frame difference, and click OK. Your animation is now 42 frames in length.

11. Choose Options, Create Alpha Channel, as shown in Figure 20.13. If you forget to do this, the still frames will not contain selection information that Photoshop needs.

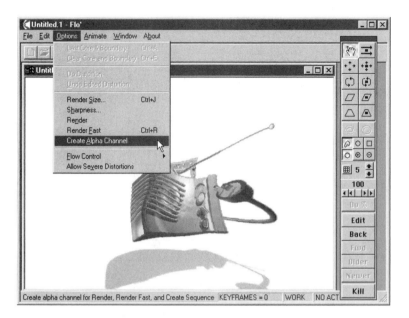

FIGURE 20.13 *Flo' will write animations or still frames with or without an alpha channel. Definitely choose Options, Create Alpha Channel!*

12. Choose Animate, Create Sequence (Macintosh: Animate, Create Numbered PICTS).

13. The Save Sequence dialog box appears, and by default you're presented with a default name, followed by five zeros. If you're using a commercial copy of Flo', in Windows, type **Aqu00000.tga** in the File name box, and choose TGA 32 in the Save as Type drop-down list, as shown in Figure 20.14. On the Macintosh, you don't need a file extension, but you do need to start a sequence from frame zero by having five zeros after the file's distinguishing name. Flo' will automatically increase the file number by 1 as it writes the in-between frames of the animation. Choose the folder to which Flo' should write the still frames, and then click Save.

14. In the Render Size dialog box, click OK to accept the default of 100% rendering size of the original boombox image. You can specify different percentages (size of the frames) for your own work, but this has already been worked out in this example, so the still frames will correspond to the Aquaback.tif image dimensions.

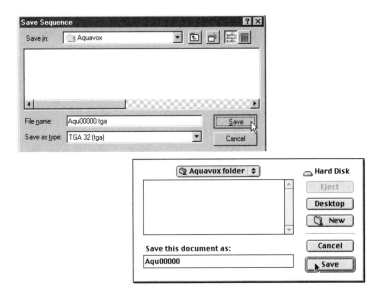

FIGURE 20.14 *Use three distinguishing characters, followed by five zeros, to begin the sequence of files that Flo' writes.*

It's get-up-and-stretch time as Flo' writes the animation stills. Actually, Flo' is one of the fastest animation generators in its category—42 frames took less than four minutes to generate on the author's Pentium 166. The image window will display some strange stuff as it writes the files.

15. Flo' renders 50 percent black in empty areas of the frame; this color is discarded in Photoshop after you load the saved alpha selection and move the image to a new layer. When the image in the document window loses this 50 percent black frame, the animation is complete. Save the resource file (as MYFILE.FLO, or something more creative), and then close Flo'.

Now it's time to create a new batch file, using the Actions list in Photoshop.

ADDING A BACKGROUND, WITH A TWIST

First, you'll load the boombox and the semitransparent shadow by loading the alpha channel within each frame; there's an alpha channel in every saved image from Flo'. Second, you will fill the background layer with the Aquaback scene after the boombox has been cut to a new layer.

There is only one caution in the following steps. Windows users will save the edited files to BMP format, and Adobe's implementation of the BMP Export filter doesn't support alpha channels. Therefore, the alpha channel will have to be discarded as part of the Actions script. Macintosh PICT files can be either 16-bit or 32-bit (24-bit with an 8-bit alpha channel), however, and Macintosh users *must* take one extra step to ensure that the saved, edited stills can be compiled, using MooVer: you need to specify that the edited files are in 16-bit color mode. MooVer will refuse to load a PICT image that contains an alpha channel.

If you didn't create the files in Flo', use the Aquavox folder images you copied earlier to your hard disk for the following steps; also create an "Aqua-finished" folder on your hard disk for the edited files.

The following steps take you through the script writing in Photoshop, and then it's off to the movie-compiling phase:

PROGRAMMING THE ACTIONS PALETTE FOR ALPHA CHANNEL EDITING

1. In Photoshop, press F9 to display the Actions palette.

2. Open the Aquaback.tif image from the Examples/CHAP20 folder on the Companion CD; press Ctrl(⌘)+A to select all, and then choose Edit, Define Pattern. Close the file now.

3. Open any one of the boombox files from the Aquavox folder.

4. On the Actions palette, choose New Action from the flyout menu. In the New Action dialog box, type **Taking boombox outdoors**, and then click Record.

5. On the Channels palette, press Ctrl(⌘) and click the Alpha 1 channel to load the visual information as a marquee selection, as shown in Figure 20.15.

6. With a selection tool currently chosen (the Lasso tool is fine), right-click (Macin-tosh: hold Ctrl and click) inside the marquee selection, and then choose Layer Via Cut from the context menu.

7. On the Layers palette, click the Background layer title, and then choose Edit, Fill, Pattern from the menu. Next—and this is *very* important—choose Pattern from the Use field, set the Opacity to 100%, and choose Normal from the Mode drop-down list.

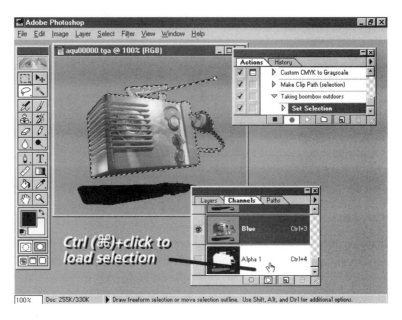

FIGURE 20.15 *Press Ctrl(⌘) and click to load a selection that Flo' created in the Targa or PICT image.*

Make sure that you do not skip the last part of step 7; if you do, you will mess up the Actions list programming. Photoshop retains previous settings in some dialog boxes, and you might have altered these settings during independent experimentation!

8. Click OK; the background plops behind the boombox, and the shadow looks convincing on the Aquaback scene. Choose Flatten Image from the Layers palette's menu flyout, as shown in Figure 20.16. Trash the Alpha 1 channel at this point.

9. Press Ctrl(⌘)+Shift+S (File, Save As); then...

   Windows users: Choose the Aqua-finished folder as the destination for the file, and choose BMP in the Save As drop-down list. The File sequence number is preserved; only the format and extension have changed.

   Macintosh users: Choose the Aqua-finished folder from your hard disk, and then click Save. Make sure to choose 16-bits/pixel in the PICT options box, and then click OK.

10. *Everyone:* Press Ctrl(⌘)+W to close the file, and then click the Stop button on the Actions palette.

FIGURE 20.16 *Photoshop will not allow you to save an image in PICT or BMP format unless it consists of only a single layer.*

LAUNCHING THE ACTIONS LIST BATCH EDITING

You have only a few more decisions to make—telling the Actions palette where to find the files and where to put the copies after they have been edited. Watching Photoshop run a batch edit is about as interesting as watching grass grow! After you see that one or two files have been successfully processed, you might want to organize the top drawer of your desk—the one with the ketchup packets, three pennies, and a broken ballpoint pen—while you wait.

Here's how to get Photoshop to edit all the frames in the animation exactly the way you did earlier:

RUNNING PHOTOSHOP IN BATCH MODE

1. Choose File, Automate, and then choose Batch. Make sure that "Taking boombox outdoors" is the current selection in the Action drop-down list. (Photoshop ships with several preset Actions.)

NOTE

In General Preferences in Photoshop, Beep When Done is an especially useful feature. When Photoshop has processed all the images, the "Adding Background" action is completed, the palette's Play button changes to stop, and with a system sound enabled, you can tell from the hallway that your work is finished.

2. Click the Choose button below the Source field, and then choose the Aquavox folder from your hard disk. Click OK (Select) to return to the dialog box.

3. Click the Choose button below the Destination field. In the directory window, choose the Aqua-finished folder you created earlier. Note that the Override Action check box should only be checked if, during the programming of the "Taking boombox outdoors" script, you saved the image to a folder *other* than "Aqua-finished." If you saved AQU00000 to the Aqua-finished folder, do *not* check this box. Your Batch dialog box should resemble Figure 20.17 now.

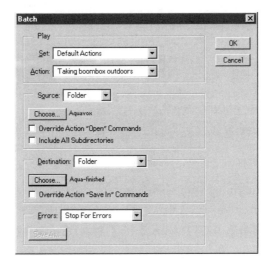

FIGURE 20.17 *Make certain that the action, the source, and the destination files are correct before you click on OK.*

4. Click OK and wait a while. You probably will not see an image rendered to an image window as Photoshop processes all the images—the commands happen far more quickly than can be redrawn to screen unless you have a powerful video card.

5. When the last file has been auto-edited, close Photoshop.

You can delete the Aquavox folder from your hard disk now, unless you have a cheaper media source on which to store it. The edited files are now in the Aqua-finished folder.

Ready for Phase Three of the Animation Pipeline? In the following section, you will use the animation compilers on the Companion CD to create your own "flicks," as we say in the "biz"...

WORKING WITH COMPRESSION, TIMING, AND FILE SORTING

Codec is the trade name for a file *co*mpressor and *dec*ompressor. Intel offers Indeo, and Microsoft and Apple have their own native compression and decompression options. However, Cinepak compression is used in the following sections because, of all the file codecs available at the time of this writing, only Cinepak is cross-platform compatible. To be able to play a QuickTime movie in Windows, and faithfully transfer a Video for Windows animation to QuickTime format with no data loss, you must use a cross-platform compression scheme.

Although *Inside Adobe Photoshop 5* is not intended as a definitive resource guide for digital animation, you should be aware of one or two more things when you use the compilers in future steps.

First, *fps* (frames per second) is completely relative when animations are shown on a computer or on the web. The length and speed of an animation depend entirely on the host machine's processing speed. The author frequently times animations at a slower rate than the standard 30 frames per second of videotape, because playback on older machines with slower processors does something called "frame dropping," when the transfer of data from an animation that is being uncompressed and played outstrips the capability of the processor to handle the data. Frame dropping makes a movie look like a Max Headroom commercial—stutters, sudden leaps from one position to another, and other unprofessional anomalies happen when you specify "real time," 30 fps for animations to be played on a personal com-puter.

Finally (and this is probably obvious), it is absolutely necessary that you sequence the files into the compiler in the order in which they were written. That's why Poser, Extreme 3D, Flo', and other animation packages add four or five digits to file names—so that you and the compiler can locate them later, and so that the Aquavox boombox looks smooth in its transitions.

This chapter's first excursion into compilers begins with a discussion of how to use MainActor for Windows to compile the Aquavox stills, followed by a discussion of MooVer for the Macintosh. Although these steps use the Aquavox sequential images, you can easily repeat the process on your own, using your own sequential image files.

MAINACTOR: PUSH-BUTTON VIDEO COMPILING

Before you do anything else, install MainActor, version 1.61, from the Companion CD to your hard disk. The installation goes quickly, and after setup, Windows 95 and Windows NT users will find a MainActor entry on the Start menu. One of the significant differences between the unregistered and the registered versions is a persistent "nag box" with a timer that frequently appears in the shareware version. This means that you will need to pay attention to the compiling process; you shouldn't duck out for a soda while MainActor is compiling.

Also, for MainActor to work, DirectX must be installed on your system. DirectX is the software portion of a software/hardware acceleration scheme that works with practically every video card manufactured in the past two years. If you have the release of Windows 95 that came preinstalled on a machine, if an application such as Extreme 3D installed it, if your video card came with DirectX software, if you upgraded Windows 95 with Maintenance Release 2, or if you're running Windows NT 4, you can run MainActor right after setup. If you don't have DirectX, you can download it from http://www.microsoft.com.

If you have both DirectX and MainActor installed, follow these steps to compile the Aquavox stills:

USING MAINACTOR TO COMPILE WINDOWS AVI FILES

1. Launch MainActor, and then click OK after the countdown "nag box" has timed out.

2. Click the File/Open icon on the toolbox to display the Multi-Select Project(s) dialog box.

3. Locate the Aqua-finished folder on your hard disk. Click the first file in the folder window, press Ctrl+A to select all the files, as shown in Figure 20.18, and then click Open.

4. After the frames have been loaded, choose Edit, Select All from the menu, right-click in the frames window, and then choose Local Timecodes. Notice that, by default, frames are measured in thousandths of a second, each frame displayed for 1000 ms; in other words, each frame is displayed for one second. The animation would be 42 seconds long—a *litttttttle* too long!

5. In the Local Timecode dialog box, shown in Figure 20.19, type **33**, and then click Accept. At 33/1000 of a second per frame, the compiled movie's frame rate is about 30 fps. The number 33 was arrived at by trial and error, using

MainActor, but it's a number you might want to use with this program if your playback is always to a personal computer's monitor.

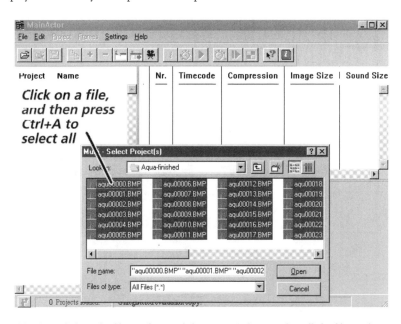

FIGURE 20.18   *Click in the file window, and then press Ctrl+A to select all the files in the Aquavox animation.*

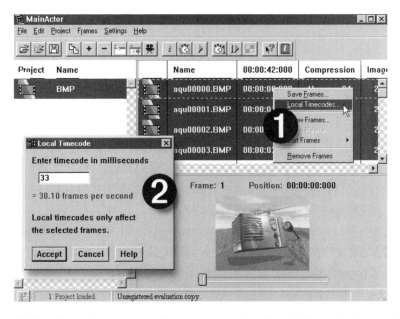

FIGURE 20.19   *The local timecode should be set anywhere from 25 to 75 thousands of a second for accurate, pleasing playback on today's machines.*

6. Click the Save button (the disk icon highlighted in Figure 20.20); another timer appears in the unregistered version of MainActor, and then the Save Window dialog box appears. Choose Millions of Colors: Cinepak, choose AVI as the Module (you could also choose QuickTime from the drop-down list), and then click Save.

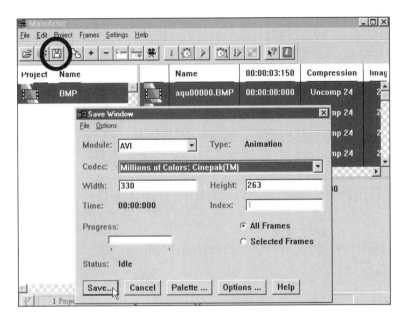

FIGURE 20.20 *Choose Cinepak compression for cross-platform compression compatibility.*

7. The Select File dialog box appears; this is where you name the file and choose a location on hard disk for the compiled movie. Call it **Aquavox.avi**, and then click Save.

8. Keep an eye on the Progress status line; at every tenth frame, the nag screen and timer prompt you to continue. When the Progress line has completed, you can close the application.

MainActor has options that this exercise did not cover; most of the defaults work fine for producing a movie.

MooVer for Macintosh QuickTime Compiling

After you install MooVer version 1.42 from the Companion CD, a folder appears on the Desktop; this folder contains the MooVer icon, documentation, a registration form, and example files. MooVer is a drag-and-drop animation compiler; you begin by dropping a single file on the MooVer icon, and then you are prompted through a series of dialog boxes for the length, color mode, and type of codec you want to use.

Here's how to use MooVer to make animations from the edited still frames:

MooVing to QuickTime

1. The still, edited frames for the boombox should be in a folder named "Aqua-finished." Open the folder, and then choose View, as List, and then Arrange, by Name from the Apple menu under System 8. This makes it easier to locate the files in sequence for dragging and dropping. Maximize the Finished folder window, being sure to leave enough room so that you can clearly see the MooVer folder window.

2. Drag AQU00000.pct on top of the MooVer program icon, as shown in Figure 20.21. This action displays MooVer's registration box. For the moment, type your name in the Your Name field, and click on Don't Register Yet. You can register *after* you have worked through this chapter.

NOTE

By the way, please don't take the popular slang "nag box" as a negative term relating to the quality of MainActor or similar programs. In fact, MainActor has the least annoying "reminder" of all the shareware compilers we found on the web. MainActor has many features you will want to try out, and if a larger commercial video editor simply isn't in your budget, MainActor is a solution that costs less than $75 (U.S.).

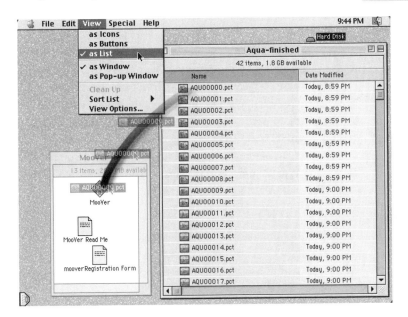

FIGURE 20.21   *Dragging a PICT file (that has no alpha channel) onto the MooVer icon begins the process of compiling a movie.*

TIP

If you choose QuickTime as the Module in the MainActor Save Window dialog box, you can then move the animation to the Macintosh, and use ResEdit (a widely distributed freeware file typer) to add a resource fork to the file, and add the correct Type and Creator data. The File Type is MooV, and the Creator type is TVOD. In the names of these types, capitalization is essential, or the movie will not play on the Macintosh.

3. You will now see the MooVer Settings dialog box, shown in Figure 20.22. Click the millions of colors button if this is not the default option, and then click the Compression Settings button. This is an important area of MooVer's configuration, and will impact the overall quality of your movie.

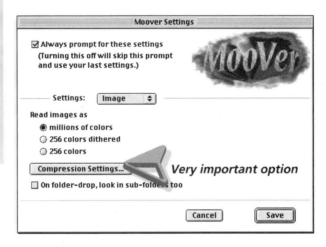

FIGURE 20.22 *Click the Compression Settings button to access transfer rate, compression type, and quality.*

TIP

Again, the author recommends using Cinepak for compression; Apple distributes QuickTime players for Windows free of charge, and unless Cinepak is used, Windows users cannot watch your movie.

4. In the Compression Settings box, choose Cinepak as the compressor, drag the quality slider to about 75–80 (75 percent compression is the default in MainActor). In the Motion field, choose 30 Frames per second from the pull-down list, and clear the Key frame every check box; you might want to limit the data transfer rate to 90 K/Second, if you intend to play your films on 68K machines. Older Macintoshes would drop frames in QuickTime movies if the amount of data decompressed and sent to the processor was greater than 90 K/second. Check out Figure 20.23 for the recommended settings in this dialog box.

5. Click OK to move to the directory box (the #2 box in Figure 20.23). Choose a name for the movie and a location on hard disk, and then click Save.

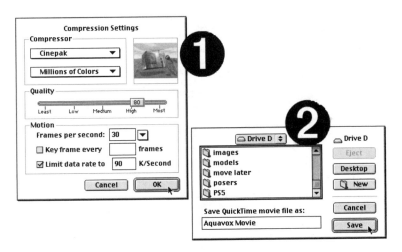

FIGURE 20.23 *Choose your compression settings, and then save the movie to hard disk.*

6. You're not finished yet! You currently have a one-frame movie. You can now marquee select the remaining files in the Aqua-finished folder window (it is recommended that you select 15 or so at a time, but not all of them at once), and drop them on the MooVer program icon, as shown in Figure 20.24. The Aquavox Movie window you see is MooVer's preview window; as you drop files on the program icon, you will see the animation progress. But this is *not* the finished movie you're viewing, nor should you try to drag a file into the preview window.

NOTE

Today's Pentiums and PPC computers with processing speeds in excess of 133 mHz can take 150 K/second easily, and this is the default value in MainActor.

7. Press ⌘+Q to quit MooVer—and seriously contemplate registering it. You now have a QuickTime movie, wherever you specified that it should be written, that you can play by double-clicking on its icon.

In Figure 20.25 you can see the Aquavox movie being played.

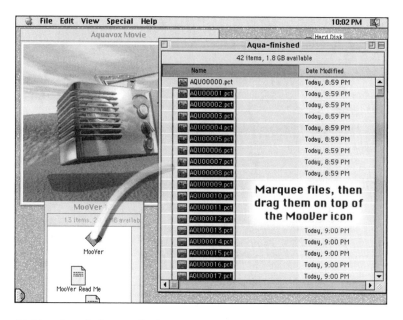

FIGURE 20.24 *Compile the movie by dropping sequentially numbered files, in order, onto the MooVer program icon.*

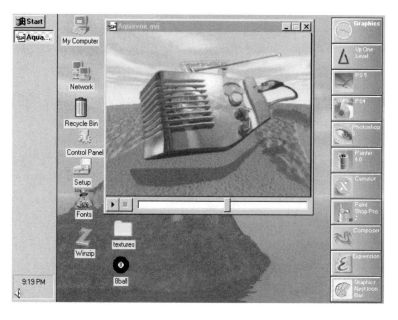

FIGURE 20.25 *The Actions palette is limited only by your own ingenuity. Use it to edit movie frames, resize web graphics, and more.*

SUMMARY

Although this is a chapter on animation, it's also a chapter on the pivotal role Photoshop plays in integrating graphics from different sources. There is hardly an assignment you could find that would not benefit in one way or another from Photoshop's tools. The Actions palette is versatile, easy to use, and when it comes to "home brew" animation, it's absolutely indispensable for taking the manual drudgery out of repetitive tasks.

In Chapter 21, we move from animation to still photography, where depth of field is examined. Suppose you used a physical camera to capture the "middle ground" of a scene. The background and foreground would be out of focus, because you used a medium aperture such as f8. Now, what if you're combining different photographs—all whose focus is perfect? How do you change the depth of field in such a composition? It's easy; your skills will make the main subject of the scene the star attraction, and the answers are awaiting you in the following chapter.

TIP

To share a QuickTime movie with a Windows user, choose the Output option on the Settings pull-down menu in the MooVer Settings dialog box, and check the Cross-Platform compatible (flattened) check box. Then compile the animation.

ADVANCED PHOTOSHOP TECHNIQUES

CHAPTER 21

SIMULATING DEPTH OF FIELD IN AN IMAGE

A lot of this book stresses the importance of creating conditions within an image, composed of many images, that will bring the composition closer to photorealism. We've gone into detail about getting shadows right, color correcting between different images to make them appear consistent when they're combined, and other optical phenomena that can make or break a retouched image. What we haven't discussed yet is an optical control on a camera called the aperture. If you're familiar with a camera, you know that specifying a low f-stop—a narrow depth of field—helps to isolate the star in the "middle ground" of an image: The foreground and background are thrown out of focus.

SOURCE IMAGES FOR A COMPOSITION ARE USUALLY TOO "PERFECT"

Unless you're intentionally capturing images that are out of focus in hopes of creating a special effect, you'll probably want your pictures focused. For single images, this is great, but it causes a problem when you go to composite them. The composition looks phony because the background, the midground, and the foreground are all in perfect focus. The images that convey the most intimate feeling are those that feature a narrow depth of field; only the subject is in perfect focus. The situation where a photographer needs f/22 (the highest depth of field on camera lenses) is when it is critical to have a large distance in focus. For example, the large rock that is six feet in front of the camera, the house that is 20 feet farther away, and the mountain in the background will all be in sharp focus with an f-stop of 22. Typically, though, when you want to take a *portrait*, and the lighting in the scene is moderate, some elements in the image should be out of focus. The eye is drawn to areas in a photograph that are in focus, and the subject matter of, let's say a person's face, is far more important that the surrounding elements. You need to open the aperture of the lens (decrease the f-stop number), and then all the elements in the scene *cannot* fall into perfect focus within the camera's imaging plane (and onto the film).

This chapter shows you how to take perfectly focused images and combine them in a way that strongly suggests the composite image was taken with a camera and a single frame of film. You'll see first how a synthetic, modeled image can be made to look more photorealistic, and then we'll move on to how photographic images can be blended, using slightly different techniques.

SETTING UP A COMPUTER-GENERATED IMAGE FOR DEPTH OF FIELD WORK

As discussed several times in this book, one of the advantages of modeling a scene instead of photographing it is that you usually can save an alpha channel, which describes the silhouette or any part of the scene. By specifying that an alpha channel is written to the rendered file, you can easily load the alpha channel as a selection marquee in Photoshop and then move the central object of interest in the scene to its own layer. Kitchen.tif is such an image; you'll work with it in the following sections. The small chrome fellow sitting on the countertop in a kitchen has a corresponding alpha channel, so you can separate him (it) from the rest of the scene.

In the steps that follow, you'll load the image, load the alpha channel selection, and then separate the star of the image from the background so that you can deal with the background as a separate element in the composition:

COPYING THE FOREGROUND ELEMENT TO A NEW LAYER

1. Open the Kitchen.tif image from the Chap21 folder on the Companion CD.

2. Zoom to about 50% viewing resolution of the image.

3. On the Channels palette (press F7 if it's not already onscreen), Ctrl(⌘)+click on the Alpha 1 title, as shown in Figure 21.1, to load the Alpha 1 channel's contents as a marquee selection.

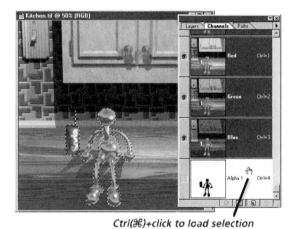

Ctrl(⌘)+click to load selection

FIGURE 21.1 *Load the Alpha 1 channel as a marquee selection that defines the tiny chrome guy and his soda can.*

4. Click on the Layers tab on the palette, and then with any tool selected, right-click (Macintosh: hold Ctrl and click) over the Background layer title on the Layers palette, and choose Layer Via Copy from the context menu, as shown in Figure 21.2.

5. Press Ctrl(⌘)+Shift+S (File, Save As), and save the work to your hard disk as Kitchen.psd in Photoshop's native file format. Keep the image open.

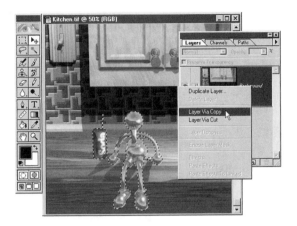

FIGURE 21.2 *Although only selection tools can be used to display the Layer Via Copy command when you right-click (Macintosh: hold Ctrl and click) over an image, any tool can be the current tool to display this command when you click on an image layer title on the Layers palette.*

Shortly, you'll apply blurring to the background of the image, but there's a problem with doing this, as the Background layer currently appears. When you use any of Photoshop's blurring commands (particularly the Gaussian Blur), image areas shift, as pixels are reassigned different colors. If the little chrome fellow weren't featured on the Background layer, applying a blur would not be a problem. He *is* on the background, however, and if you blur the background, some of the chrome guy's edge pixels will migrate outward within the image. The final composition, then, would feature the chrome guy on Layer 1 in perfect focus, with a fringe of blurred pixels from the Background layer surrounding him. The solution? Read on!

CLONING OVER IMAGE AREAS THAT WILL BE BLURRED

Part of the technique to making a convincing "middle ground" focus in this image is to apply different amounts of blurring to the background. Why? Because the countertop that the chrome guy rests on travels from the background to the front of the image. This means that there should be a gradual transition between out-of-focus areas and focused areas in the image. To accomplish this, you'll use Quick Mask mode and the Linear Gradient tool to create a selection that fades as it appears to reach the front of the countertop.

First, using samples of the wood countertop, you need to clone over part of the chrome guy on the Background layer. Then, having done this, when you apply a blur to selected areas of the image, only the wood toward the background (toward the top of the chrome guy's head) will become blurred.

Here's how to clone away unwanted areas of the chrome guy on the Background layer, and how to apply a blur defined in the image as a linear gradient created in Quick Mask mode:

REMOVING UNWANTED IMAGE AREAS AND SELECTIVE BLURRING

1. Double-click on the Zoom tool to move your view of Kitchen.psd to 100% (1:1) resolution. Maximize the window, and then scroll the window so that the chrome guy is in the center of the image. Click on the Background layer to make it the current editing layer, and click on Layer 1's eye icon on the Layers palette to hide this layer.

2. Double-click on the Rubber Stamp tool to select it and to display the Options palette. Make sure that the mode on the Options palette is Normal, cloning is Aligned, and the Opacity is 100%. On the Brushes palette (press F5 if the palette's not currently onscreen), choose the third-from-left, second row tip.

3. You might want to use the Precise cursors for the following steps (although the screen figures show the standard cursors, for clarity's sake); press Caps Lock to switch to Precise cursors. Alt(Opt)+click on the edge of the "splash" (the white trim) where it meets the wooden countertop to set the sampling point.

4. Drag the cursor, beginning to the left of the sample point, starting on the edge of the splash, and then working downward to clone over the chrome guy's head, while keeping the white edge aligned with the original area to the right of the Rubber Stamp tool. See Figure 21.3.

5. Alt(Opt)+click on an area where the wood meets the white trim to the left of your original sample point, and then click on the edge to the left of the sample point; then clone some more of the chrome guy out of the picture, along with the soda can. When all you can see on the countertop are the chrome guy's hands and the "S" on the soda can, you've cloned enough of the Background to prepare it for blurring. In other words, stop now<g>!

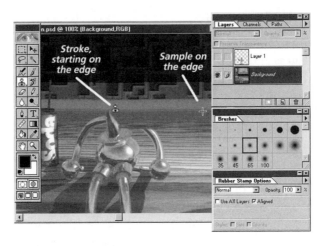

FIGURE 21.3 *Before you clone over the chrome guy's head, take a sample point at the edge of the wood, and then begin stroking to the left, at the edge of the wood, to ensure the continuity of the background in the image.*

6. Double-click on the Quick Mask Mode button toward the bottom of the toolbox, and in the Quick Mask Options dialog box, choose Color Indicates: Selected Areas if this is not the current option. Click on OK to close the box. The image is in Quick Mask mode right now.

7. Drag on the face of the gradient icon if the Linear style is not the "top" icon, and then choose it from the flyout. Double-click on the Linear Gradient tool to choose it and to display the Options palette.

8. On the Linear Gradient Options palette, choose Foreground to Background as the Gradient type; mode should be Normal, and Opacity should be 100% on the palette.

9. Hold Shift (to constrain the tool to 45-degree increments) and then drag from the point shown in Figure 21.4, releasing the cursor at the endpoint shown in Figure 21.4. What you're doing is putting the entire background in Quick Mask, while making the transition from masked to "unmasked" on the top face of the countertop.

10. Click on the Standard Editing Mode icon (to the left of the Quick Mask icon). A selection marquee appears; it does not really describe the selected and masked areas because there is a selection transition between the foreground and background. You can choose to press Ctrl(⌘)+H to hide the marquee if you like; the selection will still exist, but the dotted marquee lines won't distract you.

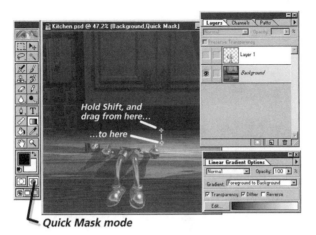

FIGURE 21.4   *Make the transition between selected areas and unselected areas by creating a steep gradient fill while the image is in Quick Mask mode.*

11. Choose Filter, Blur, and then choose Gaussian Blur. Drag the slider so that the pixels field reads about 5.4, as shown in Figure 21.5. As you can see in the image window (if you have the Preview button checked), the Gaussian Blur will blur the background but the image sharpens from back to front of the countertop. Click on OK to apply the Gaussian Blur filter. Press Ctrl(⌘)+D to deselect the marquee.

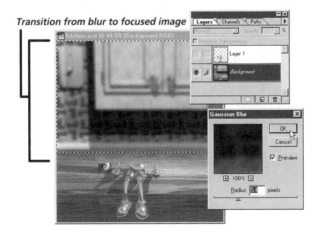

FIGURE 21.5   *Apply the Gaussian Blur filter to the selection you created while the image was in Quick Mask mode.*

12. Click on the eye icon space to the left of the Layer 1 title on the Layers palette to restore the visibility of the chrome guy on Layer 1, as shown in Figure 21.6.

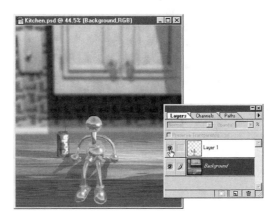

FIGURE 21.6 *The copy you made of the chrome character is in perfect focus, while the background of the image trails from focused to unfocused as the viewer looks from the front to the back of the scene.*

13. Press Ctrl(⌘)+S; keep the file open.

The amount of blurring you apply to a selection, such as the one you created in the previous example, depends entirely on the size of the overall image. A value of 5.4 for the Gaussian Blur filter is fine for the Kitchen image, which was originally 2MB if you don't count the Alpha 1 channel. For larger images, you will want to apply more blurring.

NOTE

You're finished with the Alpha 1 channel in the Kitchen.psd image, and can drag its title into the Channels palette's trash icon at any time now to conserve the system resources Photoshop uses for holding and displaying the whole image.

Now, the image of the chrome guy perched on the countertop is a fine example of a selection made by applying a gradient fill while an image is in Quick Mask mode. But from an artistic standpoint, we can push this image a little closer to photoreality by making the scene a little more complex. Many times in this book we stress that the real world is a visually complex place, and the more complexity you can add to an image (without causing needless clutter, of course) the better your work will mimic the real world.

In the next section you'll hang some pots and pans in the foreground of the image so that the audience looks "through" the kitchen utensils to see the small chrome guy.

ADDING A FOREGROUND TO THE IMAGE

When you add foreground elements to an image, they become the main attraction in the image. But you don't *want* any foreground elements to overshadow the chrome guy in the image. So the chrome guy should retain his perfect focus, and the foreground elements you add should be out of focus. The chrome guy then becomes the "middle ground" focus of attention in the composition. The audience will be peering *through* the foreground elements to see the chrome fellow.

Fortunately, we have some synthetic pots and pans on the Companion CD to help you finish the scene. Here's how to add the foreground elements and make them interact with the chrome guy:

ADDING ANOTHER PLANE OF IMAGE DETAIL TO THE COMPOSITION

1. On the Layers palette, click on the Layer 1 title to make it the current editing layer. Reduce the viewing resolution of the Kitchen.psd image to about 25%, and then open the Potspans.psd image from the Examples\Chap21 folder on the Companion CD. The pots and pans image should also be at about 25% viewing resolution, so you can see both images and the Layers palette onscreen.

2. Click on the title bar of the Potspans.psd image to make it the foreground window in Photoshop's workspace.

3. On the Layers palette, drag the Pots and Pans layer title into the Kitchen.psd image, as shown in Figure 21.7. The Kitchen.psd image now has a new layer on top of the layer that was the most current a moment ago—Layer 1.

4. Press Ctrl(⌘)+F to apply the last-used filter, the Gaussian blur filter. The pots and pans all become blurred to the same extent because you did not use Quick Mask or the Linear Gradient tool to selectively blur the utensils. And this is correct, because pots and pans hanging on a rack have a narrow depth—there should be no particular pot or pan that is in focus.

5. With the Move tool, drag on the Pots and Pans layer until one of the pots slightly overlaps part of the chrome guy's head, as shown in Figure 21.8. Unless you allow part of the blurry foreground to encroach on part of the focused middle ground in the image, there is no interaction and no visual clue that the pots and pans are in front of the chrome guy. Without this interaction, the audience could presume that the pots and pans are in the background of the image.

FIGURE 21.7 *Drag the Layer title from the Potspans.psd image into the Kitchen.psd image window to add the pots and pans to a new layer.*

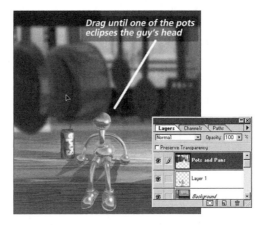

FIGURE 21.8 *Drag, using the Move tool, to position the foreground elements so they interact with the Layer 1 contents.*

6. You're finished. Press Ctrl(⌘)+S. You might want to save a flattened copy of your work to hard disk to show around to folks. To do this, choose File, Save a Copy. Then choose TIFF, BMP, or PICT from the Save As (Macintosh: the Format) drop-down list, check the Exclude Alpha channels check box (in case you still have alpha 1 tucked away in the image), check the Flatten Image check box if it's not already checked for you by Photoshop, name the file, choose a directory for the file, and then click on Save.

The preceding example was not difficult stuff, for a very obvious reason. You were working with computer-generated graphics, and the degree of reality you could add to the composition was a little limited. What do you say to applying some of the same techniques to *photographic* images in the sections to follow, so that you can see how invisibly you can blend multiple elements?

CREATING DEPTH OF FIELD IN A PHOTOGRAPH

The photographic images you'll use in the following sections were carefully selected for their matching lighting and color balance. So those are two aspects of the composition you do not need to worry about. Additionally, the hero of the composition—a fellow dressed in a knit top—has already been separated from his original background, and the image window is identical in dimensions to the background, so you can use a shortcut in Photoshop to add him to the background image.

By the way, the fellow you'll use in this composition was masked, using Extensis Mask Pro, a wonderful Photoshop plug-in that is covered in Chapter 25, "The Author's Favorite Third-Party Plug-Ins." Mask Pro made trimming around the fellow's hair a quick and simple task.

NOTE

You will get unexpected results if you use the Duplicate Layer command in Photoshop when the host image and the target image are not of identical dimensions. The target image will usually "land" in the *center* of the host image.

Here's the plot: You're going to add the Tudor guy to a background image of the Tudor house, and then add some branches of leaves to the foreground to make the Tudor guy the middle ground focus of the composition.

USING THE DUPLICATE LAYER COMMAND AND THE QUICK MASK FEATURE

Because the Tudor.tif image features a house way in the background and some shrubs and a car toward the front end of the driveway in the image, you'll use the Quick Mask tool to make a transitional selection. When the selection is blurred, the shrub and the tail end of the car will be in a little more focus than the house in the distance.

Here's how to add the Tudor guy to the house image, and use the Quick Mask tool and the Linear Gradient tool to integrate him with the background:

PUTTING A PERSON IN FRONT OF A HOUSE...WHILE CREATING A DEPTH OF FIELD

1. Open the Tudor.tif image from the Examples\Chap21 folder on the Com-panion CD. Press Ctrl(⌘)+the minus key a few times until the viewing resolution of the image is about 16.7%.

2. Open the Tudorguy.psd image from the Examples\Chap21 folder on the Companion CD, and decrease the viewing resolution of the image by pressing Ctrl(⌘)+the minus key. You should have a clear view of both images, and Tudorguy.psd should be the current foreground image in Photoshop's workspace. Some window background—about ⅛ screen inches is fine—should be visible around the Tudor.tif image.

3. On the Layers palette, click on the menu flyout button, and choose Duplicate Layer. In the Duplicate Layer dialog box, choose Tudor.tif from the Document Destination drop-down list, as shown in Figure 21.9.

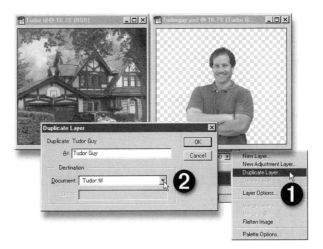

FIGURE 21.9   *Choose to duplicate the Tudor Guy layer in the Tudorguy.psd image to the Tudor.tif image.*

4. Save the Tudor.tif image as Tudor.psd, in Photoshop's native file format, to your hard disk. You can close Tudorguy.psd at any time now.

5. Click on the Background layer title on the Layers palette to make it the current editing layer.

6. Click on the Quick Mask icon toward the bottom right of the toolbox; then with the Linear Gradient tool, hold Shift and drag from about the top of the shrubs on the left of the image to the bottom edge of the image, as shown in Figure 21.10. This editing move is the reason you were asked to keep some window background visible in this image. By doing so, you've made every inch of the scene at least partially selected, so that no part of the Background image will be in perfect focus. The car and the shrub will be in what's called "soft focus" in the photography trade.

FIGURE 21.10   *Drag the Linear Gradient tool from the top to bottom indicators in this image to create the mask for blurring the background image.*

7. Click on the Standard Editing icon toward the bottom of the toolbox, and then press Ctrl(⌘)+Alt(Opt)+F to access the last-used filter (the Gaussian Blur) without applying the filter.

8. Drag the slider so that the pixels field reads about 11, as shown in Figure 21.11. The Tudor image is a little more than twice the size of the Kitchen composition, so more blurring is required to achieve the same effect.

9. Click on OK to apply the Gaussian Blur. Press Ctrl(⌘)+D to deselect the marquee, and then press Ctrl(⌘)+S; keep the file open.

Figure 21.11 *When you want to throw a background image out of focus, specify a Gaussian Blur amount that your eyes tell you is sufficient. The larger the file, the greater the amount of blurring required.*

Working with Quick Edit

The following tip doesn't really apply to the composition you're working on, but it does apply to large files in the TIFF format…and okay, the author couldn't find a good place for this tip in other areas of this book<g>!

Although a standard installation of Photoshop 5 will *not* include the Quick Edit Import feature that users have taken advantage of since its introduction in Photoshop 3, you can manually install the filter—it's on the Adobe Photoshop 5 installation CD.

To install Quick Edit, exit Photoshop 5, go to the QuickEdit folder on the Photoshop CD, and then drag the Quick Edit plug-in file (QuickEd.8BP, for Windows users) into the plug-ins folder in Photoshop on your hard disk.

For readers who have never used Quick Edit, here's how it works and what it does:

1. Choose File, Import, and then choose Quick Edit.

2. Choose a file in TIFF or Scitex format file from your hard disk. This filter is particularly useful when you want to open a small section of a huge file.

3. In the Quick Edit dialog box, marquee-select the portion of the image on which you want to work, and then click on OK. The portion of the image opens in Photoshop as a new file.

4. Perform your editing work on the image, and then choose File, Export, Quick Edit Save. The new image document is still in the workspace (and you can close it without saving it), but Photoshop has seamlessly woven the area you worked on into the file that might be too large to open as a whole.

Okay, back to the Tudor assignment. Clearly, you're working with photographic images to create a photorealistic composition. This means that we must consider some of the optics of a camera lens. Unlike the computer (a digital device) used to create the chrome guy, a camera is an analog device, and there are no clear-cut imaging planes to a camera's focus. In simpler terms, objects in the foreground (in focus) will not have sharp edges, because the focal point of a lens makes a gradual (but subtle) transition between in-focus foreground elements and out-of-focus background elements.

Therefore, you need to blur the edges of the Tudor guy ever so slightly, so that he appears to be really a part of the composition and not merely pasted into the picture. The following section guides you through a creative technique for reducing the focus of the edges of the Tudor guy.

Using the Contract Command in Combination with the Blur More Command

To define the inside edge of the Tudor guy by only a pixel or two is an easy task. In the following steps, you'll use Photoshop's Contract command to create a marquee that's two pixels inside the silhouette of the Tudor guy, and as a separate procedure, you'll invert the selection to include only the edge pixels of the Tudor guy. But you must steer a little off-course in the steps to reduce the guy's edge focus because you want a *gradual* transition between the interior of his silhouette and the background of the image. To make this gradual transition, you'll create a Quick Mask of the Tudor guy, and then use the Blur More command to soften the *Quick Mask selection*, and not the Tudor guy himself.

This will make a lot more sense when you run through the steps:

Creating a "Soft" Edge Selection by Blurring a Quick Mask

1. Ctrl(⌘)+click on the Tudor Guy layer title on the Layers palette to load the silhouette of the Tudor guy as a selection marquee. Then click on the Tudor Guy title on the Layers palette to make it the current editing layer.

2. Choose Select, Modify, and then choose Contract.

3. In the Contract Selection dialog box, type **2** in the pixels field and then click on OK, as shown in Figure 21.12. The marquee selection is now inside the silhouette of the Tudor guy.

FIGURE 21.12 *Load the silhouette of the Tudor guy as a marquee, and then make the selection two pixels smaller in diameter by using the Contract Selection command.*

4. Click on the Quick Mask Mode icon on the toolbox. You'll notice a hard-edged mask around the Tudor guy, with some pixels belonging to him lying outside the Quick Mask tinted overlay.

5. Choose Filter, Blur, and then choose Blur More.

6. Press Ctrl(⌘)+F to apply the Blur More filter a second time. Now the edges between masked and unmasked areas of the Tudor guy are soft, less well-defined, as shown in Figure 21.13.

7. Press Ctrl(⌘)+S; keep the file open.

Now that a soft edge has been defined for the selection of the Tudor guy, it's time to blur the outside edge of the selection.

FIGURE 21.13 *Put the current marquee selection into Quick Mask mode, and then apply the Blur More filter twice to the Quick Mask (not to the image itself).*

USING A LITTLE GAUSSIAN BLUR TO INTEGRATE THE COMPOSITION

The Gaussian Blur is a wonderful filter for creating soft drop shadows, and as you've seen in this chapter, it's great for creating an out-of-focus background. But the Gaussian Blur filter can also be tuned to a very small setting to apply an almost imperceptible amount of softening to the focus of a selection.

Here's how the work you performed in the previous steps leads to a very pleasing, photorealistic result in the composition:

EDGE-BLENDING, USING THE GAUSSIAN BLUR FILTER

1. Click on the Standard editing icon to the left of the Quick Mask icon to make the marquee selection active and to make the image editable. Make sure the Tudor Guy title is still selected on the Layers palette.

2. Press Shift+F7 to invert the marquee selection. Now, the Tudor guy is unselected, except for a soft boundary of about two pixels in diameter around his inside edge.

3. Choose Filter, Blur, and then choose Gaussian Blur.

NOTE

Adobe's documentation on the Blur More filter says simply that it's three to four times stronger than the Blur command. And the only information on the Blur command from Adobe is that it reduces contrast between pixels that lie on the edge of a selection or a color edge in an image.

If you really want to create a blurry image, we recommend using the Gaussian Blur filter. This filter distributes the blurring quality along a bell-shaped curve—image areas closest to the center of a selection receive more blurring than edge pixels. But if you want to soften an edge without throwing it totally out of focus, use the Blur or Blur More filters. You were asked to apply the Blur More filter twice in this example because the composition's image size is quite large.

4. Type **1.2** in the pixels field in the Gaussian Blur dialog box, and then drag the cursor around the preview box, as shown in Figure 21.14, to get a better idea of the way this blurring will affect the image. You'll see that the guy's center is still perfectly in focus, but his edges are a little soft-focus. Hint: to compare before and after applications of Gaussian Blur and many other filters, click and hold in the preview window to see the current image, and then release the cursor to see what the effect looks like when it's applied.

FIGURE 21.14   *Preview the small amount of blurring you've defined by dragging the cursor around inside the preview window.*

5. Click on OK to apply the Gaussian Blur filter, and then press Ctrl(⌘)+D to deselect the marquee. Figure 21.15 shows a 1:1 viewing resolution of part of the Tudor guy's shoulder. As you can see in this image (and on your own monitor), there is now a very natural transition between the edge of the Tudor guy and the blurry background.

6. Press Ctrl(⌘)+S; keep the file open.

Like the pots and pans you added to the Kitchen scene, there needs to be a foreground element in the Tudor scene to visually place the Tudor guy in the middle ground of the image.

FIGURE 21.15 *Sometimes, only a little blurring is necessary to create a transition between foreground elements and background elements.*

ADDING BRANCHES TO THE SCENE

A natural addition to this scene (no pun intended) would be some low branches that partially obscure the Tudor guy. This is easy enough to do in this composition, or even in one of your own, by photographing branches against a clear blue sky. There will be enough contrast between the sky and the branches for you to use the Color Range command to separate the two elements—and then you can add the branches as the top layer in the scene.

You will notice, as you follow along in the steps to come, that the Color Range command does not precisely select the sky from the leaves and branches. The branches will have a slight fringe of sky blue around them because the Color Range command isn't quite as sophisticated as Extensis' Mask Pro. But this fringe is acceptable as part of the composition because you will blur the leaves and branches, using the Gaussian Blur filter, and the blue fringe will simply vanish.

Here's how to add the first of two foreground elements to the scene:

CREATING A SELECTION OF LEAVES AND BRANCHES AND ADDING THEM TO THE SCENE

1. Open the Branch.tif image from the Examples\Chap21 folder on the Companion CD. A 33% viewing resolution is good for selecting the sky from the leaves and branches.

2. On the Layers palette, double-click on the Background image layer title, and then in the Create Layer dialog box, click on OK to accept the default name (Layer 0) for the new layer.

3. Choose Select, and then choose Color Range. Move the Color Range dialog box out of the way so that you can see the Branch image.

4. With Sampled Colors chosen from the Select drop-down list, and the Selection button clicked in the dialog box, move the cursor into the Branch image, and click on an area of sky blue.

5. Drag the Fuzziness slider up to about 115, as shown in Figure 21.16. Doing this creates a tight selection of the sky—it creates a crisp selection edge between the sky and the leaves and branches.

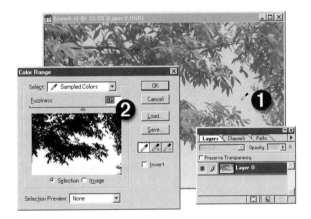

FIGURE 21.16 *Click in the sky area with the Eyedropper tool, and then drag the Fuzziness slider to the right to make a well-defined selection marquee in the image.*

6. Click on OK to apply the Color Range command, and then press Delete (Backspace). The sky is gone from the image; only leaves and branches remain. Press Ctrl(⌘)+D to deselect the marquee.

7. On the Layers palette, drag the Layer 0 title into the Tudor.psd image, as shown in Figure 21.17. The layer containing the leaves and branches is now named Layer 1 in the Tudor image.

8. Press Ctrl(⌘)+S; keep both files open. Do *not* save the Branch.tif image; soon you'll close it, without saving changes.

FIGURE 21.17 *Drag the layer title for the branches and leaves into the Tudor.psd image window*

It's time now to perform a little virtual tree-trimming and blurring, and to position the contents of Layer 1 within the composition.

COLOR AND TONE BALANCING THE ADDITION TO THE SCENE

You'll notice that the right side of Layer 1 features branches and leaves that have no place in the composition. In the steps that follow, you'll remove these unwanted areas, and in addition to blurring the branches, you'll also change the saturation and the density of the leaves on Layer 1. You need to do this because the branches and leaves are very brightly lit, and their color and tone will distract the audience, even after you've blurred Layer 1.

Here's how to integrate the branches and leaves into the picture:

MAKING THE LEAVES PART OF THE IMAGE

1. With Layer 1 as the currently selected layer, choose the Move tool, and then drag the branches up in the image window until only a few leaves intrude on the Tudor guy's head.

2. Choose the Lasso tool after the contents of Layer 1 have been positioned, and then drag a selection around the right side of the image, where unwanted leaves and branches are apparent (see Figure 21.18).

Figure 21.18 *Position the contents of Layer 1 by using the Move tool, and then use the Lasso tool to select around leaves and branches that do not belong in the image.*

3. Press Delete (Backspace) and then press Ctrl(⌘)+D to deselect the marquee.

4. Press Ctrl(⌘)+Alt(Opt)+F to display the last-used filter's dialog box without applying the filter.

5. In the Gaussian Blur dialog box, drag the slider to about 8.2, as shown in Figure 21.19. You're applying less of a blur to the leaves and branches than you did to the Background layer of the house, because you're being creative here and presenting to the viewing audience a picture in which the branches and leaves are closer to the focal point of the Tudor guy than he is to the house.

6. Click on OK to apply the blur. It should be obvious now that although the leaves are properly out of focus, they're too bright. Press Ctrl(⌘)+L to access the Levels command.

7. Drag the Black Point slider to the right until the left Input Levels field reads about 46, as shown in Figure 21.20. This adds density to the contents of Layer 1, but also creates a problem. As the leaves become deeper in tone, their green color becomes more intense—*too* intense, in fact, for this composition.

8. Click on OK to apply the Levels command change on Layer 1, and then press Ctrl(⌘)+U to display the Hue/Saturation dialog box.

FIGURE 21.19 *Use a smaller amount of blurring to the leaves than you did for the house to make the leaves appear closer to the Tudor guy.*

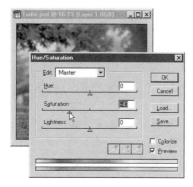

FIGURE 21.20 *Increasing the Black Point makes the pixels close to this tonal area more dense. Doing this can also increase the saturation of the pixels that are changed.*

9. Drag the Saturation slider to the left, to about –43, as shown in Figure 21.21. You've now removed some of the overly intense color from all areas on Layer 1. Click on OK to apply the change.

10. Press Ctrl(⌘)+S; keep the file open.

A single branch intruding on the scene doesn't really force the audience to look at the Tudor guy as the focus of the image. In the following steps, you'll add another branch to the scene.

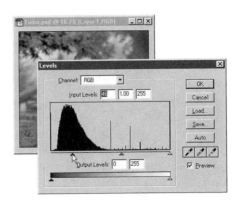

FIGURE 21.21 *Decrease the amount of predominant color on Layer 1 by dragging the Saturation slider to the left.*

MORE EMBELLISHMENTS = MORE PHOTOREALISM

NOTE

The authors can't overemphasize the fact that the best Photoshop work is "invisible." Even with impossible fantasy scenes you'll work with in this book, reality must be preserved, and your primary concern in image editing is getting a composition to look real. This sometimes means adding imperfection to a piece, as in this case, to make the audience wonder about the photographer's competence instead of the retouching that goes into the scene.

The whole idea behind adding branches to the composition is to reinforce the idea that this composition was taken as a single photograph. And the photographer of the scene, although he got the Tudor guy in focus, wasn't awfully careful about the framing of the picture. Many times, you'll find that by adding an "imperfection" to a scene—like amateurish cropping—you add a human element that tends to negate the truth that the image was assembled in Photoshop.

There's no reason why the same branch layer you brought into the composition can't be reused to create a second branch intruding on the Tudor guy's elbow. In the steps to follow, you'll create a rough selection edge around the top of one of the branches in Branch.tif, drag the selection into the Tudor composition, position the selection, and then apply the same blurring/Levels command/Hue /Saturation procedures you used with the first layer of branches you added to the scene.

FINALIZING THE TUDOR COMPOSITION

1. With Tudor.psd in the foreground in Photoshop, click on the Layers palette's menu flyout and choose Flatten Image.

2. Choose Edit, Purge, and then choose All. Click on OK in the attention box. Then press Ctrl(⌘)+S. Doing this dramatically reduces the saved file size of the image, and thus reduces the system resources Photoshop requires for saving multiple copies of your work for Undo purposes. You've also purged the History (the "undo") list, even though you can't see the History palette onscreen.

3. With Branch.tif in the foreground, drag a selection around the right, bottom, and left of the bottom branch with the Lasso tool, as shown in Figure 21.22, but make sort of a zigzag line at the top of the branch to close the selection. When this selection is blurred, the top—although you haven't precisely made the selection between the leaves—will appear natural.

FIGURE 21.22 *Use the Lasso tool to encompass the three "clear" sides of the branch, and then make a zigzag pattern along the top to suggest leaves growing at the top of the selection.*

4. Hold the Ctrl(⌘) key; this toggles the Lasso and other tools to the Move tool. Drag the selection into the Tudor.psd image window. The branches are now on a new Layer 1, and Layer 1 is the current editing layer.

5. Close the Branch.tif image without saving it.

6. Press V (Move tool), and then position the contents of Layer 1 so that the second branch is located in the area shown in Figure 21.23.

7. Press Ctrl(⌘)+F to apply the Gaussian Blur filter at its last setting (8.2 pixels).

8. Press Ctrl(⌘)+L to display the Levels command, and then drag the Black Point slider to about 46, as shown in Figure 21.24. The amount you increase the Black Point is a "trial-and-error" figure, and depending on your monitor's calibration and your system's video display, you might find that anywhere from 38 to 50 will make the branches appropriately dense.

FIGURE 21.23 *Choose the Move tool by pressing V, and then move the branches so they encroach on the Tudor guy's elbow and forearm.*

FIGURE 21.24 *Make the branch look as though it's in the foreground and in the shade by increasing the Black Point.*

9. Press Ctrl(⌘)+U to display the Hue/Saturation command.

10. Drag the Saturation slider to the left until the leaves and branch on Layer 1 lose some of their color intensity and blend in more with the overall image. Click on OK to apply the Hue/Saturation command. Press Ctrl(⌘)+S to save your work up to this point.

11. On the Layers palette, click on the menu flyout, and choose Flatten Image.

12. Choose Edit, Purge, and then choose All. Click on OK in the attention box.

13. Choose File, Save As, and then choose a more common file format than Photoshop's native PSD. TIF, BMP, and PICT are all good formats, and you can show your work around on different computers with users who don't own Photoshop.

14. You're finished! You can close the file at any time now.

In Figure 21.25 (and in the second color section of the book), you can see the finished image. It's attractive, but there's nothing outstanding about it...except that a camera was never used to capture the moment!

FIGURE 21.25 *With the right resource material and the steps shown in this chapter, you can create your own reality—complete with depth of field—to add to your "invisible" collection of Photoshop work.*

Hopefully, you can go off now and create your own composite images that feature a shallow depth of field. Depth of field is one of the many ways you can draw attention to the main attraction in an image. Use the techniques shown in this chapter with examples in other chapters, and you're well on your way to making more believable, more complex compositions an everyday part of your work.

Summary

Depth of field is only one of many aspects of photorealism, but like shadows, reflections, highlights, and consistent color balance among the images you integrate, it's the "supporting cast" of visual effects that makes a scene look real.

It's on to shadow creation and how to make a dull surface as reflective as a mirror in Chapter 22, "Creating Reflections and Shadows." If you have an image that's dull looking or otherwise not as appealing as you want it to be, we've got the answers for you.

CREATING REFLECTIONS AND SHADOWS

If you were to break down, by profession, a list of those individuals who constantly use Photoshop, you'd have:

- *Photographers*

- *Artists and designers*

- *Pre-press folks*

The talented people who perform pre-press corrections using Photoshop generally are concerned with correcting the density of images, color casting, and cropping, among other tasks. But usually a pre-press professional is not asked to change the visual content of an image.

Similarly, photographers dodge and burn areas of digitized photos, they cut and paste elements into different photos, and the images they work with typically already contain accurate highlights, reflections, and shadows.

The artist and designer are the people who will benefit the most from this chapter. These are the people who *build* images, using Photoshop and other applications. And when you build an image from the ground up, there are several photorealistic properties you'll want to add to the image.

This chapter will be of interest to *all* types of Photoshop users, however, because it shows the principles behind photorealistic content in an image, and the methods for adding realism to your work. And there will be times when an image needs a reflection or a shadow; this chapter shows how to illustrate these optical phenomena. Reflections and shadows are as important to the realism of an image as the elements of perspective and composition and the shape of objects in a scene. Reflections and shadows are products of the lighting in a scene.

THE ANATOMY OF REFLECTIONS

When you look into a properly hung mirror, what you see is the image of yourself, flipped horizontally. If someone is looking at you (while you're looking at yourself) from a viewpoint that is close to the wall upon which the mirror's hung, they too will see a horizontally flipped reflection of you. To create this sort of reflection in Photoshop is not a challenge; to create the mirror image, you'd duplicate your image and then choose Edit, Transform, and Flip Horizontal. You'd then place the mirror image in the frame of the mirror. Simple stuff.

You would seldom come across such an ideal setup for creating a reflection, however. And there are two important reasons this chapter needs to cover the creation of accurate reflections:

- The viewer of a scene in which a reflection is cast is almost never directly next to the *mirror plane* of the scene. The *mirror plane* usually is defined as the x,z coordinates (the width and depth), where an image reverses itself to create the reflection in a surface. Still ponds, a shiny table, and a wet road are all examples of a mirror plane that you do not look at directly, but instead look *into* at an angle, because your viewpoint is superior to the height of the mirror plane.

- The way an object is poised is seldom perfectly perpendicular to your line of sight. When you gaze into a mirror, you usually see a reflection that's perpendicular to your line of sight because your eyes are in the front of your head, and turning your head too much would prevent you from seeing yourself. In most tabletop photography, the product in the photo is usually angled from left to right (this is called the y rotational axis in modeling and CAD programs). The reason for turning an object clockwise or counterclockwise as it perches on a tabletop—to make one side closer to the camera than the other side—is for visual interest. An objects seems more dimensional when you can see at least part of all three of its dimensions.

It is when your viewpoint on an object is higher than the object, and when the object is turned, that creating a reflection on the shiny tabletop involves more than simply flipping a copy of the original object along the vertical axis. Figure 22.1 is an illustration of a camera viewing a perfume bottle that's resting on a shiny surface. As you can see in this figure, the left side of the perfume bottle is closer to the camera than the right; in the reflection, it's *still* the left edge of the perfume bottle that is closest to the camera. This means you cannot flip the image of the perfume bottle vertically and call it quits. The flipped image also needs to be *skewed*—the vertical edges need to move in opposing directions. By skewing the reflected duplicate of the bottle, you cause the ridges on the bottle to descend from left to right in the reflection, the same as the ridges appear on the bottle. Additionally, in optically correct reflections, the perspective from top to bottom of the object is continuous from the top of the object—through the mirror plane—to the bottom of the reflection. The *vanishing point*—the point at which the sides of an object viewed in perspective would coincide if the sides were extended far enough—is consistent throughout the scene of the object and its reflection.

The author acknowledges that some of these lofty terms in the absence of an example can be a tad abstract. And this is why you'll run through the steps needed to reproduce a reflection, as seen from the camera's point of view in Figure 22.1.

In Figure 22.2, you can see the example image used in the following section of this chapter. The "Timeless" perfume bottle is not a photograph; it was modeled in a graphics program—if the bottle were real, it would probably cast a reflection on the shiny marble, and there would be little point to the steps to come!

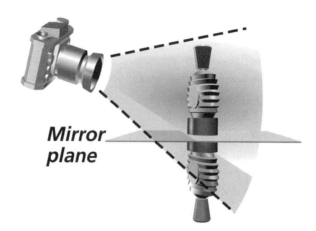

FIGURE 22.1 *When your viewpoint is much higher than the mirror plane, and an object is rotated, some aspects of the reflection (such as text) are mirrored, whereas other aspects, such as the vanishing point, are consistent.*

FIGURE 22.2 *We often see the reflection of objects that rest on a highly polished surface such as marble. The image you'll work with is synthetic, however, and one of the effects of real lighting—a reflection—has been left out of the composition.*

You'll notice in the real world that a perfume bottle or a soda bottle has *transparency*. In the timeless.tif image you'll work with, you can see some of the marble tabletop through the amber glass. This means that to create a truly authentic reflection, some of the reflection must also have some transparency. No problem; because the image was modeled and rendered, the author took the opportunity to have a partially transparent image mask rendered into an alpha channel of the image.

WORKING WITH A PARTIALLY OPAQUE ALPHA CHANNEL MASK

In this chapter the term "opacity" simply means the converse of "transparency," so don't be thrown by references to a "partially transparent" area. For all intents and purposes, a partially transparent area is also a partially *opaque* area.

Although a few shortcomings arise from the use of a modeling program to make an image (total photorealism, even with expensive modeling software, is almost never achieved), there are a few advantages to modeling a product such as the perfume bottle. The greatest advantage to modeling this "timeless" scene is that the modeling application is "smart" and knows how to write an alpha channel that contains opaque, transparent, and *partially* transparent areas, depending on the opacity of the bottle at any given point. In Figure 22.3, you can see the alpha channel—called "Masking channel"—in the timeless.tif image. The callouts indicate that white areas (such as the bottle cap) are totally opaque, and an area such as the background is 100% black; this area will not be selected at all (it's 100% transparent). The alpha channel of the bottle also contains *intermediate* areas of opacity. These are areas where the glass bottle with its perfume inside allow some light to pass through the object, and the alpha channel's interpretation of these areas is to render *percentages* of black. Photoshop knows how to read this information, and will only *partially* select the intermediate tones in the alpha channel.

Armed with the preceding theoretical background information (which *will* make sense shortly<g>!) and the image on the Companion CD, let's get down to the business of reflection-making. Making a copy of the original bottle, flipping it, and positioning it are at the top of the agenda.

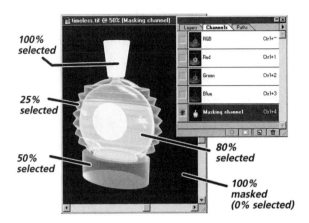

100% selected

25% selected

50% selected

80% selected

100% masked (0% selected)

Figure 22.3 *The alpha channel information that Photoshop uses to create selections is composed of fully, partially, and totally unselected bottle areas.*

Creating a Reflection Image from the Original

1. Open the timeless.tif image from the Chap22 folder on the Companion CD, type **50** in the Zoom Percentage field, and then press Enter (Return). You can drag on the window borders to minimize any window background area.

2. Press F7 if the Channels palette isn't onscreen. Ctrl(⌘)+click on the Alpha 1 title on the Channels palette to load the visual contents of the channel as a selection marquee.

   Now, you might notice that something weird is going on with the selection marquee; there's a marquee inside the base of the bottle. This does not mean that this area is unselected—it's simply a visual indicator that this area of the bottle is less than 50% opaque. *Never* trust a selection marquee to give you accurate feedback on partially opaque areas loaded from an alpha channel.

3. With a selection tool chosen (the Rectangular Marquee tool is fine), right-click (Macintosh: hold Ctrl and click), and then choose Layer Via Copy from the context menu, as shown in Figure 22.4.

4. Double-click on the Layer 1 title on the Layers palette, and then in the Layer Options dialog box, type **Upright perfume** in the Name field and click on OK. You will need a copy of the bottle in its original orientation to go on top of the reflection image (so the base of the bottle covers some of the reflection image).

FIGURE 22.4   *Create a copy of the nontransparent areas of the bottle by using the Layer Via Copy command.*

5. Drag the Upright perfume layer title into the Create New Layer icon at the bottom of the Layers palette. This creates a copy of the layer, with the name Upright perfume copy; it's the top layer in the composition.

6. Drag the copy layer to beneath the original, double-click on the title, and type **reflection perfume** in the Name field of the Layer Options dialog box. Click on OK to apply the name change. The "reflection perfume" layer is the current editing layer.

7. Ctrl(⌘)+click on the reflection perfume layer title to select the nontransparent areas of the layer, and then choose Edit, Transform, Flip Vertical, as shown in Figure 22.5. Although this version of Photoshop no longer tells you that you have a floating selection in an image, you have a mirrored floating selection now, and the flipped bottle can be repositioned by using *either* a selection tool or the Move tool.

8. Press Ctrl(⌘)+D to deselect the vertically flipped bottle; as a floating selection, there is the possibility of removing some of the image when a selection tool is active. Press V (Move tool), and then press Ctrl(⌘)+the minus key to zoom out to 33.3% viewing resolution.

9. With the Move tool, drag the upside-down perfume bottle so that the left edge of the bottom of the bottle lines up with the left edge of the bottle on the Upright perfume layer, as shown in Figure 22.6.

Edit, Transform, Flip Vertical

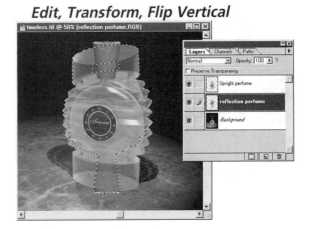

FIGURE 22.5   *Flip the selection vertically.*

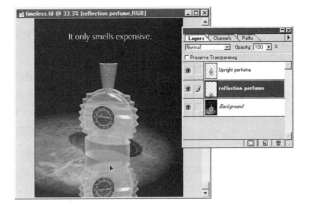

FIGURE 22.6   *Horizontally align the bottom of both bottles by using the Move tool to move the reflection image.*

10. Double-click on the Zoom tool to move your view to 100% resolution of the image. Maximize the image window, hold down the Spacebar to toggle to the Hand tool, and then drag in the window so you can see the bottom edge of both bottles.

11. With the Move tool and the keyboard's arrow nudge keys, line up both the left and right edges of the reflection to the Upright perfume layer, as shown in Figure 22.7. Line up the left bottom edges of the bottles so that the reflection layer and the upright image layer touch each other. This will cause the right edge of the reflection image to overlap the right bottom side of the upright image, but this is okay. Notice also that the edges of the bottom of the reflection image are *not* perfectly

parallel to the edges of the upright image layer. This is something you'll correct shortly.

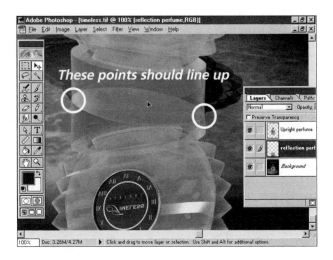

FIGURE 22.7   *Line up the edges of the bottom of the reflection to meet the same bottom points on the Upright perfume layer.*

12. Press Ctrl(⌘)+Shift+S, and save the work as timeless.psd—in Photoshop's native file format—to your hard disk. Keep the image open.

The bottom edges of the perfume bottles don't align properly because of perspective. When you mirrored the reflection layer, the bottle's perspective was mirrored also, and as mentioned earlier, perspective is consistent between object and reflection.

The most glaringly obvious fault in this assignment, however, is the direction in which the ridges of the bottle are traveling. The ridges in the reflection, like the perspective of the piece, should be the same as those in the top layer image. In the following section, you'll use the Skew Free Transform mode to correct the angle of the ridges in the reflection layer.

CREATING SIMILARITY IN THE DIRECTION OF LINES IN AN OBJECT

Because you need to work at the bottom of the timeless.psd image, which is a relatively small area, you'll use Photoshop's New View (called the New Window command in previous versions) to provide in the workspace both a complete view of the image and a close-up, so you can work with precision. Changes in one window are updated in the other window.

In the steps to follow, you'll use the Skew command to change the direction of the ridges on the bottle's reflection, and also to make the oval bottom of the reflection match the oval bottom on the Upright perfume layer.

Here's how to use the Skew command and multiple views of the composition to precisely align the bottom of the reflection with the bottom of the top layer's bottle:

USING THE SKEW COMMAND TO CORRECT A REFLECTION

1. Type **25** in the Zoom Percentage field, and then press Enter (Return). Position the timeless.psd window to the right of the workspace. Drag the window borders away from the image so that you can see some window background on the bottom of the document. You'll be working directly on the bottom edge of the image at times in the steps that follow.

2. Choose View, New View. A new view of the same document appears. Anything you do in one window is duplicated in the other one. Double-click on the Zoom tool to increase the viewing resolution of this new window to 100%. In the new image window, scroll down to where the bottle and the reflection meet.

3. Click on the title bar of the 25% viewing resolution window to make it the current editing window.

4. Press Ctrl(⌘)+T to display the Free Transform bounding box around the bottle on the reflection perfume layer.

5. Right-click (Macintosh: hold Ctrl and click), and then choose Skew from the context menu, as shown in Figure 22.8.

6. Drag downward on the middle, right handle on the Skew bounding box, as shown in Figure 22.9. Your close-up view will show you when you have the right side of the oval bottom traveling at more or less the same angle as the top layer perfume bottle. Don't worry if the two ovals aren't at exactly the same angle—you haven't dragged on the middle-*left* bounding box handle yet.

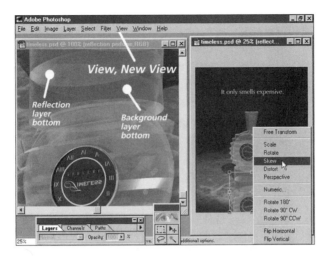

FIGURE 22.8 *Choose to Skew the selected reflection.*

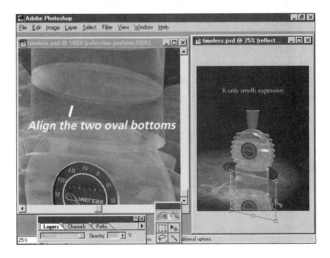

FIGURE 22.9 *Perform your editing work at a comfortable "distance," while you preview the changes you make at a 1:1 viewing resolution in the New View window.*

7. Drag the middle-left bounding box handle upward, as shown in Figure 22.10. If both the ovals appear to be at the same angle, but one is higher or lower than other, place your cursor in the middle of the bounding box, and drag up or down to move the entire selection. You can also use the keyboard's arrow keys to precisely nudge the selection in any direction before applying the transformation.

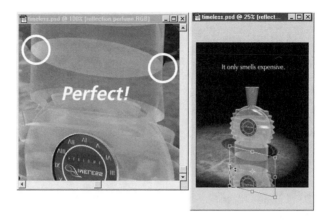

FIGURE 22.10 *The oval bottoms of the top perfume bottle and the reflection bottle should be at the same angle, and they should overlap perfectly so that the edges of the base of the bottle meet.*

8. Double-click inside the bounding box to apply the transformation (or press Enter/Return).

9. Press Ctrl(⌘)+S; keep the file open.

The skewing part of this assignment wasn't too hard, and the reflection image has a lot more credibility now. The reflection picture is still larger at the top than at the bottom, however, so you've still got a little perspective work to do.

CREATING AND USING YOUR OWN GUIDELINES

Without question, Photoshop 5's Grid and Guides features are a blessing, particularly for users who are accustomed to using guides in drawing programs such as Illustrator. Photoshop does not offer *slanting* guides, however; guides are always at a right angle to the image window.

The problem here is that you need slanted guides to create a template for the next transformation you'll apply to the reflection bottle. As mentioned earlier, perspective is continuous between object and reflection. In the steps that follow, you'll create guides by using the Pen tool, and then you'll use the Perspective transformation to align the base edges of the reflection bottle with your home-brew guides.

PAIRING GUIDES WITH PERSPECTIVE LINES IN THE IMAGE

1. Close the 25% viewing resolution window, and maximize the 100% viewing resolution window.

2. Hide both the Upright perfume and the reflection perfume by unchecking their eye icons on the Layers palette. Click on the Background title to make this the current layer.

3. Choose the Pen tool from the Pen tool flyout on the toolbox.

4. Click a point at the top of the left edge of the base of the perfume bottle, and then click a second anchor point at the bottom of the base's edge.

5. Hold the Ctrl(⌘) key so the Pen tool toggles to the Direct Selection tool. Drag the second anchor point a good 2 screen inches below its original position, keeping the line between the anchor points directly on the left edge of the bottle base.

6. While holding the Ctrl(⌘) key, click on an area of the image to deselect the path you've drawn. Then perform step 5 with the right edge of the bottle base, as shown in Figure 22.11. Notice that these paths are *not* parallel to the image window border.

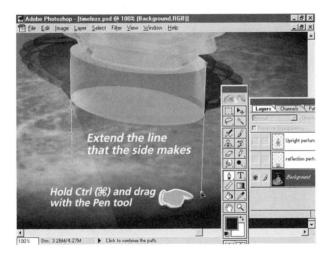

FIGURE 22.11 *Create your own guides by using the Pen tool.*

7. While you're still holding Ctrl(⌘) the Direct Selection tool is still chosen. Click on a vacant area of the background image to make sure that the second path is deselected. Otherwise, you'll be applying a transformation to a path, and not to the image layer's contents.

8. Click on the Upright perfume and reflection perfume's eye icon column on the Layers palette to restore visibility of these layers. Click on the reflection layer title to make it the editing layer. Press Ctrl(⌘)+T to display the Free Transform bounding box, and then right-click (Macintosh: hold Ctrl and click) and choose Perspective from the context menu.

9. Drag the bottom right handle a little toward the center of the image. Release the handle, and see how closely the reflection base's right edge matches the right guide path you created. Unfortunately, as you can see from Figure 22.12, the edge of the reflection base does not coincide with the bounding box edge (the bounding box includes the much wider middle of the bottle), or you'd have this perspective thing licked in one or two moves.

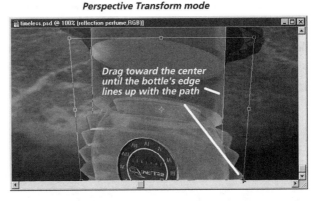

FIGURE 22.12 *Drag the bottom right handle left, toward the center of the bounding box, to change the perspective of the reflection bottle.*

10. If necessary, drag in the center of the bounding box to reposition its contents. The Perspective command moves the opposing control handles both away from and toward the edge of the bounding box in equal, opposing directions. And this might throw the left side of the reflection base off its currently centered position with respect to the top layer perfume bottle.

11. When the base edges of the reflection bottle match the guides you drew with the Pen tool, double-click inside the bounding box (or press Enter/Return) to apply the effect.

12. On the Paths palette, drag the Working Path title into the trash icon.

13. Press Ctrl(⌘)+S; keep the file open.

Congratulations are in order. You now have transformed a flipped copy of the perfume bottle into an accurate reflection of the bottle. But it's the little details that make a piece look professionally executed.

Next, you'll see how to create some embellishments to the reflection work to both enhance the work and disguise the fact that the reflection is artificial.

REMOVING UNNECESSARY DETAILS AND ENHANCING THE REFLECTION

There are a number of ways to go about finishing the reflection. As you'll see shortly, you have options, even when you think your editing work is completed.

One thing is a "must," though, in the image. The oval bottom of the perfume bottle is in the image three times: once on the Background layer (which is okay, and you'll keep it), once on the reflection layer (which might not be pixel-perfect in its alignment to the Upright perfume layer), and once on the Upright perfume layer. The bottom of the bottle is getting to look a little denser than a glass bottle would look.

Let's address the oval at the bottom of the bottle before enhancing the image.

AIRBRUSHING AWAY PART OF THE BOTTLE'S BOTTOM

In Layer Mask mode, you can selectively hide—and then discard—part of the bottle's bottom on the reflection layer. The best tool to use for this assignment is the Airbrush tool, which leaves no brush edge.

In the steps that follow, you'll tune the Airbrush tool to exactly the right strength and then "lighten up" the base of the bottle in the composition.

REMOVING PART OF THE REFLECTION—WITH SUBTLETY

1. Press Ctrl(⌘)+the minus key twice to zoom out to 50% viewing resolution on the image.

2. Click on the reflection perfume layer title on the Layers palette to make it the current layer.

3. Click on the Add Layer Mask icon at the bottom of the Layers palette to put the reflection perfume layer in Layer Mask mode. Applying black will hide areas, and applying white will restore hidden areas.

4. Double-click on the Airbrush tool to select it and to display the Options palette.

5. Drag the Pressure slider for the Airbrush to about 30%, and then on the Brushes palette, choose the 45-pixel diameter tip.

6. Drag briskly over the top edge of the oval bottom, and then stroke a second time below your first stroke. You will not see a dramatic change, but rather, a subtle reduction in color density in the oval area. When you think the oval looks more natural in the image, as it does in Figure 22.13, stop! You're finished with the Airbrush tool.

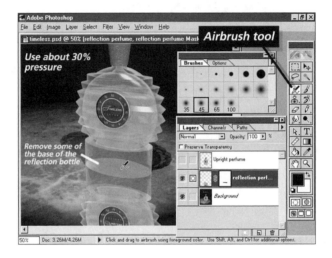

FIGURE 22.13 *Apply the Airbrush tool while the layer is in Layer Mask mode to remove some of the oval perfume bottle bottom.*

7. Click on the Layer Mask thumbnail to the right of the image thumbnail on the reflection perfume title on the Layers palette (whew!), and then drag the thumbnail into the trash icon. Click on Apply in the attention box to permanently erase the areas you hid with the Airbrush tool.

8. Press Ctrl(⌘)+S; keep the file open.

Here's the easy way to conclude your reflection work:

A PERFUNCTORY BUT UNINSPIRED CONCLUSION TO REFLECTION CREATION

1. With the reflection perfume layer highlighted on the Layers palette, drag the Opacity slider on the Layers palette to about 65%.

2. Choose Screen mode from the drop-down list on the Layers palette.

3. Consider yourself finished. *Boring!* Forget steps 1 through 3!

Check out the following section for a more creative way of suggesting a reflection in the composition.

FROM SHINY TO SLICK: WORKING WITH THE WAVE FILTER

Perhaps you've seen in automobile ads a reflection of the car on the surface upon which it rests. This reflection is usually accomplished by wetting down some dark-colored cement or blacktop; a fraction of an inch of water creates the reflection.

This method of reflection creation does not have to be limited to reflecting cars, whose weight sort of prohibits featuring the car on a mirror. You can turn the marble in the image from its present shiny appearance to a "wet" look by adding waves to the reflection. Doing this accomplishes two things:

- It makes the overall image more visually complex. Hint: modeled scenes lack the visual complexity of the real world, and can use all the visual "business" you can lend to these types of images.

- Sending waves through the reflection helps disguise the fact that the reflection layer is not as sharp as the Upright perfume layer. Whenever you transform areas of a composition—by skewing and then using Perspective, for example—you change the order of the component pixels in the image, and thereby lose some focus.

The next set of steps shows you how to work with the features in the Wave filter and offers a little explanation of what each control does, so that you won't be as reluctant to use this mind-boggling dialog box with your own work:

APPLYING THE WAVE FILTER

1. Choose Filter, Distort, and then choose Wave.

2. In the Wave dialog box, type **0** in the Vert(ical) Scale box. All the waves in this reflection will be horizontal (from left to right).

3. In the Number of Generators field, type **8**. Eight is *not* the number of waves the effect will render; the number refers to the number of different *types* of wave signals

that will distort the image. Simply put, eight different wave signals will be sent horizontally through the reflection image to produce uneven amounts of waviness, from crest to crest. This is a more realistic look than waves whose widths are all identical.

4. In the Wavelength field, drag the Min(imum) slider to 1, and drag the Max(imum) slider to 20. This creates a fair amount of difference in distance from one wave crest to the next—again, a more realistic touch than wave crests that are equally spaced.

5. In the Amplitude field, drag both the Min. and Max. sliders to 7. Amplitude determines how far in any direction a wave travels. For our purposes here, you want a small amplitude, so the shape of the reflection bottle is still recognizable after applying the effect. Greater amounts turn a layer's contents into something that visually resembles frozen silly putty that's been struck with a hammer. When the dialog box looks like the one shown in Figure 22.14, it's time to press the OK button to apply the filter.

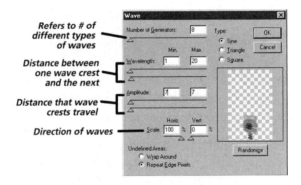

FIGURE 22.14 *The Wave filter has many parameters for controlling the shape of the distortion. Use the values listed here to produce a moving water effect.*

6. Turn the Opacity on the reflection perfume layer to about 65–75%, and choose Screen mode on the Layers palette's drop-down list. Your image should look something like the one in Figure 22.15.

7. If you're unhappy with the Wave effect, press F9 to display the History palette, and then drag the marker up to one editing move before Wave. You've got your standard reflection back again, and come to think of it, it's not such a boring "look" after all, as shown in Figure 22.16. It's simply one of the *many* looks you can add to an image when you understand the principles behind reflective objects. Press Ctrl(⌘)+S; you can close the image at any time now.

FIGURE 22.15 *Although you've distorted the reflection layer, it is the marble surface that takes on a new look.*

FIGURE 22.16 *Through the use of perspective and a host of Photoshop features, you can create realistic reflections on any type of surface.*

All right; we've covered the illustration of a reflection, the visual result of something resting on a shiny surface. But what is the visual effect in an image when a surface is *dull*? Answer: you see a *shadow*, and shadow-making is the topic of the pages to come.

EXAMINING DIFFERENT TYPES OF SHADOWS

Photoshop 5's Layer Effects includes Drop Shadow. As the name implies, this type of shadow is created when a light source is almost directly above a floating object—the silhouette of the object making the shadow is dropped onto the surface that receives the shadow. Drop shadows are cool for Web graphics and the text on most issues of *PC Magazine*. In the realm of photorealism, however, objects almost never float above a surface, and lighting is almost never so perfectly directed at an object that the object's silhouette is the shape of the shadow.

In Figure 22.17, you can see two examples of shadows: the *drop* shadow and the *cast* shadow—sometimes called a *perspective shadow*.

Drop shadow   Cast shadow

FIGURE 22.17   *Shadows from floating objects are often drop shadows; shadows that add a casting plane to the image are called cast shadows.*

As you can see in this figure, the cartoon fellow with the cast shadow seems anchored to the ground—drop shadows tend to add height to the object, whereas cast shadows add *depth* to a scene. In the sections to follow, you'll learn how to add a photorealistic shadow to several images, and in the process, you'll learn a trick or two about adding accurate shading to modeled scenes or to digitized photographs.

CALCULATING WHERE A SHADOW SHOULD FALL

The first example image in this section is called Ball.psd. The image has several layers, so slipping a shadow behind the hero of the image—the ball—is no problem. You must decide what shape the shadow should be for the ball, however, and this involves some detective work.

In Figure 22.18 you can see Ball.psd (which you'll open and work with shortly). The sky is light but cloudy—there's not much chance that the ball will receive enough illumination from behind to cast a shadow in front of it. But the rough surface upon which the ball is resting appears to be illuminated from the front of the scene, and to the left. The main highlight on the ball confirms this observation; you can see a distinct highlight toward the ball's upper left. This means that the shadow that's lacking from this scene needs to fall to the right and slightly behind the ball. Highlights fall in the opposite direction of shadows cast by an object.

NOTE

The author added a weak secondary highlight on the ball at about 4 o'clock. This was *not* done to make the assignment here more complicated; in fact, let's pretend that there *is* no secondary light source in the image creating the second highlight. The reason for the second light in the scene is to illuminate the far edge of the ball. Round objects look more dimensional when there is *catch lighting* in areas that would otherwise completely fall into shadow. And a good photographer would position the catch light so that it illuminates the round object without casting a second shadow in the scene.

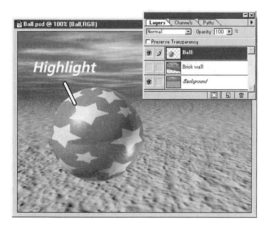

FIGURE 22.18 *The highlight on the ball is a good indicator of where a shadow in the scene should be created.*

Here's how to create a cast shadow for the ball:

CREATING A CAST SHADOW FOR A ROUND OBJECT

1. Open the Ball.psd image from the Chap22 folder on the Companion CD.

2. Type **70** in the Zoom Percentage field, and then press Enter (Return).

3. Click on the Background layer on the Layers palette, and then click on the Create New Layer icon at the bottom of the palette. An empty Layer 1 appears above the Background layer.

   The author was running short on pixels in this chapter, and the Ball.psd image is actually two tutorial images in one. Do *not* make the Brick Wall layer visible and do not click on its title to make it the current editing layer. We'll get to the Brick Wall layer in a little while…

4. Press D (default colors), and then choose the Elliptical Marquee tool from the fly-out on the toolbox. The options for the tool, located on the Options palette, should be Feather: 0 pixels, Style: Normal, and the Anti-aliased check box should be checked.

5. Drag an ellipse in the image window on Layer 1. Drag in the center of the marquee selection to position the ellipse as shown in Figure 22.19, and then press Alt(Opt)+Delete (Backspace) to fill the marquee with foreground black.

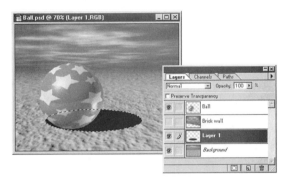

FIGURE 22.19   *The highlight on the ball is to the top and left, so the shadow should be to the bottom and right.*

The shadow you've created is close, but not precisely what a shadow would really look like if it were cast by an actual ball, with the light coming from the upper left. The shadow's angle would be a *combination* of the amount of height and the degree of left-sidedness, as suggested by the highlight.

6. Press Ctrl(⌘)+D to deselect the marquee, and then press Ctrl(⌘)+T to display the Free Transform bounding box around the shadow.

7. Right-click (Macintosh: hold Ctrl and click) and choose Rotate from the context menu.

8. Drag upward, ever so slightly (by about 12 degrees), the bottom-right corner handle of the bounding box, as shown in Figure 22.20. Now the shadow has a width and a height, and it also has *depth*, as it recedes by a small amount into the distance.

FIGURE 22.20 *Cast the shadow into the scene by rotating it so that its far side travels into the horizon.*

9. Double-click inside the bounding box to apply the transformation.

10. Choose Filter, Blur, and then choose Gaussian Blur.

11. Type **6** in the Pixels field and then click on OK to apply the Gaussian blur.

12. Choose Multiply on the Layers palette's drop-down list, and drag the Opacity slider to about 73%.

13. Save the composition as Ball.psd, in Photoshop's native file format, to your hard disk. Keep the image open.

There will be occasions in your imaging adventures when a shadow should be cast on *both* the ground plane and on a wall behind the object or person. In the next section, you'll create a shadow that bends sharply as it casts onto a plane and also onto a surface that is perpendicular to the ground plane.

TIP

The sharpness of shadows depends on the closeness of the light source to the object, the closeness of the object to the plane upon which it rests, and most important, the type of surface that receives the shadow. Clearly, the surface beneath the ball is rough, and therefore a shadow casting from the ball would have diffuse edges as the shading is scattered on the surface.

CREATING A COMPOSITE SHADOW

Perhaps, if you've taken a moonlight stroll, you've noticed that the streetlamps cast a long shadow—yours—on the sidewalk, only to change direction when the shadow hits a wall or the side of a house. This type of shadow is sort of half drop shadow and half cast shadow. You'll notice in the steps to come that creating such a shadow in your work adds visual complexity to the piece, and also reinforces the aspect of depth.

Here's how to add a brick wall to the scene, and create a shadow that falls both on the wall and on the ground:

BUILDING A "BENT" SHADOW

1. Double-click on the Layer 1 title, and name the layer **Shadow 1**. Hide the Shadow 1 layer by clicking on the eye icon next to its title on the Layers palette.

2. Click on the Brick Wall title on the Layers palette to make it visible and active for editing.

3. Click on the Create New Layer icon at the bottom of the Layers palette. Because all the other layers are named, you don't really need to name this layer—the default name of "Layer 1" is easy to locate.

4. Using steps 5–9 in the previous set of steps, "Creating a Cast Shadow for a Round Object," create on Layer 1 a tilted ellipse that represents the shadow of the ball cast upon the ground. Do *not* blur the shadow or change the Opacity or Blending mode for this layer.

5. Ctrl(⌘)+click on the Brick Wall title on the Layers palette to load the nontransparent areas of this layer as a marquee selection. Layer 1 should still be the current editing layer.

6. Press Delete (Backspace), as shown in Figure 22.21. This action removes the part of the shadow on Layer 1 that falls on the brick wall, because the perspective of the shadow on the wall is incorrect.

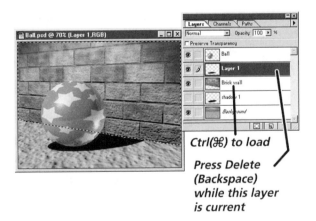

Ctrl(⌘) to load

Press Delete
(Backspace)
while this layer
is current

FIGURE 22.21 *Remove the unwanted part of the shadow by loading a selection marquee of the wall and then deleting part of the shadow on Layer 1.*

7. With the Elliptical Marquee tool, drag an oval that is a little taller and a little narrower than the ball.

8. Drag inside the marquee selection to reposition the selection so that the middle of its right edge lines up with the right edge of the shadow on Layer 1 (see Figure 22.22).

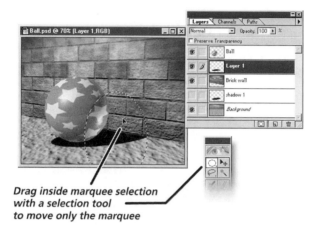

Drag inside marquee selection with a selection tool — to move only the marquee

FIGURE 22.22 *Move the selection marquee so that the middle of its right side touches the right side of the shadow on the ground.*

9. Click on the Quick Mask mode icon toward the bottom right of the toolbox. The selection marquee should turn into a tint overlay of the shape of the marquee.

   If everything *except* the interior of the marquee becomes tinted, check the Quick Mask Options by double-clicking on the Quick Mask icon. Color Indicates: Selected Areas should be the option. If your Quick Mask in the scene is inverted, click on the Selected Areas button, and then click on OK.

10. With Layer 1 still selected, Ctrl(⌘)+click on the Brick Wall layer title, and then press Shift+F7 to invert the marquee selection.

11. Press Delete (Backspace), as shown in Figure 22.23. Press Ctrl(⌘)+D to deselect the marquee selection.

12. Click on the Standard Editing mode icon (to the left of the Quick Mask icon), press D (default colors), and then press Alt(Opt)+Delete (Backspace) to fill the marquee with black foreground color, as shown in Figure 22.24.

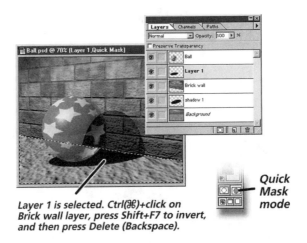

Layer 1 is selected. Ctrl(⌘)+click on Brick wall layer, press Shift+F7 to invert, and then press Delete (Backspace).

Quick Mask mode

FIGURE 22.23 *Delete the part of the Quick Mask that will not be used in the shadow.*

FIGURE 22.24 *Create the other half of the ball's shadow by filling the marquee selection with foreground color.*

13. Press Ctrl(⌘)+D to deselect the marquee, and then press Ctrl(⌘)+F, which applies the last-used filter (the Gaussian Blur filter, which will blur the shadow, using the same settings you specified when you last used the filter).

14. Choose Multiply from the Modes drop-down list on the Layers palette, and then drag the Opacity slider on the Layers palette to about 75%, as shown in Figure 22.25.

15. Press Ctrl(⌘)+S. You can close the file at any time now; you have stored away in this file two different scenes, with two different shadows!

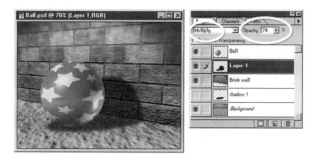

FIGURE 22.25 *Allow some of the ground and some of the wall to show through the shadow by decreasing Layer 1's Opacity.*

You've had quite a workout with all this shadow-creation stuff, and now it's time for a breather. You'll soon see how to use third-party plug-ins for Photoshop to automate the making of shadows.

SHADOW CREATION AND THIRD-PARTY PLUG-INS

Within the past two years, a few third-party Photoshop plug-in manufacturers have decided to take this shadow-creation business to a more complex level of sophistication. Alien Skin's Eye Candy 3 filters features a Perspective Shadow filter, and Andromeda Software also has an intricate shadow-making filter.

In the examples to follow, you'll see how both Eye Candy's Perspective Shadow filter and Andromeda's Shadow filter work. If you own either (or both) of these filters, example files are provided on the Companion CD for working with the filters. If you don't own the filters, demo versions of both filters are on the *Limited Edition* CD. To install the demos, quit Photoshop, take the Companion CD out of your CD-ROM drive for a moment, insert the *Limited Edition* CD, and then install the filters from the Software/ANDROMED and the A_Skin folders. These demo versions will *not* enable you to render the shadows you design into an image file, but you *can* experiment with the features and watch the results in the preview window of each filter (and then perhaps decide to add them to your artist's toolkit by *buying* them!).

Put the Companion CD back in your CD-ROM drive after you've installed the demo version of these programs.

USING THE EYE CANDY PERSPECTIVE SHADOW FILTER

The unique property of the Eye Candy Perspective Shadow filter is that you can create a shadow—with transparency that corresponds to the transparency of the selection—on *any layer* you like. You load a selection, choose a different layer, and the Perspective filter will render the complete shadow of the selection to the chosen layer. What this means for the designer is that you can experiment with the opacity, Blending mode, and even the color of the shadow as a discrete element in the image file.

Here's an example of how to use the Eye Candy Perspective Shadow on a cartoon image in a file we've provided for you:

ADDING A PERSPECTIVE SHADOW ON A LAYER

1. Open the Smirk.psd image from the Chap22 folder on the Companion CD. Type **70** in the Zoom Percentage field, and then press Enter (Return). Resize the image window so that very little window background is showing.

2. Press F7 to display the Layers palette if it isn't already onscreen.

3. Click on the Background layer title, and then click on the Create New Layer icon. Layer 1 will be created above the Background layer and below the Smirk layer. Layer 1 is now the current editing layer.

4. Ctrl(⌘)+click on the Smirk layer to load the nontransparent areas of this layer as a selection marquee, as shown in Figure 22.26. Layer 1 is still the current editing layer.

❷ Ctrl(⌘)+click to load marquee selection

❶ Click on Create new layer

FIGURE 22.26 *Load the silhouette of the cartoon character as a marquee selection. The Perspective Shadow filter will use this marquee information to create a shadow.*

5. Choose Filter, Eye Candy 3.01 Demo (or Eye Candy 3.01 if you've purchased the filters), and then choose Perspective Shadow. The Perspective Shadow interface appears.

   Unlike the highlight in the Ball.psd example, the highlight here is more toward the center of the cartoon character's head. This means that a shadow should be cast to the right of him (it), but also more into the distance than the shadow you manually created earlier with the ball.

6. Drag the Vanishing Point Direction ring to about 28 (degrees). A vanishing point of 0 degrees would cast the shadow at three o'clock (way too flat for an accurate shadow), and a vanishing point direction of 90 degrees would place the shadow directly behind the cartoon character (at 12 o'clock). So 28 degrees represents an angle measured from the ground plane of about a 30-degree elevation.

7. Drag the Vanishing Point Distance ring to about 52. This amount is about half the maximum distance of 100 that the filter offers. A vanishing point distance of zero would place the shadow directly behind the cartoon character.

8. Drag the Length ring to about 82 (99 is the maximum). This control determines the shadow's length from top to bottom and is *not* the same as the Vanishing Point Distance.

9. Drag the Opacity ring to 64, drag the Blur ring to 10, and then click on the Draw Everywhere button. The Perspective Shadow is "smart"—it knows where there are opaque areas on layers above the current layer. With Draw Everything turned off, the feet part of the shadow would be clipped out of the rendering of the shadow, because the cartoon character's feet cover the area in which the shadow and the bottom of the character's feet coincide. If the controls in the Perspective Shadow box look like those shown in Figure 22.27 (and you own the product), click on the check mark in the upper right of the interface to render the shadow. If you're working with the demo copy of Eye Candy, take a look at the preview window, examine how the shadow shortens and skews to the right, and then click on the international "no" symbol to cancel out of the interface. Or click on OK (the check mark) to display a splash screen telling you how to order Eye Candy.

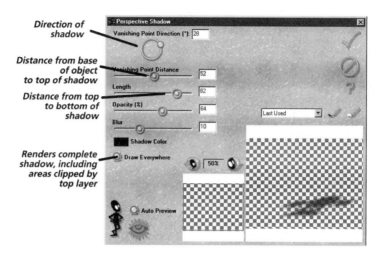

Direction of shadow

Distance from base of object to top of shadow

Distance from top to bottom of shadow

Renders complete shadow, including areas clipped by top layer

FIGURE 22.7 *The interface to Perspective Shadow offers a wealth of controls for determining direction, length, and opacity of the shadows it renders.*

10. If you don't own the retail version of Eye Candy, you can open Smirk2.psd from the Chap22 folder on the Companion CD to examine the quality of the shadow, reposition it slightly if you feel like it, and even change the color of the shadow by checking the Preserve Transparency box for Layer 1, selecting all by pressing Ctrl(⌘)+A, selecting a foreground color by clicking on the foreground color box on the toolbox, and then pressing Alt(Opt)+Delete (Backspace). If you own Eye Candy, you can certainly perform the same experiments as those mentioned here. One of the author's favorite tricks is to put the layer into Multiply mode, and then play with the opacity of the layer. In Figure 22.28, you can see the finished image.

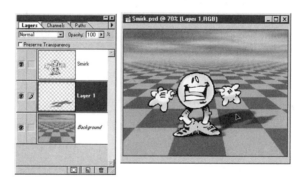

FIGURE 22.28 *When you render a shadow to its own layer, you can manipulate it independently of the object casting the shadow.*

11. You can choose to save the file to your hard disk, or not. You can close the cartoon image at any time now.

In the following section, you'll work with casting shadows from a type of object that has not yet been covered in this chapter: a semi-transparent object. You'll create a shadow whose transparency is both geometrically complex *and* tinted.

USING THE ANDROMEDA SHADOW FILTER ON TRANSPARENT OBJECTS

Andromeda Software cannot be accused of skimping on the features with its Shadow plug-in for Photoshop. With this filter, you have an entire gallery of preset shadows that cast in every conceivable way, in three dimensions; you can define a camera setup for the scene into which the shadow casts, and you can specify lighting sources—and this is an *overview* of the product!

To be fair, Alien Skin's Perspective Shadow filter and Andromeda's Shadow plug-in can *both* write varying transparency into shadows, and this is what you'll do shortly in a set of steps. Andromeda's product is a little different than Alien Skin's, however, (as you'll soon see), and any comparison between the two products would be misleading.

It should be noted before we begin that creating a realistic object on a layer in Photoshop that contains semitransparent areas—such as the wine bottle and glass in this section—is best performed in a modeling application that will write transparency to an alpha channel, as was shown in the perfume bottle example earlier in this chapter. In theory, you *could* photograph a wine bottle, carefully select it and place it on its own layer, and then use a painting tool at partial opacity while the layer is in Layer Mask mode to achieve an image similar to the Wine.psd file you'll work with shortly. Realistically, however, that would be too much labor to accomplish too little—when many Photoshop users also own modeling programs that write alpha channel transparency.

The one photorealistic touch that Andromeda's Shadow filter does not re-create is the different colors cast on a surface from vessels containing different colored liquids. This touch is something that you can create manually, however, as the following sections will show you.

NOTE

There are 21 plug-in filters in the Eye Candy suite. Although Perspective Shadow isn't a fully working plug-in, Drop Shadow and Antimatter can indeed be used to render their effects to an image. Drop Shadow is particularly handy because, unlike Photoshop's Layer Effects Drop Shadow filter, Eye Candy's filter will write a shadow to *any* layer that has a marquee selection active, or any layer that contains opaque or partially opaque elements. So let's thank Alien Skin for giving the computer graphics designer two filters for free.

Let's get down to business with the Shadow plug-in and the file on the Companion CD:

WORKING WITH THE SHADOW FILTER

1. Open the Wine.psd file from the Chap22 folder on the Companion CD. Type **50** in the Zoom Percentage field, and then press Enter (Return).

2. On the Layers palette, drag the Wine Bottle & Glass layer title into the Create New Layer icon at the bottom of the Layers palette, as shown in Figure 2.29. Andromeda's Shadow filter will either render a shadow to the same layer as the objects casting the shadow (and there goes your chance to manipulate the shadow independently) or it will render a shadow to a layer *overwriting* the current visual information. So this duplicate layer you created will soon have the bottle and glass erased, only to be replaced by a shadow on the layer.

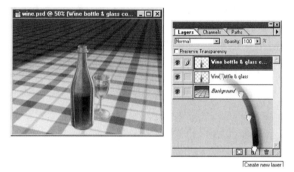

FIGURE 22.29   *Duplicate the Wine Bottle & Glass layer by dragging the icon into the Create New Layer icon. You'll use one layer for the image of the bottle and glass, and one layer in which to create the shadows.*

3. Click on the Wine Bottle & Glass layer title; this is your current editing layer, and the duplicate layer is above the current layer.

4. Choose Filter, Andromeda, and then choose Shadow Demo. Click on the splash screen telling you that the demo program will not render to file, and then the interface for the Shadow filter appears.

5. Click on the upper-left drop-down list (it's the only drop-down list in the interface!); choose Andromeda, Selected, Casting plane; then choose Studio90. A shadow will appear to the left of the bottle and glass, and the shadow will be very squat (not what is needed for this assignment).

6. Click on the Shadows Lights button, as shown in Figure 22.30, and then drag in the preview window, from left to right, until the shadow is casting as you see it in Figure 22.30. The highlights on the bottle and glass are almost face-forward, so the shadow for this scene should fall slightly to the right, and it will extend far into the distance in the image.

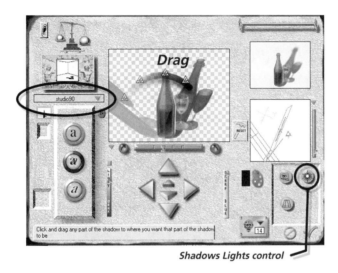

Shadows Lights control

FIGURE 22.30   *Choose a preset. Then modify the direction of the shadow by choosing the Shadows Lights button and then dragging in the preview window.*

7. Because the glass is slightly behind the bottle, the intersection of the casting plane and the objects is *not* at the bottom of the bottle. A single shadow casting plane for the bottle *and* glass should intersect the objects a little higher than the base of the bottle. Click on the Move casting plane intersection button (labeled in Figure 22.31), and then drag the blue horizontal line in the preview window until it's aligned with the base of the wine glass, as shown in Figure 22.31. If the shadow intersection (the blue horizontal line) is not visible in the preview window, drag a little upward on The Elevator control; when the blue line is visible, position it to meet the base of the glass.

8. Click on the shadow only button (the italicized "a"); the glass and bottle disappear, and only the shadow can be seen in the preview window, as shown in Figure 22.32. Click on the Shadow Lights button, and then drag the lightness slider so the marker is on the "g" in "light." Drag the sharp/blur slider until its marker is on the "h" in "sharp." Unlike Alien Skin's filter, the shadow is clipped at the blue intersection

line. This is okay—the bottle and glass on the top layer in the composition will hide the clipping.

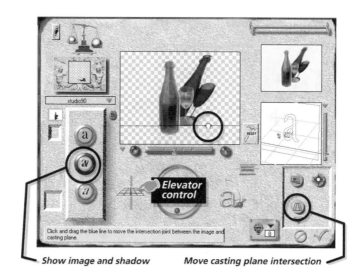

Show image and shadow   **Move casting plane intersection**

FIGURE 22.31 *Choose an intersection area for the shadow and the bottle and glass by dragging on the blue line in the preview window.*

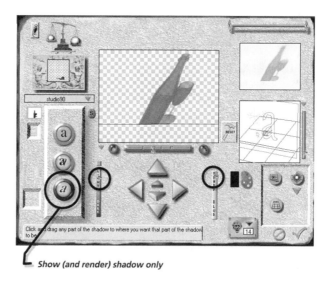

Show (and render) shadow only

FIGURE 22.32 *Click on the shadow only button to render the shadow you see in the preview window to the current editing layer in the image.*

9. If you own Andromeda's Shadow filter, click on the check mark icon to apply the filter. If you're running the demo, click on the cancel icon (play with this filter some more in the future to see its other features), and open Wine2.psd from the Chap22 folder on the Companion CD. This file contains the shadow rendered by the Shadow filter, and owners and nonowners are now at the same point in this assignment. We're not finished yet; keep the file open.

It's important to keep in mind that this Shadow filter includes a virtual camera, and that the shadow rendered to the Wine Bottle & Glass layer might not align with the bottle and glass on the duplicate layer. The reason is that the duplicate layer is static, whereas you can position the angle and location of the shadow in the Shadow filter's preview window any place you like. In fact, if you were to render a shadow to a layer that contains the objects casting the shadow, you might find that the Shadow filter repositions the objects along with the shadows!

Aligning the shadows to meet the bases of the bottle and glass is not difficult:

1. First, rename the layer that contains the shadow to Shadow (for easy reference) by double-clicking on the layer's title on the Layers palette, and then typing the name in the Name field. Click on OK to apply the name change.

2. With the Move tool, drag the Shadow layer until the shadows are beneath the glass and bottle on the top layer, as shown in Figure 22.33. The Wine2.psd image also contains a misaligned shadow, so even if you don't own the retail version of this filter, you can still practice your Photoshop skills by aligning the shadow with the objects.

Drag shadow so that its bottom is covered by the bottle and glass

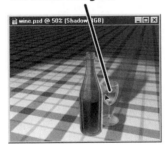 

FIGURE 22.33 *Use the Move tool to reposition the shadows so that they fall beneath the bottle and glass.*

As mentioned earlier, the shadow looks very nice and is optically accurate, but a tinted bottle and some table wine in a glass would *not* cast a grayscale shadow. Ready for some fun here?

TINTING SHADOWS

Because there is a fair degree of blurriness to the shadow you created, precision is not necessary as you tint the shadow in the following steps. The *presence* of color is more important than the exact *location* of the color you'll add to the shadows.

Here's how to add more realism to the shadows:

MASKING AND TINTING THE SHADOW LAYER

1. Double-click on the Zoom tool to move your view of the Wine.psd scene to 1:1 viewing resolution, and then maximize the image window.

2. Click on the eye icons for the Background and the Wine Bottle & Glass copy layers on the Layers palette to hide them. All you should see now are the shadows.

3. Double-click on the Quick Mask icon toward the bottom right of the toolbox. In the Quick Mask Options dialog box, make sure that the Color Indicates: Selected Areas button is chosen, and then click on OK to exit the dialog box. The image is in Quick Mask mode now, and everywhere you apply foreground color, the foreground color will appear as a tinted overlay in the image.

4. Choose the Paintbrush tool, and then on the Brushes palette click on the second row, far-right tip. On the Options palette, the mode should be Normal, Opacity: 100%, and Fade: 0. The current foreground color on the toolbox should be black.

5. Stroke over the denser area of the wine glass—the area that holds the wine in the top layer image (see Figure 22.34).

6. Click on the Standard Editing mode icon to the left of the Quick Mask mode icon. The selection you painted becomes a marquee selection, and the contents within the selection are available for editing.

7. Press Ctrl(⌘)+U to display the Hue/Saturation command box.

8. Click on the Colorize check box, drag the Hue slider to 0, and drag the Saturation slider to 74, as shown in Figure 22.35.

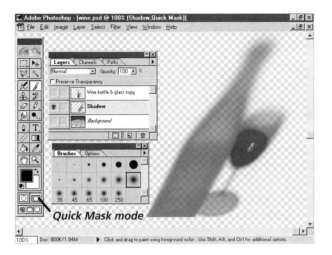

FIGURE 22.34 *Select the wine from the wine glass by stroking over it with the Paintbrush tool and a soft-edge brush tip.*

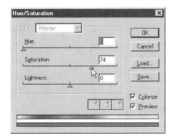

FIGURE 22.35 *Colorize and increase the saturation of the selection area to turn a grayscale tint to a red area, more accurately casting a shadow through semitransparent wine.*

WARNING

New to Photoshop 5 is the Auto Select Layer option on the Options palette. In versions 4 and 5, you can select a layer in a composition with a right-click (Macintosh: hold Ctrl and click) over an area, and pick the layer from the context menu. When this new Auto Select Layer feature is turned on, however, it enables you to choose a layer by clicking on the contents of a layer with the Move tool.

If you have the Layers palette open at all times, and you know exactly which element is located where, the Auto Select Layer feature can be welcome. But if you've grown accustomed to dragging *anywhere* on a layer to move the layer's contents, *un*check the Auto Select Layer option on the Options palette when the Move tool is chosen. If you don't, you'll be moving layer contents in all sorts of odd directions!

9. Click on OK to apply the color change, and then press Ctrl(⌘)+D to deselect the selection.

10. With the Lasso tool, create a marquee selection around the top of the wine bottle shadow, ending the selection above the top of the wine in the bottle's shadow. Peek ahead to Figure 22.36 for the shape of the selection you should create.

11. Press Ctrl(⌘)+U to display the Hue/Saturation command. Click on the Colorize check box, drag the Hue slider to 140, as shown in Figure 22.36, and drag the Saturation slider to about 70. Click on OK to apply the change, and then press Ctrl(⌘)+D to deselect the selection.

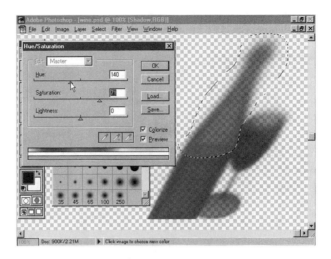

FIGURE 22.36 *Tint the top of the wine bottle shadow a rich green. The remainder of the shadow is okay as a grayscale area; a light casting through red wine in a green bottle would not cast a shadow with much color.*

12. Click on the areas next to the Background layer and the Wine Bottle & Glass Copy layer where there used to be eye icons. Doing this restores the visibility of the layers.

13. With the Shadow layer selected on the Layers palette, choose Multiply from the Mode drop-down list, and drag the Opacity slider to about 90%, so you can see some of the tablecloth through the shadow.

14. You're finished! Press Ctrl(⌘)+S to save the file one last time. For some perverse reason, the author has included Figure 22.37 in this book—these steps have had everything to do with color, and obviously Figure 22.37 is in black and white! No matter; check out the second color section in this book to see the finished assignment in color.

Through the preceding example of the wine glass and bottle, you've worked through the process by which a design of something becomes an integrated part of a whole composition. Only on the most overcast of days will an object fail to cast a shadow, and those are days when you would not want to be taking photographs anyway! Sharpness, perspective, density, color, and shape are all elements in the recipe for creating realistic shadows.

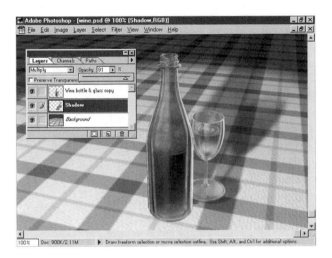

FIGURE 22.37   *Filters are a terrific timesaver. Filters plus your own artistic input add up to outstanding images.*

SUMMARY

Okay, the author reread this chapter before submitting it to the publisher, and he must correct himself. This chapter is *not* solely for the artist, even though all the example images were computer generated. If you're a photographer (or even if you like playing with photographic images as a hobby), you now know how to turn a dull surface into a reflective one. You also know how to create shadows of many different types, which can be a career saver if you work in a production department and you're handed a badly retouched photograph. Reflections and shadows are as important to a design or photo as the main elements, because they are the supporting elements. Without shadows and reflections, a picture or a rendered model will look flat, and the audience, on some level, will say to themselves, "Eh. There's something wrong with this picture."

In Chapter 23, "Playing with Perspective," we get back to photography and photo-retouching, but with a novel twist. "Perspective" is usually something we think of as what an audience sees in a scene. But what about the *subjects* in the scene? Don't they have their own perspective—their own point of view—of the scene, too? Come along to the next chapter, where you'll learn how to create different scene perspectives that are perfectly correct from the subject's point of view, but are totally impossible—yet photographically accurate—from your audience's point of view. Chapter 23 shows you how to manipulate images to create a composition that's an homage to the famous surrealist artist M.C. Escher.

PLAYING WITH PERSPECTIVE

Totally amazing imaging software programs have hit the market and achieved great success in the past few years. Progressive technology and consumer demand have driven vendors to create powerful programs that were inconceivable only a handful of years ago. Within the reach of any designer or photographer is the ability to create an image of an implausible reality or to alter an existing reality. If putting a new twist on reality interests you, one approach is to create multiple perspectives within the same image.

One master of altering reality was the artist M.C. Escher. Among his most famous works are images that show two or more perspectives simultaneously. In one such piece, called Relativity, *the "ancestors" of Poser 3 models are walking on stairs that are at various angles—left, right, upside-down, right-side up—yet all these views seamlessly tie together to*

create an image that looks real but at the same time seriously challenges the viewer's concept of logical spatial order.

This chapter's assignment takes two average-looking photographs and creates two points of view within one image relative to the people in the scene. To help you visualize this, Figure 23.1 shows the completed image, Park Bench. The model on the left is sitting on the backrest for the model on the right, and vice versa. The newspaper is also perplexing—it's on the seat but also on the backrest. Because the newspaper is on the backrest, shouldn't it fall down? Then again, which way *is* down? The same goes for the glass of soda held by the model on the right. Why doesn't the soda spill, if it is on the edge of the seat? Or is it?

FIGURE 23.1 *This chapter's assignment contains two points of view in one image.*

You might wonder where the idea for Park Bench came from and how you can develop ideas of your own. There's an old saying, "There is nothing new under the sun." If you examine any creative work, you will find signs of influence from other artists no matter how original the work appears—in this case, Park Bench is an offspring of Escher's *Relativity*. If ideas for images haven't been dropping in your brain, study work from your favorite artist(s) to help get the creative juices flowing. Now, let's take a look at the work involved in getting the Park Bench images into the computer.

PARK BENCH—BEHIND THE SCENE

You should be aware that all the example images in this book and on the Companion CD were *not* conceived of and created in only minutes or hours. Also keep in mind that the steps you will be going through were written after many days of trial and error and of fine-tuning the image—before the author started writing this chapter! Several things were necessary before the actual Park Bench photo shoot could happen: a sunny summer day, an available model, locating (actually *purchasing*) an 8-foot ladder, and finding a wooden bench that was in good condition.

Notice in the Park Bench image that symmetry is needed between the seat and the back of the bench. This symmetry required photographing the model at 45° off the ground plane, or in other words at an angle that bisects the angle formed between the seat and back. With a tall ladder and a nuclear engineer (the model's dad) to guide the author, the axis of the camera lens was fairly close to the target angle, as you can see in Figure 23.2.

FIGURE 23.2 *Placing the camera's lens axis at 45° above the ground helps achieve symmetry between the seat and back of the bench.*

TIP

If you have access to a film scanner, you can save a lot of money by requesting "Develop only, no prints" at a one-hour lab. For example, the author pays $1.79 per 24-exposure roll; if prints were included, the cost would be $9.99.

Be sure to read Chapter 2, "Getting Stock Images," for more information on scanning.

NOTE

Throughout this chapter, you may need to hide or show all palettes or only specific palettes. To hide or show all palettes, press the Tab key. To hide or show a specific palette only, select it from the Window item on the menu bar.

Also, Park Bench is the only image in this chapter. At the end of each set of steps you will save your edits to disk, and the following steps will pick up at that point. In other words, leave the image open after each procedure if you are going through this chapter without taking any detours.

The props—newspapers, magazines, and a glass of soda—were placed in different locations for each of the two pictures. The model was also repositioned throughout the shoot, and clothing was changed occasionally. Two rolls of 100 ISO film were shot to ensure enough good resource material to work with. In your own imaging, don't ever hesitate to burn lots of film—it's a lot cheaper in time and money than having to reshoot.

After the photo shoot, both rolls were developed at a one-hour lab. No prints were made because the negatives would be scanned. A scan from a negative provides far more image detail than a scan from the photograph printed from that negative.

This chapter is about seamlessly merging two pictures and working with the details to create a simple yet perplexing image. The operative word here is "seamless," and matching the color of the two images is most important, so let's get to Photoshopping!

COLOR-MATCHING TWO IMAGES

Unless you create your images totally in the computer by using, for example, a painting or modeling program, you will need to perform some color correcting—the perfect scan rarely happens. Photoshop has many commands to adjust color, and the best one to use is the one that works for each specific assignment.

In the following steps you will combine two files, digitized by a film scanner, into one document. The color of one of the images requires correcting, and you will use the other image as a reference for the adjustments.

COMBINING AND COLOR-MATCHING TWO IMAGES

1. Open the Rghtside.PSD and the Leftside.PSD images from the Chap23 folder on the Companion CD. (In the Open dialog box, Windows users can press the Shift key and select both files; then click OK. This will open both files with just one trip to the Open box.)

2. With the Leftside.PSD image active, choose Layer, Duplicate Layer from the menu bar. In the Duplicate Layer dialog box, type **Left Side** in the As: field and choose Rghtside.psd from the Document list (see Figure 23.3). Click OK.

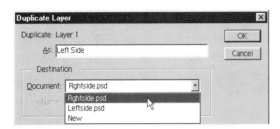

FIGURE 23.3 *Use the Duplicate Layer feature to place a copy of the layer in Leftside.PSD into the Rghtside.PSD image.*

3. Close the Leftside.PSD image now. Notice that the Rghtside.PSD image has an additional layer with the title you gave it: Left Side. Double-click on the Layer 0 title in the Layers palette and type **Right Side** in the Name field. Click on OK.

4. Type **50** in the Zoom percentage box, press Enter (Return), and drag the document window edges away from the image so the window background is slightly larger than the image.

5. Press Alt(Opt)+] to make the layer (Left Side) above the current layer active for editing. Choose the Rectangular Marquee tool and select the left half of the image. Figure 23.4 shows the selection area.

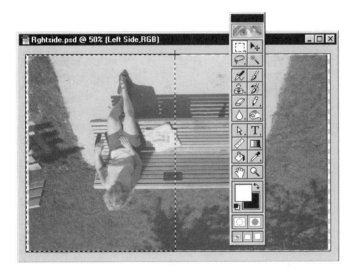

FIGURE 23.4 *Select the left half of the image with the Rectangular Marquee tool.*

6. On the Layers palette, click the Add Layer Mask icon at the center bottom of the palette. The rectangular selection you created prohibited Layer Mask from hiding the left side of the layer. At this point, your image should look like Figure 23.5.

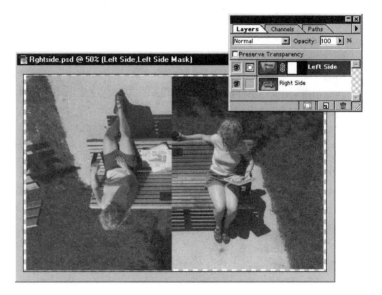

FIGURE 23.5 *Using Layer Mask, hide the right half of the top layer.*

The layer mask you just created is temporary. The purpose for the mask is to make visible, simultaneously, the two areas on each layer that will meet each other in the final composition—the bench and the concrete. By doing this, you'll constantly have a reference to color correct from within a single image.

7. The Right Side layer needs the color adjustments. Click on its layer title on the Layers palette to make it active for editing.

Notice the difference in color between the left half of the image and the right half. The bench on the right contains too much magenta and yellow. The concrete is too green and blue.

8. Choose the Color Sampler tool (I) and press Enter (Return) to show the Options palette. Change the Sample Size to 3 by 3 Average on the Options palette's Sample Size drop-down list. Press the Tab key to hide all palettes—you'll need to see as much of the image as possible.

9. On the left half of the image, click a Color Sampler point just above the seat's shadow on the concrete (the Info palette appears). Click another Sampler in the middle of the wood slat located just above the plaque on the bench. You can see both locations in Figure 23.6. Alert: Your color values shown in the Info palette for samples #1 and #2 should be close to those shown in this figure, but do not need to be exactly the same!

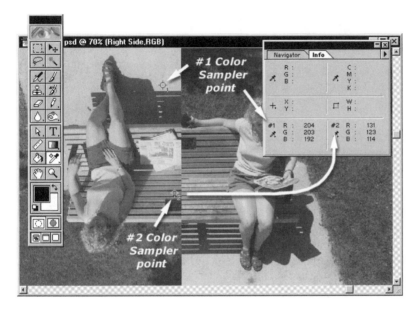

FIGURE 23.6   *Click a Color Sampler at the two locations shown here.*

10. Press Ctrl(⌘)+B to display the Color Balance dialog box. Uncheck the Preserved Luminosity box.

11. With the Midtones selected, enter the following in the Color Levels fields: **−6, +13, +14**. With Shadows selected, enter: **−5, +9, +18**, and for the Highlights, enter: **+12, −10, −11**. Click OK to apply the color adjustments.

12. Place the Color Sampler tool over the concrete area just below the bench shadow in the Right Side layer and compare the RGB readout in the Info palette with the #1 point sample values. As you can see in Figure 23.7, the numbers are very close, indicating that the corrections in the highlights are quite accurate! Note: your values might not be exactly the same as the values you see in this figure.

NOTE

The Color Sampler tool is new in Photoshop 5. You can use a maximum of four sample points; the points will remain in the image, even after the document is closed, until you delete them. There are two ways to delete a sample point: with the Color Sampler tool active, press Alt(Opt) and click on the point, or drag the point outside the image window. You can also move a point by dragging it with the Color Sampler tool.

FIGURE 23.7 *Place the Color Sampler tool over the concrete area and compare the Info palette's readout with the #1 sample point.*

TIP

In your color correcting adventures, adjustment layers (Layer, New, Adjustment Layer) will serve you better than the process used in these steps. You can repeatedly re-enter the dialog box to fine-tune your settings or totally discard the adjustments without ever altering the pixels in your image.

13. Place the tool over the wood slat just below the plaque on the same layer, and compare the RGB values with the #2 sample point.

The readout values are lower than those for #2, *but* they are almost identical in difference *between* colors. In other words, the difference between R:113 and G:106 (see Figure 23.8) is 7. For #2, the difference between the red and green is 8. And when you compare the difference between G: and B: in both the live readout and #2, the value is the same: 9. This indicates that the colors are virtually identical, but the brightness is different. Due to the edits that will be performed on this image later in this chapter, we will stop here with color correcting. Further tweaking would be a waste of time because the corrections would not be noticed.

14. Press the Alt(Opt) key and click on each of the sample points to delete them. Press the Tab key to show the palettes that were hidden.

15. Click on the layer mask thumbnail (*not* the image thumbnail) for the Left Side layer, drag the thumbnail into the trash icon, and then choose Discard in the attention box.

16. Save the file as Park Bench.PSD to your hard disk and leave the image open.

FIGURE 23.8 *The difference between each color value is almost identical to those of the #2 sample point.*

The preceding steps only touched on the power of using the Color Sampler tool to help adjust the color of an image. If you master this method, you can color correct "by the numbers" without even having to look at the image!

Now that Right Side is color balanced to Left Side, it's time to begin the actual blending of the images. You will use one of Photoshop's most popular features—the Layer Mask.

PAINTING WITH THE LAYER MASK TO CREATE A SEAMLESS COMPOSITE

Some of the most favorite features of any software program are those that enable the user to go back repeatedly and change edits that were applied earlier in the creation process. Among Photoshop 5's features are adjustment layers, Layer Effects, the Type layer, the History palette, and of course, the layer mask. The price of most of these features is RAM usage. The author uses a machine with 128 MB of RAM (RAM is so cheap these days, I encourage all Photoshop users to buy and install as much as possible). By stocking up on RAM, you can take full advantage of these editable features by setting the History States to 100, not applying a layer mask, and not merging an adjustment layer until the very end of the creative process, if ever.

In the following steps, you will move the Left Side layer to make the lines in the bench align with the lines on the Right Side layer. Then you will apply a layer mask to the bench area to begin the compositing process.

MOVING A LAYER AND PAINTING LAYER MASK

1. Press V (Move tool) and click on the Left Side layer in the Layers palette. Type **200** in the Zoom percentage box and press Enter (Return).

2. Type **5** to reduce the layer opacity to 50%. Toggle to the Hand tool by pressing the Spacebar, and pan the image so you can see the newspapers and glass of soda. Using the arrow keys, nudge the Left Side layer to align at the edge of the bench near the glass (see Figure 23.9).

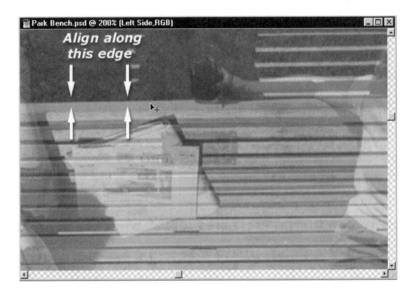

FIGURE 23.9   *Align the two benches along the top/bottom edge, as shown here.*

3. Press 0 to return the layer opacity to 100%. Press Ctrl(⌘)+[to flip the layer stack order in the Layers palette. Click on the top layer, Right Side, and then click on the Add Layer Mask icon at the bottom of the Layers palette. Your Layers palette should look like Figure 23.10.

FIGURE 23.10 *After flipping the order of the layer stack and adding a layer mask, your Layers palette should look like this.*

4. Move to a 100% magnification and choose the Polygon Lasso tool (L). Create a selection that encompasses most of the bench area. Do not include the top side of the top slat. Refer to Figure 23.11 to see the shape of this marquee.

FIGURE 23.11 *Create a selection that encompasses most of the bench area.*

5. With black as the foreground color, press Alt(Opt)+Delete to fill the selection with layer mask. Press Ctrl(⌘)+D to deselect the marquee. Your image should look like Figure 23.12.

FIGURE 23.12 *After filling the selection with layer mask, the bottom layer is visible.*

TIP

The brush tip you use when you apply a layer mask along a border area should produce an edge that most closely matches the image's visual content. In other words, a 35-pixel brush with 0% Hardness would create an extremely fuzzy edge in this example, whereas the 3-pixel brush with 100% Hardness would produce an edge identical to those seen in the image. Experimenting with various brush sizes and settings to find the best brush for the situation is a standard procedure.

6. Zoom to 300% and scroll the image so you can see where the model's right leg meets the edge of the bench seat on the Right Side layer. Press B (Paintbrush) and choose the second-from-left brush on the top row of the Brushes palette.

You will not apply this mask until the end of this chapter. The reason you are keeping the mask is that as you progress with the image, you may need to make additional edits. For this reason, at any time during the steps, add or subtract from the layer mask as you see fit.

7. Paint along the model's right side to reveal the bottom layer's bench, as shown in Figure 23.13. Add a mask from the seat's edge all the way to the beginning of the shadow under the model's arm—stop there.

8. Choose the Polygon Lasso tool and create a selection that follows the line of the shadow and extends into the model. Figure 23.14 shows the shape of this selection.

9. With the Paintbrush, continue to paint a layer mask along the underside of the model's arm.

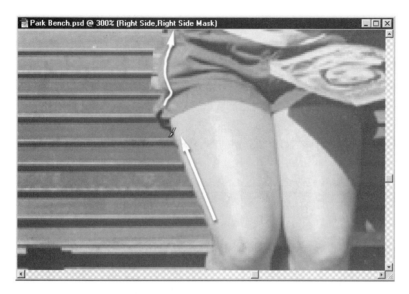

FIGURE 23.13 *When applying a layer mask, always use the brush size that produces an edge that looks identical to the edges in the image.*

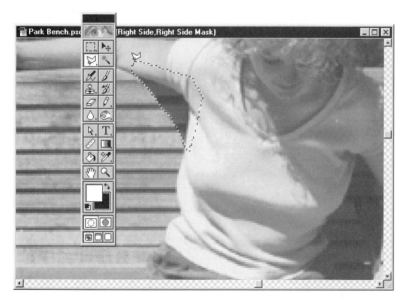

FIGURE 23.14 *Create a selection that follows the edge of the shadow and extends into the model.*

10. On the Layers palette (F7), click on the Left Side title, and then click the Create New Layer icon. A new layer titled Layer 1 is placed above the bottom, Left Side layer.

11. With black as the foreground color, press Alt(Opt)+Delete to fill the selection. Press Ctrl(⌘)+D to deselect the marquee.

12. On the Layers palette, change the mode of Layer 1 to Multiply from the drop-down list and set the Opacity to 60%. This will create a shadow effect on the bottom layer similar to the original shadow (see Figure 23.15).

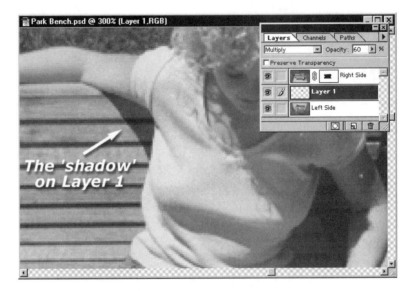

FIGURE 23.15 *Create on Layer 1 a shadow effect that resembles the original shadow.*

13. Press Ctrl(⌘)+E to merge this layer with the Left Side layer.

14. Click on the layer mask thumbnail on the Layers palette to return to editing the layer mask on the Right Side layer. Toggle to the Hand tool (Spacebar) and pan the image so that the glass is at the right of the image window and the leg of the model (Jaci) on the bottom layer is visible at the left.

15. Paint along the top of the bench from the shadow created by Jaci's hand all the way left to her leg at the left of the image. Painting into the grass area is okay— you'll mask that entire area later.

16. Press Ctrl(⌘)+S to save your changes. Leave the image open.

Although the masking task is not complete yet, you have covered a lot of ground in these steps and deserve a break. Treat yourself to a cool beverage (or a hot one, if you prefer)!

You might have wondered why the bench seat and back on the Left Side layer were made visible all the way across the bench. Why not some other configuration? As mentioned early in this chapter, experimentation is used extensively in design, and Park Bench required lots of it! The author tried just about every imaginable way to complete the Park Bench concept, and the steps you are following are those that created the most surreal-looking image.

So let's continue and finish adding the layer mask to the Park Bench image.

DEFINING AND FILLING A SELECTION ON THE LAYER MASK

1. While the layer is still in Layer Mask mode, paint along the outside edges of the glass, Jaci's arm and hair, the small bench area, and finally down her other arm until you reach the concrete area. Refer to Figure 23.16 for this area (note: this figure is at 200% zoom so you can see the entire area).

Due to the color of the background, it is difficult to distinguish where Jaci's hair line begins and ends. Apply mask using your own artistic eye, keeping in mind that green is not a color in Jaci's hair!

FIGURE 23.16 *Add layer mask around Jaci, all the way to the concrete area.*

2. Move to a 200% zoom. With the Pencil tool (N) and the third brush from the right on the top row of the Brushes palette, follow the line you made in the previous step, being careful not to paint into Jaci. You are widening the mask line to make it easier to work with in the next step.

3. Press Ctrl(⌘)+0 to fit the image view to your screen. Choose the Polygon Lasso tool and click within the *center* of the pencil line you created in step 2. Continue selecting the top half of the image, as shown in Figure 23.17. Try to follow the figure's marquee lines as closely as possible.

FIGURE 23.17 *Create a selection shaped like this, using the Polygon Lasso tool.*

4. With black as the current foreground color, press Alt(Opt)+Delete to fill the marquee with layer mask. Press Ctrl(⌘)+D to deselect the marquee.

Your image should now look dramatically different. But before someone peeks over your shoulder and asks whether you've found the next headless woman for the circus, continue applying layer mask.

5. Zoom to a 200% view of the missing-head area. Select the Paintbrush and, using the brush of your choice, apply mask in the area where you should see Jaci's head, shoulders, and arms. Let the mask extend beyond Jaci so you can see exactly where her silhouette starts and stops. Refer to Figure 23.18 to see what your image should look like at this point.

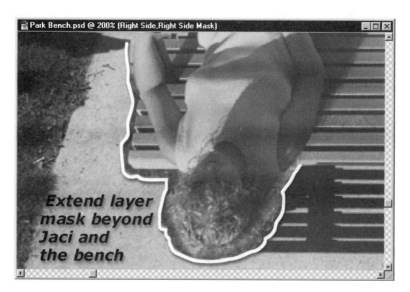

FIGURE 23.18 *Apply enough layer mask to reveal the areas that surround Jaci (the white line is a guide).*

6. Press D (default colors); then press X (switches foreground/background colors), and choose the far-left brush on the second row of the Brushes palette. Paint with white to remove the layer mask around Jaci's hair.

Because the grass is in the sun, distinguishing the hair line is easier here. Don't try to mask around the loose strands of hair; just follow the outside edge of her hair as best you can.

7. Choose the second-from-left brush on the top row and continue removing the grass area along Jaci's arm and the left side of the bench.

8. Use the Hand tool (hold the Spacebar) to pan the view to her left arm, and add or remove layer mask as necessary.

9. Press Ctrl(⌘)+0 to move the view to fit in Photoshop's workspace without window scrollbars. Your image should look like Figure 23.19.

10. Press Ctrl(⌘)+S to save your changes.

FIGURE 23.19   *Even at this point of the assignment, your image should look confusing!*

Clearly you have dramatically changed Park Bench by carefully applying layer mask to visually integrate the two layers. Now let's take a look at the image and decide what other changes would make this image have a stronger visual impact.

A good question to ask yourself when designing is, "Are there any unnecessary elements in the image?" By eliminating superfluous areas, you make your image visually stronger. In Park Bench, the biggest distractions currently are the shadows cast by the bench—*both* top and bottom shadows. Here is a situation that calls for artistic license. Park Bench is supposed to preserve as much realism as possible (okay, perspective is something you're *not* preserving) and shadows are elements that shout "This is real!" So, if you remove the shadows, you are losing an aspect of the image's credibility. After all, there is a shadow cast from Jaci's head. A workaround? Do a little trickery that most, if not all, viewers won't notice. Here's how: Remove all shadows cast by the bench, yet retain the shadows cast by the model. This will work very well to simplify the image, yet require some fancy Photoshop footwork.

REMOVING THE SHADOW AREAS

When the author was first learning Photoshop, the version was 2.5. Photoshop was a simple world then—no layers and layer masks, no History palette, no Actions, and very few native filters. You could learn all the features a lot faster, simply because there was less to learn. So in 1993, when confronted with a design problem, you had to make do with the few commands you had. Today, in version 5, you have much more latitude in problem-solving *as long as* you know all the features at your disposal. Once you learn all of Photoshop's features, those seemingly impossible problems become very easy to solve.

To remove the bench shadows as easily as possible, you will use a number of different techniques and tools in the steps to follow. Starting with the shadow in the upper half of the image, you will modify the shadow cast from Jaci's legs and then remove the bench's shadow.

USING SELECTIONS AND LAYERS TO REMOVE A SHADOW

1. Zoom to a 100% view of the upper bench shadow. Double-click the Magic Wand tool and type **20** in the Tolerance field in the Options palette. Be sure the Anti-aliased box is checked and Use All Layers is *un*checked.

2. Choose the bottom layer, Left Side, on the Layers palette and click on the right side of Jaci's right calf area. Press the Shift key and click on the right side of her thigh area. Holding Shift adds to the current marquee selection. Depending on exactly where you click, you might not need the second click or you might even need a third click. Refer to Figure 23.20 for the shape of this selection.

3. Hold down the Shift key and press the right-arrow key three times to move the marquee (see Figure 23.20). Holding the Shift key when using the arrow keys moves the marquee in 10-pixel increments. With the marquee selection, you are matching the outside line of her leg to create the shape of the shadow for her leg.

4. On the Channels palette, click the Save Selection as Channel icon.

5. Choose the Polygon Lasso tool. Hold down the Shift key again, but this time click a selection that includes the bench's shadow and part of Jaci's arm and head, and that goes through the center of the selection you created in step 2. Be sure to carefully select along the edge of the bench, as shown in Figure 23.21.

FIGURE 23.20 *Move the selection of the leg to the right.*

FIGURE 23.21 *Using the Polygon Lasso tool while you press and hold the Shift key, create a selection that encompasses the shadow.*

6. Choose the Rectangular Marquee tool, hold down the Alt(Opt) key, and select most of the marquee that extends into the bench area. This action will remove this part of the selection. Do not select any area that is higher than the bench itself.

7. Press the Page Up key to view the uppermost area of the image.

8. Click inside the marquee and drag upward and slightly to the right so that only those concrete areas that are fully illuminated (no shadows) are within the selection area. Don't worry if an area in the upper left goes beyond the concrete.

9. Press Ctrl(⌘)+J to copy this area to a new layer. Choose the Move tool and drag the concrete area down and to the left until it touches the top (or is it bottom?<g>) of the bench.

10. On the Channels palette, Ctrl(⌘)+click on the Alpha 1 channel to load the selection. Press the Delete (Backspace) key, then Ctrl(⌘)+D to deselect the marquee. Drag the Alpha 1 channel to the trash icon. Figure 23.22 shows the Park Bench image at this point.

The visible line at the top of the "new" concrete area—caused by the lighter concrete being next to darker concrete—is a telltale area that needs to be removed.

FIGURE 23.22 *After copying the concrete area and moving it over the shadow, your image should look like this.*

11. Choose the Rubber Stamp tool (S) and, on the Options palette, be sure Use All Layers and Aligned are checked. On the Brushes palette, click on the 35-pixel tip.

12. Alt(Opt)+click just above the line to define a sampling point. Click and drag along the line to clone in darker concrete there.

From steps 9-12, you might duplicate some of those stains or marks on the concrete—this is something to avoid because it says "Sloppy Photoshop work here!" After you have eliminated the line, go back over those stains after you have defined a different sampling point for the Rubber Stamp tool.

13. Zoom in to a 200% view of the leg area you worked on earlier. Press E and then press Enter (Return) to activate the Eraser tool and bring up the Options palette. Set the mode to Paintbrush and use the third brush on the top row of the Brushes palette. Remove any concrete area that spills over the bench.

14. Choose the Blur tool and a setting of 40% Pressure on the Options palette and the second brush on the second row of the Brushes palette. Slowly drag once over the line where the leg and shadow meet. This will blur the line to mimic the other shadow edges.

15. Press Ctrl(⌘)+S to save the edits. Figure 23.23 shows the shadow area at this point.

FIGURE 23.23 *Copying the concrete area onto a new layer and placing it over the shadow is a quick and effective way to remove the shadow.*

After you outlined the shadow to define the area of concrete to copy, covering the shadow was relatively easy. Having the Right Side layer was helpful because you could slide the concrete area under Jaci's head and arm—you had already defined that area with the layer mask. Speaking of the layer mask, now that you've replaced the dark grass with the bright concrete, you might notice a few areas of grass that need touching up, using Layer Mask mode. Do this now before proceeding with the image.

Four small shadow areas still need to be removed from the top bench shadow. As in the previous steps, you will select each area before you use the Rubber Stamp. This way, you don't have to be concerned about spilling into other areas.

USING SELECTIONS AND THE RUBBER STAMP TO REMOVE THE SMALLER SHADOWS

1. Zoom to a 300% view of the two small shadow areas at the right of the bench.

2. With the Polygon Lasso tool, click along the edge of the bench and Jaci's arm where the shadow borders. Then click well into the sunlit concrete area and return to your first click. See Figure 23.24 for a guide of this marquee.

You don't want to select along the right edge of the shadow because doing so will create a hard edge. You want a hard edge only at the bench and bench arm. A sharp edge in the concrete area would display something that would ruin your cloning work with the Rubber Stamp tool, as mentioned earlier.

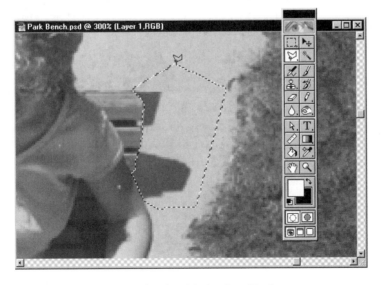

FIGURE 23.24 *Carefully select along the edge of the bench and Jaci's arm.*

3. Press Ctrl(⌘)+H to hide the marquee. This will enable you to see, as you clone, how well you selected the bench and arm.

4. Press Ctrl(⌘)+Alt(Opt)+Spacebar, and click once inside the image window to zoom out to 200%.

5. Select the Rubber Stamp tool and the far-right brush on the second row on the Brushes palette.

6. Alt(Opt)+click a sample area above the marquee and toward the grass, and then click and drag over one shadow. The concrete is somewhat darker near the grass, and the area you are cloning into also features the darker concrete.

7. Alt(Opt)+click to sample another area above the marquee, and then click and drag over the other shadow.

8. Type **300** in the Zoom percentage box, and then press Enter (Return).

9. Toggle to the Hand tool (hold the Spacebar) and pan the document view to the right so you can see the shadows near Jaci's legs.

10. Using the same technique for the other shadows, remove these two shadows, one at a time.

11. Choose the Blur tool, and set the Pressure to 20% in the Options palette. Using the second brush on the second row of the Brushes palette, slowly drag once over any skin area edges that look sharper than other edges.

12. Press Ctrl(⌘)+S to save your changes.

You have successfully removed the bench's upper shadow area. The techniques you used are the same as those used to remove the bench's lower shadow area, yet the process is shorter because there are fewer elements to work around and only one shadow area to remove—the shadow at the far right should remain because it is Jaci's shadow.

Can you remove the lower shadow without directions? If so, give it a try! If you're not too sure, then follow these steps as a guide:

REMOVING THE BENCH'S LOWER SHADOW

1. Zoom to a 200% view of the lower shadow area.

2. Click on the Right Side layer thumbnail or title on the Layers palette to make it active for editing. Do not click on the Layer Mask thumbnail.

3. Select the left half of the left calf and foot. You can use the Magic Wand, Pen tool, or Polygon Lasso.

4. Create a channel of the selection.

5. Ctrl(⌘)+click on the Layer Mask thumbnail. This creates a marquee selection based on your layer mask painting work. Press Ctrl(⌘)+Shift+I to invert the selection.

6. Ctrl(⌘)+Shift+click on the Alpha 1 channel to add it to the selection. Save this selection as a channel. Drag the Alpha 1 channel to the trash icon.

7. Deselect the selection and zoom out to a 100% view.

8. Loosely select the shadow area with the Polygon Lasso tool (see Figure 23.25). Click inside the marquee and drag the selection down until it encompasses only sunlit concrete. Copy this area to a new layer and then move the layer contents over the shadow area.

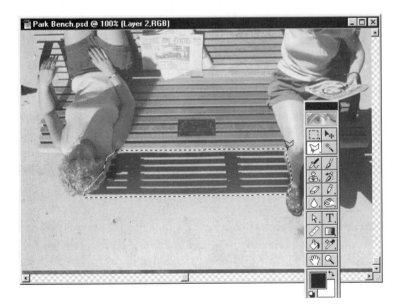

FIGURE 23.25 *Loosely select the shadow area with the Polygon Lasso tool.*

9. Load the Alpha 2 channel and press the Delete (Backspace) key.

10. Deselect the selection and use the Rubber Stamp tool to eliminate any lines and repeated stain marks.

11. Use the Blur tool to soften any edges that appear too hard.

12. Delete the Alpha 2 channel.

13. Save the changes. Your image should look like Figure 23.26.

FIGURE 23.26 *Even with both bench shadows removed, the image still retains a sense of realism.*

Voila! Using several Photoshop features, you have created a visually stronger image by removing the unnecessary shadows.

Now is a good time to take a critical look at Park Bench. A lot has been accomplished, but more can be done. Can you see at least one area that is begging for attention? If you said, "the grass," you are correct. But before discussing how to handle the grass area, can you find two more areas that need Photoshop surgery? Aside from the fact that the image needs to be cropped (visible transparency isn't very attractive), you have grass showing through the glass of soda and under Jaci's hand, where you should see concrete. And you have quite a bit of touch-up work throughout the image—stray white specks, stains on the concrete, and a cigarette butt, to name a few. Let's tackle the grass areas first.

REDESIGNING THE GRASS AREAS

The first question to ask is "What should be done with the grass areas?" There are some unattractive shadows on the left side of the image, and two different shades of grass on the right side. Do we want to retain that funky angular look or design a different shape (Photoshop does *landscaping,* too)? Or should we totally remove the grass? Perhaps the quickest, easiest, and best design is to create a vertical line of grass on each side of the image. So, get out your virtual shovel and landscaping gloves and let's get digging!

USING LAYERS TO MANIPULATE THE GRASS AREAS

1. Move the view of the image to fit on your screen (Ctrl(⌘)+0). Click on the Left Side title in the Layers palette to make it active for editing.

2. Choose the Polygon Lasso tool and select a portion of grass and concrete from the upper-right area of the image. Don't worry if the selection includes part of Jaci (refer to Figure 23.27).

FIGURE 23.27 *Select part of the grass and concrete area with the Polygon Lasso tool.*

NOTE

The frequency and color of the gridlines you see could be the default settings or settings you might have entered previously. As long as you have one line at approximately every .25 inch, your screen is set for the next step.

If you do not like the frequency or the current color of the grid, press Ctrl(⌘)+K, and then press Ctrl(⌘)+6 to access the Guides and Grid preferences.

3. Press Ctrl(⌘)+J to copy the selected area to a new layer.

4. Press Ctrl(⌘)+' (apostrophe) to show Grid Lines.

5. Press Ctrl(⌘)+T to launch the Free Transform command. A bounding box now surrounds the area you copied to the new layer.

6. Place the cursor outside the box and move the cursor's position around any bounding box handle (the boxes at the corners and the middle of the bounding box) until the cursor becomes a bent double-headed arrow. Click and drag to rotate the layer contents until the grass line is parallel with one of the grid lines (see Figure 23.28).

7. Press Enter (Return) to apply the rotation. Press Ctrl(⌘)+' (apostrophe) to hide the grid lines.

8. On the Layers palette, drag this layer, Layer 3, to the top of the layer stack. Then drag this layer to the Create New Layer icon at the bottom of the Layers palette. Repeat this procedure one more time so that you have three layers of this grass and concrete section.

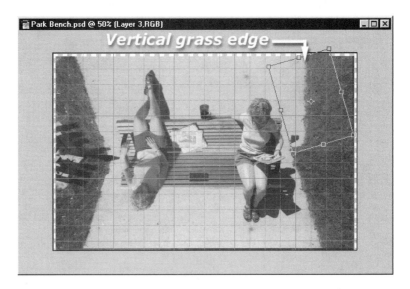

FIGURE 23.28 *Rotate the grass and concrete area until the grass line is parallel with a grid line.*

9. With the Auto Select Layer option active, all it takes is a click in the image window to switch between active layers. If you click on a nontransparent area, the layer that contains the area you clicked on instantly becomes the current editing layer.

10. Click and drag the top copy of the grass and concrete layer (Layer 3 copy 2) downward until the top of this copy touches the bottom of the Layer 3 copy (see Figure 23.29). You can hold down the Shift key to constrain the movement to 45° increments, such as this perfectly vertical direction.

FIGURE 23.29 *Move one copy of the grass and concrete layer downward.*

11. Click once on the next grass and concrete copy in the image; then hold the Shift key and drag the contents downward until this copy lines up with the bottom of the layer you moved in step 10.

12. On the Layers palette, click on the Layer 3 copy 2 title. Press Ctrl(⌘)+E two times to merge all three layers.

13. Press the Alt(Opt) key and click on the eye icon for Layer 3, the grass and concrete layer, in the Layers palette. This will hide all *other* layers, making it easier to see the edits you will make in the next step. Place a check in the Preserve Transparency box.

NOTE

The reason you had to click once on the next copy of the grass and concrete layer is to make that layer active. If you were to hold the Shift key first and then click, you would create a link between that layer and the currently active layer—the layer you just moved—and then both would move.

14. Using the Rubber Stamp tool and the 35-pixel brush, clone over any lines and shadows that make this layer look as though it were actually three identical layers (see Figure 23.30). Then, Alt(Opt)+click on the eye icon in the Layers palette to show all layers.

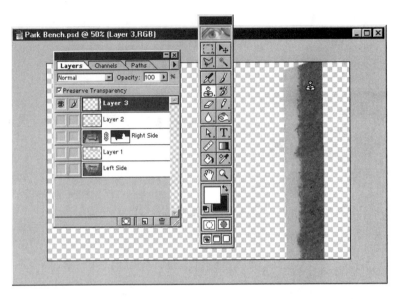

FIGURE 23.30   *Use the Rubber Stamp tool to remove the lines and shadows that indicate that this was three identical layers.*

15. On the Layers palette, uncheck the Preserve Transparency box and drag the layer to the Create New Layer icon. From the menu bar, choose Edit, Transform, Flip Horizontal.

16. Choose the Move tool, hold the Shift key and drag this layer to the left side of the image. The exact placement is not important at this time.

17. Double-click on the Layer 3 copy title in the Layers palette and name the layer Grass Left. Perform the same procedure for Layer 3, but call it Grass Right. Press Ctrl(⌘)+S to save the changes. Your image should look like Figure 23.31.

Whew—after all this yard work, you deserve a snack break!

You have taken Park Bench a long way on its journey to completion. In your own image-creating process, you might want to save a copy of the document at various stages. This way, you can go back and create multiple versions of your first concept, or take the image in a totally different direction than you originally intended.

FIGURE 23.31   *A little Photoshop landscaping, and the image looks more organized.*

INTEGRATING THE GRASS AREAS WITH THE MAIN IMAGE AREA

The procedures to make a seamless transition between the grass layers you just created and the concrete area surrounding the bench are very similar to the steps you used earlier in this chapter to create the first composite.

After cropping the image in step 4 of the next set of steps, feel free to continue on your own to complete the image. The end result should be the bench surrounded by the concrete areas, with a vertical strip of grass on both sides. The areas you want to pay particular attention to are the stray shadows on the left and the model's shadow on the right. The stray shadows should be removed and the model's shadow should be completely visible. Finally, you'll merge the two grass and concrete layers. Let's begin…

USING LAYER MASK AND THE RUBBER STAMP TOOL TO CREATE A SEAMLESS COMPOSITE

1. With your image view fit to screen (Ctrl(⌘)+0), press Ctrl(⌘)+R to show the rulers.

As noted earlier in the chapter, you will want to hide all palettes if you need an unobstructed view of the image. Hide or show palettes as necessary by pressing the Tab key.

2. Click inside the zero origin box located at the intersection of the rulers, and drag down and to the right until the vertical cross hair is in the middle of the plaque (dark rectangle) on the bench (see Figure 23.32). This sets the horizontal ruler to 0″ at this location, which is extremely close to the center of the image.

FIGURE 23.32 *Reset the zero point to the middle of the plaque.*

If your rulers are not displaying inches, double-click on either of the rulers to display the Preferences dialog box, make sure that inches is chosen, and then click on OK.

3. Using the Move tool with Auto Select Layer on, position the two grass layers so that the grass edge lines up at 1 3/4″ at each side of the image (refer to Figure 23.33).

4. Press C for the Crop tool, uncheck the Fixed Target Size box on the Options palette if it's checked, and drag a rectangle that includes the outer edge of the grass layers as well as the outer edge of the top and bottom concrete areas (see Figure 23.34). Double-click inside the marquee to apply the crop. Press Ctrl(⌘)+R to hide the rulers.

FIGURE 23.33   *Align the grass edge to the 1 3/4" mark on the horizontal ruler.*

FIGURE 23.34   *The Crop tool provides anchors that you can drag to tweak your cropping area.*

NOTE

You can also crop an image by using the Rectangular Marquee tool and then choosing Edit, Crop from the menu bar. Using the Crop tool, though, allows you to easily reposition your crop lines. You can individually move any of the four sides by dragging on the center anchor, or you can change the size of the rectangle by dragging on any of the four corner anchors.

5. Click on the Grass Left layer in the Layers palette to make it active for editing. Double-click the Rubber Stamp tool to choose it and display the Options palette. Place a check in the Use All Layers box. On the Brushes palette, choose the far-right brush on the second row.

6. Zoom to 100% view of the Grass Left layer near the bench. Alt(Opt)+click on a concrete area near a shadow to create a sample point. Click and drag over a section of the shadow.

Continue this technique to replace all shadows in this area with concrete (see Figure 23.35). When you get to the area close to Jaci's wrist, change the brush size to the second-from-left brush on the second row on the Brushes palette.

FIGURE 23.35 *Use the Rubber Stamp tool to clone the concrete area over the shadow areas.*

7. Press the Page Up key (to move your view to the top of the image) and clone over any visible line between the Grass Left layer and the layer containing the concrete. Press the Page Down key to move your view to the bottom, to remove the visible line in the bottom half of the image. Your goal is to remove the shadows and visually blend the concrete on the two layers.

8. Press the End key to move the view of the image to its lower-right corner area. You can see that the shadow Jaci casts is partially covered by the Grass Right layer. Click on the Right Side layer in the Layers palette.

9. Double-click the Magic Wand tool and, in the Magic Wand Options palette, type **22** for the Tolerance, and make sure that Anti-aliased is checked and Use All Layers is unchecked. Click inside the shadow. The marquee will extend into the concrete area, as you can see in Figure 23.36.

FIGURE 23.36 *The entire shadow (and more!) is selected on the Right Side layer.*

10. From the menu bar, choose Selection, Feather, and type **1** in the Feather Radius field. Click OK.

The value of 1 was determined from trial and error. The Feather value that most closely matches the edge of the shadow is the goal.

11. Click on the Grass Right layer in the Layers palette, and then press the Delete key. This will delete the concrete area within the marquee. Press Ctrl(⌘)+D to deselect.

12. Press S (Rubber Stamp tool) and, using the second-from-right brush on the second row of the Brushes palette, remove the visible line created by the two different shades in the concrete.

Be sure Use All Layers is checked on the Rubber Stamp Options palette. When you're working next to the shadow area, place a check in the Preserve Transparency box in the Layers palette. This will prevent cloning into the shadow area. Remember to *un*check this option when you're working on the other concrete areas.

13. Click on the top layer, Grass Left, and press Ctrl(⌘)+E to merge it with the layer below it, Grass Right. Press Ctrl(⌘)+0 to view the entire image; then press Ctrl(⌘)+S to save your changes.

Whether you followed all the preceding steps or completed the exercise on your own, your Park Bench should look like Figure 23.37. You have removed all lines created from different shades of concrete on each of the layers. You have also deleted part of the Grass Right layer so that the entire shadow from Jaci is visible.

FIGURE 23.37 *Park Bench, just a few edits before completion.*

APPLYING THE FINISHING TOUCHES TO PARK BENCH

Let's wind up this chapter with the finishing touches. Two edits remain: Concrete, not grass, should show through Jaci's glass, and there are white specks, stains, and a cigarette butt that must be cloned out. You will create a path to outline the area inside the glass and place concrete in this area. Finally, you will use a tool you should be quite familiar with by now—the Rubber Stamp tool—to remove blemishes throughout the image.

CREATING THE VISUAL EFFECT OF CONCRETE BEHIND GLASS

1. Zoom to 500%, with the glass of soda in the middle of the image window.

2. Choose the Pen tool. If you know how to use the Pen tool, draw a path inside the glass, just below the lip and around Jaci's fingers (see Figure 23.38). If you need a little help using the Pen tool, click at the 9 o'clock position inside the glass. Click the second anchor at 12 o'clock and don't release the mouse button. Drag away from the point until the line between the first and second points is curved along the inside of the glass's lip. Release the mouse button. Click the third anchor at the 3 o'clock position and use the same technique to create a curved segment between this and the previous anchor point. Continue this process, working around the fingers until you reach the first anchor point, and then click once on the first anchor to close the path. Your path should look like the one in Figure 23.38.

FIGURE 23.38 *The Pen tool is ideal for selecting curved areas.*

3. Ctrl(⌘)+click on the Work Path in the Paths palette to load the path as a selection. Click on the empty area below the Work Path title on the palette to hide the path.

4. Click on the Right Side layer in the Layers palette and press the Delete key. You should see the concrete area on Layer 1.

5. Click the Create New Layer icon at the bottom of the Layers palette (this layer will be named Layer 3). Choose Select, Feather from the menu bar, type **1** in the Feather Radius field, and then click OK. You are going to create a smoked-glass effect and the edges here should be slightly soft, just like other edges in this area.

6. With black as the foreground color, press Alt(Opt)+Delete to fill the selection with black. Press Ctrl(⌘)+D to deselect.

7. Okay, so the inside of the glass looks like the area filled with soda—this is easy to fix. On the Layers palette, change the blending mode to Soft Light (see Figure 23.39).

FIGURE 23.39 *Change the blending mode to Soft Light.*

8. There's also a small patch of grass area immediately below Jaci's hand, where only concrete should be visible. This is not a complex area to select, so use the Polygon Lasso tool to create the selection (be sure to make the Right Side layer active), and then press Delete. Deselect the marquee (Ctrl(⌘)+D).

If you find the edges a bit too sharp, use the Blur tool at a low pressure setting (20%) to blur the edges until they are similar to other edges in this area.

9. If you look at the top half of the glass, you can see areas of green from the original grass. Choose the Sponge tool. On the Sponge Options palette, set the mode to Desaturate and the Pressure to 100%. Select the first brush on the second row on the Brushes palette.

10. Click and drag over the greenish areas until the green is desaturated to gray (see Figure 23.40).

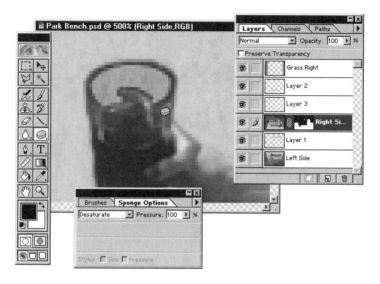

FIGURE 23.40   *Desaturate the green areas with the Sponge tool.*

11. Choose Layer, Flatten Image from the menu bar. The layer mask is applied (and you won't see an attention box).

12. Hold down the Ctrl(⌘) key and press the – (minus) key twice. This will zoom the view out to 300%. Press the Home key to move the view to the upper-left corner of the image.

13. Use the Rubber Stamp tool to clone over any white or dark specks that should not be in the image. The first brush on the second row of the Brushes palette is a perfect size for most of these spots. Don't forget the cigarette butt, and feel free to "heal" the bruise on Jaci's knee, using the Rubber Stamp tool. Navigate throughout the image with the Hand tool (press the Spacebar) in a "slowly but surely" fashion, straight up and down, perhaps, moving the view by one window width when you reach the top or bottom.

14. Press Ctrl(⌘)+S to save your changes. See Figure 23.41 (and the second color section of this book) for the completed Park Bench image.

TIP

The Park Bench image will be completed after the next four steps. After all the layers are flattened, any significant editing you may want to do will not be as easily accomplished as it is in this layered version. In your own imaging, it is a good practice to Save a Copy at this stage so you will have a layered version to go back to if necessary.

FIGURE 23.41 *The finished Park Bench.*

SUMMARY

You have used only a few of Photoshop's tools to create Park Bench. Although many techniques are shown in this chapter, the use of Photoshop's features was but a pittance when you consider its total power. The first and foremost reason this is a visually fascinating image is its concept. To bring photorealistic work beyond the "gee-whiz" stage (such as relying on filters to "make" the image), always begin with a strong idea. The execution of that idea is also very important, of course, but knowing everything about Photoshop is not a prerequisite to creating a masterpiece.

If you, like the author, enjoy finding clues to the way effects were created in either images or movies, you may have noticed one element in the Park Bench image that gives away its secret. After you flipped the left side vertically, the text in the newspaper was mirrored—the legible headline "AUTO" is flipped. You can handle this three ways: blur the text until it's no longer legible, flip the text so it's readable, or leave the text as is. This is an artist's call; you are familiar with the Blur tool and with using the Flip Vertical command and are welcome to handle the headline as you choose.

Early versions of Photoshop (pre-3.0) were more edit oriented—they had few illustration capabilities. In the next chapter, you will be introduced to the more robust illustrating power of Photoshop 5. Whether you want to add a splashy graphic to an existing image or start with a new document, Chapter 24, "Making Your Own Chrome Lettering," will teach you how.

CHAPTER 24

MAKING YOUR OWN CHROME LETTERING

Ron, a friend of the author, is an absolute wizard at using modeling and rendering programs—his work is photorealistic down to the last detail and inviting in content, and his understanding of what makes things look real is absolutely complete. But Ron confided to the author that he can't draw a straight line with a physical pencil, and that he has a hard time with drawing and painting applications. How can this be? Isn't he doing something more difficult than drawing, so drawing should naturally be tucked under his creative belt?

As mentioned earlier in this book, computer graphics is an art of "bootstrapping"; we designers learn what we can from informal education, and doing this frequently leaves gaps in one's talents. Photoshop 5 is a perfect example of a graphics tool that anyone can access, but the results can be quite limited if you think of and treat Photoshop solely as an application in which you paste together parts of digitized images. Photoshop is also a great *illustration* tool, and whether you believe you can paint or not, this chapter is going to walk you through the steps needed to create a fairly realistic illustration of chrome lettering.

NOTE

The font used in Chrome.tif was patterned after the chrome lettering on vintage cars, such as a 1954 Chevy. The "Ol' 54" font was created by Jonathan Smith, a gifted designer who has allowed the author to provide you with the font, in TrueType and Type 1, for Windows and the Macintosh. If you'd like to create chrome text using a phrase other than "Chrome," close all applications, and then add the font to either your system/fonts folder if you want to use TrueType, or load the font into Adobe Type Manager if you prefer to work with PostScript fonts.

This distinctive typeface can be found in the Examples/ Chap24/1954 folder on the Companion CD. Please don't forget to read the READ54.pdf file in this folder, so you can register the font with Mr. Smith if you decide to keep the font on your machine for future use. This is a shareware "try before you buy" typeface. It is *not* freeware.

BEGINNING AN ILLUSTRATION WITH A TEMPLATE

There are few things as intimidating as beginning an illustration without a framework already laid down—a template of sorts. Therefore, this section shows you how to create a template for your chrome illustration work. Chrome.tif in the Examples/Chap24 folder on the Companion CD is what you'll work with, if you like, in the sections to follow.

In the next section you'll create an alpha channel based on the lettering in the image, so you can add a gradient that looks like chrome to a layer in the composition.

CREATING AN ALPHA CHANNEL FROM GRAYSCALE ARTWORK

Granted, with the advent of layers in Photoshop, one's need for alpha channels is quite reduced, but there are times in a design assignment when you'll want to leverage the power of both layers and channels.

The chrome illustration is exactly such an occasion. You want the chrome lettering to be located in an alpha channel, so you can load it at any time to then paint within the selection marquee on a layer.

Here's how to set up the Chrome.tif piece so you can add a blend of colors that simulates chrome:

CREATING A TEMPLATE FROM A GRAPHIC

1. Open the Chrome.tif image from the Examples/Chap24 folder on the Companion CD.

2. On the Channels palette (press F7 if it's not presently onscreen), click on the Blue channel title and then drag the title into the Create New Channel icon, as shown in Figure 24.1. Actually, you can use any channel to duplicate as an alpha channel because this image consists of grayscale information only—equal amounts of density in the Red, Green, and Blue color channels.

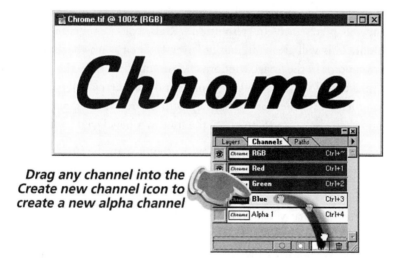

FIGURE 24.1 *Create an alpha channel of the visual content of the image by dragging one of the image's color channels into the Create New Channel icon on the Channels palette.*

3. With the RGB channel view as your current view of the image, double-click on the Background layer title on the Layers palette. This displays the Make Layer dialog box.

4. Type **Chrome** in the Name field of the Make Layer dialog box, and then click on OK to return to the workspace.

5. Press Ctrl(⌘)+A to select the entire image, and then press Delete (Backspace) to remove the opaque areas of the image. Then, press Ctrl(⌘)+D to deselect the marquee selection.

6. Click on the Create New Layer icon on the Layers palette, and then drag the layer title on the palette to beneath the Chrome layer. This new layer is by default named Layer 1.

7. Press Ctrl(⌘)+Shift+S (File, Save As), and then save your work to hard disk as Chrome.psd, in Photoshop's native file format. Keep the image open.

USING YOUR OWN FONTS FOR THE CHROME TEXT DESIGN

If you intend to use Jonathan Smith's font or any other font instead of the Chrome.tif template, the steps for creating the template are a little different than those described in the previous steps.

Begin with a new document window whose settings are 500 pixels wide, 199 pixels high, 72 pixels/inch in resolution, RGB color mode, and Contents: Transparent. This will create an empty Layer 1. Then, with the Type Tool, click an insertion point in the image window, choose your font from the Type Tool dialog box (make the font size about 100 points and black in color), type your phrase (we recommend Chrome, for consistency with the rest of this chapter's example steps), and then click on OK to apply the font to a new layer, named Chrome.

Then drag the type, using the Move tool to center it in the image window, and choose Layer, Type, Render Layer—you can't apply custom fills while the text is still editable text.

Except for the fact that you have text on a layer instead of in an alpha channel, the layers' names and positions are identical to those created in the previous steps. In future steps, you'll use a different technique for applying color to the text, and it will be called out for you in the steps.

Users of the Chrome.tif template and users who've decided to make their own text now have the outline of the chrome lettering saved. But lettering that looks like chrome is made up of far more than mere outline. Chrome has detail, specifically the detail that is reflected from the chrome's environment. The following section takes you through the process of customizing a linear gradient that ships with Photoshop (to make it more realistic-looking) and gets into a little artistic discussion about what makes chrome look like chrome, so the steps in this chapter will make a lot more sense!

BUILDING UPON AN EXISTING GRADIENT FILL

Photoshop comes with a lot of nifty preset gradient fills, one of which is called Chrome. Adobe gets points for creating a fairly sophisticated gradient simulation of what we usually perceive as the "chrome look." Traditional illustrators generally use the same blend of colors, in the same order, when using an airbrush. You will customize the default Chrome gradient to suit your *own* illustration needs in the steps to follow, however, for the reasons described next.

Chrome and other highly reflective surfaces don't really have a surface look of their own. These surfaces depend on the visual interest of the outside world to give the interior of their shape some rich visual complexity. If, for example, you were to take a chromed wrench into a completely white tent and look at it, you'd see only the silhouette of the wrench, and it wouldn't really look like a wrench because we anticipate some visual "business" going on within the interior of the wrench's shape.

Because a designer can't render *every* type of scene reflection within the shape of a chrome object, a convention has been used for more than 20 years that makes things you paint or draw look like chrome. At the top of the interior of the chrome object is sky blue, which gradually fades to a sunset color at the horizon within the chrome. Then, abruptly, a deep brown enters the scene directly below the horizon. This is the ground in the reflected scene, and it fades vertically to a lighter shade of brown, as light closest to the viewer illuminates the chrome object. So, basically, what traditional illustrators illustrate and what Adobe has set up in the Chrome gradient fill is a reflection of a desert scene.

Usually, the more visual detail you add to illustrations, the closer the work comes to looking like a photorealistic piece. This is particularly true of chrome, which needs all the detail you can lend to it, because the world is a visually complex place and chrome merely reflects the world's complexity.

In the steps that follow, you'll duplicate Photoshop's Chrome gradient fill and add to it, so you can embellish the text in this assignment with detail that mirrors the world.

CREATING A CUSTOM CHROME GRADIENT FILL

1. Double-click on the Linear Gradient tool on the toolbox to display the Options palette.

2. Click the arrow to the right of the Gradient field on the Options palette, choose Chrome from the drop-down list, and then click on Edit.

3. In the Gradient Editor, click on Duplicate, as shown in Figure 24.2. In the Gradient Name dialog box, type **My Chrome** and then click on OK to create the new gradient.

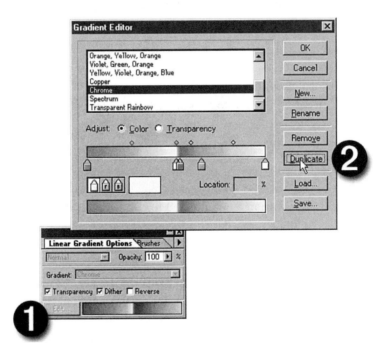

FIGURE 24.2 *Choose the preset gradient and then click on Edit to display the Gradient Editor, where you can duplicate, and then customize any of the presets.*

4. Double-click on the far-left, blue marker on the gradient strip to display the Color Picker.

5. In the Color Picker, drag the color field circle so the value of the blue is deeper, as shown in Figure 24.3. H:205, S: 96%, and B:51% is a good color. Click on OK to apply the change and return to the Gradient Editor.

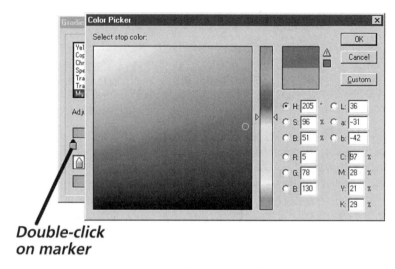

Double-click on marker

FIGURE 24.3 *Change the beginning color of the "sky" in the My Chrome gradient by double-clicking on the color marker to display the Color Picker.*

Okay, so why are we making the sky a deeper color than the perfectly fine default blue? Because you're going to combine the sky area with fractal clouds to increase visual detail in the illustration, and the clouds will need a dense color to contrast against. Trust me on this one…

6. The second-to-left color marker is white. You'll want to "ease" the visual transition between horizon illumination and the now deep blue sky with an additional color, such as a light blue, on the gradient strip. Hold Alt(Opt) and drag the white marker slightly to the left. This duplicates the white marker, as shown in Figure 24.4. (You can also single-click directly below the gradient strip to create a new marker—there are at least two ways to do just about anything in Photoshop.)

7. Double-click on this new white duplicate marker to display the Color Picker. In the Color Picker, choose a blue that is approximately H:202, S:70%, and B:100%. Click on OK to apply the new color and exit the Color Picker.

8. Double-click on the white marker, and in the Color Picker, make the new color a sunset shade. H:59, S:14%, and B:100% is fine. Click on OK to exit the Color Picker.

9. Double-click on the brown horizon marker, and then in the Color Picker, choose H:44, S:74%, and B:27%; click on OK to apply the color change.

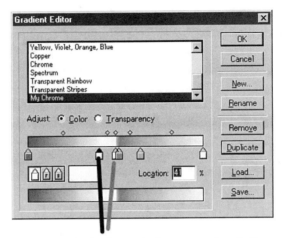

**Hold Alt (⊼) and drag to the left
to duplicate the marker**

FIGURE 24.4   *Duplicate the color marker by holding Alt(Opt) and dragging.*

10. Drag the second-to-right color marker by about $^1/4$ screen inch to the right, as shown in Figure 24.5. What you're doing is creating less of a steep color transition between the "horizon" and the "foreground" in this chrome blend. As a result, the foreground of the Linear gradient when you use it will feature denser shades toward the bottom of the text.

11. Finally, double-click on the far-right color marker, and in the Color Picker, choose H:52, S:91%, and B:91%. Click on OK to apply the change and return to the Gradient Editor.

12. Click on OK in the Gradient Editor to add your custom fill to the drop-down list on the Options palette and return to the workspace.

Whether you have the chrome lettering in an alpha channel or it's currently rendered to a layer, the following section will show you how to apply a "base coat" of chrome shading to the lettering.

Drag to the right

FIGURE 24.5 *Decrease the speed of transition between the horizon color and the ground color by moving the color marker to the right.*

ADDING CHROME COLORS TO THE LETTERING

You've got your custom fill, and you've got the shape of the design saved—it's time to put the two together. Here's how to apply the custom My Chrome fill to the image window:

APPLYING SHADING

1. The Chrome layer should be the current editing layer; click on its title on the Layers palette to make this layer active. If you're using the chrome design from the Companion CD, on the Channels palette, Ctrl($\mathcal{H}$)+click on the Alpha 1 channel title to load the design as a marquee selection, and then press Shift+F7 to invert the selection so the lettering, and not the background, is selected. If you've created your own design using text, click on the Preserve Transparency icon on the Layers palette for the Chrome layer.

2. With the Linear Gradient tool, begin at a little beneath the top of the lettering, hold Shift (constrains fill direction to 45-degree increments, one of which is 90 degrees—perfectly vertical), and then drag down to a little below the bottom of the lettering, as shown in Figure 24.6. Ideally, the horizon of the fill should be at the vertical halfway point of the lowercase letters. If your fill doesn't look like that shown in Figure 24.6, try again, overwriting the previous fill.

FIGURE 24.6 *Hold Shift, and then drag vertically from top to bottom of the lettering or the marquee selection.*

3. Press Ctrl(⌘)+D to deselect the marquee; folks who've used their own typeface on a layer should uncheck the Preserve Transparency check box on the Layers palette now.

4. Press Ctrl(⌘)+S; keep the file open.

Now that the basic shape and contents of the shape have been established, it's time to get into the illustration portion of this assignment. First on the agenda is adding a faint layer of clouds to the upper part of the lettering.

ADDING FRACTAL CLOUDS AND MERGING IN COLOR MODE

Here's the deal: In the following steps, you'll use the Layer 1 in the composition to add a fractal cloud illustration. You'll modify it by using the Levels command to bring out the white in the rendering and stretch the cloud rendition by using the Scale command. Then you'll assign the Chrome layer a Color mode attribute, so the clouds on Layer 1 will merge with the chrome text but retain the overall color you've defined for the fill. Ambitious? Yes, but as mentioned earlier, the world's a visually complex place, and the more detail you add to the illustration, the more lifelike it will look.

CREATING AND MODIFYING CLOUDS FROM THE RENDER COMMAND

To use the Clouds command, you must set up on the toolbox the foreground and background colors that the filter will use to render wispy clouds. Unfortunately, wispy clouds are too subtle for this striking composition, so what you'll do in the following steps is create a Clouds render, and then use the Difference Clouds filter a number of times on the same area to produce bolder clouds with more visual interest. The Difference Clouds filter requires that a selection be filled (which you'll do), and with every successive application of Difference Clouds, the clouds will invert in color scheme (as the Difference mode on the Layers palette inverts colors), so it will be important to apply the Difference Clouds filter an *even* number of times.

Here's how to fill a working area on Layer 1 with fairly intense clouds:

RENDERING CLOUDS AND DIFFERENCE CLOUDS INTO A SELECTION

1. Click on the Layer 1 title on the Layers palette to make this the current editing layer.

2. With the Rectangular Marquee tool, drag a rectangular selection that encompasses the "Ch" in Chrome and whose bottom edge lies a pixel or two above the horizon of the chrome fill of the lettering.

3. Type **D** (Default colors), and then choose Filter, Render, Clouds.

4. Choose Filter, Render, and then choose Difference Clouds.

5. Press Ctrl(⌘)+F to apply the last-used filter (Difference Clouds) an odd number of times until you see some intense cloudlike areas in the marquee selection, as shown in Figure 24.7. Make sure that there is an even amount of black and white in the selection before you stop pressing Ctrl(⌘)+F.

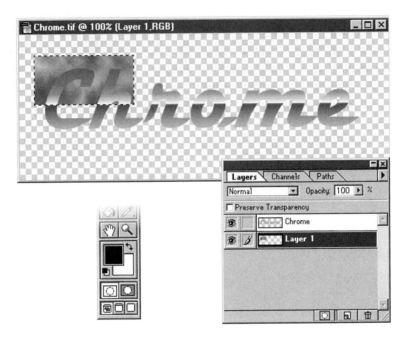

Figure 24.7 *First, use the Clouds filter to create white clouds on black, then use the Difference Clouds filter a number of times to make the rendered selection area look like really intense clouds.*

6. Press Ctrl(⌘)+T to put the selection into Free Transform mode. The middle handles of the bounding box are used to perform the Scale function on the selection in a non-proportional way. In other words, dragging on a middle handle scales the width of the selection in this example, but it does not scale the height of the selection in the bounding box.

7. Click on the middle, right handle, as shown in Figure 24.8, and then drag the selection so that it covers the entire top of the Chrome lettering.

8. Double-click inside the selection marquee to apply the transformation, and then press Ctrl(⌘)+L to display the Levels command.

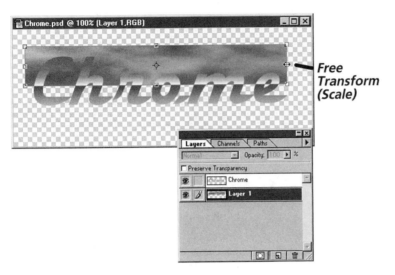

Free
Transform
(Scale)

FIGURE 24.8   *Stretch the selection so the clouds appear to be experiencing some wind, instead of lying static within the composition.*

9. Drag the midpoint slider to about .90 in the Levels command dialog box, so the midtones of the cloud selection contain a little more contrast. Then drag the white point slider to the left until you can see a lot of white in the clouds, as shown in Figure 24.9.

10. Click on OK to apply the tonal changes to the selection, and then press Ctrl(⌘)+D to deselect the marquee selection. Press Ctrl(⌘)+S; keep the file open.

Okay, you've got the synthetic clouds behind the top half of the Chrome lettering; it's now time to apply the clouds to the sky portion of the lettering.

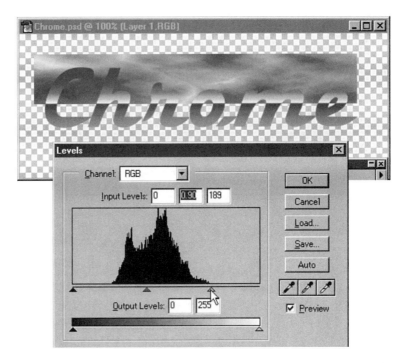

FIGURE 24.9 *Increase the amount of contrast in the cloud selection, and emphasize white by using the sliders in the Levels command.*

USING COLOR MODE AND TRIMMING AWAY SUPERFLUOUS CLOUD AREAS

The next set of steps takes you through the integration of the clouds layer with the Chrome lettering. You'll use the outline shape of the Chrome lettering to trim away the areas you don't need on the clouds layer (Layer 1) and put the Chrome lettering in Color mode so it will shade the clouds with the original colors you used in the custom gradient fill.

Here's how to refine the composition:

COLOR MODE AND TRIMMING A SELECTION

1. Ctrl(⌘)+click on the Chrome layer title on the Layers palette to load the opaque areas on this layer as a marquee selection.

2. Press Ctrl(⌘)+Shift+I (or Shift+F7) to invert the marquee so everything except the lettering is selected.

3. Click on the Layer 1 title to make it the current editing layer.

4. Press Delete (Backspace) and then press Ctrl(⌘)+D. The clouds on Layer 1 have now been trimmed so they conform to the top half of the Chrome lettering.

5. Click on the Chrome layer title on the Layers palette.

6. Choose Color from the Modes drop-down list on the Layers palette, as shown in Figure 24.10. What you should see on your own monitor is the gentle blending of clouds with the deep blue on the upper half of the lettering.

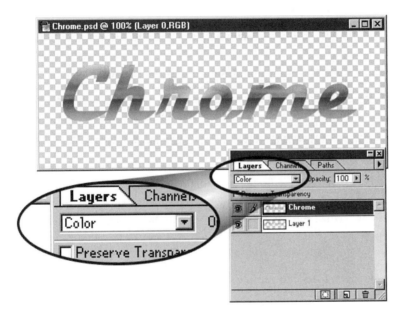

FIGURE 24.10 *Apply the upper layer—the Chrome lettering—to the lower layer of clouds in Color mode, so the color of the Chrome lettering blends with the brightness values of the clouds.*

7. Click on the menu flyout button on the Layers palette, and then choose Merge Visible. There should be only one layer, named Chrome, in the image now.

8. Press Ctrl(⌘)+S; keep the file open.

The chrome lettering looks a little flat, doesn't it? This is because we can't see an edge to the lettering, and most car chrome lettering has depth. You need to create the illusion of depth by adding a bevel edge to the illustration. It's easier than you think; read on!

USING THE EXPAND COMMAND ON A SELECTION

Because your viewpoint on the chrome lettering is directly perpendicular to its face, any depth you might add to the lettering must be applied equally around its outline. This is no problem. In fact, Photoshop has the perfect command for expanding a selection edge—oddly enough, it's called the Expand command!

In the steps that follow, you'll apply the Expand command to the opaque areas of the Chrome layer, and then apply your My Chrome linear fill to the selection to create an outer edge to the design.

Here's how to add still more visual complexity to the chrome lettering:

ADDING AN EDGE TO THE DESIGN, USING THE EXPAND COMMAND

1. On the Layers palette, click on the Create New Layer icon at the bottom of the palette (the page icon with the turned-over corner).

2. Drag this new layer title to beneath the Chrome layer title on the Layers palette. The layer is, by default, named Layer 1.

3. Ctrl(⌘)+click on the Chrome layer title on the Layers palette. This loads a selection marquee based on the opaque pixels on the layer. Layer 1 should still be the current editing layer (because you selected and moved it in step 2).

4. Choose Select, Modify, and then choose Expand. In the Expand dialog box, type **8** in the Pixels field, and then click on OK to apply the expansion of the selection marquee. Figure 24.11 shows what the image window should look like right now.

5. Choose the Linear Gradient tool. On the Options palette, the My Chrome fill should still be chosen.

6. Hold Shift, and then drag from the top of the marquee selection to just below the bottom.

Now, the goal is to get the horizon line in this "outer chrome" selection not to fall at the same vertical point as the "inner chrome" on the Chrome layer. It needs to be a fraction of an inch lower or higher than the chrome horizon on the Chrome layer. It will make the chrome lettering far more legible, and it's also optically correct for the side of a reflective object to have its own horizon, apart from the front-facing facet. If the horizon of the fill falls exactly where the horizon line is on the inner chrome, try holding Shift and dragging from a different start point to a different end point within the selection. This will overwrite the previous fill (see Figure 24.12).

TIP

If you've gone through the trouble of naming layers, there's a way to preserve the names when you merge them with other, untitled layers. It's simple: Make sure the layer with the name you've applied to it is the current editing layer when you merge the layers. For example, you can have, in descending order, Layer 5, Layer 4, MyLayer, Layer 2, and Layer 1. As long as the MyLayer title is highlighted when you merge layers, the single layer will still have the title MyLayer. Otherwise, *any* current editing layer's name will be applied to the merged layers, and it's sort of useless to refer to "Layer 3" in a composition, when all default layers added to a composition are given a numbered name.

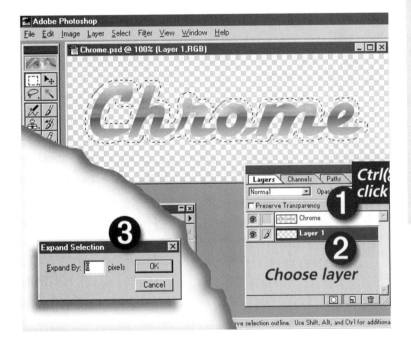

FIGURE 24.11   *Use the Expand command to increase the size, equidirectionally, of the current marquee selection.*

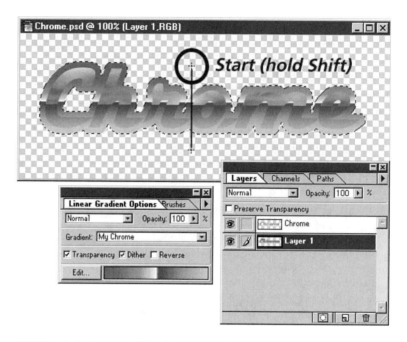

FIGURE 24.12 *Apply the custom fill to the marquee selection on Layer 1. Make sure the horizon line of the fill does not coincide with the fill on the Chrome layer.*

7. Press Ctrl(⌘)+D; press Ctrl(⌘)+S; keep the file open.

Clearly, the lettering is not as legible as it was before you added the outside edge to it, but this will be corrected through a set of enhancements you'll apply later. Right now, what you need to do is apply the same sort of clouds effect to the top portion of the outer chrome lettering.

PAYING A SECOND VISIT TO THE DIFFERENCE CLOUDS COMMAND

Because the steps in this next set are the same as those you followed with the Chrome layer—been there, done that—the outline here is brisk and to the point, because I notice a few of you in back there nodding off!

Ready?

SHADING THE OUTER CHROME

1. Click on the Create New Layer icon on the Layers palette. A Layer 2 is added to the title list on the palette.

2. Drag this Layer 2 to the bottom of the palette list. It's now the current editing layer.

3. With the Rectangular Marquee tool, drag a selection that encompasses the top half of the "Ch" in Chrome on Layer 1.

4. Choose Filter, Render, and then choose Clouds.

5. Choose Filter, Render, and then choose Difference Clouds.

6. Press Ctrl(⌘)+F to reapply the Difference Clouds filter; do this an *odd* number of times so the clouds will *not* be color inverted.

7. Press Ctrl(⌘)+T to display the Free Transform bounding box, and then drag its middle right handle to the right so the clouds selection covers the top half of the outer chrome lettering (see Figure 24.13). Double-click inside the bounding box to apply the transformation.

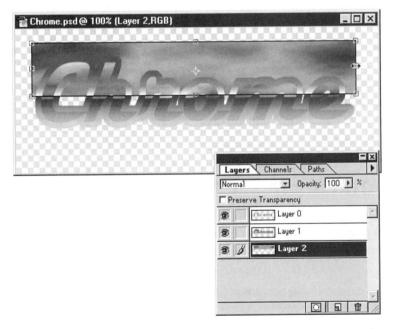

FIGURE 24.13 *Drag the selection handle of the Free Transform box to the right to cover the entire upper half of the outer chrome lettering on Layer 1.*

8. Press Ctrl(⌘)+L to display the Levels command; drag the midpoint slider slightly to the right to increase contrast, and then drag the white point slider from the far right to the left to increase the whiteness of the clouds on Layer 2. Click on OK to exit the Levels command box and to apply the changes.

9. Ctrl(⌘)+click on the Layer 1 title on the Layers palette to load nontransparent pixels as a marquee selection. Then press Shift+F7 to invert the selection. Layer 2 should still be the active layer.

10. Press Delete, and then press Ctrl(⌘)+D to deselect the marquee.

11. Click on the Layer 1 title; then, on the Layers palette, choose Color from the Modes drop-down list.

12. Click on the eye icon next to the Chrome layer to hide it. Layers that can't be seen can't be merged.

13. Click on the menu flyout on the Layers palette and choose Merge Visible. Now you have an invisible Chrome layer, and underneath the invisible layer, an outer chrome layer titled Layer 1.

14. Click on the eye icon area to the left of the Chrome layer to restore the Chrome layer's visibility.

15. Press Ctrl(⌘)+S; keep the file open, and go get a cold beverage—you deserve it.

We're getting to our goal here. The front and sides of the chrome lettering have been created, but there are a number of enhancements that you'll add to your creation that will add dimension to these two layers, which are currently flat in appearance.

CREATING A STAMPED METAL LOOK

Often, with actual stamped lettering that is reflective, we'll see highlights or even a visible edge where the side meets the front of the object. In the steps to follow, you'll create this effect, and as a side benefit, you'll restore legibility to your creation.

USING THE STROKE COMMAND TO CREATE AN EDGE EFFECT

The author has to admit that he does not use the Edit, Stroke command frequently as a tool, but it does serve a valuable purpose when you want to emphasize a visual element in a composition. Your next step is to add a graphic separation between the outer chrome and the inner chrome, using the Chrome layer's opacity information to build a marquee selection that you'll stroke on a new layer. Then you'll duplicate the new layer and make the stroke a contrasting color. Finally, to create an embossed effect for the strokes, you'll offset the top layer by one pixel down and to the right. You'll be surprised how this simple set of steps will add to the visual richness and depth of the piece.

Here's how to create an edge to the Chrome layer text:

USING THE STROKE COMMAND TO CREATE AN EDGE TO THE LETTERING

1. Press D (Default colors). Click on the Chrome layer title on the Layers palette.

2. Click on the Create New Layer icon at the bottom of the Layers palette. Doing this creates a new layer—Layer 2—directly above the current editing layer, so Layer 2 is on the top of the layer stack now.

3. Ctrl(⌘)+click on the Chrome layer to load the opaque areas as a marquee selection. Layer 2 should still be the current editing layer.

4. Choose Edit, Stroke. The Stroke dialog box appears.

5. Type **1** in the Pixels field, choose Location: Center, and choose Multiply from the Mode drop-down list. Click on OK, as shown in Figure 24.14.

6. Press Ctrl(⌘)+D to deselect the marquee, and then drag the Layer 2 title into the Create New Layer icon at the bottom of the Layers palette, as shown in Figure 24.15.

7. Layer 2 copy is the title of the current editing layer. Click on the Layer 2 title on the Layers palette to make it the current editing layer.

8. Click on the Preserve Transparency check box on the Layers palette.

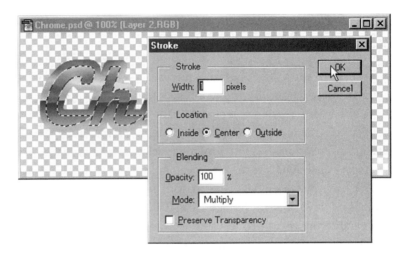

FIGURE 24.14 *Stroke the marquee selection to create a one-pixel outline in black on Layer 2.*

FIGURE 24.15 *Dragging the layer title into the Create New Layer icon duplicates the layer.*

9. Press X (switch foreground/background colors), and then press Ctrl(⌘)+A to select all.

10. Press Alt(Opt)+Delete (Backspace). The opaque contents of Layer 2 are now white. Press Ctrl(⌘)+D to deselect the contents of Layer 2. Uncheck the Preserve Transparency check box now.

11. With the Move tool active, press the down-arrow key and the right-arrow key once on the keyboard, to nudge the white outline away from the underlying black outline. Your composition should look like Figure 24.16 now.

Nudge the white outline down and to the bottom using the keyboard arrow keys while the Move tool is active

Figure 24.16   *Use the keyboard arrow keys to nudge the contents of the current editing layer down and to the right.*

12. Press Ctrl(⌘)+S; keep the file open.

Okay, you've got four "players" in this piece now, and it's time for a little recap of what is located where. In Figure 24.17 all the layers in the design are labeled.

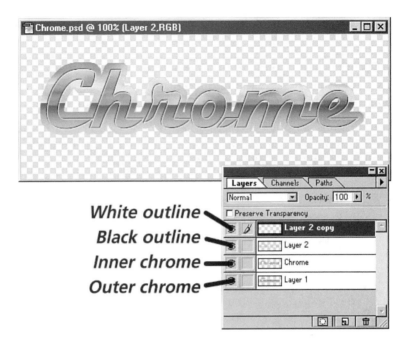

FIGURE 24.17 *Because you will be modifying the elements of this composition individually, it's a good idea to keep the elements on separate layers.*

In the next section you'll distort the horizon of the chrome lettering to add realism to the piece. Ever play with the Smudge tool? You'll soon see an innovative use for it.

EMBELLISHING THE CHROME WITH THE SMUDGE TOOL

The Smudge tool is a powerful Photoshop feature. That is not to say that it's diverse—it's not. It simply treats the pixels in an image as though they're wet paint. But a little smudging goes a long way. As you'll soon see, you don't need a very large brush tip to create a bending, swooping horizon within the lettering.

BENDING THE FACE AND EDGE OF THE CHROME LETTERING

One visual effect that distinguishes actual chrome from a poorly illustrated rendition of chrome is that chrome tends to be applied to metal surfaces a little unevenly, and as a result, on real chrome there's more of a fun house mirror reflection instead of a planar mirror reflection.

In the following steps, you'll use the Smudge tool to bend the horizon of the chrome text downward, creating the optical illusion of the chrome bulging out toward the viewer. This effect needs to be applied to both the inner and outer chrome layers, so hang on tight, choose the Smudge tool, and let's get to work…

BENDING THE CHROME HORIZON, PART I

1. Type **200** in the Zoom Percentage field, and then press Enter (Return). Drag the image window edges away from the image so your view of the lettering is maximized.

2. Click on the Layer 1 title (the outer chrome layer) to make it the active layer.

3. With the Smudge tool selected, check the Options palette to make sure the mode is Normal and the Pressure is at the default of 50%.

4. On the Brushes palette, choose the fourth-from-left tip on the second row.

5. Click on the Preserve Transparency check box on the Layers palette. You do not want to accidentally smudge the shading on the layer outside its outline. Starting at the far left of the illustration, drag downward on the horizon. Wait for the effect to process and display onscreen. One application of the Smudge tool should be enough to drag the horizon downward in a bowed fashion.

6. Smudge downward at the next visible horizon of the outer chrome. Continue this process, as shown in Figure 24.18, until all the visible horizon on Layer 1 has been smudged downward.

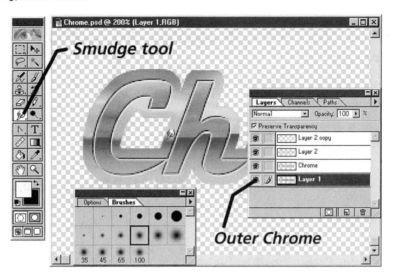

FIGURE 24.18 *The Smudge tool causes a smearing effect. The visual content of the affected layer will lose a little focus, but overall, you will accomplish a photographic effect by smudging the horizon of the outer chrome.*

7. Uncheck the Preserve Transparency check box when you finish working on Layer 1.

8. Click on the Chrome layer's title on the Layers palette, and then click in the Preserve Transparency check box on the Layers palette.

9. Perform the same Smudge tool maneuvers on the inner chrome as you did in steps 5–6, as shown in Figure 24.19.

10. Uncheck the Preserve Transparency check box when you're through smudging the Chrome layer. Press Ctrl(⌘)+S; keep the file open.

The text looks detailed, but it still looks a little flat, doesn't it? This is because the outer chrome, if this were a real chrome object, would not be angled parallel to the audience, but instead would be at a 45-degree angle, give or take a few degrees. And an angled object shows highlights where its parts face the light source in the scene, whereas areas that face away from the light source fall into shadow. In the next section, you'll shade the outer chrome layer to suggest lighting. And you'll see exactly how dimensional works of art you produce can be when accurate lighting is added.

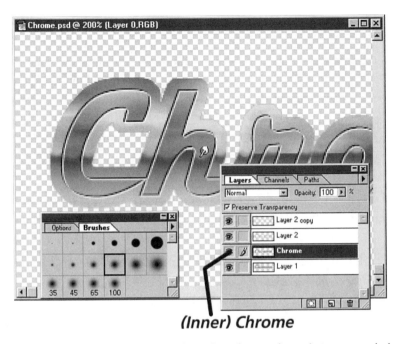

(Inner) Chrome

FIGURE 24.19   *Smudge the horizon of the Chrome layer downward to make it appear to be bowing outward.*

ADDING LIGHTING TO THE COMPOSITION

Let's decide right now that a light source is pointing into the composition from a steep, upper-left angle. This means that the reflective chrome's sides will be brilliantly illuminated and take on highlights along the top-left of every curve on the side. Conversely, light will be hidden from the bottom-right sides of the composition. In the following section, you'll use the Burn and Dodge tools to create consistent shading on the outer chrome layer, the layer containing the text that should be angled away from the viewer.

USING THE BURN TOOL TO SHADE THE OUTER CHROME

Photoshop's Burn tool operates in three modes—it can affect the Highlights, the Midtones, and the Shadows of any region of the artwork you stroke over. When

NOTE

Because the Burn tool, like all of Photoshop's Toning tools, does not displace pixels, but instead merely shades them, the Preserve Transparency option is not needed for your work here.

used on image areas that display a medium tonal quality, the Burn tool intensifies (adds saturation to) the areas when it's set to Shadows. Set to Midtones, the Burn tool does the same thing it does in Shadow mode. Applying the Burn tool in Highlight mode produces exactly the effect you want—the tool adds neutral density to areas of mid to high tonal values. If you use the Burn tool excessively in mid to lighter tonal areas, the areas eventually become black, so a "light" application of the tool is all you need in the steps to follow.

Get in a visualization frame of mind before you begin the steps. Try to "see" where the lower-right areas of the outer chrome lie, and then apply the Burn tool.

WORKING WITH THE BURN TOOL TO PRODUCE SHADING EFFECTS

1. At 200% viewing resolution, hold down the Spacebar and drag to the right in the image so you can see the beginning of the lettering.

2. Make sure the bottom layer in the composition—the layer containing the outer chrome—is chosen, by clicking on its title on the Layers palette.

3. Drag on the face of the Toning tools group on the toolbox, and then choose the Burn tool. It's the tool whose icon is a tiny hand making an "OK" gesture.

4. On the Options palette, choose Highlights from the drop-down list, and leave the Exposure at 50%.

5. On the Brushes palette, choose the second-from-last tip in the second row.

6. Stroke over an area on the outer chrome lettering, to the bottom or to the right of the first letter. Apply the Burn tool enough times to make the area you stroke over visibly darker than the neighboring image areas.

7. Choose another area to the bottom or the right, or that lies on the bottom-right area of the lettering. Apply no more than three strokes of the Burn tool. In Figure 24.20, the circled areas are target areas for the Burn tool. There are other areas than the ones called out in this figure, but after you detect and apply the Burn tool to three or four areas, the areas that need shading will become more apparent to you.

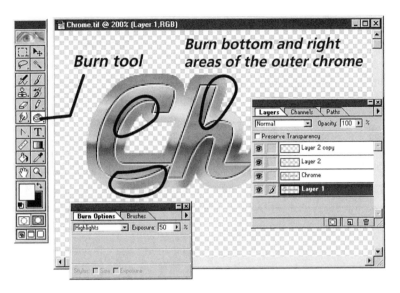

FIGURE 24.20 *Apply the Burn tool in Highlight mode to the lower- and rightmost areas of the outer chrome lettering on Layer 1.*

8. When you've finished burning in all the lower and right areas on Layer 1, press Ctrl(⌘)+S; keep the file open.

Shading is only half the reflection game. In the following section, you'll apply the Dodge tool to create specular highlights on the outer chrome.

USING THE DODGE TOOL TO LIGHTEN AREAS

Real chrome is so mirrorlike that it casts specular reflections at the viewer. *Specular reflections* are intense highlights that the viewer sees when she or he is close to the "mirror angle" of a reflective object. The *mirror angle* is seen in reflective objects when the angle of light striking the object is very close to the angle the viewer sees.

The Dodge tool has three settings, exactly like the Burn tool's options, for brightening different tonal ranges. But only the Highlights setting takes light-colored areas and creates brilliant, pure tones in the area where you apply the Dodge tool.

In the following steps, you'll apply the Dodge tool to the outer chrome areas that lie in the opposite direction to where you performed the shading in the previous section. Upper and left-side areas of the Layer 1 object need brightening up to make viewers definitely think that the light source in the image is in the upper left.

Here's how to use the Dodge tool on the chrome piece:

ADDING YOUR OWN HIGHLIGHTS TO THE CHROME

1. Hold the Spacebar and drag to the right in the image window until you have a clear view of the beginning of the text. You should still have the Layer 1 (outer chrome) layer active.

2. Choose the Dodge tool by dragging on the Toning tools flyout on the toolbox to choose it.

3. On the Options palette, choose Highlights if it's not already chosen. Keep the same Brushes palette tip size for your work here.

4. Stroke, no more than three times, over the areas to the top and left of Layer 1's chrome. You can see the work in progress in Figure 24.21; circles have been drawn around a few of the upper and left areas to give you an idea of where the lightening work should occur. The upper and left edges of the design become brighter (some areas might actually turn white, depending on the density of the clouds you layered with this image), and the areas will take on what is close to a pure hue of cyan.

5. Scroll the image window and continue working with the Dodge tool until all the upper and left areas are significantly brighter than the rest of the composition.

6. Press Ctrl(⌘)+S; keep the file open.

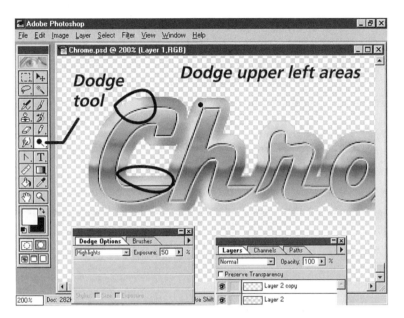

FIGURE 24.21   *Stroke over the top and left areas of Layer 1's chrome design until a highlight appears in these areas.*

In Figure 24.22, you can see the chrome image at this point in your work. You might ask yourself (or the author), "Why don't I repeat the dodging and burning steps with the inner chrome layer (the layer labeled Chrome)?" The answer has to do with the viewer's perspective on the piece. The outer chrome is supposed to be angled away from the inner chrome design. And if you angle a reflective surface, that surface will pick up highlights and take on shading that's in synch with the direction of the light source in the image. Conversely, the inner chrome is supposed to be directly facing the viewer. There should be no highlights or shaded areas when a plane is not angled perpendicular to the light coming into the image. Therefore, the chrome piece is realistic right now.

FIGURE 24.22   *The lighting, the embossed edge, and the dips in the chrome's horizon all add up to a fairly faithful rendition of real-world chrome.*

Among traditional airbrush artists a typical embellishment is to place a distant light or two at the horizon of paintings of chrome. Distant lights add depth to the image; the lights suggest that there is something reflective toward the horizon, such as a tin roof on a shack or a piece of metal on a telephone pole, that is too small to see in the picture. In the following section, you'll add a few highlights to bring out the true depth of the illustration.

ADDING "INTERIOR" HIGHLIGHTS

The steps for casting highlights from within the chrome lettering are really quite simple—you pick up the Paintbrush tool, specify a fairly small size for the tip, and then, using the tool sparsely, apply white foreground color.

Here are the steps you need to integrate the outer chrome with the inner chrome and add depth to the picture:

CREATING DISTANT LIGHTS WITHIN THE CHROME

1. Click on the eye icons for both the Layer 2 and the Layer 2 copy titles on the Layers palette, to hide the contents of these layers—those that contain the edge outlines—from view.

2. Click on the Chrome layer title, and then click on the menu flyout button on the Layers palette and choose Merge Visible. The outer and inner chrome designs have been merged, and the title on the Layers palette for this single layer is Chrome because the Chrome layer was the current editing layer when the Merge Visible command was made.

3. Click on the areas where the eyes were for the Layer 2 and Layer 2 copy titles on the Layers palette to restore their visibility. The Chrome layer should still be the current editing layer; you have to click on the title or the thumbnail of a layer on the Layers palette to switch layers.

4. Choose the Paintbrush tool, and then on the Brushes palette, choose the second-from-left tip in the second row.

5. Press D (Default colors) and then press X (switch foreground/background colors) so the current foreground color is white.

6. Click, do not drag, a point on the horizon, on the edge of the inner chrome. Because the outlines are on separate layers, you cannot accidentally paint over them.

7. Click another point, on a different character, on the horizon, close to the edge of the inner chrome.

8. Choose the second-from-left tip in the top row on the Brushes palette, and then click a point on the horizon, on the opposite edge of the character where you made the highlight in step 7. In Figure 24.23, you can see the location of the highlights. As mentioned earlier, do not overdo this inner highlight stuff. One click, perhaps two, per character is sufficient to simulate a distant light that's reflecting in the chrome. As you proceed, alternate between the top and second row brush tips.

TIP

You can also hold Alt(Opt) and press the left or right square bracket keyboard key to switch to different layers. Alt(Opt)+ left bracket ([) moves to one layer down and Alt(Opt)+ right bracket (]) moves to one layer up in the image.

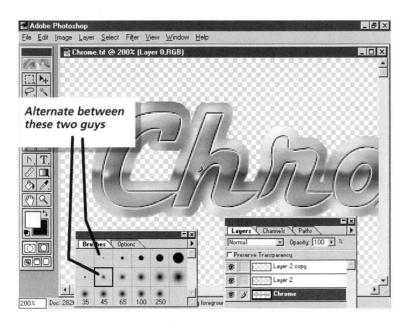

FIGURE 24.23 *Alternate brush tip sizes and click points along the horizon, near the edge of the inner chrome.*

9. Feel free to click a point or two on the horizon of the outermost chrome on the Chrome layer. Simply make sure, when you do this, that you are not close to any transparent areas on the layer. Otherwise, you'll be painting into transparency, and the piece will look phony when you're finished.

10. When you have about 12–14 highlights on the chrome and all the layers are visible, choose Merge Visible from the Layers palette's flyout menu, as shown in Figure 24.24. The name of the current—and only—layer should be Chrome, because it was the current layer on which you last worked.

FIGURE 24.24 *With the Chrome layer as the current editing layer, choose Merge Visible to condense all the layers to a single one.*

11. Press Ctrl(⌘)+S; keep the file open.

Shortly, you will add another layer to the composition, because chrome floating in space doesn't look awfully realistic. You'll use the Pen tool to create an abstract template for variations in the color you apply to the new layer, and before you know it, this chrome will look as though it's on the rear fender of a 1954 Chevy!

CREATING A NONDESCRIPT METAL BACKGROUND

To borrow yet another convention from traditional airbrush artists, you'll create variations in tone on a flat color behind the Chrome layer. If you look closely at almost any highly reflective surface—such as a water faucet—you'll notice gradual transitions in color, as well as very sharp transitions where something is displaying an edge in the reflection.

To imitate this "sharp and soft" metal finish effect, you'll use the Pen tool in the following steps to create a template. Then you'll apply foreground color, using the Airbrush tool to get a soft edge on one side of the metal background in the composition.

Here's how to give the elegant chrome you've created a background that complements the overall design:

CREATING A METALLIC BACKGROUND FOR THE COMPOSITION

1. On the Layers palette, click on the Create New Layer icon, and then drag this Layer 1 title below the Chrome layer so that the Chrome layer is on top in the image.

2. With the Eyedropper tool, click on a lighter area of the blue in the chrome lettering; then click on the foreground color swatch on the toolbox, and add some saturation to the current color, using the Color Picker. The author discovered that H:187, S:100%, and B:100% works well against the chrome lettering. Click on OK to select the new color and exit the Color Picker.

3. Press Ctrl(⌘)+A, and then press Alt(Opt)+Delete (Backspace). Press Ctrl(⌘)+D to deselect the marquee. You've got a nice "vintage" blue as the background now.

4. Type **100** in the Zoom Percentage field, and then press Enter (Return). Drag the window edges away from the canvas of the image so you can see the image window background. You'll be working outside the image window to create the marquee selection that in turn will be used to create the streaks of accent color on Layer 1.

5. Choose the Pen tool, and then click a point slightly outside the upper-right corner of the image, about $1/2$ screen inch down from the absolute corner. Sneak a peek at Figure 24.25 to see the shape of the path you'll be creating.

6. Click and drag on a point at the top of the "o" in Chrome. Continue dragging until the path segment between the first and current anchor points bows upward.

7. Click a point just outside the lower-left corner; click a point outside the lower-right corner, and then close the path by clicking on the first anchor point you created.

8. Hold Ctrl(⌘) to toggle the Pen tool to the Direct Selection tool, and then click on the anchor over the "o" to select it and to expose its direction lines and points.

9. Hold Alt(Opt) to toggle to the Convert Point tool, and then drag upward on the left direction point at the end of the direction line coming from the anchor point. As you can see in Figure 24.25, this action changes the anchor point's property from smooth to cusp (break in the continuity of the path segments), and by continuing to drag upward without releasing the mouse button, you've created two segments that bow upward. This shape you've created will serve as a template for an authentic-looking piece of metal background.

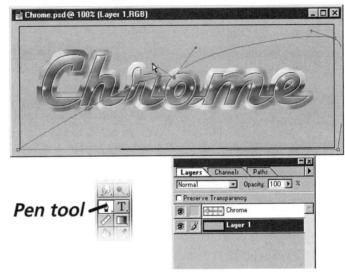

FIGURE 24.25 *Use the modifier keys in combination with the Pen tool to create a closed path that has an interesting inflection at its center.*

10. On the Paths palette, click on the Loads Path as a Selection icon at the bottom of the palette, and then click on an empty area of the palette to hide the path.

11. Click on the foreground color box on the toolbox, and then in the Color Picker, choose a slightly darker color for the shading work you'll perform. H:187, S:100%, and B:80% is a good color—*verrrry* 1950s! Click on OK to return to the workspace.

12. Choose the Airbrush tool. On the Options palette, make sure the mode is Normal, the Pressure is 50%, and there is no Fade option. On the Brushes palette, choose the 100-pixel tip.

13. Stroke along the top, bowing edge of the marquee selection, and then make a few quick strokes below your original strokes to blend the new color into the background color (see Figure 24.26).

FIGURE 24.26 *Create a hard edge in the composition, and then make it fade into the background color by using the Airbrush tool slowly, and then quickly, as you travel downward in the selection.*

14. Press Ctrl(⌘)+D to deselect the marquee, and then make a fast stroke in the upper left of the image, going from about eight o'clock to one o'clock, touching both the left and the top edges, respectively, of the image window. This adds a very subtle amount of color variation to the background, as you'll often see in real chrome.

15. Press Ctrl(⌘)+S; keep the file open.

Clearly, you now have a nice piece of chrome and a metallic background in Chrome.psd. These two elements don't seem to combine properly, however; the chrome looks as though it's floating *above* the background, instead of being stamped *into* the background. The folks in Detroit have their metal presses, and we Photoshoppists have the Layer Effects command to produce the same visual results. Read on!

NOTE

Regardless of the Pressure setting you choose for the Airbrush tool, the longer you linger over an area, the more foreground color is deposited there. This is why you can create subtle color changes by moving the cursor quickly, and why you can totally cover other areas with foreground color by lingering over those areas with the Airbrush tool.

USING A PILLOW EMBOSS TO IMITATE STAMPED METAL

If you've read this book linearly, from the first page up 'til here, you're already familiar with the Layer Effects command from Chapter 16, "Creatively Working with Filters," where you created a pillow-embossed Web button. But if you leapt right into this chapter after ripping the bag off this book, let's walk through the steps for creating a soft "punched-in" look for the chrome lettering. It's fun and it's fast:

CREATING A STAMPED LOOK, USING LAYER EFFECTS

1. Click on the Chrome layer title on the Layers palette to make it the current editing layer.

2. Choose Layer, Effects, and then choose Bevel and Emboss.

3. In the Effects dialog box, choose Pillow Emboss from the Style drop-down list. You might want to drag the Effects box away from your illustration so you can preview the effect you're creating in the image.

4. In the Highlight area of the Effects box, drag the Opacity slider to about 88%. Drag the Opacity slider to about 55% in the Shadow area of the Effects dialog box.

5. Click on the arrow to the right of the Angle text entry field. When the direction pop-up appears, drag the angle of the line in the circle until the text field reads 125. Alternatively, you can type **125** in the text field and then press Tab twice to move to the Depth field.

6. Leave the Depth at the default of 5 pixels, and drag the Blur slider so the text field reads 8, as shown in Figure 24.27. You're not striving for a "knock out" effect here; your composition needs a subtle amount of pillow embossing to make the chrome look stamped into the background. Too much effect will overwhelm all the well-balanced "business" you've created with the chrome lettering.

7. Click on OK to apply the effect, and then press Ctrl(⌘)+S.

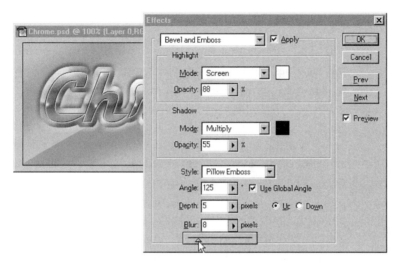

FIGURE 24.27 *Add a pillow emboss at about "3/4 strength" to bring out the dimension of the piece and to visually unite the background with the chrome lettering.*

8. You're finished! However, and this is optional, you might want to save a flattened copy of the composition, to TIFF or JPEG format. If this is your wish, press Ctrl(⌘)+Alt(Opt)+S, choose the file format from the Save As (Macintosh: Format) drop-down list, and check the Flatten Image, the Exclude Alpha Channels, and the Exclude Non-Image Data (such as the path you have in the image) check boxes. Name the file and choose a directory for it in the Save A Copy dialog box, and then click on Save. You can close Chrome.psd at any time now.

In Figure 24.28 (and in the second color section of this book), you can see the completed assignment. It's hard to believe that you began with some ornamental text against a white background, isn't it?

FIGURE 24.28 *Variation in color, highlights, shading, distortion, faint secondary light sources, the right amount and shape of tonal variation on the background, and—whew!—a little embossing can transform text into chrome-plated, dimensional text!*

SUMMARY

NOTE

Remember all the settings you used for the Smudge tool, the Dodge and Burn tools, the Paintbrush tool and the Layer Effects? If not—*good*! The amount of enhancement you apply to any text or other shapes is directly related to the file size of the design you intend to embellish. Do not, for example, use a small brush to create interior lighting effects on a 6 or 7MB image.

Let the size of the file you work with dictate the size and number of features you apply in Photoshop. The larger the image, the larger the amounts for the settings, and the exact numbers need to be arrived at by experimenting. Everything you do to a piece can be undone through the History palette.

The author thinks that you've gone "beyond chrome" by following the examples in this chapter. That's right; you can certainly whip up an outstanding chrome headline for your next Web site assignment, and even illustrate a company logo for a magazine advertisement. But that's not all. You now understand the interplay between shape and surface texture, you know how to reinforce an embellished piece with an embossed outline, and you have a pretty good handle on lighting effects you can create manually. If you put all these nuggets of wisdom together, you can create rough or polished chrome, you can create gold lettering (hint: use shades of gold instead of the My Chrome gradient preset you created), you can light your work from different angles, and more. When you understand the *principles* behind why things look realistic, the sky's the limit.

It's not often that the author gets to indulge himself, while at the same time showing you, the reader, some ultra-advanced uses for tools, but this one time, it's called Chapter 25. Come along and see how third-party plug-ins for Photoshop can be pushed to the extreme, to create designs you might have only *seen* on the Web or in print. No secrets, everything's step-by-step, and it's all about as dull as a roller coaster ride!

THE AUTHOR'S FAVORITE THIRD-PARTY PLUG-INS

Author's Warning: Do not give this chapter to small children. Do not attempt to swallow the contents of this chapter all at once! Recommended serving size is one topic per day!

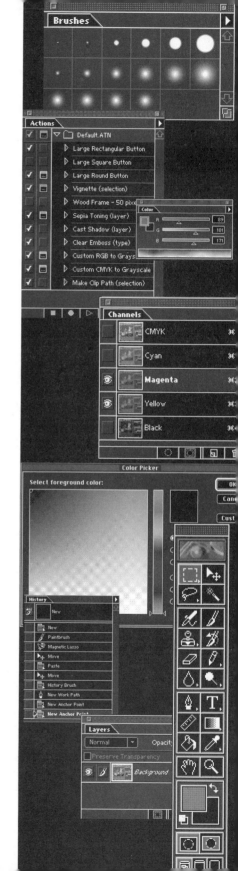

It's hard for an author who is also an illustrator *not* to have favorite third-party plug-ins for Photoshop. But in the past three years, the third-party plug-in field has exploded, with more enhancements to Photoshop than we, as designers, could imagine. There's everything from photorealistic shadow filters to 3D modeling plug-ins; there's even a plug-in that helps you select around human hair in a photograph!

Because this Limited Edition book is an extension of *Inside Adobe Photoshop 5*, the author tried to see how *far* he could extend this book. Happily, this chapter provides you with a fairly comprehensive list of exciting plug-ins for Photoshop that'll advance your work from great to *incredible*. And it documents all the author's favorite plug-ins in tutorial style. The sections in this chapter are modular, so you can pick and choose what you want to read first. Demo versions of all the plug-ins can be found on the *Limited Edition* CD-ROM.

INTRODUCING XAOS TOOLS FOR THE MAC— AND WINDOWS

XAOS|tools has been manufacturing Photoshop plug-ins for the Macintosh for several years, but not until 1998 did XAOS port Paint Alchemy 2, Terrazzo 2, and TypeCaster 1.5 (collectively sold as the bundle "Total XAOS") for Windows users. Corel Corporation licensed the rights to distribute Paint Alchemy and Terrazzo for their product Corel PHOTO-PAINT, so some Windows users have seen and used XAOS|tools' products, but Corel's implementation of the filters was limited to work within PHOTO-PAINT. With Total XAOS, XAOS tools has opened the door to *all* Photoshop users to get in on the creative fun these filters bring to design work.

The first stop on our tour of XAOS|tools products is Paint Alchemy 2. If you own the filter, come along and see some unique uses for it. If you don't own Total XAOS, take the Companion CD out of your CD-ROM drive for a moment, put in the *Limited Edition* CD-ROM, and run the installation program from the Xaos folder.

PAINT ALCHEMY: PAINTING WITH SMALL DRAWINGS AND PHOTOS

The concept behind Paint Alchemy is not unlike Photoshop's Assorted Brushes palette. In Paint Alchemy, you can choose from a number of small bitmap images to apply to an image. But where Paint Alchemy departs from the Assorted Brushes palette is in the control it gives you over the coverage of the brush strokes, the different colors, the angle of the stroke, size, opacity, and a host of other features.

Now, Paint Alchemy comes with several attractive presets, but to make the plug-in work for *you* (instead of the other way around), the following steps show you how to design your own brush tip, and how to apply the brush strokes in a way that creates a pattern you can use as a texture map in Photoshop.

Let's begin by defining two brush strokes for Paint Alchemy 2 to use:

CREATING BRUSH TIPS FOR PAINT ALCHEMY

1. In Photoshop, press F5 to display the Brushes palette if it's not already onscreen.

2. Click on the menu flyout button on the Brushes palette, and choose Save Brushes. In the Save directory box, locate on your hard disk Photoshop5, Goodies, Brushes, and then save your current set of brushes (with a unique name such as My1998Brushes) to this folder. You're doing this because shortly you'll load a new set of brushes from this folder, and any custom brush tips you might have created on your own will be lost forever if you load new brushes without first saving your current set.

3. Click on the menu flyout button on the Brushes palette, and choose Replace Brushes. In the directory box that appears, locate on your hard disk Photoshop, Goodies, Brushes; then click on the Assorted Brushes file, and then click on Load (Macintosh: click on Open). Your default brushes are replaced by really weird, small patterns and drawings. Do *not* worry that your default set of brushes has been replaced—you'll see by the end of this example how to restore the default set of brush tips.

4. Press Ctrl(⌘)+N, and in the New dialog box, type **2** (inches) in the Width field, type **2** (inches) in the Height field, type **72** in the Resolution field, choose Grayscale from the Mode drop-down list, choose White as the Contents of the new image, and then click on OK.

5. Press D (default colors), and then choose the Paintbrush tool.

NOTE

You might want to install *all* the third-party filters from the *Limited Edition* CD-ROM right now, so you won't have to keep swapping CDs as we cover different plug-ins. The tutorial files are all on the Companion CD.

Also, Photoshop 5 installs with a folder called "plug-ins," with a hyphen. Because Photoshop can only read from one directory to run plug-in filters, it's important that you do *not* create a plugins folder within the Photoshop 5 folder, even if a demo application offers to create such a folder. If you install the demo programs to anything other than the plug-ins folder— the folder with the hyphen— Photoshop will not list this filter in the Filters menu.

6. Click on the snowflake design on the Brushes palette to select it, and then click in the new document window. The result is a black snowflake against the white background, as shown in Figure 25.1. Hint: You cannot change the size of the tips on the Assorted Brushes palette, so the snowflake is of a fixed size.

Assorted Brushes

FIGURE 25.1 *Click, do not drag, a Paintbrush tip in the image window to create source material for Paint Alchemy.*

7. With the Rectangular Marquee tool, drag a tight selection area around the snowflake design, and then press Ctrl(⌘)+I to make a negative version of the design, as shown in Figure 25.2.

FIGURE 25.2 *Press Ctrl(⌘)+I to invert the tonal scheme within the selection marquee.*

8. Choose Image, Crop.

9. Save the file to hard disk as Flake. Macintosh users should choose the PICT file format, 8 bits/pixel, no compression. Windows users should choose the BMP file format with 8-bit selected in the Options dialog box as the color capability of the image. If you intend to create a lot of your own brush tips for Paint Alchemy, it's probably a good idea to designate a specific folder for your work. A good place might be Photoshop/Goodies/Brushes.

10. Perform steps 4–9, using the scattered lines pattern on the Assorted Brushes palette, as shown in Figure 25.3. Call the image Lines.bmp (Macintosh: Lines.pict). Now you have two unique brush tips that you'll use in the sections that follow.

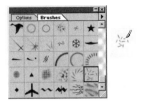

FIGURE 25.3 *Create a second design for Paint Alchemy to use as a brush tip.*

11. You can close the two files at any time now.

Now that you've designed your own brush tips, it's time to use them in Paint Alchemy. Through the process, we'll run down what the features in Paint Alchemy do to an image.

WORKING WITH PAINT ALCHEMY'S CONTROLS

The concept here is that you'll apply both the snowflake and the lines brushes to a new document window, with varying size, density, and angle of the brush strokes. By doing this, you'll set up an image to be ideal for Photoshop's Lighting Effects Texture channel to produce an embossed image whose height varies in different areas of the image. Remember that with the Lighting Effects Texture channel, a slight tonal variation compared to the background of the image produces a more subtle embossed effect than an image area that contrasts strongly against the background.

Here's how to apply the first of two Paint Alchemy patterns to a new image in Photoshop:

NOTE

Paint Alchemy will accept brushes in Grayscale or Indexed color mode. The color index must consist of 256 colors. You specify this by choosing the System palette under Image, Mode, Indexed Color, and then picking either System (Macintosh) or System (Windows) from the Palette drop-down list.

Whether you decide to create a colored brush tip or a grayscale tip, the "proper" arrangement of colors in the image is that the design should be in color (or a light or white grayscale tone), and the background of the image to be used as a brush tip should be black.

APPLYING A SNOWFLAKE PATTERN, USING PAINT ALCHEMY

1. Press Ctrl(⌘)+N, and then in the New dialog box, type 7 (inches) in the Width field, type **5** (inches) in the Height field, type **72** in the Resolution field, choose RGB Color from the Mode drop-down list, and then click on OK to create the new image.

2. Choose Filter, XAOS Tools, and then choose Paint Alchemy 2.0. If you're using the demo program, the filter listing is Paint Alchemy 2.0 demo, and a splash screen telling you that you cannot render effects you create to file is displayed before the Paint Alchemy interface appears.

3. Alt(Opt)+click on any of the default brushes. Doing this displays the Load/Save dialog box. Click on Load New Brush, as shown in Figure 25.4.

**Alt (⭜)+click on any brush
to display the dialog box**

FIGURE 25.4   *To load, save, or restore the default brushes, Alt(Opt)+click on any of the brush previews within the interface.*

4. In the directory box, locate Photoshop, Goodies, Brushes, and then choose the Flake.bmp (Macintosh: Flake in the PICT format) image, and then click on Open. The image file loads as a thumbnail on the default brushes area on the interface, but it's not loaded as the current brush yet. Click on the Flake icon to load it as the current brush.

5. Click on the Color icon. In the Color dialog box, click on the Solid Color swatch, which will then display the system color picker. Choose black in the color picker, and then click on OK to return to the Color dialog box.

6. Under Background Color, click on the From Image button. With this setting, the foreground color of the brush that's selected will render to the image but leave empty those areas that do not contain the snowflake pattern. It's as though you're rendering opaque areas to a transparent layer in Photoshop.

7. Drag the Lightness Variation slider to about 92, as shown in Figure 25.5. As you can see in the preview window, by mixing different Lightness values for the rendered image, you achieve an effect that makes all the snowflakes that will be rendered a different percentage of black.

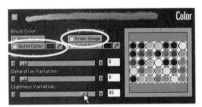

FIGURE 25.5   *The snowflake brush will now render snowflakes of different tonal values.*

8. Click on the Close box in the upper left of the Color dialog box, click on the Preview button, click on the brush icon below the right preview window (so that it turns orange), and then drag in the left preview window. As you can see in Figure 25.6, the snowflake rendering will feature different shades of the brush design, but the strokes are too evenly spaced, and there's no variation in size. You'll correct this shortly.

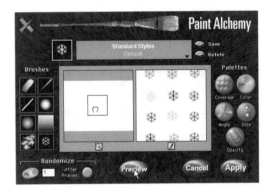

FIGURE 25.6   *Preview the image by clicking on Preview. Move the zoomed-out preview window around to see more of the image by first clicking on the brush icon, and then dragging the zoom box around in the left preview window.*

9. Click on the Coverage button, and then either very carefully drag the Brush Density slider so the number field reads 75 or (much more simply and precisely) type **75** in the Brush Density number field. The proxy box at the right of the dialog box is *not* a fair indicator of how many snowflake strokes will appear in the finished image; you should always preview the proposed application of strokes, and soon you'll learn how to do so.

10. Drag the Horizontal Placement Variation slider to about 77, and then drag the Vertical Placement Variation slider to about 65, as shown in Figure 25.7. By adding variation to the placement of the snowflakes, the design becomes less stagnant and more visually interesting.

FIGURE 25.7 *Keep the density of snowflake strokes sparse, and don't let them appear in neat columns and rows. You'll be adding a second coat of Paint Alchemy design to this image, so leave space in the image for the second application of strokes.*

11. Click on the Close box, and then in the main interface, click on the Angle button.

12. Drag the Variation slider to about 100, as shown in Figure 25.8. As the proxy box depicts, the snowflake brush tip will appear in the finished image with many different degrees of rotation.

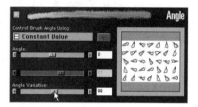

FIGURE 25.8 *Add Variation to the angle at which the snowflake pattern is rendered to the image file.*

13. Click on the Close box, and then click on the Size button in the main interface.

14. In the Control Brush Size Using drop-down list, choose Random Values.

15. Drag the Size is Between This Value slider to the right, to about a tenth of the slider's length. Drag the And That Value slider to about two thirds the length of the slider to the right, as shown in Figure 25.9. Don't concern yourself with the number fields—the amounts shown are handy to copy on a piece of paper so you can duplicate the Size setup in the future, but they are not an indication of how many different sizes of snowflakes will render to the image. (How, for example, can you have a minimum/maximum difference in size of 7,000, when you're only rendering around 200 snowflakes to the image?)

The important point here is that the snowflake strokes don't overlap each other by too much. If they do, you'll wind up with dense lumps of varying tones instead of distinct design elements in your work.

NOTE

You can preview a limited area of the whole image by clicking on Preview; you don't absolutely need to click on the Brush icon and then drag in the left preview window to see different areas on the image to which Paint Alchemy will render.

If you've clicked on the magnifying glass icon in the left preview window, the interface is in "zoomed in" mode, and you cannot drag in the window to see different areas of the image. So to check out how the entire image will look, click on the Brush icon, but do not click on the magnifying glass icon.

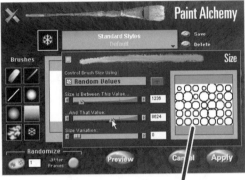

Don't let different sizes overlap

FIGURE 25.9 *Create different sizes of snowflake designs, but don't let the strokes overlap each other by too much. Use the proxy window as your guide to specifying the settings in the Size dialog box.*

16. Drag the Size Variation slider to about 31. It might seem odd to add variation to random values (almost a redundant effort!), but this control specifies the difference in size between strokes, based on their current size. So, yes, you *will* be applying a variation based on an existing variation!

17. Click on the Close box in the dialog box, and then preview what the image will look like. If you followed the steps up until now, the preview should look much like that shown in Figure 25.10, and you can click on the Apply button.

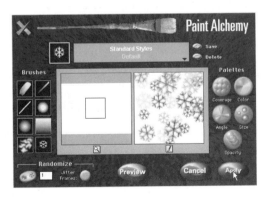

FIGURE 25.10 *Preview the design you've created one last time before applying it to the document window.*

18. Your new image should look something like that shown in Figure 25.11. Save the file as Weird Bumps.psd in Photoshop's native file format to your hard disk. Keep the file open.

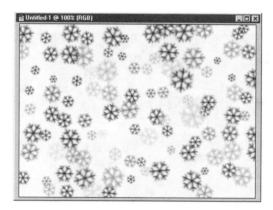

FIGURE 25.11 *From a single image file used as a Paint Alchemy brush tip, you can create a multitude of design elements of different sizes, angles, and tones.*

In the following section, you'll apply the second of the two brushes you saved earlier to the composition. Because Paint Alchemy retains previously defined settings, the steps to follow to complete the image will be short and easy.

APPLYING A SECOND COAT OF PAINT (ALCHEMY) AND CREATING A TEXTURE MAP

It's time to scatter the Lines brush tip into the snowflake image. There is no reason you cannot accept the same Color, Angle, Size, and Coverage settings you defined in the filter's interface. All you really need to do is shift where the brush tip strokes appear, so they are not directly on top of the snowflake strokes.

Here's how to finish the design and then set up the document for Photoshop's Lighting Effects filter, which will emboss your creation:

COMPLETING THE PAINTING AND CREATING AN ALPHA CHANNEL FROM IT

1. Press Ctrl(⌘)+Alt(Opt)+F to open the last-used filter dialog box without applying the effect.

2. Alt(Opt)+click on the snowflake image in the default brush tips area of the interface. The Load/Save dialog box pops up; click on Load New Brush.

3. In the directory box, choose Lines.bmp (Macintosh: Lines, in the PICT format), and then click on Open.

4. Click on the thumbnail image in the default brushes columns to the left of the interface. This makes the Lines brush the current brush. All other settings are currently the same as those you used for the snowflake image. The reason you'll be able to apply the Lines brush over the snowflake pattern you have in Weird Bumps.psd is that earlier you specified that the background for the Paint Alchemy effect is the image. You did this shortly after you selected the Brush Color in the Color dialog box.

5. Click on the pair of dice icon at the bottom left of the interface. As the name above it clearly states, you're changing the current pattern of the brush strokes to a random variation of the current position they will be rendered to in the image. Click on the brush icon under the right preview window, and then drag in the left window to preview the effect of the lines on the current composition. If, in any area, the lines seem to be clumping over the snowflakes pattern, click on the dice again, and then preview the proposed changes to the image, as shown in Figure 25.12.

NOTE

The Jitter Frames option is meaningless when Paint Alchemy is used as a plug-in for Photoshop. This option is used when Paint Alchemy is plugged into Adobe Premiere; it displaces the pixel colors in the brush strokes you apply over a number of video frames to achieve an animation effect.

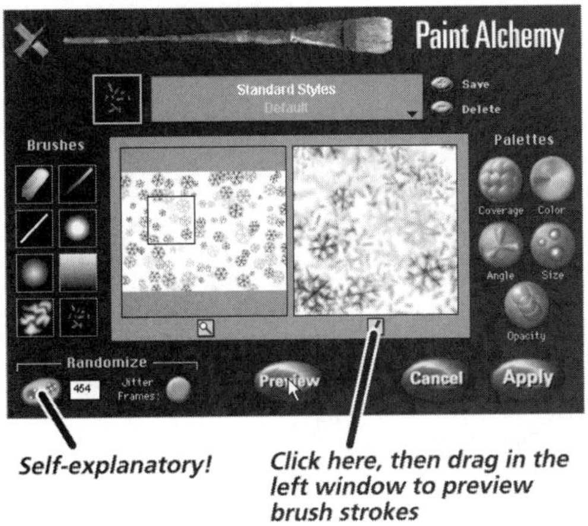

Self-explanatory!

Click here, then drag in the left window to preview brush strokes

FIGURE 25.12 *Create a variation on the current position of the brush strokes you'll apply to the image by clicking on the dice icon.*

6. Click on Apply. The Lines brush tip image is scattered around the Weird bumps.psd image at different angles, sizes, and degrees of density.

If you're using the demo version of Paint Alchemy, you obviously cannot continue with the following steps because the demo version won't allow you to render to an image window. For designers who don't own the retail version of Paint Alchemy, open the Weird.psd image from the Chap25 folder on the Companion CD, save the file as Weird Bump.psd to your hard disk, keep the image open, and let's continue…

7. Press F7 if the Channels palette isn't currently onscreen.

8. Drag the Green channel into the Create New Channel icon at the bottom of the Channels palette, as shown in Figure 25.13. Doing this creates an alpha channel in the image. Actually, you can drag any of the three channels into the Create New Channel icon, because this image is grayscale in content—it uses equal amounts of red, green, and blue.

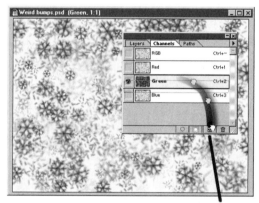

Create new (alpha) channel

FIGURE 25.13 *Drag a color channel into the Create New Channel icon to create an alpha channel for the image.*

9. Press Ctrl(⌘)+S; keep the file open.

Now that you have a copy of the visual information that makes up Weird bumps.psd, you can do anything you like to the composite color channel of the image. Next, you'll add a flat color to the composite color channel, and then use the alpha channel you created as a texture map for the image.

A TEXTURE CHANNEL IS A BUMP MAP

One of the most visually exciting products of Photoshop's Lighting Effects filter is the Texture Channel controls. Unfortunately, computer graphics programmers seem to lend different names to the same visual effect. The effect produced by the Texture channel in the Lighting Effects filter has a more common name, one that is based on what the effect looks like in modeling applications. Simply put, the Texture channel is a *bump map* that creates changes in the color composite image in Photoshop. A bump map is a grayscale image that creates the effect of bumps and recesses in an image (or on the surface of a 3D model), depending on the brightness values found in the alpha channel.

Now, if you think back to several paragraphs ago, you'll realize why the Paint Alchemy filter was set up to render different tones of the brush strokes. The alpha channel you created in the previous steps contains various tones. These different tones will create different heights in the color composite image when the different tones are used as a Texture channel (bump map).

Here's how to use the Lighting Effects filter to create a visually interesting "topology" in the Weird Bumps.psd image:

CREATING A BUMPY IMAGE, USING THE LIGHTING EFFECTS FILTER

1. Press Ctrl(⌘)+~(tilde) to move your view of Weird Bumps.psd to its color composite channel.

2. Click on the foreground color box on the toolbox, and choose any color you like in the Color Picker. The author went with a dull lavender for this example because he didn't want the color of the image to fight for interest with the bumps that will be created in the image. Click on OK in the Color Picker to choose the color and return to Photoshop's workspace.

3. Press Ctrl(⌘)+A to select the entire image, and then press Alt(Opt)+Delete (Backspace) to fill the image with foreground color. Press Ctrl(⌘)+D to deselect the marquee selection.

4. Choose Filter, Render, and then choose Lighting Effects.

5. In the Lighting Effects box, choose Directional from the Light Type drop-down list. Drag the light source point in the proxy window—the dot on the far end of the light direction line—away or toward the window until the color of the image in the proxy window is about the same as the color with which you filled the image in step 3.

6. Leave the White Is High check box unchecked (the effect you're creating uses blacks and denser tones in the alpha channel, and not on the white areas to make bumps). Choose Alpha 1 from the Texture Channel drop-down list, and drag the Height slider to about 3, as shown in Figure 25.14. Generally, "less is more" with the height of a Texture channel image, unless the alpha channel contains extremely subtle variations in tone.

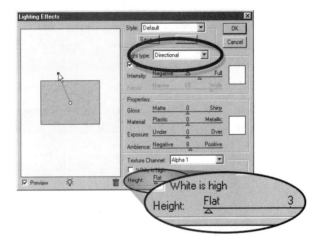

FIGURE 25.14 *Choose Alpha 1 as the Texture channel to be used in the Lighting Effects filter, and drag the Height slider to the left until it reads about 3.*

7. Click on OK to apply the filter. Although Figure 25.15 is not in color, you can see that the Lighting Effects filter has produced an intricate, 3D sort of image, whose elements appear to rise above the surface of the image with different elevations.

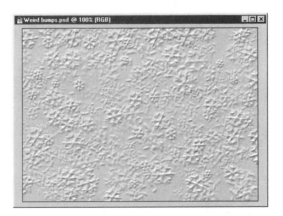

FIGURE 25.15 *By applying the Lighting Effects filter's Texture Channel option to the image, you now have bumps in the image—some higher than others.*

8. Press Ctrl(⌘)+S; you can close the image at any time now.

9. On the Brushes palette, click on the menu flyout button, and then choose Reset Brushes (or choose Replace Brushes if you saved a custom collection of brushes earlier in the chapter). If you choose to reset the brushes to their default, you'll see an attention box now that asks you whether you want to go ahead with the action, or to Append (add to) the current brushes on the palette. Click on OK, and your Brushes palette returns to normal. If you want to retrieve you custom palette, clicking on Replace Brushes will present you with a directory box in which you can locate My1998Brushes (or whatever you named the saved set), and then click on Load (Macintosh: click on Open).

Certainly, there is more to explore with the XAOSItools Paint Alchemy filter. Whether you own the retail (fully functional) filter or only the demo version, you can, and should, experiment with different settings. One of the most useful ways to gain knowledge with Paint Alchemy is to click on the Standard Styles area in the interface, which is a drop-down list of preset styles. Choose one of these styles, and then check out the Coverage, Color, Angle, and Size settings, to see how a specific preset is designed. You can then create a number of brush tips for use with Paint Alchemy, apply similar settings to those used for the presets, and create original patterns. The author's favorite to play with is the Standard Styles, Abstract Styles, Autumn. You don't need to limit your adventures with Paint Alchemy to producing bump map images—there are lots of attractive things you can do by adjusting the Hue Variation slider in the Color dialog box. The preceding example simply shows how you can use third-party filters in combination with Photoshop filters to produce art that the competition out there might not have thought of!

Our next stop is XAOS | tools' Terrazzo filter. Prepare yourself for some kaleidoscopic effects!

USING THE TERRAZZO FILTER TO CREATE TILE EFFECTS

One of the most appealing features for designers who use the Terrazzo plug-in is that they can create seamless tiling textures by using only the simplest of artwork for the base image, and one or two clicks in the Terrazzo interface. With the Terrazzo filter, you have the option of filling an image window with a repeating pattern while, additionally, saving the design as a small, seamless texture—ideal for a Web page background.

In the sections that follow, you'll use Terrazzo to create a seamless tiling texture and then embellish it, using Photoshop's native features.

Creating the Most Interesting Art for the Terrazzo Plug-in to Use

The Terrazzo filter acts as a kaleidoscope, mirroring a selected area in a design you've already created in Photoshop. But Terrazzo goes beyond the traditional physical kaleidoscope, with options for the shape of the mirrored pieces, the center of the artwork you've created that Terrazzo mirrors, and the size of the center of the kaleidoscopic effects, plus other options.

Through a lot of trial and error, the author has discovered that the best piece of art you can design for use with the Terrazzo filter is a collection of different, simple shapes that overlap and have slightly different colors. By painting a bunch of different, simple, overlapping shapes, as shown in Figure 25.16, you can produce at least three or four different Terrazzo tiles from a single base image. The different patterns are a result of shifting the center and the size of the target pattern area within the Terrazzo filter.

Figure 25.16 *Different shapes and different colors, all of which overlap one another, are the key to producing several different and interesting tiles, using the Terrazzo filter.*

Here's how to create some base artwork for the Terrazzo filter to use:

Creating Abstract Art to Transform into Kaleidoscopic Art

1. Create a new file in RGB color mode, one that's about 4 inches in both Height and Width and has a resolution of 72 pixels/inch.

2. Click on the Foreground color box on the toolbox, and then in the Color Picker choose a color that will be the background of the image. Click on OK to exit the Color Picker, and then press Alt(Opt)+Delete (Backspace) to fill the image window with the color you chose.

3. With the Polygon Marquee tool, create a polygon selection (four or five sides are plenty for this example); click on the Foreground color box on the toolbox, and then choose a color that contrasts well with the background color. Click on OK to exit the Color Picker, and then press Alt(Opt)+Delete (Backspace) to fill the selection marquee. Press Ctrl(⌘)+D to deselect the marquee.

4. With the Elliptical Marquee tool, drag an oval shape in the image window. Then click and drag inside the selection to position it so that it overlaps the polygon area slightly.

5. Click on the Foreground color box on the toolbox, choose a new color for the selection, click on OK to exit the Color Picker, press Alt(Opt)+Delete (Backspace) to fill the oval, and then press Ctrl(⌘)+D to deselect the marquee.

6. With the Paintbrush tool selected, choose the top, far-right tip on the Brushes palette. Choose a new color from the Color Picker for the foreground color, and then draw a squiggle that overlaps the other shapes in the design.

NOTE

If you'd like to use the design shown in figure 25.16 in combination with the Terrazzo filter, the image is called Design.tif, and it's located in the Examples\Chap25 folder on the Companion CD.

Design.tif is a grayscale image of low contrast because the author wants to produce a grayscale texture using Terrazzo—too many different, intense colors would make the Terrazzo tile unsuitable as a background texture for a Web page. If you are not interested in creating Web pages, use any colors you like in the following steps, but keep to simple, overlapping shapes for the best results using the Terrazzo filter.

What you've done here is create different shaped edges to the colors you've added to the image window. The Terrazzo filter's target control can now be moved around to different areas where the color edges overlap to produce entirely different kaleidoscopic patterns.

7. Choose File, Save As, and then save the work as Design.tif in the TIFF file format to your hard disk. Keep the design open.

Now, it's time to run the Terrazzo filter and see what can be created from your design.

WORKING WITH THE TERRAZZO FILTER'S FEATURES

The Terrazzo filter is about as intuitive as interfaces get, so the instructions in this section might seem a little facile. But just to make absolutely sure you get it, here's how to create a seamless tiling image using the filter:

CREATING A TERRAZZO SEAMLESS TILE

1. With Design.tif open in Photoshop's workspace, choose Filter, XAOS Tools, and then choose Terrazzo 2.0 (or Terrazzo 2.0 demo).

2. By default, the Pinwheel style (called the *Symmetry*) is activated in Terrazzo. Let's go for something a little more elaborate; click on the Pinwheel icon to display the different Symmetry styles, click on Whirlpool, and then click on OK.

3. Drag in the center of the polygon target shape (called the "motif" in XAOS documentation) in the left window in the Terrazzo interface. This moves the target zone for the pattern; watch the right preview window as you move the motif, and stop dragging the motif when you think you have an interesting pattern.

4. Take a look at the Tile preview window, and check to see whether this pattern will be interesting as a seamless tiling pattern. If so, click on the Save Tile button, as shown in Figure 25.17. If you want to experiment a little more, drag the corner handle on the motif toward or away from the center of the motif. Doing this increases or decreases the sampling size of the motif. When you're happy with (or at least intrigued by) the pattern, click on Save Tile.

Although it's easy to look up later, you might want to make a physical note of the dimensions of the tile, which are displayed directly above the Tile preview box.

5. In the Save Tile dialog box, save the image as pattern.bmp (or pattern in the PICT format on the Macintosh); decide on an easy-to-find hard disk location for the file, and then click on Save.

6. Click on Cancel to exit the Terrazzo filter's interface.

7. Open the pattern image in Photoshop and close the Design.tif image.

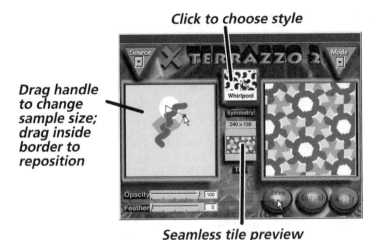

Click to choose style

Drag handle to change sample size; drag inside border to reposition

Seamless tile preview

FIGURE 25.17 *Defining a pattern is as simple as placing the motif over an area in the preview of the image and then resizing the motif by dragging on its control handle.*

TERRAZZO FEATURES THAT WE DIDN'T HAVE THE SPACE TO COVER THOROUGHLY

Useful features in the Terrazzo filter that were not covered in the example are

- The Source drop-down list, which enables you to create a pattern from an image other than the current image in Photoshop. This feature is useful when you want to layer a pattern shaped from an "outside" image source on top of the current image in Photoshop. You'd drag the Opacity slider to the left, look at the preview of this combination of images, and then click on Apply instead of Save Tile.

- The Feather option, which enables you to soften the edges of the motif and create an image—or an image tile—whose edges are indistinct.

Although the pattern tile you created in the previous steps can be used "as is" without any additional steps, the author thought you might like to know how to embellish the tile so that it looks more dimensional and has more "business" going on within the pattern. In the Boutons/Textures folder on the *Limited Edition* CD-ROM, many of the seamless texture files were created by using Terrazzo and then post-processing the pattern, using Photoshop and MetaCreations' Painter.

Building "into" a Seamless Tiling Pattern

The seamless tiles that Terrazzo produces can be real eyecatchers. With the retail version of the product, your only limit to the different patterns you can produce would appear to be your life span! This chapter, however, focuses on the way native Photoshop filters can work in *combination* with third-party filters, and indeed there is some manual tuning you can perform on a Terrazzo tile that will make it more complex and more dimensional.

In the steps that follow, you'll use Photoshop's Glass filter to distort the pattern so it looks a little more handcrafted. Then you'll use the Offset filter to relocate the center of the pattern and look for (and correct) any edges in the pattern that might be produced by the Glass filter.

The reason you need to retouch a perfect seamless pattern that's been passed through the Glass filter is that the Glass filter uses hard-coded image files (you can't access these files) of specific dimensions to displace the target file. You have no way of knowing how large the hard-coded image file is, and it's almost certain that the displacement created by the Glass filter won't line up with the visual content of the Terrazzo tile.

Here's how to add a touch of glass to the Terrazzo tile:

Adding Visual Interest to a Seamless Tiling Image

1. If you don't have the retail version of Terrazzo 2.0, then you don't have a tiling image in Photoshop yet! Open the pattern.tif image from the Examples\Chap25 folder on the Companion CD. If you own the retail version and have created a pattern of your own, ignore everything in step 1 except this sentence; simply open the pattern file in Photoshop.

2. Choose Filter, Distort, and then choose Glass.

3. In the Glass Filter dialog box, leave the Texture at its default of Frosted, and leave the Scaling at the default of 100%. Drag the Distortion slider to 2, and then drag the Smoothness slider to 4, as shown in Figure 25.18. This produces a mild but visible distortion of the pattern.bmp, pattern.pict, or the CD's pattern.tif image.

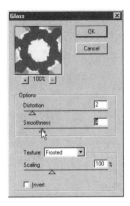

FIGURE 25.18 *Add a small amount of Glass distortion to the image to make it look more hand-drawn.*

  4. Click on OK to apply the effect.

If you're using a tile you created in Terrazzo, the author has no way of knowing what the dimensions of the file are. The dimensions of the tile are determined by the size of the motif in Terrazzo. If you're using the pattern.tif file from the Companion CD, its dimensions are 240 pixels wide by 138 pixels high. You will use approximately half the height and width values in the following step, in combination with the Offset filter.

  5. Choose Filter, Other, and then choose Offset. The Offset filter turns images "inside-out," so that the center of an image lies at the edges of the image window, and the edges of the image converge at the center of the design.

  6. In the Undefined Areas part of the Offset dialog box, click on Wrap Around. You should move the dialog box so that you can preview changes in the pattern.tif image in the workspace.

  7. Type half the image's width in the Horizontal field, and type half the image's height in the Vertical field, as shown in Figure 25.19. You can see in this image that there are some straight lines within the pattern. This happened because the Glass filter only displaced the pattern image according to its own internal displacement pattern, which is not the same size as the pattern image.

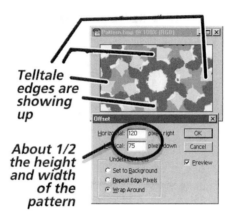

Telltale edges are showing up

About 1/2 the height and width of the pattern

FIGURE 25.19 *Use values of about half the height and width of the pattern.tif image in the Offset dialog box.*

8. Click on OK to apply the Offset filter.

9. Zoom into a 200% viewing resolution of the pattern.tif image.

10. With the Paintbrush tool selected, choose the third-from-left tip in the top row on the Brushes palette.

11. Alt(Opt)+click over an area that's close to the edge of a straight line in the image. This samples the foreground color, and you can now use it with the Paintbrush tool.

12. Carefully stroke an irregular, wavy line across the straight edge in the image, as shown in Figure 25.20. This disguises the telltale edge in the image.

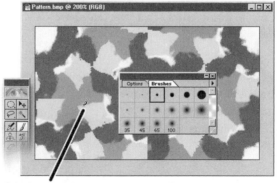

Remove hard edges. Hold Alt(⌥)+click to sample an area's color, then stroke over the hard edge area.

FIGURE 25.20 *Stroke over the edges of a straight line in the image, using a color sampled from either side of the edge.*

13. Perform steps 11 and 12 with the remaining straight edges in the image.

14. Press Ctrl(⌘)+S; keep the file open.

The author believes that a little more user input can be lent to the pattern image. How about adding texture to the image? Read on!

WORKING WITH THE POINTILLIZE AND LIGHTING EFFECTS FILTER

We are going to pay another visit to the Lighting Effects filter to add texture to the pattern image. *This* texturing assignment has a twist, however. Instead of using the pattern you created in Terrazzo as the Texture channel in the Lighting Effects filter, you'll *filter* a copy of the pattern.tif image and then apply the results—which will look *nothing* like the pattern image—to the color composite channel.

Here's how to apply a texture to the pattern that makes it look like the skin of some impossible fruit or vegetable:

USING THE POINTILLIZE FILTER FOR ADDING TEXTURE

1. On the Channels palette, drag the Green channel into the Create New Channel icon at the bottom of the palette, as shown in Figure 25.21. This creates a copy of the Green channel, with the name Alpha 1, and it's the current editing channel.

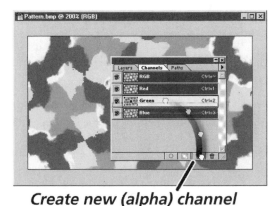

Create new (alpha) channel

FIGURE 25.21 *Create a copy of the tile pattern to a new alpha channel in the document.*

2. Choose Filter, Pixelate, and then choose Pointillize.

3. In the Pointillize dialog box, drag the Cell Size slider to 3, as shown in Figure 25.22, and then click on OK. All the solid fields of tones in the Alpha 1 channel have now become patterns of dots of the original tonal values.

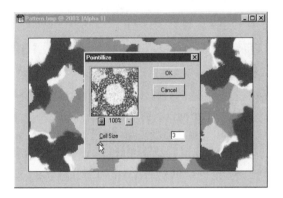

FIGURE 25.22 *Create dots in the alpha channel that are of the same tone as the original areas in the channel.*

4. Press Ctrl(⌘)+˜(tilde) to move your view to the color composite of the channel, and then choose Filter, Render, Lighting Effects.

5. In the Lighting Effects dialog box, choose Directional from the Light type drop-down list, drag the Gloss slider to 0, and drag the Material slider to 0. Drag the light source handle at the end of the light direction line in the proxy box to about 11 o'clock and slightly outside the box to make the brightness of the image in the proxy box about the same as that in the pattern image.

6. Choose Alpha 1 from the Texture Channel drop-down list, as shown in Figure 25.23; check the White Is High check box, and then drag the Height slider to about 20.

7. Click on OK to apply the filter. Click on the Alpha 1 channel on the Channels palette, and then drag it into the trash icon at the bottom of the palette.

Once again, you have lost the seamless tiling property of the pattern image by adding the Pointillize effect. The Pointillize effect does not render into an image—or image channel—seamless tiling information.

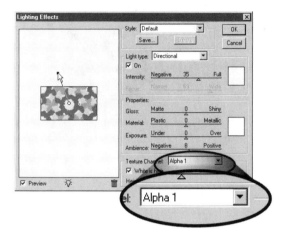

FIGURE 25.23 *Use the pointillized alpha channel as the bump map for the pattern.tif image.*

8. Choose Filter, Other, Offset. Click on OK to accept the values you entered the last time you used this filter. Choose the Rubber Stamp tool. On the Options palette, make sure that the mode is Normal, that the Opacity is 100%, and that the Aligned check box is checked. On the Brushes palette, choose the second-from-left tip in the second row.

9. Look for a telltale edge in the image, and make a note of its color (or tone). Then find an area of identical color or tone and Alt(Opt)+click on it to specify the starting point for the Rubber Stamp tool's sampling feature.

10. Carefully stroke over the edge in the image while watching the traveling sampling point; make sure that the traveling sampling point does not go into areas of color or tone other than the one you want (see Figure 25.24). Reset the sampling point by Alt(Opt)+clicking on an image area if you're running out of sampling space while you clone over the edge in the image.

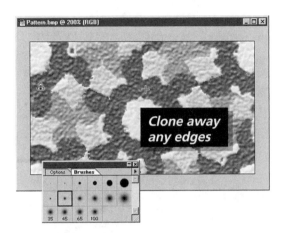

Figure 25.24 *Set a sampling point for the Rubber Stamp tool in an area whose color is identical to the area in the image that contains the hard edge.*

11. Repeat steps 9–10 on other areas of the pattern until there are no more edges. Congratulations! You now have a "hand-painted," textured, seamless image tile.

12. To test the seamless tiling property of your work, press Ctrl(⌘)+A to select all, and then choose Edit, Define Pattern. Press Ctrl(⌘)+N, and in the New dialog box, type **640** (pixels) in the Width field, type **480** (pixels) in the Height field, type **72** in the Resolution field, choose RGB Color as the mode from the drop-down list, and then click on OK to create the new image.

13. Choose Edit, Fill, and then in the Fill dialog box, choose Pattern from the Use drop-down list, and click on OK. In Figure 25.25, you can see how the pattern tiles in a large image area.

14. Save the image as pattern.tif in the TIFF file format to your hard disk for future use, and then close the file. Close the Untitled-1 image without saving it.

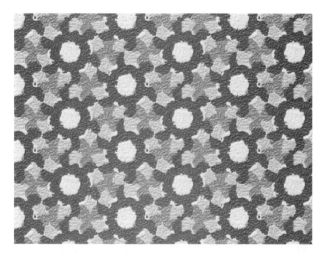

FIGURE 25.25 *This intricate pattern began as a sampling of some geometric doodles by the motif in the Terrazzo filter. Think of the other patterns you can create simply by following the steps and changing the size and location of the motif and selecting different Symmetry styles!*

The sections that follow show in comprehensive detail the options you have as a designer, equipped with Photoshop's native filters and Andromeda Software's 3D filter, to build a photorealistic scene. No modeling programs are involved; you'll create in Photoshop's workspace an image that approaches realism in lighting, shading, and surface textures. Roll up your sleeves now!

BUILDING A PHOTOREALISTIC SCENE: THE CONCEPT COMES FIRST

The author has an idea for taking a simple math symbol—the division sign (÷)—and embellishing it so that it looks three dimensional and as though it is made of wood, and so that it has a backdrop with a spotlight illuminating the scene. The dots in the division symbol will become spheres, and the dividing line will become a flat slab turned at an angle.

If this sounds impossible, it's not. You're going to dig deeply into Photoshop's features and use Andromeda's 3D filter in combination with a rendering of some wood to accomplish exactly what has been described. The demo version of the 3D filter on the *Limited Edition* CD-ROM will not render an image to an image window, but the trial version is still a lot of fun to play with. Suggestion: Take the Companion CD out of your CD-ROM drive right now, install both the 3D demo and the Shadows demo from the ANDROMED folder on the *Limited*

Edition CD, and then put the Companion CD back in your drive. At some point in the steps in the following sections, you will definitely need the rendered spheres and slab. If you do not own the retail version of Andromeda's 3D filter, the finished rendered images are in the Examples\Chap25 folder on the Companion CD—so you most assuredly can complete the assignment as outlined.

CREATING A CURTAIN GRADIENT AND A DISPLACEMENT MAP

You've seen in other chapters in this book how the Gradient Editor in Photoshop can be used to create some pretty sophisticated blends. In the steps to follow, you'll create a gradient that *suggests* a wafting curtain in front of which will be the 3D division symbol. The word "suggests" is stressed in the preceding sentence because the Gradient Editor alone cannot produce an image area that truly looks like a curtain. You also need a pattern for the curtain, and the curtain needs to sag at regular intervals to suggest some stress from the fabric being hung.

So, to begin, you'll create a custom gradient and then create a displacement map for the curtain background that you'll apply to the entire image later in this section.

CREATING A CUSTOM BACKGROUND BY USING THE GRADIENT EDITOR

1. Click on the Linear Gradient tool; then on the Options palette, click on Edit.

2. Click on New in the Gradient Editor, and then in the Gradient Name dialog box, type **Curtains**. Click on OK to return to the Gradient Editor.

3. Double-click on the far-left color marker below the gradient preview strip, and then in the Color Picker, choose black. Click on OK to return to the Gradient Editor.

4. Double-click on the far-right marker, and then in the Color Picker, choose a dull but light tone that will work well contrasted against wood tones. H:31, S:30%, and B:91% is a good choice. Click on OK to return to the Gradient Editor.

5. Alt(Opt)+drag on the far-right marker and bring it close to the left (black) marker. Holding Alt duplicates a selected marker.

6. Alt(Opt)+drag on the black marker and move it to the right of the second (dull wood-colored) marker.

7. Perform step 6 about nine more times, and then drag the far-right marker to the left, and drag a black marker to the far right. Equal spacing between markers is not necessary or even wanted in this example. A curtain has uneven fold widths when hung. See Figure 25.26 for what the Curtains gradient should look like.

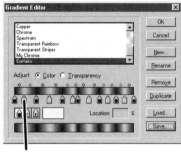

H:31°, S:30%, B: 91%

FIGURE 25.26 *Create alternating colors in the Curtains gradient to make the gradient look like folds of cloth.*

8. Click on OK; the new gradient appears on the Options palette's list.

9. Press Ctrl(⌘)+N, and then in the New dialog box, type **1000** (pixels) in the Width field, type **1000** (pixels) in the Height field, type **72** in the Resolution field, choose RGB Color as the mode from the drop-down list, and then click on OK to create the new image.

10. Zoom out of the new image so you can see the entire image without scrollbars. Drag the image window borders away from the image so you can see some window background.

11. With the Linear Gradient tool chosen, hold Shift (constrains the tool to 45-degree increments), and then drag from the leftmost edge of the image to the rightmost. This fills the image window with the Curtains fill you created.

12. Save the file as Division.psd in Photoshop's native file format to your hard disk.

13. Click on the Red channel on the Channels palette, click on the menu flyout on the Channels palette, and then choose Duplicate Channel, as shown in Figure 25.27.

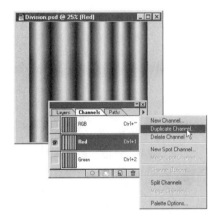

FIGURE 25.27 *You can choose to duplicate a channel within a document or send the duplicate to a new image window.*

14. In the Duplicate Channel dialog box, click on the Document drop-down list and choose New; in the Name field, type **Displace.psd**, and then click on OK.

15. Press D (default colors), and then choose Foreground to Background as the Gradient style on the Gradient Options palette.

16. With the Rectangular Marquee tool, select the leftmost "band" of tones in the image, where from left to right, the image's tones make a transition from black to white to black again. Sneak a peek at Figure 25.28 to see the location of the marquee.

17. With the Linear Gradient tool, hold Shift and then drag from the leftmost point of the selection marquee to the rightmost point, as shown in Figure 25.28.

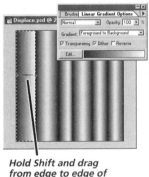

Hold Shift and drag from edge to edge of the selection

FIGURE 25.28 *Create a black-to-white gradient in the area of the first "fold" in the curtain design.*

18. Press Ctrl(⌘)+M to display the Curves dialog box. Drag the left and right markers to the bottom of the graph, and drag the middle of the graph line to the top of the graph, as shown in Figure 25.29. You're creating a distribution curve for Photoshop's Displace command; the darker areas will displace the curtain image downward, and the lighter areas will displace the curtains image upward. Click on OK to apply the change to Displace.psd.

The shape in the image created by the displacement template will match the curve

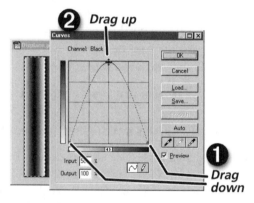

FIGURE 25.29 *The shape of the Curves graph represents the shape of the displacement you'll apply to the Curtains image after you add a pattern to the curtains.*

19. Repeat steps 16–18 with the rest of the bands in the Displace.psd image. Your image should look like Figure 25.30 when you're finished.

FIGURE 25.30 *This is the displacement map you'll use later to make the curtain image look as though it's swooping downward in different areas.*

20. Save the Displace.psd image to your hard disk in Photoshop's native file format. You can close it now, but keep the Division.psd image open.

The Displace command will not do anything that's visually noteworthy unless there's a pattern on the curtain background in the composition. Therefore, you'll create a simple pattern on the curtains in the following section, using the Texturizer filter and a handcrafted pattern.

CREATING YOUR OWN TEXTURIZER SOURCE MATERIAL

The Texturizer command, like many of the Gallery Effects that Adobe has included in the Filters menu, has hard-coded patterns, but also has the option to use your own pattern. As long as the pattern is in the PSD (Photoshop) format, you can pick the pattern while the Texturizer dialog box is displayed.

Here's how to create a small pattern that you'll apply to the Background image:

ADDING A PATTERN TO THE CURTAINS BY USING THE TEXTURIZER FILTER

1. Press Ctrl(⌘)+N, and then in the New dialog box, type **25** (pixels) in the Width field, type **25** (pixels) in the Height field, type **72** in the Resolution field, choose Grayscale as the mode from the drop-down list, and then click on OK. The 25-pixel–wide design will tile in the 1000-pixel–wide Division.psd file nicely; if you want to follow the steps in the future with an image of your own, scale the new tile image to the host image accordingly. If the host image is smaller than 1000 pixels wide, choose to create a tile image smaller than 25 pixels.

2. Press D (default colors). Press Alt(Opt)+Delete (Backspace) to fill the small image with foreground black.

3. Choose the Move tool. Use the up-arrow key to nudge the image up by one pixel, and then press the left-arrow key once to move the image to the left by one pixel, as shown in Figure 25.31. Whenever an image that contains only a Background layer is moved with the Move tool or nudged, the Background layer turns into a transparency layer. Choose Flatten Image from the menu flyout on the Layers palette and save the image as Tile.psd in Photoshop's native file format to your hard disk. You might want to place this file in the Photoshop/Goodies/Patterns folder for easy access later. Close the file.

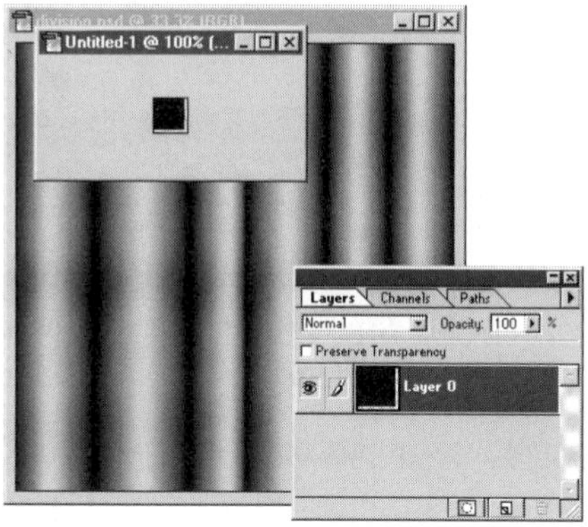

Nudge up once, nudge to the left once

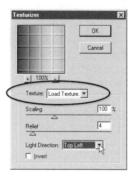

FIGURE 25.31   *Create a small tile image by nudging the contents of the layer up and to the left, and then flatten the image.*

4. With the Division.psd image in the foreground, choose Filter, Texture, and then choose Texturizer.

5. In the Texturizer dialog box, scroll to the bottom of the Texture drop-down list and choose Load Texture.

6. In the directory box, click on Tile.psd and then click on Open.

7. Drag the Relief slider to 4. Now you're going to define the direction of light coming into the scene (which you'll have to stick to with the rest of the objects you add to the composition). Click on the Light Direction drop-down list, and choose Top Left, as shown in Figure 25.32. Click on OK to apply the texture to the curtains.

FIGURE 25.32   *Choose your own image to create the texture in the image, using the Texturizer filter.*

The texture looks sort of flat on the curtain's Linear Gradient fill. As mentioned earlier, when curtains are hanging there should be a downward "swoop" to the folds of cloth. Let's fix this now:

8. Choose Filter, Distort, and then choose Displace.

9. In the Displace dialog box, type **15** in the Vertical Scale percentage box, as shown in figure 25.33, and type **0** in the Horizontal Scale percentage box. What you've done here is specify that the displacement map you created earlier should only displace the curtain image vertically—up and down.

The Displace filter has a maximum displacement effect of 128 pixels in any direction. Why? Because there can be only 256 shades of black in a saved displacement map; 50% black, in the middle of these 256 possible tones, produces no displacement. So you're telling the filter to displace, vertically, the black pixels in the displacement map by 15% of 128 pixels—about 19 pixels in a down direction. The white pixels in the displacement map will push the image pixels up by about 19 pixels, and shades between black and white will diminish and increase the Displace effect across the curtain image to produce dips in the folds of cloth.

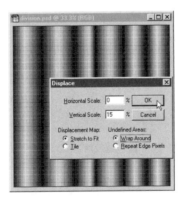

FIGURE 25.33   *Use these Displace settings to alter the pattern in the Division.psd image.*

10. Click on OK; then, in the directory box that appears, locate the Displace.psd image you created earlier. Click on it, and then choose Open.

11. The curtain image now looks more realistic. Press Ctrl(⌘)+S; keep the file open.

A spotlight would really make the scene come alive, and in the following section, you'll see how to create shading that makes the curtain image look positively three dimensional.

CASTING A SPOTLIGHT INTO THE IMAGE

The author discovered a fun and fast technique for adding spotlight illumination—and shading—in a two-dimensional image. If the curtain were real, the folds of cloth that make up the curtain would distort a spotlight cast into the scene in areas where the curtain folds come toward the viewer. You'll create this waving shading effect in the image by using a new layer, the Pen tool, and the Add Anchor Point tool.

NOTE

The other options in the Displace box are not relevant to the preceding steps. Stretch to Fit is not a relevant option because the Displace.psd file is the same size as the Division.psd image. Similarly, the Wrap Around and Repeat Edge Pixels options are useful only when your displacement map is smaller than the image receiving the displacement.

Here's how to define the area of the spotlight in the image:

USING PHOTOSHOP'S VECTOR TOOLS TO CREATE A SPOTLIGHT SHAPE

1. Press Ctrl(⌘)+the plus key or the minus key to make your viewing resolution of the image 33.3%. Drag the window borders away from the image so you can see a little image background.

2. With the Pen tool, create a shape, starting at the upper right of the image that widens as it travels to the bottom left of the image. Before you begin doing this, there should be several anchor points along the closed path, and they should all be located in the densest areas of the image, as shown in Figure 25.34. Do not worry that this shaft of light shape is not perfect; it doesn't need to be perfect (the example in Figure 25.34 is fine). You'll be adding curves to the closed path, and visually, no one will detect or criticize the imperfection of the spotlight shape here.

3. Choose the Add Anchor Point tool from the flyout on the toolbox (don't you wish Adobe would stop changing the names of the Pen tools with every version?!??). It's the Pen Tool icon with a tiny plus symbol in the upper right of the toolbox.

4. In the lightest areas of the Division.psd image, click a point, and then drag the point away from the center of the image, so the path segment swoops outward, as shown in Figure 25.35. The curved path segments you're creating should not be identical; let some of the curves be more shallow than others.

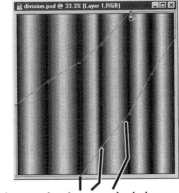

Click an anchor in every shaded area

FIGURE 25.34 *Try to create a closed path that is diagonal and narrower at the top right than at the bottom left. Be sure to click an anchor every place there's a deeply shaded area.*

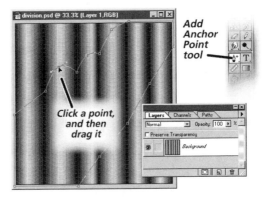

FIGURE 25.35 *First click on the path segment to add the anchor point, and then drag away from the center of the image to create an arc path segment.*

5. On the Layers palette, click on the Create New Layer icon. On the Paths palette, click on the Work Path thumbnail, and then click on the Loads Path as a Selection icon. Click on an empty part of the Paths palette to hide the path, so only the marquee selection is visible in the image.

6. Press Ctrl(⌘)+Shift+I (or Shift+F7, if you're a seasoned Photoshop user—these are the same commands for Select, Inverse). Press Alt(Opt)+Delete to fill the selection with foreground black color, as shown in Figure 25.36.

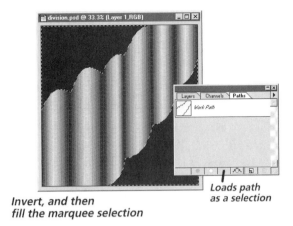

Invert, and then
fill the marquee selection

Loads path
as a selection

FIGURE 25.36 *Select the inverse of the marquee and then fill it with foreground color.*

7. Press Ctrl(⌘)+D to deselect the marquee, and then choose Filter, Blur, Gaussian Blur.

8. Type 7 in the Pixels field and then click on OK.

9. Drag the Opacity slider for this Layer 1 to about 50%, as shown in Figure 25.37. Your spotlight rendering is *beautiful*! And it adds dimension to the scene, too!

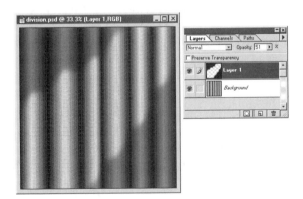

FIGURE 25.37 *Although you used many filters to create a 3D background for the composition, it is you who chooses the filters, and you who decides the amounts, the source material, and the order in which filters are applied.*

10. Press Ctrl(⌘)+S; keep the file open.

"Okay," you might ask at this point, "so where's the third-party filter in this composition?" The answer is: Andromeda Software's 3-D filter will be used in the next section, extensively, to create the dimensional foreground shapes for this piece.

USING THE ANDROMEDA 3-D FILTER

Andromeda's 3-D filter is not one of the current crop of advanced design tools; in fact, it was created in 1994. But to date, no other manufacturer has even attempted to write what Andromeda Software has created. The 3-D filter is a little like Photoshop's 3D Transform filter, but Andromeda's product far surpasses the 3D Transform filter in features, flexibility, and the capability to render three-dimensional primitives (cubes, spheres, and cylinders) that look photorealistic.

To begin with, you'll create the diagonal slab that will play the part of the division line in a division symbol. And you'll make it out of a wood texture. Here's how to begin using the 3-D filter:

CREATING A 3D WOODEN SLAB

1. Choose a background color on the toolbox that is the color of wood. The reason you're doing this is that the 3-D plug-in will render, with antialiasing, against the current background color in Photoshop. By choosing a medium wood color (H:30, S:80%, and B:71% is good), you will find that it will be less of a hassle to separate the rendered 3D object from its background when the color of the wood and the background color are similar.

2. Open the Wood.tif document from the Chap25 folder on the Companion CD. This image is 900 pixels by 900 pixels, so fitting the resulting 3D image into the Division.psd image will be no problem.

3. Choose Filter, Andromeda, and then choose 3-D (or 3-D 32 Demo if you're using the demo filter from the *Limited Edition* CD-ROM).

4. Click on Surface, and then in the second-to-left field click on Box. Click on Wrap Corner, so the Wood.tif image will wrap around the corner of the object without telltale seams.

5. In the X, Y, and Z Size fields, type **205** in the X field (the length of the box), type **124** in the Y field (the width of the box), and then type **21** in the Z field (the depth of the box). You can see in the wireframe preview window that the box is now a slab.

6. Click on the Viewpoint button; the fields for the X, Y, and Z dimensions turn into coordinate fields, where you specify how the object should be angled toward your view. Click on the Spherical button, which then provides Latitude, Longitude, and Distance fields (which are more intuitive to work with than the Rectangular or Cylindrical options).

7. Type **17** in the Longitude field, type **56** in the Latitude field, and type **341** in the Distance field. Doing this will make your view of the top and right sides of the slab very steep, while visually emphasizing the front of the slab.

8. Now, chances are that the slab has fallen outside the dotted box in the wireframe preview window, which means that the whole slab will not render to the Wood.tif image file. Click on the Display button; this option orients the 3D object relative to the borders of the image to which it renders the 3D object. Click on the Shift button, type **–47** in the Horizontal field (moving the object to the left), type **23** in the Vertical field (moving the object up within the dotted bounding frame), and most importantly, type **21** in the Angle field, so the slab's length dimension runs diagonally within the wireframe preview window.

9. Click on Preview. You'll notice that the wood image only partially covers the slab. To correct this, click on Photo and then click on Scale.

10. Drag the Horizontal slider to about 25, and then drag the Vertical slider to about 25. You'll notice that a heavy black outline in the wireframe view of the filter is expanding to meet the edges of the slab. It's important to keep the horizontal and vertical values the same; otherwise, the wood grain will look too fat or too skinny when mapped to the slab object. Drag the Overall slider to about 77, so the black edge of the image surfacing the slab travels over the top right side of the slab wireframe. Click on Preview again, and the slab will be covered with wood grain, as shown in Figure 25.38.

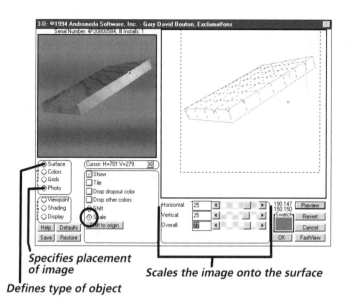

Specifies placement of image

Scales the image onto the surface

Defines type of object

FIGURE 25.38 *Adjust the dimensions, the view, and the placement of the object in the image window, and then use the Photo options to cover the wireframe with the wood texture in the image.*

11. Click on the Shading button, and then click on the Light Source (p.o.l.) button. Using the Spherical settings, as shown in Figure 25.39, drag the p.o.l. lat(itude) slider to –8.8, drag the p.o.l. long(itude) slider to 158.8, and then drag the p.o.l. dist(ance) slider to 250.

TIP

If the dotted preview bounding box is not centered relative to the slab wireframe, drag inside the border to center it.

If you'd like to increase the size of the slab when rendered to the image file, drag on a corner of the dotted bounding box to scale it.

These values are trial and error to get the cross in the wireframe view to rest on the right edge of the front plane of the object. This cross indicates where the highlight should be on the slab (and your lighting in the Division.psd image is from the upper right); the solid green line indicates where direct lighting should fall on the slab. If the cross has a white inside, you know that the highlight is not falling on the surface of the object. If the green line turns into a dotted line as you drag the slider for the position of the light, you know that direct illumination is not falling on the object.

Click on Preview one more time, and if you have the retail version of this filter, click on OK. If you're running the demo version, click on Cancel.

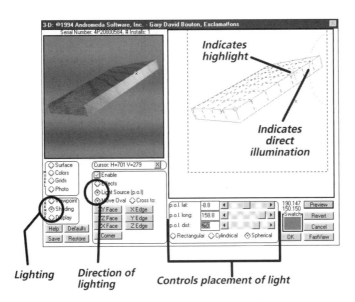

Figure 25.39 *Drag on the Light Source controls to position the light in the scene to fall on the upper right of the front face of the slab.*

12. If you're running the retail version of Andromeda's 3-D filter, save the image now as dividing line.tif, in the TIFF format, to your hard disk. Keep the image open. If you're running the demo version, open the divide.tif image now. Save it to your hard disk as dividing line.tif.

Clearly, many steps are necessary to get the shape, the texture, and the lighting source for the slab correct for use in the composition. But the author has news for you readers who do not use modeling applications: It takes way more than 11 steps to create a 3D slab in a modeling program!

It's time now to select the slab from the background of the image file and add it to the Division.psd image.

Using the Polygon Lasso Tool and the Toning Tools to Enhance the Image

In the following steps, you'll select the slab from its background and copy it to a new layer in the Division.psd image. Also, because the 3-D filter can produce only a single light source, you'll add a little contrast to the left face of the slab so that it doesn't blend into the Background layer. As mentioned frequently through this book, lighting an area of an object in a scene that clearly has no secondary light source might not be technically correct, but the designer's goal is to make scenes look artistically correct. And the audience will accept the "flaw."

Here's how to bring the first of three objects into the Division.psd scene:

BRINGING WOOD INTO THE DIVISION COMPOSITION

1. Zoom into a 200% viewing resolution of the dividing line.tif image. Hold the Spacebar and drag down and to the left until you can see the upper-right corner of the wooden slab.

2. Choose the Polygon Lasso tool from the toolbox, and click—ever so slightly—inside the bottom front-face edge of the slab.

3. Click a second point where the front face meets the top face of the slab on the right side.

4. Hold the Spacebar to toggle to the Hand tool, and drag in the image window to the right until you can see the back, right corner of the top face of the slab. Then release the Spacebar. The Hand tool reverts to the Polygon Lasso tool, and you can click on this corner of the slab, as shown in Figure 25.40.

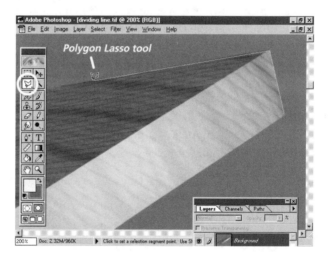

FIGURE 25.40 *You need a close-up view of the image to precisely select the slab's edges, but you also need to pan the window so you can view different areas. Toggle between the Polygon Lasso tool and the Hand tool by holding the Spacebar.*

5. Repeat step 4, moving counterclockwise around the slab, until the selection marquee is complete.

6. Press Ctrl(⌘)+– (the minus key) until your view of the dividing line (the slab) is at 33%. Make sure you can see both the slab and the Division.psd document windows. Reposition the windows in the workspace, if necessary.

7. With the Move tool, drag inside the selection marquee, and move a copy of the slab into the Division.psd window, as shown in Figure 25.41.

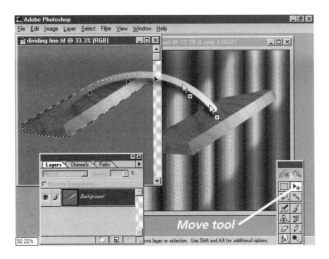

FIGURE 25.41 *Use the Move tool to copy the selected slab area to the Division.psd document window.*

8. Close the dividing line.tif image. Then, with the Move tool, position the slab so it's about in the center of the image. Right-click on the Layer 2 title on the Layers palette (Macintosh: hold Ctrl and click), and choose Layer Options. In the Layer Options dialog box, name the layer **Division line**, and then click on OK.

9. With the Polygon Lasso tool, click points around the left face of the slab (you don't need to be precise with the bottom edge, because it's surrounded by transparency).

10. Choose the Burn tool from the flyout on the toolbox, choose Shadows on the Options drop-down list, and on the Brushes palette choose the 100-pixel–diameter tip.

11. Make one or two strokes toward the top of the selection marquee, as shown in Figure 25.42. By doing this, you're visually creating contrast between the top and left faces of the slab.

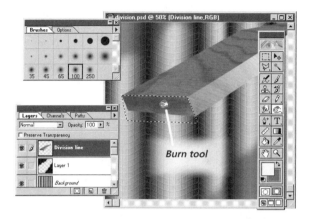

FIGURE 25.42 *Bring out some saturation and add tonal density to the top edge of the left face by using the Burn tool.*

12. Switch to the Dodge tool (on the flyout on the toolbox). Make sure Highlights is chosen on the Options palette, and use the same 100-pixel Brushes palette tip. Stroke once or twice over the bottom of the left face of the slab. This creates a little brightness in this area, which separates the face's edge from the background of the image (see Figure 25.43).

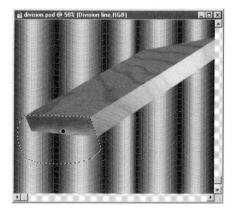

FIGURE 25.43 *Use the Dodge tool to lighten the bottom edge of the left face of the slab.*

13. Press Ctrl(⌘)+D to deselect the marquee. Press Ctrl(⌘)+S; keep the file open.

Now you'll add the top and bottom "dots" that make up a division symbol.

A RETURN TRIP TO THE 3-D FILTER

Creating a properly illuminated sphere by using the 3-D filter is less demanding than creating the wooden slab. Your primary concerns are the size of the sphere and the point of illumination of the sphere's surface.

Here's how to create the first of two spheres for the composition:

HAVING A (WOODEN) BALL WITH THE 3-D FILTER

1. Open the Wood.tif image from the Chap25 folder on the Companion CD.

2. Choose Image, Canvas Size. Type **450** (pixels) in both the Width and the Height fields, and then click on OK. An attention box appears telling you that you're going to clip the image; click on Proceed.

3. Save the file as Ball1.tif to your hard disk. Keep the file open.

4. Choose Image, Duplicate, and then name the image Ball2.tif in the Duplicate Image dialog box. Click on OK.

5. Choose Image, Rotate Canvas, and then click on 90 degrees CW (clockwise). Save this image as Ball2.tif to your hard disk and keep the image open.

6. Click on the Ball1.tif image's title bar to make it the current image.

7. Press Ctrl(⌘)+Alt(Opt)+F to access the last-used filter without applying it.

8. In the 3-D filter's interface, click on Surface, and then click on Sphere.

9. Drag the corners of the dotted bounding box in the wireframe view so that the sphere takes up most of the space in the window. Click on the Photo button, click on the Scale button, and then increase the size of the image on the surface of the sphere by using the Horizontal, Vertical, and Overall controls so that the black outline of the image extends to outside the wireframe of the sphere.

10. Click on the Shading button, and then click on the Effects button. Uncheck the Bright-Photo check box. This feature increases the brightness of the image on the surface, and what you want to do here, instead, is play with the brightness of the *surface* of the sphere.

You'll note that the highlight is in the upper right of the wireframe view. You did not change the direction of the light source after you created the slab, so you do not need to direct the Light Source in these steps.

11. Drag the Amb-Surf slider to 17.6. This controls the ambient light that is rendered to the surface of the object.

12. Drag the Amb-Photo slider to about 28. This adds a little ambient light, which covers the surface of the image. Ambient light is light that seems to emanate from everywhere in a scene; it's indirect lighting. This is *not* the same as brightening the image, as you had the option to do in step 10. Ambient lighting has a definite fall-off across the surface of an object, whereas brightening the photo (the wood image) uniformly increases its brightness.

13. Drag the Spread slider to 21.4, as shown in Figure 25.44, and then drag the Glare slider to 100%. The Spread slider controls the size of the direct illumination area on the surface of the sphere, whereas the Glare feature controls how much of a surface is completely wiped out with a white highlight.

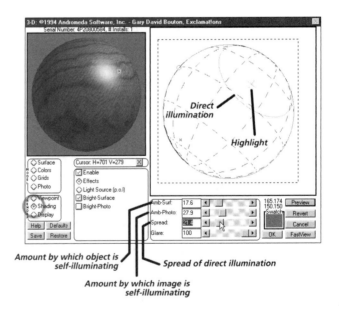

FIGURE 25.44 *Create a wooden sphere that has the same highlight direction as the slab and opposes in direction the spotlight effect in the Division.psd image.*

14. Click on OK to apply the 3D object to the Ball1.tif image. If you do not have the retail version of the 3-D filter, click on Cancel, and open Ball1.tif from the Examples\Chap25 folder on the Companion CD now. Save the image as Ball1.tif to your hard disk.

15. Click on the Ball2.tif image's title bar to make it the current foreground image.

16. Press Ctrl(⌘)+F to apply the 3-D filter, using the last-used settings, to the Ball2.tif image. Earlier, you were asked to rotate the image so that you can have two spheres of equal size but with grain running in different directions. The Ball2.tif image, although lit identically to the Ball1.tif image, looks like a different sphere. If you do not have a working copy of the 3-D filter, you can use Ball2.tif in the Examples\Chap25 folder, but don't open it now; you won't use it until later in this chapter. Keep the Ball1.tif and Division.psd images open.

It's very easy to select the Ball1 sphere from its background. In the following section, you'll do exactly that and add the sphere to the main composition.

Using Guides to Precisely Select an Image Area

Photoshop's Guides feature is useful in general, but it's particularly welcome when you need to precisely select a circular area from an image. In the steps that follow, you'll use the guides and a modifier key in combination with the Elliptical Marquee tool to select and then copy the Ball1 sphere to the Division.psd composition.

Creating a Selection, Using Guides and the Elliptical Marquee Tool

1. If you're running the demo version of the 3-D filter, open Ball1.tif from the Chapter 25 folder on the Companion CD. With Ball1.tif in the foreground in Photoshop, type **67** in the Zoom percentage field, and then press Enter (Return).

2. Press Ctrl(⌘)+R to display rulers to the left and top of the Ball1.tif image window.

3. With the Move tool, drag guides out of the top and left rulers to meet the top and left sides of the sphere in the image, as shown in Figure 25.45.

Drag guides to top and left

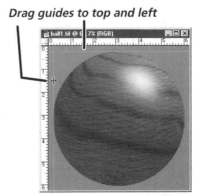

FIGURE 25.45 *Align horizontal and vertical guides to the edges of the sphere.*

4. With the Elliptical Marquee tool, start at the crossing of the guides in the upper left of the image, hold Shift (constrains the tool to circular selections), and then drag down and to the right until the bottom and right of the selection touch the edges of the sphere.

With the Elliptical Marquee tool, you have the option (on the Options palette) to create antialiased or aliased selections. Its default state is antialiased. Now, you don't want any of the background in the selection, so what is the harm in contracting the selection by 2 pixels? No one will ever know that the sphere is a fractional amount smaller than was rendered.

5. Choose Select, Modify, Contract. In the Contract Selection dialog box, shown in Figure 25.46, type **2** in the Pixels field, and then click on OK.

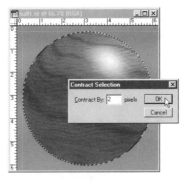

FIGURE 25.46 *Move the selection marquee inward so there is no possibility that some of the background, even antialiased areas, will be included in the selection.*

6. With the Move tool, drag inside the selection, into the Division.psd document. You can close Ball1.tif without saving it. Press Ctrl(⌘)+R again to remove the rulers from current document windows.

7. Double-click on the sphere's title on the Layers palette, type **Ball1** in the Name field, and then click on OK. The Ball1 layer is on top of the Division Line layer, and this is correct. With the Move tool, drag on the sphere on the Ball1 layer so that it is positioned in the horizontal center of the image.

8. Press Ctrl(⌘)+S; keep the file open.

It's one ball down and one to go. In the following section, you'll add the second ball and use the Dodge tool to brighten the edges of both spheres that are farthest from the spheres' highlights.

FINISHING THE GEOMETRY IN THE DIVISION COMPOSITION

There are no new steps in the next example. Let's briefly run through what you need to do to complete the geometric aspect of this image. Then, in the following section, you'll work with lighting the scene.

POLISHING OFF THE ELEMENTS IN THE DIVISION COMPOSITION

1. With Ball1 as the current layer, choose the Dodge tool from the toolbox and stroke once or twice, in an arcing motion, along the bottom left edge of the sphere, as shown in Figure 25.47. Use the same 100-pixel brush tip as you used earlier on the front edge of the division line element.

FIGURE 25.47 *Stroke the ball in an arcing motion, using the brush you used on the division line.*

2. Open Ball2.tif from either your hard disk or the Chap25 folder on the Companion CD. Use the steps listed in the previous example to add guides to the image; use the Elliptical Marquee tool to select the sphere; use the Select, Modify, Contract command to decrease the size of the selection by two pixels. Then, with the Move tool, drag the sphere into the Division.psd composition. Close the Ball2.tif file without saving it. Use the Dodge tool on the bottom left of the second sphere.

3. Name the layer for the second sphere Ball 2, and then drag its title on the Layers palette down until it's beneath the Division line layer.

4. Play with the elements—move them—on their respective layers until you have a composition that looks like that shown in Figure 25.48.

FIGURE 25.48 *Move the layer elements until you have a 3D division symbol.*

5. Press Ctrl(⌘)+S; keep the file open.

It's shadow-creating time! In the following section you'll use the Pen tool to create an ellipse that you'll fill with a wood color. You'll blur the fill and then trim it, using the opaque areas on the Division line layer.

CREATING A SHADOW FOR THE TOP SPHERE

All the shadows that you will create in this section and the ones to follow will have a very definite shape, dictated by the fact that the spotlight in the background is casting at a steep angle. Think "diagonal" and think "oval"; this is the orientation and the shape of the shadow you'll now build.

Here's how to use the Pen tool to create a shadow outline, and how to fill it with a color that is consistent with the rest of the composition:

CREATING A SPHERE SHADOW

1. Click on the Division line title on the Layers palette, and then Alt(Opt)+click on the Create New Layer icon. In the New Layer dialog box, type **Ball 1 shadow** in the Name field, and then click on OK. This creates a Ball 1 shadow layer directly above the Division line but beneath the top sphere.

2. With the Pen tool, create on the Ball 1 shadow an ellipse that tilts at the same angle as the slab in the image, as shown in Figure 25.49. Do not worry that the ellipse goes over the far edge of the slab. Hold the Ctrl(⌘) key to toggle to the Direct Selection tool to finesse the closed path you've drawn.

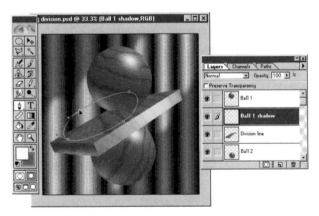

FIGURE 25.49 *The spotlight in the scene is casting at a diagonal angle. Therefore, a shadow cast on the slab by the sphere would be distorted at the same angle as the spotlight.*

3. With the Eyedropper tool, sample a color from the densest region of the wood sphere. This will be the color of the shadow you'll create.

4. On the Paths palette, click on the Loads Path as a Selection icon, and then click on an empty space on the palette to hide the path. Press Alt(Opt)+Delete (Backspace) to fill the selection, and then press Ctrl(⌘)+D to deselect the marquee.

NOTE

If your machine feels sluggish and you think you're running low on system resources right now, hide the spheres and the slab by clicking on their eye icons on the Layers palette, and then choose Merge Visible from the Layers palette's menu fly-out. Then Press Ctrl(⌘)+S. You've merged the shadow layer with the Background layer; doing this reduces the saved size of the file as held in system memory and hard disk.

Click on the eye icon slots next to the spheres and slab layers on the Layers palette to restore their visibility.

TIP

If you're not comfortable drawing ellipses at angles with the Pen tool, you can simply draw a horizontal ellipse. Then, press Ctrl(⌘)+T to display the Free Transform bounding box around the path, and drag on a corner handle to rotate it. Press Enter (Return) to finalize the transformation.

The Free Transform feature in Photoshop works with selections, paths, and even Quick Mask overlays.

5. On the Layers palette, choose Multiply from the Modes drop-down list, and then drag the Opacity down to about 65%, as shown in Figure 25.50.

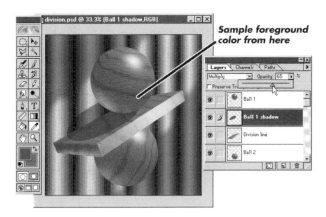

FIGURE 25.50 *Sample a foreground wood color from the image, and then fill the selection you created from the path with this color.*

6. Choose Filter, Blur, and then choose Gaussian Blur. Type **5** in the Pixels field, and click on OK to apply the blur to the shadow.

7. Ctrl(⌘)+click on the Division line layer title to load the outline of the slab as a marquee selection. Press Shift+F7 to invert the selection. The Ball 1 shadow layer should still be the current editing layer.

8. Press Delete (Backspace). As you can see in Figure 25.51, the areas outside the slab have been deleted, and the shadow looks as though it's casting correctly on the slab now. Press Ctrl(⌘)+D to deselect the marquee.

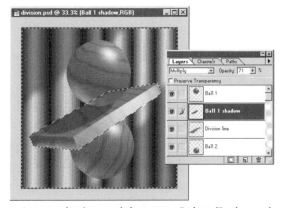

Invert selection, and then press Delete (Backspace)

FIGURE 25.51 *Delete the shadow areas that do not fall on the slab.*

9. Press Ctrl(⌘)+S; keep the file open.

Creating a shadow on the sphere underneath the slab is a tough one. The shadow that a slab would cast on a sphere, when the light is coming into the scene diagonally, creates a unique shape.

The next section guides you through the creation of the shadow for the bottom sphere.

CREATING AN ARCING SHADOW

The optically correct shape of the shadow cast on the bottom sphere would be an arc; the shallowest area of the shadow would be toward the front of the sphere, and the shadow would gradually increase in depth in areas that are farther from the slab. Admittedly, it's tough to "think" in 3D, which is why we'll run through the steps now for creating this shadow:

CREATING THE SHADOW CAST BY THE SLAB

1. Click on the layer title for Ball 2 on the Layers palette. Then Alt(Opt)+click on the Create new layer icon. Name the layer Ball 2 shadow in the New Layer dialog box, and then click on OK.

2. With the Pen tool, click a point at about two o'clock relative to the second sphere, slightly outside the sphere. Then, drag toward the middle of the sphere, creating a curve between the first and second anchor points, and allow this curve to overlap the front face of the slab slightly. Sneak a peek at Figure 25.52 for the shape of the path segment.

3. Drag a third anchor point at about a six o'clock position slightly outside the bottom sphere. The two path segments should form an "eclipse" of the top and left edges of the sphere.

4. Click, don't drag, anchor points that encompass the left side of the bottom sphere, and then close the path by clicking once at the first anchor point. It is important that the "eclipse" curve of the path be smooth, so hold Ctrl(⌘) and drag on the direction points of the second anchor to ensure that the curve is smooth (see Figure 25.52).

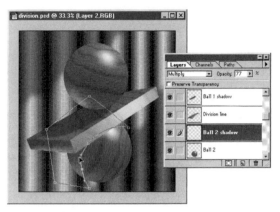

Hold Ctrl(⌘) to toggle to Direct Selection tool

FIGURE 25.52   *A convex, curved path describes the area where the bottom sphere will be shaded.*

5. On the Paths palette, click on the Loads Path as a Selection icon and then click on an empty part of the palette to hide the path.

6. With the same deep brown foreground color you defined in the previous set of steps, press Alt(Opt)+Delete (Backspace), and then press Ctrl(⌘)+D to deselect the marquee. You now have a shape on the Ball 2 shadow layer that overlaps the bottom sphere.

7. Press Ctrl(⌘)+F to apply the last-used filter—the Gaussian Blur.

8. Ctrl(⌘)+click on the Ball 2 title on the Layers palette to load the sphere outline as a marquee selection, and then press Shift+F7 to invert the selection. The Ball 2 shadow layer should still be the current editing layer. Press Delete (Backspace) to remove areas of the shadow that do not fall on the bottom sphere. Press Ctrl(⌘)+D to deselect the marquee.

9. Choose Multiply from the Modes drop-down list on the Layers palette, and then drag the Opacity slider down to about 65%.

10. Press Ctrl(⌘)+S; keep the file open.

You now have shadows that fall on the curtains in the background of the image, you have a sphere casting a shadow on the slab, and you have the slab casting a shadow on the bottom sphere. What's missing? Let's suppose that the division symbol here is very close to the curtain background. It would cast a shadow on the curtains. In the following section, you'll see how to create this effect.

CASTING A STEEP SHADOW

As mentioned earlier, everything shading this scene is at a diagonal, because the spotlight effect in the composition is casting diagonally. Therefore, if the division symbol is to cast a shadow on the curtains, the shadow's shape should be elliptical in shape and diagonal in direction.

Here's how to use the Layers palette in combination with the Channels palette to create the shadow cast by the division symbol:

CREATING A COMPOSITE SHADOW

1. Ctrl(⌘)+click on the Ball 1 title on the Layers palette to load its outline as a selection marquee.

2. On the Channels palette, click on the Save Selection as Channel icon, as shown in Figure 25.53.

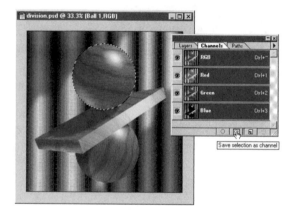

FIGURE 25.53 *Save that circular shape to a new channel in the image.*

3. Back on the Layers palette, Ctrl(⌘)+click on the Division line title to load the slab's outline as a marquee selection.

4. On the Channels palette, click on the Alpha 1 title to move your view to the saved selection area of the top sphere.

Now, saved selections can appear as either black against white or white against black. This arrangement is specified by double-clicking on an alpha channel title and then choosing Color Indicates: Selected Areas or Masked Areas. The author has Color Indicates: Masked Areas defined, so the author's alpha channel is black with a white circle in it.

5. If your alpha channel is black with a white circle in it, fill the marquee selection of the slab with white (by pressing Delete/Backspace), as shown in Figure 25.54. When you view an alpha channel, the foreground/background colors on the toolbox change to black foreground and white background. If your alpha channel is white with a black circle, fill the marquee selection with black. Whether the saved selection is tonally inverted or not does not matter; the alpha channel will load correctly whether it's black on white or white on black.

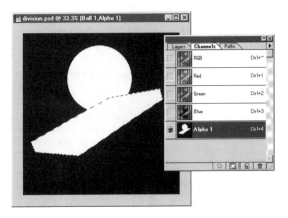

FIGURE 25.54 *Fill the marquee selection with the same color as the outline of the sphere.*

6. On the Layers palette, Ctrl(⌘)+click on the Ball 2 layer title, and then switch your view back to the alpha channel. Fill the marquee selection with the same color you see in the sphere and slab outlines. Press Ctrl(⌘)+D to deselect the marquee, and then Ctrl(⌘)+click on the Alpha 1 channel title to load its visual contents as a marquee selection. Press Ctrl(⌘)+~(tilde) to move your view back to the color composite of the composition.

7. Click on the Background title on the Layers palette, and then click on the Create New Layer icon. A new layer appears above the Background layer but beneath all the other layers.

8. Press D (default colors), and then press Alt(Opt)+Delete (Backspace) to fill the new layer with foreground black, as shown in Figure 25.55. You'll see the black shape as a thumbnail on the Layers palette, but it won't appear in the image window because it is directly behind the division symbol.

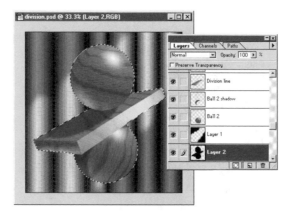

Load the channel, and then press Alt(⌥)+Delete (Backspace)

FIGURE 25.55 *Load the alpha channel, and then fill the selection marquee with foreground black color.*

9. Press Ctrl(⌘)+D to deselect the marquee, and then choose the Move tool. Drag the shadow shape down and to the left so that the bottom sphere shape in the shadow is mostly outside the image window.

10. Drag the image window borders away from the image so you can see some of the window background. You'll be working directly on the image edge in the following step.

11. Press Ctrl(⌘)+T to display the Free Transform bounding box around the part of the shadow that is within the image. Logically, if this division symbol were real and close to the background, the shadow that it would cast would fall partly outside the image window (the image *frame*, if a camera were involved).

12. Right-click (Macintosh: hold Ctrl and click) and then choose Distort from the context menu, as shown in Figure 25.56.

13. Drag the four corner handles of the Distort box, one at a time, so that a diamond shape is created. Notice that in Figure 25.57, the shape of the Distort bounding box roughly corresponds to an ellipse at a diagonal angle—the "theme" of the shadow-creation steps in this assignment. When the bounding box looks like the box in Figure 25.57, press Enter (Return) to finalize the distortion.

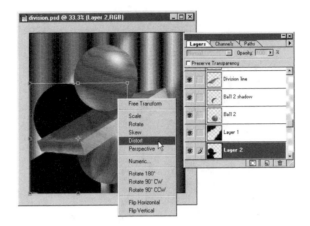

FIGURE 25.56 *Choose to distort the shadow within the Free Transform bounding box.*

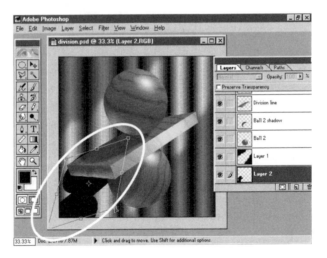

FIGURE 25.57 *Create a Distort bounding box that is at a diagonal angle and diamond-shaped by dragging on the corner handles of the bounding box.*

14. Press Ctrl(⌘)+F to apply the Gaussian Blur filter. Drag the Opacity slider on the Layers palette down to about 65%, and choose Multiply from the Modes drop-down list on the Layers palette. Your image should look like the one in Figure 25.58.

FIGURE 25.58 *The shadows in the scene are all handmade, and they're all visually correct!*

15. Press Ctrl(⌘)+S; keep the file open.

GETTING PICKY WITH DETAILS

For all the wonderful lighting, composition, shading, highlights, and so on, the composition looks a little artificial, mostly because the slab and the spheres are so perfect. To add a little imperfection to the scene, the author suggests putting some nicks in the slab; almost as though the delivery people were clumsy and banged the slab against the doorway on its way to your living room!

Here are a few quick steps for putting some finishing, photorealistic touches into the scene:

ADDING DETAIL TO THE SURFACE OF THE DIVISION LINE

1. On the Layers palette, click on the Division line title (or the title of the merged foreground elements if you chose to conserve system resources by merging all the foreground elements), and then click on the Create New Layer icon on the Layers palette.

2. Choose Multiply from the Modes drop-down list on the Layers palette, and drag the Opacity slider down to about 75%. Take a moment to name this layer Nick shadow, to keep track of all the layers in the composition.

3. With the Eyedropper tool, click over a dense area of the image to sample a deep brown.

NOTE

Again, if you want to conserve system resources, you might want to merge the shadows with the spheres and the slab. To do this, hide the Background layer and shadow, hide the distorted shadow you created in the previous steps, and then choose Merge Visible from the Layers palette's flyout menu. Then restore the visibility of the Background layer and the two shadow layers and save the file.

Photoshop will not free up resources used to store images on hard disk and in RAM until you've saved the file.

4. Zoom into a 100% viewing resolution of the image, and then scroll the window until you can see the front edge of the slab.

5. With the Polygon Lasso tool, click around the front edge of the slab to create a polygon shape like the one shown in Figure 25.59. Then press Alt(Opt)+Delete (Backspace) to fill it with foreground color. Note that this is part of a nick on the surface of the slab that is facing away from the direction of the spotlight in the scene. Therefore, this area should be darker than the surface of the slab. Press Ctrl(⌘)+D to deselect the marquee.

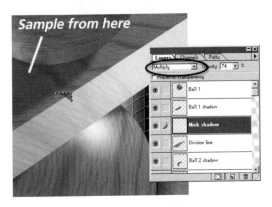

Figure 25.59 *Create one-half of a nick shape on the new layer, and then fill it with the sampled foreground color.*

6. Click on the Create New Layer icon at the bottom of the Layers palette, and then choose Screen from the Modes drop-down list on the Layers palette. Name the layer Nick highlight.

7. With the Polygon Lasso tool, create the other half of the nick. Sample a light area of the wood in the image, using the Eyedropper tool, and then press Alt(Opt)+Delete (Backspace) to fill the marquee selection, as shown in Figure 25.60. This is the area of the nick that faces the light source in the image, and therefore it should be a light color. Press Ctrl(⌘)+D to deselect the marquee.

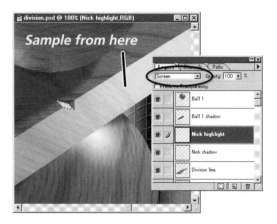

FIGURE 25.60 *Create an irregularly shaped highlight on the layer to suggest a highlight on the slab caused by a nick picking up light.*

8. Ta-dah! You're finished! Save the file one last time. You can either close it (with all the layers in the image) or save a flattened copy of the design in TIFF format (which most users can open and view) by choosing Save a Copy from the File menu. You'll then have a "take around" piece, plus the working image file that you can go back to at any time and experiment with some more.

In Figure 25.61, you can see the author's rendition of the 3D division sign (it's also in color in the second color section in this book). The author added a second nick next to the first one and then took a triangular piece out of the far edge of the slab to suggest more imperfections—more reality.

The art of creating dimensional objects demands a recipe that includes not only the "stars" of the scene, but also supporting elements. Think of how visually boring the division symbol piece would be without a background and the shading you applied. Conversely, the piece would be a tad lacking if it didn't contain any foreground elements interacting. So what we can conclude from the previous sections and steps is that there always needs to be a balance in a work of art; the background supports the foreground, and the foreground yields attention somewhat to what's going on in the background!

FIGURE 25.61 *The Andromeda 3-D filter provided the objects, but your own skills fleshed out the piece to look both dramatic and realistic.*

In the following section, you'll take a look at a Photoshop plug-in that does only one thing, but does it exceedingly well. Have you ever come across a photo or artistic composition whose foreground elements are attractive, but whose sky is dismal? Then there's a company and a plug-in to which you need an introduction!

FOUR SEASONS FOR PHOTOSHOP

RAYflect has created a product called "Four Seasons" that does nothing but render awesome sky images to a selection area in an image, or to an entire layer. If you'd like to get hands-on experience with this plug-in, swap the Companion CD for the *Limited Edition* CD-ROM in your CD-ROM drive, and install the demo version of the plug-in from the Software\4Seasons folder on the *Limited Edition* CD-ROM. Then put the Companion CD back into your CD-ROM drive.

EXAMINING AN IMAGE FOR THE TYPE OF SKY IT REQUIRES

In the steps to follow, you'll work with a rendered 3D scene that lacks a sky—but you might as well be working with a photograph whose sky is dull and uninteresting. The reason for using a modeled scene is that it was easy to separate the ground elements from the sky areas. walk.psd on the Companion CD is an image of a chrome cartoon fellow strutting along a brown, textured ground, with green mountains and palm trees in the distance. Open walk.psd from the Examples\Chap25 folder now, and let's take a look at what type of sky should be added to the scene.

If you look carefully at the reflections in the chrome cartoon character, the sky reflecting into his surface is blue, with clouds. Therefore, using Four Seasons, you need to create a blue sky with clouds. Additionally, shadows are casting sharply to the left in the image, so the sun in the sky should be to the far right, and perhaps not visible at all (it might fall behind the mountains). In any event, the sky itself should be illuminated from the right.

WORKING WITH FOUR SEASONS' FOG AND OTHER FEATURES

Four Seasons has a feature-filled interface, but it's logically laid out, so even a computer graphics novice can quickly get results from the program. The only thing that needs to happen before you can use the filter is that an opaque layer must exist in the image file—Four Seasons does not write to transparent layers.

Here's how to begin an appropriate sky for the walk.psd scene:

CREATING FOG AND ANGLING THE CAMERA IN FOUR SEASONS

1. With the walk.psd image open in Photoshop at about a 70% viewing resolution, click on the Create New Layer icon at the bottom of the palette.

2. Drag the new Layer 1 title to beneath the Walk layer title on the Layers palette.

3. Press Alt(Opt)+Delete (Backspace) to fill the new layer with color, as shown in Figure 25.62. It does not matter which color is the current foreground color; Four Seasons will render over the pixels on Layer 1.

4. Choose Filter, RAYflect, and then choose Four Seasons.

5. Click on the Haze eye icon to turn off Haze in the picture. Click on the eye icon for Fog. Presently, you should have only the Fog and Cloud Layer 1 active in the interface; click on the Fog title to make it the active layer.

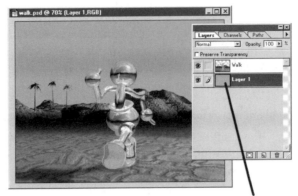

Four Seasons needs an opaque layer upon which to render

FIGURE 25.62   *Add an opaque layer to the composition, so Four Seasons can render a sky into the layer.*

6. To the left of the Fog Color title is a small color swatch. Drag on it to reveal a color picker, drag in the color picker until the cursor is over a light blue, and then release the cursor.

7. Drag the Fog Intensity to 100%. Doing this obscures the horizon in the rendered sky (which, as you'll notice, also includes some ground). Drag the Fog Start slider to 0% (ground level). Drag the Fog End slider to about 38%. Doing this will render fog that diminishes at 38% of the height of the rendered image, above the ground plane.

8. Drag the Fog Distance slider to 48%. This control determines how far in the distance the fog is rendered. At low values, the fog is close to your view of the sky and fuzzes out the sky. So 48% places the fog about halfway between the horizon and your viewpoint.

9. Drag on the camera that is located at the bottom right of the Preview section until Four Seasons' status line tells you that the camera angle is about 7 degrees off the horizon. You're looking up in the preview window, and there's less ground in the framed image. The dotted outline tells you how much of the preview scene will be rendered to the image.

10. Drag the sun in the left sphere in the interface to about a three o'clock position, slightly above the horizon and slightly to the front, as shown in Figure 25.63. Notice the difference positioning the sun creates in the preview window. Make sure that the arrow to the upper left of the sphere is pointing to the right. This means that the sun is illuminating the scene from the front.

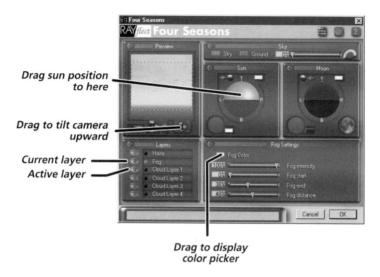

Drag sun position
to here

Drag to tilt camera
upward

Current layer
Active layer

Drag to display
color picker

FIGURE 25.63 *Working with fog, positioning the camera, and positioning the sun in the image are only the beginning of creating a complex sky image.*

Now that the sun and fog have been set up, it's time to move to the cloud layer controls…

11. Don't click on OK yet! Instead, read the following section!

ADDING CLOUDS TO THE FOUR SEASONS SKY MODEL

Every time you start a session with Four Seasons, a default sky appears in the preview window. Because (although it might not seem like it) this book is finite, we can't really get into the mixing of different cloud layers in Four Seasons. Instead, the following section focuses on how to create a single cloud layer scene that will work well with walk.psd.

Here's how to create a single layer sky for the composition:

ADDING CLOUDS TO THE SKY

1. Click on the Cloud Layer 1 title to make it the active layer. You'll see six thumbnail boxes in the Cloud Layer 1 field. Peek ahead to Figure 25.64 to see what you'll be working with here.

NOTE

Four Seasons comes with a number of beautiful preset skies. If you'd like to see how they are created, load one by clicking on the preset button (the checkered box in the upper right of the interface), click on a type of sky (Day, Night, Sunrise, and so on), pick a sky to load, and then click on the active layers that make up the sky, and see which values are used.

2. In the upper left thumbnail box, drag all the way to the right on the cloud. This sets the lumpiness of the clouds in the sky (as opposed to soft, subtle clouds.

3. In the second thumbnail box, drag to the left or right until the status line tells you that the layer thickness is about 50%. This control actually specifies whether dark or light clouds will appear in the sky. At 50%, and at the current sun angle, the clouds will be dark on the bottom, with some highlights toward the top of the image.

4. In the third thumbnail of this row, drag to the left or to the right until the status line tells you that the cloud coverage is 75%. This places plenty of clouds in the image.

5. In the bottom far-left thumbnail, drag to the left or the right until the status line tells you that the cloud rotation is at 38°. At this angle, the sun will cast light on the clouds in such a way that all the clouds are horizontal.

6. In the middle thumbnail on the bottom row, drag up or down to specify the Y (the height) size of the clouds; make the figure around 54. Then, drag to the left or to the right until the first figure on the status line—the X value (width)—is about 50. The clouds in the image will be horizontal, with no distortion.

7. In the bottom right thumbnail, drag up until the status line tells you that the layer altitude is 54. With this value and the camera pointed slightly upward, you will see several clouds in the image.

8. Drag in the Sun aura circle, as shown in Figure 25.64, until it is as bright as possible. Doing this will add white highlights to the right of the rendered sky (and the walk.psd scene is lit from the right, so this is a correct move).

9. Click on OK. The unregistered version of Four Seasons will render the sky to the layer, but there will be a violation—"where to order" text—on the sky, so the image really can't be used. If you have the registered version, however, the clouds will render to Layer 1 in the walk.psd composition.

The only physical phenomenon that's missing from the image is a bumpiness to the edge of the clouds. Reality is easily enhanced in the following step:

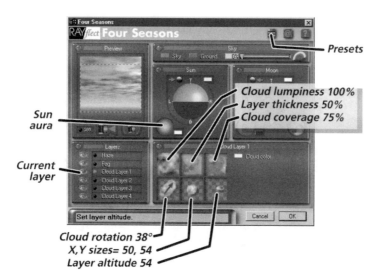

Presets

Cloud lumpiness 100%
Layer thickness 50%
Cloud coverage 75%

Sun aura

Current layer

Cloud rotation 38°
X, Y sizes= 50, 54
Layer altitude 54

FIGURE 25.64 *Specify the type, height, and other parameters of the clouds on the layer, so that the rendered sky will look appropriate when placed behind the Walk layer.*

10. Choose Filter, Distort, and then choose Glass. In the Glass dialog box, keep the Texture as Frosted, and keep the Scaling to 100%. Drag the Distortion slider to 2, and then drag the Smoothness slider to 6, as shown in Figure 25.65.

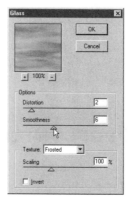

FIGURE 25.65 *Add a mild amount of Glass distortion to the sky image to make the edges of the clouds a little rough.*

11. Click on OK, and wait a while for the filter to render to the layer. You're finished! The image should look like Figure 25.66. You can save and close the image at any time now.

FIGURE 25.66 *With Four Seasons, the weather in a picture can be anything you render.*

In the second color section in this book is the same scene, except the author added three different cloud layers to the composition. As you build up layers in Four Seasons, the cloud patterns become more complex, and as a result, they look more realistic.

To round out the gallery of the author's favorite plug-ins, the following section takes a look at the Extensis Mask Pro plug-in. It's not really an effects plug-in, and it's more like a full-blown application than a filter. The best part, as you'll discover, is that Mask Pro is fully functional for 30 days after you install the demo. So you can indeed follow the steps to come and see how useful Mask Pro can be in your selection work.

EXTENSIS MASK PRO: COMPLEX AND EASY SELECTION WORK

One of the most attractive qualities of Extensis Mask Pro is its capability to auto-select around human hair. This book has shown you many workarounds for masking around a head of hair, and the following sections show you how you can take much of the effort out of this task.

THERE'S A PLUMBER IN MY SINK!

To conclude this chapter, and the book, the author thought it would be amusing to put a goofy-looking plumber *in* a sink—not in front of or beneath, but actually coming out of a bathroom sink. To accomplish such an image, you need two photos: one of a sink, and one of a plumber (or a friend, or whomever will pose for you). It's important from the beginning—the photography stage—that you get the orientation and field size of the sink and the plumber the same. We took about two rolls of film, and then decided on the best two images that would integrate well.

In sink.psd, in the Chap25 folder of the Companion CD, we used a wide angle lens to capture the sink and its surroundings. The viewpoint looks into the sink, and therefore the image of the plumber must also look as though he's leaning forward. Additionally, the width of the plumber should be about the same as the width of the sink. This was a trial-and-error effort made by the authors: Before the two images were cropped for you, both the plumber and the sink took up about two-thirds the width of the frame. Finally, the sink and the plumber images feature flat lighting. Shadows are cast almost directly downward, so the shading in both images is basically the same.

As you'll see, the plumber needs to be separated from the background of the image. His hair is all messed up from being in the sink pipe, and ordinarily, accurately masking such an image would present a laborious challenge. But Mask Pro will make the work easy, as soon as you learn how the features work.

MASKING THE PLUMBER

Before continuing, if you haven't already installed Mask Pro, look for the Extensis folder on the Companion CD, and run the install program (while Photoshop is *not* running!). Then, launch Photoshop, and then…

DEFINING DROP AND KEEP COLORS AND SPECIFYING A BRUSH TIP

1. Open plumber.tif from the Examples\Chap25 folder on the Companion CD. On the Layers palette, double-click on the Background layer, as shown in Figure 25.67; accept the default name in the Make Layer dialog box, and then click on OK. Mask Pro needs to work on a layer; it cannot work on the background of an image.

**Double-click on
Background title**

FIGURE 25.67 *Create a layer from the Background image so that Mask Pro can be used on the image.*

2. Choose Filter, Extensis, Mask Pro. Photoshop's interface will disappear, only to be replaced by the Mask Pro interface.

3. On the toolbox, click on the Zoom tool, and then drag a selection around the top of the plumber's head. This is the first area in which you'll work.

4. Click on the right Eyedropper tool on the toolbox. This is the Drop Color tool; everywhere you drag the tool, color is recognized by Mask Pro as an area that will be dropped out (masked) by the other tools.

5. Drag the tool over the pale blue areas near the plumber's hair, as shown in Figure 25.68. Do *not* click with the tool—drag with it. Mask Pro will then come up with an average of several different tones that will be dropped out of the image. On the Drop palette, you will see the average of colors that you've sampled.

6. Carefully (as in "*Carefully!*"), drag the Keep Color tool—the left eyedropper on the toolbox (the green one) around the strands of hair in the image, avoiding the blue background. This is the greatest challenge when you use these tools on an image like this. The strands of hair are only two or three pixels wide. As shown in Figure 25.69, the Keep palette displays a blend of brown hair color and (too much) gray hair color.

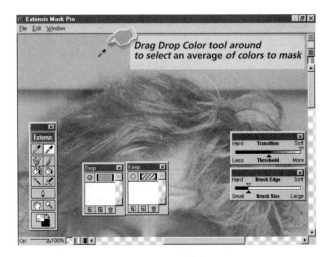

FIGURE 25.68 *Drag with the Drop Color tool to sample an average of colors that will be masked out of the image.*

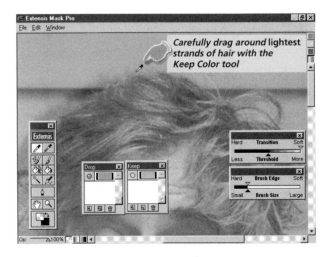

FIGURE 25.69 *Make certain that you drag the Keep Color tool through only the loose strands of hair.*

7. On the Transition/Threshold palette, drag the Threshold slider to the middle, and drag the Transition slider all the way to the right. You're defining the way the Magic Brush will operate in the image. It will make gradual transitions between masked and visible areas, and the threshold between masking areas and keeping areas is medium.

8. On the Brush Edge/Size palette, drag the Brush Edge to about the 25% mark, and drag the Brush Size slider to the same point, about 25%.

9. Choose the Magic Brush tool from the toolbox—the icon of a brush with stars all around it.

10. Make a few strokes along the edge of the plumber's head. As you can see in Figure 25.70, the blue background is turning transparent, while the strands of hair are left in the image.

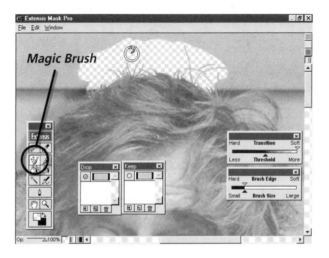

Figure 25.70 *Drag the Magic Brush tool through the areas of color in the image that you've defined as "drop" and "keep."*

11. Keep painting into the area in the image that contains colors you've defined as Drop colors and those that are Keep colors. Eventually, you'll run into areas of darker hair and darker siding on the building behind the plumber. At this point, stop. Do not close the Mask Pro interface.

The Drop and Keep palettes in Mask Pro operate very much like Photoshop's Layers palette. But instead of keeping track of layers, the Keep and Drop palettes keep track of colors you've specified to mask or keep. In the following section, you'll see how to work with some of the other features in Mask Pro.

Using the Brush Tool, the Keep and Drop Palettes, and the Pen Tool

As mentioned in step 11 in the preceding section, you can go only so far in defining the edge of the plumber's head with one averaged sampling of Keep Color and one averaged sampling of Drop Color. Extensis is way ahead of us on this one.

You can create new Keep and Drop colors as you work around an image area in which the colors change. Additionally, there will be areas that contain no Keep colors; you'll want to simply use the Brush tool to mask away these areas.

To top it off in the next set of steps, there are areas in the plumber image that will be best selected by using a Vector Pen tool. Let's take a crack at all three of these features:

USING MASK PRO'S EXTENDED FEATURES

1. Click on the bottom, middle icon on the Drop Color palette. This creates a new, empty color slot that you can fill by dragging the Drop Color tool around a new area. Choose the Drop Color tool, and then drag around the deeper blue areas to the left of the image, near the plumber's head. The new averaged color appears in the new slot you created on the palette. It is highlighted, which means that areas you brush over with the Magic Brush will drop out *this* color, and not the unselected color at the top of the palette.

2. Click on the bottom, middle icon on the Keep Color palette. This creates an empty slot that you'll fill, using the Keep Color tool. Choose the Keep Color tool, and then drag around the darker areas of the plumber's hair that are closest to the deeper shades of blue you defined in step 1 as Drop colors.

3. With the Magic Brush tool, drag through the image area you've defined for Keep and Drop colors.

You can keep adding to the Keep and Drop Color palettes, and you can even go back to your original colors by clicking on their icons on these palettes. But your work has proceeded pretty well so far, and it's time now to clear away areas of the image that are of no use to you—the blue paneling that contains none of the plumber's hair.

4. Choose the Brush tool, and then click on the Mask mode toggle—the bent-arrow icon at the bottom of the palette—until the checkerboard swatch is in the foreground. This means that you'll be masking with the Brush tool. The other swatch is the Restore mode—when the black swatch is in the foreground, every transparent area you stroke over with the Brush tool is restored to opacity. This feature is very much like Photoshop's Layer Mask mode.

5. Brush over areas of the blue paneling that you do not want to appear in the finished image, as shown in Figure 25.71.

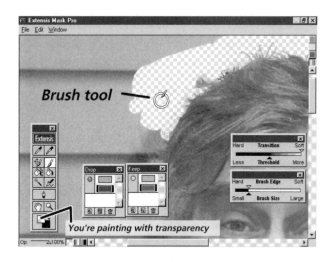

FIGURE 25.71 *Using the Brush tool in Mask mode, mask over areas that you do not want to appear in the finished image.*

6. Use the Brush tool technique, and then use the Magic Brush in combination with your Keep and Save colors to completely mask around the plumber's head. You might need to sample additional colors to drop and keep; if this is the case, click on the new Keep and new Drop icons at the bottom of their respective palettes, and then drag in the areas you want to keep or drop, using the Keep and Drop tools.

7. When you get to the shirt area in the plumber image, you'll want to create a sharp edge between the masked background and the shirt. Instead of making the Brush tool's Edge control harder, choose the Pen tool.

8. Click a point on the edge of the shirt. Then, drag with the Pen tool until there's a sharp turn in the shirt's direction, and click another anchor. Mask Pro's Pen tool uses a combination of modifier keys to feature several of the Pen tools you find in Photoshop. Click anchors around the area shown in Figure 25.72. If any of the anchor points are misplaced, hold Ctrl(⌘) and place the cursor directly over the anchor you want to move, and then move it. This modifier represents the Direct Selection tool in Photoshop. Holding Alt(Opt) toggles the Pen tool to the Convert Anchor Point tool, and will make sharp anchors into smooth ones and vice versa when you hold the cursor over an anchor. When you've got the area perfectly outlined with the Pen tool, click inside the path. The cursor turns into a gavel, and with Mask mode active on the toolbox, the area becomes transparent.

FIGURE 25.72 *Create a path, and with Mask mode in the foreground on the toolbox, click inside the closed path to mask the interior of the path.*

The hard part of this assignment is over—you've masked around the plumber's hair. You can continue to use Mask Pro to mask out the rest of the image areas around the plumber, or you can close Mask Pro and finish your masking work in Photoshop. If you choose to stay with Mask Pro, the general instructions for completely masking around the plumber are to use the Pen tool on the edge of the shirt and the wrench, use the Brush tool for the areas of the plumber's arms and pants, scroll the window to make sure you've got every edge masked, and then zoom out and finish the masking in the corners of the image, using the Pen tool.

When you're ready to return to Photoshop:

9. Press Ctrl(⌘)+Q; in the attention box click on Yes to apply the changes, click on No Path in the Clipping Path dialog box (you don't need a path created in this image), and you're back in Photoshop with your masking work completed.

10. Choose File, Save As, and then save the image as plumber.psd in Photoshop's native file format to your hard disk. Keep the image open.

The authors of *Inside Adobe Photoshop 5, Limited Edition* set out to accomplish two goals:

- To demonstrate the use of tools and their value in your work

- To work completely through an example so that you get a better idea of what it's like to begin with a concept and end with a finished composition

To meet one of these goals, an alpha channel exists in the plumber.tif image you opened from the Companion CD. The alpha channel precisely divides the unwanted areas of the image from the areas you want to keep. The alpha channel was created using Mask Pro. So if you feel you've spent enough time masking the image, you've gained experience using Mask Pro, and you can automatically complete the masking process. To do so, Ctrl(⌘)+click on the Alpha 1 title on the Channels palette, and then on the Layers palette, right-click (Macintosh: hold Ctrl and click) on the Layer 0 title, and choose Layer Via Copy. You can then drag the Background layer into the trash icon.

This is not to suggest that the authors are "cheating" for you. Mask Pro is an invaluable tool, as you've seen in the preceding examples. And if your line of work consists of selecting complex shapes, we suggest that you work a little more on your own with Mask Pro and your own images, and then register it. The reason for the built-in mask in plumber.tif is that we'd simply like you to be able to continue with this humorous composition at any point you like!

SETTING UP THE SINK

The plumber is going to obscure the back of the sink image, so to put him into the sink, all you need to do is define an accurate selection around the front lip of the sink.

In the steps that follow, you'll see how to create an accurate selection edge of the sink lip, save it to an alpha channel, and add the plumber. Then, after the plumber is added to the scene, you'll load the selection, increase the selection to include more of the plumber, and trim away the areas of the plumber that should not show in the composition.

DEFINING AND SAVING A SELECTION OF THE SINK'S INTERIOR

1. Keep plumber.psd open, and open sink.tif from the Examples\Chap25 folder of the Companion CD.

2. Double-click on the Zoom tool to move the sink to 100% viewing resolution. Then scroll the window so that the sink is in the center of the window. Maximize the image window.

3. With the Pen tool, starting at the left middle edge of the sink, click and drag an anchor. Click and drag a second anchor in the middle front of the sink (the lip of the sink). Before you stop dragging, steer the path between the first and second anchor points so that the path aligns with the front lip of the sink.

4. Click and drag a third anchor point to the right of the first, on the lip of the sink. Then click and drag another anchor on the far right middle of the sink.

5. Click, don't drag, a point above and to the left of the previous anchor point, and then click another above and to the left of that one, as shown in Figure 25.73; then close the path by clicking on the first anchor. If the path segments that define the front edge of the sink aren't exactly on the lip, hold Ctrl(⌘) to toggle to the Direct Selection tool, click on an anchor, and move it. You can also correct the curve of the path segment by Ctrl(⌘)+clicking on an anchor to reveal the direction lines, and then dragging on a direction point.

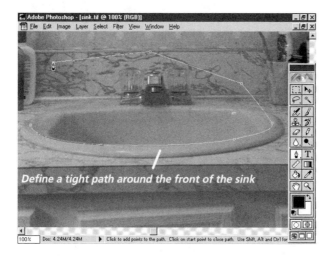

FIGURE 25.73 *Create an accurate path around the front lip of the sink; the rest of the path can be loosely defined.*

6. On the Paths palette, click on the Loads Path as a Selection icon, and then on the Channels palette, click on the Save Selection as Channel icon. Drag the path title on the Paths palette into the trash icon, and press Ctrl(⌘)+D to deselect the marquee selection.

7. With the Move tool, drag the plumber into the sink, as shown in Figure 25.74. Position the plumber (using the Move tool) so that part of the bottom of his image overlaps the sink's front lip.

FIGURE 25.74 *Copy the plumber image to the sink.tif file, and then position the plumber so that the bottom of him overlaps the front lip of the sink.*

8. Save the image as sink.psd, in Photoshop's native file format, to your hard drive, and close the plumber image without saving it (him).

9. Ctrl(⌘)+click on the Alpha 1 channel on the Channels palette to load the selection you saved, and then with the Lasso tool, hold Shift (to add to the current selection), and drag around the top of the plumber to include him in the selection, as shown in Figure 25.75.

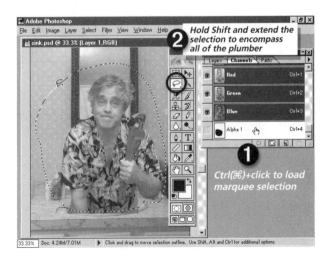

FIGURE 25.75 *Add to the loaded selection by holding Shift in combination with the Lasso tool.*

10. Press Shift+F7 to invert the selection marquee, and then press Delete (Backspace). Doing this removes the area of the plumber that extends below the front lip of the sink. Press Ctrl(⌘)+D to deselect the marquee, and then press Ctrl(⌘)+S. Keep the image open.

Regardless of the quality of the image editing tools you use (and Photoshop and Extensis Mask Pro *are* of the highest quality), you will fall short of your goal of perfectly integrating an object from one scene to another for a very simple reason. Unless images are taken in exactly the same location (sink.tif and plumber.tif were not), some ambient light is going to fall on an image area and influence the color of a selection edge. A perfect example of this is the plumber's loose strands of hair. Although they were carefully selected, using Mask Pro, the strands do not blend into the sink image because some of the light blue siding in the plumber.tif image cast the blue color into the plumber's hair.

In the next section, you'll correct this; you'll keep the plumber's hair messed up, but you'll make it appear as though he really is in the bathroom sink.

USING THE BLUR TOOL AND COLOR MODE

First things first; you'll notice at a 200% view of the image that the plumber's hair is sharp and crisp. This is because Mask Pro did what it was supposed to do—accurately selected the strands of hair from the blue background. The focus of the bathroom is soft, however, and hair that you'd photograph against a scene like the sink would blend into the background.

In the steps that follow, you'll use the Blur tool and the Paintbrush tool in Color mode to better integrate the plumber's hair with his new surroundings.

FIXING THE PLUMBER'S HAIR

1. Type **200** in the Zoom percentage field, and then press Enter (Return). Scroll the window so that you can see the loose strands of hair on the plumber's head.

2. Choose the Blur tool from the Focus Tools flyout on the toolbox. On the Options palette, Normal mode and 50% Pressure should be the settings. On the Brushes palette, choose the far-left tip in the second row. You might want to press Caps Lock to toggle the Blur tool from its icon appearance to the precise crosshair for this assignment.

3. Stroke once, twice at most, over a hair, in the outward direction of the hair.

4. Repeat step 3 with other strands that appear too sharp in the image (see Figure 25.76).

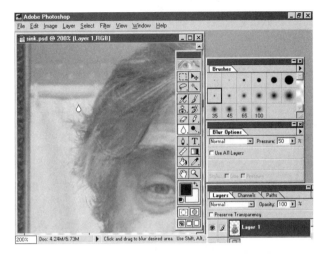

FIGURE 25.76 *Blur slightly the loose strands of hair so they blend into the background of the image.*

5. Once the strands have been blended into the image, it's hair-coloring time. Choose the Paintbrush tool, choose the far-left tip in the second row on the Brushes palette, and choose Color from the Modes drop-down list on the Options palette.

6. Alt(Opt)+click over a dark brown area of the plumber's hair. This specifies the color with which you'll be painting. On the Layers palette, check the Preserve Transparency check box.

7. Stroke over the strands of hair that appear to have a bluish tint. The bluish cast will be replaced by the brown color you sampled. Color mode does not change the *brightness* of areas on a layer, so don't expect deep brown hair as a result of this step. In a way, you're color-correcting the hair.

Another problem in the composition, one that's easy to correct, is the difference in color balance between the plumber, who was photographed outdoors, and the sink, which probably was photographed indoors under tungsten lighting—so it has a warm color cast. Here's a very simple solution:

8. Press Ctrl(⌘)+B to display the Color Balance command. With Midtones selected on the Color Balance command, drag the bottom slider to about –28, toward yellow and away from blue, as shown in Figure 25.77.

FIGURE 25.77 *Warm up the plumber by using the Color Balance command to move the midtones of this layer away from blue.*

9. Press Ctrl(⌘)+S; keep the file open.

It's time to pay attention to the subtle shading found in the sink background in the image. You'll notice that light is casting down from overhead. And yet the plumber is evenly illuminated. If the plumber really were leaning forward out of the sink, the bottom of his shirt would fall into partial shading from the upper part of his body.

CREATING A COMPLEX SELECTION AND ADDING SHADING TO THE PLUMBER

Here's a challenge (one that we help you solve): The plumber's left hand holding the wrench is coming toward our view, and his arm and wrench should not be shaded. His shirt and jeans are definitely in the background of the image, however, so they need to be toned down a little.

To accomplish this, you'll create a path around the wrench handle, drag a rectangular marquee around the bottom part of the plumber, put the selection in Quick Mask mode, and remove the wrench handle and the guy's arm from the selection. Then you'll save the selection as a template from which you'll create a Linear Gradient selection, so the shading on the bottom of the plumber's shirt gradually lightens as we look upward in the image.

Challenges don't have to be complicated. Here's how to achieve the fading shading effect:

CREATING A PARTIAL MASK AND APPLYING SHADING

1. Zoom out to about 100% viewing resolution of the sink.psd image. Scroll the window so you can see the handle of the wrench.

2. With the Pen tool, click and drag a path that runs along the edge of the wrench handle, as shown in Figure 25.78. The top of the closed path can be straight; this area will not come into play in your selection and shading work.

FIGURE 25.78 *Create a path on the edge of the bottom of the wrench.*

3. Double-click on the Work Path name on the Paths palette, accept the default name for the saved path by clicking on OK, and then click on an empty area of the Paths palette to hide the path.

4. Zoom out to about 70% viewing resolution so you can see the entire bottom of the plumber.

5. With the Rectangular Marquee tool, drag a selection like the one shown in Figure 25.79. Then, choose the Lasso tool, hold Alt(Opt) (to subtract from the current selection), and drag around the plumber's forearm, so it isn't in the marquee selection.

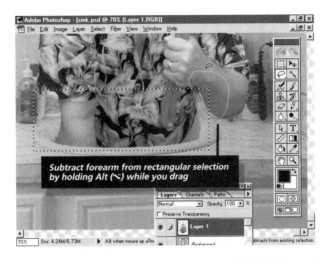

FIGURE 25.79 *Create a rectangular marquee of the area to be shaded, and then subtract the plumber's forearm from the selection, using the Lasso tool.*

6. Click on the Quick Mask mode button on the toolbox; then, on the Paths palette, click on the Loads Path as a Selection icon. Click on an empty area of the Paths palette to hide the path, and then press Delete (Backspace), as shown in Figure 25.80. Press Ctrl(⌘)+D to deselect the marquee.

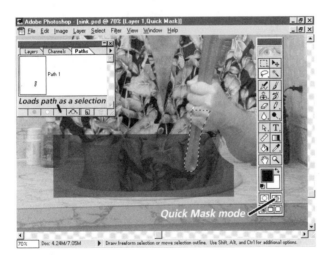

FIGURE 25.80 *Remove part of the Quick Mask overlay by deleting the selection created by the path.*

7. Click on the Standard Editing Mode icon (to the left of the Quick Mask icon); then on the Channels palette, click on the Save Selection as Channel icon at the bottom of the palette. Press Ctrl(⌘)+D to deselect the marquee.

8. Click on the Alpha 1 title on the Channels palette, and then click on the Channels palette's menu flyout and choose Channel Options. Click on the Color Indicates: Selected Areas button in the Channel Options box, and then click on OK.

9. Ctrl(⌘)+click on the Alpha 1 channel title on the Channels palette to load the selection. Then click on the Create New Channel icon. Click on the Alpha 2 title to move your view to this empty white channel with a marquee selection loaded.

10. Press D (default colors), and then choose the Linear Gradient tool. On the Options palette, choose Foreground to Background from the Gradient drop-down list.

11. Drag in the marquee, from bottom to top, as shown in Figure 25.81. You've created a selection in Alpha 2 that makes a smooth transition between selected areas in the image to protected (masked) areas.

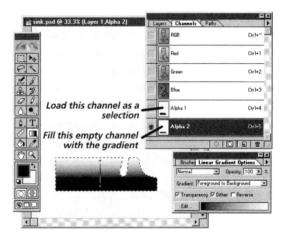

FIGURE 25.81   *Load the channel that contains the solid selection. Then use the Linear Gradient tool in the Alpha 2 channel to make a transitional selection.*

12. Ctrl(⌘)+click on the Alpha 2 channel title to load the visual information as a marquee, and then press Ctrl(⌘)+˜(tilde) to move your view to the RGB composite view of the image. Zoom out to about 33% viewing resolution so you can see the entire image.

13. Choose Image, Adjust, and then choose Brightness/Contrast.

14. Drag the Brightness slider down to about –36, as shown in Figure 25.82. You've successfully made the bottom of the plumber's shirt and jeans darker. Click on OK, and then press Ctrl(⌘)+D to deselect the marquee.

FIGURE 25.82 *Decreasing the Brightness in the selection makes a gradual transition between the upper ⁴/₅ of the plumber's shirt and the bottom.*

15. Press Ctrl(⌘)+S; keep the file open.

At any time now, you can drag the Alpha 1 and Alpha 2 titles on the Channels palette into the trash icon. You no longer need them, and doing this decreases the saved file size. Press Ctrl(⌘)+S once more after you do this.

ADDING A SHADOW TO THE SINK COUNTERTOP

If you look at the far right of the image, you can see an electrical cord and a cup that are casting shadows slightly to the right of the image, but mostly straight down onto the sink countertop. The plumber's arm and wrench should cast shadows on the countertop, too.

Here's how to complete the scene by adding some subtle shadows:

ADDING YOUR OWN SHADOWS TO THE SCENE

1. Click on the Background layer on the Layers palette and then click on the Create New Layer icon. A new Layer 2 appears on the Layers palette's list, between the Background and the plumber on Layer 1.

2. Choose the Airbrush tool, set the Options to Normal Painting mode and 50% Pressure. On the Brushes palette, choose the third tip from the left, second row.

3. Alt(Opt)+click on the shadow area next to the electrical cord in the image. This samples the color you will use to paint shadows in the image.

Okay, a quick conference meeting here on the shape of the shadows. The plumber's elbow is closest to the countertop, so it will be the densest shadow area. The monkey wrench extends forward in the image, so its handle area will create the densest shadow, and the shadow will get lighter where the wrench is closest to the plumber (the farthest from the countertop). Finally, the plumber's forearm extends also, so you need to create a lighter shadow beneath his forearm, as it becomes farther from the countertop. Hup, hey: let's go—

4. On the Layers palette, choose Multiply from the Modes drop-down list, and drag the Opacity slider to about 75%.

5. Paint a circle below the plumber's elbow, on the countertop.

6. Paint a wide line from the front of the countertop into the sink (peeking at Figure 25.83 will help you here). This is the shadow of the wrench.

7. Decrease the Pressure of the Airbrush on the Options palette to about 20%, and then paint the forearm shadow, as shown in Figure 25.83. Do not worry about painting over the front edge of the countertop; you'll fix this in a moment.

8. Choose Filter, Blur, and then choose Gaussian Blur. In the Gaussian Blur dialog box, type 4 in the Pixels field, and then click on OK to apply the blur effect. You'll notice that the real shadows on the Background layer are extremely diffuse; this is why you applied the Gaussian Blur filter to your shadow work.

Sample color here

FIGURE 25.83 *Paint the densest areas first; the elbow and wrench shadows should be the deepest. Then decrease the Pressure of the Airbrush tool, and paint in a shadow for the plumber's forearm.*

9. With the Polygon Lasso tool, click points along the edge of the countertop, and then close the selection toward the bottom of the image, as shown in Figure 25.84. Press Delete (Backspace) and then press Ctrl(⌘)+D to deselect the marquee. You're doing this to remove any of the shadow you painted that extends beyond the edge of the countertop.

FIGURE 25.84 *Remove the shadow parts that don't belong on the front face of the countertop.*

10. Press Ctrl(⌘)+S. You're finished, and so is this chapter! You might want to save a flattened copy of your creation so you can save it to TIFF, BMP, or PICT file format. If so, press Ctrl(⌘)+Alt(Opt)+S, and then save a copy of the image to your hard disk. Choose the file format from the Save As (Macintosh: the Format) drop-down list, click in the Exclude Alpha Channels and the Exclude Non-Image Data check boxes, pick a good location on your hard disk for the copy, name it, and then click on Save. You can close the sink.psd image at any time now.

In Figure 25.85 (and in the second color section of this book), you can see the finished image. If you *really* want to have some fun and duplicate this unlikely scene, photograph the bathroom sink at an angle, take a picture of the *back* of your plumber's head in addition to his front, and add a reflection of the back of his head to the mirror.

FIGURE 25.85 *If he didn't fix that leak once and for all, we should shove him back down the drain.*

SUMMARY

Clearly, there are many important third-party plug-ins that you can add to your personal collection, and in the process, speed up your work and enhance your work in a way you presently might not have the skills to perform. Like Photoshop's native filters, however, third-party filters should *not* act as a replacement for inspiration or a concept. The very best third-party plug-ins add a special something to your designs, but the very best designer knows how and when to use them.

There seem to be a few pages still under your right thumb. Chapter 25½ contains some closing thoughts the author would like to share with you, and oddly, they have *nothing* to do with Photoshop. But they have *everything* to do with you, your creativity, and where artistic adventures beyond the covers of this book can lead.

WHERE DO WE GO FROM HERE?

CLOSING THOUGHTS

Unfortunately, Inside Adobe Photoshop 5, Limited Edition *must come to a close now, because the publisher has run out of paper. Onnnnly kidding! Seriously, though,* Inside Adobe Photoshop 5, Limited Edition *was not the beginning of your computer graphics education—you began when you developed enough interest in graphics to go out and look for a book— and it is not the end of your education, either. The authors will certainly be back with a version 6 book in good time, but until then, be sure to keep this chapter in mind, because there's still a lot more to learn.*

LEARNING FROM LIFE

In the same way that you must occasionally take your face away from the monitor to catch a breath of fresh air, you should also seriously consider taking a day or two off from the computer. Go outdoors, visit a friend you respect and haven't spoken with in a while, and even stick your head into a continuing education classroom that looks interesting. The creative mind is always looking for outside stimulation—you see a beautiful scene, your mind filters it, and you eventually express what you feel about this scene, using Photoshop or even (gasp) a pencil on paper. When the creative urge strikes (and it has historically been a very strong urge), you should do two things:

- **Realize firmly in your mind what the concept is.** It can be as commercial as a stunning graphic to sell a car, or as personal as creating a graphic to tell your spouse that you love her.

  A concept is an elusive thing. Many people presume, for example, that a concept is "Okay, we get this elephant to stand on one leg next to a clothes washer." This describes what someone wants to see in a composition, but it is not the concept. Why is the elephant there? Why is the elephant next to a clothes washer? If there's no reason, there's no concept, and as we would traditionally say, it's "back to the drawing board."

  A fair example of a concept (the author doesn't want to give away *too* many free concepts!) would be a clown, in color, walking down an urban street that's in black and white. The picture is saying that there is humor in the cold, serious world; *that's* the concept. Do you see the difference between the clown and the elephant?

- **Gather stock photography, but also gather stock ideas, and write them down.** There's a yin/yang to ideas. You give an idea life, but the idea also provokes you on an emotional level, and then more ideas are created. There's nothing sadder than sitting down in front of Photoshop without an idea. It's time wasted, better spent examining the geometric complexity of a flower, or how clouds can create specific moods.

We, as a civilization, are so caught up in the day-to-day machinery we call a working life that we often deprive ourselves of inspiration and really good ideas. After this book has been written, the author intends to mow the lawn, inspect all the flowers his spouse has planted, look at the sky, look at an insect crawling around for food—and then open Photoshop or another application and see where these impressions of life lead. To be an artist means being able to see life with the widest vision you permit yourself, and then filter what you saw into a graphical composition. It doesn't get much easier than that. Don't feel intimidated about the outcome of your work. Simply immerse yourself without shame or fear that other people won't like your work, and gaze upon what you've done as a way of expressing yourself.

Learning How to Learn

It's not easy to know instinctively how to learn. Schools tend to make you recite instead of invent, and we tend to be conditioned, not taught, by even the best-meaning but opinionated scholars. The authors feel differently about books than about any other medium of communication because you, the reader, have the option of closing the book and taking a break any time you feel like it. Additionally, try as we may, *Inside Adobe Photoshop 5, Limited Edition* is an information guide above all things, so this puts the authors in the position of being fellow artists second, and "information vendors" first. Hopefully, we've set a conversational tone in this book, but not at the expense of our prime goal, which is teaching.

Inside Adobe Photoshop 5, Limited Edition is the eighth book the authors have written on Photoshop. Through the years, we've received mail from our friends and readers with questions (and a scattered complaint here and there). Like other artists, the authors depend on feedback to influence what we document, and how we communicate with you, the reader. The most useful feedback we've received has been on how readers approach this book.

Many readers never actually perform the tutorials; instead they skip around in the book looking for a magic recipe or technique here and there. For many readers, this approach works when they need to quickly solve a specific problem. But the most "successful" readers—the ones who have increased their overall relationship with art and increased their skill levels—are the ones who found time to sit with the book for an hour or two at a time and work their way through a chapter. Like most things in life, mastery of an art comes from doing. It's only then that the principles behind the steps become tangible. If you've passed over chapters on your way to this paragraph, please invest in your own talent and work completely through a favorite chapter. Follow the steps, and then do something similar with images of your own. Make the knowledge truly yours.

Also, it should be known that the authors actually *read* sometimes(!), and even a tutorial-based book has some "good stuff" lodged between the pages that might not be a formal set of steps to arrive at a finished piece. What we do when we discover a nugget of wisdom is outlined in (you guessed it) a numbered list—

INDEXING A NUGGET OF WISDOM IN A BOOK

1. Take out a pad of fluorescent sticky notes.

2. Detach one leaf.

3. Place it between the pages in the book that contain a morsel of interest.

For all the information organized into procedures found in this book, however, please *don't* treat *Inside Adobe Photoshop 5, Limited Edition* as a workbook. We've tried to make this book an excellent *resource* guide, and a book on art, too.

Whether you are an imaging enthusiast who simply wants to retouch photos as a pastime, a designer in a large enterprise who is forced to measure output in volume, or a fine artist who is looking for that "special something" to refine your work, you might not immediately know where you're going creatively. But we all pack toolkits for our artistic voyages, both virtual and physical. You've seen in this book that Photoshop is not only a necessary part of your computer graphics toolkit, but also that it should be located at the *top* of the toolkit.

This author has had the career privilege of never having to write about an application he does not believe in. To bring all the examples in this book, the tricks, tips, techniques, and secrets together, took being able to learn correctly. But it also took an imaging program as capable as Photoshop to be the vehicle of the author's expression. You've got the right application, you've got the right book (we think), and now it's simply up to you to create your own gallery of ideas.

PART VII

BACK O' THE BOOK

WHAT'S INCLUDED IN THE BACK OF THIS BOOK?

On the pages to follow, you'll glean some important information concerning special offers, what some of the Companion CD's contents are, and instructions on how to load Acrobat Reader 3. Reader is an all-important component to the Companion CD, because it enables you to browse more than 200 textures, 25 scenes, and custom fonts the authors have designed by loading the FST-7.pdf file. If you follow the directions on installing Acrobat Reader 3, you'll also gain access to IP5Gloss.pdf in the root of the Companion CD. This is an online glossary, illustrated in full color with more hyperlinks than you can believe, to skip from section to section of explanations about Photoshop 5 and computer graphics in general. There are more than 250 pages in the Glossary that you won't want to miss. Additionally, the *Limited Edition* CD-ROM contains Acrobat files that guide you through the collection of scenes, clipart textures, and other valuable stuff in the Boutons folder.

Check out the following pages to see what Extensis Vector Tools can do, what Extensis PageTools looks like (in case you own PageMaker), and take a gander at the new fonts in the Boutons folder. Additionally, we provide a glimpse here of Three-D Graphics' Texture Creator; a demo of this program is on the CD and although it doesn't contain as many presets as the retail version, you can most certainly experiment with the program for 30 days and create some beautiful, photorealistic images of wood, stone, marble, and other natural textures.

Finally, the publisher and the Boutons (and Gary K., too) are out to save you some bucks with firms we've known and trust as being outstanding in their respective fields. Graphics Masters can save you up to $250 on film recording work, Conde—who makes the best inkjet transfer paper in the world—wants to send you a free mouse pad, and i/us has a special Filter Factory offer, where you can get 300 plug-ins for Photoshop for under $30 when you mention this book.

And, oh yes, the authors have our Web sites listed in this section. If you have problems, suggestions, or (most importantly) high marks for this book, we'd like to hear about it. Who knows? You could have a quotable quote featured in *Inside Adobe Photoshop 6* book (puh-*lease* don't write to us asking about when it'll be coming out), like other readers have their *bon mots* listed in the front of *this* book!

DaVinci Caps

Folks

Haxton logos

...and many more!

In the Boutons/Fonts folder on the Companion CD, you'll find original one-of-a-kind typefaces in both TrueType and Adobe Type 1 formats. These are display and symbol fonts that can be used to spruce up a headline or add a simple piece of art-work to a layout in Photoshop, Illustrator, and any application that can read a type-face. Create Web buttons and more with hands-on typography lessons in this book.

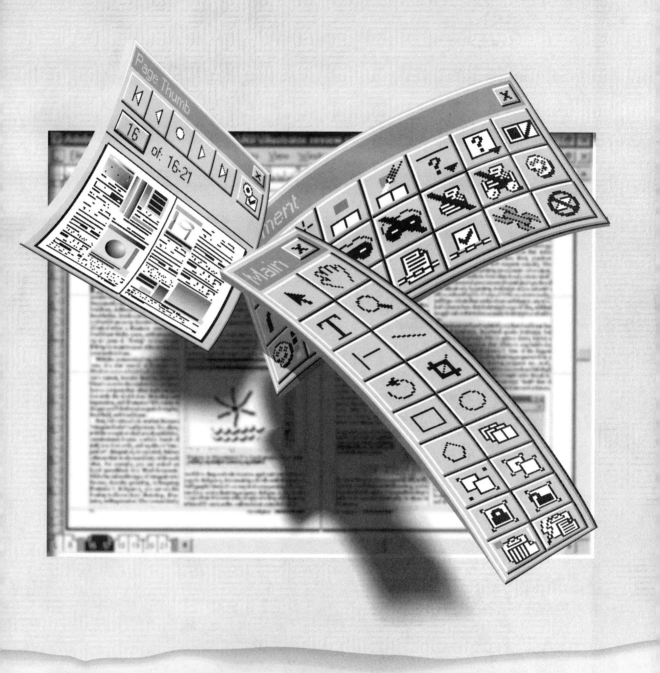

Extensis PageTools is exclusively designed for Adobe PageMaker. This 30-day fully functional trial version puts commands at your fingertips, provides character styles, and has other enhancements to help you work more efficiently. Also in the Extensis folder on the Companion CD for Photoshop are PhotoFrame—a framing effect; Intellihance 3—for creating perfectly exposed images; and Mask Pro 1—for defining selections that are far too complex to mask manually.

Extensis has graciously provided VectorTools, among other plug-ins for Adobe products on the Companion CD. These 30-day trial, fully functional plug-ins can warp text in Illustrator 6 or 7, in addition to providing commands at the click of a palette button. Check out the Extensis folder on the Companion CD.

Three-D Graphics' Texture Creator is the ideal companion to your Web work. Generate natural textures such as wood and stone to any resolution, and make the patterns tile. A demo version of Texture Creator can be found on the Companion CD.

INSTALLING ACROBAT READER 3.01

The *Inside Adobe Photoshop 5* Companion CD contains a number of Adobe Acrobat files, of particular importance the FST-7.psd file, which is your guide to the scenes, textures, and fonts in the Boutons folder, and IP5gloss.pdf, the Online Glossary.

If you already have Acrobat Reader 3.01 or later installed on your machine, you can ignore this text, but be sure to check out the ads in this section! If you do not have Acrobat Reader 3.01 installed, and you've chosen not to use the Companion CD's install program, it's really quite simple to install Acrobat Reader.

FOR THE MACINTOSH

Go to the Reader3 folder on the Companion CD, and then double-click on the Reader 3.01 Installer icon. Click on Continue on the splash screen, and then click on Accept in the End User License Agreement screen. You should be aware that you are accepting the terms and conditions of installing Reader 3.01. The "short version" of this agreement states that you can install and use the Reader utility on your machine (only Power Macintoshes can use the Reader; it's not designed and will not run on 68K machines). Additionally, you can share a copy of Reader 3.01 with friends, but you cannot distribute Reader 3.01 as part of a sales tool. You also cannot decompile the program or alter it in any way. These are pretty liberal terms by anyone's measurement, right?

After you've clicked on Accept, the Installer will display options for where you want the program installed. Click on Select Folder, select an installation folder (or choose to create a new one), and then click on Select. Click on Install; if you have any applications running in the background, click on Continue, and Acrobat will automatically close the application(s).

That's it. Restart your computer when prompted after installation is completed, and you now have a gateway to all the information on the Companion CD.

WINDOWS USERS

Double-click on the Ar32e301.exe file in the Reader3 folder on the Companion CD. The file is the same for Windows 95 and NT users. Click on Yes when prompted to continue the installation. Click on Next in the Welcome screen, click on Yes in the End User License Agreement screen (check the Macintosh section that precedes this section for an explanation of what the Agreement entails), click on Browse in the following screen to specify a directory for Acrobat Reader 3.01, click on OK once you've specified a current or new directory, and then click on Next. After installation is complete, you'll see a screen that prompts you to read the ReadMe file that accompanies Reader. You can uncheck this option box, and click on finish. Click on OK in the dialog box thanking you for choosing Adobe Acrobat. You do not have to restart your computer; you can get to checking out the PDF files on the Companion CD right away.

Transfer Paper and more!

Conde offers free technical support to its customers and expert advice to those looking to purchase color printers.

7851 Schillinger Park West
Mobile Al 36608
334 633-5704
1 -800- 826-6332
FAX 334 633-3876

CondeWear™ transfer paper works on many brands of printers including large format, dye-sublimation, laser, and inkjet printers. Hot letter, legal and ledger sizes; 24" and 36" wide rolls, or Cold Peel letter and 11" by 17" sizes. Our papers can be applied to fabric, coasters, mugs, and hats.

A **free mouse pad** with the first order from any customer who mentions this advertisement in *Inside Adobe Photoshop 5*. The blank pad is suitable for printing.

Conde products are available through our website at **http://www.conde.com**.
International orders are welcome!

All the graphics on this page were drawn in XARA version 2 for Windows. A fully-working, 15 day trial version of this vector program that thinks it's a bitmap program can be found in the XARA folder on the Limited Edition CD. CorelXARA™ is small (7MB), fast, and one of the perfect companion applications to Photoshop, for the Web and commercial printing uses. For a limited time, you can purchase this amazing program online, for **$99⁹⁵** U.S., at i/us. **http://www.i-us.com**. Look in the XaraXone on i/us.

SYMBOLS

A

1034 Inside Adobe Photoshop 5, Limited Edition

T

W–Z

WHAT'S ON THE COMPANION CD?

The Companion CD contains everything you need to work through the tutorials in this book—and more. Here's exactly what the CD includes:

- Nine one-of-a-kind decorative typefaces in both TrueType and Adobe Type 1 formats, designed by the authors
- More than 200 seamless tiling textures and bump maps, including a gallery of thumbnail images in Acrobat format
- 50 high-resolution scenes—everything from country settings to out-of-this-world landscapes
- Sample images and example files for every project in the book
- A 250+ page, full-color online glossary, complete with cross references, in Adobe Acrobat format
- And the following software:
    - A fully functioning trial copy of Extensis PageTools, PhotoFrame, Intellihance, and Mask Pro 1 for Windows and the Macintosh
    - A fully functioning trial copy of Extensis VectorTools for the Macintosh
    - Adobe® Acrobat® Reader 3.01
    - A fully functioning trial copy of Three-D Graphics' Texture Creator, a natural texture-making program for Windows and the Macintosh
    - A trial version of The VALIS Group's Flo'™, a program that twists images as though they were made of putty
    - MooVer, an animation compiler for the Macintosh
    - MainActor, an animation compiler for Windows 95 and NT
    - Earthlink Network, Inc.'s Dialer for Windows
    - StuffIt Expander for the Macintosh
    - Winzip compression program for Windows
    - BBEdit Lite, a powerful text editor for the Macintosh
    - TextPad®, a mega-text editor for Windows

What's on the CDs in the Back of the Book?

More than you might imagine, and we *know* that you have a healthy imagination! One-of-a-kind, original Bouton textures, stock art, typefaces, and trial versions of exciting programs that work with Photoshop 5 is the "terse" description of the CDs' contents. Let's expand on this…

What's on the *Limited Edition* CD-ROM?

It was hard to top the offerings on the Companion CD, but as you'll see, we came up with *a lot* of fun, useful, and occasionally necessary items with which you can enhance your work in Photoshop 5. To be specific…

- Clip art—The Boutons have created more than 75 files of common, and not so common, images on Photoshop layers. All the files are in Photoshop's PSD format, and all the selection work has been done for you. All you need to do to add a clip art element to a composition is drag the title of the object (on the Layers palette) into your composition window.
- Close-ups—143MB of high-resolution, color-corrected scans of everything from candy to yarn. There are 34 close-up files, and we're sure you can use many of them as backgrounds for compositions.
- Five new typefaces, in both Type 1 and TrueType for Windows and the Macintosh. The Boutons have created a font we're particularly proud of called "Sympols" that's ideal for Web button-making or modifying to use as a corporate logo.
- Scenes—Everyone needs a good background to complement a good foreground element. We offer 42 files, almost all of them 2.5MB or larger, for high-quality output. You'll find everything from sunsets to textures of wood, gears, and brick walls. All images are either digitized photos or are synthetic, computer-generated pictures.
- Textures—204 seamless tiling textures, not to be found anywhere else! Many of the textures have corresponding bump maps, so you can enhance a texture by using the Lighting Effects filter's Texture channel in combination with the bump map files in the Textures folder.
- In the root of the Boutons folder, you'll find FST-8.PDF, an illustrated Acrobat document that enables you to preview and access the files in the Boutons folder quickly. Please read the User Agreement in this file before distributing files in the Boutons folder.
- And the following software in the Software folder:
  - Four Seasons, a Photoshop plug-in that creates beautiful skies for Windows and the Macintosh.
  - XAOS|tools' Total XAOS, for the Mac and Windows. This suite of Photoshop plug-ins contains Paint Alchemy, Terrazzo, and TypeCaster (for creating 3D text). This trial version does not allow you to write your creations to file, but we *do* document what each program does in the *Limited Edition* book…and perhaps you'll spring for the commercial version after test-driving these amazing filters!
  - Andromeda Software's fantastic Shadow and 3D filters. These versions are documented in chapters later in this book, and you'll be astounded at how photorealistic your creations can be with these plug-ins.
  - Alien Skin's Eye Candy 3 plug-ins, for Mac and Windows. Two of the 21 filters are completely functional, and the rest offer previews of what you can do with a specific plug-in. Check them out, and see what they can do for your Photoshop work!
  - CorelXARA version 2 for Windows. This state-of-the-art vector drawing program creates bitmap images on-the-fly, features transparency blends for photorealistic effects, and is the perfect companion to Photoshop. This is a 15-day, fully functional trial version, so don't install it until you have a couple of weeks to spare, to experiment!

Read This Before Opening Software

By opening this package, you are agreeing to be bound by the following: